Leonhard Schmitz, Connop Thirlwall

A history of greece

From the earliest times to the destruction of Corinth

Leonhard Schmitz, Connop Thirlwall

A history of greece
From the earliest times to the destruction of Corinth

ISBN/EAN: 9783742809582

Manufactured in Europe, USA, Canada, Australia, Japa

Cover: Foto ©ninafisch / pixelio.de

Manufactured and distributed by brebook publishing software
(www.brebook.com)

Leonhard Schmitz, Connop Thirlwall

A history of greece

A

HISTORY OF GREECE

FROM THE EARLIEST TIMES

TO THE DESTRUCTION OF CORINTH (B.C. 146)

MAINLY BASED UPON THAT OF

CONNOP THIRLWALL, D.D.

BISHOP OF ST. DAVID'S.

BY DR. LEONHARD SCHMITZ, F.R.S.E.

RECTOR OF THE HIGH SCHOOL OF EDINBURGH.

SIXTH EDITION

WITH SUPPLEMENTARY CHAPTERS ON LITERATURE AND THE ARTS

BY C. KNIGHT WATSON, M.A.

TRINITY COLLEGE, CAMBRIDGE.

ILLUSTRATED WITH NUMEROUS WOODCUTS

BY GEORGE SCHARF, JUN., F.S.A., F.R.S.L.

LONDON:

LONGMAN, GREEN, LONGMAN, ROBERTS, & GREEN.

1863.

LONDON

PRINTED BY SPOTTISWOODE AND CO.

NEW-STREET SQUARE

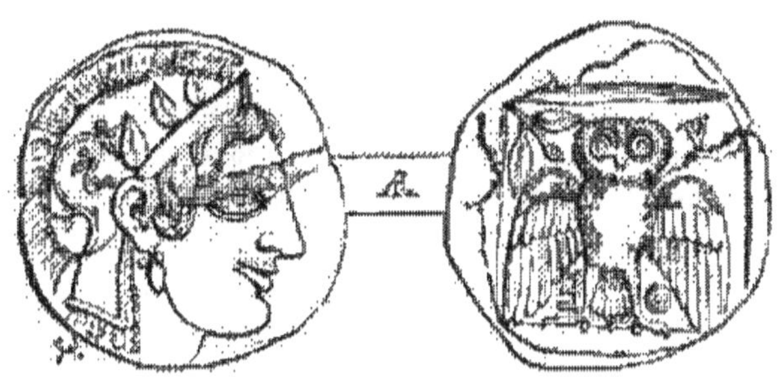

Athenian Coin of an early period.

PREFACE.

Within the last fifty years more has been done by both English and foreign scholars to elucidate the History of Greece than at any former period since the revival of learning; and the results of all these labours are two English works on the History of Greece such as no other nation can boast of. For although the Germans possess in their literature a countless number of treatises and dissertations upon almost every subject connected with Greek antiquity, yet they seem to lack either the will or the power to produce some one great work combining the treasures dug out by the numberless workers in the quarries of Greek lore, and exhibiting to the modern student a complete picture of the Greek nation. This task, requiring, perhaps, more practical knowledge of free political institutions than continental scholars generally can be expected to possess, has been left to English scholars, and has been executed by Bishop Thirlwall and Mr. Grote in a manner which throws all previous attempts of a similar nature completely into the shade.

Under such circumstances, it appeared desirable that the results arrived at in the voluminous works of these authors should be made available for educational purposes. The History of Greece is taught, more or less, in all schools and colleges which profess to give a liberal education; and as by far the greater number of young students want either the means to procure or the time to study the great works on this subject, it has been thought advisable to prepare a manual containing, within a reasonable compass, an accurate and complete outline of the subject, and not unworthy to serve as an introduction to the masterpieces of classical historical literature produced in our own age and country.

With this view the present work has been undertaken. It is mainly based upon Bishop Thirlwall's Greek History, especially in the first part, down to the account of the Peloponnesian war. As this portion of the bishop's work enters less into the minute details of the subject, it was possible, and was at the same time thought expedient, to preserve, to a considerable extent, the form and diction of Dr. Thirlwall's work, of which the first half of this manual is, therefore, in every sense, an abridgment. But of the affairs of Greece from the Peloponnesian war the bishop's work contains such a detailed account that, although the period over which it extends is not quite three centuries, it occupies six volumes out of the eight of which the whole history consists. Here, therefore, the process of abridging could not be conveniently adopted, and it became necessary to proceed more freely; especially as it was not requisite that the later portions of the History of Greece should be treated, in this manual, with that minuteness which it seemed desirable to preserve in the accounts of the earlier and more brilliant period of Greek History, which ends at the time when the kings of Macedonia began to interfere in, and to exercise influence upon, the affairs of Greece; for this reason, the narrative of events subsequent to the time of Philip is more brief than that which relates to the preceding period; and as, moreover, the history of Macedonia and of her conquests in the East does not, properly speaking, form part of the History of Greece, it is introduced in the present work only so far as is necessary to enable the student to understand the main subject.

In conclusion, the author would fain indulge a hope that this manual may meet with the same kind and indulgent reception which has been accorded to his little work on Roman History. His most ardent desire is, that it may contribute towards keeping alive love for, and admiration of, a people which, although it is the first we meet with at the dawn of European history, still stands pre-eminent in all matters connected with literature and the arts, and to whose spiritual influence all civilised nations owe a vast debt of gratitude.

L. SCHMITZ.

Edinburgh, Oct. 1850.

The supplementary chapters, containing, besides a sketch of the history of the literature and the arts among the

Greeks, a succinct view of their civilisation and religious development, have been entirely re-written and expanded for this, the fifth, edition. The illustrations interspersed throughout the work are copies from the antique; those representing scenes memorable in the history of Greece are taken from Sir William Gell's original sketches, now in the British Museum, to the Trustees of which the Author's best thanks are due for their permission to make free use of that valuable collection. The coins also have been drawn from the originals in the British Museum. AV signifies gold; AR, silver; Æ, brass.

Edinburgh, June, 1858.

Dionysus returning from India, received as a guest by Icarius.
(A bas-relief in the British Museum.)

Head of the youthful Dionysus in the style of Praxiteles.
(From the Museum of the Capitol at Rome.)

CONTENTS.

SUPPLEMENTARY CHAPTERS.

(From a Pompeian Painting.)

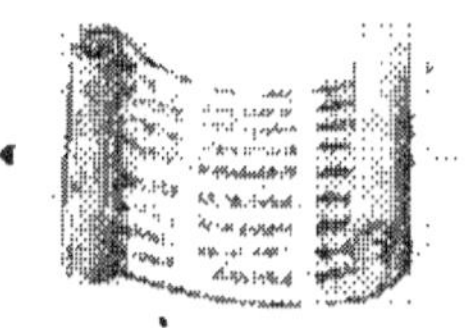

A Volume, showing the Mode in which Books were written

LIST OF ILLUSTRATIONS.

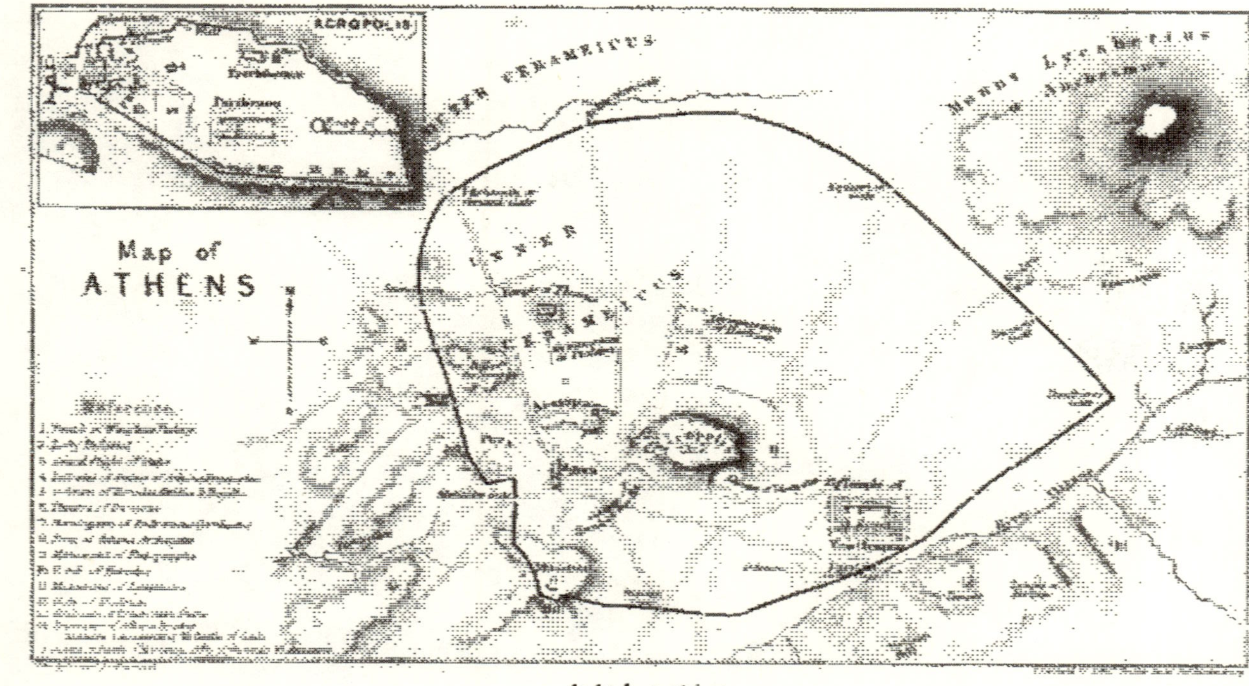
Map of
ATHENS
ACROPOLIS
Parthenon
Erechtheum
CERAMEICUS
INNER
CERAMEICUS
Reference.

Olympian Zeus.

INTRODUCTION.

At the very threshold of European history, before any other nation of our continent is known even by name, we meet in its south-eastern portion with a people which presents to us mankind in its beautiful and poetical infancy, and gradually rises to the full vigour and restless intellectual activity of early manhood. Much beyond this state it never proceeded, for its career was cut short by internal dissensions and the all-absorbing power of Rome. The history of Greece in her best days, therefore, is the history of European mankind in the age of its youth, when all its mental and physical powers displayed a vigour, activity, and fertility which will never cease to awaken the admiration of those who know how to appreciate the noblest attributes of humanity. To dwell upon and study such a history is as delightful, refreshing, and invigorating, as that exercise of the imagination when, in times of trouble and adversity, we try to forget the actual world by which we are surrounded, and betake ourselves to the fair regions of our youth, so full of poetry, beauty, and happiness. But it is not pleasure and recreation only that we seek and find in the history of Greece; its pages, like those of the history of all civilised nations, abound in wholesome and useful lessons for states as well as for individuals, especially in regard to every thing connected with the cultivation of intellect and taste. We there hold communion with a people which not only was inspired with a glowing love of its country and its liberty, but has produced in the arts, in poetry, in oratory, and in philosophy, the noblest and sublimest works to which the human mind has hitherto given birth, and which have ever been, and probably always will be, the highest models for study and imitation. A nation in which all these excellencies attained so great a degree of perfection and were so harmoniously blended together, has existed only once in the history of the world; and the fairest flower of humanity is assuredly entitled to claim the deepest interest and the most earnest attention of those who aspire to what is highest in man, and do not allow the merely physical wants of our nature to engross their whole being. Although the Greek nation has long since departed from the scene of history, yet its glory is immortalised by the deeds of its heroes, the writings of its poets and sages, and by the works of its artists, which still excite the admiration of those who are most competent to judge of their beauties, and still exercise their influence upon the best literary and artistic productions of our own time.

The interest inspired by the history of Greece is very different from that which we feel when studying the history of Rome. In the latter there is a unity from beginning to end, the city of Rome always forming the centre, as it were, around which all the events of Roman history are grouped, and upon which they always have a more or less direct bearing. The history of Greece presents no such unity, except in a few isolated cases. Greece, small as it was, consisted of almost as many independent states as it contained cities, so that, properly speaking, a history of Greece is almost an impossibility; the history of many of its numerous little states having come down to us in so fragmentary a condition, that we catch a glimpse at their internal affairs, or hear of their doings, only now and then, when they come in contact with one or other of the leading states. What, therefore, is generally called the history of Greece, is in reality not much more than the history of Athens and Sparta. During a short period, Thebes also emerges from its condition of comparative obscurity; but the other states occupy a prominent place only in proportion as they are connected with Athens and Sparta, between which cities the supremacy in Greece was divided, and on which the other states were more or less dependent. This want of unity, however, is sufficiently compensated for by the variety in social and political institutions, as well as in literature, to which the peculiar circumstances of Greece naturally gave rise; for, each town or tribe being left to itself and following the bent of its own genius and inclination, a freedom of development was allowed in every particular state, of which there is no example in any other nation. Greece, therefore, is a little world by itself, in which the attentive observer has opportunities of seeing all the varieties and shades of difference that exist in a great nation developed in such a manner as to keep each tribe distinct, and yet so far united with the rest as to form with them but one great family.

Some persons believe that the history of Rome is more practically useful than that of Greece; and reasons in support of this opinion are certainly not wanting, especially as Rome and her institutions may, in a more direct manner, be regarded as the basis upon which most of our social and political institutions have been reared, and of which they are, in fact, further developments. But in every thing that ennobles man—mentally, morally, and aesthetically, the history of Greece possesses numerous examples of the most striking kind; and it may be safely asserted that human life, in all the variety of its manifestations, is nowhere more completely exhibited than in the history of the Greek states. If, further, the importance of the history of a nation is to be estimated by the influence which it has exercised upon contemporary nations and upon posterity, and if we allow intellectual influence a higher place than that which is the result of military conquest, then the history of no other nation can compete in usefulness and interest with that of Greece. Greece did not conquer the world by the sword, indeed; but she subdued it by the superiority of her genius in art and literature, and has thereby acquired an empire more vast and more enduring than that which was established by the arms of the Romans, who, themselves, cheerfully owned that the Greeks were their masters in all the nobler achievements of the human mind. The Greeks extended and communicated to other nations the blessings of civilised life by means of peaceful colonisation along the shores of the Mediterranean and the Black Sea, in Asia, Africa, Sicily, Southern Italy, Spain, and Gaul; while the conquests of Alexander spread Greek culture and literature from the Mediterranean to the Indus: so that, about the beginning of the Christian era, every man of rank and education, from the Indus to the shores of the Atlantic Ocean, was familiar with the language and literature of Greece. Providence seems to have chosen this as one of the great means for facilitating the extension of Christianity; inasmuch as the documents of the Christian religion, being composed in Greek, thus became accessible at once to all educated persons throughout the civilised world.

In studying the history of Greece, we go back to the perennial spring from which all truly great men in all subsequent ages have deeply drunk. Persons unacquainted with the noble productions of the Greek mind may sneer at our enthusiastic admiration; but it is more than a mere consolation to know that the greatest poets, philosophers, orators, and artists, of all ages and countries, have willingly and humbly acknowledged their obligations to the Greeks, from whose teachings and examples they have derived great and powerful assistance in the production of their greatest and sublimest works. The history of Greece is so rich in every thing that can claim our admiration, esteem, and affection, that we cannot help approaching it with a feeling of joy and delight.

The political existence of Greece ceased at the time when the Romans became the rulers of the country, but its intellectual sovereignty survived even the fall of Rome in the fifth century of the Christian era; nay, a faint shadow of Greek independence continued to exist in the Byzantine empire down to the middle of the fifteenth century; and although the real spirit of ancient Greece had disappeared from the trifling and dissolute capital of the eastern or Greek empire, still a veneration for the great minds and masters of antiquity was kept alive there, and, after the conquest of Constantinople by the Turks, was communicated by the exiles whom that event drove forth from their native land to the people of south-western Europe. There the seed fell upon a fertile soil: a love of the noble and beautiful in art and literature was its first fruit; and the sources of learning being now thrown open, the darkness which had been hanging over Europe for a thousand years was soon dispelled. The revival of letters, which then commenced, was the beginning of a new era in the history of Europe; the free spirit of Greece rose from its tomb, drove away the mists of ignorance, broke the chains of superstition, emboldened the mind of man to assert its right of independent thought, and thus opened that career of intellectual life and activity which is the pride and glory of modern times.

Sitting Figure of Athene.

(From a very ancient statue discovered on the Acropolis at Athens.)

Entrance to the Treasury of Atreus, at Mycenae.
(From Sir William Gell.)

CHAPTER I.

GREECE AND ITS EARLIEST INHABITANTS.

Greece forms the south-eastern extremity of Europe. It is situated between the thirty-sixth and fortieth degree of northern latitude, and its whole extent is considerably less than the small kingdom of Portugal. In form, Greece is distinguished among the countries of Europe by the same features which distinguish Europe itself from the other continents; that is, by the great range of its coast compared with the extent of its surface, exceeding in the former respect the whole of Spain and Portugal. Greece is a peninsula, which projects from the main trunk of Europe, grows more and more finely articulated as it advances towards the south, and terminates in the peninsula of Peloponnesus, which resembles an outspread mulberry-leaf, whence its modern name Morea.* The position of Greece between the two neighbouring continents, and opposite one of the most fertile regions of Africa, presented

* Μορέα signifies a mulberry tree.

to human activity more advantages than any other country on earth; for the surrounding sea afforded the most convenient communication with the civilised nations of the ancient world, and the numerous islands scattered over it offered agreeable and commodious resting-places to the sailor who navigated it. In addition to this, Greece abounded in excellent harbours and spacious bays; it was watered by numerous rivers, and, being in the enjoyment of a serene and delightful climate, though the winter was often very severe, it was a country no less rich than beautiful. Its productions were as various as its aspects, some parts being more fertile in grain, wine, olives, and many valuable fruits, while others afforded abundant pastures. In precious metals the country was, perhaps fortunately, poor; but plenty of iron and copper was found in various districts: so that the land provided its inhabitants with everything required for the perfect development as well of their physical as of their intellectual powers.

This land was called by its own sons *Hellas*, for which we have adopted the Roman name *Greece* (*Graecia*). The word Hellas, that is, the land of the Hellenes, however, did not at all times apply to the same extent of country; according to some*, it was originally the name of a town or district in the south of Thessaly, which was afterwards called Phthiotis. From that territory the name is said to have gradually extended to the whole of Thessaly. But, according to others, the most ancient Greeks were the Selli (Σελλοι = Ἑλλοί = Ἕλληνες), who dwelt in and about Dodona †, bearing the name of Graeci (*Γραικοί*). ‡ The Greeks themselves traced their national name to a mythical hero, Hellen, just as the Graeci derived theirs from a hero, Graecus, who is called a son of Thessalus, while Thessalus is said to have founded Dodona. Another tradition represents a son of Graecus as ruler of Thessaly, for the Graeci are said to have migrated from the country of the Molossians, in the neighbourhood of Dodona, to Thessaly, and to have there been called Hellenes. In later times, when the Hellenes spread farther south, the name Hellas embraced a wider extent of country, and might properly be considered to reach as far as the national features of the Hellenes, so as to include Peloponnesus, and even the islands and colonies occupied and founded by the Hellenes; though, in a more limited sense, the ancients apply it to the region south of Macedonia as far as the Corinthian isthmus, the southern peninsula deriving its separate designation,

* Steph. Byz., s. v. Ἑλλάς. † Aristot. *Meteor.* i. 14.

‡ This name seems to have become known through Tyrrhenian navigators to the nations of the west, who transferred it to all the inhabitants of the country commonly called Greece, who continued to be designated by it even when the ancient tribe of the *Γραικοί* had ceased to exist.

according to tradition, from the Phrygian Pelops. In a somewhat loose acceptation, the name Hellas embraced even Macedonia and Epirus. After the destruction of Corinth, in B. C. 146, the Romans gave to the whole of Greece the name Achaia, and subsequently constituted it as a Roman province. If we understand by the term Greece merely the country between the Cambunian range of mountains in the north and the southern extremity of Peloponnesus, it denotes a land of small extent; but if we include under it the adjacent islands, the numerous colonies established by the Greeks on the coasts of Thrace, Asia Minor, Africa, Southern Italy, and Sicily, it becomes the designation of a vast empire; and still more so, if we include the conquests of Alexander in the East, into which, through him, the Greek language and civilisation were introduced.

Greece Proper seems to have acquired its present shape by violent convulsions and changes of the earth's surface, which belong to an extremely remote period, and of which only very obscure and vague traditions were preserved among the ancients. The country lies in a volcanic zone, extending from the Caspian to the Azores, and although history informs us of no volcanic eruptions in Greece, still there were many permanent traces of volcanic agency scattered over its surface, in the hot springs of Thermopylae, Troezen, Aedepsus, and other places. The sea between Peloponnesus and Crete has always been the scene of surprising changes, wrought by volcanic forces. Not long before the Christian era a new hill was thrown up on the coast, near Troezen, and within a short period three small islands were formed in the neighbourhood of Thera.* Earthquakes and inundations have, in all ages, been frequent in Greece, especially in Peloponnesus. It is said that in the earliest times the plains of Thessaly were covered by water, until an earthquake separated the mountains Ossa and Olympus, and, opening an outlet for the river Peneus, formed the celebrated valley of Tempe. Similar catastrophes seem to be implied in the legends about the quarrels of Poseidon with Athene, for the possession of Athens and Troezen, and with Hera for that of Argos; as well as in the stories relating that the islands of Delos, Anaphe, Rhodes, and Cyprus were at one time covered by the sea, and rose at the bidding of some god. There was, lastly, a tradition that no connexion existed between the Euxine and the Aegean, until the Euxine, breaking through its barriers, formed the Hellespont and Propontis. Another stated that Asia was anciently connected with Greece, until the intervening country, which bore the name of Lycaonia or Lyctonia, being struck by

* Plin. *H. N.* iv. 12. 23.; Strab. i. p. 57.

Poseidon with his trident, formed with its scattered fragments the islands in the Aegean. There is nothing unreasonable in the belief of such violent convulsions of the earth's surface; but no one can say with certainty whether these accounts were actually ancient traditions, or mere opinions, arrived at by the speculations of the philosophers of a late period of Greek literature. All authentic information must be drawn from a careful examination of the geological nature of the country and its surrounding islands; and this certainly leads us to the belief that Greece owes its present appearance to the operation of mighty volcanic forces.

In the earliest times, before Greece was occupied by the Greeks or Hellenes, we meet with the names of many races which were afterwards considered by the Greeks as barbarous, or foreign to themselves in manners and language. Among them the Pelasgians were by far the most important; they were the most widely spread, and their name appears in Crete and Asia Minor as late as the fourth century before the Christian era, when all the other ancient tribes had entirely disappeared. Their name and origin have been the subjects of much speculation, which, however, has yielded no definite results; all that we can say with certainty is, that they must have immigrated into Europe, from Asia Minor, perhaps across the Hellespont and Propontis, and that they gradually spread, under different names, over nearly the whole of south-eastern Europe, and the west of Asia Minor. All Greece is said to have been inhabited by them, and to have borne the name of Pelasgia.* In some parts of Greece, however, they appear to have been mixed with other tribes; in others, no traces whatever of them are found. The first distinct mention of the Pelasgians in Greece itself is met with in the south-east of Thessaly, where a district or town is called the Pelasgian Argos †; and on the banks of the Peneus we find a town of the name of Larissa ‡, which is said to signify a fortress, and is probably a Pelasgian word. There are, however, many indications which seem to prove that at one time the whole of Thessaly was occupied by Pelasgians, though they were not distinguished by that appellation in all parts of that country, for the Perrhaebians also were Pelasgians. In the west of Greece we meet with Pelasgians in Epirus at Dodona, where Zeus was worshipped as the *Pelasgian king*. There they were called *Helli* or *Selli*, *Graeci* and *Chaones*, and constituted a very extensive tribe, by which nearly

* Strab. v. p. 220. Herod. ii. 56.; viii. 44.

† *Argos* signified a plain.

‡ Towns or fortresses so named, as well as towns bearing the name of Argos, occur in many parts of Greece, and in every instance may be clearly traced to the Pelasgians.

all Epirus was occupied before it came under the rule of the Molossians. South of Epirus, in Acarnania and Aetolia we lose sight of the Pelasgians, and the names of other races occur, as Leleges, Taphians, Teleboans, and Curetes, which are not known to have belonged to the Pelasgian stock. So, too, in the countries south of Thessaly, no Pelasgians present themselves until we come to Boeotia, where they appear as one of a great number of barbarous tribes, such as Aones, Temmices, Leleges, and Hyantes, and where they are said to have settled after the expulsion of the Phoenician colony of Cadmus. Being afterwards driven out of Boeotia, they are stated to have settled in Attica, though Attica had been peopled by Pelasgians long before that time. They were believed to have dwelt in Attica from time immemorial, without undergoing any change, except by successively assuming new names and adopting a new language, until at length they called themselves Ionians, after Ion, one of their chiefs.*

In Peloponnesus, as in the north of Greece, the Pelasgians appear to be confined to particular districts, though, according to some authorities, the whole peninsula was at one time called Pelasgia. The parts in which their presence is attested by direct evidence, are Argolis, Arcadia, and Achaia. The plain and city of Argos, with its fortress Larissa, were distinguished from the Thessalian Argos by the epithet Achaean, and were regarded by the ancients themselves as the district from which the Pelasgians spread northward over Greece. The first settlers in Achaia are called Pelasgians, and are said to have subsequently assumed the name of Ionians, from Ion, the son of Xuthus, who came among them. On the confines of Elis and Achaia, also, we find a town Larissa, and a river Larisus, which confirms the belief in Pelasgian settlements in those parts. Arcadia was so celebrated as a Pelasgian land, that it disputed with Argolis the honour of being the mother-country of the whole nation.

These are the places in Greece where the Pelasgians are expressly mentioned in ancient traditions, and from the review we have just taken, we must conclude that the name Pelasgians was a general one, like that of Saxons, Franks, or Alemannians, but that most, if not all, of the Pelasgian tribes, had also specific names peculiar to themselves. Hence it is quite probable that branches of the same race may have existed in countries where no tradition mentions its name; and we must often look for other evidence in order, on the one hand, not to separate kindred races, and, on the

* It must, however, be observed, that the Pelasgian wall on the Acropolis of Athens was believed to be the work, not of those primitive inhabitants of the country, but of a Pelasgian tribe, who, at a later time, made only a transitory stay in Attica.

other, not to confound those which were really distinct. But here everything is so obscure that it is impossible to come to any definite and satisfactory conclusions. The most probable opinion, however, is, that most of the tribes which we find scattered among the acknowledged Pelasgians were connected with them, and branches of the same great stock. Among the most ancient inhabitants of Boeotia were the Hectenes, Temmices, Aones, and Hyantes, of whom we know scarcely anything beyond their names; but the Caucones, who once occupied a large portion of the western side of Peloponnesus, were undoubtedly a Pelasgian race, and the Leleges, whom we meet with on the coasts of the Aegean and in Peloponnesus, were, no doubt, allied either to the Pelasgians or to the Hellenes. The Thracians, who occur in Phocis, and are mentioned among the barbarous inhabitants of Boeotia, the possession of which they are said to have shared with the Pelasgians, were likewise a branch of the Pelasgian race; and the relationship between them and the Pierians, in the north of Greece, is well attested. These Thracians, though the later Greeks style them barbarous, appear to have cultivated a certain kind of poetry, as is implied in the story of Thamyris, even if we set aside the names of Orpheus and Musaeus, which, as well as the productions assigned to them, are probably forgeries of a later age. In Asia Minor, Pelasgians are expressly mentioned along the western coast, and three ancient towns in that tract bore the name of Larissa. In the Trojan war Pelasgians are included among the allies of the Trojans, who themselves belonged to the Pelasgian race. In the Aegean, the islands of Lesbos, Chios, Lemnos, and Imbros were occupied by them.

We have already intimated that in the earliest traditions we meet with the Pelasgians in Greece; but it is quite certain that they did not originate there, or, to use the Greek expression, were not Autochthones (earth-born); by which term the Greeks merely indicated that they were both unable and unwilling to trace their origin any further. They must have come into Europe from the quarter where mankind made its first appearance. We are not, however, to suppose that the Pelasgian race immigrated into Greece at once, or at one particular point; their migration may have lasted for many years, nay for centuries; and while some crossed over the Hellespont in the north, others may have sailed directly across from more southern parts of Asia, and at a different time; so that there is no necessity for considering the Pelasgians in one part of Greece as the ancestors of those in other parts; and the same supposition may also account for the different names and other peculiarities of the various Pelasgian tribes, though their fundamental character was the same everywhere.

The first well-established fact in the history of Greece, then, is, that the great bulk of the population consisted of Pelasgians; and as we hear of no subsequent immigration of foreign tribes, nor of any convulsions or revolutions by which its ancient inhabitants were wholly or mostly exterminated or dislodged, we must further infer that the Pelasgians constituted the main body of its inhabitants during the whole historical period. How, then, is it that the later Greeks looked upon themselves as a different race, and speak of the language of the Pelasgians as barbarous, or not Hellenic? And what was the difference between the Pelasgic and the Hellenic or Greek language? To answer the latter question would not be difficult if many distinct remnants of the Pelasgian language had been preserved; but, unfortunately, almost all that have come down to us consist of names of persons and places, many of which, moreover, are very doubtful, it being uncertain how far they may have been changed and adapted to Greek ears. Herodotus, who heard a language, called Pelasgian, spoken in two places near the coast of the Propontis, and at a town which he calls Creston, the site of which is uncertain, though it was probably not very far from the isthmus of Mount Athos, says that it was barbarous*; but in discussing the matter further, he uses an expression which he also employs when comparing the language of the Ionians in Lydia with that of the Ionians in Caria.† Hence we must indeed infer that the Pelasgian which he heard, had something strange and foreign about it; but we cannot by any means conclude that the two languages were as distinct as, for example, the German and the French, or even as the English and the German. If we assume this to be the case, which still leaves a wide field for speculation where all the details are so uncertain, we may easily conceive how the Pelasgian language passed into or became amalgamated with the Hellenic or Greek, without any great convulsions among the inhabitants of Greece; and it also becomes probable, that the Greek language, as it has been handed down to us, contains more Pelasgian elements than is commonly supposed. This view is confirmed also by what we know of the Pelasgians in Italy, of which they occupied the whole of the south, and both the eastern and western coasts; for the languages there spoken by them, such as the Latin and other dialects, have the strongest resemblance to, and in innumerable instances a perfect identity with, that of the Greeks. We must therefore consider the Pelasgian language as the basis, or rather as an early phasis, of the Greek. With the knowledge of this general fact we must be content, for all attempts to define more exactly the relation between the two languages rest on nothing but arbitrary assumptions.

* I. 57. Βάρβαρον γλῶσσαν ἱέντες.

† I. 142.

The question which here naturally presents itself to us is, in what relation did the Hellenes or Greeks, who afterwards gave to the nation its tone and character, stand to the Pelasgians? They are said to have originally occupied the district on and about Mount Pindus, where they took refuge during the flood of Deucalion; and this would imply that previously to that catastrophe they had possessed a larger extent of country. From Mount Pindus they may afterwards have spread farther south, and extended their power; but this subject will be more fitly discussed in another chapter, and we shall here add only a few observations respecting the traditions about the state of civilisation among the Pelasgians.

The idea that the Pelasgians in Greece, like the Aborigines in Italy, were half savages, living without laws, without fixed habitations, and without any knowledge of agriculture, is merely an application of the speculative notion that man at first was little better than the brute creation, and only by degrees emerged from the savage state into any degree of civilisation. That they were not savages may be safely taken for granted; but how their civilisation was acquired is a matter of uncertainty. According to some, it was of a spontaneous and gradual growth; while, according to others, it was the effect of foreign influence. The testimonies of ancient authors are not safe guides, as we do not know how far they report genuine traditions, and how far they give us only the results of philosophical or historical speculations. According to the legends of Arcadia, Pelasgus taught his people to build rude huts, to clothe themselves with skins, and to substitute the fruit of the oak for the leaves and wild herbs on which they had before subsisted. His son, Lycaon, founded the first town, Lycosura; and under Arcas, the fourth king from Pelasgus, from whom the country derived its name of Arcadia, the people learned the use of bread, and began to exchange their skins for woollen garments. This account is probably nothing more than the result of a speculation as to the manner in which man may be supposed to have emerged from his primitive state, and is of no historical value. The legends of the earliest condition of Attica are of the same nature, and opposed to the more trustworthy traditions, which assign to the Pelasgians tillage and the useful arts as their proper and original pursuits. We are told that they loved to settle on the rich soil of alluvial plains; so in Thessaly, Pelasgus hastened to take possession of the country formed by the withdrawal of the waters which had forced a passage for themselves between Mounts Ossa and Pelion. The oldest Pelasgian divinities, moreover, seem to have been those powers which preside over husbandry, and protect the fruits of the earth, and the growth of the flocks and herds.* In the plains they seem to have been engaged in agriculture, while in mountainous districts, such as Arcadia, they naturally adopted a pastoral life. As some portion, at least, of the Pelasgians had come to their new country by sea, we must suppose that those, at all events, who inhabited the coast, were acquainted with the rudiments of navigation, and continued to cultivate it. Hence we find the islands of the Aegean peopled by Pelasgians (Leleges), and the Tyrrhenian Pelasgians, as pirates, infested the seas far and wide. It is, further, a fact beyond all doubt, that in many places the Pelasgians dwelt together in fortified towns (Larissa), had regular political and religious institutions, and were perhaps even acquainted with the art of writing. Some of the most ancient architectural monuments in Europe, which may probably outlast all that have been reared in later times, clearly appear to have been the works of their hands; we allude to the huge structures known by the singular name of Cyclopaean†, which are found in many parts of Greece, Asia Minor, Epirus, and Italy. In what remains of these buildings, we can still trace the progress of the art, from the rudest and most unsightly beginnings, to edifices like the lion-gate of Mycenae, and the treasury of Atreus.

* It is, therefore, not improbable, that Πελασγοί (from ἄργος and πέλω) was expressive of this national character, and described them as the inhabitants or cultivators of the plain.

† The name Cyclopaean probably expresses nothing more than the wonder which these gigantic works excited in the Greeks of a more refined age.

Lion-Gate, at Mycenae. The Plain of Argos and Gulf of Nauplia to the right.

From an original sketch by F. C. Penrose, Esq.

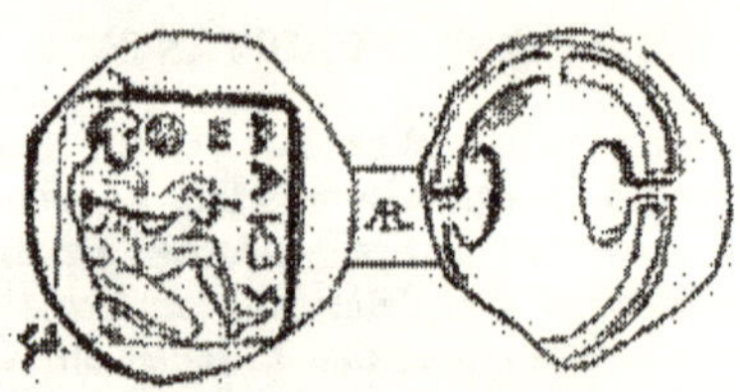

Coin of Thebae, in Boeotia.

CHAPTER II.

FOREIGN SETTLERS IN GREECE.

At a comparatively late period, when an historical literature had sprung up in Greece, it was generally believed that, in ages of very remote antiquity, before the name and dominion of the Pelasgians had given way to that of the Hellenes, foreigners from distant countries had landed on the shores of Greece, and had there planted colonies, founded dynasties, built cities, and introduced useful arts and social institutions, before unknown to the ruder natives. This belief was prevalent, not only among the mass of the people, but even among philosophers and learned men, and has maintained its ground with some, even in our own days. But the current stories about these ancient settlements afford great room for distrust, not merely in the marvellous features which they exhibit, but in the still more surprising fact, that with the lapse of time their number seems to increase, and their details to be more accurately known; and that the farther we go back the less we hear of them, till, on consulting the Homeric poems, our most ancient records, we lose all traces of their existence. These circumstances have led some historians to discard the traditions altogether, and to deny that any foreign influence was exercised upon the development of the national character of the Greeks. Now, although even a slight inspection of these stories will show that neither the authority on which they rest, nor their internal evidence, is such as to satisfy a cautious inquirer, yet it would be rash to deny that, during those Pelasgian times, foreign adventurers, especially Phoenicians, landed on the inviting coasts of Peloponnesus for the sake of commerce, and in some instances planted colonies there. But the mythical stories of Cecrops, Danaus, Cadmus, and Pelops, must be rejected as devoid of the characteristics of history, and as fictions which sprang up in Greece itself, although they were afterwards believed as history. Let us here briefly notice their leading features.

The principal colonies brought to Greece from the east are said to have been planted in Argolis and Boeotia. The Pelasgians were still masters of the plain of Argos, when Danaus, driven out of Egypt by the fifty sons of Aegyptus, landed with his fifty daughters on the coast, was raised to the throne by the consent of the natives, and founded a town, afterwards the citadel of Argos (Larissa). He is said to have given his name to the warlike Danai, who were once so celebrated, that Homer uses this as a general appellation for the Greeks, when that of Hellenes was still confined to a narrow range. Herodotus, who relates this story without any distrust, even mentions the Egyptian town from which Danaus came; and he recounts a Rhodian tradition, that Danaus, on his way to Greece, touched at Rhodes, and founded a temple of Athena at Lindos; the Danaids, moreover, instructed the Pelasgian women of Argos in the mystic rites of Demeter. To them, too, was ascribed the discovery of the springs, or wells, which relieved the natural aridity of a part of the Argive soil, with the peculiar character of which the legend is thus intimately connected; and this gives some colour to the conjecture of those critics who believe that the whole story of Danaus was of purely Argive origin, and sprang out of local circumstances and accidents. At Megara, also, we find a king Lelex, who, according to one author *, had come from Egypt, founded a dynasty, and given his name to the Leleges.

In Attica we meet with reports of more than one Egyptian colony. The first, led by Cecrops, is said to have found Attica without a king, and desolated by the deluge which befel it, more than a century before, in the reign of Ogyges. Some of the latest Greek writers state that Cecrops also gave his own name to the land, and on the Cecropian rock founded a new city, which he called Athenae, after the goddess Athene. To him is ascribed the introduction, not only of a new religion of pure and harmless rites, but even of marriage, the first element of civil society. Notwithstanding, however, the confidence with which this story has been repeated in modern times, the Egyptian origin of Cecrops is extremely doubtful; the early Greek poets and historians do not mention the tradition; and even at the time when it became current, it was contradicted by some of the Greeks themselves, who regarded Cecrops as an autochthon, or earth-born being, half man, half serpent. The Egyptians, however, evinced such anxiety to represent the Athenians as their kinsmen, as to excite doubts even in the minds of the most credulous; they went so far as to assert, that on one occasion they sent Erechtheus with a supply of corn for their kinsmen in Attica, and that he was rewarded there by

* Paus. i. 39. § 6.

receiving the kingly dignity, in return for which he founded the mysteries of Eleusis on the model of those of the Egyptian Isis. A third Egyptian colony was said to have been led to Attica by Peteus, shortly before the Trojan war. The arguments by which the Egyptians supported these tales, were as weak as their assertions were bold; and though that which is derived from the oriental character of some of the primitive institutions of Attica seems to be somewhat better entitled to a careful consideration, yet it is unaccountable that early writers, who might have been expected to be best informed on this subject, are utterly silent about it. In fact, all mythological inquiries tend to show that Cecrops and Erechtheus are fictitious personages, and belong entirely to a homesprung Attic fable.

The tradition about a foreign settlement in Boeotia is undoubtedly supported by much better authority. That Cadmus led a Phoenician colony into the heart of the country, and founded a town called Cadmea, which afterwards became the citadel of Thebes, was a tradition which had been current in Boeotia long before the time of Herodotus, whose judgment was not biassed in this case by the Egyptian priests; it also derives support from some collateral circumstances, which show that the Phoenicians had very early gained a footing on the islands and shores of Greece. The Thebans believed that they had received the art of writing from the Phoenicians, and pointed out traces of what was thought to be Phoenician worship. Modern writers, on the other hand, find in the legends of Cadmus and his wife Harmonia, and in their connection with Samothrace and the mysterious Cabiri, decisive marks of a Pelasgian origin; urging, further, that it is not likely that the Phoenicians should have founded a settlement in a place like Thebes, in the very heart of a country.

A tradition, supported by the authority of Herodotus and Thucydides, states that Pelops crossed over from Phrygia to Greece with treasures which afforded him the means of founding a new dynasty. His descendants ruled at Argos for three generations; their power was acknowledged throughout Greece, and the southern peninsula was called after him Peloponnesus, or the island of Pelops. The details of the story are entirely mythical, and it may be mentioned that Homer nowhere alludes to the Asiatic origin of the house of Pelops, whence there naturally arises a suspicion, that the connection of Pelops with the east is a mere fiction, which it was easy to devise at the time when Greece sent forth her colonies to Asia Minor.*

* The name Pelops is, perhaps, connected with Pelasgus, and identical with it; the Phrygians did not occupy the country from which Pelops is said to have come till a much later time, so that he cannot have been a Phrygian.

All attempts to elicit out of these legends anything deserving the name of history must prove abortive, and yet there are points which seem to justify the belief that they cannot have been wholly destitute of historical foundation. We have already mentioned as probable that the Pelasgians, in their migrations from east to west, did not all cross over into Europe at once, nor from the same points; on the contrary, these migrations must have continued for many generations, and it therefore appears highly probable that the stories of the foreign settlers which we have just enumerated, are only so many forms of the impressions which a dim and vague recollection of those migrations had left on the minds of the Greeks, and which were wrought by them into the poetical tales for which their natural genius so peculiarly fitted them. But at the same time, we must not forget that Greece, so far from being secluded from the rest of the world, was particularly open and inviting to foreign settlers; and on examining the stories of the various colonies said to have been planted in Greece, we are now and then struck by coincidences which cannot have been the result of design. Thus, at the period which is commonly given as the date of the foundation of those colonies, we generally hear of some great feud or convulsion in the countries from which they are said to have come. But all we contend for is, that if Egyptian or Phoenician adventurers or fugitives did settle in Greece, they were not sufficiently numerous to build cities, still less to exert any considerable influence upon the development of the religious, social, or political institutions of the Greeks. Herodotus, indeed, represents the greater part of the religious notions and practices of his countrymen, the objects and forms of their worship, as derived from Egypt; and when we consider that in Greece, as elsewhere, it was religion that called forth the arts, poetry, and even philosophy, it is clear that many of the most interesting questions depend upon the ascertainment of the degree in which the religious and intellectual culture of the Greeks was derived from foreign sources; but our knowledge of the Egyptian and Greek religion has not yet arrived at such a stage, as to enable us to draw the line of demarcation between what was foreign and what was of home growth.

With regard to Phoenician settlements in Greece, an intercourse between the two countries may have existed, even several centuries before the age of Homer; we know that the Phoenicians were attracted by the mines of Cyprus, Thasos, and Euboea, and this intercourse seems to have been the most powerful of all the external causes that promoted the progress of civilised life in Greece. The Phoenicians must have had many stations on the coasts, and it is not improbable that some names we meet with in the mythical stories, are their popular designations. For instance, one of these names is that of Telchines, whose mythical pursuits and occupations seem to embody recollections of arts introduced or refined by foreigners. The objects of the Phoenicians can scarcely have been to establish permanent settlements in Greece, but rather to found commercial depôts and factories, which they abandoned, as soon as their attention was diverted to a different quarter. It is highly probable also, that these Phoenicians not only introduced their arts and the products of their industry, and thus made themselves really useful to the districts which they visited, but at the same time imparted religious superstitions of a very injurious nature; and many of the horrid rites which are described as prevailing at an early period in Greece may have been derived from the Phoenicians, whose religious ceremonies are known to have been particularly impure and atrocious. But whatever extent we may allow to the intercourse with Phoenicia or any other country, it was certainly not sufficient materially to alter the natural progress and development of the Greeks themselves, in whose history, so far as it is attested by authentic evidence, there is nothing which cannot be explained, on the supposition that their culture and civilisation were in all essential points of native growth.

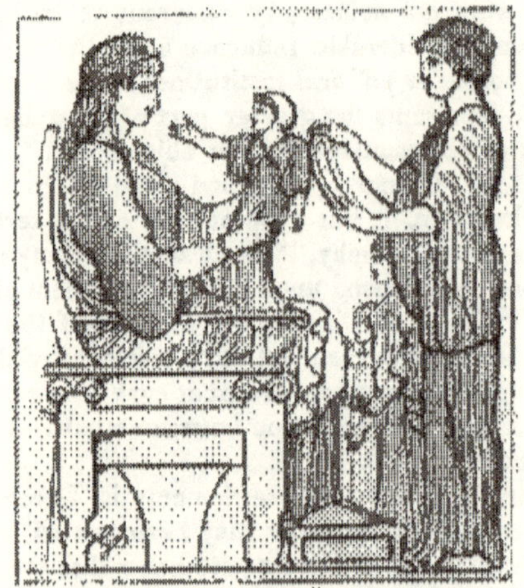

Specimen of Early Greek Sculpture.
(From a bas-relief in the Villa Albani at Rome.)

Temple of Theseus, at Athens.
(Drawn on the spot by G. Scharf, jun.)

CHAPTER III.

THE HELLENIC NATION AND ITS EXTENSION.

During the period when the Greeks had a literature of their own, they showed on all occasions an extreme proneness to create fictitious persons for the purpose of explaining names, the real origin of which was lost in remote antiquity. Thus almost every nation, tribe, city, mountain, sea, river, and spring was supposed to have been named after some ancient hero, of whom very often nothing but this fact is recorded. Such fictions were the natural growth of the poetical genius of the Greeks, which always endeavoured to embody the spiritual and to personify the indefinite. But clearly as we may perceive this tendency in innumerable instances, we should yet be going too far if we were to attribute to it alone all legends in which the name of a tribe is referred to that of an individual. Accurate discrimination alone can guide us, and it may be regarded as a safe rule, that we must withhold our belief from such traditions whenever they are not supported by trustworthy authorities, and when the period or the person referred to belongs to remote antiquity. This remark applies with full force to the heroes whom the Greeks believed to have been the founders of their whole nation and its main branches. All the Greeks no doubt held the opinion that the name of Hellenes was derived from Hellen; but on such a subject the authority of the best Greek writer is of very little weight, and Hellen must be regarded as a pure fiction or abstraction from Hellenes. But in the account of Hellen's progeny we may nevertheless trace the propagation of the main branches of the Hellenic nation, and it is for this reason that we cannot leave it unnoticed.

Hellen is commonly called a brother or a son of Deucalion, who with his wife Pyrrha, escaped from the flood which happened in his time, and replenished the desolated earth with a new race, which sprang up from the stones which he and his wife, by the command of the Delphic oracle, threw behind them on Mount Parnassus.* Thence he crossed over with his new people into Thessaly, taking with him a host of Curetes, Leleges, and other tribes. This leads us to the belief that the people afterwards called Hellenes came from the west, a belief which is confirmed by the fact that we find names differing but slightly from that of the Hellenes among the most ancient tribes of Epirus; for there, according to Aristotle, lay the ancient Hellas†; and there also we meet with the Hellopes, inhabiting the country of Hellopia, perhaps only another form of Hellas. It is, therefore, much more probable that the Hellenes derived their name from this tribe than from a hero Hellen, though the form Hellenes may have been first used in Thessaly. Beyond this we cannot go, and all that we can say with any degree of probability is, that the Hellenes and Hellopes were akin to each other and to the Pelasgians, the ancient possessors of all Epirus. What connection there was between the Hellenes in Epirus and those in Thessaly, it is impossible to ascertain; but that there was a connection, may be inferred from the fact that Achilles, in the Iliad‡, invokes the Pelasgian Zeus of Dodona as the protector of his family. The Leleges and Curetes, whom Deucalion took with him to Thessaly, are met with among the earliest inhabitants of Acarnania, Euboea, Boeotia, and Laconia. The Leleges are said to have been called Locrians from their leader Locrus, and that the Locrians were Hellenes is admitted on all hands.

The first known seats, then, of the Hellenes lay in the south of Thessaly, near the foot of Mount Othrys, a district which was called Hellas. Before the name of Hellas had extended beyond this limited tract of country, the Hellenes themselves seemed to have gained a footing in almost every part of the land afterwards so called. This diffusion of the Hellenic race must have effected important changes in the condition and character of the inhabitants of Greece, though we have but scanty information as to the nature and progress of this revolution. But before we proceed to trace its course, we shall endeavour to set forth the most characteristic features of the Hellenes. There can be no doubt that the Hellenic

* This legend may have arisen from an etymological speculation about the word λαὸς (people), which was connected with λᾶας (a stone).

† See above, p. 6.

‡ xvi. 234.

population included some new elements, not indeed absolutely foreign to the Pelasgian race, but yet very slightly connected with it: and it is evident that the peculiar stamp which distinguished the Greeks from all other nations was impressed upon them by the originally small tribe of the Hellenes. We must, therefore, look upon them not as strangers, such as the Phoenicians and Egyptians, but as a branch of the Pelasgian family, containing its best and purest blood, and destined to unfold the noblest faculties of the race, and to raise the national existence to the highest stage it was capable of reaching.

The transition from the Pelasgian to the Hellenic period was not effected by conquests or migrations only, for it seems that previously to the general diffusion of the warlike and powerful descendants of Hellen, they were frequently called in as auxiliaries to other states, during the civil feuds which in those early times arose in all parts of Greece in proportion to the growth of power and opulence. Hence, in many parts of the country the transition was the result of a natural development of circumstances in the social state of the Pelasgians; and it is manifest that no exact line can be drawn between the two periods. The population of Greece must, in fact, from the very earliest times, have been in continual, though often not unobstructed, progress: at first it was probably almost wholly engaged in struggling with the obstacles opposed by nature to the cultivation of the soil, and the separate tribes lived more or less isolated. But before the diffusion of the Hellenes, the intercourse of the tribes with one another must have been greatly increased, and those on the sea-coast had no doubt made considerable advances in civilisation through foreign navigators and adventurers; while those settled in the interior and secluded parts of the country remained more in their primitive condition under patriarchal or sacerdotal forms of government, which exercised a severe control over their actions and mode of life. The wealthier class had begun to seek its chief distinction in the use of arms, and where a sacerdotal caste existed, a military one rose up by its side. We have every reason for believing that, when the diffusion of the Hellenes commenced, they were not superior in any respect to the Pelasgians, except in their martial qualities, their active and enterprising genius, their love of arms, and skill in warfare; and these were the qualities most prized among their descendants for many generations. The ascendant which they thus gained among the weaker but more civilised Pelasgians, placed them at once in possession of all the stores, material and intellectual, which the latter had amassed, and in a situation the most favourable for increasing them. Accordingly they everywhere constituted the ruling class; and their spirit was more or less communicated to all parts of Greece, throughout which it produced a similar state of society. It is this general predominance of a warlike tribe, raised above the need of labour, rude in its manners, impatient of inactivity, and eager for adventures, yet endowed with a boundless intellectual capacity, and, gradually softened by the arts and pleasures of peace, submitting to the restraints of religion and of social order, that seems to constitute the characteristic feature of the Hellenic period in its earliest stage.

Of the four Hellenic tribes which traced their origin to Hellen, and accordingly represent the main branches that issued from the general stock, two, the Aeolians and Dorians, derived their descent from two sons of Hellen, Aeolus and Dorus. The third son, Xuthus, is not regarded as the direct representative of any tribe; but his sons, Ion and Achaeus, were considered as the ancestors of the Ionian and Achaean tribes. The Aeolians were the most widely spread in Greece; the Achaeans are most celebrated in epic poetry, and Homer commonly uses their name to designate all the Greek tribes which took part in the Trojan war. The Dorians and Ionians rose later to celebrity; but their fame and power far surpassed that of the other tribes. In order to understand the relations of these four branches of the Hellenic nation to one another and to the more ancient inhabitants of the country, we must not only form a clear idea of their geographical bonndaries, but must follow them, as far as we can, into the localities in which we find them at the beginning of the historical period, when a new series of convulsions changed their relative condition.

Hellen is said to have left his kingdom to Aeolus, and to have sent forth his other sons, Dorus and Xuthus, to make conquests in distant lands. The dominion of Aeolus was bounded by the rivers Asopus and Enipeus, and comprised the tract afterwards called Phthiotis, at the northern foot of Mount Othrys. That part of Thessaly called Aeolis, in Thessaliotis, between the Enipeus and the Peneus, was probably one of the first settlements of the Aeolians.

In Boeotia, also, mention is made of Aeolians, who are traced either to Amphictyon, the son of Deucalion, or to a daughter of Aeolus*; but they did not settle in Boeotia till sixty years after the Trojan war, when, on being driven from Thessaly, they proceeded to Boeotia, expelled the Pelasgians, and gave to their new country the name of Boeotia, which had belonged to the district where they originally dwelt. To Aeolus himself no conquests are

* Paus. ix. 1. § 1.; 40. § 5. Diod. iv. 67.

ascribed; but his sons and their descendants spread the Aeolian and Hellenic name far and wide, and in their history we must seek that of the people. The principal settlements of the Aeolids in Thessaly lay round the shores of the Pagasaean Gulf, and in the fertile plains near the coast: there Cretheus, the son of Aeolus, was said to have founded Iolcos; and Pherae was believed to have received its name from Pheres, another Aeolid. The district called Magnesia, from Magnes, probably contained many Aeolian towns; and the Athamanes, in another part of Thessaly, traced their origin to the Aeolid Athamas, who is said to have dwelt in the Thessalian town of Alos. The Aeolians on the Gulf of Pagasae appear inseparably blended with the Minyans, a race very celebrated in early times, but almost forgotten at the period when the real history of Greece begins. The adventurers of the Argonautic expedition are all called Minyans, though they were mostly Aeolian chieftains. Their fabulous progenitor Minyas is described as a descendant of Aeolus, and we find them in such places as are known to have been occupied by Aeolians. Whether these Minyans were originally a Pelasgian tribe subdued by the Aeolians, who afterwards assumed their name, or whether Minyes was only a title of honour, equivalent to heroes, is uncertain. The most flourishing of the Aeolian Minyans are met with in the north of Boeotia, where the city of Orchomenos rose to great power and opulence in the earliest period of which any tradition has been preserved. Its most ancient monument, the treasury of Minyas, was, in the eyes of the Greeks themselves, inferior to none of its kind; and the kings of Orchomenos ruled over a great part of Boeotia, Thebes itself seeming to have been at one time subject to them. The extraordinary wealth of the Minyans and of their rulers arose, no doubt, from their dominion over a fertile country; and their magnificence may have been owing to their intercourse with more cultivated foreigners. Their native traditions, however, pointed to Thessaly as their mother country, where we also meet with a town, Minya, and with another called the Minyan Orchomenos. The people consisted of two tribes, the Eteoclean and the Cephisean: the former seems to have comprised the warlike chiefs; the latter, the industrious people who cultivated the plain watered by the Cephisus. Along with them are mentioned the Phlegyans, a fierce and godless race, who were destroyed by the gods for their infamous deeds against the Thebans and the temple of Delphi. This mythus appears to allude to the violent resistance made by the natives to the new settlers, and their final extirpation or expulsion. In the south of Boeotia, too, we meet with traces of the Aeolians; for the towns of Tanagra and Hyria were Aeolian settlements, their dynasties being connected in the legends with Aeolus. But it is not in Hellas proper only that we can trace the diffusion of the Aeolian tribe; we find them also at Ephyra, the city afterwards more celebrated under the name of Corinth, where the dynasty of the wily Sisyphus ruled over the Aeolians; and his grandson, Phocus, gave his name to the Phocians, which intimates that the Phocians too were Aeolians. Some of the more remote descendants of Aeolus spread his name over the western parts of Peloponnesus, such as Elis, where Salmoneus is said to have founded Salmone, in the territory of Pisa. From him, again, were descended Pelias and Neleus, to the latter of whom was ascribed the foundation of the kingly dynasty at Pylos, probably the Pylos in Triphylia. During the formation of these little Hellenic kingdoms, the ancient inhabitants of the land formed perhaps the bulk of the population; but many of them, driven from the coast into the hills on the borders of Arcadia, preserved their independence for several centuries. What happened in Messenia during that early period is not quite certain; but, according to one tradition, it, too, fell under the dominion of Aeolian princes, the first of whom was Perieres, whom Hesiod calls a son of Aeolus, while others represent him as a son of Lelex, king of Laconia; however this may be, that Aeolians did establish themselves in Messenia is clear from the fact that the names of three Messenian towns, Oechalia, Ithome, and Tricca, are found in Thessaly also. One of the princes of Elis, Aetolus, is said to have been driven from his dominion, to have settled in Aetolia, which derived its name from him, and to have there founded the towns of Calydon and Pleuron; while his brother Paeon was the progenitor of the Paeonians on the river Axius. In Aetolia, however, the Aeolians seem to have occupied only the maritime districts, the interior being possessed by different tribes. The Locrians claimed a higher antiquity than any of the other Greeks; and Locrus, their progenitor, was described as a descendant of Amphictyon, a son of Deucalion. The national traditions of the Locrians connect them with the Aeolians of Thessaly and Elis.

The sketch we have here given of the diffusion of the Aeolians, shows that in the greater part of northern Greece, and on the western side of Peloponnesus, the beginning of a new period is connected more or less closely with the house of Aeolus, or with the tribe represented by his name. The legends, through which alone we can follow the gradual extension of this tribe, furnish indeed but scanty information; yet it is worthy of notice, that most of the Aeolian settlements were founded in maritime districts; places like Iolcos, Corinth, and Orchomenos, are the luminous points from which rays shoot out in all directions, while Poseidon is the god most frequently mentioned in the fabulous genealogies.

In this respect the Aeolians present a strong contrast to the Dorians, to whose traditions we shall now direct our attention.

The Dorians are distinctly stated by Herodotus to have been a Hellenic race, while he describes the Ionians as Pelasgians.* The former, moreover, are said to have gone through many wanderings, whereas the Ionians never changed their ancient seats. In the time of Deucalion, the Dorians inhabited Phthiotis; under Dorus, the son of Hellen, the country at the foot of Mount Ossa and Olympus, called Hestiaeotis; afterwards, being expelled by the Cadmeans, they occupied the heights of Pindus, and assumed the name of Macedonians. Thence, again, they passed first into Dryopis, and from Dryopis into Peloponnesus, where they were called Dorians. In this account, Herodotus must be mistaken in stating that the Dorians originally inhabited Phthia, the earliest seat of the Aeolians; for the legends present no traces of any such connection between the two tribes, but, on the contrary, the people who were the first and bitterest enemies of the Dorians are described as the friends and brothers of the Aeolians. Herodotus, however, regarding Aeolus and Dorus literally as brothers, could not well avoid representing their respective races as issuing from the same country. Their primitive seats must have been in Hestiaeotis, west of Mount Pindus, and then at the foot of Oeta, where we meet with Aegimius, the great hero and lawgiver of the Doric nation. He had to struggle against the Lapithae, and being unable to defend himself, called in the aid of Heracles, which he agreed to repay with a third of his kingdom. The invincible hero delivered him from his enemies, and slew their king, Coronus, whom we find mentioned among the chiefs of the Argonauts, and must accordingly regard as a Minyan or Aeolian. It seems that at a very early period Dorians, being expelled from Thessaly, migrated to Crete, where, as everywhere else, they lived divided into three tribes.† The statement of Herodotus, that the Dorians were ejected from Hestiaeotis by the Cadmeans, that is, the Thebans, is extremely obscure; and it is equally difficult to determine his meaning, when he says that the Dorians were a Macednian or Macedonian race, for with the Macedonians the Dorians had nothing in common, either in their language, their religion, or their social institutions. Other convulsions of which we likewise know nothing compelled the Dorians to seek a home in the south of Thessaly, the country of the Dryopes, which now received the name of Doris. Some of the Dryopes submitted to their conquerors, while others migrated to Euboea and Peloponnesus, where they established themselves on the coast of Argolis, in the towns

* Herod. i. 56.; comp. viii. 43. † Hom. *Od.* xix. 174

of Asine, Hermione, and Eion. In their newly conquered territory, the Dorians continued to live for a considerable time, and on good terms with the Heraclidae, in conjunction with whom they ultimately conquered Peloponnesus, an event of which we shall speak hereafter.

The two remaining Hellenic tribes, the Ionians and Achaeans, derived their origin from Ion and Achaeus, the sons of Xuthus; and even from this genealogy, fabulous as it is, we may infer that these two tribes were more closely connected with each other than with either the Aeolians or the Dorians; a presumption which is greatly strengthened by the traditions which have come down to us concerning them. Xuthus, the third son of Hellen, is said to have been expelled from Thessaly by his brothers, because he had taken more than his due share of their common patrimony. He found shelter in Attica, where he established himself, and founded what was called the Attic tetrapolis, or the four united townships of Oenoë, Marathon, Probalinthos, and Tricorythos. He wedded Creusa, the daughter of Erechtheus, king of Attica, and became, by her, the father of Achaeus and Ion. Some traditions add, that, on the death of Erechtheus, he was chosen to decide the disputed succession, and that the preference he gave to Cecrops provoked the other sons of Erechtheus to expel him from Attica. Thereupon, he went with his children to Peloponnesus, to the district then called Aegialos (the coast), but which afterwards received in succession the names of Ionia and Achaia. From this point, the story of his two sons is parted into separate lines.

Achaeus, according to some accounts, was forced to quit Aegialos, or Athens, in consequence of accidental bloodshed, and led his followers to the eastern side of Peloponnesus, where they mingled with the Pelasgians of Argolis and Laconia, or subdued them; and thus arose the Peloponnesian Achaeans, from whom the whole of Peloponnesus was sometimes called the Achaean Argos, to distinguish it from the Pelasgian Argos of Thessaly. Others relate, that after his father's death, Achaeus, with a band of adventurers from Aegialos and Athens, went to Thessaly, and recovered the patrimony of which his father had been wrongfully deprived. Accordingly we find, that at a later period Phthia bore the name of Achaia also*; and it is an established fact, that Achaeans existed both in the east of Peloponnesus and in Thessaly: the latter country seems to have been their primitive abode, whence they spread southward, and settled in Peloponnesus; for, independently of other traditions, there is one which states that Arch-

* Homer commonly uses the name of Achaeans for the Greeks in general, but more particularly designates by it the subjects of Achilles, who reigned in Phthia.

ander and Architeles, the mythical sons of Achaeus, came from Phthiotis to Argos, and married two daughters of Danaus, whose names, Automate and Scaea, are indicative of the relation of dependence into which the original inhabitants fell. The questions, however, who the Achaeans were, and whether they were connected with the Hellenic race as closely as the current genealogy seems to suggest, still remain to be solved. For in some traditions, Achaeus is called a brother of Phthius and Pelasgus, and a son of Larissa and Poseidon; according to which, the Achaeans would seem to be the ancient Pelasgians of Phthia. Hence it is not surprising to find, that when they were expelled from the Thessalian Argos, they met with a kindly reception in the Pelasgian Argos, and did not attempt to set themselves up as rulers there, as the Aeolians did everywhere. If we take this view, the Achaeans in the north were no other than the Aeolians, who were sometimes called by the name of the people among whom they established their sway. Hence Strabo and Euripides call the Achaeans an Aeolian race.* To these Aeolian Achaeans, belong also the Myrmidons, the subjects of Achilles, whose fabulous origin from ants (μύρμηκες, μύρμοι) is transferred by tradition to Aegina, where Aeacus is said to have prevailed on his father Zeus to people the island with a new race, but where, more probably, an Aeolian or Achaean colony from Phthia established itself. Afterwards, however, Aeolian chiefs from the western side of Peloponnesus settled in Argolis. The manner in which the Achaean name was introduced into Laconia is very obscure; according to some, Achaeus himself settled there, while others relate that Achaeans came into Peloponnesus with Pelops; but the stories about intermarriages between the dynasties of Sparta and Argos suggest the idea that there existed an original natural affinity between them. At a subsequent period, the Achaeans being driven from Argos and Laconia by the Heraclidae, migrated to the north of Peloponnesus, to Aegialos, which was thenceforth designated by the name of Achaia.

The early history of the Ionians, though peculiarly interesting on account of its connection with the ancient institutions of Attica, is, perhaps, more obscure than that of any of the other tribes. In the current genealogy, Ion is represented as a grandson of Hellen; but the Athenians gladly listened to a tradition more flattering to their national vanity, according to which he was the son of Apollo; a story which furnished Euripides with the subject of one of his most ingenious plays. But all the variations from the common story, which were devised to gratify the Athenians, tend to confirm

* Strab. viii. p. 383. Eurip. *Ion*, 64.

the substance of the received tradition, which is never entirely suppressed in them. According to the most generally entertained opinion, the Ionians were a Hellenic tribe, who took forcible possession of Attica and a part of Peloponnesus, and communicated their name to the ancient inhabitants. In Thessaly, however, to which their genealogy points, no trace of the Ionian name is met with; Herodotus considers the Ionians as Pelasgians, and distinguishes them from the Hellenic Dorians. He further states that the inhabitants of Attica were originally Pelasgians; and although we know that afterwards the Athenians formed a part of the Hellenic nation, yet the historian remarks, that the Attic Ionians had never changed their seats. The only way of reconciling these statements seems to be, to suppose that a body of Hellenic settlers established themselves among the old Pelasgian population, and gave it a new name, and a new nature. The time when this great change took place may have been that in which the legend places the arrival of Ion, to whom is attributed, not only the introduction of a new national name, but also the institution of the four tribes into which the people of Attica was anciently divided. One of these Attic tribes consisted of warriors, and down to a very late period we find in Attica a powerful body of nobles, possessing the best part of the land, commanding the services of a numerous dependent class, and exercising the highest authority in the state. Hence we must suppose, that the warrior tribe and the noble class were the Hellenic conquerors who overpowered the native Pelasgians. By this violent revolution, an end was put to the Pelasgian line of kings, and the conquerors took possession of the throne: this is, in fact, implied in the story, that Poseidon, the national god of the Ionians, destroyed Erechtheus and his house; and in the statement, that Ion was the founder of a new dynasty.* On the other hand, however, there are reasons for believing, that the name of the Ionians is of much higher antiquity than the common legend ascribes to it, and that it prevailed in Peloponnesus and Attica, even before the Hellenes made their appearance in Thessaly.† The name is used as synonymous with Pelasgian, and Peloponnesus seems to have been one of the earliest Ionian seats, or, at least, as ancient a one as Attica. Distinct traces of the Ionians also occur at Troezen and Epidaurus. The inhabitants of the former town distinguished themselves, even in the historical times, as the friends and kinsmen of the Athenians; and, at Epidaurus, the last king before the Dorian invasion was said to be a descendant of Ion, and took refuge with his people in Attica. On the eastern side of Peloponnesus, the name of the Ionians appears

* Apollod. III. 15. 5. Eurip. *Ion*, 284. † Herod. VIII. 73.

indeed to have at one time extended much further; and Argos, before it bore the name of the Achaean, was designated by the name of the *Iasian*.*

But how is this view of the Pelasgian character of the Ionians to be reconciled with the known state of society in Attica, and with the various indications which it seems to disclose of a foreign conquest, and of two distinct races? Of the four Attic tribes, one is said to have been a caste of priests, who may originally have had the supreme power in their hands. The relation between this tribe and that of the warriors appears to be indicated by the tradition, that at the death of Pandion, his twin sons, Erechtheus and Butes, divided their inheritance, and that the former succeeded to the throne, while the latter obtained the priesthood of Athene and Poseidon. From this tradition we may perhaps infer two periods in the ancient history of Attica, one of which might be called the priestly, the other the heroic, in the former of which the priest-

Metope from Selinus, representing Hercules carrying the Cercopes, or two Thieves of Ephesus.

hood was predominant, while in the latter the warriors gradually rose to power. The latter period would be the Ionian as contrasted with the Pelasgian, which preceded it, not indeed because

* Hom. *Od.* XVIII. 246.

the Ionians were foreign to the Pelasgians, but because at that time, in consequence of migrations from Peloponnesus, the Ionian name became established in Attica, and the warrior class received additional strength from the new adventurers. This second period must have formed the transition to a condition which may be termed Hellenic, inasmuch as it was one of gradual approximation to the purely martial and heroic character of the genuine Hellenic states; and also, perhaps, because strangers of Hellenic origin now gained some footing in Attica. For this, at least, seems to be implied in the story of Xuthus and the establishment of the Attic tetrapolis. In later times the Ionians of Attica founded numerous colonies in the island of Euboea, which, until then, had been occupied by Leleges, Curetes, and Abantes. The transition by which the Pelasgian language spoken in Attica gradually became Hellenised was, no doubt, greatly facilitated by the close affinity of the two dialects, and by the growing intercourse between Attica and the neighbouring Hellenic states; not to mention the influence which must have been exercised by the Attic tetrapolis, if it was Hellenic, which there is reason for believing.

Paris conveying Helen to Troy.
(From a terra-cotta in the British Museum.)

Battle between the Gods and Giants.
(From a painted vase at Berlin, belonging to the finest period of art. The figures are yellow upon a black ground.)

CHAPTER IV.

THE HEROIC AGE OF GREECE.

The period between the first appearance of the Hellenes in Thessaly and the return of the Greeks from Troy, is commonly designated by the name of the *heroic* age or ages. The real chronological limits of this period cannot be defined, for the chronology of the history of Greece, previously to the first Olympiad, that is, the year B.C. 776, is involved in utter obscurity; and all the dates of events given in modern works being either mere guesses, or based upon doubtful calculations, are anything but certain. But still, so far as its traditions admit of anything like a chronological connection, the duration of the heroic period may be estimated at about two hundred years, perhaps, from about B.C. 1400 to B.C. 1200. We have already seen how the warlike race of the Hellenes spread from the north over the south of Greece, founding new dynasties in a number of small states; and how a similar state of things arose even in countries which were not immediately occupied by the invaders; so that everywhere a class of nobles, entirely given to martial pursuits, and the principal owners of the land*, became prominent above the mass of the people, which they held in various degrees of subjection. The history of that age is in reality the history of the most illustrious persons belonging to this class, who are commonly termed heroes.† It is filled with

* Their station and character may be fitly compared to that of the chivalrous barons of the middle ages.

† The real meaning of this term is doubtful; it seems to contain the

their wars, expeditions, and adventures, which form the great mine from which the materials of Greek poetry were almost entirely drawn; but its very richness in poetical materials deprives it of much value to the historian, who can extract from it but little. For this reason we shall confine ourselves to those legends which are most worthy of notice, either for their celebrity, or for the light which they throw on the general character of the period, or for their connection with subsequent historical events.

The most celebrated of all the heroes is Heracles; but the legends about him are so varied and complicated, that the ancients themselves saw no way of removing the difficulties which they involve, except by assuming the existence of a number of fabulous persons of the same name; and on examining the exploits ascribed to him, we must agree with them, at least so far as to be convinced that the actions said to have been performed by him must be divided into two classes, which manifestly belong to two different periods in the history of Greece. The one carries us back to the infancy of society, when it is engaged in its first struggles with nature for existence and security: we see the hero cleaving rocks, turning the course of rivers, opening or stopping the subterraneous outlets of lakes, clearing the earth of noxious animals, and, in short, effecting works which belong to the united labours of a young community, and are accomplished only by the efforts of successive generations. The other class of Heracles' exploits exhibits a state of things comparatively settled and mature, when the first victory has been gained, and the contest is between one tribe and another, for possession or dominion: we see him maintaining the cause of the weak against the strong, of the innocent against the oppressor, subduing tyrants, exterminating his enemies, and bestowing kingdoms on his friends. It would be an idle undertaking to inquire whether such a person as Heracles ever really existed, but it is interesting to investigate whether the first conception of such a being was formed by the unassisted imagination of the Greeks themselves, or was suggested to them by a foreign people. A single glance at the fabulous adventures called the labours of Heracles suffices to show, that a part of them, at least. belongs to the Phoenicians and their wandering god, to whom they built temples in all their principal settlements along the coasts of the Mediterranean. To this god must be ascribed all the journeys of Heracles around the shores of western Europe, which did not

same root as the Latin *herus*, *hera*, the Greek Ἥρα, and the German *Herr*. Homer applies it as a title to the leaders and their followers. Afterwards it was restricted to persons of a superhuman, though not divine, nature, who were honoured with sacred rites. In the course of time, however, it came to signify men of extraordinary strength and gigantic stature.

become known to the Greeks for many centuries after they had been explored by Phoenician navigators. Twelve, the number of his labours, points to an astronomical period, or the course of the sun, which luminary the Phoenician god represented. The closing event in the career of the hero, who rises to immortality from the flames of a pile on which he lays himself, may safely be believed to be borrowed from eastern mythology. Such tales may, indeed, have been subsequently engrafted upon the Greek legend, but it is a remarkable coincidence, that the birth of Heracles is assigned to Thebes, the city of Cadmus the Phoenician; and that the great works ascribed to him correspond better with the arts and industry of the Phoenicians than with the skill and power of a less civilised race. But whatever we may think of this, the legends which we have distinguished as belonging to the second class, clearly represent Heracles as a Greek hero: and here it may be asked, did all or any part of the adventures they describe really happen to a single person?

We must, first, briefly mention the manner in which these adventures are linked together in the common story. Amphitryon, the father of Heracles, was the son of Alcaeus, who is named first among the children of Perseus at Mycenae. The hero's mother, Alcmena, was the daughter of Electryon, another son of Perseus. In the reign of Electryon, the Taphians, a piratical people, landed in Argolis, and carried off the king's herds. While Electryon was taking vengeance on the robbers, Amphitryon and Alcmena were forced by Sthenelus, a third son of Perseus, to quit their country and take refuge at Thebes. There Alcmena gave birth to Heracles, who thus, although the legitimate heir to the throne of Mycenae, was, as to his birthplace, a Theban. Hence Boeotia is the scene of his earliest exploits: he delivered Thespiae from a lion which made havoc among its cattle; freed Thebes from the yoke of Orchomenos, slaying its king Erginus, and compelling the Minyans to pay tribute to Thebes. In the meantime Sthenelus had been succeeded by Eurystheus, at whose command Heracles undertook his famous labours, in expiation for the murder of his wife and children, committed by the hero in a fit of rage. The supposed right of Heracles to the throne of Mycenae was the ground on which, some generations later, the Dorians claimed the dominion of Peloponnesus. During the prodigious and supernatural adventures which he undertook at the bidding of Eurystheus, the hero is also described as engaged in expeditions which are only accidentally connected with these marvellous labours. He appears in the light of an independent prince, and a powerful conqueror: he leads an army against Augeas, king of Elis, and, having slain him, bestows his kingdom on one of his sons, who had condemned his father's injustice. So also he invades Pylos, and slays Neleus with all his children, except Nestor, who was absent. He further carries his conquests into Laconia, where he exterminates the family of king Hippocoon, and places Tyndareus on the throne. All this he is said to have done while he suffered himself to be excluded by a weak usurper from his own kingdom! To discover anything like history in such accounts is impossible.

It was the fate of Heracles to be incessantly forced into arduous and dangerous enterprises; hence every part of Greece, in its turn, becomes the scene of his achievements. Thus in Thessaly, we find him bringing about an alliance between the Dorians and his own descendants; in Aetolia he appears as a friend and protector of the royal house in the war with the Thesprotians. These wanderings and sufferings are perfectly intelligible in poetry, which describes them as the consequence of the implacable hatred with which Hera persecutes him as the son of her husband Zeus by Alcmena; and they might even be taken as historical, if the various enterprises were supposed to be quite independent of one another, and connected only by being referred to one fabulous name. The safest way will be, after rejecting those features in the legend which evidently belong to eastern mythology, to distinguish the Theban Heracles from the Dorian and the Peloponnesian hero. The story of each of them may possibly contain some historical groundwork, but what that is, it is impossible to say; poetry and the love of the wonderful, here, as in the early history of other nations, have been so busily engaged in assigning marvellous deeds to their favourite hero, that in the end it has become impossible to discern the slender foundation upon which the magnificent structure has been raised.

Attica had its own Heracles in the person of Theseus, who was conceived as his younger contemporary, and is described as only second to him in renown. The exploits assigned to him likewise include events which were probably the work of ages. His legend is interesting to us, inasmuch as it furnishes an outline of the mythical history of Attica. The list of the kings who are said to have preceded him is a fabrication upon which no reliance can be placed. Their reigns are as barren of events as their existence is questionable. Two occurrences only are mentioned which may seem to bear marks of a really political character. One is the war with Euboea, in which Xuthus aided the Athenians; the other a contest between the Attic king Erechtheus, and the Thracian bard Eumolpus, who had become the priestly sovereign of Eleusis. In this war Erechtheus is said to have perished, and to have been succeeded by a second Cecrops, who migrated to Euboea, leaving his hereditary throne to his son Pandion II. The latter was expelled from Attica and went to Megara, where he became the father of four sons. The eldest was Aegeus, who recovered his father's kingdom, and shared it with his brothers. A mysterious oracle afterwards brought him to Troezen, where he formed an intimacy with Aethra, the daughter of king Pittheus. At parting from her, he showed her a huge mass of rock, under which he had hidden a sword and a pair of sandals; when her child, if a boy, should be able to lift the stone, he was to repair to Athens with the tokens it concealed, and to claim Aegeus as his father.*

The story of Theseus is composed of three main acts, — his journey from Troezen to Athens, his victory over the Minotaur, and the political changes which he was believed to have introduced in Attica. When he set out to claim the throne of Athens, the young hero resolved to signalise his journey by clearing the wild road that skirted the sea of the monsters and savage men who haunted it, and had thus interrupted almost all intercourse between Troezen and Athens. In the neighbourhood of Epidaurus he won the brazen mace with which Periphates had been wont to surprise the unwary passenger. On the Isthmus he inflicted on Sinis the punishment with which he had tortured his victims, whom he used to rend to pieces between two pines; and he celebrated this victory by renewing the Isthmian games. Before leaving that district he also destroyed the wild sow of Crommyon. In the territory of Megara, Sciron, who delighted in thrusting travellers from a rock into the sea, met with a similar fate from his hands, and thus the Scironian road was freed from the dangers and obstacles which had beset it. Thus, struggling and conquering, he forced his way to the banks of the Cephisus, where he was purified from bloodshed by the Phytalids. Recognised by Aegeus, he crushed a conspiracy of his kinsmen, who treated him as an intruder, and then sailed to Crete, to deliver Attica from the thraldom of Minos, king of that island, who, every ninth year, exacted a tribute of Athenian youths and maidens, and doomed them to perish in the jaws of the monster called the Minotaur. With the aid of Ariadne, Minos' daughter, he vanquished the monster, and retraced the mazes of the Labyrinth. But on his way home he abandoned his fair guide on the coast of Naxos, where she was consoled by Dionysus for the loss of her mortal lover. At Delos he left memorials of his presence in sacred and festive rites, which continued ever after to be religiously observed. His arrival at Athens proved fatal to his father Aegeus, who was deceived by the black sail of

* According to other and, perhaps, more genuine legends Theseus was a son of Poseidon, the great divinity of the Ionians.

the victim-ship, which Theseus had forgotten to exchange for the concerted token of victory, and in despair threw himself down from the Cecropian rock. Many cheerful festivals in after times commemorated the return of Theseus, and the happy state of things which was regarded as his work. We might mention a great many other adventures which adorn the legend of Theseus; but passing them over, and reserving the tradition about his political reforms for another chapter, we shall here offer only a few remarks on the legends of which we have just given a sketch.

The account of his journey from Troezen to Athens seems to show that the coasts of the Saronic Gulf were occupied by kindred tribes of the Ionian race; hence Poseidon is called the father of Theseus, the national hero.* His successful struggles on the road are, perhaps, typical of a period when the union of the Ionian tribes of Attica and the opposite coast of Peloponnesus was cemented by the establishment of periodical meetings in honour of the national god, not without opposition and interruption. The same legend seems to indicate also that at that time a change took place in the ruling dynasty at Athens; for both Aegeus and Theseus appear as strangers to the line of Erechtheus, both coming from Megara to take possession of Attica. The only historical fact distinctly suggested by the story of the expedition to Crete, is a temporary connection between that island and Attica; but it is impossible to determine the nature of this connection, or of the tribute said to have been paid by the Athenians. The part assigned to Minos in these transactions, leads us to inquire a little further into the traditions respecting this celebrated personage, who is represented by the general voice of antiquity as having raised Crete to a higher degree of prosperity and power than it ever reached at any subsequent period. He appears in the twofold character of a victorious prince who exercises a salutary dominion over the sea and the neighbouring islands, and of a wise and just lawgiver, who exhibits to the Greeks the first model of a well-ordered state. In the former character he unites all the tribes of Crete under one sceptre, raises a powerful navy, scours the Aegean, subdues the piratical Carians and Leleges, makes himself master of the Cyclades, plants various colonies, undertakes a successful expedition against Megara and Attica, and imposes tribute on his vanquished enemies. He is even said to have carried his arms into Sicily, where his people founded a settlement, which preserved his name. The leading features of this account are attested by the best authorities, and they may, perhaps, not be

* The name of *Theseus* is probably no more than an epithet of the great Ionian deity, Poseidon.

very greatly exaggerated; for the situation of Crete is most favourable to the exercise of influence over Greece, and its insignificance during the historical times is, in reality, more surprising than the transient lustre which falls upon it in the mythical ages. That the Cyclades were subject to Minos, is confirmed by numerous traces; and the general belief of the ancients was, that he founded colonies even in Lemnos and Thrace. But we need not on that account assume that these settlements were the work of one person; for here, as in the case of Heracles and Theseus, that which must have been the result of the efforts of ages, is ascribed in the legend to a single personage. The question, to what race Minos and his people belonged, is a more interesting subject, because, according to a common opinion, they possessed institutions which subsequently became the model of those of Sparta.

Homer calls Minos a son of Zeus, by the daughter of Phoenix, whom all succeeding authors name Europa; but in a genealogy found only in later writers, he is likewise the adopted son of Asterius, a descendant of Dorus, and is thus connected with a colony said to have been led into Crete by Teutamus or Tectamus, son of Dorus, who is stated either to have crossed over from Thessaly, or to have embarked at Malea, after having led his followers by land into Laconia. His son Asterius married Europa, and left his kingdom to her son Minos. This account of his connection with the Dorians, though not expressly mentioned by any very weighty author, is apparently supported by Homer's description of the various tribes inhabiting Crete, and would be entitled to consideration, if it could be shown that Minos left any monuments of his reign which can be ascribed only to a Dorian prince or people. There are indeed many points connected with the religion of the Dorians, especially with the worship of Apollo, which have induced modern writers to look upon Minos as a Dorian, and to conclude that in his days a colony of Dorians was established in Crete. But, in the first place, the origin of all such institutions in Greece, is extremely obscure; and, in the second, there are some indications which point to a different conclusion. The stories of Minos' birth, and of the mythical personages by whom he is surrounded —Europa and Pasiphaë, Ariadne and the Minotaur—transport us to a region wholly foreign to the Dorians and their national god Apollo. Minos is described as a son of Zeus, from whom, and not from Apollo, he is said to have derived his political wisdom. If Dorians existed in Crete, in the days of Homer, what is there to prevent us from supposing that their settlement was comparatively recent? If, then, Minos was not a Dorian, his political institutions can have been but slightly connected with those which afterwards existed in the Dorian states of Crete; and we therefore reour account of the latter for the period when they were most probably first introduced into the island. The Cretan Dorians, finding the fame of Minos, as a powerful king, a wise lawgiver, and a righteous judge, widely spread over their new country, may naturally have been inclined to attach so glorious a name to their own institutions. Moreover, the system of government ascribed to Minos, his powerful navy and foreign conquests, are scarcely compatible with what we know of the Dorians both in the earlier and in the historical times. It therefore seems to us most probable that the maritime greatness of Crete was principally attributable to the Phoenicians, with whom Minos appears to have been much more closely connected than with the Dorians. What we mean, is this: it is not improbable that the age of Minos may represent a period, when the arts introduced by Phoenician settlers had raised one of the Cretan tribes, under an able and enterprising chief, to a temporary pre-eminence over its neighbours, which enabled it to establish a sort of maritime empire. The progress of the Phoenicians in the west also seems to be alluded to by the account of Minos' death in Sicily, whither he had gone in pursuit of Daedalus. The disaster of Minos was believed by the Cretans to have been attended with the complete downfal of Crete's maritime power; and it would seem that it was only after this event that Crete was occupied by a branch of the Hellenic race.

We might here enumerate many other wars and adventures of the heroic age, which were highly celebrated in Greek poetry, such as the quarrel in the royal house of Thebes, which terminated in the destruction of that city by the Argives, and the expulsion of the Cadmeans; and the story of the renowned hunt of the Calydonian boar; the principal agents in which occurrences are not individual heroes, but bands of chiefs leagued together for a common object. But we must confine ourselves to a notice of two celebrated expeditions, which were conducted by confederate chieftains with their followers, and were directed against distant lands; we mean the expedition of the Argonauts, and the siege and capture of Troy.

The Argonautic expedition, as commonly related, seems to be of a thoroughly poetical nature, with little or no historical substance; the adventure is incomprehensible in its design, astonishing in its execution, grounded on a peculiar form of religion, connected with no conceivable cause, and is attended with no sensible effect. The story, reduced to the form in which it is usually told, runs as follows:—In the generation before the Trojan war, Jason, a young Thessalian prince, incurred the jealousy of his kinsman Pelias, king of Iolcos. The latter persuaded the adventurous youth to embark in a maritime expedition, full of difficulty and danger. It was to be directed to a point far beyond the most remote which Greek navigation had hitherto reached, to Colchis, on the eastern corner of the Black Sea, the coasts of which were inhabited by such ferocious barbarians, that it is said to have borne the name of the Inhospitable (Axeinus), before it acquired the opposite appellation of Euxeine (the Hospitable) from the civilisation which was ultimately introduced there by Greek settlers. From the land of the Colchians, Jason was to fetch the golden fleece. Having built a vessel of uncommon size, and manned it with a band of heroes from various parts of Greece, he sailed to Colchis, where he not only succeeded in the main object of the expedition, but carried off Medea, the daughter of the Colchian king Aeetes.

This is the skeleton of the story reduced to what, in an age of faith, might seem to be natural and probable. But it still contains many points which can scarcely be explained or believed. The period to which the undertaking is ascribed, was that of the infancy of navigation, and yet we are told that the adventurers at once went far beyond the boundaries attained in much later times. The story presupposes a knowledge of Colchis, and how could that have been obtained? The object of the undertaking is still more mysterious, and can be explained only by conjectures. Such an explanation was attempted by some of the ancients themselves, who thought that the golden fleece referred to the particles of gold swept down by the mountain torrents of the country, and which the natives detained by fleeces dipped in the streams. But the name *golden* is only a poetical and ornamental epithet of the fleece, and indicates no more than the epithets *white* or *purple*, by which it is sometimes described. The main thing in the story is the *fleece*, and not the circumstance that it was golden. According to a genuine tradition, the fleece was a sacred relic, and its importance arose entirely from its connection with the tragic story of Phrixus, who was rescued from his father's vengeance by a marvellous ram, which transported him over the sea to Colchis. On his arrival there he sacrificed the ram to Zeus, who had favoured his escape; and the fleece was nailed to an oak in a grove of Ares, where it was kept by Aeetes as a sacred treasure or palladium.

The religious practice from which the legend seems to have sprung, was this:—The town of Alos, near the Gulf of Pagasae, in the Thessalian Achaia, was celebrated for the worship of the Laphystian Zeus. The eldest among the descendants of Phrixus was forbidden to enter the council-house at Alos, though Athamas, their ancestor, had built the town. If the head of the family was detected on the forbidden ground, he was led in solemn procession, like an ordinary victim, and sacrificed. Many members of the family were said to have quitted their country to avoid this danger, and to have fallen into the snare on their return after a long absence. The origin assigned to this rite was, that after the escape of Phrixus, the Achaeans had been on the point of sacrificing Athamas himself to appease the anger of the gods; but that he was rescued by the timely arrival of the son of Phrixus, who had returned from Colchis. Hence the curse, unfulfilled, was transmitted for ever to the posterity of Phrixus. It seems to have been from this religious belief of the people among whom the Argonautic legend sprang up, that it derived its peculiar character; and the expedition, as far as the fleece is concerned, appears to have had no connection with piracy, commerce, or discovery. The historical foundation of the story was probably a series of maritime enterprises which may have been the employment of several generations. The Argonauts are Minyans, who were very early given to maritime pursuits; and the form which the tradition assumed, was probably determined by the course of their earliest naval expeditions. These expeditions were certainly not carried so far as stated in the legend, but poetry and the credulity of the Greeks might, in after ages, without difficulty extend the wonderful voyage at pleasure. As to the principal personages of the story, Jason and Medea, they are both ideal or fictitious characters, and Jason is, perhaps, no other than the Samothracian god or hero Jasion (whose name is sometimes written in the same manner, Jason), the protector of mariners. Medea seems to have been only another name for Hera, and to have descended, by a common transition, from the rank of a goddess to that of a heroine, when an epithet had been mistaken for a distinct name. A Corinthian tradition claimed her as properly belonging to Corinth, one of the principal seats of the Minyans, where she was honoured with religious rites until the city was destroyed by the Romans, and the murder of her children was expiated by annual sacrifices to Hera. The Argonautic expedition may also indicate the beginning of an intercourse between the inhabitants of northern Greece and those of the opposite coast of Asia; and in this sense it was, perhaps, not without some reason that the ancients stated that the expedition of the Argonauts gave rise to the celebrated conflict between Europe and Asia, or the Trojan war, which we shall now proceed to notice.

Of all the enterprises of the heroic age of Greece, the Trojan war is the noblest and greatest, and this renown it owes to the immortal poetry which bears the name of Homer. We have already seen* how Sthenelus usurped the kingdom which belonged of right to Heracles. Sthenelus had reserved Mycenae and Tiryns for himself; but had bestowed the neighbouring town of Midea on Atreus and Thyestes, the sons of Pelops and uncles of Eurystheus. On the death of Heracles, Eurystheus pursued his children until they found a place of refuge in Attica. Theseus refused to surrender them, and Eurystheus then invaded Attica in person; but his army was routed, and he himself slain by Hyllus, the eldest son of Heracles. Atreus succeeded to the throne of his nephew, whose children had all perished during his unfortunate expedition. Atreus was followed on the throne by Agamemnon, who now ruled over an ample realm. Heracles had bestowed Laconia on Tyndareus, the father of Helen; and when Agamemnon's brother, Menelaus, had been preferred to all other suitors by this beautiful princess, Tyndareus resigned his dominions to his son-in-law. In the mean while a flourishing state had risen up on the eastern side of the Hellespont. Its capital Troy, or Ilium, had been taken by Heracles with the assistance of Telamon; but had been restored to Priam, the son of its conquered king, Laomedon. Priam reigned in peace and prosperity over a number of little tribes, until his son Paris, or Alexander, attracted to Laconia by the fame of Helen's beauty, abused the hospitality of Menelaus by carrying off his queen in his absence. To avenge this outrage, all the chiefs of Greece combined their forces under the command of Agamemnon, and sailed with a great armament to Troy, which after a siege of ten years they took and razed to the ground, according to the common belief, in the year B.C. 1184.

Such is the brief outline of a story familiar to all. The reality of the siege of Troy has often been questioned, though without sufficient ground, and against some strong evidence; and even if the story is unfounded, it must still have had some historical groundwork. If the legend, as some believe, arose out of the Greek colonies in Asia Minor, it would be difficult to explain its universal reception in Greece itself. The leaders of the earliest of these colonies, indeed, claimed Agamemnon as their ancestor; but if this had suggested the story of his victories in Asia, those very colonies would probably have been made the scene of his glory, and not a neighbouring country. On the other hand, the earliest (Aeolian) colonies seem to be a natural consequence of previous conquests by the Greeks in those parts. We cannot, therefore, avoid admitting the reality of the Trojan war as a general fact, whatever we may think of the details which have been handed down in poetry. What is most unaccountable in the whole

* See p. 33.

narrative, leaving the character of the persons out of the question, is the intercourse between Troy and Sparta implied in it. Helen, according to all appearance, is a merely mythological person; she is classed by Herodotus with Io, Europa, and Medea, and all the particulars of her legend, such as her birth, her relation to the divine twins, Castor and Polydeuces (Pollux), and the religious honours paid to her at Sparta,—point in the same direction. Moreover, Theseus also is said to have carried off Helen, and, according to a third story, the same exploit was achieved by Idas and Lynceus, two Messenian heroes, who answer to the Spartan Dioscuri. These variations of the legend seem to show that her abduction was a theme for poetry originally independent of the Trojan war, but which might easily be associated with that event.

If then we must reject the traditional occasion of the war, we are bound to show its connection with preceding events. We have already observed that the Argonautic expedition was sometimes represented as having given rise to the conflict between Greece and Troy; for, according to some legends, Heracles, one of the Argonauts, rendered a service to the Trojan king Laomedon, on the voyage to Colchis, but was afterwards defrauded of the promised reward, in consequence of which Troy was taken and sacked by the hero. Here, then, we have an event which may have provoked the enmity, or tempted the cupidity, of the Greeks in the next generation, especially if Troy, as the story relates, soon rose again to power and opulence. We may, perhaps, even go so far as to doubt whether the common legend of the Trojan war did not arise out of that of Heracles against Troy; for there is a singular resemblance in the two accounts; and the historical groundwork of the legend may have been a series of attacks made by the Greeks on the coast of Asia, either merely for the sake of plunder, or with a view to permanent settlements.

All the details of the expedition which ended in the fall of Troy, are so uncertain, that it is quite hopeless to form any distinct conception of them; even those which appear to involve no impossibility cannot be considered to be more historical than the most marvellous incidents, for all are alike the products of the poet's imagination. Thus the expedition is said to have consisted of 1200 ships, and 100,000 men, headed by the flower of the Greek heroes; the siege lasted for ten years, and the besiegers were often ready to abandon the enterprise in despair, until in the end they were indebted for victory to an unforeseen favourable turn of affairs. And yet we are told that, one generation before, Heracles achieved the same thing with no more than six ships and a few men. This contrast cannot be explained by any supposed prosperity and power which Troy might have acquired in the interval;

on the other hand, it is credible enough that, whatever were the motives of the expedition, the spirit of adventure may have drawn warriors together from most parts of Greece, among whom the southern and northern Achaeans, under Pelopid and Aeacid princes, took the lead, and that it may thus have deserved the character of a national enterprise. There is no doubt that the expedition accomplished its immediate object: but it is nevertheless clear, that a Trojan state survived for a time the fall of Ilium; for we have it on good authority that Troy was finally destroyed by an invasion of the Phrygians, a Thracian tribe which crossed over from Europe to Asia after the Trojan war.* This statement is confirmed by Homer himself, who introduces Poseidon predicting that the posterity of Aeneas should long continue to reign over the Trojans after the race of Priam should be extinct.

To the conquerors the war is represented as no less disastrous in its consequences than to the vanquished; for the returning heroes found their thrones occupied by usurpers, or their dominions in a state of anarchy. Many did not return at all, but perished on their way homeward.† This calamitous result of a successful enterprise seems to have been an essential feature in the Trojan legends; for Heracles also on his return was persecuted by the wrath of Hera, and driven out of his course by a tempest. It appeared as if the jealousy of the gods had been roused by the greatest achievement of the Achaeans, to afflict and humble them. The question as to the antiquity and original form of the poems which contain the earliest memorials of these events, does not affect the opinions here advanced, and may, therefore, for the present, be left untouched. The poet, if he was a single one, evidently did not allow himself to be fettered by his knowledge of the facts. For aught we know, he may have been a contemporary of Achilles, whom he nevertheless describes as the son of a marine divinity. His poem must have had a popular tradition for its basis, without which it would have been hollow and insipid; but his work was not chiefly valued as the recital of real events, the main object being to exalt the glory of his heroes. But, although in regard to persons and events, we can allow very little weight to the authority of Homer, yet his accounts of the state of society, of institutions, manners, and opinions must, as in all similar kinds of national poetry, be founded on truth, since otherwise they could not have excited any interest in his hearers, who were competent and unbiassed judges in these matters. For the age in which he sang,

* Xanthus in Strab. xiv. p. 680. Comp. xii. p. 572.

† The returns of the heroes formed a distinct circle of epic poetry called [illegible], of which the Odyssey includes only a small part; they were generally full of tragic adventures.

cannot have been parted from that which he described by any wide break in thoughts, feelings, or social relations. He may, perhaps, be supposed to have sometimes transferred to an earlier age, that which was peculiar to his own, and he no doubt still oftener heightened and embellished the objects which he touched; but there is no ground for believing that he anywhere endeavoured artificially to revive an image of obsolete simplicity, or suppressed any superior knowledge or refinement which he and his contemporaries possessed. Hence we must suppose that he gives a true picture of the society of Greece near to his own time, if we make due allowance for the privilege he enjoyed as a poet. With the help of his productions, examined by the light of historical analogy, and compared with other accounts and vestiges, we shall now endeavour to give some idea of the main features of the heroic age, its manners, religion, knowledge, and arts.

Plain of Troy.
(From an original drawing by Sir William Gell, preserved in the British Museum.)

Electra.
(From a painted vase.)

Hero in War Chariot.
(From an ancient painted vase in the possession of Mr. Rogers.)

CHAPTER V.

THE GOVERNMENT, MANNERS, RELIGION, KNOWLEDGE, AND ARTS OF THE GREEKS IN THE HEROIC AGE.

The political condition of the Pelasgians is unknown to us, having been thrown into the shade by the lustre of the heroic age. There are only a few allusions from which we may infer that, in the earliest times which we call Pelasgian, the government was of a patriarchal nature; and in some cases seems to have been in the hands of priests; in others, those of chieftains or kings. In the heroic age, the institutions of which did not owe their origin to legislators, but grew spontaneously out of natural causes, we must not expect to find the same state of things everywhere. How the transition from the Pelasgian to the Hellenic period was made, we have no means of ascertaining; in what relation the warlike and adventurous race of the Hellenes stood to the former inhabitants, and what changes they introduced, are matters only to be conjectured from the social institutions which we find subsisting in the later period. These do not generally present traces of violent revolutions and conquests; yet it is natural to suppose that such events occasionally occurred, and now and then we meet with facts confirming this suspicion.

The distinction between slaves and freemen seems to have obtained generally, though not universally, and in the age described in the Homeric poems, slaves seem to have been used only in the houses of the great; but there is no evidence that the servile condition anywhere owed its origin to an invasion which deprived the natives of their liberty. Slaves were generally persons taken prisoners either in war or by pirates, or they were bought. They were employed in the house and about the person of their master or mistress. Husbandry was carried on by free labourers (θῆτες) who did not disdain to serve the wealthier for hire. A broad distinction, however, was drawn between the common freemen and the chiefs, who formed two distinct classes. The essential quality of persons belonging to the higher order was noble birth, that is, a pedigree connecting their ancestors with the gods themselves, to whom every princely family seems to have traced its origin; but, in addition to this, a legitimate chief was distinguished from ordinary mortals by a robust frame, a lofty stature, a majestic bearing, a sonorous voice, and still more by skill in warlike exercises, patience under hardship, contempt of danger, and love of glorious adventures. Prudence in council, readiness in invention, and fluency of speech were likewise highly valued. The great wealth by which the nobles were distinguished from the rest of the people, furnished them with the means of undertaking their adventures, and was increased by the booty which rewarded a successful expedition.

The kingly form of government appears to have been the only one known in the heroic age, and probably arose from the patriarchal, with and out of the warlike and adventurous character of the period. Where the people were almost always in arms, the office of leader naturally became permanent, though sometimes royal houses may have been founded by wealthy and powerful strangers. Divisions, answering to the Roman *gentes* and the Scottish clans, seem to have existed in every Greek community; and not to be a member of such a community was the mark of an outlaw or vagrant. These clans (γένη) were bound together by certain sacrifices which were probably performed on behalf of the body by the chief of the principal family; and these priestly functions afterwards became one of the important branches of the kingly office. But the relation of these clans to one another, and their political character, lie beyond the reach of history. Obscure, however, as is the origin of regal power, the prerogatives of the sovereigns in the heroic age are tolerably well known. Their principal functions were the command in war, the performance of those sacrifices which did not belong to particular priests, and the administration of justice. From the first of these they must have derived the greatest part of their power. In the division of the spoil their share was usually increased by a present previously selected from the common mass. The sacrifices performed by the kings were those offered to the gods in behalf of the whole people; and their jurisdiction was shared either with a council of assessors or elders, or even with a popular assembly; so that the kings would seem to have occupied only the most distinguished seats in the courts of justice, as well as in the assemblies of the people. The kingly power accordingly was not unlimited; for the sovereign took no measures, and transacted no business in an official capacity, without the assistance and sanction of the chiefs of the people. The kings were the first among their equals, rather than men of a higher order, and many of the nobles, if not all, bore the name of king, and in case of a vacancy of the throne, might aspire to the supreme dignity. But as the kingly power was not accurately determined or circumscribed by custom or law, it must have varied in particular cases according to the personal character of the ruler and other circumstances. One of the principal advantages connected with the dignity of a king, consisted in the facility with which he might enrich himself and his house; he was the possessor of the domain land, which was originally the gift of the people, and seems to have been, not the private property of the person, but attached to the station. Another part of the royal revenue consisted of presents; but it is uncertain whether they were stated and periodical, or merely voluntary and occasional. The administration of justice, however, appears to have always been requited with a present from the parties.

The kingly power appears to have been everywhere hereditary, according to general usage; which is confirmed by the cases in which an aged parent resigns the reins of government to his son, as Odysseus reigned over Ithaca in the lifetime of Laërtes, and Achilles over the kingdom of his father Peleus; but when the legitimate heir did not possess the requisite qualities of a ruler, he might be reduced to a state of dependence on the nobles, or even deprived of his exalted station. Most of the nobles seem to have resided in the town containing the royal palace, though we also find mention of their lonely rural habitations.

In the state of society described in the Homeric poems, the word answering to *law* in the language of the later Greeks, does not occur; nor did laws in our sense of the term exist; for all rights, human and divine, were fixed only by immemorial usage, confirmed and expounded by judicial decisions; but it is clear, that where the king was unable to afford protection and redress, the rich and powerful could not always be restrained, and were checked only by the fear of divine wrath or of public opinion. The state does not appear to have interfered in private quarrels and disputes, unless the parties agreed to submit their cause to a public tribunal. But among a people of quick and strong passions, there would have been an endless succession of bloodshed, had there not existed, by common agreement, a more peaceful mode of atoning for crimes committed against persons. Thus, if a member of a family had been injured or even slain, the offender might be redeemed, or redeem himself, by a stipulated price, and thus appease the vindictive spirit of his victim's kinsmen. A religious feeling also assisted in maintaining this custom, it being believed that bloodshed was loathsome to the gods themselves. Hence a manslayer usually withdrew into a foreign land, and did not return to his country, till he had been purified by some expiatory rites. The person of such an exile even seems to have been looked upon with a kind of reverence, and it was deemed almost sacrilegious to refuse him shelter. Offences against the community were probably of rare occurrence, and it was only in extraordinary cases that they were visited with capital punishment, which in such instances seems to have generally been inflicted by stoning criminals to death, burying them alive, or hurling them down a precipice, — all modes of punishment suggested by the dread entertained by the ancients of polluting their hands with the blood of man.

The mutual dealings of independent states were regulated by principles not more fixed than those which applied to the intercourse of individuals. Consciousness of a distinct national existence, and of certain rights and duties incident to it, showed itself only on particular occasions, and does not seem to have restrained members of one community from attacking those of another, even though there existed no hostility between their respective states. But when two states were in alliance, or on terms of intimate friendship, the case was different. Piracy was everywhere an honourable occupation: and although in some cases restitution was demanded, in the name of the state, for piratical aggressions, yet, when the injured parties were not persons of high rank or station, they were usually left to right themselves as they could. Communication between hostile states was carried on by heralds, whose persons were considered sacred and inviolable.

In the earliest times there existed no national bond of unity among the several tribes and numerous little independent states of which Greece was composed, though there were partial associations, for religious and also for political purposes, among neighbouring states. In the legend of the Trojan war we have the first trace of a national enterprise; and that legend, no doubt, greatly contributed to awaken the feeling of a distinct nationality among the Greeks. The name Hellenes does not occur in the Homeric poems, as a designation of all the Greeks; its place is generally supplied by that of Achaeans.

We shall now proceed to touch on a few of the social relations of the Greeks, in which their national character is most clearly unfolded.

The intercourse between the sexes, though not as free as in modern European society, appears to have been less restricted in the heroic age than in later times. The conduct of the stronger sex towards the weaker displays great truth and simplicity, though it is entirely destitute of the chivalrous devotion which characterises the history of the middle ages, and the influence of which upon modern manners is still visible. Maidens, even of the highest rank, not unfrequently had to discharge various household duties, which in later times were performed by slaves; thus we find them spinning, weaving, embroidering, fetching water, washing, and even attending upon male visitors while bathing and dressing; and these things were no more degrading to them than it was for a prince to tend his father's flocks. A father disposed of his daughter's hand with absolute authority; at the marriage, presents were interchanged by both parties, according to their means; and if a wife was obliged without her fault to return to her father's house, she was entitled to carry her portion back with her. In this age of heroic enterprise, however, wealth, and even noble birth, did not recommend a suitor more powerfully than strength, courage, and skill in manly sports and martial exercises. In many parts of Greece, as among the Romans, the nuptial ceremony was a symbolic representation of a forcible abduction of the bride,—probably an allusion to the fact that, in the earliest times, the suitor had to win his bride by some deed of skill or courage. Many of the female characters delineated in the Homeric poems command our respect and admiration, and must be reckoned among the noblest conceptions of the poet; but if we were to conclude that Nausicaa, Penelope, Arete, or Andromache, is a representative of the average class of women in that age, we should be estimating it too favourably. The numerous stories of the loves of gods, and the adventures of a crowd of heroines, indicate that the later Greeks did not think very highly of female purity in the heroic age; the faithlessness of a wife does not seem to have been an event of rare occurrence, or to have been regarded as an enormous offence. Witness the manner in which Helen is treated by all parties in the Iliad, and still more in the Odyssey.

It was a natural consequence of the unsettled state of society, that every stranger was looked upon as either an enemy or a guest. If he threw himself with confidence on those among whom he came, he was sure to meet with a hospitable reception. No question was asked as to who he was, until he had partaken of the best cheer which the house could furnish; and then the inquiries addressed to him implied friendly curiosity rather than suspicion or distrust. When the stranger came in the character of a suppliant, he commanded still greater respect; Zeus himself was regarded as the protector of all strangers, and of the rights of hospitality; and the gods were believed to visit occasionally the abodes of mortals in the garb of strangers, for the purpose of seeing how the laws of hospitality, which applied to the lowest as well as to the highest classes, were observed. The convivial usages of the Greeks appear in a much more favourable light than those of our ancestors during the middle ages. The wine was always diluted with water; the guests had their places ranged along the walls of the banqueting-room, and a separate table was set before each. The fare, even in the noblest houses, was of the simplest kind; and although after the wants of nature were satisfied, the bowls were replenished with wine, from which libations were made in honour of the gods, yet the glory of the feast was not held to depend on a lengthened carouse. The song and the dance were regarded as its appropriate ornaments, and the presence of the minstrel was almost indispensable at every great entertainment. After the repast, the guests frequently amused themselves with trying their strength in gymnastic exercises, and with the dance. Drinking to excess is hardly ever mentioned.

In their conduct towards inferiors the Greeks appear to have been kind and amiable. This we must infer from the many instances of the noblest friendship subsisting between the heroes and their personal attendants, and also from the kindness with which the aged Laërtes and his wife treated their slaves. Severity towards slaves was never wanton, but seemed rather to imply that their condition still left them a title to a certain degree of respect, which they could forfeit only by their own misconduct. It is necessary for the sake of justice, to bear in mind this kindly disposition of the Greeks, as it must be owned that if their friendship was warm and their hospitality large, their anger was fierce and their enmity ruthless. At the same time they were not vindictive, but were usually willing to accept a pecuniary compensation for any wrong which had been done to them. In war, on the other hand, we find them indulging in the most ferocious cruelties, which seem hardly consistent with what we know of their social conduct in times of peace. In battle, quarter was never given, except with a view to get a large ransom for a prisoner. The armour of the slain was regarded as a valuable part of the spoil, and was always stript off by the conqueror. Even the naked corpse sometimes became the object of an obstinate struggle; if it remained in the power of the enemy, it was deprived of burial and exposed to the vultures and ravenous beasts, and was not unfrequently mutilated.

Usually, however, an armistice was granted to the defeated, for the purpose of enabling them to give an honourable burial to the slain. The fate of a captured city was generally decided in a merciless spirit; all the males capable of bearing arms were put to death; the women and children were dragged away, to be divided among the victors as the most valuable part of the spoil: by this means the members of a family were often torn asunder, and scattered over distant quarters of a foreign land, and thus separated for ever. The temples of the gods, however, sometimes afforded an asylum to the conquered who escaped into them, and were then respected as suppliants.

In regard to religion we have reason to believe that the Greeks of the heroic age were not very different from their descendants. The Greek was formed to sympathise strongly with the outward world: nothing was to him absolutely passive and inert; in all the objects around him he found life, or readily imparted it to them out of the fulness of his own imagination. This was, in fact, the popular mode of thinking and feeling, cherished, no doubt, by the bold forms, abrupt contrasts, and all the natural wonders, of a mountainous and sea-broken land. The teeming earth, the quickening sun, the restless sea, the rushing stream, the irresistible storm — every display of superhuman power which the Greek beheld, roused a distinct sentiment of religious awe. Everywhere he found deities, which, however, may not for a long time have been distinguished by name from the objects in which their presence was manifested. Thus in the Iliad we find Agamemnon calling upon the gods, but naming among the Olympians Zeus only, after whom he invokes the all-seeing and all-hearing sun, the rivers, the earth, and lastly the gods below. In like manner we may suppose the Pelasgians to have worshipped the powers, which, according to the primitive belief, animated the various forms of the visible world. Herodotus attempts to trace the steps by which this simple belief in the divine powers of nature, was transformed into the complicated system of the Greek mythology. He seems to assume two great causes of the change: first, the introduction of foreign divinities and rites; and secondly, the inventive imagination of the Greek poets. His belief on the first point is, that nearly all the names of the Greek gods had been brought into Greece from Egypt; but this supposition, which was formerly adopted without scruple, and was believed in as firmly as the establishment of Egyptian colonies in Greece, has in modern times been the subject of very earnest controversies; and, although it is not to be denied that eastern nations, and even Egypt, present some striking coincidences with the religion and rites of the Greeks, yet the accounts contained in Herodotus and others who followed him, are little more than dreams. As to the second point, Herodotus states that Homer and Hesiod were the authors of the Greek theogony, gave titles to the gods, distinguished their attributes and functions, and described their forms. From this it is evident that he considered those poets to have effected an important change in the religious belief of their countrymen; but this opinion can be regarded as reasonable only on the supposition that Homer and Hesiod were viewed by Herodotus as the representatives of a whole line of poets who were the organs and interpreters of the popular creed, and thus gradually determined its permanent form; for all that we find in those poets, seems to be founded on conceptions of the divine nature which had long been familiar to the people. The religion of the Greeks was, in the main, purely home-sprung; but the mythology which has come down to us, must have had two important phases in its formation. The one was that by which the invisible powers of nature were invested with human forms—the process of personification; the other, that by which the local deities of the several tribes were reconciled and united in one family. Each of these steps must have occupied a very long period; and it is not necessary to suppose that the one began only after the other had ended. The Greek religion, then, may in general be correctly described as a worship of the powers of nature, and most of its deities corresponded either to certain parts of the outward world, or to certain classes of objects comprehended under abstract notions; but it is at the same time clear, that several tribes worshipped tutelary gods of their own, who were neither embodied powers of nature, nor personified abstractions, but represented the general consciousness of dependence on superior beings. Yet the conception of the gods as beings with human forms led to a belief also that they were subject to the same passions and frailties as mortal beings, that they were sensible to pleasure and pain, that they needed the refreshment of ambrosial food, and inhaled with delight the savour from the sacrifices of their worshippers. But with all this, they were believed to punish men for their negligence and offences, both in this world and in the world to come; and, in this respect, religion exercised a salutary moral influence. The idea of retribution, however, was not generally associated with that of a future state. The soul and the body were viewed as distinct, though not wholly dissimilar, substances; the latter had no life without the former; the former, no strength without the latter. The souls of the heroes descended into the realm of Hades (the Invisible), while they themselves, that is, their bodies, became a prey to dogs and birds. The soul could enjoy no rest in the nether world, until the funeral rites had been duly performed: it was regarded as a mere shadow of its former self, and as pursuing only the empty image of its former enjoyments and occupations.

The favour of the gods was believed to be obtained by worship and sacrifices. The simple feeling of dependence on the divine bounty was naturally expressed in the form of an offering, which, however trifling in itself, might be an adequate symbol of the religious sentiment. But in the course of time the notion arose that the efficacy of a sacrifice depended upon its value; and that the feeling which prompted the offering, was not merely to be expressed, but also to be measured by it. Accordingly, the greater the guilt for which a mortal wished to atone, the more sumptuous was the sacrifice offered to the gods; and this naturally led to the belief that, on extraordinary occasions, the divine wrath could be appeased by no oblation less precious than the life of man. Human sacrifices, accordingly, are met with in the legends of the earliest times, and traces of this dreadful practice occur even in the most brilliant period of Greek history.

Besides the temples in which they were worshipped, some gods had territories or domains (κλῆροι) on earth, where they sometimes loved to sojourn; a piece of land assigned to a divinity (τέμενος), was rarely cultivated; but if any portion of it was tilled, its produce seems always to have been applied to some purpose connected with the worship of the deity to whom it belonged. All the sacred functions prescribed by religion, were performed by priests; but we must beware of being misled by this name; for the ordinary worship of the gods, consisting of sacrifices and prayers, and all other domestic religious rites, were celebrated by the father of the family; and in the Homeric poems the heroes and kings perform priestly offices, without being priests in the proper sense, their sacerdotal character being merely incidental to their public station. A priest, strictly speaking, was a person whose functions were connected with the worship of one particular god, and who was attached to a certain temple or locality; such priestly offices were often hereditary in the same family. In some cases the power of divination also was believed to be transmitted from father to son in these priestly families. The offices of elective priests were bestowed sometimes for life, sometimes for a very short term. The priestly office involved no civil exemptions or disabilities, and was not thought to unfit a person for discharging the duties of a senator, a judge, or a warrior; but where the continual residence and presence of a priest were required at a temple, he was in effect excluded from every other employment, and from the ordinary pursuits of his fellow-citizens. The Greek priests never formed one organised body or hierarchy, for which they had neither the means nor the motives; nor are there any traces of a party-spirit or fellow-feeling among them, although there were times when such a feeling might have been called forth by the attacks of philosophy on the popular religion. But every individual priest, as well as every local corporation of priests, had the greatest interest in maintaining their influence and authority. Priestcraft had inducements as effectual, and a field as large, in Greece as elsewhere, and it was not less fertile in profitable devices, such as the invention of legends and other modes of imposture. The qualifications required for the priesthood varied according to circumstances; female ministers of religion were as numerous, perhaps, as those of the other sex: in some cases boys or maidens of a certain age were appointed to the priesthood, in others only persons advanced in years; in some cases they were allowed to marry, in others obliged to live in celibacy. It was no part of a priest's duties to expound theological dogmas, or to deliver moral precepts; nor was his conduct viewed as a model for others, though the gods were supposed to demand clean hands and in some degree a pure heart.

The most important branch of the Greek religion grew out of the belief that, through the divine favour, man might obtain a knowledge of the future, which his natural faculties could not reach. The means by which this knowledge was communicated were very different: sometimes the prophetic power was thought to be conferred upon a certain favoured person or family; sometimes it was attached to a particular locality where a god was believed to be ever present. Such places were termed oracles. All prophetic power emanated from Zeus, of whose will, however, Apollo was considered to be the general interpreter, and hence the latter possessed the greatest number of oracles. The most ancient and renowned of these oracles were that of Zeus at Dodona in Epirus, and that of Apollo at Delphi in Phocis. The shades of the dead also were consulted in some places, but they were seldom resorted to. The interpretation of casual sights and sounds was likewise employed as a means of ascertaining the future; and this superstition was all the more readily believed because it offered ample food for the excited imagination. Every variation from the ordinary tenor of life was regarded as an omen denoting some remarkable event about to happen. The interpretation of innumerable occurrences of this kind afforded, in later times, employment for a large class of soothsayers. Dreams were believed to be sent by Zeus, and the art of interpreting them gave a name to a distinct class of diviners (ὀνειροπόλοι).

The worship of heroes, which was so common in later times, is not mentioned in the Homeric poems. It was an expression of religious veneration for departed excellence, whereby the deceased mortal was exalted above the level of his kind. Some such heroes as Heracles were believed to have been raised into the society of the gods; and the piety of surviving friends and kinsmen displayed itself, at an early period, in costly offerings at the funeral pile. The tomb of such a mortal gradually became the site of an altar or of a temple (ἡρῷον). This reverence and awe for departed greatness were enhanced by the belief that many thousand spirits of heroes were continually walking over the earth, watching the deeds of men, and dispensing weal or woe. These were termed demons, a name which afterwards also comprised a variety of personifications of abstract ideas and relations. The belief in demons, in the sense of spirits of departed heroes, approaches very nearly to that in fairies and goblins, which we meet with in the mythology of other nations.

The character of the Greek religion remained essentially the same at all times, the changes which took place affecting its outward aspect, rather than its real nature. Commerce with foreign regions occasionally introduced new divinities and forms of worship; the progress of wealth and art multiplied and refined religious rites; but the substance and character of every important religious principle and institution is found in the Homeric poems.

These poems also furnish us with a pretty complete view of the state of knowledge and the arts in the heroic age; but we must confine ourselves to selecting a few of the most striking features, which mark the limits of the progress which the Greeks of this period had made in intellectual acquirements, and in their application to the purposes of life.

Their geographical knowledge, so far as we can trace it in the poems of Homer, was almost confined to Greece, the Aegean, and the north western portion of Asia Minor; beyond this circle all is foreign and more or less obscure, in treating of which the poet evidently depended on vague rumours and reports, which he moulded according to his pleasure. His descriptions of distant countries in the east and south, though full of marvellous circumstances, yet always have some truth for their foundation, and are well fitted to excite curiosity in his hearers. The northern and western parts of the world, on the other hand, are wrapped in obscurity, or presented under a forbidding aspect, as approachable only through the midst of perils which made the courage of even the hardiest quail. Homer seems to have known so little about the Black Sea, that he imagined it formed the northern boundary of Greece and Italy, and was connected with the Adriatic, nay, even with the Atlantic Ocean; so that the northern part of the world was occupied by one vast sea. Sicily and the south of Italy appear to have been known to him only from reports, and he accordingly describes them with all the licence of a poet, though his marvellous accounts were, perhaps, suggested by some real features in the nature of the scenes described, as the dangers of the straits dividing Italy and Sicily, and the volcanic islands in the neighbourhood. The part of the earth exposed to the rays of the sun, was considered to be a plane surface, only varied by its heights and hollows, and its form was thought to be determined by that of the visible horizon. This whole orb was girt by the ocean, a deep and broad river, circulating with constant but gentle flux, and separating the world of light and life from the realms of darkness, dreams, and death. All the other rivers, all springs and wells, and the Mediterranean itself, are described as issuing from the ocean stream, which may have been supposed to feed them by subterraneous channels. Within the earth the poet conceives a vast hollow which is a receptacle for departed spirits, and perhaps the proper abode of Hades. Beneath this, and as far below the earth as heaven was above it, lay the still more murky pit of Tartarus, secured by its iron gates and brazen floor; the dungeon reserved by Zeus for his implacable enemies.

In the eastern part the ocean river formed a large lake, out of which the sun rose every morning; and, after having performed his journey across the vault of heaven, he descended into the same river in the west; and the belief probably was, that he floated in a golden bowl along the river to the east, where he found another chariot and fresh steeds ready to receive him and again to transport him across the heavens.* The regions in the extreme east and west are described as shores or islands blessed with a double portion of light and heat, and as teeming with inexhaustible fertility. The people who inhabit these two parts of the world are (as their name, Ethiopians, denotes) of a swarthy complexion, from their neighbourhood to the sun; they are the favourites of the gods, and are sometimes honoured by visits from the celestials. The extreme north likewise was believed to be inhabited by a happy and long-lived race, which was sheltered from the blasts of Boreas by a barrier of mountains. Mount Olympus was regarded as the highest point on the earth; but it is not always carefully distinguished from heaven or the aërial region above it, both being often blended in the poet's mind. The vault of heaven seems to have been considered by him as a solid vault of metal, supported by Atlas, who kept heaven and earth asunder.

Navigation in the heroic age was in its very infancy; even small

* This idea of the golden bowl is not mentioned in Homer. It first occurs in a fragment of Mimnermus, who lived between the seventh and sixth century before Christ; but it may have been a popular notion at a much earlier period.

distances in the Aegean are spoken of with dread, and were avoided as much as possible by coasting. It is stated that the largest ships which sailed against Troy, contained 120 men; but it seems more probable that they did not accommodate more than fifty. These vessels were half-decked boats with a moveable mast; at night they usually put into port, or were hauled up on the beach. Engagements at sea are never mentioned by Homer, though he frequently alludes to piratical excursions. In winter all navigation ceased. Astronomy, as a science, can hardly be said to have existed in the heroic age of Greece: the regular succession of light and darkness, the recurring phases of the moon, and the vicissitudes of the seasons naturally forced themselves upon the attention of every one, and were observed for agricultural and religious purposes, as well as by seamen. The Greeks, from the earliest times down to the age of Solon, divided their year into twelve lunar months; and the defect of the lunar year, as compared with the duration of the annual course of the sun, seems to have been compensated for by the occasional addition of an intercalary month. In the division of the seasons Homer makes no distinction between summer and autumn; and the different parts of the day are named from the civil occupations belonging to them.

Commerce was carried on indeed, but was not held in great esteem; it was deemed more honourable for a person to enrich himself by war and piracy than by the peaceful pursuits of commerce. Homer does not allude to anything like money, and hence we must infer that commerce was carried on by barter. The precious metals are mentioned only as commodities, the value of which was always determined by weight. The Phoenicians appear to have carried on a considerable trade with the Greek ports. In regard to the arts which contribute to the comforts and the refinement of life, it would seem that the opulent lived, not only in rude plenty, but in a high degree of luxury and splendour; their dwellings, furniture, clothing, armour, and other such property, are commonly described as magnificent, costly, and elegant, as to both the materials and the workmanship. We must not, however, suppose that in these descriptions Homer represented what he had actually seen; for he, as a poet, had the inexhaustible stores of his imagination to draw from; a very rude and simple reality might in his mind assume a stately and magnificent appearance. The most distinguished works of art he mentions, are the productions of the divine artist Hephaestus, or importations from the East, especially from Phoenicia. Homer, moreover, being in all probability an Asiatic Greek, may have been familiar with many things which were little known to his European countrymen before the

Trojan war; the arts of Europe were evidently in a state of infancy when compared with the skill and ingenuity of some eastern nations. We need not, however, conclude that in these points the Greeks were altogether dependent upon foreigners. Homer may have highly coloured his pictures of the heroic style of living, but the main features must have been drawn from life; he may have been somewhat too lavish of the precious metals, but copper, iron, steel, and tin were, no doubt, extensively used; and the industry of the Greeks had long been employed upon these materials. The ruins of Mycenae and other ancient cities present us with specimens of architecture which were probably contemporary with the events which the poet describes; they also sufficiently attest that, in general, we may rely on the accuracy with which he represents the character of the heroic age; and they show that Greek buildings, even of that early age, bore the stamp of the national genius. Yet such arts had not then been long familiar to the Greeks, nor were they very commonly practised; hence a skilful artificer, such as a carpenter, was viewed with great admiration and occupied a high rank in society; nay, the heroes themselves did not disdain to be admired for their skill in the crafts of artificers.

Although war was the chief business and delight of the heroic ages, it appears to have been very far from being reduced to any form deserving the name of an art. In the Iliad we hear much of the combats of the chiefs, but little or nothing about the engagements of the armies; the common warriors serve only as figures in the background to fill up the picture; for the contests are invariably decided, either by the interposition of the gods, or by the valour of the heroes, who sometimes put a whole army to flight. The principal chiefs always used chariots or cars, the drawing of which was the only purpose for which horses were employed; the warrior stood in his chariot by the side of his charioteer, and sometimes fought in that position, but he more commonly alighted from it to attack his opponent, and mounted it again for pursuit or flight. No traces occur of the art of besieging towns; if besiegers could not venture to scale the walls, they usually waited for an opportunity of effecting an entrance by surprise or stratagem. The skill of a chief appears to have consisted more in concerting ambuscades and other stratagems and surprises, than in providing against them. The contest before Troy frequently offered opportunities to the surgeon for the practice of his art, which consisted chiefly in extracting arrows, applying herbs or charms to stop the blood and ease the pain of wounds. The principal physicians were sons of Asclepius; Achilles, too, is said to have been instructed in the healing art by Chiron. The south of Thessaly, the territory of Ephyra, and Egypt, were supposed to be the countries particularly favourable to the growth of medicinal herbs. The healing art itself was practised by women as well as by men, but it does not appear to have been in a more advanced condition among the Greeks than among the savage tribes of the American Indians.

It is the more interesting to trace the gradual development of poetry and the fine arts, as in later times they became the highest glory of Greece, and raised her to a position demanding the admiration of all civilised nations. The poems bearing the name of Homer are the most ancient specimens of poetry in Europe; and from them we may collect some hints as to its earlier condition. It was held in the highest honour among the heroes, and the bard was one of those persons who were sent for from very distant parts; his presence was welcome at every feast; and it would seem that a bard was attached to every great family, and treated with almost religious respect. Nay, one might almost infer that poetry and music formed an essential part of a princely education; for both Achilles and Paris were skilled in them. Most of the poetry to which allusion is made in Homer, is, like that which bears his name, of the narrative kind, and its materials are the exploits of renowned men. Another species of poetry which was cultivated at the same period, was of a religious nature, and consisted of hymns intended to soothe the anger of the gods. Music, as in later times, was inseparably connected with poetry, though subservient to it, being employed to prepare the audience and heighten the inspiration of the bard. Dancing also was frequently united with poetry and music, and seems to have been carefully cultivated, in order that the youths of both sexes might, on festive occasions, delight the beholders with their agility in graceful and harmonious movements. The pleasure which the Greeks took in the dance, no doubt greatly contributed to their subsequent excellence in statuary, as it made them familiar with the most beautiful forms and attitudes of the human body.

The Homeric poems hardly enable us to arrive at a distinct notion of the general state of architecture in the age of their author. The temples of the gods and the palaces of the chiefs afforded ample room for the display of architectural skill; though in the latter, strength and convenience were probably more aimed at than beauty or elegance. The temples probably did not materially differ from the princely mansions; they were, in general at least, partially roofed; some contained great treasures which had been presented as offerings, consisting of robes, vessels, and other valuable productions of art, which required safe custody and shelter, and must accordingly have contributed to determine the form of the building. Representations of the human form, though on a small scale, are frequently mentioned by the poet, both in embroideries and in relief; but throughout the Homeric poems there is only one distinct allusion to a statue as a work of human art *; for all the other statues, such as those in the palace of Alcinous, must be regarded as works of the artist-god Hephaestus, and as purely imaginary; they prove, however, that the poet was not a stranger to such objects. Statuary in the most ancient times was applied exclusively to the service of religion; the earliest objects of adoration were not imitative, but symbolical; not idols, but either rude stones, or wooden staffs or beams, bearing no resemblance whatever to the human form. Such symbols were held in high esteem even in the most brilliant period of Grecian history. The transition from the worship of symbols to that of idols is traditionally ascribed to the influence of Egyptian settlers; but it is not improbable that the custom of making rude images for devotional purposes sprang up in Greece itself, during the period of transition from the Pelasgic to the Hellenic age. As religion itself was stationary, admitting fewer changes than any other part of either public or private life, it was thought necessary that the forms of old idols should remain unaltered, so that they might retain their original sanctity in the eyes of the people. Thus it happened that, although in the course of centuries statuary made great progress, there was no improvement in temple statues. These ancient idols appear to have been all clothed, and the drapery and symbolical ornaments naturally occupied the artist's attention more than the features. The earliest statues were made of clay; the first one of bronze was probably much later than the age of Homer. Pictures, in the proper sense of the word, are not mentioned in Homer, though, if we may judge from the descriptions which the poet gives of embroidered works, the art of design must have been known and practised.

The most important of all the arts is that of writing, and it is, therefore, highly interesting to inquire whether the Greeks in the age of Homer were acquainted with it. The names of most of the Greek letters, their order, and the forms which they exhibit in the most ancient monuments, leave no doubt of the truth of the tradition, that the Greek alphabet was derived from Phoenicia. Considerable modifications must of course have taken place to adapt the foreign signs to the native sounds. At what time the Greeks adopted the Phoenician alphabet is a question to which no certain answer can be given. Herodotus connects the event with the settlement of Cadmus at Thebes. The Homeric poems suggest that commerce between Phoenicia and Greece had been established for some generations; but this commerce was a passive one on the

* Hom. *Il.* vi. 303.

part of the Greeks, so that it might have been carried on by them without a knowledge of the art of writing. Still it is possible that they became acquainted with it through their intercourse with the Phoenicians. But let us see what we can learn from the Homeric poems on this subject. The first question is, Does Homer in any way mention or allude to the art of writing? for the fact that later poets speak of written documents in the heroic age, is of no historical value whatever. There is one passage in the Iliad* which can hardly be explained without supposing that it alludes to alphabetical writing; but this only proves that the poet knew of the existence of the art, which is no more than might be naturally conjectured, seeing that intercourse between Greece and Phoenicia had already existed for a long time. But if we consider that, in the whole range of the two great Homeric poems, the art of writing is alluded to only once, and that very obscurely, we must necessarily conclude that, although known, it was yet in its infancy and very little practised. Whether the Homeric poems themselves were originally composed in writing is a question of considerable literary interest and instruction. The early Greeks never doubted that Homer was the author of both the Iliad and the Odyssey; and, although there was much dispute about his birthplace, yet it was commonly believed that he was an Asiatic Greek; and the ancients generally seem to have taken it for granted that his poems were written from the first. Many reasons, however, may be adduced for the contrary opinion; and the difficulty which we experience in conceiving such long poems to have been composed without the aid of writing, had no existence for the ancients, whose memory, unsupported by books, was much stronger and far more tenacious than that of the moderns. Some critics have endeavoured to show that each poem is an aggregate of several poems composed by different authors, and afterwards more or less skilfully put together in the way in which they have come down to us. That both poems are the productions of one mind is not now very generally maintained, and was denied by some even of the ancient critics; but the original unity of each poem is recognised by most persons competent to form an opinion upon the question. It is said that, after these poems had been created by their author, they were perpetuated by the rhapsodists, a class of men who recited parts of them on festive occasions, and transmitted them orally to their descendants, until at last they were fixed by writing. But this, as well as the origin of the Homeric poetry, are questions which we cannot discuss here. It may seem wonderful that the earliest poems are models of perfection in so

* vi. 168, foll.

many respects; but this will cease to surprise us, if we recollect that, although they are the oldest productions with which we are acquainted, they were preceded by others, which were eclipsed and thrown into the shade by the magnificent and sublime compositions which bear the name of Homer.

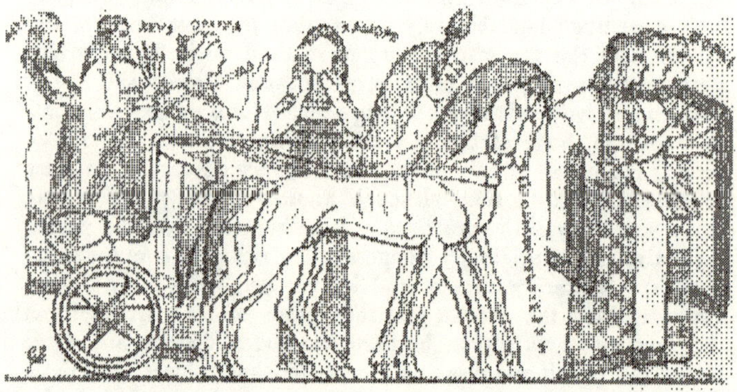

Zeus and Hera in a chariot, attended by Urania, Calliope, and the Horae or Seasons.

(From a painted vase in the Museum at Florence. The name of the artist, Ergotimos, is written in front of the horses, in retrograde characters.)

Daedalus at work.

(From a bas relief in the Louvre.)

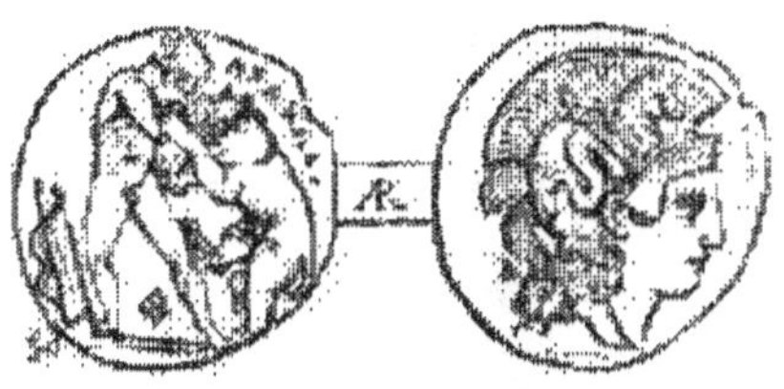

Coin of Heracleia, in Lucania.

CHAPTER VI.

THE RETURN OF THE HERACLEIDS, AND FOUNDATION OF THE DORIC STATES.

After the return of the Greek heroes from Troy, which forms the conclusion of the heroic age, Greece might have continued as before and without experiencing any material influence resulting from the great national expedition. But the heroes who in the war against Troy had been aided and protected by the gods, had in the end incurred their wrath, in consequence of which some perished at sea, and others did not reach their homes till they had encountered many perils during a long course of wanderings. In some instances they are said to have found their thrones occupied by usurpers, or their dominions distracted by revolutions, and in other cases the royal or noble families are stated to have emigrated. But, though it may be justly doubted whether any of the numerous stories connected with the return from Troy have an historical foundation, this much seems certain, that the expedition must have diffused among the Greeks a more general knowledge of the isles and coasts of the Aegean, and left in their minds a lively recollection of the beauty and fertility of the country which was the scene of the protracted contest. This would naturally direct the attention of future emigrants towards the same quarter; and the fact that the first tide of emigration actually set in this direction, may seem to confirm the truth of the story of the Trojan war.

For sixty years after the fall of Troy no great change appears to have taken place in Greece; but about the end of that period there began a long succession of wars and migrations, which finally introduced a new order of things in Greece and the surrounding countries. The detail of these migrations may be altogether of a mythical nature; but the great fact that, about half a century after the Trojan war, there commenced a revolution, arising out of a series of migrations, cannot be doubted. The first of these occurrences is the migration of the Thessalians from Epirus into the plains on the banks of the Peneus, where they began the conquest of the country which finally derived its name from them; before that time it had been called Haemonia. It seems probable that these Thessalians were Pelasgians; for, though they never rose to a degree of civilisation equal to that of the other Greeks, they spoke the same language. Their success in Thessaly was very gradual and slow, as the Achaeans, Perrhaebians, and Magnetes offered a long resistance. The Boeotians, in the territory of Aeolis, were the first to give way before the invaders, in consequence of which a general emigration of the freemen from Aeolis took place; all who remained became the serfs of the conquerors, under the name of penests (πενέσται, labourers). The emigrants took forcible possession of the country afterwards called Boeotia. Here again many were driven from their homes; and being joined by bands of adventurers from Peloponnesus, led by descendants of Agamemnon, they embarked for Asia. These expeditions are called the Aeolian migration, from the race which took the principal part in it. Many families also sought refuge in Attica and Peloponnesus. In Athens they are said to have fortified the Acropolis. The Thracians, the allies of the Boeotians, settled in the neighbourhood of Mount Parnassus, and afterwards entirely disappear from history.

A far more important migration is that of the Dorians, from their seats at the northern foot of Parnassus, to Peloponnesus. It is said to have happened twenty years later than the expulsion of the Boeotians from Thessaly; but how far the Dorian migration was connected with the earlier event is uncertain. The migration itself is historical, but the manner in which it is interwoven with the return of the Heracleids is altogether fabulous. The whole of Peloponnesus changed its character and population, with the exception of the Pelasgians in Arcadia, who retained their political independence, though they were unable to resist the Hellenising influence of the language and manners of their neighbours. The little country known in later times by the name of Doris, probably formed only a part of the district occupied by the Dorians, and as we do not hear of its having been exposed to hostile inroads, it seems probable that those Dorians who migrated southward, were the inhabitants of other parts of Doris. Our authorities, however, unanimously connect the Doric migration with the story about Heracles. After that hero's death, his children, it is said, being persecuted by Eurystheus, took refuge in Attica, whither they were pursued by the tyrant, whom they there defeated and slew; after which they resumed possession of their birthright in Peloponnesus. But not long afterwards a pestilence, in which they recognised the finger of Heaven, drove them again into exile; and

Attica once more afforded them a refuge. Some years later, by the advice of an oracle, they attempted to return to Peloponnesus by the Isthmus of Corinth; but were met by the united forces of the Achaeans, Ionians, and Arcadians. Their leader Hyllus, the eldest son of Heracles, proposed to decide the quarrel by single combat. The proposal was accepted; and as Hyllus fell by the hand of Echemus, king of Tegea, the Heracleids were bound by the terms of the agreement to abandon their enterprise for a hundred years. Nevertheless, attempts continued to be made from time to time by the son and grandson of Hyllus; but with no better fortune, until his great-grandsons, Aristodemus, Temenus, and Cresphontes, were assured that the time alluded to in the oracle for recovering their lawful inheritance had come. They were to enter Peloponnesus, however, not by the Isthmus, but across the mouth of the western gulf. Thus encouraged, and aided by the Dorians, Aetolians, and Locrians, they crossed the straits at Naupactus, vanquished Tisamenus, the son of Orestes, and divided the fairest portions of Peloponnesus among them.

It was the belief of all antiquity, that the Dorians were led into Peloponnesus by princes of Achaean blood; this was the current tradition as early as the age of Hesiod, and was universally received; at Athens poets and orators, down to the latest times, boasted that their ancestors had given protection to the exiled Heracleids. There is nothing incredible in this story; but it may nevertheless be a mere invention made up at a time when the true history was forgotten; a process which occurs so frequently in Greek history, that in this case, where there are sufficient motives to account for such a fabrication, there can be little doubt as to the real origin of the story. That the royal family of Sparta, though of Dorian blood, should claim Heracles for their ancestor, cannot surprise us, if we admit that there was a Dorian, as well as an Achaean and a Theban, Heracles. But leaving the discussion of this doubtful point, we proceed to relate the issue of the expedition. The invaders arrived at Naupactus, where they were perhaps strengthened by the Aetolians, Hyllus being the son of an Aetolian princess, Deianira. According to the common legend, the Heracleids were guided into Peloponnesus by Oxylus, an Aetolian chief and their kinsman, who alleged a title to Elis, and claimed that kingdom as the price of his guidance, which an oracle had declared to be indispensable to the success of the Heracleids. Oxylus became master of Elis by the successful issue of a single combat between one of his Aetolian followers and Degmenus, an Epean chief. Oxylus is said to have used his victory wisely and mildly; to have permitted the ancient inhabitants, after resigning a share of their lands to his Aetolian companions, to retain the remainder as independent owners; and to have treated the deposed king Dius with generosity. A friendly union between the followers of Oxylus and the subdued Epeans may indeed have been established; but the new settlement was, no doubt, the cause of emigrations here as elsewhere. But no other revolution was produced in the peninsula by this conquest, and even the kingdom of Pisa, though attacked by the conquerors, maintained its independence for several centuries.

Oxylus, wishing to divert the attention of the Heracleids from the fertile land which he himself desired to retain, led them through Arcadia into the country subject to the house of Atreus, which was then governed by Tisamenus, the son of Orestes. This prince, with those of the Achaeans who were unwilling to submit to the conquerors, went to the northern coast of Peloponnesus, inhabited by the Ionians, and offered to settle among them, if they would cede to him a fair share of their land; but fear and jealousy prevented the realisation of this scheme. The question was decided by arms, and victory was on the side of the Achaeans. The Ionians, besieged in Helice, at length capitulated, and obtained leave to quit their country, which henceforth received the name of Achaia. The dislodged Ionians sought and found shelter among their kinsmen in Attica; but as the land was too narrow for them, they followed the example of the Aeolians, and being joined by swarms of adventurers of various races, sailed to the coast of Asia Minor. After the death or retreat of Tisamenus, the Heracleids, according to the legend, were busied only with the partition of his kingdom. Aristodemus, as was believed everywhere, except at Sparta, had not entered Peloponnesus, but had been killed at Delphi: his twin sons, Procles and Eurysthenes, claimed, as his successors, an equal share with Temenus and Cresphontes. The dispute which thus arose, was decided in the following manner:— Three lots were cast into an urn filled with water; they were to be of stone, and the first drawn was to give possession of Argos, the second of Lacedaemon, the third of Messenia. Cresphontes, to secure the fairest portion, threw into the vessel a clod of earth, which, being dissolved, remained at the bottom while his competitors were drawing their lots. The descendants of Heracles accordingly took quiet possession of their allotted shares.

The poetical legend, of which the above is only an outline, combines events which probably occupied many generations. The revolution, by which a foreign yoke was imposed upon the brave Achaeans, was certainly not effected by a momentary struggle. The Dorian conquerors, of whom there cannot well have been more than about 20,000, were inferior in numbers to their enemies; the issue of the contest, however, does not appear to have been decided by pitched battles or sieges; but the invaders occupied a strong position near the enemy's city, and wore them out by a series of harassing excursions. That Argos was gradually subdued in this manner is confirmed by the story about the monument of Temenus, which was situated on a hill near the city*, against which his attacks are said to have been directed from the hill in question. At the time of the Trojan war, Messenia was subject to the house of Atreus, and formed a part of the dominions of Menelaus; but after his death it came under the rule of the kings of Pylos. At the period of the Dorian invasion it was governed by Melanthus, a foreigner, towards whom the people were disaffected, so that they offered no resistance to the Dorians. Melanthus withdrew to Attica, where he became the founder of an illustrious family. The Messenian Pylos, however, seems to have remained independent of the Dorians, and to have been ruled for several centuries later, by a branch of the family of Neleus, while the rest of the country submitted to Cresphontes, though probably not as quietly as is commonly related.

According to some accounts, the conquest of Laconia was as easy as that of Messenia. The Achaeans, it is said, were collected at Amyclae, which was besieged and obliged to capitulate; Eurysthenes and Procles divided the country into six districts, over which they set governors with the title of kings, while they themselves fixed their residence at Sparta. During the reign of Eurysthenes, the conquered Achaeans were admitted to an equality of political rights with the Dorians; but his successor Agis deprived them of this privilege, and reduced them to the condition of subjects of the Spartans. All submitted without resistance, except the inhabitants of the town of Helos, who however were compelled to yield, and lost, not only their political independence, but their personal liberty, giving rise and name to the class of serfs called Helots. This story, which no doubt pleased the later Spartans, contains several points which are contradicted by more trustworthy authorities, though they allow us only a glimpse at the real state of affairs. It is in the highest degree probable, that the Dorians became masters of Laconia only gradually and after a long struggle. Amyclae, which in the legend is said to have been given to Philonomus, appears to have formed an independent state for nearly 300 years after the invasion. It was not conquered till towards the close of the ninth century B.C., and had probably never before submitted to Sparta.† Now, what happened at Amyclae, must have happened also in other parts of Laconia, which were more remote from Sparta. Helos, in parti-

* Paus. II. 38. § 1. † Ibid. III. 2. § 6, 9. § 12

cular, seems to have preserved its independence down to the reign of Alcamenes, the son of the conqueror of Amyclae.* It would appear that the Dorians invading Laconia were accompanied by a clan of Cadmeans, who had been driven from Thebes by the Boeotians.† Minyans, also, are said to have been settled for a time at Sparta, until, owing to the haughtiness of the Spartans, they emigrated to the country henceforth called Triphylia, where they formed six independent little states or towns.

The sons of Temenus, the Dorian ruler of Argos, plotted against his life; and Ceisus, the eldest, succeeded him on the throne. Deiphontes, the son-in-law of Temenus, who had entertained hopes of the crown, now drew a part of the Dorians over to his side, and with their aid undertook the conquest of Epidaurus. The invader met with no resistance; the principal families withdrew to Athens, and Epidaurus at once became a Dorian state. At Troezen, Agraeus, the youngest son of Temenus, established himself without opposition from the natives. Phalces, another son of Temenus, subjected Sicyon to the Dorian sway; but shared the government of the place with its lawful king, because the latter traced his origin to Heracles. In the next generation, the Dorian arms were carried against Phlius, by Rhegnidas, a son of Phalces. The town is said to have submitted without a struggle; but a party headed by Hippasus, animated by a spirit of independence, quitted the place and joined the Ionian emigrants who were embarking for Asia Minor.

The more important conquest of Corinth was reserved for another dynasty of Heracleids. When the Dorians were on the point of embarking at Naupactus, a pestilence had broken out; and Hippotes, a descendant of Heracles, being believed to be the cause of the divine wrath, was forced to quit the camp, and accordingly took no part in the conquest of Peloponnesus; but his son Aletes collected a band of Dorian adventurers, and attacked Corinth. How he became master of the place is variously related; but the race of Sisyphus was dethroned, and some of the Aeolian inhabitants of the place are said to have migrated to foreign lands. The fall of Corinth brought the Dorians into conflict with Attica. When the Boeotians had completed their conquest, they began to threaten their southern neighbours, and made inroads upon the Attic border, claiming some towns as belonging to their territory. The Boeotian leader proposed to decide the dispute by a single combat; but as the Athenian king, Thymoetes, shrank from it, Melanthus, the late king of Messenia, came forward to accept the

* Paus. III. 2. § 7.
† Herod. IV. 149. Schol. *ad Pind. Pyth.* V. 101., *Isthm.* VII. 18.

enemy's challenge, and by a stratagem was enabled to slay his opponent. The victor was rewarded with the kingdom of the cowardly Thymoetes, the last in the line of Erechtheus. Melanthus was succeeded by his son Codrus, who was still reigning, though at an advanced age, when some Dorian states, impelled by a general scarcity, the natural consequence of long-protracted wars, united their forces for the invasion of Attica. Aletes was the chief mover of the expedition, in which the Messenians also, actuated by jealousy of the Neleids, joined. The Dorian army encamped under the walls of Athens. The Delphic oracle had promised Aletes success, provided he spared the life of the Athenian king. This oracle had been disclosed to the Athenians, and Codrus resolved to devote himself for his country's welfare. Disguised in a woodman's garb, he went out of the city, and falling in with two Dorians, he killed one with his bill, and was himself killed by the other. When the Athenians sent heralds to claim the body of their king, the Dorian chiefs, deeming the war hopeless, withdrew their forces from Attica.

Such is the story which continued for centuries to warm the patriotism of the Athenians; its details, however, though there is nothing impossible in them, cannot be vouched for. Another, though less credible, tradition is, that the Dorians found their way into the city by night; but being surrounded by their enemies, they took refuge at the altars of the Eumenides, and were spared by the piety of the Athenians.*

About this time Megara was finally separated from Attica, being occupied by a Dorian colony from Corinth, with which it remained long closely connected, or rather was held in subjection by it. Aegina, which had hitherto been the seat of an Aeolian population, was likewise transformed into a Dorian island by a colony from Epidaurus. The most important Dorian colonies were those which, in the third generation after the conquest, were established in the island of Crete. These colonies, though they may not have been the first Dorian settlements in that island, deserve our special attention, because to them the influence which Crete is commonly believed to have exercised on the institutions and destinies of the mother country, may, so far as it really existed, be most justly ascribed. It is only to be regretted that our information about those colonies is so scanty and unsatisfactory. One of them came from Laconia, under the following circumstances:—The Minyans established at Amyclae are said to have revolted against the Dorians, and in consequence to have migrated anew from Laconia to Crete, but accompanied

* Paus. VII. 25. § 2.

by many Spartans. In Crete they made themselves masters of Gortyna or Lyctus, and other cities. The leaders in this expedition are called Pollis and Delphus, or Crataidas. The fact that Sparta was looked upon as the mother city shows, that either the number of Spartan emigrants was considerable, or that the emigration took place with the sanction of Sparta. A second expedition to Crete proceeded from Argos, in consequence of domestic feuds in the family of Temenus. It was conducted by Althaemenes, and consisted chiefly of those Dorian adventurers who, after the failure of their enterprise against Attica, found themselves without a home and without employment. Althaemenes is said to have been invited by the emigrants from Laconia under Pollis to join them; but he determined to pursue the course marked out by an oracle, which commanded him to seek the land of Zeus and the Sun. Rhodes was the land of the Sun, Crete the land of Zeus; and accordingly Althaemenes, while bending his course to Rhodes, left a part of his followers in Crete, where they made considerable conquests, probably on the western side of the island.

The general fact that Dorian colonies were established in Crete cannot be doubted, though the number of Dorians who took part in them must have been very small compared with the extent of the island: but the state in which they found the country enabled them to gain a firm footing and make steady progress; for Crete is said to have been desolated by plague and famine during the period subsequent to the Trojan war, and to have remained in that condition until it was replenished by the race which finally retained possession of it. Nevertheless, the conquest there, as in Peloponnesus, must have been gradual; and a long time must have elapsed before the Dorians spread over the whole island, if no part of it was previously inhabited by a kindred race.

Some authors represent the Spartan institutions as borrowed from those of Crete, while others maintain that the Cretan towns, some of which were colonies of Sparta, derived their political institutions from the mother city: in the accounts of the former kind Minos is described as the original author of those institutions. This belief may have arisen from the ambition of the Dorian settlers, who wished to hallow their own usages by the revered name of Minos; but it may, at the same time, have been erroneous only in extending to the whole system that which was true of no more than a few of its parts, in which vestiges might be preserved of a more ancient polity. It can hardly be believed, however, that the whole social fabric of Crete, which so closely resembled that of Sparta, was already standing in the time of Minos. The Cretan institutions are described as being so similar to those of Sparta, that it will be sufficient here to give a brief outline of the former.

The inhabitants of Crete were divided into three ranks, — slaves, freemen, and an intermediate class, nearly equally removed from the degradation of the one and from the privileges of the other. This class probably consisted chiefly of the old proprietors of the land, who had submitted without a struggle to the invaders. They were called *perioeci* (περίοικοι), a name indicating a rural population dwelling in open towns or villages, in contrast with the citizens who resided in the capital of each district. Their lands were subject to a peculiar tax; but their persons were free and their industry unrestricted. The privileges reserved for the citizens, that is, the members of the superior class, consisted in the power of making legal enactments, the administration of justice, the government of the state, the exclusive use of certain arms, and the exercises in the public schools by which the citizens were trained to use them. The bow was the ordinary weapon of the perioeci, who in all ages supplied the Greek armies with their best archers. They retained most of their ancient usages, and their condition was, on the whole, not very oppressive.

The slaves were probably divided into two classes, namely those who were already in a state of servitude at the time of the conquest, and those of the ancient free inhabitants who were taken with arms in their hands, and who purchased their lives by the sacrifice of their liberty. Besides the lands which were left to their former owners, and those which were occupied by the citizens, each state reserved a domain for itself, which was cultivated by public slaves, who constituted a separate body called *mnoa* (μνῶα, probably connected with δμῶες). Every individual freeman had his own slaves, who tilled his land, and whom he might sell, but not carry out of the country. A third class of slaves, employed for the most menial labours, was purchased from abroad, as is indicated by their name χρυσώνητοι (bought with gold). The Dorian citizen or freeman had no occupation save warlike exercises; he lived upon the toil of his subjects and slaves; he knew no care but the defence of his station, and to secure to himself the enjoyment of its privileges.

The form of government was very nearly the same in all the Dorian colonies in Crete; a circumstance which shows that it everywhere sprang out of the character of the age and of the people, and was not the result of accident or design. The state of things closely resembles that described in the Homeric poems, the only great difference being that the royal dignity seems to have been unknown in any of the Cretan states. The place of kings was occupied by magistrates, who bore the title of cosmos (κόσμος), and were ten in number; the first in rank, the proto-cosmos, gave his name to the year. They were elected by the whole body of citizens from certain privileged families, and held office for only one year, at the end of which those whose conduct seemed worthy of it, might aspire to fill up vacancies in the council or senate (*γερουσία* or *βουλή*). The number of this senate seems to have been limited to thirty; its members were elected by the people from among those who had filled the supreme magistracy, and they retained their office for life. They formed the council of the ten magistrates, and administered the internal affairs of the state.

This brief outline shows that the Cretan constitution was strictly aristocratic, like those of Greece in the heroic ages. The assembly of the people, consisting of the Dorian conquerors and their fellow-adventurers, might be convoked by the magistrates, whenever they had any measures to lay before it; but the individual members of the assembly were not allowed to discuss these measures; they could only accept or reject them as a body; nay, it is even doubtful whether they really did possess the right of rejecting a measure brought before them. The principal duties of the citizen were to be discharged in the field of battle.

The most important feature in the Cretan mode of life is the usage of the syssitia (*συσσίτια*), or public meals, of which all the citizens partook, without distinction of rank or age. The origin of this institution is commonly ascribed to Minos; but its prevalence in all the Dorian colonies of Crete renders it probable that they did not adopt it from the conquered people, but brought it with them from the mother country. In most Cretan cities, the expense of these syssitia was defrayed by the state out of the revenues of the domain-lands, and the tribute paid by their subjects. Each citizen received his share, out of which he paid his contribution to one of the public tables, and provided for the females of his household. These public meals derived their Cretan name from the men (*ἄνδρες*), who partook of them, being called *ἀνδρεῖα* or *ἀνδρία*. There is another regulation peculiar to the Cretans, and characteristic of the friendly intercourse among the Dorian cities of the island: in every town there was a public building for the reception of strangers; and in every banqueting-room two tables were set apart for foreign guests. These syssitia, whatever their origin may have been, answered several important ends; they maintained a strict separation between the ruling and the subject classes; they kept alive in the former the full consciousness of their superior station and their national character; they bound together the citizens by ties of the most endearing intimacy; taught them to look on one another as members of the same family; and gave an efficacy to the power of public opinion, which must have almost superseded the necessity of any penal laws. We may add, that they provided a main part of the education of the young. Till the boys had reached their eighteenth year, they accompanied their fathers to the public board, with the orphans of the deceased. The younger waited at the table. All the young people might thus listen to the conversations of their elders, and were under the eye of an officer appointed by the state to superintend them, and who seems to have watched over their conduct. On other occasions, also, they were early inured to hardship and laborious exercises, and their strength and spirit were tried by frequent combats between rival companies. The intervals between these occupations were filled up with simple lessons in poetry and music, and in later times, in the rudiments of letters. From their eighteenth year, they were placed under stricter rules; they were now divided into troops, headed by some youth of noble family, who was himself placed under the control of an elder person, generally his father, who directed the exercises of the troop in the chase, the course, and the wrestling school. When the youths entered into the society of men, they were compelled by law to choose a bride, who, however, seems to have continued to live with her parents until she was found capable of discharging the duties of a wife and mother. A comparison of these institutions with those which we afterwards find at Sparta, cannot fail to show their common origin, and to convince us that they were devised neither by Minos in Crete, nor by Lycurgus at Sparta, but that in both cases they were the offspring of the characteristics of the Doric nation.

Plain of Sparta.

(From an original sketch by Sir William Gell in the British Museum.)

Cyclopaean Arcade of Tiryns.
(From Sir William Gell's Itinerary of Greece.)

CHAPTER VII.

THE LEGISLATION OF LYCURGUS.

The history of the Dorian states of Peloponnesus during the first centuries after the conquest, is extremely obscure; and the little information we possess, is so mixed up with fable, that it is almost impossible to discern truth from falsehood. This much, however, is certain, that Sparta was from the beginning the chief Dorian state in the peninsula, and that there the national character of the Dorian race assumed the most permanent forms in all the relations of public and private life. These circumstances, and the conquest of Messenia, ultimately raised Sparta to the supremacy not only of Peloponnesus, but of the whole of Greece. The gradual development of Spartan power and influence, and of the social and political institutions by which that power was maintained, sheds, down to a certain time, a lustre over the history of Sparta, which has dazzled both ancient and modern historians, and filled them with an admiration which, in many instances, is not very well deserved. The chief feature in the Spartan constitution was a rigid conservatism, which, clinging to ancient forms, even when their soul had departed, could not avoid frequently coming in conflict with existing realities, made the people hypocritical, and gradually undermined the foundations of the political and social fabric.

It has been usual, both in ancient and in modern times, to consider the Spartan constitution as the work of a single man, Lycurgus, who is generally supposed to have had the merit, if not of inventing, at least of introducing and establishing it among his countrymen. According to an opposite view, it was not an artificial fabric, but the spontaneous growth of the national character of the Dorians, which required at the utmost only a few slight touches from the hand of an individual; and in this view of the subject, the agency of Lycurgus shrinks into so narrow a compass, that even his personal existence becomes a question of much doubt and of little moment. Our safest course will probably be to steer between these two extreme opinions, and to admit that there is some, but not the whole, truth on each side.

The discrepancies in the statements respecting the time at which Lycurgus lived are so great, that while some make him a contemporary of the Heracleids and the Doric invasion of Peloponnesus (about B. C. 1104), others place him only 108 years before the beginning of the Olympiads, that is, B. C. 884, a date which has been adopted by most modern writers. Similar disagreement prevails in the accounts of his parentage; but all these differences afford no satisfactory reason for doubting the historical existence of a Spartan lawgiver. We have already seen that, after the death of Aristodemus, the throne of Sparta was shared by his two sons, Eurysthenes and Procles, in whose line the kingdom remained hereditary. The royal families of Sparta, however, did not derive their distinguishing appellations from these twin-kings; the elder house was called the Agids, from Agis, a son of Eurysthenes; and the younger, Eurypontids, from Eurypon, a grandson of Procles. Agis was followed by Echestratus and Labotas; and according to some, it was during the minority of the latter, that Lycurgus, as his guardian, employed the power thus placed in his hands to establish his institutions.* This tradition, however, does not agree with the received chronology, nor with another better authenticated statement that Lycurgus belonged to the family of the Eurypontids; for he was commonly believed to have been a son of Eunomus, a grandson of Eurypon. Eunomus being killed in a fray, was succeeded by his eldest son Polydectes. As the latter died childless, Lycurgus was apparently entitled to the crown; but soon afterwards his brother's widow gave birth to a son, and Lycurgus, who had directed that the child

* Others call Lycurgus' ward Eunomus.—Dionys. Hal. II. 49.

should be brought to him the moment it was born, at once proclaimed it king of Sparta, and called it Charilaus, that is, the joy of the people, as its birth was hailed with universal delight. Hereupon Lycurgus is said to have left his country, from fear of being plotted against by the young king's mother, whose proposal to give him her hand and to kill the child he had skilfully evaded. Thus the future lawgiver spent the best part of his life in voluntary exile, notwithstanding the repeated invitations of his countrymen to return. But he employed his time, it is said, in maturing a plan for remedying the evils under which Sparta had long laboured, by a fundamental change in its constitution and laws. With this view he visited many foreign lands, observed their institutions and manners, and conversed with their sages. Crete and the laws of Minos are said to have been studied with particular care; the Egyptians also claimed him as their disciple, and the later Spartans even fabled that he had sat at the feet of the wise Brahmins of India. On his return to his country, he found the disorders of the state worse than they had been before, and the need of a reform more generally felt. Having strengthened himself by an oracle of the Delphic god, who declared his wisdom to be above that of ordinary mortals, and having secured the aid of a large body of the leading men, who were ready to support him in all his undertakings, he successively procured the enactment of a series of solemn ordinances or compacts (ῥῆτραι), by which the civil and military constitution of the state, the distribution of property, the education of the citizens, the rules of their daily intercourse, and of their domestic life, were to be fixed on a hallowed and immutable basis. He carried his measures against violent opposition, and finally triumphed over all obstacles, living to see his great idea developed in all its beauty. His last act was to sacrifice himself to secure the perpetuity of his work. He set out on a journey to Delphi, having previously bound his countrymen by a solemn oath to make no change in his laws before his return. From this expedition he never returned; but he transmitted to the Spartans an oracle which declared that Sparta should flourish as long as she adhered to his laws. The place and manner of his death are veiled in an obscurity befitting the character of the hero: Delphi, Crete, and Elis, claimed his tomb, and the Spartans, down to the latest times, honoured him with a temple and yearly sacrifices as a god.

Such are the outlines of the story of the most renowned lawgiver of antiquity; a renown which he would certainly deserve if he had devised the constitution which is ascribed to him, or if he had collected the materials for it during his travels. But such a belief cannot be maintained, for there is no doubt that every important part of the institutions ascribed to him, was in existence long before his birth. This was the case especially with those regulations which were common to Crete and Sparta: these were the property and characteristics of the Doric race, and are found with more or less modification in all parts of Greece occupied by the Dorians. What then becomes of Lycurgus on this view of the subject? If the institutions bearing his name are not the work of a single man, there scarcely remains room for the intervention of Lycurgus, and this was perhaps the reason why one Greek author*, passing over Lycurgus altogether, ascribed the Spartan institutions to the founders of the state, Eurysthenes and Procles. But the concurrent testimony of all other writers prevents us from concluding that Lycurgus was only an imaginary or symbolical person. One fact seems to be supported by all accounts, however discrepant they may otherwise be, namely, that by him Sparta was delivered from the evils of anarchy or misrule, and that from this date she began a long period of tranquillity and order; but what was the nature of these evils, or the precise aim of his remedies, is nowhere distinctly stated. Our authorities do not agree in their descriptions of the condition of Sparta which Lycurgus is said to have so successfully remedied; but a reform of some kind must have been effected by him, and this reform must have determined, not merely the relations of the Dorians among themselves, or to their kings, but also that in which they stood to their subjects, the provincials of Laconia. This supposition is supported by the tradition that the legislator extended his agrarian regulations over the whole country. We have already intimated that the conquest of Laconia by the Dorians proceeded very gradually, and it seems to have been reserved for Lycurgus finally to settle the relative position of the several classes of its inhabitants. The difficulty of this task will appear to have been very great, if we recollect that besides having to deal with the conquered Achaeans, the Dorians had also to satisfy the claims of those foreigners who had aided them in their enterprise, and who perhaps demanded equal political rights. The legends of Eurypon, Eunomus, and Charilaus seem to support the belief that one of the royal houses favoured those claims. The inequality of property said to have existed among the Dorians, may have been the natural result of the gradual conquest of the country, of encroachment and usurpation, some of the leading men availing themselves of the successive subjugation of Achaean towns for the purpose of enriching themselves at the expense of the ancient proprietors, and to the exclusion of their less fortunate brethren.

* Hellanicus in Strabo, viii. p 866.

If these suppositions are correct, it will not be difficult to understand the double aspect which the legislation of Lycurgus presents. His objects must have been to maintain the sovereignty of Sparta over the rest of Laconia, and to unite the Spartans among themselves by the closest ties. It seems that all that it was necessary for him to do was to lead Sparta back into the ancient track, from which she appears to have been drawn partially aside; to induce his fellow-citizens to resume the habits of their forefathers, to sacrifice all artificial distinctions, and to live together as brothers in arms, under the rigid but equal discipline of a camp. To effect this, it was requisite that that which until then had been only an undefined usage, should henceforth assume the character of strict law, solemnly sanctioned and consecrated by religion. In this view of the matter, which we give as a mere hypothesis, Lycurgus loses a portion of the glory commonly attached to his name; but he still retains the honour of having judiciously and successfully employed the simplest and most efficacious means which the circumstances of the case afforded, for the attainment of a great and arduous object. The occasion, then, which called forth his legislation, was, in all probability, the danger which threatened the Spartan Dorians, while divided among themselves, of losing the privileges which raised them above their subjects, the common freemen of Laconia; so that the basis of all his regulations was a new distribution of property, to remove the causes of discord, and to facilitate the reform of other abuses. This was accompanied by an exact determination of political rights, and by regulations to bind the higher classes more firmly together.

According to Plutarch, Lycurgus divided the whole of Laconia into 39,000 parcels, of which 9000 were assigned to as many Spartan families, and 30,000 to their free subjects. In this account, all the shares are supposed to be equal, but such a division would have been impracticable, owing to the nature of the ground, not to mention that all Laconia was not subject to Sparta in the days of Lycurgus. Another account stated, that he assigned only 6000 lots to the Spartans, and that 3000 more were added at the end of the first Messenian war; while a third asserts that Lycurgus assigned only 4000, and that this number was afterwards doubled. The last of these statements seems, for several reasons, the most probable; for it is not likely that the number of free Spartan families was much greater than 4000. It is probable also that the lots assigned to the Laconians did not amount to more than 15,000. There is reason, moreover, for supposing that the shares were not all of equal extent or value; Aristotle * expressly

* *Polit.* II. 6.

states that the greater part of Laconia belonged to the Spartans, and their portion no doubt contained the most fertile and valuable lands. And this, indeed, they required for the maintenance of their families and numerous slaves. The whole of the country, however, was not in private hands; the state remained in possession of a considerable domain, while another part was reserved for the service of the numerous temples. It is uncertain how far, in making these agrarian regulations, Lycurgus was obliged actually to undertake a new division of property, and whether in many places he might not retain the ancient land marks which had been established by the conquerors immediately after their occupation of the country.

The inhabitants of Laconia must be divided into three classes: the Dorians of Sparta; their serfs, the Helots; and the subject people of the provincial districts, that is, the Laconians. The last were a mixed race, consisting partly of the conquered Achaeans, partly of strangers who had accompanied the Dorians during their invasion, or had been invited by them to supply the place of the old inhabitants; some of them may have been Dorians, but their number must have been very small. Sparta's policy towards these subjects was to weaken them by dispersing them over a great many small townships, the number of which is said to have amounted to one hundred. They were always viewed with peculiar jealousy by the ruling city, and were not permitted to attain any high degree of strength or opulence. The provincial land was tributary to the state, and its occupants were subjects, sharing in none of the political privileges of the Spartans; yet they bore the heaviest share of the public burdens, and had to fight the battles, the principal object of which was to gratify the pride and ambition of the Spartans. Beyond this, they had not much reason to complain; and, on the whole, they may have seen little ground for envying the Spartans themselves. Their political dependence was compensated by their exemption from many irksome restraints to which the ruling class was forced to submit. They enjoyed undivided possession of the trade and manufactures of the country. It is true, the Spartan constitution being adverse to luxuries of every kind, did not allow much scope to artificers; but the public buildings and the festivals of the gods must have furnished ample employment. The higher as well as the lower arts, which were looked upon as alike degrading to a Spartan, were left to the provincials, many of whom distinguished themselves in the annals of Grecian art.

Very different was the condition of the Helots *; they were

* Their name was believed by some to be derived from Helos (Ἕλος), a town in the south of Laconia, which held out resolutely and for a long time

persons who had lost their personal liberty, and were in all probability the descendants of those Achaeans, who, in consequence of their obstinate resistance to the Dorians, were reduced by them to slavery. Their lot was the most wretched and degrading kind of servitude. They were always viewed with suspicion by their masters, as enemies who only waited for an opportunity to revolt; they were accordingly placed under the inspection of a vigilant police; and it cannot be denied that atrocious violence was sometimes used to reduce their strength or to break their spirit. They were bound to the soil, and could not be torn from it, or sold into another country; a regulation which must have made their lot, hard as it was, bearable in comparison with that of the slaves in other parts of Greece, who might be sold or dragged from their homes at the pleasure of their masters. Some were employed in public works; others in domestic service; and by zeal and industry they might obtain their freedom. Their compulsory attendance in the camp, and their share in the dangers of war, were sweetened by the opportunities of enriching themselves with booty. But in all other respects, the treatment of these slaves seems to have been adopted with a view to render the distinction between the freemen and the Helots as conspicuous and as deeply felt by each party as possible. The members of the ruling class were held to be profaned by the touch of the unfortunate outcasts; the latter are said to have sometimes been forced to make themselves drunk, that in this state they might be exposed to the derision and insults of their young lords, as a practical lesson of sobriety. This and similar stories may be much exaggerated; but there can be no doubt that the account of the famous *Cryptia* is, in the main, correct. It consisted in this: a commission was given every year to a select number of young Spartans to range the country in certain directions, secretly and armed with daggers, for the purpose of assassinating those Helots, wherever they might be found, who by eminent qualities of body or mind had excited the jealousy or fear of the government. That no scruples of justice or humanity influenced the Spartans in their conduct towards the Helots is but too evident from that deed of blood over which Thucydides draws a veil of mystery, which only serves to heighten its horror. On one occasion, he says, when the weakness of Sparta gave reason to dread an insurrection of the Helots, all those whose past services seemed to entitle them to claim their emancipation, were publicly invited to come forward and receive their reward. The bravest and most deserving presented themselves, and 2000 were selected as the worthiest. They joyfully crowned them-

against the Dorian conquerors (see p. 67.); it is more probably, however, connected with αἱρεῖν, ἑλεῖν, and signifies men taken in war.

selves, and went round the temples to offer their thanks to the gods; they were then secretly despatched, so that the historian could not learn the exact manner in which the horrible crime was committed. Sometimes, however, the government restored Helots to freedom; but it would seem that there were several degrees between bondage and the freedom of a Spartan citizen. The treatment of Helots, moreover, seems to have been different at different periods; and there can be little doubt that, in later times, the Spartans were more cruel to their slaves than in the earlier ages.

The servitude of the Helots was the basis on which the existence of the Spartans, as a body, rested; for the districts cultivated by the slaves, and their services in the field and in the city, afforded the ruling class that leisure which was the essential condition of all the Spartan institutions: the Helot had to work and toil, while the fruits of his labours were enjoyed by the Spartan, and used by him in the service of the commonwealth. Among themselves the Spartans were all equal, and formed a class which we may term noble. In later times, indeed, we find a disparity of rank among them, which it is difficult to trace to its origin; for it is uncertain how far the ancient division of the ruling class into tribes implied any distinction of rank or privileges. Wherever the Doric race was established, we find them divided into three tribes, just as the Ionians were always divided into four. Thus three Dorian tribes are mentioned, even at the time of the conquest. The tribe of the Hylleans (from Hyllus) to which the royal families belonged, may have had some precedence in dignity over the tribes of the Dymanes and Pamphylians. Besides this political division into three tribes, there appears to have been a division into four local tribes, probably according to the villages or hamlets of which the capital was composed. As Sparta itself is not mentioned among these four, it perhaps constituted the fifth tribe or region. The next subdivision of the tribes was that into thirty obae (ὠβαί), villages or districts, though it is uncertain whether these obae were a subdivision of the three political, or of the five local tribes. The fact that all free Spartans, with the exception of the two kings, had equal rights and privileges, constitutes Sparta itself a democracy, with two hereditary magistrates at its head; but in its relation to the subject towns and country it was a rigid aristocracy.

At Sparta, as in all the ancient republics, the sovereign power resided in the assembly of the people, where a descendant of Heracles had no advantage over a common Dorian.* According

* In later times we find two assemblies, a greater and a lesser.

to a regulation ascribed to Lycurgus, though it was no doubt an ancient custom, the assemblies were held periodically in a field near the city. The magistrates who convened the people, had the right of proposing measures, and the people might either adopt or reject them; but no one, except persons in office, was allowed to express an opinion, or propose an amendment, though the latter right was for a time assumed by the people, until it was formally abolished. The subjects brought before the assembly must have been few; its business was probably confined to the election of magistrates and priests, to questions of war and peace, to imposts, treaties, and the like. Other subjects must have come before the people very rarely.

As it cannot be doubted that assemblies of the people had been held at Sparta long before the time of Lycurgus, so there is the strongest reason to believe, that there, as in all the ancient republics, a council of elders, or senate (*γερουσία*), had existed from time immemorial, and that in regard to this council, as to the assembly of the people, Lycurgus only regulated and defined more accurately that which had long been customary. The Spartan senate consisted of thirty members, corresponding to the thirty obae, two of the obae being represented by the two kings, whose twenty-eight colleagues were elected by the people, without regard to any qualification except age and personal merit. The age, before which no one could aspire to obtain a seat in the senate, was sixty years; and the senators held their office for life, no provision being made to supply their places even when they were in a state of decrepitude or dotage. They were not subject to any regular responsibility, but were liable to punishment if convicted of misconduct. They had to prepare the measures which were to be laid before the assembly of the people; and exercised a criminal jurisdiction, in which, without being confined by any written laws, they had power over the lives of their fellow-citizens. The exact limits of the power of the senate in the days of Lycurgus cannot be ascertained; but it must have been more extensive than at a later period, when part of the functions of the senate were assumed by the ephors, a magistracy which reduced the influence of both the senate and the kings to comparative insignificance.

The twenty-eight senators were the colleagues of the kings. The royal dignity of Sparta is the more remarkable, because it continued to exist at a time when royalty had been abolished in all other parts of Greece, and because, though resembling the kingly dignity in the heroic ages, its power was more tempered and restrained. Most of these restrictions, however, seem to have been the consequences of the growing powers of the ephors, and in the time of Lycurgus things may have been very different. The origin of the institution of two kings was ascribed in the Spartan tradition to the accidental circumstance of Aristodemus having left twin sons; but design had probably as great a share in this arrangement as accident, for diarchies appear to have been rather common during the latter period of the heroic ages; and the two kings at Sparta, like the two consuls at Rome, may have been instituted in order that the one might be a check upon the other. Their power can never have been very great. In the senate the voice of a king was of no more weight than that of any other senator. They had some kind of jurisdiction, which was afterwards confined to certain questions of inheritance and legal forms, connected with the patriarchal character of the kings. As in most ancient states, they also were the high priests of the nation, both being priests of Zeus. But the most important of all their prerogatives was the command of the armies, whence the royal majesty was seen in its greatest lustre in times of war. The people, indeed, had the power of decreeing war and peace; but the kings seem originally to have had the uncontrolled direction of all military operations, only assisted by a council of war. It was long before any inconvenience was felt to arise from their taking the field together and sharing the supreme command between them. The honours attached to the royal dignity, however, were greater than its powers, and the former suffered little diminution even after the latter had been considerably reduced. They were revered, not only as the chief magistrates, but as connected with the gods by their descent. They were not distinguished from their subjects by pomp and ceremonies, or by their dress and mode of living; but ample provision was made for the maintenance of their household, and for a species of hospitality which they exercised rather in their character of priests than as kings. Besides their demesnes in various districts of the country, they received certain payments in kind, which enabled them to offer rich sacrifices to the gods, and to entertain their friends. At every public sacrifice the kings were the most honoured guests; they occupied the foremost place in every assembly, and all rose at their approach. In the camp they were guarded by a band of a hundred men, and no officer was allowed to enter on any undertaking without their express command. Both the accession and the decease of a king were celebrated with solemn rites and observances, some of which resemble Oriental rather than Hellenic customs.

Little is known of the functions of the inferior magistrates, the most important of whom were the ephors, whose name and office also occur in other Doric states, and were therefore probably more ancient than Lycurgus, though some referred their origin to him, and others even to a later period. Their number, five, was perhaps connected with the five local tribes or quarters of Sparta. They were elected annually, and from the first exercised superintendence and jurisdiction over the civil affairs of the Spartans. In the institutions of Lycurgus their power seems to have remained what it originally was; their political importance, at all events, belongs to a later period, and arose out of the peculiar circumstances of the times, which we shall have to relate hereafter.

In the institutions hitherto mentioned, Lycurgus probably did no more than modify and correct that which had existed among the Dorians from time immemorial; but there can be no doubt that he added much that was new, though it would be difficult to draw a line between the two kinds of institutions. The principle which pervaded the whole Spartan constitution — that a citizen was born and lived only for the state, that his substance, time, strength, faculties, and affections were to be dedicated to its service, and that its welfare and glory should be his happiness and honour — was certainly not introduced by Lycurgus; it was the necessary result of circumstances by which a handful of men were placed in a country of which they occupied only a single point, surrounded by enemies far more numerous than themselves, over whom they were nevertheless determined to rule as masters. It is probable, however, that Lycurgus may have been the first really to comprehend this position of his countrymen, and to adopt it as a principle of legislation; and that thus he made the Spartans conscious of what they had before followed by a kind of instinct.

The allotment of landed property assigned to every Spartan, was an indivisible and inalienable patrimony which descended to the eldest son, and, in default of a male heir, apparently to the eldest daughter. This fixed number of allotments rendered it necessary to prevent the increase of the heads of families; but how this was effected is altogether unknown. Notwithstanding the penalties inflicted on celibacy, and the rewards offered to fathers of numerous families, we find the number of Spartans continually decreasing, so that the stock of property always remained sufficient for the community, and only required to be regulated from time to time, so as to prevent excessive wealth on the one hand, and extreme poverty on the other.

The restraint put upon every kind of profitable industry, obliged the Spartan to depend entirely upon the produce of his land and of the chase, so that he needed little money for the support of his household. Hence, when money had long been coined in the other parts of Greece, the want of it was not felt by the Spartans in the affairs of ordinary life. The precious metals were regarded as dangerous, and the possession of them was forbidden. Iron, the native produce of Laconia, at first in little bars, afterwards in a more convenient form, continued, down to the latest times, to be the only legal currency at Sparta.* This restriction, which has often been ascribed to Lycurgus, must have been introduced at a later time, as the coinage of silver money appears to have been unknown to the Greeks for more than a century after him. Gold was altogether out of the question, as there was extremely little of it in Greece down to the Persian wars. It must, however, be observed, that the prohibition of the precious metals applied only to the Spartans, for the provincials were not debarred from commerce, nor can such a restriction have affected the state itself. This regulation must certainly have contributed to preserve the simplicity of the ancient manners; but it was unable to check the tendency of human nature to hanker after everything which is forbidden. Hence, although outward forms were scrupulously observed, it is notorious that in no other Greek state were men so avaricious as at Sparta; and money, for which a Spartan had scarcely any use, became to him an almost irresistible bait.

The character of the Spartan system is nowhere more conspicuous than in its mode of determining the relations of the sexes. The freedom which women enjoyed, and the deference paid to them at Sparta, while in other parts of Greece they were confined by strict regulations, were remnants of the ancient customs described in the Homeric poems. The education of young women was conducted with a view, not so much to the discharge of domestic and household duties, as to the citizens they were to give to the state. They were to be the mothers of a robust race, and hence were subjected to the same athletic exercises as the harder sex. Notwithstanding the freedom enjoyed by women, and their exposure in their exercises in a manner which would shock the feelings of a modern, we do not find that in the sexual relations the Spartans were less pure than any other ancient or modern people. The bride was considered as a prize to be gained by courage and address, and was always supposed to be carried off from the parental roof by force or stratagem. After marriage, the women appeared much less in public than before; but, although they were not allowed to enjoy much of the society of their husbands, they were treated with a respect, and exercised an influence which to the rest of Greece seemed extravagant and pernicious. In the latter period of Spartan history, they alone among the Greek women show a dignity of character which renders them worthy rivals of the noblest of the Roman matrons.

* Some authors relate that leather was applied to the same use. Seneca, *De Benef.* v. 14.

From his birth every Spartan belonged to the state, which decided whether he was likely to prove a useful member of the community, and extinguished the life of the sickly or deformed infant, which was exposed in a glen of mount Taygetus. Up to the age of seven, a boy was left to the care of his natural guardians, though not without some control to prevent mischievous parental indulgence. At the end of his seventh year, he began a long course of public discipline, which grew more and more severe as the boy approached manhood. Though the elders exercised a more or less direct influence over him, his training was under the special superintendence of an officer (παιδονόμος) selected from the men of most approved worth. He divided the boys into classes, which were commanded by the most distinguished among them. All offences were rigorously punished. The whole system of education aimed at nothing beyond training men who were to live in the midst of difficulty and danger, and who could be safe themselves only while they held rule over others. The citizen was to be equally ready to command and to obey; and this system, narrow as it was, was carried to such perfection, that it is impossible not to admire it. A young Spartan might not be able to read or write, nor be possessed of any of those qualifications which we deem essential to the character of a man; yet he could run, leap, wrestle, hurl the disc or the javelin, and wield every other weapon with vigour, agility, and grace. But above all things, he was distinguished for the firmness and perseverance with which he endured hardships and sufferings; for from his infancy his life was one continued trial of patience. One test of this passive fortitude, the διαμαστίγωσις, was particularly celebrated among the ancients. The origin of this is explained as follows: from the earliest times human sacrifices had been offered in Laconia to Artemis, whose image Orestes was believed to have brought from Scythia. These bloody rites, it is said, were abolished by Lycurgus, who substituted for them a contest little less ferocious, in which the most generous youths, standing on the altar, presented themselves to the lash, and were sometimes seen to expire under it without a groan. This and similar usages, such as the cryptia, prepared the Spartan youths for all the hardships of a military life.

But, although bred in this manner, the Spartan warrior was not a stranger to music and poetry. He was taught to sing and to play on the flute or lyre; but the strains to which his voice was formed, were either sacred hymns or breathed a martial spirit; and it was because they cherished such sentiments that the Homeric poems, if not introduced by Lycurgus, became popular among the Spartans at an early period. For the same reason Tyrtaeus was held in high honour, while Archilochus was banished because he had not been ashamed to record his own flight from the field of battle. The mental training of boys consisted chiefly in cultivating a moral taste and imparting to them presence of mind and promptness of decision; and hence the Spartans became proverbial for ready, pointed, and sententious brevity in their ordinary conversation. Modesty, obedience, and reverence for age and rank were inculcated more by example than by precept, and upon these qualities above all others the stability of the commonwealth reposed; since that respect for the laws of his country, which rendered the Spartan averse to innovation, was little more than another form of the reverence and awe with which in earlier years he had regarded the magistrates and the aged. During the interval between the age of twenty and thirty, the Spartan was not yet permitted to appear in the public assembly, and seems to have been chiefly employed in military service in the camp or on the frontier. When he had attained the age of full maturity, he was a soldier in time of war, and in time of peace enjoyed the leisure which was believed to be essential to the dignity of a freeman; but, in order that he might not become unfitted for war, his amusements were the palaestra and the chase, from which he rested only at the public meals. These public meals (συσσίτια), like many other institutions, Sparta had in common with Crete*, though they were not entirely the same in the two countries. The sixtieth year closed the military age, and the period which followed was one of peaceful repose, though not of wearisome inaction: it was cheered by respect and authority, and was employed either in the direction of public affairs, or in the superintendence of the young.

The institutions of Sparta had all more or less a warlike tendency, and this one-sidedness is justly censured even by their admirers. A prominent feature of the Spartan character was caution; and this, together with their observance of the maxim not to pursue a routed enemy farther than was necessary for securing the victory, may sometimes have supplied the place of humanity and softened the ferocity of warfare. The same end was gained by the regulation that, during certain religious festivals, there should be a cessation from all hostilities. War seems to have been the element in which a Spartan breathed most freely and enjoyed the fullest consciousness of his existence; he dressed his hair and crowned himself for a battle as others did for a feast; and advanced to the mortal struggle with a mind as calm and

* Comp. p. 72.

cheerful as that with which he commenced a contest for a prize at the public games.

The warlike spirit of the Spartans was maintained by their ancient system of tactics. The main strength of the army consisted in its heavy-armed infantry, the only mode of service which was thought worthy of a free Spartan. Hence little value was set upon the cavalry, which in fact never acquired any great efficacy. Three hundred picked young men indeed, who served as the king's body-guard, bore the name of horsemen as a title of honour; but in battle they fought on foot, using their horses only on the march and in executing the king's commands. The Spartans, moreover, always shrank from besieging a fortified town, and the sea was never a congenial element to the spirit of their warfare. At sea the Helots were mostly employed, as on land they formed the light-armed infantry or followed their masters in the capacity of menial servants. Promptness and punctuality in the execution of the various evolutions and movements and in their harmonious combinations, distinguished the Spartan armies at all times; and these movements were greatly facilitated by the warlike dance, called the Pyrrhic, in which the Spartan youths were habitually exercised. The tidings of an important victory were celebrated with the sacrifice of a cock, and their bearer was rewarded with a dish of meat from the table of the ephors. During the most brilliant period of Spartan history, the warrior's watchword was "victory or death;" and the coward who saved his life by flight, was degraded from all the privileges of society, and became a butt for public scorn and insult.

It was no doubt felt from an early period, that the security of the Spartan constitution depended, not on its being written on stone or parchment, but on the national feeling in which it lived: and hence Lycurgus is said to have forbidden the use of written laws. It was, perhaps, chiefly with the view of preserving this feeling in its full strength and purity, that citizens were not allowed to go abroad without leave of the magistrates, and that the presence of foreigners at Sparta was discouraged; but, previously to the rivalry between Athens and Sparta, this latter regulation appears to have been rarely enforced, and distinguished foreigners were not only permitted, but even invited, to sojourn at Sparta.

From all that has been said about the Spartan institutions, it is clear that the greater part of them were only a continuation of the Hellenic, and especially the Doric, institutions, such as they existed in the heroic ages. Among the Dorians this Hellenic character maintained itself in comparative purity, in consequence of the circumstances by which they were surrounded in Peloponnesus after the conquest; nay, in many points it may even have become more marked and developed, and all that a legislator like Lycurgus had to do, was to arrange and regulate that which previously had been only customary.

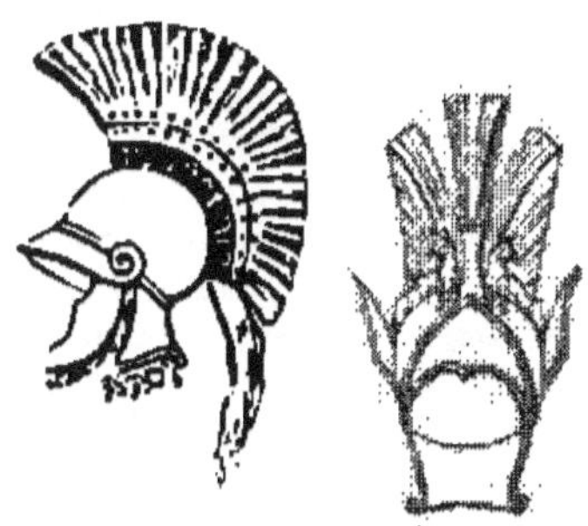

Greek helmets.

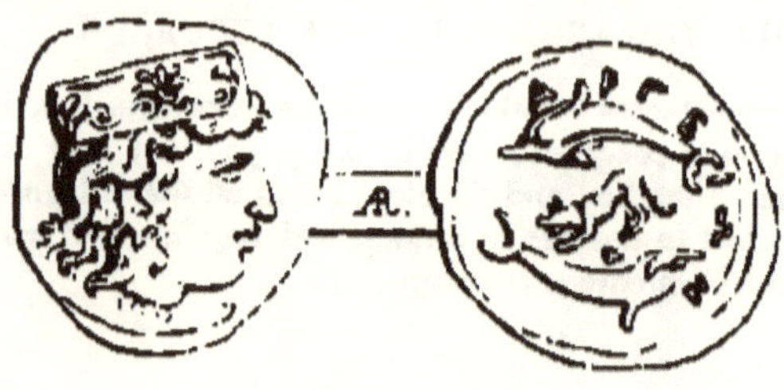

Coin of Argos.

CHAPTER VIII.

THE MESSENIAN WARS AND AFFAIRS OF SPARTA DOWN TO THE SIXTH CENTURY BEFORE CHRIST.

About the first Olympiad, B.C. 776, all Laconia was subdued and tranquil. The Spartans, united and made strong by the institutions of Lycurgus, and long accustomed to war, were perhaps impatient for fresh enterprises. Their first undertaking seems to have been directed against Arcadia; but the account of the expedition of king Sous against the Arcadian town of Cleitor* is not supported by sufficient authority. Jealousy appears to have soon sprung up between Sparta and Argos. Originally, the whole of the eastern coast of Laconia, as far as Cape Malea, belonged to Argos, and bore the name of Cynuria. Of this district the Spartans had made themselves masters in the reign of Echestratus, the son of Agis, and this led to a series of hostilities between the two states. Charilaus and Nicander, joined by the Dryopes of Asine, made inroads into the Argive territory; and Charilaus, deceived by an oracle which seemed to promise the conquest of the important town of Tegea, marched into Arcadia also; but he was defeated, and the captured Spartans were obliged to serve as slaves in the chains which they had brought with them for the Tegeatans.† The struggle with them was often renewed, but always with ill success.

An easier and more inviting conquest, however, offered itself to them in the west. It was probably not without jealousy and envy that the Dorians of Laconia observed that Messenia, which had fallen to the lot of Cresphontes and his followers, was a much fairer country than their own, and under the influence of such feelings a pretext for war is easily found. The Dorians in Mes-

* Plut. *Lycurg.* 2.

† Herod. i. 65, &c.; Paus. iii. 8. § 3.

senia, moreover, had become a very different people from their kinsmen in Laconia. The Achaeans in Messenia seem to have submitted without much resistance to their new sovereigns, and the kings appear to have adopted a wise and moderate policy towards the vanquished. Cresphontes himself, who made Stenyclerus his capital, was thwarted in his plan to amalgamate the Dorians and Achaeans into one people, by a conspiracy among the Dorians, who are said to have cut him off with his whole family except one son. This son Aepytus fled into Arcadia; but at a riper age, with the assistance of other Heracleid princes, he recovered his hereditary throne, and now carried out the generous policy of his father with better success. He seems to have abolished all distinctions between the Dorians and the Messenian commonalty, and to have maintained the ancient religious and political institutions of the country, whereby he attached the original population to himself and his house. His successors, the Aepytids, followed the same policy; thus the country prospered, the arts of peace flourished, and no class of the people aimed at ruling over the others, whence, perhaps, in military skill the Messenians were inferior to the Spartans.

In the struggle which soon ensued, the Spartans charged the Messenians with having been the aggressors, and the Messenians retorted the charge; but it is probable that the Spartans were only too anxious to obtain a fair pretence for directing their arms against their neighbours. The story of the origin of the quarrel runs thus:—In the reign of Teleclus, the seventh king from Agis, the Spartans sent a company of virgins to celebrate a festival at the temple of Artemis Limnatis, on the confines of the two countries. The temple was a sanctuary common to both nations, and Teleclus accompanied the procession. Some Messenians offered violence to the maidens, and a fray arose, in which the king himself was slain. Such is the Spartan tale; whereas the Messenians related, that Teleclus had laid a plot to assassinate some of the noblest Messenian citizens at the festival, and that for this purpose he had disguised a band of Spartans as maidens with daggers hidden under their dresses; but the plot being detected, both the king and his followers fell by the hands of their intended victims. The Spartans, conscious of their king's guilt, made no demand of reparation.

The grudge arising from this affair was scarcely healed, when the wrongs and the revenge of a private man kindled a fatal war between the two nations. Polychares, a Messenian of great note, possessed some cattle for which he had no pasture, and contracted with a Spartan, named Euaephnus, to feed them on the land of the latter. Euaephnus sold both the cattle and the herdsmen in one of the Laconian ports, and went to Polychares with a plausible tale of pirates who had landed and carried them all off. At this very moment, however, one of the herdsmen who had made his escape, came back to his master and related the truth. Euaephnus, overwhelmed with shame, entreated Polychares to be satisfied with the price of the oxen, and to send his son along with him to receive it. The Messenian good-naturedly consented, and the youth went with Euaephnus; but when they had crossed the Laconian frontier, the Spartan, instead of making restitution, killed his companion. The injured father first sought redress at Sparta; but, finding the kings and ephors deaf to his complaints, he took his revenge into his own hands, waylaid passengers on the border, and spared no Lacedaemonian that fell into his power. The Spartans now demanded the surrender of Polychares. Androcles, one of the Messenian kings, was willing to give up Polychares; but Antiochus, the other, refused to comply with the demand. A bloody contest ensued in Messenia between the two opposite parties; Androcles was slain, and his children fled to Sparta. Antiochus, now sole king, sent envoys to Sparta proposing to have the dispute decided by some impartial tribunal. The Spartans made no reply, but silently determined to settle the matter by force. Meantime Antiochus died; and, in the beginning of the reign of his successor Euphaës, B. C. 743, the Spartans bound themselves by an oath not to cease warring against Messenia until the country should be made their own by the right of conquest. Soon afterwards they crossed the border without having declared war, and under the command of Alcamenes marched against the fortified town of Amphea. The Messenians were taken by surprise, and the invaders massacred the defenceless inhabitants. There the Spartans established themselves, as in a strong post from which they might at all times attack their enemies.

Such is the story about the beginning of the first Messenian war, which is said to have lasted for nineteen years, from B. C. 743 to 724, and of which we have a tolerably minute account in Pausanias. This author seems to have derived his information mainly from Myron of Priene, who probably lived after the time of Alexander the Great, and wrote a history of the first Messenian war, which does not appear, however, to be very trustworthy. That the first, as well as the second, Messenian war is a real historical event cannot be doubted, though the simple facts have been embellished by ancient popular poetry, which kept alive in the conquered race the hope of better days. The account of the second Messenian war in Pausanias is based upon the poetical history of Rhianus, of Bene in Crete, and in its details is certainly not more authentic than that of the first.

When Euphaës, the king of the Messenians, heard of the surprise of Amphea, he trained his people in military exercises; but not venturing to take the field against the enemy, the Messenians sheltered themselves behind the walls of their towns, which the Spartans were unable to force. But while the Spartans, in their sallies from Amphea into the heart of the country, carried away the fruit, corn, cattle, and slaves, the Messenians were not inactive, but made incursions into Laconia and infested its coasts. At length, in the fourth year of the war, when Euphaës thought his men sufficiently trained in arms, he took the field. The indignation of the Messenians had risen to the highest pitch, but still the king did not venture to meet the Spartans on even ground, and after a few skirmishes, the armies parted as they had met. The next year, a great battle is said to have been fought, in which the Spartans were assisted by Cretan archers and by the Dryopes whom the Argives had expelled from Asine. But the victory again remained undecided. The Messenians, exhausted by the necessity of keeping their towns constantly garrisoned, whereby the husbandmen were drawn away from their occupations, were also afflicted by diseases such as commonly attend upon war and scarcity; and they now resolved to collect their forces in an impregnable hold, where they might keep the enemy in check and cover the country which lay behind them. With this view they enlarged the small town on the summit of the lofty rock of Ithome on the river Pamisus, which commanded the plain of Stenycleros. While the work of extension and fortification was going on, the king sent to Delphi to consult the oracle. The god declared that an unsullied virgin of the blood of Aepytus, selected by lot, must be sacrificed to the gods below. When the oracle became known, all the maidens of the royal family immediately drew lots, and the result was that a daughter of Lyciscus was to be the victim. But during an investigation to ascertain whether she was really a descendant of Aepytus, her father fled with her to Sparta. Hereupon Aristodemus, an Aepytid also, freely offered his own daughter, although she was already betrothed and the day for her marriage fixed. Her lover, after many useless remonstrances, alleged that the maid would not be an unsullied victim, for that she was about to become a mother. Aristodemus, enraged at this information, killed his daughter with his own hand and proved her innocence. But the soothsayer declared that a murder was not a sacrifice, and that a fresh victim must be sought. The king, however, who was a friend of the lover, persuaded the people that the oracle had been duly obeyed, and the event was celebrated with joy and feasting.

The report of this awful deed discouraged the Spartans, and it was not till the sixth year after Ithome had been fortified that their king Theopompus led an army against it. Without waiting for the arrival of his allies, he offered battle; but as before, although the fight lasted till nightfall, no victory was gained. Euphaes himself fell while attacking Theopompus, and died soon after of his wounds, without leaving an heir to the throne. Aristodemus, who was now elected by the people to succeed him, won the hearts of all by his wise government, and gained over the Arcadians as his allies. The war was continued with petty inroads and ravages which were made every year at the harvest season.

In the fifth year of the reign of Aristodemus a pitched battle was again fought at the foot of mount Ithome, in which the Lacedaemonians and the Corinthians, their allies, were defeated by the Messenians. Their spirit now began to sink, and they sought advice from Delphi. The god promised success to stratagems, and Sparta tried many in vain. Aristodemus, on the other hand, was warned to beware of Spartan cunning; other advice brought from Delphi was so obscure that it could not be understood. Meantime the twentieth year of the war had commenced when Apollo declared to the Messenians, that their land should belong to the nation which should first dedicate a hundred tripods at the altar of Zeus in Ithome. While they were preparing the offering a Spartan, who had heard of the oracle, stole into the temple by night and placed a hundred small earthen tripods round the altar. Aristodemus himself was dismayed by many visible signs of impending ruin, and at length understood the obscure expressions of the oracle. His daughter, too, appeared to him in a dream; and, showing her wounds, took away his arms and adorned him, as for his obsequies, with a golden crown and a white robe. Thus certain that his end was near at hand, and that he could not avert the fate of his country, he slew himself at his daughter's tomb. The Messenians, who had now lost their hopes, but not their courage, chose Damis for their commander in the war, and some time afterwards made a vigorous sally from Ithome; but their bravest leaders fell, and at length they fled from the fortress, leaving their rich fields in the possession of the conquerors. Thus ended the first Messenian war, in B. C. 724.

Many of the unfortunate Messenians sought and found refuge in foreign lands, and the priestly families withdrew to Eleusis; but the bulk of the people dispersed from Ithome to the districts whence they had come. Ithome was razed to the ground, and the Spartans soon made themselves masters of all the other Messenian towns, and disposed of the country at their pleasure. The Dryopes were rewarded for their assistance with a portion of the coast of Messenia, where they founded a new Asine. The condition of the subject Messenians, who were allowed to dwell on their former estates as labourers of their new lords, was that of serfs; like the Helots in Laconia, they were obliged to pay to their masters half the produce of their fields. Tyrtaeus, in the third generation after these events, reminds the Spartans that their ancestors had forced the Messenians to stoop like asses under wearisome burdens.

The conquest of Messenia contributed more than any other event towards determining the character and subsequent history of Sparta. The additional territory was divided among the Spartans: but it would seem that those who received lands were not the old Spartan citizens, but Laconians who were now for the first time admitted to the franchise, since it would appear that, during the war, marriages between Spartans and Laconians had, contrary to earlier usage, been legalised. These new citizens, however, were probably not raised to a footing of equality with the old ones, and hence their discontent, which led many of them to emigrate, and found the colony of Tarentum in Southern Italy, B.C. 708.* In later times we find all the Spartan citizens divided into two classes, the Equals (ὅμοιοι) and the Inferiors (ὑπομείονες); and it is not impossible that this distinction arose at the time when Laconian subjects were admitted to the franchise, which seems to have entitled them to vote in the general assembly, but not in the election of the senate, which appears to have been reserved for a more select assembly (ἡ μικρὰ ἐκκλησία).

This supposition of the enlargement and consequent graduation of the franchise, may also serve to reconcile the different accounts of the origin of the ephoralty, which is ascribed by some to Lycurgus, whom later generations naturally loved to regard as the founder of all their political institutions, while others, apparently with better reason, describe the ephoralty as an innovation introduced by king Theopompus, the colleague of Polydorus. The Spartan kings, from motives of policy, were always favourable to an extension of the franchise, and this was apparently the natural tendency of the ephoralty also. Theopompus, therefore, not being able to foresee the character which the new magistracy afterwards assumed, may have regarded it at first as a useful ally, though by instituting it he sacrificed a considerable part of the royal prero-

* According to the common story, the founders of Tarentum were the offspring of an illicit connection between the wives of the soldiers engaged in Messenia and young Spartans who had remained at home. After the conquest of Messenia, the youths thus born out of legal wedlock are said to have threatened the safety of Sparta by conspiring with the Helots, in consequence of which the government induced them to emigrate and seek a new home. They are called Parthenii, and, under the guidance of Phalanthus, founded Tarentum. Strab. vi. p. 278. foll.; Athen. vi. p. 271.

gative. The college of the ephors (overseers) consisted at all times of five members, and exercised the civil jurisdiction, while the senate was the supreme court in criminal cases. Their general superintendence over the execution of the laws must have brought them into frequent collision with the kings, and might easily enable a dexterous and enterprising ephor to raise his power above that of the kings themselves. It may have been by virtue of this that the college exacted an oath from the kings that they would govern according to law, while they bound themselves and the nation only to a conditional obedience. Another prerogative of the ephors was that, at the end of every eight years, they might suspend the functions of the kings. The ceremonies observed on such occasions, however, show that this was a religious, rather than a political measure, and that on such occasions the ephors acted merely as the executors of the divine will, being guided by the suggestions of certain heavenly signs If the gods were found to be displeased with a king, the ephors forthwith interdicted him from the discharge of his office, and he could be restored only by the intervention of an oracle. In later times the ephors also acquired the right of convoking the assembly of the people, of laying measures before it, and of acting in its name; and this character of representatives of the people enabled them in many ways to encroach on the royal prerogatives, and to draw the whole government of the state into their hands. Whether they acquired this power during an accidental absence of the kings in time of war, or whether the admission of new citizens to the franchise brought about the change in their relation to the senate and kings, cannot be decided with any degree of certainty. The power of the ephors was democratical in its form, and tyrannical in extent, never having been accurately defined; whence its limits probably varied with the character of the men who held it and with the circumstances of the times. The ephors, moreover, not only possessed the substance of supreme power, but also assumed its outward signs; thus the royal dignity was forced on all occasions to bow to them; and as they could control the proceedings of the kings, could fine them for slight offences at their discretion, and could even throw them into prison, so they alone among the Spartans kept their seats while the kings were passing. But notwithstanding all this, the kingly station, even when the power of the ephors was at its height, continued to confer important prerogatives and means of extensive influence.

During the first Messenian war, Argos seized the opportunity of recovering the country of Cynuria from Sparta. The plan succeeded, and Argos became the mistress, not only of the eastern coast of Laconia as far as Cape Malea, but even of the island of

Cythera. These conquests seem to have been made in the reign of Pheidon, a Heracleid king of Argos, who broke through all the restraints which had been put upon his power, and deprived the Eleans of their presidency at the Olympic games. His brother Caranus is said to have founded a little kingdom in the north of Greece, which became the nucleus of the Macedonian monarchy. Pheidon introduced a new system of weights and measures, and established a mint in Aegina, which formed part of his dominions. After his death, Argos seems to have been deserted by its good fortune; for his conquests were lost, and Sparta ruled over the south of Peloponnesus from the eastern to the western coast.

But in the mean time a new generation sprang up in Messenia, which, while groaning under a degrading yoke, remembered nothing of the evils of the war which their fathers had waged, but heard of their heroic deeds. Many also who had been born in exile, longed to recover their patrimony. While all hearts were thus full, and all spirits roused, it only required one man to come forward as the champion of the oppressed, and this man appeared in the person of Aristomenes. He was of noble descent, like Aristodemus the hero of the first Messenian war, whom in strength and courage he even surpassed. He cheered the hopes of the exiles, fanned the indignation of his enslaved countrymen, and solicited the aid of foreign cities. Argos and Arcadia were more than ever hostile to Sparta, and Elis too was willing to assist in the deliverance of Messenia. Under these circumstances the second Messenian war broke out, in B. C. 685.

From Andania, his birthplace in the Messenian highlands, Aristomenes began his attacks, penetrating as far as the plains of Stenycleros, and the first battle was fought before any succours had come from abroad. Although he did not gain a decisive victory, yet his valour struck fear into his enemies. His countrymen offered him the crown; but he declined the honour, and contented himself with the supreme command of the Messenians In order to terrify the Lacedaemonians, he one night crossed the mountains, went to Sparta, and fixed a shield which he had taken in battle, against the temple of Athene Chalcioecos, with an inscription stating that Aristomenes dedicated it to the goddess as a sign of his victory over the Spartans. Such an adventure is not altogether impossible, considering that Sparta was an open place, and that it was forbidden by law to light the city at night.* The Spartans, seeing that they had no common enemy to contend with, sent to Delphi for advice. The god bade them seek an Athenian counsellor. No connection appears to have existed between

* Plut. *Lycurg.* 12.; *Inst. Lac.* 3.

Athens and Sparta from the most ancient times; but the town of Aphidnae in the north of Attica, whence the Dioscuri are said to have carried back their sister Helen, now sent Tyrtaeus, a martial poet, to the aid of Sparta.* Contradictory as the statements about Tyrtaeus are, it is nevertheless certain, that by his poetry he revived the spirit of the Spartans, and that he came from Attica. But what led him to devote his muse to the service of Sparta is doubtful; though it may possibly have been owing to the mythical connection between the Spartan Dioscuri and Aphidnae; for Aphidnus, the founder of the town, was said to have adopted Helen's brothers as his sons; hence the Aphidnaeans, induced by a feeling of kindred, may have sent Tyrtaeus to aid the Spartans either with his arm or with his voice.

The Spartans were also joined by auxiliaries from Corinth and Lepreum in Triphylia, and by a few ships from the island of Samos. The Messenians, on the other hand, were reinforced by their exiled countrymen, and by allies from Sicyon, Argos, Arcadia, and Elis; and as a counterpoise to the influence exercised by Tyrtaeus on the Spartans, the Messenians were cheered by the prophecies of their soothsayer Theocles. A great battle was fought in the plain of Stenycleros, where Aristomenes broke the Spartan forces and routed the enemy. Unmindful of the warnings of the soothsayer, he pursued the fugitives too far and lost his shield, which was carried off by an invisible hand. But Messenia was freed for a time from her enemies, and Aristomenes on his return to Andania was received with unbounded enthusiasm as the deliverer of his country. His shield he afterwards recovered in the cave of Trophonius at Lebadea, into which he descended by the command of Apollo. On his return from Lebadea, he again acted on the offensive, and with the suddenness of lightning fell upon the towns and villages of the Laconians. With a chosen band of companions he plundered Pharae, put to flight the Spartan king Anaxander who came to its relief, and was only stopped in his progress by an accidental wound. After this was cured, he planned an attack on Sparta itself, from which however he was deterred by the Dioscuri and their sister Helen, who appeared to him in a dream. But he did not allow himself to be prevented from making inroads into Laconia. On one occasion he carried off a number of maidens who were celebrating with festive dances a solemnity of Artemis at Caryae. He protected them, however, from the violence of his companions, and restored them for a heavy ransom

* Others call Tyrtaeus a Milesian or Spartan. The witty Athenians ridiculed the Spartans, by saying that they had sent them a lame schoolmaster as a counsellor. Paus. VIII. 15. § 8. The story about Tyrtaeus is almost as mythical as that of Aristomenes.

to their kinsmen. At Aegila he himself fell into the hands of the women who were celebrating the rites of Demeter; but in the night he escaped, either by his own courage and strength, or through the compassion of the priestess.

In the third year of the war, Sparta again prepared for battle, but she now had recourse to treacherous means. On this occasion the Messenians were assisted only by the Arcadian Aristocrates, who was induced by Spartan bribes to draw off his men in the heat of the battle, and leave his allies to their fate. On his retreat the Messenians found themselves surrounded on all sides by a superior force, and many of them were slain. Aristomenes assembled the survivors at Andania, and advised them to concentrate their strength in one place, as their ancestors had done. As Ithome was probably in the hands of the enemy, they chose Mount Eira, on the frontiers of Triphylia. There they fortified themselves, while the Spartans, masters of nearly the whole country, lay encamped at the foot of Eira, hoping soon to reduce it by force or famine. But Aristomenes continued to sally forth in defiance of the besiegers, and brought back booty into the fortress. The Laconians now determined to change the surrounding country into a desert, until the enemy should be compelled to surrender by famine. The opposition of the owners of the land, who by this measure became themselves impoverished, was overcome by Tyrtaeus, who impressed on their minds the blessings of concord and of obedience to the laws.

Aristomenes, emboldened by his success, one night went as far as Amyclae, and returned laden with booty before sunrise. In a second inroad he was less successful; the Spartans were better prepared, and his little band was surrounded by their army commanded by both kings. Aristomenes long kept his enemies at bay, until he was stunned by a stone and taken prisoner with fifty of his companions. All were condemned, like the vilest malefactors, to be thrown down from a high rock into a pit called the Ceadas. Aristomenes alone came to the ground unhurt; the rest were dashed to pieces by the fall. He saw no means of escape, however, and prepared himself for death; but on the third day a sound caught his ear, and, uncovering his face, he perceived that a fox had found its way into the pit through a passage by which he might escape. He awaited the animal's approach, caught hold of its tail, and, guided by it as it struggled to escape, he crept on till he came to an opening in the rock. The next day he was again at Eira.* It would lead us too far to relate in detail the many other

* The fox, it must be observed, was the symbol of Messenia. Paus. iv 6. § 4, 32. § 5.

wonderful adventures which are assigned to the hero; how he cut to pieces a Corinthian army on its march to join the Spartans; and how, being taken by a band of Cretan archers, he broke his bonds and escaped. Thrice he offered to Zeus Ithomates the sacrifice called Hecatomphonia, because it was reserved for the warrior who had slain a hecatomb of foes. But he had provoked, it is said, the anger of the Dioscuri by counterfeiting their appearance and disturbing with bloodshed a festival celebrated by the Spartans in their honour. The gods accordingly turned against Messenia. The siege of Eira lasted till the eleventh year, when a portent indicated that the end of the contest was approaching and that the Messenians were about to be conquered. An oracle had declared that, when a goat or a wild fig-tree* should drink the water of the Neda, the destruction of Messenia would be at hand. The Messenians tried to prevent their goats from approaching the Neda; but a wild fig-tree, which overhung the stream, at length stretched its boughs down to the water, and when Theocles saw this, he knew that the oracle was accomplished, and that the end of Messenia was approaching.

The will of the gods was accomplished by treachery and female weakness. A Spartan herdsman had gone over to the enemy with his master's cattle; and one day while feeding his flocks on the banks of the Neda, he was seen by a Messenian woman who admitted him into her house while her husband was guarding the citadel. One night the husband returned home and was overheard by the herdsman, while he was relating to his wife the cause of his coming home. The herdsman immediately determined to make the best use of his information, and, as a means of obtaining forgiveness and favour, communicated it to his master, who happened to command the Spartan army at Eira. Aristomenes was ill of his wounds, and being unable to make his usual rounds at night, the sentinels neglected their duty, and left their stations. The Spartans now under the herdsman's guidance scaled the walls of the fortress, and before the alarm was given were already within. The Messenians with Aristomenes at their head made the assailants pay dearly for every inch of ground they gained. Even the women took part in the conflict. But it was useless to fight against destiny. A thunderstorm raging during the contest sounded to the Messenians like the voice of the angry deity. The struggle was nevertheless continued for three days and nights in the streets and open places of Eira, until Theocles, after having advised Aristomenes to desist from the hopeless struggle, rushed into the

* The Greek word is τράγος, which, in the Messenian dialect, signified a goat and a wild fig-tree.

thickest of the fight that he might not survive his country's fall. Aristomenes rallied his men around him, bade them form themselves into a hollow square inclosing their wives and children, and advancing towards the enemy, by his gestures demanded a free passage. The Spartans, fearing to drive their enemy to extremities, opened a road through their ranks and allowed the Messenians to depart. The unfortunate men turned their steps towards Arcadia, where they were hospitably received. The faithful Arcadians were willing even to share their lands with the exiles; but Aristomenes was bent on a new enterprise and meditated an expedition against Sparta itself, with 500 Messenians and 300 Arcadians. This design, however, was betrayed by the faithless Aristocrates, whose cowardly conduct was now proved by an intercepted letter from the Spartan king, who thanked him for his past and present services. When the assembly of the Arcadian people learned this, they stoned the traitor to death. After this disappointment, fifty of the exiles, with a kinsman of Aristomenes at their head, crossed the border, fell upon the Spartans, and died sword in hand in the land of their fathers.

Thus ended the second Messenian war, which had lasted for seventeen years, from B.C. 685 to 668; on the termination of it, all the Messenians who remained in their country were degraded to the rank of Helots; but most of the people probably emigrated. The inhabitants of Pylos and Methone sailed to Cyllene the Elean port, and Methone was given by the Spartans to the Nauplians, whom the Argives had expelled from their own town. The Messenians, on their arrival in Elis, begged Aristomenes to lead them to a new country; but his mind being bent upon continuing the war against Sparta, he sent them his two sons. Under these guides a band of Messenians sailed to Rhegium in Italy, where they found some of their kinsmen who had settled there at the end of the former war. Afterwards they made themselves masters of the town of Zancle, and named it Messene (the modern Messina).

Aristomenes is said to have gone to Delphi, where the Pythia was at that very time advising Damagetus, the ruler of Ialysos in Rhodes, to marry the daughter of the most illustrious among the Greeks. He accordingly became the son-in-law of Aristomenes, who was taken by him to Rhodes, where, after his death, he was honoured with a splendid monument and heroic honours. According to another tradition, Aristomenes was captured by the Lacedaemonians, who on opening his breast found his heart covered with hair.*

The yoke appeared now to be fixed on the neck of Messenia for

* Plut. *De Herod. Malig.* 2; Plin. *Hist. Nat.* xi. 70.

ever, and henceforth Sparta continued to rise towards undisputed pre-eminence in Peloponnesus and throughout Greece. She was now in a position to reward her friends, humble her rivals, and punish her enemies. Soon afterwards she stepped in to decide an ancient quarrel betwin Elis and Pisa respecting the presidency at the Olympic games, and decided in favour of the former. The old contest between Sparta and Tegea, from which Sparta had hitherto reaped only shame, was now brought to a successful termination. About the middle of the sixth century B.C., an oracle bade the Spartans bring the bones of Orestes, the son of Agamemnon, to Sparta; and another oracle directed them to search for the relics at Tegea. Some gigantic remains were accordingly dug up there and carried away. Tegea, having thus lost its palladium, fell and became a dependent ally of Sparta. Argos was a more formidable rival, and could ill brook the loss of Cynuria; but the submission of that district was finally secured by Sparta, about the same time that Tegea was compelled to yield. The fame of Sparta now spread so far, that even Croesus, the great king of Lydia, sent ambassadors to court her alliance. Sparta willingly entered into an alliance with him, and would, perhaps, have assisted him against Cyrus, had not his sudden ruin frustrated her intentions.

Mount Ithome.

From a sketch by Sir William Gell

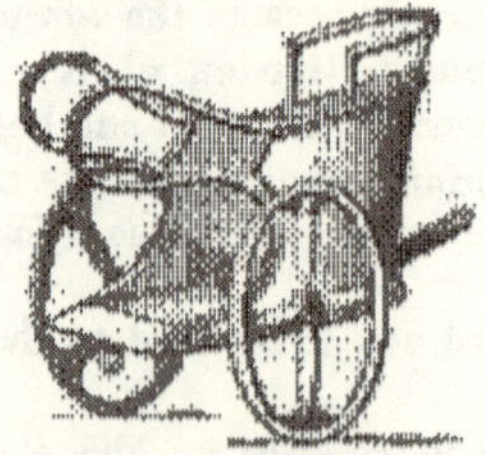

War chariot.

(From a painted vase.)

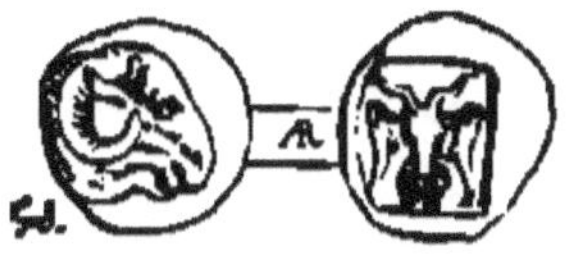

Coin of Delphi.

CHAPTER IX.

NATIONAL INSTITUTIONS AND FORMS OF GOVERNMENT.

The migrations and conquests which we have hitherto described, produced a variety of changes in Greece itself and led to the establishment of numerous colonies abroad. The changes brought about in Greece, consisted partly of modifications of ancient national institutions, and partly of political reforms or revolutions.

The Greeks were at all times united by the bonds of their common language and religion; in the Trojan expedition alone they are said to have been also united under one commander and in a common enterprise; but this was only transitory, and was not followed by any political consequences, the several tribes being enabled to balance one another and to preserve their independence. There existed, however, partial associations for religious and political purposes, some of which, in the course of time, assumed the appearance of national associations or confederacies. Of these associations, the principal class was that designated by the Greek term Amphictiony.* It was believed to have derived its name from Amphictyon, the son of Deucalion, who founded the most celebrated confederacy of this kind; but this account is as mythical as a hundred others of the same nature, and the name probably signifies a local union among a number of places or tribes, with a common centre, which was always a religious one, such as a temple, at which the periodical meetings for the celebration of a common worship were held. National affinity may have drawn neighbouring tribes into such associations, though it does not seem to have formed an essential requisite. Many such Amphictionies probably existed in Greece, but few of them are known; one is mentioned as having held its meetings at Onchestos, in Boeotia, another met in the island of Calaurea, a third had Delos for its centre; but the most celebrated and important Amphictiony, which is known by the name of *the* amphictionic league or council, was that which held its meetings, in the spring at Delphi, and in the

* The name is also, though less correctly, spelt Amphictyony.

autumn near the town of Anthela within the pass of Thermopylae, at a temple of Demeter. The council was composed of the deputies sent by the several states, according to very ancient rules. The two places of meeting seem to suggest that this amphictiony was formed out of two originally independent associations, one perhaps consisting of inland, the other of maritime tribes. The council is said to have originally consisted of deputies sent by twelve tribes, each of which might include several independent states. The names of these tribes are not the same in all accounts, but the most probable list contains the following names:—Thessalians, Boeotians, Dorians, Ionians, Perrhaebians, Magnetes, Locrians, Octaeans (or Aenianians), Phthiots, Malians (Melians), and Phocians, to which must be added either the Dolopians or the Delphians. This list comprises no nation south of the Corinthian isthmus, and seems to take us back to a period previous to the return of the Heracleids. After this event the number of tribes remained the same; but the extent of the league was increased by that part of Peloponnesus which was occupied by the Dorians, so that the confederacy included most of the states of Greece: and thus exercising its influence over the whole country, it might be looked upon as a true national confederation; but the nature of its constitution and the range of its functions did not allow it ever to assume that character. The tribes represented in the council stood to one another in a relation of perfect equality, each having two votes in the congress. If the subjects discussed and decided upon by such an assembly had affected any important political interest, it is evident that the league could not have existed long. But it was not commonly viewed as a national congress for such purposes. Its ordinary duties were chiefly connected with religion, and it was only by accident that it was ever made subservient to political ends. Its two main functions were to guard the temple of the Delphic god, and to restrain mutual violence among the states belonging to the league. There is nothing to suggest that the object of the confederacy was protection against foreign enemies. Even the chief objects of the institution were at no time strictly carried into effect; for we find members of the confederacy inflicting the worst evils of war upon one another, without remonstrance being made on the ground of the oath which bound them together. The league was, in fact, powerless for good, and active only for purposes which were either unimportant or pernicious. Its most important sphere of action, was in cases where the honour and safety of the Delphic sanctuary were concerned; in which it might safely reckon on general co-operation from all the Greeks. One of the most celebrated instances of such intervention is that which gave rise to the Crissaean or first sacred war, in B.C. 594. The inhabitants of Crissa (also called Cirrha) were charged with extortion and violence towards the strangers who landed at their port, or passed through their territory, on their way to Delphi. The Amphictions decreed war against the city, and it was carried on vigorously by the Thessalians and Cleisthenes, tyrant of Sicyon. By the advice of Apollo, the Amphictions resolved to dedicate the Crissaeans and their territory to the god, by enslaving them and making their land a waste for ever. The war is said to have lasted for ten years, till B.C. 585, and was at length terminated by a stratagem ascribed to Solon, who is said to have poisoned the waters of the Pleistos from which the city was supplied. When the town was taken, the vow of its enemies was literally fulfilled. Crissa was razed to the ground, its harbour choked up, and its fertile plain changed into a wilderness. This success is said to have given rise to the institution of the Pythian games, which thenceforth supplanted a more ancient and simple festival.

The Delphic oracle, through which the Amphictions might have exercised an extensive influence over the affairs of Greece, was not under their management, but under that of the leading citizens of Delphi, who had constant and more efficacious access to the persons employed in revealing the supposed will of the god.

Another class of national institutions consisted of the great festivals, which were celebrated at certain places and at fixed intervals of time, and were open to all who could prove their Hellenic blood. The most important of these festivals was that solemnised every fifth year on the banks of the Alpheus, in Elis. It lasted four days, and was called the Olympic contest or games, from the place of its celebration; the period which intervened between its returns was called an Olympiad. The origin of this institution is involved in great obscurity; it was believed to have been founded, and at various periods renewed, by gods and heroes long before the Trojan war. In the time of Lycurgus, Iphitus, it was said, in concert with the Spartan lawgiver, and with the sanction of the Delphic oracle, revived the solemnity, and ordained a periodical suspension of hostilities throughout Greece, to enable all tribes to attend without hindrance or danger. There had, no doubt, existed at Olympia from very early times an oracle and worship of Zeus, and festivals had undoubtedly been celebrated there from time to time. The Dorian conquest of the peninsula must long have interrupted the celebration of the solemnity, and its renewal, which is ascribed to Iphitus and Lycurgus, may have been suggested by political as well as religious motives. It was not till B.C. 776, however, that the Olympic contest began to be used as a chronological era, and it may have been long before the institution came to be regarded as a real national festival. The Eleans presided at the games, and their territory was regarded as sacred and inviolable during the period of the contests, which at a very early time were frequented by spectators, not only from all parts of Greece itself, but also from the Greek colonies in Europe, Asia, and Africa; this assemblage, however, was not brought together by the mere fortuitous impulse of private interest or curiosity, but was in part composed of deputations, which were sent by most cities as to a religious solemnity, and were considered as guests of the Olympian god. The contests carried on at these games consisted of exhibitions displaying almost every mode of bodily activity; they included races on foot, and with horses and chariots; contests in leaping, throwing, wrestling, and boxing, and some in which several of these exercises were combined; but no combats with any kind of weapon. The contests in the chariot race were naturally confined to the wealthy, but the greatest part were open to all Greeks without distinction. Towns and families regarded it as the highest honour for one or more of their members to gain a victory in any of the contests at Olympia. In the earliest times, valuable prizes appear to have been given to the victors in all the public games; but after the seventh Olympiad, the prize at Olympia consisted of a simple garland of the leaves of the wild olive. Other honours, however, were frequently bestowed upon the victor; he was sometimes honoured with the franchise of a foreign city, and in his own with statues and other distinctions. By a law of Solon, every Athenian who gained an Olympic prize was rewarded with 500 drachmas, and with the right to a place at the table of the magistrates in the prytaneum; the Spartan law or custom honoured the victor with a conspicuous place on the field of battle. The Altis, the place where the games were carried on at Olympia, was adorned with numberless statues of the victors, erected by themselves, their families, or at the expense of their fellow-citizens. The joyful event, moreover, was celebrated both at Olympia and in the victor's native place, by a triumphal procession, in which his praises were sung and were commonly associated with the glory of his ancestors and his country. Thus sports, originally as simple as any in our villages, gave birth to masterpieces of sculpture, and to the sublimest strains of the lyric muse.

The celebrity of the Olympic games led to the institution of several other festivals of a similar nature, such as the Pythian, which were celebrated in every third Olympic year; the Nemean and Isthmian, which were celebrated each twice in every Olympiad, the former in the plain of Nemea, in Argolis, and the latter on the Corinthian isthmus These four contests, which in various degrees rose to the dignity of national festivals, were distinguished from other similar institutions chiefly by the nature of the prize, which was in all cases a simple garland. The importance of such solemnities depended partly upon the degree in which they answered the purpose of a bond of national union, and partly on the share they had in forming the national character. In the former point of view, it is clear that the Olympian games were of very little efficacy. The short periodical cessation of hostilities hardly diminished the effusion of blood. The Greeks must, indeed, on such occasions, have become conscious of their distinction from all foreigners, whom they called barbarians; but they did not find in them the means of merging their local and domestic patriotism in the more comprehensive sentiment of a common country and nationality. The business of the festival, in fact, rather nourished the selfish passions of rival cities and states, each of which felt its own honour concerned in the success or failure of the individual competitors; and at every step there was as much to recal to their remembrance the political disunion of the Greeks, as their national union. The accidental and contingent effects produced by these meetings were probably much more important. The scene of the Olympic festival was a mart of busy commerce, where productions, not only of manual, but of intellectual labour, were exhibited and exchanged. Thoughts, inventions, and discoveries were thus communicated, and produced an equable diffusion of knowledge among the Greeks. Literary productions were read and published there, and poetry and sculpture in particular received a great impulse from the events of the contests. It may be said, that at those solemnities the animal powers were the chief instruments by which a Greek was raised so far above his countrymen and rose almost to heroic honours. The exercises which were held in such high esteem, consisted indeed principally in the development of the bodily faculties; but it cannot be denied that they at the same time contributed to the healthiness, freshness, and vigour of the Greek intellect. All public amusements in the Roman amphitheatres, and in the tournaments of our ancestors, appear little better than barbarous and bloody shows when compared with the Grecian spectacles.

Each of the institutions which we have been considering, might have become instrumental in uniting the Greeks into a political confederacy, but they do not seem to have even suggested the idea of such a thing. Mutual jealousy stifled this natural thought, and was early heightened by the great diversity of the forms of government, which rose up in the several states of Greece. The same cause, indeed, at a later period led to partial alliances; but such combinations, as they widened the breach out of which they arose, only served to render a general union more hopeless, and war the habitual state of Greece. The form of government universally prevalent in the Homeric age appears to have been a monarchy, limited by ancient custom as well as by a body of powerful chiefs who were almost the king's equals; it was in fact an aristocracy, with an hereditary prince at its head. But during the first two or three centuries after the Trojan war, various causes were at work, which tended to reduce the power, and abolish the title of royalty, in almost every part of Greece. Military expeditions or violent internal revolutions often displaced a dynasty, leaving its place unoccupied; and in all cases the power of the nobles increased at the expense of that of the kings. The great migrations of the Thessalians, Boeotians, and Dorians, contributed greatly to the same end; for in most parts of Greece they dislodged or destroyed the lines of ancient kings; and the migrating tribes themselves, though accustomed to monarchy, naturally tended to reduce the regal power, by constantly reminding those who held it that they were dependent upon the people, and owed everything to the men in arms. But all such things were the occasion, rather than the cause, of the decline of monarchical power; that result was attributable to the energy and versatility of the Greek mind, which prevented it from ever stiffening in the mould of Oriental institutions, and from stopping short in any career which it had once opened, before it had passed through every stage.

Royalty, however, was very rarely, if ever, abolished by a sudden and violent revolution; the title often long survived the substance, and the latter was extinguished only by slow successive steps, which consisted in abolishing its hereditary character, and making it elective, first in one family, then in more—first for life, then for a certain number of years, and lastly, in separating its functions and distributing them into several hands. In the course of these changes the king became more and more responsible to the nobles, and the title itself was frequently exchanged for one simply signifying a ruler or chief magistrate.* The form of government thus substituted for monarchy, might be termed either an aristocracy, or an oligarchy; that is, the government of the nobles distinguished from the multitude by birth, military valour, and skill, and by such personal merits as in a simple age will gain for their possessor the esteem of his fellow-men. These nobles were in most cases the descendants of the warlike conquerors, who had subdued the original inhabitants of the country, and distributed their landed property among themselves. In the course of time, while the ruling body remained stationary or was even losing

* Such as archon (ἄρχων) or prytanis (πρύτανις connected with πρῶτος).

strength, the commonalty—the class which, though personally free, was at first excluded from all share in the government—was constantly growing in numbers and wealth, was becoming more united in itself, more conscious of its resources, and more disposed to put forward new claims. This was the case especially in the larger cities, which were at all times the most formidable opponents of oligarchies. Various means were devised by the nobles to prevent the overthrow of their power; such as restraints upon the sale of landed property, and regulations guarding against any material increase or decrease in the numbers of the privileged body. But the utmost that an oligarchy could effect by such means, was to keep itself stationary; it could neither prevent the continual growth of the commonalty, nor keep pace with it by a corresponding expansion of its own frame. Under such circumstances, it often became necessary to make a compromise between the nobles and the commonalty; the former appeasing the latter by allowing them some small share in the management of affairs, or by altering the basis of the constitution in such a way that wealth was substituted for birth as a qualification for the higher privileges of citizenship. A constitution in which property was the standard of civic rights and duties, was called a *timocracy*. As the nobles were generally the wealthiest also, such a reform might produce little or no real change. When, however, the property standard was low, so that members of the middle classes also might participate in the administration of affairs, the constitution became what the Greeks called a *polity*, and was considered the best and most durable democracy. In the feuds between the two parties in a state, recourse was often had to the appointment of an individual with unlimited power, to restore order and tranquillity. This, however, was only a temporary measure, and rarely produced lasting effects.

The Greek oligarchies were sometimes overthrown by a disastrous war, but more frequently by revolutions or dissensions within their own body; and then it not rarely happened that one of the nobles, who by superior skill or prudence had conciliated the commonalty, raised himself with its assistance above his brother nobles. Such a usurper was designated by the name of tyrant (*τύραννος*). Most of the tyrannies which we meet with in Greek history, down to the time of the Persian wars, owed their origin to feuds between the ruling class and the commonalty, or among the rulers themselves. Some of the tyrants abused the power thus acquired, while others acted with caution and prudence, and thus kept their subjects in quiet submission, though they had a watchful eye upon whatever might prove dangerous to their power. Partly to keep the lowest classes in good humour, and partly to gratify their taste and magnificence, the tyrants often adorned their cities with costly buildings, which required years of labour from numerous hands. For the same reason they were not reluctant to engage in wars, which afforded them opportunities of relieving themselves both from troublesome friends and from dangerous enemies, as well as of strengthening their dominion by conquest. By these and similar means, many a tyrant contrived to reign in peace, and transmit his power to his descendants, as if he had possessed an hereditary right to the sovereignty. But still scarcely one instance is known in which a tyrannical dynasty lasted beyond the third generation; for the sons of a tyrant rarely possessed the prudence necessary to keep them in their usurped position; and even if they did possess it, they did not think it necessary to exercise it. A variety of impolitic steps generally obliged the ruler to have recourse to foreign troops, by whose aid he destroyed or exiled the most illustrious among his subjects. By such means he made himself universally odious and despised; and one cruel act leading to another, he at length fell a victim to a conspiracy which his own deeds had instigated and matured. Whenever Spartan aid was sought against a tyranny it was readily granted; partly because Sparta dreaded evil consequences to her own constitution from such examples, and partly because she was always glad of an opportunity to extend her own influence by taking an active part in the revolutions of other states, which would afterwards naturally look upon her as their defender and protector. Accordingly most of the tyrannies which existed in Greece previously to the Persian wars, are said to have been overthrown by the exertions of Sparta; and this, no doubt, greatly contributed to the acquisition by her of that paramount influence which is commonly called the supremacy of Sparta in the affairs of Greece.

Sparta, however, was not generally satisfied with simply overthrowing tyrannical power; where circumstances permitted it, her object was to establish a constitution as similar as possible to her own; but she was sometimes unintentionally instrumental in promoting the triumph of principles more adverse to her own views than those of tyranny itself; for when, after the temporary usurpation, the struggle between the nobles and the commonalty was renewed, the two parties were usually no longer in the same relative position as before, the commonalty having gained in strength and spirit even more than the oligarchy had lost; and consequently there was always a strong leaning towards democracy, which in many cases succeeded in establishing a timocracy, substituting wealth for birth. The standard of property was then gradually lowered until it was wholly abolished, and the constitution became truly democratic. An instance of this process will be seen in the history of Attica. It would lead us too far to enter here into a description of the various shades of the republican and democratic forms of government which were established in the different states of Greece. What happened at Athens and Sparta was repeated in the other states, with more or fewer modifications according to local and political circumstances. Suffice it to say that, in all the states of Greece, with the exception of Sparta, royalty was abolished about the same time, and that this change was everywhere brought about by similar causes.

Circe giving the cup to Ulysses.
(From a Pompeian painting.)

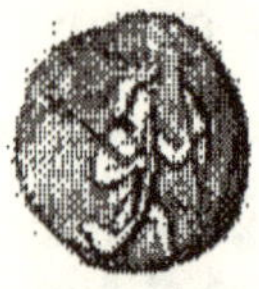

Gold Daric.

CHAPTER X.

CIVIL HISTORY OF ATTICA TO THE EXPULSION OF THE PEISISTRATIDS.

THE early history of Attica is much less attractive than that of the Doric nations, being almost entirely destitute of those grand poetical stories which are interwoven with the traditions of the Doric tribes.

The territory of Attica is said to have been originally divided into a number of little states, each of which was governed by a chief bearing the title of king. Cecrops is described as the first who established a confederacy among these petty states, for the purpose of defending them against the Carian pirates and the Boeotians. For this purpose he divided the country into twelve districts*, a number which we find predominating in the Ionian institutions. Athens, under the name of Cecropia, appears to have been at the head of the confederacy, whose council probably held its periodical meetings in the temple of Athena, the tutelary divinity of Attica and Athens. Other accounts state, that the whole country or people was divided into four tribes, which changed their names under several successive kings; thus under Cecrops their names are said to have been Cecropis, Autochthon, Actaea, and Paralia; under Cranaus, Cranais, Atthis, Mesogaea, and Diacris; while under Erichthonius we find the names Dias, Athenais, Posidonias and Hephaestias,—all of which are derived from names of divinities; whereas some of the names in the two preceding lists refer to the natural features of the country, and others to the origin or political relations of its inhabitants. But these divisions, whatever historical value we may attribute to them, were superseded by one much more celebrated and lasting, which is said to have been instituted by Ion, the founder of the Ionian race, and to have derived the names of its tribes from his four sons, namely,

* Or he is represented as sovereign of Attica, and as the founder of twelve townships.

the Teleontes (Geleontes or Gedeontes), Hopletes, Aegicores, and Argades. These names, however, are evidently descriptive of certain occupations; and hence the tribes have been regarded by some modern writers as castes, and their names as indicative of their respective employments. The second, no doubt, denotes a class of warriors; and the third those inhabitants of the country who tended their flocks on the Attic hills. From this alone we might infer, that the names of the first and fourth tribes, likewise, had reference to the occupations of their members; but their precise meaning is still the subject of controversy. The name Argades seems to denote labourers in general, and must have been applied either to a class of husbandmen, or to one employed in other laborious occupations. Which of these is the correct explanation might be easily decided, if the meaning of the name of the first tribe were ascertained. But that name, which appears in three different forms, admits of different explanations. Some consider the Teleontes or Geleontes as a sacerdotal caste; while, according to others, they were peasants who tilled the lands of their lords, and paid a tribute or rent for the use of them. If they were a priestly caste, they would probably occupy the hallowed territory of Eleusis, and this notion seems to be confirmed by the fact, that their name stands first in the list. The country of Attica would thus be divided into four geographical districts, one of which belonged to the warriors, who may be conceived as the descendants of a conquering race. The opinion that the Geleontes were a class of dependent husbandmen is incompatible with the idea of a geographical division of the country, which cannot be well set aside; for how could these husbandmen have inhabited a distinct district of Attica, if they had to till the lands of their lords on whose estates they must have lived?

If we designate these four divisions by the name of castes, we must be careful what meaning we attach to it. Certain occupations may at one time have been hereditary in the same families; but we are nowhere informed that such a separation and exclusion were ever sanctioned or enforced by either a religious or a civil ordinance. Such castes, if they existed at all, were only the result of circumstances, and were certainly not defined and constituted like the castes of India or Egypt. On the contrary, it is probable, that as they became more closely united into one body, the primitive distinctions, to which they owed their names, were gradually obliterated by mutual intercourse. It still, however, remains difficult to say by what circumstances a priestly caste could have lost its sacred character, and become so diffused among the nation, that every trace of its having once formed a caste was completely effaced, as we find it to have been in the earliest history of Attica.

A great revolution might have effected the change, but of such a revolution there is no vestige in the history of Attica.

The four tribes of Ion were, perhaps, originally not members of one body, but distinct communities, long kept apart by differences of descent, of situation, of pursuits, and of religion, yet still connected by neighbourhood, by affinities of blood and language, and by the occasional need of mutual assistance. Their gradual union was thus prepared and promoted; and the superiority of the race which occupied Athens, naturally disposed all to look upon that city as the natural head and centre of political union. The effect of all these causes is commonly described as the work of Theseus, who is said to have consolidated the national unity, and thus to have laid the foundations of the future greatness of Athens. The legend represents him as having collected the inhabitants of Attica into one city, and as having thus for ever put an end to the discord and hostility which until then had prevented them from considering themselves as one people. It cannot, indeed, be conceived that the whole population of Attica, or even any considerable portion of it, should have migrated to Athens; all that appears to be meant is, that Attica was united into one state, of which Athens became the head and the seat of the government, all the other towns sinking from the rank of sovereign states into that of subjects. This union was cemented by religion, perhaps by the mutual recognition of deities which had hitherto been honoured only in particular localities, and was certainly celebrated by public festivals, at which the whole people paid their homage to the tutelary goddess of Athens.* The city is said to have been enlarged on that occasion, and the lower city was added to the ancient one, which had covered little more than the rock of the acropolis.† The families, which by this new order of things were induced to take up their abode at Athens, were, no doubt, chiefly those of the highest rank, whose members had formed the ruling class in their respective states, and who were admitted to a similar station under the new constitution.

Theseus is described by the ancients as the founder of the political institutions of Athens, and later orators and poets went so far as to hold him up as the parent of Athenian democracy. This, however, arose only from their natural desire to represent that form of government, which was dear to all, as venerable by its antiquity, just as at Rome the plebeians were always inclined to look upon Servius Tullius as the author of all their political rights

* Such at least is said to have been the origin of the Ξυνοίκια of the Panathenaea, and of the festival of Aphrodite Pandemos.

† Hence perhaps the plural name Ἀθῆναι, which Theseus is said to have given to the sovereign city.

and privileges. The constitution of which Theseus is called the founder, remained, for many centuries after him, rigidly aristocratical. Theseus is said to have accomplished his object by a promise made to the nobles (for with the lower classes he found no difficulty) that all of them should be admitted to an equal share in the government, and that he would resign his royal prerogatives, except the command in war and the administration of justice. To guard, on the other hand, against democratical confusion, he instituted a gradation of ranks and a proportionate distribution of power. Accordingly he divided the people into three classes, nobles (εὐπατρίδαι), husbandmen (γεωμόροι), and artisans (δημιουργοί); to the first of which he reserved all the offices of the state, with the privilege of regulating the affairs of religion, and of interpreting the laws, human and divine. These privileges were no doubt the same as the nobles had enjoyed in their respective states before the union; but by concentrating that class, its powers were in fact increased. The king himself was only the first among his equals, the four kings of the tribes (φυλοβασιλεῖς) were his constant assessors, and his colleagues rather than his counsellors, the chief difference being that they did not, like the king, hold their office for life.

In one sense, the constitution ascribed to Theseus had a democratic tendency, inasmuch as a number of isolated townships were by it united into a single body, and made to feel their strength more than before; so that they might thus begin more effectually to resist the encroachments of the nobles. In later times we meet with subdivisions of the tribes, which, although not attributed to Theseus, must have originated at the time when Attica was formed into one state. Each tribe contained three phratriæ * or fraternities, and each phratria was subdivided into thirty sections, called γένη, equivalent to the Latin *gens*, and nearly so to our word *clan*. The members of each γένος were called γεννῆται, and are said to have been thirty in number. That these gennetae cannot have been heads of families is clear from the simple fact, that families cannot be limited in their number, but are constantly either increasing or decreasing; unless, indeed, care was taken to regulate the number, by excluding certain families and admitting them only when vacancies occurred.

It is evident that the change of the Attic constitution which is ascribed to Theseus cannot have been the work of one man, but must be regarded as the gradual result of circumstances which may have required more than a century for fully working out their consequences, though we do not mean to deny that a par-

* Φρατρία or φράτρα, etymologically connected with *frater* and *brother*.

ticular person, perhaps called Theseus *, may have done much to bring about the reform, and establish it on a firm basis.

We are not informed in what relation the three classes of Athenians stood to one another. The name of the second may signify that it consisted of free landowners or peasants who cultivated the land of their masters; but it is probable that it contained neither class of men exclusively. The third class consisted of all those who subsisted on any kind of industry besides that connected with agriculture. It accordingly included a great variety of occupations, which were held in very different degrees of esteem. Whether there existed any political distinction between the second and third class, is uncertain; it is possible that there was none at all, the distance which separated both from the first class being so great that all minor gradations may have been lost in it.

Notwithstanding the absolute power of the nobles, there probably existed at Athens, as in most ancient states, an assembly of the people, though it may have exercised as little influence as that of Sparta. The first contests of the nobles were not waged with the people, but with the king. The legend represents the kingly power as on the decline even in the time of Theseus; for that hero himself is said to have been compelled, by a conspiracy of the nobles, to go into exile with his family, and to leave the throne to Menestheus, a descendant of the ancient kings. At a subsequent period, Thymoetes was forced to abdicate in favour of Melanthus, a stranger, who had no claim but his superior merit. After the death of Codrus, the nobles, taking advantage, perhaps, of the opportunity afforded by the dispute between his sons, are said to have abolished the title of king, and to have substituted for it that of archon (ἄρχων, ruler). This change does not seem to have affected the nature or extent of the royal prerogatives, except that the office became a responsible one. It was still held for life; and Medon, the son of Codrus, was the first archon. The office continued hereditary in his family; but it would appear that within the family of the Medontids, the succession was determined by the choice of the nobles. The responsible character of the archonship implies that those who elected, had also the power of deposing the chief magistrate. This power, however, did not satisfy the more ambitious spirits among the nobles, and they gradually but steadily advanced towards the accomplishment of their final object — a complete and equal participation in the sovereignty. After twelve reigns, ending with that of Alcmaeon,

* The etymology of the name Theseus, however, seems to justify the inference that it is a mere fiction, invented to describe a man who arranged and settled the affairs of the state.

in B.C. 752, the duration of the archonship was limited to ten years; but it still continued to be held by the descendants of Medon, until, through the guilt or misfortune of Hippomenes, the fourth decennial archon, they were deprived of the privilege. This change was soon followed by one of much greater importance, for in B.C. 682, the term of the archonship was reduced to a single year, and at the same time the various powers which had hitherto been possessed by one, were distributed among nine new magistrates. The first of these bore the distinguishing title of *the* archon, and the year was marked by his name.* He represented the majesty of the state, and exercised that kind of jurisdiction which had formerly belonged to the king, as the common parent of his people, the protector of families, the guardian of orphans and heiresses, and of the general rights of inheritance. The second archon received the title of king (ἄρχων βασιλεύς) †, because he represented the king in his capacity of high priest of the nation. He regulated the celebration of the most solemn festivals, decided all causes connected with religion, and protected the state from the pollution which it might incur through the heedlessness or impiety of individuals. The third archon bore the title of polemarchus (πολέμαρχος, commander in war), and supplied the place of the king as the leader of the people in war, and the guardian of its security in time of peace. He had jurisdiction over strangers who settled in Attica and over freedmen. The remaining six archons received the common title of thesmothetae (θεσμοθέται, legislators) ‡, not because they made the laws, but because, in the absence of any written laws, they, by their decisions as judges, established precedents equivalent to laws in a variety of cases, which did not fall under the cognisance of their colleagues.

This gradual increase of the power of the nobles, and their final triumph are almost the only events which fill the meagre annals of Attica, for several centuries. That period, however, was not, as might be supposed, one of peace and happiness for the people of Attica; on the contrary, whenever we catch a glimpse of what was going on, we perceive a very different state of things. The reign of Hippomenes, the last archon of the family of Codrus, was made memorable by the shame of his daughter, and by the extraordinary punishment which he inflicted on her and her seducer:

* Whence he was also called ἄρχων ἐπώνυμος, or ὁ ἐπώνυμος.

† In like manner, the title of *rex sacrorum* was retained at Rome after the abolition of the kingly power; probably because in matters relating to the gods it was thought impious to make any important change, even if it should be merely a matter of form.

‡ Before the time of Solon laws are said to have been called θεσμοί or statutes; whereas Solon called his laws νόμοι.

he is said to have shut her up to perish of hunger or by the fury of a wild horse, the companion of her confinement; while the seducer was put to death by being yoked to a chariot. The nobles seized the opportunity, deposed Hippomenes, and razed his house to the ground. This story might seem to indicate austerity and purity of manners in that age, but we are at the same time informed that Hippomenes was urged to this severity by the extreme dissoluteness prevailing in his family. Another event which breaks through the obscurity of that period, is the legislation of Draco, the accounts of which do not lead us to suppose that the people enjoyed any great degree of happiness under the government of the nobles, or that their manners were particularly innocent and mild.

The immediate occasion which led to Draco's legislation in B.C. 624 is not recorded, nor are we informed of the motives which induced him to give it that character of severity to which it owes its chief celebrity. We know, however, that he was the author of the first written laws of Athens; and as such a measure necessarily limited the authority of the nobles, the sole expositors and administrators of the customary law, we may reasonably conclude that the innovation was extorted from them by the growing discontent of the people. On the other hand, Draco no doubt framed his code as much as possible in conformity with established usage and with the wishes of the ruling class, to which he himself belonged; and the extreme rigour of his laws, which, as Demades said, were written in blood, was probably designed to overawe and repress the popular movement. The substitution of a written law for fluctuating and flexible customs, however, was an important step. Draco made no change in the constitution, but he transferred cases of murder or accidental homicide from the cognisance of the archons to magistrates called ephetae (ἐφέται). Although Draco himself is reported to have said, that in his opinion all offences, even the smallest, deserved to be punished with death, still there were some for which he provided a milder sentence. Thus an attempt to change his laws was to be punished with the loss of franchise; and on another occasion, we hear of a fine of the value of ten oxen. Hence we may perhaps infer, that the accounts of the extreme severity of his legislation have been somewhat exaggerated; but the obscurity in which the subject is involved precludes us from forming a correct opinion respecting it. Draco is said to have made himself so odious to the people of Athens, that he was obliged to quit the city and go to Aegina, where he died.

The power of the aristocracy had thus received a shock instead of a support from the legislation of Draco, and the discontent of the people rose to such a height, that it would willingly have submitted to a tyrant in order to get rid of the intolerable rule of the nobles, who were now threatened from a quarter where they probably thought themselves most secure. In B.C. 612, twelve years after Draco's legislation, a conspiracy was formed by one of their own order for overthrowing the government. It was headed by the eupatrid Cylon, distinguished by his wealth and by a victory at the Olympic games. He was married to a daughter of Theagenes, the tyrant of Megara, and conceived the design of making himself master of Athens. In this dangerous undertaking he relied on the general dissatisfaction of the people with the rule of the nobles, which in other cities of Greece also had led to the establishment of tyrannies. At this period scarcely any great enterprise was undertaken in Greece without the sanction of an oracle, and accordingly Cylon consulted the Delphic god, who answered, that he must seize the citadel of Athens during the principal festival of Zeus. Cylon having gained a prize at Olympia, naturally interpreted this to mean the Olympic games, forgetting that the great Attic festival in honour of Zeus, the Diasia, occurred at a different period; and he proceeded to carry his plan into effect in accordance with this incorrect notion of the meaning of the oracle. With the aid of a body of troops furnished by Theagenes and of his partisans, he made himself master of the acropolis. But Cylon, who seems to have lost the confidence and support of the people by employing foreign auxiliaries, soon found himself besieged by the forces which the government had called in from all parts of the country. During the blockade Cylon and his brother made their escape, but their adherents were not so fortunate. When their provisions were all spent and some had died of hunger, the remainder abandoned the defence of the walls and withdrew into the temple of Athene. The archon Megacles (the son of Alcmaeon) and his colleagues induced them to surrender, on condition that their lives should be spared, for it was apprehended that they might die in the temple and thus pollute the sanctuary. But the archons, disregarding their promise, put their prisoners to death when they had quitted their asylum, and some were even killed at the altars of the Eumenides or Furies, at which they had taken refuge.* As this crime was committed with the sanction of Megacles, who had thereby become guilty of a gross act of sacrilege, he and his whole family were looked upon as accursed persons, whose lives were forfeited to the gods. All public disasters were thenceforth attributed to them and inter-

* The account of this affair is not the same in all authors. We have adopted that of Thucydides, i. 126.: but comp. Plut. *Solon*, 12.; Herod. v. 71.; and Paus. vii. 25. § 1.

preted as signs of the divine wrath. The surviving partisans of Cylon did not fail to foster such a belief, and urged that the gods would never be appeased until vengeance should have been taken on the offenders. The excitement thus produced was another ingredient in the ferment which the conflict of political parties had called forth, and some extraordinary remedy for the evils of the state had now become absolutely necessary.

To soothe this excitement, to conciliate the hostile elements of society, and to apply a thorough cure for all the evils from which Athens was suffering, required a man, who by his birth as well as by mental superiority, by calm wisdom and freedom from prejudice, could raise himself above the strife of parties and secure respect for the reforms which he might think it necessary to introduce. That man was Solon, the son of Execestides, a descendant of the house of Codrus. In his youth he is said to have embarked in commercial adventures in order to repair his fortunes, which had been reduced by his father's imprudent liberality. It was, however, probably not more the desire of affluence than the thirst of knowledge, that impelled him to seek distant shores; and the most valuable fruit of his travels was the experience he collected of men, manners, and institutions. He had become acquainted and formed friendships with the most illustrious men of the age, such as Thales of Miletus, and Anacharsis the Scythian. On his return to Athens, probably not long after the Cylonian conspiracy, he found his country in a deplorable condition, distracted by exasperated parties, and scarcely able to resist the attacks of its least powerful neighbours. An old enmity existed between the Dorians of Megara and the Athenians, and the former had succeeded in wresting the island of Salamis from the latter, who had been repeatedly baffled in their attempts to recover their rightful possession of the island. These losses had broken the spirit of the Athenians, and had induced them to pass a decree which forbade any one, under penalty of death, to propose the renewal of so desperate an undertaking. Solon, who was himself a native of Salamis, was indignant at this pusillanimous policy, and is said to have devised an extraordinary plan for rousing his countrymen from their despondency. He was endowed with considerable poetical talent, and now composed a poem on the loss of Salamis. To elude the prohibition, he assumed the demeanour of a madman, and rushing into the market-place recited his poem to a crowd of bystanders.* It contained vehement censure of the disgrace which the Athenians had incurred, and a summons to take the field again

* The beginning of this poem, and many other fragments of his numerous works, are still extant. See Bach, *Solonis Atheniensis quae supersunt*, Bonn, 1825.

and vindicate their right to the lovely island. The people, stirred up by his enthusiasm, which was seconded by the applause of his friends, and especially by the eloquence of his young kinsman Pisistratus, immediately repealed the law, and it was resolved once more to try the fortune of arms.

Solon was entrusted with the command of the expedition, in which he was assisted by Pisistratus. In a single campaign he recovered Salamis by a stratagem, and drove the Megarians from the island, B.C. 604; Nisaea also appears to have fallen into the hands of the Athenians at that time. The Megarians, however, did not give up their pretensions, but while the Athenians were occupied with their internal troubles, recovered Nisaea and Salamis, where 500 Athenian colonists had formed settlements. Both parties now agreed to refer the matter in dispute to the arbitration of the Lacedaemonians. Solon, who acted as spokesman for the Athenians, satisfied the Lacedaemonian commissioners by his arguments, and by a reference to a passage in the Iliad *, that the claim of his countrymen was just. Athens thenceforth remained in undisturbed possession of Salamis, for Megara was soon eclipsed by the vast rising power of her old rival. Solon's fame rose still higher in consequence of the part which he afterwards took in the sacred war against Cirrha, which began in B.C. 594.†

Athens continued to be the scene of feuds between Megacles and his associates on the one hand, and the friends of Cylon on the other. Solon now, with the assistance of the moderate nobles, prevailed on the party of Megacles to submit their cause to the decision of a court of 300 men of their own order. The court pronounced them guilty; all the survivors were sent into exile, and even the bones of the deceased were taken out of their graves and carried beyond the frontier. This happened in B.C. 597. Party feuds however continued to rage with unabated fury at Athens; for the evil from which the state was suffering lay deeper and required a very different remedy, which was to be found only in a new organisation of the state. But before this could be undertaken, it was necessary to purify the city by religious ceremonies, and to allay the fears of the superstitious people, who thought that enough had not yet been done to propitiate the anger of the gods. For this purpose Solon, by the advice of the Pythia, invited Epimenides of Crete, who was renowned far and wide for his wisdom and magic powers, to come to Athens. This venerated person was received with a reverence which insured his success. He performed certain religious rites which soothed the fears of the

* He is said to have committed the patriotic fraud of forging the line in the Iliad, ii. 558, to which he appealed.

† See above, p. 105.

people, and among which a human sacrifice is mentioned; he founded a temple to the Eumenides on the Areopagus, and two altars to Hybris and Anaideia, the two malignant powers under whose influence Athens had been suffering for years. He further imposed restraints on the profuse expense with which private persons celebrated the worship of the gods, and on the extravagant signs of grief which women used to display at funerals. When he had accomplished his great work, he was dismissed with tokens of the warmest gratitude; but he declined all the honours which the Athenians were ready to shower upon him, and the only boon he requested was, for himself, a branch from the sacred olive-tree, which was believed to have been planted on the acropolis by Athena, and for his country, perpetual friendship between Athens and Cnossos.

By this preliminary process the minds of the Athenians were tranquillised, and they were enabled to consider their affairs with calmness and without angry passions. It had removed the imaginary evils, but the real ones yet remained to be remedied. The nobles, who wielded all the powers of government, had reduced a great part of the class engaged in agriculture to a state of abject dependence; the political rights of this class were little more than nominal; they held even their personal freedom by a precarious tenure, and were frequently reduced to actual slavery. The smaller proprietors, impoverished by bad times or casual disasters, were compelled to borrow money at high interest, and to mortgage their lands to the rich, or to receive them back as tenants upon hard terms. A noble was enabled by law to seize the person of his insolvent debtor and to sell him as a slave. Numbers had thus been torn from their homes and families and condemned to end their days in the service of a foreign master. Others were even obliged to sell their own children. This state of things must have affected Solon in the same way as, at a later period, a similar condition of society at Rome did the elder Gracchus, who was thus aroused to take his stand against the insatiable avarice of the Roman grandees. Those who groaned under this tyranny were eager only for a change, and unconcerned about the means by which it might be effected. But the population of Attica was not simply composed of these two classes. The eupatridae or noble landowners, who as a faction were called πεδιαῖοι or πεδιεῖς, because their estates lay mostly in the fertile plains, were anxious to keep things in their existing state. The hilly districts in the north and east of Attica were occupied by shepherds and poor peasants (διάκριοι or ὑπεράκριοι) who, though they do not seem to have suffered any of those evils which the rapacity and hard-heartedness of the powerful had inflicted on the lowland peasantry, were of a more democratic temper, and wished for a revolution which should place them on a level with the rich. The men of the coast (πάραλοι), in the port towns from Piraeus to Cape Sunion, who probably consisted mainly of those who subsisted by commerce and by the exercise of the mechanical arts, were averse to violent measures, but were desirous of a reform in the constitution, which should remove all reasonable grounds of complaint, and should admit a larger number to the enjoyment of those rights which were now engrossed and abused by a few.

Solon's reputation pointed him out as the man most capable of remedying the disorders of the state. He was therefore chosen, with the unanimous consent of all parties, to mediate between them; and under the legal title of archon he was invested with full authority to frame a new constitution and code of laws, B.C. 594. Such an office under such circumstances conferred almost unlimited power, and an ambitious man might easily have abused it to make himself tyrant of the state. His friends are said to have suggested this plan to him, but he was not tempted to betray the sacred trust reposed in him; instead of harbouring any selfish scheme, he bent all his thoughts and energies to the execution of the great task he had undertaken.

This task consisted of two parts: the first and most pressing business was to relieve the present distress of the commonalty; the second, to provide against the recurrence of the same or similar evils, by regulating the rights and duties of all the citizens according to just principles. In regard to the first, he adopted a middle course between the revolutionary schemes of the people and the selfish views of the privileged class, who wished to retain all that they had hitherto enjoyed. His first measure was a *disburdening ordinance* (σεισάχθεια), which relieved the debtor, partly by a reduction of the rate of interest, and partly by lowering the standard of the silver coinage, whereby a debtor saved more than one-fourth in every payment.* He also released the pledged lands from their incumbrances, and restored them in full property to their owners. Finally, he abolished the cruel law by which a creditor might enslave his debtor, and restored those who were pining at home in such bondage, to freedom. Those who had sold their debtors into foreign countries, seem to have been compelled to ransom them at their own expense. If any one should think that in these regulations Solon did not pay sufficient regard to the rights of property, he must remember that Solon had been chosen as an arbitrator, to whom all parties had volun-

* Plut. *Sol.* 15, states that he made the mina, which before contained 73 drachms, to contain 100; that is, that he made 73 old drachms to be worth 100 new ones.

tarily submitted their claims, and to whom they had given full power to act in the manner which he thought best for the good of the state.

After this Solon entered upon his second and more difficult task. He began by repealing the laws of Draco, except those which concerned the repression of bloodshed and murder. It was, perhaps, in consequence of this abolition, that he published an amnesty, which restored those citizens who had been deprived of their franchise for lighter offences, and recalled those who had been sent into exile. This act of grace seems to have included the members of the family of Megacles, or the Alcmaeonids, as they are more commonly called. The four ancient tribes were retained with all their subdivisions; but it would appear that Solon admitted as new citizens such foreigners as had settled in the country with their whole family and substance, and had given up all connection with their native land. But the distinguishing feature of his constitution was the substitution of property for birth, as the standard to determine the rights and duties of the citizens. This change, though its consequences were most important, probably produced little alteration at the time, as wealth and birth generally concurred in the same person. According to their property then, Solon divided all Athenian citizens into four classes. The first consisted of persons whose estates yielded a net yearly income or rent of 500 measures of dry or liquid produce (πεντακοσιομέδιμνοι*); the second class contained those whose income amounted to 300 measures, and who were called knights (ἱππῆς or ἱππεῖς), as being accounted able to keep a war-horse. The members of the third class had an annual revenue of 200, or more probably 150 measures, and were termed ζευγῖται, because they were supposed to keep a yoke of oxen for the plough. The fourth class, called θῆτες, comprehended all whose incomes fell below that of the third, and appears to have consisted of hired labourers in husbandry. The highest offices of the state were accessible only to members of the first class; some lower offices were no doubt left open to the second and third classes; but it is uncertain whether the second had any rights or privileges not belonging to the third. These classes, however, were distinguished from each other by the mode of their military service; the second class furnished the cavalry, and the third the heavy-armed infantry. As their rights were inferior to those of the first class, so their burdens were lighter; for they were assessed, not in exact proportion to the amount of their incomes, but at a much lower rate, the nominal value of their property being

* The measure, μέδιμνος, here spoken of, is about six pints more than a bushel.

for this purpose reduced below the truth, that of the knights by one-sixth, and that of the third class by one-third. The fourth class was excluded from all public offices, and served in the army only as light troops; in later times they were employed in manning the fleets. They paid no direct contributions, but were allowed to take part in the popular assembly as well as in the courts in which justice was administered by the people.

This classification takes no notice of any other than landed property; and it is probable that all those whose wealth consisted in capital, were placed on a level with the members of the fourth class. In this manner, every order of citizens had its place assigned to it, the object of the legislator being to give to the commonalty such a share of power as would enable it to protect itself, and to the wealthy as much as was necessary for maintaining their dignity, or for ruling the people without oppressing them. The magistrates retained their ancient powers, but became responsible for the exercise of them, not to their own body, but to the governed. The judicial functions of the archons were, perhaps, preserved in their full extent, but appeals were allowed from their jurisdiction to popular courts, numerously composed, and filled indiscriminately from all classes. The democratic element which was powerful in the assembly and in the judicial courts, and which in the end overruled every other power in the state, was, in the legislator's opinion, to be checked by two great councils, that of the Four Hundred, and that of the Areopagus.

The institution of the senate (βουλή) of Four Hundred is uniformly assigned to Solon; but there can be no doubt that before his time a senate or council of nobles existed, though we do not know its number, nor whether it represented the four tribes; Solon increased this council to the number of four hundred, and gave it a more popular constitution by ordaining that its members were to be taken from the first three classes, each of the four tribes furnishing one hundred. As the members of this council were in all probability elected, and as a large portion of the population was excluded from it, the body must have been of an aristocratic, rather than of a democratic temper. Besides the fitness for their office, as inferred from their property, age also was taken into consideration, none being eligible under thirty. They held their dignity for only one year, at the end of which they were liable to render a general account of their conduct, and to meet the charges which might be brought against them. As the senate was mainly designed to restrain and guide the enlarged powers of the popular assembly, the principal part of its business was to prepare the measures which were to be submitted to the votes of the people, and to preside over its deliberations. The senate was divided into sections called prytanes (πρυτάνεις), succeeding one another throughout the year, as the representatives of the whole body. Each section during its term assembled daily in its session-house (πρυτανεῖον) to attend to its duties. The members were entertained at a common table, together with the guests of the state, who enjoyed that privilege either by virtue of some office, or as a reward of merit. Besides the functions above mentioned, the senate also possessed powers connected with the finances and other subjects of administration. Thus it had the power of issuing ordinances or edicts, which continued in force for the current year, and of inflicting fines to a certain amount at discretion.

The Areopagus likewise is said to have been founded by Solon, though it is certain that he only made some changes in its constitution; but of this we shall speak hereafter. According to Solon's theory, the people in its assembly was little more than the organ of the senate, as it could act only upon propositions (προβουλεύματα) laid before it by the latter. But, unlike the Spartan assembly, that of Athens had not only the right of adopting and rejecting, but also of modifying or amending the measures proposed, without sending them back for the acceptance of the senate in their altered form. The ordinary assemblies seem to have been held at most once in every month, and certainly did not at first excite as lively an interest as in later times; it was even found necessary to punish those citizens who neglected the duty of attending the meetings. The votes were taken by show of hands (χειροτονία) and without any distinction of classes; the vote of the humblest Athenian being of as much weight as that of the wealthiest noble, and every voter was allowed to speak. The exercise of the right of taking part in the assembly began at the age of twenty; but those who were past fifty, were called upon to express their opinion first. No fixed number of voters appears to have been necessary, except in a few cases which required the presence of at least 6000 citizens.

For the purpose of exercising the judicial power which Solon gave to the people, a body of 6000 citizens was every year created by lot to form a supreme court, called heliaea (ἡλιαία), which was divided into several smaller ones, not limited to any precise number of persons. Every citizen who had the right to take a part in the popular assembly, and had attained the age of thirty, might become a member of this court. It was thus a select portion of the larger body, and Solon seems to have viewed it rather as the guardian of the constitution, than as the minister of the laws, as we must infer from the oath prescribed to the heliastae. The peculiar sphere of action of these popular courts, as representatives of the people, lay in questions relating to political offences, especially in prosecutions instituted against authors of illegal measures. For any one who had caused a decree to be passed, which was afterwards found to be inconsistent with existing laws, or with the public interest, was held responsible for his conduct, and if convicted within a year after the passing of his measure, was liable to punishment. A decree of the popular assembly might thus be reversed by the heliaea.

Solon was too wise a man to believe that the laws which he enacted could remain in force at all times, and under altered circumstances; accordingly he made regulations subjecting them to perpetual revision. At the first popular assembly in every year, proposals were received from any person for a change in the existing laws. If such a proposal seemed to be useful or desirable, the third ordinary meeting of the year might appoint a committee of legislation (νομοθέται), drawn by lot from the heliaea, to examine the merits of the proposal. This committee then proceeded according to the forms of a legal trial; and if the proposal was approved of, it came immediately into force, but its author was still responsible for it. The thesmothetae also were enjoined constantly to keep a watchful eye on the laws, and to bring before the committee of legislation any imperfections which they might discover.

Solon's legislation was of so simple a nature, that he thought every man endowed with the ordinary degree of intelligence qualified to sit in judgment on his fellow-men. Lawyers in our sense, therefore, did not exist at Athens, nor was there any distinction between the province of the judge and that of the jury. Solon considered that every citizen ought to be interested in the maintenance of order and justice; and hence he encouraged every one to come forward as prosecutor in cases affecting the interest of the state; but that he did not intend to promote a spirit of litigation in general, is clear from his institution of the public arbitrators (διαιτηταί), a body of persons past the age of sixty, who were annually appointed by lot. Before them all private causes might be brought, and from them, when they were chosen with the consent of both parties, no appeal was allowed.

The council of the Areopagus, or the Hill of Ares, so called from an eminence on the western side of the acropolis, where its sittings were held *, had from time immemorial been a highly revered court of criminal justice, which took cognisance of cases of wilful murder, maiming, poisoning, and arson. It was held in the open air. Its forms and modes of proceeding were peculiarly

* Hence it is sometimes called ἡ ἄνω βουλή, "the upper council," to distinguish it from the senate, or council of four hundred.

rigid and solemn; and the defendant was kept closely to the point at issue. Both parties were obliged to affirm the truth of their allegations with the most awful oaths; but before sentence was passed the culprit might evade its consequences by going into voluntary exile. It is not certain whether the constitution of the Areopagus, such as we find it subsequently, is the work of Solon, or whether he only retained the ancient regulations. Henceforth the vacancies occurring in the council were filled by the archons who had discharged their office with approved fidelity, and they held their seats for life. Solon, moreover, extended the powers of this venerable body, by erecting it into a supreme council, with a superintending and controlling authority over almost every part of the social system. Thus it became the guardian of the public morals and religion, and kept watch over the education and conduct of the citizens. It is, however, extremely difficult precisely to define the limits of its powers, and it was probably Solon's intention to leave them in that obscure and undefined state, with a view to magnify its authority in the eyes of the people; for its strength rested on public opinion, not on any written law. When the votes of the council were equally divided in any case, the herald cast a white stone into the urn in favour of the accused, just as Athene was believed to have procured the acquittal of Orestes; and hence this vote was called the vote of Athene (ὁ Ἀθηνᾶς ψῆφος).

Our knowledge of the civil and penal codes which Solon introduced, is very scanty and fragmentary, and we shall draw attention to a few points only, connected with education and the state of manners at Athens. He did not think it desirable to exercise that minute control over the citizens which Lycurgus had established at Sparta. Up to the age of sixteen, the education of the Athenian youth was left entirely to his parents or guardians. During the next two years he was obliged to be trained in gymnastic exercises, under publicly appointed masters, who kept him subject to a discipline little less severe than that of Sparta. At eighteen he might become master of his patrimony, and entered upon his apprenticeship in arms; he had to keep watch in the towns and fortresses on the frontier and the coast, and perform any task which might be imposed upon him for the protection of his country. It appears that at this stage his name was entered in the list of citizens (ληξιαρχικὸν γραμματεῖον), and he had to take the military oath, by which he pledged himself never to disgrace his arms, nor to desert his comrade; to fight to the last in defence of Attica, its altars, and its hearths; to leave his country not in worse, but in better, plight than he found it; to obey the magistrates and the laws, and resist all attempts to subvert them; and to respect the religion of his ancestors. At the end of these two years he was admitted to all the rights and duties of a citizen for which the law did not prescribe a more advanced age. Till the end of his sixtieth year he was liable to be called out to perform military service. The general object of Solon's regulations regarding the female sex was to restrain the license it had hitherto enjoyed, and often abused; and officers were appointed to enforce the observance of them. Women were forbidden to go abroad with more than three changes of apparel and a certain quantity of provisions, to pass through the street by night, otherwise than in a carriage and with a light carried before them, and to wail with frantic or studied vehemence at funerals. These regulations seem to show, that in the time of Solon women were not subject to that jealous seclusion with which, in later ages, they are generally believed to have been confined to their homes.

Solon appears to have been the first to perceive the advantageous position of Athens for becoming a maritime power, and to have laid the foundation of the Attic navy. He charged the forty-eight sections, called naucrariae (ναυκραρίαι), into which the tribes had been divided for financial purposes, each with the equipment of a galley, as well as with the mounting of two horsemen. He also gave active encouragement to trade and manufactures, and with this view invited foreigners to settle in Attica, by the assurance of protection and large privileges. These resident aliens (μέτοικοι), however, were still kept distinct from the citizens; they were not allowed to acquire landed property in Attica; their burdens were heavier, and some of them were peculiar. Each had to pay a small alien-tax (μετοίκιον), and to place himself under the guardianship of a citizen, who was his representative in the courts of justice. Certain duties, also, were imposed upon them, which seem to have been devised to remind them of their position. Many, however, were admitted to the franchise, and others, who had gained the favour of the people, were exempted from their peculiar burdens as aliens.

The condition of slaves in Attica was, at least in later times, less wretched than in other parts of Greece; but it is unknown how far Solon may have contributed to this state of things. It is certain, however, that at an early age a slave was entitled to claim the protection of the law against the cruelty of a brutal master, who might be compelled to transfer him to another owner. But there can be little doubt that Solon sanctioned the atrocious abuse to which a slave was subject in the Athenian courts, where, at the discretion of either party, evidence might be wrung from him by torture; and his evidence, even when offered freely, was deemed worthless until it had been sifted by the rack. On this point Solon did not rise above his age and country, for even aliens were exposed to the same treatment.

The laws of Solon were inscribed on wooden tablets, arranged in pyramidal blocks, turning on an axis*: at first they were kept in the acropolis; but afterwards, for greater convenience of inspection, were brought down to the Prytaneum. It is said that, after the completion of his legislation, Solon, to escape from over-curious inquirers and cavillers, withdrew from Athens for a period of ten years, and visited Asia Minor, Cyprus, and Egypt. During his travels he is reported to have become acquainted with Croesus, king of Lydia, and Amasis, the ruler of Egypt; but as neither of these princes can have ascended the throne before B.C. 572, Solon's travels, if they are an historical fact, must be assigned to a much later date; and it is, in fact, far more likely that, after the completion of his work, the legislator remained at Athens for some years, to watch its working and to see its principles gaining hold of the popular mind, than that he immediately quitted his country.

On his return to Athens, about B.C. 562, he found that faction had been actively engaged in attempting to pervert and undo his work. The three parties of the Plain, the Coast, and the Highlands, had revived their ancient feuds. The first of them was now headed by Lycurgus, the second by Megacles (a grandson of the archon who had brought the curse upon his house), and the third by Pisistratus, Solon's kinsman and the friend of his youth. Solon had early detected the designs of Pisistratus, but in vain endeavoured to avert the danger by attempting to reconcile the chiefs of the factions; and Pisistratus waited only for an opportunity to carry out his plans. He had resolved to renew the enterprise of Cylon, in which his noble birth, his eloquence, and munificence towards the poorer citizens, promised him better success. When his scheme appeared to be ripe for action, he was one day drawn in a chariot into the public place, his own person and his mules disfigured by recent wounds, inflicted, as the sequel showed, by his own hands; these he displayed to the multitude, telling them that he had narrowly escaped a band of assassins, who had been employed to murder the friend of the people. While the indignation of the multitude was fresh, an assembly was called by his partisans, in which one of them brought forward the motion, that a guard of fifty citizens, armed with clubs, should be appointed to protect the person of Pisistratus. Solon was the

* Ἄξονες, κύρβεις. According to some, the ἄξονες contained the civil laws, and the κύρβεις the religious ones.

only man who ventured to oppose this proposal; but as all who thought like him did not dare to brave the danger of expressing their opinion, the body-guard was decreed. As the people did not pay much attention to the manner in which Pisistratus made use of the means thus placed at his disposal, he raised a force and made himself master of the acropolis. Megacles and the Alcmaeonids left the city. Solon, after an ineffectual effort to rouse the people against the tyrant, laid his arms before his door, as a sign that he had made his last exertion in behalf of liberty and the laws. Lycurgus and his party seem for a time to have quietly submitted to the authority of Pisistratus, waiting only for a favourable opportunity of overthrowing him. This happened in B.C. 560.

Like most of the Greek tyrants, Pisistratus was satisfied with the substance of power, avoiding all display of it. He made no visible changes in the constitution, affected in his own person the demeanour of a private citizen, and submitted to the laws by appearing before the Areopagus to answer a charge of murder, which, however, the accuser did not think fit to prosecute. He even continued to court the friendship and to ask the advice of Solon, who seems to have endured the usurpation, because he saw no alternative between tyranny and anarchy. According to the most authentic account, Solon died in B.C. 559, the very year after this revolution. In the mean time, Lycurgus formed a coalition with Megacles, and their united efforts compelled Pisistratus to quit Athens. How long his first tyrannis lasted is uncertain, though it was probably not much more than one year.

How little the coalition could depend upon the people, however, soon became evident; for when the property of the exiled tyrant was exposed to public sale, no one could be found to bid for it, but Callias, an ancestor of Alcibiades. The union between Lycurgus and Megacles, moreover, could not last long; and at the end of five years, Megacles, finding himself unable to secure all the advantages he had expected, made overtures of reconciliation to Pisistratus, and offered to bestow on him the hand of his daughter and to assist him in recovering the station which he had lost. Pisistratus accepted the proposal, though he was long past the prime of life, and the father of three sons and a daughter by a former marriage. A plan was now concerted for the restoration of Pisistratus, which struck even Herodotus by its childish simplicity. A tall comely woman, named Phya, was arrayed in a complete suit of armour, and riding in the same chariot with Pisistratus, brought him back to Athens, where she was believed to be the goddess Athene, conducting her favourite to her own citadel. This spectacle, however, was probably devised only to add unusual solemnity to the entrance of Pisistratus, and to suggest the reflection that he was restored by the especial favour of heaven. But the probability of the story is diminished by the addition, that Pisistratus rewarded the woman, who is said to have been a garland-seller, for her services, by giving her in marriage to one of his sons. Pisistratus himself, according to the compact, married the daughter of Megacles; but it was soon discovered that he did not treat her as his wife, and that he had no intention of really uniting his blood with that of a family which was believed to lie under a curse. The Alcmaeonids were indignant at the affront, and determined once more to make common cause with Lycurgus. Pisistratus, unable to resist the combined power of his enemies, was again driven into exile, and went to Eretria in Euboea. The second tyrannis had probably lasted not more than two years, and he now deliberated with his sons whether he should not abandon all thoughts of returning to Attica. But Hippias, the eldest, prevailed on his father again to make head against his enemies. He had large possessions in Thrace, and had great interest in various parts of Greece, especially at Argos and Thebes, which latter distinguished itself by the liberality of its subsidies. By the end of ten years he had completed his preparations; a body of mercenaries was brought to him from Argos, and Lygdamis, one of the most powerful men in the island of Naxos, came to his aid with all the troops and money he could raise. With these he sailed from Eretria, and landed on the plain of Marathon. The government of his enemies had not been popular at Athens during his absence, and his numerous friends in the city and country flocked to his camp as soon as he arrived. Megacles and Lycurgus hastily collected their forces, but at noon they were taken by surprise on their road from Athens to Marathon, for they showed as little of watchfulness in the field, as of forethought in their counsels. Pisistratus, instead of following up his victory and slaughtering his flying enemies, proclaimed a general amnesty on condition of their dispersing quietly to their homes. The leaders of the hostile factions finding themselves deserted by nearly all, abandoned the city, and left their opponent undisputed master of Athens.

What he had so hardly won he determined to hold henceforth with a firm grasp: he no longer relied on the affections of the people; but surrounded himself with a body of foreign mercenaries, and seizing the children of some of the nobles who had opposed him, he sent them to Naxos, to be kept as hostages. By these means, and by the great popularity which he contrived to gain at Athens, he succeeded in maintaining his position for fourteen years, until his death, in B.C. 527. The fact that he is said to have raised his friend Lygdamis to the tyrannis in Naxos, presupposes the existence of a naval force; and this force he also employed in the recovery of Sigeum on the Hellespont, which was then in the possession of the Mytilenaeans, and about which Athens and Mytilene had been at war nearly half a century before, when it is related the sage Pittacus gained a memorable victory over the Athenians, having come into the field armed with a casting-net, a trident, and a dagger; and having first entangled the Athenian general Phrynon with the net, he then dispatched him with the dagger. In a later battle of the same war the poet Alcaeus lost his shield. At length the war had been brought to a close, through the mediation of Periander of Corinth, who awarded Sigeum to Athens. The Mytilenaeans, however, refused to surrender the town, and Pisistratus now took it from them by force, entrusting it to the keeping of his bastard son, Hegesistratus, who successfully defended it against long-continued attacks. By this conquest he not only increased his reputation at home, but secured a place for himself, if fortune should again turn against him.

Pisistratus, as the ruler of the chief city of the Ionian name, undertook the purification of the island of Delos, which an oracle had commanded, and which was effected by the removal of all the dead bodies that had been buried within sight of the temple of Apollo. At home, he still maintained the institutions of Solon, and courted popularity by munificent largesses, and by throwing open his gardens to the poorer citizens. The law of Solon, which required every citizen to give an account of his means of gaining a subsistence, enabled him to remove from the city a great number of the poorer class, and to compel them to engage in rural occupations, in which, however, he is said to have assisted them with money, cattle, and seed. By this means he got rid of his most restless subjects, and gained the praise of a benefactor of the poor. He also adorned Athens with many useful and magnificent works. Among the latter was a temple of Apollo, and one dedicated to the Olympian Zeus, of which, however, he lived to complete the substructions only, and which was not finished till 700 years later, in the reign of the Emperor Hadrian. Among the monuments in which splendour and usefulness were combined, was the Lyceum, a garden at a short distance from Athens, sacred to the Lycian Apollo, where stately buildings for the exercises of the Athenian youth rose amid shady groves; and the fountain of Callirhoë, which, from the new channels in which Pisistratus distributed its waters, received the name of the Nine Springs (Ἐννεάκρουνος). The expenses of these works were defrayed out of the revived tithe on the produce of the land, which was thus a tax levied on the rich for the purpose of employing the poor, and with which the former were naturally not a little discontented. Pisistratus is also believed to have been the author of a wise and beneficent law for supporting, at the public expense, citizens disabled in war.

According to a tradition once very generally received, posterity has been indebted to him for a benefit greater than any which he conferred on his contemporaries, in the preservation of the Homeric poems, which until then are said to have been scattered in unconnected rhapsodies. He was probably not the first collector, but his collection was no doubt superior in extent and accuracy to all that had preceded it. His taste for literature appears to have been genuine; he was the first Greek who formed a library, and he imparted its contents to the public with great liberality. On the whole, it must be owned that he made princely use of the power he had usurped; and Athens was indebted to him for a season of repose, during which she gained much of that strength, which she finally unfolded. He died at an advanced age, B.C. 527, thirty-three years after his first usurpation.

His power was so firmly rooted, that his sons Hippias, Hipparchus, and Thessalus, succeeded him in the government without any opposition. Hippias, as the eldest, took his father's place at the head of affairs; but the three brothers seem to have lived in great unanimity, and to have worked together with little or no show of outward distinction. Hippias seems to have been distinguished as a statesman; Hipparchus inherited his father's literary taste, but was addicted to pleasure; of Thessalus we hear only that he was a spirited youth. For some years the Pisistratids followed the footsteps of their father, and seem to have directed their attention to promote the internal prosperity of the country and the cultivation of letters and arts. To Hipparchus is attributed the merit of having erected a number of Hermae, or stone busts of Hermes, along the roads leading from the capital, inscribed on one side with an account of the distance which it marked, and on the other with some moral sentence in verse. These verses were either the compositions of Hipparchus himself, or of one of the many distinguished poets whom he hospitably entertained in his house. He is also said to have established the order in which the Homeric poems continued in after times to be recited at the Panathenaic festival. Although the three brothers, like their father, made no display of power, yet they were not always scrupulous about the means which they employed to get rid of persons who had incurred their hatred or their jealousy. Thus they hired the assassins who murdered Cimon, the father of Miltiades. They kept up a standing force of mercenaries; they made no change in the constitution indeed, but took care that the most important offices were filled by their own friends. The wealthy citizens were conciliated by a reduction of the tithe imposed by Pisistratus, to one twentieth. No new taxes were levied, although the great works commenced by their father were continued. The sober-minded Thucydides states that these tyrants cultivated virtue and wisdom, whence we cannot wonder that later writers describe their reign as a sort of golden age. There seems, in fact, to have been no discontent in the country, and the Pisistratids might have maintained their ascendancy for many generations, had not an event occurred which led to their overthrow and to a complete change in the government.

This revolution was brought about by two young men, Harmodius and Aristogeiton, who were connected by intimate friendship. Harmodius was grossly insulted by Hipparchus, and, instigated by his friend, he meditated revenge. Hipparchus then tried to cast dishonour upon the family of Harmodius, which stung the youth to the quick. The two friends resolved, not only to wash out the disgrace in the blood of the offender, but to overthrow the ruling dynasty, a plan which Aristogeiton had formed even before these occurrences. They were secretly joined by many friends, and the conspirators fixed on the day of the great Panathenaea for effecting their purpose. It was intended to kill Hippias during the procession, in which the citizens took part in arms; but the conspirators, imagining from some circumstances that their scheme was betrayed, hastened back from the Ceramicus to the city, with their daggers concealed under branches of myrtle. On meeting with Hipparchus, they killed him before his guards could come up to his assistance. Harmodius, however, fell in the fray. Aristogeiton escaped for the moment among the crowd, but was afterwards taken. When Hippias was informed of the event, he commanded the armed men who formed the procession, and who were yet ignorant of what had happened, to lay aside their arms, and meet him at an appointed place. His guards then searched all persons, and those who were found with daggers, or were otherwise suspected, were arrested on the spot. This occurred in the year B.C. 514.

Aristogeiton was put to death, perhaps even with cruel torture; but before he died he revenged himself by accusing the truest friends of Hippias. Hippias had hitherto acted as a wise and good ruler; but fear and suspicion now turned him into a stern and cruel tyrant; and instead of conciliating his subjects, he aimed only at cowing them by rigour. Executions were things of common occurrence, extraordinary taxes were levied, and various artifices were resorted to for the purpose of filling the tyrant's coffers at the expense of all classes of the people. At the same time, seeing that he was hated and detested at home, he entered into a foreign alliance in order to provide for himself a place of retreat, whenever he should be compelled to seek it. He gave his daughter in marriage to a son of Hippoclus, the tyrant of Lampsacus, who stood high in the favour of Darius, king of Persia.

While Hippias was thus surrounded by dangers at home, he was also threatened from without by the machinations of the banished Alcmaeonids, who were in a position to command any aid that money could purchase. They were encouraged by the unpopularity of Hippias to renew their attempts at revolution, but his vigilance repulsed them, although they had taken possession of a frontier town. They now secured the services of the Delphic oracle, by rebuilding the temple, which had been accidentally burnt, in a style far more magnificent than was stipulated in the agreement which they had made with the Amphictions. Thus Cleisthenes, now at the head of the Alcmaeonids, made the Pythian priestess the instrument of his designs. Henceforth whenever Spartans came to consult the oracle, they received but one answer, bidding them restore Athens to freedom. Owing to these repeated exhortations, the Spartans at length resolved to send an army into Attica to expel Hippias and his family. Anchimolius led the Spartan forces, and landed at Phalerum. The Thessalians, being allied with Hippias, sent him 1000 horse under Cineas, who routed the Spartans, slew their commander, and drove them to their ships. A greater force, under King Cleomenes, now invaded Attica by land. This time the Thessalians were defeated, and though their loss was small, they returned home. Hippias might still have maintained himself: but he was so alarmed that he ordered his children to be sent out of the country; on their way they fell into the hands of the enemy, and he could redeem them only on condition of quitting Attica within five days. Accordingly, in B. C. 510, he set sail for Asia, where for a time he took up his residence in his hereditary principality of Sigeum.

After his departure, severe measures were taken against his adherents: some were put to death, others sent into exile, and others deprived of their political privileges. The tyrant and his family were condemned to perpetual banishment. The fortunate tyrannicides, Harmodius and Aristogeiton, on the other hand, received almost heroic honours: statues were erected to them, and their names never ceased to be repeated with affectionate admiration. Much of this enthusiasm was evidently misplaced; for their crime had not been committed in the service of freedom, but at the suggestion of private vengeance; the latter years of Hippias' government, however, seemed to the Athenians to justify all the praise bestowed upon those who had first, though unsuccessfully, attempted to deliver the country from his tyranny.

After the expulsion of the Pisistratids, the democratic party at Athens was without a leader. The Alcmaeonids had always been regarded as its opponents, though they were no less hostile to the faction of the nobles, which seems at this time to have been headed by Isagoras. It was still so powerful, that Cleisthenes and his party were unable to cope with it. He accordingly shifted his ground, and attached himself to the popular cause, which Pisistratus had used as his stepping-stone; and to secure for himself a lasting advantage over his rivals, he planned an important change in the constitution, which should for ever break the power of his own order. With this view, having gained the confidence of the commonalty, and obtained the sanction of the Delphic oracle, he abolished the four ancient tribes, and made a fresh geographical division into ten local tribes (φυλαί), each of which bore a name derived from some Attic hero. The ten tribes were subdivided into ten districts of different extent called demi (δῆμοι), each of which contained some town or village as its centre. At a later time, we find the number of demi increased to 174, some of the earlier demi having perhaps been subdivided for the sake of convenience. The phratriae continued to exist, but lost all political importance, and retained no power but that of watching over the legitimate succession of their members, and registering their title to their hereditary civil rights. Each township was governed by its local magistrate called demarchus (δήμαρχος), who held its assemblies for the transaction of its own affairs, and for ascertaining and recording the number of its members. Every citizen was obliged to be a member of a demos, without which he could exercise no political rights. Cleisthenes at the same time increased his strength by making a great many new citizens; and is said to have admitted not only aliens, but even slaves. If this account is true, it shows that there was still a considerable portion of the people on whom he could not rely, and that he was compelled to adopt that measure for the purpose of strengthening his own party among the commonalty.

We are too little acquainted with the machinery which the new system of Cleisthenes broke up, to form an accurate notion of the importance of the latter, which however was certainly not suggested by the mere love of novelty or innovation: it transformed the commonalty into a new body, furnished with new organs and breathing a new spirit, which was no longer subject to the slightest control of the old nobility. The whole reorganisation of the state was made to correspond with the new geographical division of the country. Accordingly, the senate also was increased from 400 to

500: so that fifty were drawn from each of the ten tribes; and the rotation of the presidency was adapted to this change, the fifty representatives of each tribe filling that office for thirty-five or thirty-six days in rotation; and nine senators were elected, one from each of the other tribes, to preside in the council and the assembly of the people, which was now called regularly four times in every month, certain business being assigned to each meeting. The heliaea, also, was distributed into ten courts, and the same division prevailed in most other public offices, though the number of the archons remained unchanged. To Cleisthenes is also ascribed the institution of the ostracism; a summary process, enabling the people to rid itself of any citizen who had made himself formidable, or an object of suspicion, without any proof or even imputation of guilt. This is another proof of the weakness of the government; but at the same time it proved a useful check upon ambitious and aspiring individuals, and allayed the public fear whenever the ascendancy of one man threatened to endanger the liberty of the people.

These reforms so much increased the power and influence of their author, and reduced the party of Isagoras to such utter weakness, that the latter had no hope except in foreign aid. They accordingly solicited the assistance of Sparta, whose king, Cleomenes, had received some very equivocal favours from Isagoras, and who now sent heralds to Athens, requiring the expulsion of the accursed race of the Alcmaeonids. Cleisthenes, either dreading the cry which had so often been disastrous to his family, or unwilling to expose his country to a hostile invasion, withdrew from Athens. But this concession did not satisfy Cleomenes, who was bent upon reducing Athens under the dominion of Isagoras. He came with only a small force; but, during the dismay of the people at the absence of their leader, was allowed to act as if he were absolute master. He banished 700 families marked out by Isagoras, and then took steps to abolish the senate of 500, and to place the government in the hands of 300 of his friend's partisans. This measure roused the people; and Isagoras and Cleomenes, having taken refuge on the acropolis, were besieged by the people. On the third day, however, they capitulated; Cleomenes and Isagoras were permitted to depart with the Lacedaemonian troops, but were compelled to leave their adherents to the mercy of their enemies. All were put to death; and Cleisthenes, with the 700 exiled families, triumphantly returned to Athens, in B.C. 508.

As it soon became known that Cleomenes was preparing to avenge his humiliating defeat, the Athenians in their alarm sent envoys to Sardis, to seek the protection of Persia. This embassy had no immediate effect; and while Cleomenes, accompanied by his colleague Demaratus, invaded Attica on the side of Eleusis, the Thebans, who had promised to join him, took the towns of Oenoë and Hysiae; and the Chalcidians from Euboea ravaged the eastern coast. The Athenians directed all their forces against the Spartans; but before battle was joined, the Corinthians, who with other Peloponnesians served in the Spartan army, ashamed of being used as tools to crush the liberty of Athens, returned home; and Demaratus, for some unknown reason, also refused to co-operate. The rest of the Peloponnesians then followed the example of the Corinthians, and Cleomenes was obliged to abandon his enterprise. The dispute between the two kings on that occasion, led the Spartans to enact a law that both kings should never in future take the field together.

The Athenians, on being delivered from their most formidable enemy, marched towards the Euripus to chastise Chalcis. In Boeotia they met the Thebans, whom they defeated and took 700 prisoners. The same day they crossed the straits, and gained a victory over the Chalcidians, from which they derived great advantages; for they were enabled to distribute the estates of the great Chalcidian landowners among 4000 Attic colonists, who settled there, but retained their Attic franchise. This acquisition gave the means of subsistence to many poor families; and enabled Athens to raise a body of cavalry, the force in which Attica was most deficient. All the captive Chalcidians, and the 700 Thebans, were put in chains, but were afterwards ransomed for two minas a head. The chains with which they had been fettered were hung up on the walls of a temple on the acropolis; and a brazen chariot was dedicated to Athene as a tenth of the ransom, with an inscription recording this first achievement of the liberated commonwealth.

In the enjoyment of civil freedom Athens now became strong and powerful; under her noble rulers she had surpassed none of her neighbours in feats of arms, but now got far ahead of them all. This is the best proof that Cleisthenes, though he no doubt acted from selfish motives, yet understood the temper and character of the people, and saw that the half measures of the Solonian constitution satisfied neither the nobles nor the people, and might become dangerous to the safety of Athens, which under an aristocracy or a tyrant would undoubtedly have become a Persian province.

The Thebans, burning to revenge their disgrace, but unable to do anything, allied themselves, by the advice of an oracle, with the Aeginetans, who bore an ancient grudge against Athens and were then at the height of their power. While the Thebans invaded Attica from the north, the Aeginetans with their fleet plundered many of the maritime towns. The Athenians were preparing to retaliate on Aegina, when they perceived that they were threatened from another quarter. The Spartans had in the mean time learned, that Cleisthenes and the Delphic oracle had imposed upon them in inducing them to ruin the Pisistratids. The resentment thus roused, and the conviction that the growing power of Athens would become a match for Sparta, led them to invite Hippias to come from Sigeum to Sparta. A congress of deputies from the Peloponnesian allies was at the same time summoned to consider a plan for restoring Hippias. The greater part of the allies, however, appear to have perceived, that, though it might suit the interest of Sparta to keep Athens subject to a creature of her own, they should reap nothing but shame from such an act of injustice. No one, however, ventured to declare his opinion, till the Corinthian Sosicles vehemently remonstrated with the Spartans for wishing to set up a tyrant in direct opposition to the spirit of their own constitution. Encouraged by his eloquence, all the other deputies declared with one accord against the proposal of Sparta. The design was thus abandoned; Hippias soon afterwards returned to Sigeum, and thence proceeded to the court of Darius. The war with Aegina was continued up to the time of the Persian war, during which the Aeginetans joined the common enemy of Greece, until in B.C. 457, the Athenians succeeded in destroying their fleet and making themselves masters of the island

Astragalizontes, or Players at Knuckle-bones.
(From a painting discovered at Herculaneum.)

Central Statues from the Western Pediment of the Temple of Athena, at Aegina.

CHAPTER XI.

THE COLONIES OF THE GREEKS, AND THE PROGRESS OF ART AND LITERATURE FROM THE HOMERIC AGE TO THE PERSIAN WAR.

The history of Greece would be incomplete without some account of her colonies; but we must in this place content ourselves with a brief sketch of their general character, and of the influence which they exercised upon the ancient world at large. It is one of the most pleasing spectacles in the history of antiquity to behold the establishment of the Greek colonies on all the coasts of the three ancient continents, by means of which the Greek language, manners, and culture, were spread among barbarous nations. The Greeks seem to have been destined by Providence to become the civilisers of the ancient world, and this destiny they fulfilled by their wide-spread colonial settlements, which exercised an influence upon mankind far greater than any they could have acquired, had they confined themselves to the narrow boundaries of their mother country.

We need not dwell upon the mythical colonies said to have been founded by the Greeks on or after their return from the siege of Troy; the most ancient historically attested colonies are those connected with the Aeolian migration; that is, with the first of the great movements produced by the eruption of the Aeolians into Boeotia, and of the Dorians into Peloponnesus. Achaeans, driven from their homes, and seeking new seats in the east, are believed to have been joined in Boeotia by a part both of its ancient inhabitants and of their Aeolian conquerors. From the latter, who were probably predominant in influence, the migration is called the Aeolian, but sometimes also the Boeotian. The emigrants were headed by chiefs claiming descent from Agamemnon, and their main body embarked at Aulis. Their first settlements were in Lesbos, where they founded six cities. Other detachments occupied the opposite coast of Asia Minor, from the foot of Mount Ida to the mouth of the river Hermus. This is the real origin of the greater part of the Aeolian colonies; but there is reason for believing that the Achaeans had begun to migrate from Peloponnesus eastward, even before the time of the Dorian conquest. The countries of which they took possession were still in the hands of the Pelasgians; who, however, were in a state of great weakness. Cuma became the principal of the Aeolian cities in Asia. It is highly probable, that the current of emigration towards those beautiful and fertile countries continued for more than a century; the results of this were eleven Aeolian cities on the mainland of Asia; and Cuma and Lesbos founded thirty others in the territory of Priam.

The country to the south of Aeolis, from the river Hermus to the Maeander, which enjoyed a still happier climate, fell to the lot of the adventurers who embarked in the Ionian migration. They were mostly Ionians, who, when dislodged by the Achaeans from their seats on the Corinthian gulf, took refuge in Attica, and probably assisted in repelling that invasion of the Dorians in which Codrus is said to have devoted himself for his country. Here they were joined by other fugitives and adventurers, especially Phocians; and as Attica could not afford permanent abodes for them, Neleus, the son of Codrus, with several of his brothers and clansmen, put himself at their head and emigrated. On their passage across the Aegean, many formed settlements in the Cyclades and other islands; and in process of time Delos became a common sanctuary of the Ionian race. The Asiatic coast, henceforth called Ionia, and the neighbouring islands of Chios and Samos, were at this time inhabited by various tribes, such as Carians, Leleges, descendants of Cretan colonists, and adventurers from various parts of Greece. The new invaders readily united with all except the Carians and Leleges, who were expelled or exterminated. Twelve independent states were gradually formed, all of which assumed the Ionian name, and were regarded as parts of the same nation, although they were composed of very different elements and spoke different dialects. At Miletus the settlers might boast of the purest Ionian blood, and Neleus chose that place for his residence. All its male inhabitants, Carians and perhaps Cretans, were massacred, and the women were forced to marry the invaders. Myus and Priene were likewise wrested from the Carians. Androclus, a son of Codrus, led his followers to Ephesus, which was inhabited chiefly by Leleges and Lydians, who were expelled by the Ionians; but the temple of the Asiatic Artemis afforded an asylum to a considerable number of suppliants, among whom were women said to have been descended from the Amazons, its reputed founders. Colophon was inhabited by Cretans, with whom the Ionians, under two sons of Codrus, agreed to dwell on terms of equality. Andraemon or Andropompus, another son of Codrus, drove the Carians out of Lebedos. Teos had been previously occupied by Minyans from Orchomenos, intermingled with Carians; and the Ionians were peaceably admitted to a share in the colony, which soon afterwards received a fresh band of adventurers from Attica and Boeotia. Erythrae seems to have become a member of the Ionian body at a later period, being colonised by settlers from all the Ionian cities, who found there Cretans, Carians, Lycians, and Pamphylians, with whom an amicable union was formed.

All the cities here enumerated were in existence before the Ionian migration, but Clazomenae and Phocaea owed their origin to that event. The former was founded by Ionians, mixed with a larger body of emigrants who had quitted Cleonae and Phlius after the Dorian invasion. Phocaea was built on ground obtained from Cuma, by a colony of Phocians. The island of Chios most probably received its colonists from Erythrae, it having previously been inhabited by Abantes and Carians from Euboea, and by Cretans; the Erythraeans and Chians were distinguished from all the other Ionians by a peculiar dialect. Samos had received an Ionian colony originally sprung from Epidaurus, which shared it with its ancient inhabitants, the Leleges. The Ephesians made war on the new settlers, and drove them out of the island. A part of them crossed over to Samothrace, and there united with the Tyrrhenian Pelasgians; but another body seized Anaea, on the opposite coast of Asia, and there waited for an opportunity of returning to Samos. Ten years later they succeeded in this, and ejected the Ephesians. After this event they must have become members of the Ionian confederacy. The dialect of Samos was peculiar to itself. To these twelve cities Smyrna was afterwards added. It is said to have been at first occupied by Aeolians, and to have been treacherously seized by a body of exiles from Colophon; but another, and more probable account represents it as having been founded by Ionians from Ephesus. There a part of the ancient town once bore the name of Smyrna. Smyrna is stated to have succeeded to the place of a town called Melite, the thirteenth in the list, which was destroyed by the common consent of the other twelve.

The south-western corner of the peninsula of Asia Minor, and the neighbouring islands, were occupied nearly at the same period by colonists of the Doric race. Some of the Dorian conquerors themselves were drawn into the tide of migration, and led bands of their own countrymen, and of the conquered Achaeans to the coast of Asia. The most celebrated of these expeditions was that of the Argive Althaemenes, who leaving one division of his followers in Crete, proceeded with the rest to Rhodes, where the Heracleid Tlepolemus was believed to have founded the towns of Lindos, Ialysos, and Cameiros, before the Trojan war. About the same time Halicarnassos was founded by Dorians from Troezen, and Cnidos by others from Laconia. A third band from Epidaurus took possession of the island of Cos. These six colonies formed an association, from which several others in their neighbourhood were excluded, and which, after Halicarnassos had been obliged to withdraw from it, was called by the name of the Dorian pentapolis. Rhodes was probably the parent of most of the Greek colonies on the south coast of Asia Minor. She may also have contributed to the Greek population of Lycia, though it was unquestionably of Cretan origin. Traces of Greek adventurers occur even far inland, for Selge, a great Pisidian town, and Sagalassos, boasted a Laconian origin.

The Greek colonies in Cyprus may likewise be referred to the century following the Dorian conquest, though most of them claimed a higher antiquity, and ascribed their foundation to some of the heroes who fought at Troy.

A long interval seems to have elapsed after this before the state of Greece gave occasion to new migrations; for it was not till the century following the beginning of the Olympiads that the Greeks established themselves on the coast of Sicily, and spread so far over the south of Italy, that it acquired the name of Great Greece (Magna Graecia). These colonies, like those of Asia, were of various origin, some Aeolian or Achaean, some Dorian, some Ionian. The Ionians led the way, and the city of Chalcis in Euboea, sent out, if not the first adventurers who explored the Italian and Sicilian coasts, yet the first who gained a permanent footing there; for, according to a generally received tradition, Cuma in Campania was founded by a Chalcidian colony, about the middle of the century following the return of the Heracleids. Some accounts even make it an earlier settlement than the Aeolian Cuma, from which it was erroneously believed to have derived its name and a part of its population; but in these its antiquity was, no doubt, greatly exaggerated. It is singular, however, that for three centuries no adventurers followed in the same track; and that, even at the end of that time, the first Greek settlement in Sicily was the result of a fortunate chance, which revealed the richness of the island and the weakness of its inhabitants to Theocles, an Athenian, who was driven upon its coast. On his return to Greece, he persuaded the Chalcidians, after having tried his fellow-citizens in vain, to send out a colony to Sicily. The great landowners of Chalcis seem to have had political motives for encouraging emigration among the poorer citizens; and Chalcis had probably already planted colonies in the Thracian peninsula, which hence acquired its name of Chalcidice, though a great part of its Greek population was derived from Eretria, the neighbour and rival of Chalcis. In the colony which Theocles led to Sicily in B. C. 735, the island of Naxos took so important a part, that the name of Naxos was given to the town which it founded, though Chalcis was always recognised as its parent. Sicily was at that time inhabited by various tribes, Sicanians, Sicels, Phoenicians, Elymians. The Sicels and Phoenicians gradually retreated before the Greeks, whose colonies, in the course of a century, covered the eastern and southern coasts of the island. The Chalcidians of Naxos soon afterwards planted the colonies of Leontini and Catana; Messana and Rhegium likewise, the two cities which command the straits, were of Chalcidian origin.

But the Greek cities in Sicily which rose to the highest renown were of Dorian foundation. Of these Syracuse was founded in B. C. 734, by Corinthians under a leader named Archias, a Heracleid, who seems to have been obliged to quit his country in consequence of an outrage which he had committed on a humble family. His companion, Chersicrates, was left with a division of his followers in Corcyra, from which the inhabitants were expelled. Corcyra was the most important of a series of Corinthian colonies on the eastern coast of the Adriatic and the Ionian sea; and Syracuse became the parent of other Sicilian cities, of which Camarina was the greatest. Megara, now independent of Corinth, followed her ancient sovereign in this field of enterprise, though her most flourishing colonies lay on the coasts of the Propontis and Bosporus, where about a century after the foundation of Rome, B. C. 658, she planted Byzantium, the future rival of the eternal city. In Sicily, Megarian adventurers succeeded in establishing themselves at Hybla, which became the parent of Selinus, B.C. 629. Gela was founded in B.C. 690, by a band collected from Crete and Rhodes; and about a century later, B. C. 582, it sent forth settlers, who built Agrigentum (Acragas), on the banks of the Acragas. Himera, on the north side of the island, was peopled by a colony from Messana and by Dorians, who had been banished from Syracuse.

Within half a century after the Greeks first set foot in Sicily they founded most of the great cities in southern Italy. The rivals Sybaris and Croton were both of Achaean origin, though in the foundation of the former Troezenians also took part; and in the latter Dorians from Laconia may have had a share. Such seems also to have been the origin of Locri, which was founded either by the Locrians of Opus or by those on the Crissaean gulf, who were joined by Achaeans, and perhaps by Dorians from Laconia. Tarentum was founded by Laconian settlers (Parthenii)*, at the end of the first Messenian war, though it appears to have been occupied by Greeks even before that event. Metapontum, said to have been colonised by followers of Nestor after the return from Troy, seems to have been subsequently in the possession of Greeks from Crissa. These great cities extended and secured the dominion of the Greeks in Italy, by a number of new colonies, among which we need only mention Posidonia (Paestum), the ruins of which still attest its former greatness.

Another field of enterprise was opened to the Greeks on the north coast of Africa. The island of Calliste had in early times received a colony from Laconia, chiefly consisting of Minyans, from whose leader, Theras, the island is said to have been named Thera. Many centuries later, Battus, a leading citizen of Thera, undertook an expedition to the coast of Africa, the fertility of which had long been known to the Greeks. The Theraeans formed a settlement there on the table-land which arises on the western border of the Great Syrtis, at the distance of ten miles from the coast. This was Cyrene, so called from the gushing spring of Cyre in the neighbourhood. The country was one of inexhaustible wealth, and possessed a most salubrious climate. Cyrene itself founded four colonies in the adjoining district, with which it formed the Cyrenaic Pentapolis. The barbarians who inhabited the country before the arrival of the Greeks, seem to have made room for them without a struggle. At a later period, about B.C. 637, adventurers from various parts of Greece were invited by the Cyrenaeans to share the fertile soil. The Libyans seeing themselves thus threatened with the complete loss of their country, sought aid from Egypt, whose king, Apries, sent them succours, which, however, were repulsed with terrible slaughter, and the dominion of the Greeks became firmly established in Cyrenaica.

The colonies which we have enumerated were not by any means all that were founded by the Greeks during that period; we shall afterwards have occasion to mention others, and here confine ourselves to pointing out certain general features of the Greek colonies. As regards the relation subsisting between a colony

* See p. 85.

and its parent city it must be observed, that colonies were commonly established with the approbation and encouragement of the states from which they issued, the latter often finding it expedient to rid themselves of superfluous hands or discontented and turbulent spirits. There was in most cases, however, nothing to suggest the feeling of dependence on the one side, or a claim of authority on the other; a claim which it would generally have been impossible to enforce, on account of the great distance between the mother-country and the colony. Hence the only connection which continued to exist, was one of filial affection and religious reverence. Except in the few cases where the emigrants were forced as outcasts from their native land, they cherished the remembrance of it as a duty prescribed by religion as well as by nature. The tutelary deities of the mother-city were invited to share the newly conquered land, and temples were commonly dedicated to them in the new acropolis, resembling as nearly as possible those with which they were honoured in the mother-country; their images were made after the old models, and it would seem that the priests who ministered to them were sometimes brought from their ancient seats. The sacred fire which was kept constantly burning on the public hearth of the colony, was taken from the altar of Hestia, in the senate-house of the elder state. The founder of a colony, as the representative of the parent city, was after his death honoured as a being of a higher order; and when the colony, in its turn, became a parent, it usually sought a leader from the original mother-country. The same reverential feeling manifested itself more regularly in embassies and offerings sent by the colony to honour the festivals of the parent city, and in the marks of respect shown to its citizens who represented it on similar occasions in the colony. The natural result of all this was a disposition to mutual good offices in seasons of danger and distress.

In most cases the colonists established themselves as conquerors in lands already inhabited and cultivated, and dispossessed either partially or entirely the ancient owners of the soil. The condition to which the latter were reduced varied, according to circumstances, between absolute slavery and an equality of political rights, though the conquerors scarcely ever admitted the vanquished to perfect equality with themselves. Subsequent adventurers, settling in the same place, generally enjoyed an inferior franchise to that of the original colonists. As most of the colonies, however, were planted on the coast, and in spots favourable to commercial enterprise, an aristocracy rarely maintained its ascendancy, and powerful commonalties soon sprung up in them, so that the tendency towards a complete democracy could seldom be restrained.

As during the period of the return of the Heracleids the monarchical form of government prevailed almost everywhere in Greece, it was probably established in the colonies founded at that time. But circumstances generally contributed to restrict the power of the hereditary chiefs, until it finally disappeared altogether. A striking instance of this gradual change is exhibited in the history of Cyrene, where the royal authority was maintained for a long time without any diminution; but after the increase of the colony, in B.C. 637, the people seem to have become dissatisfied with their institutions. A pretext for a change was soon found, and, with the sanction of the Delphic oracle, Demonax of Mantinea was invited to frame a new constitution. He defined the respective rights of the old and the new colonists, and distributed them into three tribes, of which the descendants of the original settlers formed the first. He then deprived the king of all his substantial prerogatives. Afterwards, a counter-revolution being brought about by foreign aid, the government became a tyrannis.

The Greek colonies in Asia Minor, as we have seen, were divided into three great masses, each bearing a name indicating its supposed unity of descent. The Ionians recognised Athens as their common parent, a relation which could not be claimed in so strict a sense either by Thebes in regard to the Aeolians, or by Argos or Sparta in regard to the Dorians. Each of these three divisions, strengthened by an unbroken geographical connection, might at the same time have formed a compact political body; but causes similar to those which tended to keep the Greeks in Europe asunder, also operated in Asia, and at first there was no enemy in the neighbourhood powerful enough to induce them to combine their forces. The nearest approach to anything like a confederacy consisted in periodical meetings for the celebration of festivals in honour of a tutelary god, which afforded an opportunity for discussing political matters in case of need. The Aeolians, perhaps, did not even possess such a religious centre of union. The meetings of the Dorians took place near the temple of Apollo, on the Triopian headland, and were celebrated with games, the victors in which dedicated their prizes, bronze tripods, to the god. Halicarnassos was excluded from the league, because she had not observed the rules customary at the games; a proof how loose the connection must have been. The meetings of the Ionians were held at the foot of Mount Mycale, on a spot called Panionium, and sacred to the national god Poseidon. There, also, religious ceremonies were the predominant feature; yet there seems to have existed in early times among the Ionians a tendency to a closer union than prevailed among either the Dorians or the Aeolians. All the Ionian cities except Samos were ruled by princes of the house of Codrus, and this appears to have been an indispensable condition of admission into the confederacy; there is, moreover, some ground for believing that the eldest prince of this house enjoyed a sort of supremacy over the rest, and resided at Ephesus. But there can be no doubt that the Ionian cities soon became completely isolated, without any provision being made either for defence against foreign enemies or for the maintenance of internal tranquillity; there was no common treasure, tribunal, magistrate, or laws. The only Greeks in Asia who lived in a regularly organised confederacy were those inhabiting the twenty-three cities in Lycia; their union was so framed that, although there was a common government, yet each city felt itself independent. Had all the Asiatic Greeks followed this example, their history, and even that of the mother-country, might have been very different from what it actually was.

But this want of union did not affect the prosperity of the several cities; on the contrary, they seem to have shot up all the more vigorously and luxuriantly from the entire absence of restraint. The monarchical government was abolished within a few generations after the first settlement; we hear of severe struggles between political parties and of civil wars, from which we may conclude that their history was nearly the same as that of the cities in the mother-country. During those convulsions Miletus rose to the summit of her greatness as a maritime state; her colonies and commerce extended the limits of the Grecian world, and opened an intercourse between its most distant regions. The Aeolians and Dorians did not possess the enterprising spirit of the Ionians, but remained comparatively stationary; while the progress of commerce and maritime discovery among the Ionians was coupled with the cultivation of the nobler arts, and with the opening of new intellectual fields, in which they not only outshone the mother-country, but have never been equalled, except perhaps in our own times.

Soon after the middle of the seventh century B.C. when considerable improvements in the art of shipbuilding had been introduced among the Ionians by the Corinthians, the Milesians began to plant a series of colonies on the eastern coast of the Propontis, though Cyzicus, the most important of them, is referred to an earlier date. The rivalry of the Phocaeans, who founded Lampsacus, and that of the Megarians, who occupied the most advantageous positions on the European shore, seem to have urged them to explore the coasts of the Euxine, which was now first opened for ordinary navigation by the Milesians. There they planted the greater part of their numerous colonies, which are said to have amounted to no less than eighty. These settlements, unlike most of those hitherto mentioned, were no doubt founded with a distinct view to commercial advantages. During that period the power of Miletus rendered her the common protectress of all the Greeks settled in those regions. Sinope, probably the earliest Milesian colony on the Euxine, became, in its turn, the mother of many flourishing cities.

The Euxine, or the "Hospitable Sea," formerly called the "Inhospitable," had, through the enterprises of the Milesians, lost a part of its terrors, before the recesses of the Adriatic and the sea west of Sicily were explored. The glory of having opened these new tracts of commerce belongs to the Phoenicians; but they were soon followed by bold and active rivals. The beginning of the seventh century B.C. seems to be the date of their first adventures in the Adriatic. They themselves, or other and still bolder adventurers, reached Tartessus, a town on the southern coast of Spain. The Rhodians appear at an early period to have pursued the same direction; for there is no doubt that they founded Parthenope, and we may readily believe that they established themselves at Rhode, or Rhodos (the modern Rosas in Catalonia), before the Phocaeans had gained a footing at Emporiae (Ampurias); it is even possible, that the river Rhone (Rhodanus) may have derived its name from them. If so, they there also preceded the Phocaeans, who about B.C. 600 founded their most celebrated colony of Massilia (Marseilles) in Gaul, where they maintained themselves with the aid of the Celtic tribes, whose good will they gained and requited by diffusing among them the arts of civilised life and Grecian usages and letters. Miletus likewise carried on considerable commerce with southern Italy, especially with Sybaris.

About the year B.C. 650, Egypt, which until then had been jealously closed against foreign settlers, was thrown open for permanent and friendly intercourse to the Greeks. For Psammetichus, having raised himself to the throne by the aid of a band of Ionians and Carians, who had by chance landed on the coast of Egypt, induced them to enter into his service. He not only rewarded them with grants of land on the Nile, but gave their countrymen free access to his dominions. A number of Egyptian boys, moreover, were consigned to their care, to learn the Greek language, and to form a permanent class of interpreters between the two nations. The successors of Psammetichus adhered to the same policy; and thus Greeks of various classes were drawn to Egypt, in the pursuit of knowledge as well as of gain. To this intercourse with Egypt Greece was indebted for the more general use of the papyrus, which must have become much cheaper than it had previously been, and thus supplied the Greeks with a commodious writing-material, the influence of which on the literature of Greece was no doubt considerable.

We shall, in the following Chapter, give an outline of the history of the Asiatic colonies, previously to the period of the Persian war, and here add a succinct view of the progress of art and literature, which is intimately connected with the rise of those colonies.

The arts, which had been cultivated before the time of Homer, no doubt kept pace with the advance of public and private prosperity. Among the Asiatic Greeks, wealth and refinement made more rapid progress than in the mother-country where circumstances were less favourable; and the Ionian cities were early distinguished by a degree of luxury before unknown to the Greeks; accordingly the fall of Magnesia, on the Meander, about the beginning of the Olympiads, is ascribed to the prevalence of effeminate habits. But the Ionians generally did not abandon themselves to indolence; the same spirit which led them to commercial enterprises in distant lands, found employment at home in the cultivation of the arts, which cheered and adorned their private and public life. In Greece itself, Corinth was perhaps the only city that can be compared to them; for the first steps in the arts of drawing, painting, and moulding figures in clay, are commonly attributed to the Corinthians. Other Dorian cities also had their schools of art, at a time when Athens seems to have been barren in great works, as well as in illustrious artists. But the Ionians in Asia were not behindhand, either in the richness of their productions, or in the glory of new inventions. They began early to vie with one another in the grandeur and splendour of their sacred buildings, and in all the arts which served to adorn them. The temple of Hera at Samos, the largest of all that Herodotus had seen, appears to have been begun in the eighth century B.C. Of the arts dedicated to the service of the gods the most important, next to architecture, was that of casting metal statues, which is ascribed to Theodorus of Samos. The same artist laid the foundation of the splendid temple of Artemis at Ephesus. Statuary during this period rose nearly to the summit of perfection. The fact that this art made such extraordinary strides, just at the time when Egypt was thrown open to the Greeks, proves no more than that the Greek artists perhaps became acquainted there with various technical processes, with which the Egyptians had long been familiar, and that, by this fortunate assistance, Greek art at once advanced from a state of comparative rudeness to a level with that of Egypt. But even this is very doubtful, since great works of art are spoken of in Greece at a period when Egypt was yet inaccessible to Greek artists.* The progress of the arts must, therefore, probably be ascribed to other causes than the intercourse with Egypt. Among these causes may be mentioned the preference which was generally given to brass and marble over the ancient material, wood, which henceforth, when employed, was commonly overlaid with ivory or gold. The use of marble is said to have been introduced by two Cretan artists, Dipoenus and Scyllis, but was probably promoted by the closer connection into which statuary was brought with architecture, and by the increased sumptuousness of the temples, in which marble frequently took the place of ordinary stone. Statuary received another great impulse from the enlargement in the range of its subjects, and the consequent multiplicity of its productions. So long as statues were confined to the interior of temples, and no more were seen in each sanctuary than the idol of its worship, there was little or no room for innovation, and the general practice was rather to adhere strictly to the traditionary forms hallowed by ancient custom. But insensibly piety grew ostentatious, and began to fill the temples with groups of gods and heroes; the pediments of the temples were peopled with colossal forms, exhibiting legendary scenes connected with the stories of the god worshipped within. The custom of honouring victors at the public games, and other illustrious personages, contributed perhaps still more to the same effect. For here all restraints confining the artist in making statues destined for worship, were removed. With the extension of the range of subjects the number of artists also increased; their industry was sharpened by competition and rich rewards; the sense of beauty grew steadier and quicker; and the progress made was so rapid, that the last vestiges of arbitrary or conventional forms had not yet everywhere disappeared, when the final union of truth and beauty was accomplished in the school of Phidias.

The observant and inquisitive spirit which was the inmost spring of this new life in the world of art, gave birth about the same time to new branches and forms of poetry. The first period in Greek literature is represented by the names of Homer and Hesiod, the former marking its beginning, the latter its close. In their dialect and forms of versification, they resemble each other, but in every other respect they move in different spheres. These two poets, however, represent only a very small part of the poetical produce of their age; for the names of many contemporary bards have probably been lost in the lustre of Homer's; and as their works, no doubt, often served as a basis for celebrated labours of subsequent poets, they were soon neglected and forgotten.

* See, for example, Herod. iv. 152., and Paus. v. 17. § 3.

Hesiod appears to have been a poet who exercised an influence similar to that of Homer, and the works which have come down to us under his name probably belong to different authors; for he was the founder of a poetical school, and among the works bearing his name the inhabitants of his birthplace recognised only one as genuine.* He was a native of the village of Ascra, at the foot of Mount Helicon, in Boeotia, to which his father had migrated from the Aeolian Cuma; and from the manner in which the poet speaks of himself, we must infer that at one time he was engaged in pastoral and rural occupations. The time at which he lived is nearly as uncertain as that of Homer, though it is generally supposed that he flourished after Homer, about B. C. 850. If the other works which bear his name, the Theogony and the Shield of Heracles, are not really his, we must at least believe that they correctly represent the themes of his song, since otherwise they would scarcely have been attributed to him. As Homer had been the poet of a conquering race of warriors, so Hesiod was the poet of the peaceful peasantry of Boeotia. He is a teacher of divine and human wisdom, and his name represents the whole poetical growth of the Boeotian and Locrian schools.

The two centuries which followed the beginning of the Olympiads were still very rich in epic song, though this period formed the close of that poetry which had reached its culminating point in Homer and Hesiod. Most of the epic poets of this period are usually comprehended under the name of the cyclics (κυκλικοί), or poets of the cycle, a term which denoted a collection of epic poems, the subjects of which were confined to a certain period of time, and which were so arranged as to form one compact body, though such a design probably never entered the head of any one of the poets themselves. The period over which their subjects extended began with the union of heaven and earth, or the origin of all things, and ended with the latest adventures of Odysseus in Ithaca, that is, with the close of the heroic age. The poems forming the cycle are all lost, and we know little more than the titles of some of them. Several were designed to fill up the blanks left by the Iliad and Odyssey in the story of Troy. The poetical interest, which in Homer's works is predominant, was, in the poems of the cycle, subordinate to that interest which concerned the succession of events. But while they were thus necessarily inferior to Homer in poetical merit, we must regard them as a prelude to history, which made its first appearance about the close of this period.

Lyric poetry, the expression of human feelings and emotions,

* Namely, the Ἔργα καὶ Ἡμέραι. See Paus. ix. 31. § 4.

is, no doubt, as ancient as epic poetry; but so long as the national taste inclined more towards the latter, lyric poetry was probably not much cultivated, and it was carried to its highest perfection during the last stage in the career of the epic muse. Thenceforth for more than three centuries a series of great masters of lyric song were continually enlarging and enriching the sphere of their art. The names of these masters were not obscured, like those of the cyclic poets, by the lustre of Homer's; yet of their works, those of Pindar excepted, only a few fragments remain to justify the admiration which they excited. These fragments are sufficient to show that the loss of the works of the lyric poets is not inferior to any that we have to deplore in the whole range of ancient literature; the extant works of Pindar, great and wonderful as they are, neither compensate for this loss, nor enable us to estimate its full extent. In the Dorian states, poetry and music were generally looked upon as instruments of education, whence their character was watched over and guarded by the magistrate or the law. The themes of the poets were chiefly religious, martial, and political: in Crete and at Sparta the spirit of the laws and the maxims of the constitution were expressed in verse. Though the Spartans themselves, perhaps, disdained the labour of poetical composition, they were keenly sensible of the charms of both music and poetry, and greatly encouraged such foreign poets as were willing to adapt their strains to Spartan principles. Thus Tyrtaeus was honoured, and Alcman, though a Lydian by birth, earned by his genius a rank next to that of a Spartan citizen. The tyrants also cherished the lyric muse, which cheered their banquets, applauded their success, and extolled their magnificence. The Olympic and other public games afforded constant themes for poetical panegyrics, which delicately interwove the praises of the victor with those of his ancestors, his country, its gods and heroes. In short, all the great events of human life in Greece were deemed to need the aid of song to enliven and adorn them: the war-march, the religious and convivial procession, the nuptial ceremony, the feast and the funeral, would have appeared spiritless and unmeaning without this accompaniment.

A particular and indeed the grandest species of lyric composition were the great choral odes, which were brought to perfection by Arion and Stesichorus. They combined the attractions of music and action with those of the loftiest poetry, and formed the favourite entertainment of the Dorian cities. They were the elements out of which Thespis and his successors unfolded the Attic tragedy by the introduction of recitation by a performer who, perhaps, related some simple story in a few scenes, interrupted by the intervening song of the chorus. In the Aeolian and Ionian states, sentimental lyric poetry was more cultivated; in this the resentment of Archilochus, Hipponax, and Alcaeus found vent in bitter sarcasm or open invective; Anacreon and Ibycus sang of the delights of the senses, while Mimnermus was melted into sadness by the thought of their fugitive nature, and Sappho's tenderness was as pure as it was glowing. The insight which these poems would have given us into the private and social life of the Greeks, makes their loss all the more deplorable.

All the early poetry of the Greeks was designed for exhibition, more or less public; and it was not till a late period that poets began to think of writing for the satisfaction of individual readers. This was the case when instruction instead of pleasure became the immediate object, and hence the rise of a prose literature coincides with that of historical inquiry and philosophical speculation. Pherecydes, of Syros, who flourished about B.C. 550, is said to have been the first prose-writer in Greece; and Cadmus, of Miletus, to have first applied prose to historical subjects. The first essays in history which we meet with before the Persian war seem to have been professedly mythological, and to have contained the substance of a large portion of the epic cycle. Many of the first historical works included descriptions of countries or cities, which served as a thread to connect their mythical traditions. Historical criticism, which never rose to any high degree of vigour and independence among the Greeks, was then almost entirely dormant; and the writers of this period, whom we can hardly call historians, probably had no higher aim than the desire of gratifying patriotic vanity or the popular taste for the marvellous. How far they carried their histories down is uncertain, but it is clear that before the Persian war the Greeks had no idea of the importance of their own history; and its practical uses were not understood till considerably later.

Philosophy, or the investigation of causes and effects, may be discerned in Greece in the very earliest period to which its legends go back; but it was not till the sixth century B.C. that it began to be separated from poetry and religion, with which it had before been blended; thenceforward it continued a steady and uninterrupted progress. The character of this age, in its relation to philosophy, is marked by the fame of the Seven Sages, the list of whom was variously made up, but who were all actively engaged in the affairs of public life, as statesmen, magistrates, or legislators. Their wisdom seems to have been of a purely practical nature, and to have been derived from their intercourse with the world rather than from any deep meditation or speculation.

The activity and inquisitiveness of the Greek mind led a few of the bolder spirits, at this peroid, to grapple with some of the great questions which are suggested by the contemplation of the visible universe. There is no necessity whatever for believing that this spirit was called forth or strengthened by intercourse with foreign countries; it is, on the contrary, much more probable that the first speculators were led to their researches by the ancient cosmogonies and theogonies of their own countrymen. The oldest school of philosophy, called the Ionian, was founded by Thales, of Miletus, a contemporary of Solon. He and all his followers attempted to account for the present order of nature, by tracing it back to its primeval state by such steps as they could find. Thus Thales maintained, that water or some liquid was the origin of all things; half a century later, Anaximenes, of Miletus, arrived at the conclusion that air was the universal source of life; and Heraclitus, of Ephesus, attributed the same elementary power to fire or heat. The boldness of these fathers of philosophy, who at once applied themselves to the highest problems, cannot but fill us with amazement; yet the direction which their speculations took towards the objects of outward nature was perfectly in accordance with the natural tendency of the human mind, and with the peculiar character and genius of the Ionians. These speculations, however, gradually led to the recognition of one supreme mind, distinct from the visible world to which it imparted motion, form, and order.

Nearly simultaneously with the Ionian philosophers sprang up in the western colonies the Eleatic school, so called from the town of Elea or Velia, on the western coast of southern Italy, a colony of the Phocaeans. Xenophanes, its founder, is said to have migrated about B. C. 536 from his birthplace, Colophon, to Elea. It began where the Ionian ended, with the admission of a supreme intelligence which was believed to be one with the world itself. Parmenides, the follower of Xenophanes, pursued the same direction, but set out from the idea of being, not from that of deity; he expressly grounded his system on the distinction between sense and reason, as means of arriving at truth. His disciples, Zeno and Melissus, exercised their dialectic subtlety chiefly in combating the dogmas of other philosophers, and the opinions of the vulgar; a mode of intellectual occupation which not unfrequently led them to sophistical paradoxes.

Whether Thales wrote an exposition of his doctrines is uncertain; but his disciple, Anaximander, unfolded his theory in a prose work; and his example appears to have been followed by all the philosophers of the same school. Their works are lost, but it seems that the simplicity of their style was sometimes relieved by bold poetical imagery, in which their thoughts were veiled. Xenophanes and Parmenides, on the other hand, explained their systems in verse, which appears, however, scarcely to have deserved the name of poetry. The remains of these productions breathe a strain of oracular solemnity and obscurity. Zeno expounded his views in the form of dialogues in prose, which were probably dry and unattractive. About the middle of the fifth century B.C., Empedocles, of Agrigentum, unfolded in a poetical form his system, which seems to have been suggested by the Eleatic.

The second and most celebrated of the western schools of philosophy, which, perhaps, was a few years older than the Eleatic, was founded by Pythagoras of Samos, who was born about B.C. 570. His history is obscured by a cloud of legends, through which we can scarcely distinguish the leading outlines of his life and character. There can, however, be no doubt that he travelled in the East, or at least in Egypt, and derived some instruction from Pherecydes of Syros, and perhaps also from Anaximander. To Egypt he was probably indebted for his opinion about the importance of connecting political with religious institutions. Whether he derived his doctrine of the immortality of the soul (which he taught in the form of a transmigration of souls) from some foreign country, or from the mysteries in which he had been initiated, cannot now be determined. He is said to have been the first Greek who assumed the title of philosopher, thereby describing himself as a man devoted to the pursuit of wisdom. He was distinguished by his strong bent for mathematical studies; and some great discoveries in geometry, music, and astronomy are attributed to him. He himself probably never committed his doctrines to writing, so that it is extremely difficult to decide what belongs to him, and what to his disciples and their followers. He appears to have considered numbers as representing the essence and properties of all things, a doctrine which has not yet been satisfactorily explained, and which in later times gave rise to a variety of fancies and chimeras.

After his return from the East, Pythagoras, unable to endure the tyrannical government then exercised in Samos by Polycrates, is said to have quitted his native island; seeing, no doubt, that a tyrannis would oppose insuperable obstacles to his own political designs. The fame of his travels, wisdom, and sanctity, had probably gone before him into Greece, where he stayed some time, and where he seems to have increased his reputation by various circumstances. From Greece he proceeded to Italy and fixed his residence at Croton, whose political and social condition perhaps appeared to him to present the best prospects for his exertions. Causes of discord were at work there, similar to those which produced the struggles between patricians and plebeians at Rome.

The power of the oligarchy, with its senate of 1000 members, was preponderant, but not so secure as to render all assistance superfluous; so that the arrival of a stranger like Pythagoras could not but be hailed with great joy by the privileged class. The nature of his designs has often been discussed, and various conclusions have been arrived at; but his leading thought seems to have been, that the state and the individual ought, each in its way, to reflect the image of that order and harmony by which he believed the universe to be sustained and regulated; but at the same time he was content with slowly approaching this unattainable mark, and with adapting his exertions to the circumstances in which he was placed. He does not appear ever to have assumed any public office, nor to have drawn up a constitution, such as Lycurgus, Zaleucus, and Charondas had done in other places before him; but he formed a society, or order, of which he became the general. It consisted of young men selected from the noblest families of several Italiot cities. Their number was confined to 300, and through them he probably hoped to exercise a powerful influence over all the Greek states of Italy. This society was at once a philosophical school, a religious brotherhood, and a political association; all which characters were inseparably united in the founder's mind. The utmost cultivation of the intellectual faculties in his disciples was a necessary preparation for the work to which he destined them; it was indispensable that those who were to govern the world should first comprehend the place which they filled in it. Religion was probably the centre of the Pythagorean institutions, and the main bond of union among his followers; but what kind of religion it was, is by no means clear, as all the proceedings of the fraternity, and more especially the religious ones, were enveloped in great secrecy. Pythagoras, however, professed the highest reverence for the objects of popular superstition; and the chief mystery which he inculcated on his disciples was, perhaps, the doctrine of the migration of souls. In politics his sentiments were, there is every reason to believe, rigidly aristocratic; and his plan seems to have been to exercise a moral influence through his disciples, rather than that they should come forward as lawgivers or magistrates. Any one seeking admission into his society had to pass through a period of probation and discipline, during which his mode of life was most minutely regulated by the will of Pythagoras; the restrictions which he is said to have put upon the diet of his followers were probably intended to impress some moral or religious truths, or were the results of his medical knowledge. It is stated that all his disciples brought their possessions into a common stock, and that their union was more intimate than that of kindred: many anecdotes are related of the purity and constancy of their friendship.

The failure of Pythagoras' undertaking seems to have been owing not more to the violence of the passions with which he had to contend, than to the rudeness of the instruments which he was obliged to employ. He became a party in a contest in which the right certainly did not lie all on one side; for, having acquired unbounded influence over all classes at Croton and in other cities, he endeavoured to support or restore the aristocratic government. The ascendancy gained by his order of 300 excited the hostility of the party whose interests they opposed, and probably the jealousy of that which they espoused. They were charged with attempting to abolish the popular assembly; but the main cause of their overthrow was probably an overweening confidence in their own strength. The civil feud at Sybaris, which had lasted for some time, at length broke out in a general insurrection against the oligarchs. The democratic party, guided by one Telys, compelled their lords, to the number of 500, to quit the city; and when the latter took refuge at Croton, their surrender was insolently demanded. By the advice of Pythagoras, the senate of Croton refused to comply, and prepared to defend itself by arms. The forces of Sybaris far outnumbered those of Croton; but the latter were commanded by Milo, a disciple of Pythagoras, and an able general, who in bodily strength surpassed all his contemporaries. The two armies met on the banks of the Trionto, and victory declared itself for Croton. A reaction at Sybaris, in which Telys and the leading democrats were massacred, came too late to save Sybaris from its doom. The city was swept from the face of the earth, and the river Crathis was turned through its ruins to obliterate all traces of its departed greatness, B.C. 510.

The senate of Croton, elated by this victory, ascribed the whole success to itself, and claimed the spoil and the conquered land as the property of the state, refusing any share to those who had won the victory by their toil and blood. The commonalty, which felt itself particularly endangered at this crisis, directed its fury mainly against the Pythagorean society, and fire was set to the house in which the members were assembled, B.C. 504. Many perished, and the rest found safety only in exile. Pythagoras himself is generally believed to have died soon after at Metapontum. The rise of the commonalty at Croton seems to have been followed by similar events in several other Italian cities, and everywhere the Pythagoreans were expelled; but civil bloodshed continued to prevail for many years wherever the society had had its seats. Tranquillity was at length restored by the mediation of the Achaeans of the mother-country, when sixty Pythagoreans were allowed to return from exile. But wherever they reappeared, new troubles seem to have arisen from their opposition to the democratical institutions which Croton and other cities had adopted from Achaia.

Coin of Miletus.

Amazon with the Pelta Lunata and Bipennis.
(From a Sarcophagus in the Capitol Museum at Rome.)

Croesus on the Funeral Pile.
(From a painted vase in the Louvre at Paris.)

CHAPTER XII.

AFFAIRS OF THE ASIATIC GREEKS TO THE YEAR B.C. 521.

While the Asiatic colonies were flourishing in freedom, commerce, wealth, arts, and arms, the kingdom of Lydia, which was growing by their side, gradually encroached on their territory, and in the end crushed their independence. Lydia seems anciently to have been inhabited by Pelasgians, and the Lydian monarchy to have been founded on a conquest by which the original inhabitants were either expelled or subdued. This must have happened after the time of Homer, for he nowhere mentions the Lydians. It is stated that the kingdom was governed by two successive dynasties, first by the Heracleids, and afterwards by the Mermnadae. With the commencement of the latter dynasty a new period opened for the Asiatic Greeks. Hitherto the inland districts, bordering on the territories of the Greek colonies, had been constantly disturbed by the irruption of barbarous hordes, the fiercest of which were the Treres and Cimmerians; the former destroyed Magnesia, on the Maeander, and their cruelty made the calamity of the ruined city proverbial; but their inroad was only transient. The Cimmerians disturbed the peninsula of Asia Minor during a longer period, and, issuing from their strongholds in Paphlagonia, more than once overran the fertile plains of the south; but Alyattes, who succeeded to the throne of Lydia in B. C. 617, was powerful enough to deliver Asia from their ravages. About the same time it was freed by the Medes from the Scythians, who are said to have invaded Asia Minor in pursuit of the Cimmerians.

But while the Lydians pushed their conquests far into the interior of Asia, they naturally grew impatient at being separated from the sea, and ambitious of subjecting the cities on the coast to their own empire. Accordingly, when they had got rid of the Cimmerians, they at once set about this task. Gyges is said to have taken Colophon, and to have invaded the territories of Smyrna and Miletus. His son Ardys prosecuted the war, and made himself master of Priene. His successors, Sadyattes and Alyattes, directed their hostilities chiefly against Miletus. From B. C. 623, the war was continued for eleven years; the Lydian army marched every summer into the Milesian territory, and destroyed the crops, but left the houses standing, that the enemy might not be deterred from tilling the land. Beyond this the Milesians suffered little harm: their city was secure from attack, and the sea supplied them with abundance of provisions. In the twelfth of these yearly campaigns a temple of Athene was burnt down; soon afterwards the king was taken ill, and, ascribing his sickness to the sacrilege committed by his troops, he consulted the Delphic oracle, whose answer seems to have inclined him to peace; accordingly, he concluded a treaty of peace and alliance with Miletus, in B. C. 612. Alyattes left two sons, Croesus and Pantaleon, the former of whom, in accordance with his father's wish, succeeded to the throne in B. C. 560, and accomplished all that his father had desired or undertaken.

He began by laying siege to Ephesus, which was then ruled by the tyrant Pindarus, and when the city had fallen into his hands he treated it very leniently, but compelled Pindarus to resign his power. With the same success he attacked, one after another, all the Greek cities on the continent. The mildness of the terms he offered, and the character of his government, probably facilitated his conquest. The tribute which the towns had to pay was a sign of submission rather than a sensible burden, and in every other respect Croesus appears to have permitted his new subjects to regulate their own concerns. Where tyrants had before existed, they continued to exercise their power under the safeguard of a mighty prince. Afterwards, Croesus began to cast a longing eye on the adjacent islands; but a wise Greek is said to have diverted him from the design of attacking them, by reminding him that he was about to expose his Lydians to the chances of an unequal conflict, on an element to which they were strangers. He accordingly confined himself to extending his empire towards the east, in which direction he proceeded triumphantly as far as the river Halys; so that, with the exception of Lycia and Cilicia, all Asia Minor west of the Halys obeyed his commands. The fame of Croesus resounded throughout Greece, and his kingdom was believed to be a sort of paradise. He loved the Greeks, received them at his court, and respected their oracles, which he enriched with the most munificent offerings. The Spartans sent to purchase gold of him to adorn an image, but Croesus made them a present of as much as they required. The Athenian Alcmaeon, who had once done the king a service, was invited to Sardis, and allowed to take as much gold as he could carry. The wise also were drawn to his court by curiosity, and a desire to learn and see as well as to teach. Thus it was believed that Solon, in the course of his travels, went to Sardis, and was hospitably entertained by the king; but that he gazed without admiration or envy on the wonders of the palace, and refused to declare the king a happy man so long as he was subject to the smiles and frowns of fortune The event showed that the Athenian legislator was right, for not long afterwards the kingdom of Croesus became a province of Persia.

In the reign of Astyages, king of the Medes, the Median kingdom was overthrown by the Persians, a hardy race of mountaineers, under their leader Cyrus. The immediate occasion of this conflict between the Medes and Persians, and the history of the birth of Cyrus, are concealed under a heap of fabulous traditions. The dethroned Astyages was connected with Croesus by marriage; but, independently of this connection, Croesus had other reasons for wishing to avenge the injury done to his kinsman. By a prompt and resolute mode of acting he hoped to make himself master of all Asia, while if he remained quiet his own kingdom might soon become endangered by the upstart race of Persian shepherds. After having, as he thought, convinced himself of the trustworthy character of the oracle of Delphi, he consulted the god about the result of his meditated undertaking. The answer seemed to encourage him to prosecute his designs with the assurance of success. Grateful for the advice, Croesus filled the treasury of the god with gold and silver, and even showered munificent presents on the Delphians. He then collected an army from his subject provinces, and marched against Cyrus.

Croesus crossed the Halys, challenging Cyrus to a contest, and waiting for his approach. Cyrus advanced with a superior force, but before he tried the strength of Croesus he sent envoys to the Ionian cities, inviting them to throw off the Lydian yoke. But they had found it too light to wish for a change, and turned a deaf ear to his summons. A battle was fought between the two armies, but with no decisive result; and Croesus, believing that his forces were not powerful enough to accomplish the decree of fate, returned to Sardis to reinforce his army, intending to renew the war in the following spring. He then sent to the kings of Babylon and Egypt for support, and even solicited the aid of Sparta. Croesus was leisurely pursuing this course, and had disbanded his army for the winter, when Cyrus encamped before the walls of Sardis.

Sardis.
(Drawn on the spot, by George Scharf, Jun.)

Croesus, with scarcely any means of defence, tried his fortune in a battle; but lost it, and was closely besieged by the Persians in his citadel. The fortress was taken by surprise, in B.C. 546, and the king with all his treasures fell into the hands of the conqueror. According to a legend, Croesus was at first condemned to the flames, but finally spared; it is more probable, however, that he was conveyed to Ecbatana, and there closed his chequered life.

The conqueror of Lydia soon afterwards found it necessary to deprive the people of their arms, and compel them to confine themselves to the arts of peace and luxury. But being anxious to secure and extend his eastern possessions, Cyrus left the subjugation of the Asiatic Greeks to his lieutenants. The Aeolians and Ionians, even before he left Sardis, offered to submit on the terms which had been granted to them by Croesus. Cyrus, however, gave them to understand that they must submit unconditionally; but exempted Miletus, from which city he was content with the tribute which it had paid to Croesus. The Greeks now began to prepare for resistance. The Ionians assembled at their common sanctuary, the Panionian temple, to consult for the general weal, and sent ambassadors to beg assistance from Sparta. The Spartans, not feeling sufficient sympathy with the Ionians, refused to engage in a war with Persia on their behalf; but still they were bold enough to send an envoy to Cyrus, requesting him to refrain from doing harm to any Greek city. Cyrus, who had never before heard of Sparta, sent them a taunting and contemptuous answer. In the meantime, Mazares, a Median general in the service of Cyrus, proceeded to subdue the Ionians who had aided the Lydians in an attempt to shake off the Persian yoke. But after the capture of Priene and Magnesia, he died. His successor, Harpagus, vigorously pressed the Ionian cities. The first he attacked was Phocaea, whose citizens, seeing that resistance was hopeless, availed themselves of a truce to embark with their wives and children, and steered for Chios. The Persians, on their return, found the city empty. The Phocaeans, being unable to obtain a settlement from the Chians in the neighbouring islands, determined to seek a new home in the western parts of the Mediterranean, where they had already planted several flourishing colonies. But before they did so, they once more sailed home and slew as many of the Persian garrison as they could. They then swore never to return to Phocaea, and sailed westward. Some, however, repenting of their vow, remained behind, while all the rest steered for Corsica, and settled among their kinsmen at Alalia, which had been founded twenty years before. But being attacked there by the Carthaginians and the Tyrrhenians of Agylla, they again embarked with their families, some sailing to their countrymen in Massilia, others to Rhegium in southern Italy. In the latter country they founded Elea, a celebrated seat of arts and learning, which long preserved the independence which its founders had bought so dearly.

The example of the Phocaeans was followed by the inhabitants of Teos, who, seeing no prospect of a successful defence, took to their ships and sailed to the coast of Thrace. There they took possession of a district from which a band of Ionian settlers had, some time before, been driven by the Thracians, and founded the city of Abdera. In this manner all the Ionian cities fell under the successive attacks of Harpagus, and even the islanders thought it prudent to disarm the irresistible conqueror by voluntary submission. The Persian rule was, perhaps, not much more oppressive than that of Croesus had been, but the misfortune was, that the Greeks might in future be commanded by their foreign masters to fight against their countrymen, and to assist in reducing them to the same foreign yoke.

After the conquest of Aeolis and Ionia, Harpagus pushed his conquests along the southern coast. The Carians submitted without a struggle, except Pedasa, which held out even after all around had yielded. Cnidos, which had at first meditated resistance, surrendered at the first summons. In Lycia, the spirit of freedom was more resolute. Xanthos, with its women and children, was burnt by the Xanthians themselves, and while the flames were raging the men sallied forth and died sword in hand. Caunos made a like display of unavailing courage. Whatever did not bend to the will of the conqueror, was broken and ground to dust; and, after a few struggles, the sovereignty of Persia was acknowledged throughout the whole of Asia Minor.

In the meantime Cyrus himself carried out his designs in the interior of Asia. His conquest of the effeminate city of Babylon probably contributed more than any other cause to corrupt the simple and virtuous manners for which the Persians had at first been distinguished. Cyrus' protection of the Jews was probably connected with his designs upon Egypt. But soon after the fall of Babylon, he undertook an expedition against the Massagetae, who dwelt to the east of the Caspian; and after gaining a victory over them by a stratagem, he was defeated and slain in a great battle, and was succeeded, in B.C. 529, by his son Cambyses. The first important measure of this prince was the invasion of Egypt, whose monarchy had long been ripe for destruction, and ready to fall at the first blow struck by a vigorous hand. It was then governed by the usurper Amasis, who had overpowered the Greek troops kept by his predecessor, Apries, but yet knew their value. He removed their quarters from Pelusium to Memphis, that they might guard his person, bestowed many favours upon them, and assigned the city of Naucratis to Greek settlers. He contributed towards the building of temples in Greece, cultivated the friendship of Sparta, and honoured her with presents. Against this prince, Cambyses, in the fifth year of his reign, conducted an expedition in person, and thus carried out the design which his father had meditated. The manner in which the conquest of Egypt was accomplished is variously related, though the account of Herodotus, that Cambyses was aided by a Greek who had deserted the service of Amasis, is the most probable. But before Cambyses reached Egypt, Amasis died, and his son Psammenitus (Amyrtaeus) awaited the approach of the Persians with a large army. The Egyptians were defeated with great slaughter, and their king, who threw himself into Memphis, was besieged and taken, but treated with the respect usually shown by the Persians to fallen greatness.

Cambyses was one of those rulers who aim at everything and accomplish little. Expeditions to the south and west of Egypt completely failed; but some of the Libyan tribes in the west of Egypt acknowledged his sovereignty, and their example was followed by the Greeks of Barce and Cyrene. The Phoenicians having furnished him with a fleet to second his invasion of Egypt, he even contemplated making himself master of Carthage. But the Phoenicians refused to lend their aid for the destruction of their own colony, and Cambyses was obliged to accept the plea with which the Phoenicians covered their refusal. In his conduct towards Egypt he showed no regard for national customs and institutions, which, in fact, he treated with scorn and contempt, and his wanton and sacrilegious acts aroused in the Egyptians feelings which afterwards vented themselves in several attempts to shake off the Persian yoke.

During the reign of Cambyses, the Greek cities of Asia remained quietly subject to their Persian governors. The adjacent islands, though they had made professions of obedience and paid tribute to Persia, were almost independent, as the satraps had no navy at their command. Samos, the most prosperous of these islands, was then governed by the tyrant Polycrates, who maintained himself by the aid of a thousand bowmen, forming his bodyguard, and protected the Samian commerce by a fleet of 100 galleys. He made war on Miletus, and, in a sea-fight, defeated a Lesbian armament sent to its relief. This involved him in hostilities with Persia, which he could safely defy on his own element, for his navy was the most powerful that had ever ridden on the Aegean since the fabulous maritime empire of Minos. He adorned Samos with many useful and ornamental works, lived in regal splendour and luxury, but seems, nevertheless, to have been a wise and active ruler. He cherished the arts; and poets, such as Ibycus and Anacreon, whose muse was devoted to love and wine, were the most welcome guests at his court, and companions of his leisure. His ambition suggested to him the design of uniting under his dominion all the Ionian cities, both in the islands and on the continent of Asia.

But being a tyrant, his power was based on a feeble foundation, and there was, moreover, a party in Samos which only waited for a favourable opportunity to revolt. To get rid of these malcontents, Polycrates offered to Cambyses, during his preparations for the invasion of Egypt, to assist him with a squadron of ships. Cambyses accepted the offer, and Polycrates equipped forty galleys, in which he embarked all the persons who had incurred his suspicion, and requested the Persian king to take care that they should never return. But the malcontents resolved to turn the force which Polycrates had put into their hands, against himself. They sailed back, but found him on his guard, and were defeated, though not without the greatest exertions on the part of the tyrant. They did not, however, give up their designs, but addressed themselves to Sparta, which, from its general hostility to the tyrannical form of government, was ready on every occasion to establish an oligarchy in its room. The request of the exiles for assistance was accordingly granted. The Corinthians also lent their aid, and the Samians, thus reinforced, renewed their attempt to overthrow the tyrant; but after a sharp battle, and sustaining a siege for forty days, he was still so strong that the Peloponnesians abandoned the undertaking, and their friends were obliged to resign themselves to the loss of their country, and seek a new home elsewhere. After ranging for some time as pirates over the Aegean sea, they took possession of Cydonia in Crete, and flourished there, until they were conquered and enslaved by the Aeginetans.

After the removal of this danger, the power of Polycrates seemed to be more firmly established than ever, and he again turned his views to the enlargement of his dominions. But his downfall was suddenly brought about by Oroetes, the satrap of Sardis, who by a cunning stratagem enticed him to come to Sardis, where he was arrested and hung upon a cross. The Samians who had followed in his train were dismissed, and the satrap made no attempt to gain possession of Samos. This occurred in B.C. 522.

Next year Cambyses died on his march against an impostor who had usurped the Persian throne. The usurper belonged to the sacerdotal caste, and was supported by the Magi. But a counter-revolution, headed by the Persians of the highest rank, put an end to the Magian rule, and raised Darius, son of Hystaspes, of the royal house of the Achaemenids, to the throne. Darius was the greatest and most powerful king that ever ruled over Persia, and his wisdom and prosperity shed a lustre over his reign which long continued to be remembered in Asia. He was the first who organised the vast mass of countries which had been conquered by his predecessors, but which were previously unconnected by any tie except that of being subject to the will of a common ruler. The empire of Darius stretched from the Aegean to the Indus, and from the steppes of Scythia to the cataracts of the

Nile. He divided this vast tract into twenty satrapies or provinces, and appointed the tribute which each was to pay to the royal treasury. The western coast was connected with the seat of government by a high road, on which the distances were regularly marked, and spacious buildings were placed at convenient intervals to receive all who travelled in the king's name. The satraps in their provinces were so many almost independent sovereigns, except that they were accountable for the imposts of the provinces which they ruled. These provinces were, in all other respects, governed according to their own laws and institutions, so that the burdens which were imposed on them were the only indications of

Bas-relief representation of Cyrus the Great upon a Square Pillar at Mourg-aub, the ancient Pasargadae.
(Drawn by Sir R. K. Porter.)

foreign sway. These burdens, however, must have been extremely heavy, being levied not only for the supply of the royal revenue, and the maintenance of the royal army and household, but also for the support of the satraps, each of whom kept up an army and a court, which in magnificence sometimes rivalled that of the king himself. The greatness of these viceroys was both oppressive to those whom they governed, and a source of weakness to the king's own government; for if any of them incurred the sovereign's displeasure, it was not always easy to coerce them or to deprive them of their power. We have already seen that Oroetes put to death Polycrates, the ally of Cambyses, for which he was never called to account. During the usurpation of the Magi, he was still more reckless, for he seized the governor of an adjacent province, and murdered both him and his son. Even this outrage he might have committed with impunity, had he not waylaid and murdered a courier who brought him an unwelcome message from the king. A faithful Persian servant disclosed this crime to Darius, who, with the aid of a body of 1000 Persians, put the satrap to death in his palace at Sardis.

The simple and hardy manners of the Persians, at whose head Cyrus overthrew the kingdom of the Medes, must have become considerably altered by their amalgamation with those of the Medes; and still more so after the conquest of Babylon, which Cyrus is said to have chosen for his capital. The court was cruel and luxurious; the women seem to have been of the most depraved character, and their influence was the source of most of the atrocious barbarities which fill the Persian annals. The sacerdotal caste, or the Magi, were the chief counsellors of the kings, who thus became the slaves of their priests, their eunuchs, and their wives. Such was the empire with which Greece was on the eve of entering upon a contest of life and death.

Head of Paris.
(From a Pompeian painting.)

Darius passing Judgment upon Prisoners.
(From a sculpture on the tablet-rock at Behistun.)

CHAPTER XIII.

FROM THE ACCESSION OF DARIUS HYSTASPES, B.C. 521, TO THE BATTLE OF MARATHON, B.C. 490.

DARIUS was not a conqueror like Cyrus; the ruling maxim of his government seems to have been rather to consolidate and secure his empire than to enlarge it, and all the wars of his reign are of a defensive character. Accidental causes directed his attention to the West, and there brought him into collision with the Greeks. The occasion arose out of the misfortunes of Polycrates: at the time when he was put to death at Sardis, the Samians who were in his retinue were dismissed, but the strangers were kept in prison until the death of Oroetes, when they were transported to Susa. Among these captives was a physician named Democedes, a native of Croton, whom Polycrates with his wonted munificence had attracted to his court. At Susa Democedes remained for a time unnoticed; but the king, having dislocated a foot while hunting, was informed of the skill of the Greek physician, who was summoned, and, after some reluctance, arising from a fear that his art might become the cause of a perpetual though honourable exile, undertook and effected a complete cure. The king loaded him with gold, and was ready to grant him any favour except permission to return to his own country, the very thing which he most longed for.

Some time afterwards, Atossa, the king's favourite wife, also availed herself of the services of Democedes. By his descriptions of his native land, he excited her curiosity, and a wish to have Greek damsels to wait upon her. Darius was induced by her to send Democedes home, guarded by a small number of Persians, who were directed at the same time to survey the coasts of Greece and southern Italy under his guidance, and to bring him back to Persia. Democedes, after landing at Croton, of course refused to go on board again, and his companions were unable to compel him; they were themselves wrecked on the southern coast of Italy, and made slaves, but were redeemed and carried back to Persia by a Tarentine exile named Gillus, who hoped, though in vain, to be restored to his country by the mediation of Persia.

Another consequence of the misfortunes of Polycrates was the ruin of Samos. His brother Syloson, when in exile, had conferred a slight favour on Darius while he was serving in the army of Cambyses in Egypt; and on hearing that Darius had been raised to the throne, Syloson went to the Persian court. The king bade him name a reward, and Syloson asked to be made tyrant of Samos as the successor of his brother. The island was then governed by Maeandrius, whom Polycrates, on going to Sardis, had left behind as his vicegerent. When the Persian force under Otanes arrived to restore Syloson, all resistance seemed hopeless, and Maeandrius capitulated on condition of being allowed to quit the island. But while he was withdrawing to the ship which was to carry him away, his hot-headed brother, Charilaus, suddenly fell upon the unsuspecting Persians who were waiting for the surrender of the citadel, and cut them to pieces. The main body of the Persian army, however, soon drove the Samians back into their fortress. This was reduced, and Otanes commanded an indiscriminate slaughter without regard to age or place, sacred or profane. The surviving population of the island was carried away captive, so that Syloson was put in possession of nothing but a desert. Maeandrius meantime had sailed to Sparta, hoping to prevail on King Cleomenes to espouse his cause, but he met with no success, and, in consequence of an attempt to bribe the king, was banished from Sparta and Peloponnesus.

While these events were passing on the coast of the Aegean, Darius undertook an expedition against the Scythians about the same time that the satrap of Egypt was engaged in the conquest of the Greek settlements in Africa. The Scythians, who had been driven from the north-east of Asia by the Massagetae, were now masters of the great plain between the Danube and the Don. The expedition against these nomadic hordes of savages had been delayed by a rebellion at Babylon in the beginning of the reign of Darius, but when this was quelled he set out against the Scythians. The cause, as well as the progress, of this war is involved in great obscurity; and scarcely any fact relating to it is absolutely certain, except that Darius conducted it in person, and that it failed. His object, however, seems to have been to weaken the Scythians, and thus to secure his own empire on that side. His army is believed to have consisted of seven or eight hundred thousand men. A bridge of boats was ordered to be laid across the Thracian Bosporus, and it was successfully accomplished by a Samian engineer called Mandrocles. There also 600 ships, furnished by the subject Greek cities, waited his commands; and most of the Greek tyrants, who ruled under his protection along the coast of Asia, served in the fleet. They were to sail up the Danube to a point above the head of its Delta, and there to wait for the arrival of the land force. Most of the tribes through whose territories Darius passed, yielded without resistance. On arriving at the appointed place, the troops crossed to the left bank of the river; the king then ordered the bridge to be broken up, and the Greeks to follow him into Scythia. But being reminded that the bridge might be wanted on his return, he directed it to be left standing for sixty days, after which the Greeks who guarded it were to break it down and return home.

He then proceeded against the Scythians, but the events of the campaign elude every attempt to form a clear conception of them This much only is certain, that the pursuit, in which the Persians had wasted their strength, was changed into a retreat, in which they were compelled to abandon their baggage and their sick. In the mean time the sixty days had elapsed, and the Greeks stationed at the bridge on the Danube were urged by the Athenian Miltiades, the ruler of the Thracian Chersoneus, to avail themselves of the opportunity of recovering their freedom by breaking up the bridge. But Histiaeus, the tyrant of Miletus, thought differently; his arguments brought most of his countrymen over to his side, for he reminded them that their power as tyrants depended upon that of the Persian sovereign, and that his downfall would involve their own ruin. The bridge, accordingly, was allowed to stand, and Darius escaped from imminent danger. The army which he brought back was still large enough to enable him to leave 80,000 men in Enrope, under the command of Megabazus, who was to complete the conquest of Thrace and of the Greek cities on the Hellespont. Darius himself rested some time at Sardis. Histiaeus asked and received, as a reward for his service on the Danube, a district on the river Strymon, where he founded the town of

Myrcinus, which commanded the navigation of the river. Histiaeus still retained Miletus, but committed it to the charge of his cousin Aristagoras. Miltiades, however, appears to have been left in the undisturbed possession of the Chersonesus, a circumstance which throws great doubt upon the story of his offence.

Megabazus began his operations in Thrace with the reduction of Perinthos, and then proceeded to subdue all the Thracian tribes which had not yet submitted to his master. Darius, while staying at Sardis, had become acquainted with some Paeonians, and was so struck with their manners and appearance, that he commissioned Megabazus to invade their country, the upper vale of the Strymon, and transport the whole people to Asia. They attempted to resist the aggressor, but, finding themselves unable to do so, dispersed; a part of them, however, submitted, and Megabazus carried them into Asia, where Darius assigned a district in Phrygia for their habitation.

The regions into which Megabazus had carried the Persian arms bordered on the kingdom of Macedonia; and before he led his forces from Paeonia, he sent envoys to Amyntas, the king of that country, to demand, in the name of the Persian monarch, earth and water, the customary symbols of subjection. Macedonia at this period was only a small kingdom, which had grown to its present extent by the conquest of insignificant neighbouring states. The Macedonian people were a mixture of Illyrian tribes and a more ancient Pelasgian population; but the reigning dynasty was believed to be of purely Hellenic origin, and was traced to the Heracleid Temenus, who, in the division of Peloponnesus, had obtained Argos for his share. The founder of the Macedonian dynasty was said to have been Caranus, a brother of the Argive prince Pheidon. While thus the kings of Macedonia were universally believed to be Greeks, the people are always called barbarians. Amyntas consented to become the vassal of Darius at the summons of Megabazus. A banquet was given to the Persian envoys; in the course of which, however, their outrageous conduct towards the ladies of the court roused the indignation of Alexander, the king's son, to such a point, that he caused them to be murdered in the banquet-hall. Amyntas himself took no further steps of resistance, nor did Darius ever avenge the death of his envoys.

Megabazus, while engaged against the Paeonians, perceived that Histiaeus was collecting the elements of a formidable power at Myrcinus, and afterwards communicated his suspicions to Darius. The king, resolving to deprive Histiaeus of the opportunity of doing any harm, sent for him on pretence of consulting him about some important undertaking. When Histiaeus arrived at Sardis, the king told him that he could no longer bear to be without his company and conversation, and expressed a desire to take him to Susa, where he was to share the king's table and counsels. Histiaeus was obliged to obey the command of his sovereign, and accompanied the king into a splendid captivity, in which he was to spend the remainder of his days. Before setting out for Susa, Darius appointed Artaphernes satrap of the Asiatic coast of the Aegean, and of the southern provinces of the kingdom of Croesus, whose capital, Sardis, was still the seat of government for this part of Asia. Otanes succeeded Megabazus, and was very successful in reducing the maritime cities on the north of the Aegean, such as Byzantium and Chalcedon, and the islands of Imbros and Lesbos. Towards the year B.C. 505, all the nations from the banks of the Indus to the borders of Thessaly thus rested under the shade of the Persian monarchy; and there appeared to be no power that could rival its majesty, and none from which it could not enforce submission.

While the world was thus enjoying for a short time profound repose, the aristocratic party in Naxos was driven by its victorious adversaries into exile, and now applied to Aristagoras of Miletus for succours. As they had been united by political ties with Histiaeus, Aristagoras was not unwilling to restore them; for he hoped that Naxos, when ruled by his creatures, would virtually become his own. But the undertaking was too much for him alone; accordingly he applied to Artaphernes, representing that an opportunity was now offered not only of conquering Naxos, but of making himself master of all the Cyclades. Aristagoras described the enterprise as very easy, and promised to defray all the expenses. Artaphernes was taken with the scheme; and, with the king's consent, placed 200 ships and a Persian force at the disposal of Aristagoras. The fleet, commanded by a Persian admiral, Megabates, sailed from Miletus, having taken on board the Ionian army raised by Aristagoras.

It was intended to lull the Naxians into security by making them believe that the expedition was destined for a different quarter. Megabates cast anchor off the coast of Chios; and there a dispute arose between him and Aristagoras, which provoked him to such a degree, that he determined to thwart the expedition against Naxos, on which Aristagoras had staked so much. He accordingly sent a message to the Naxians to warn them of their danger. The Naxians now made vigorous preparations to defend themselves, so that when at last the Persian fleet appeared their city was in a condition to sustain a long siege. At the end of four months, the besiegers had made no progress; the treasures of Aristagoras were exhausted, and he was obliged, in B.C. 501, to return to Miletus without having effected anything. The failure of the expedition rendered it impossible for him to discharge his debt to the Persian government, and he was a ruined man. He saw no way of extricating himself from his difficulties, except by inciting his countrymen to revolt. While he was pondering over this scheme, he received a message from Histiaeus which fixed his resolution. Histiaeus found his captivity intolerable, and had no hope of delivery except in an insurrection of his countrymen. As a safe method of conveying his wishes to his friends, he shaved the head of a trusty slave, traced some letters with a hot iron on his skin, and when the hair had grown again, sent him off to Miletus. When Aristagoras, as directed, inspected the slave's head, he found an invitation to revolt. In every city there were persons impatient of the Persian yoke, and Aristagoras forthwith assembled some of the leading men to deliberate upon a plan of action. Hecataeus, the historian, who was present at the meeting, and saw the danger of the scheme, dissuaded his friends from it; but they, being rash, though neither bold nor firm, resolved upon war without securing the means for carrying it on. It was further determined to seize the Greek tyrants who were still stationed off Myus with the Persian fleet. This was the signal of a general insurrection. Aristagoras, in order to obviate all opposition, and to gain over the democratic party, resigned his own authority, and delivered up the tyrants taken at Myus to the cities over which they had ruled. Liberty was now everywhere restored in the revolted cities, B. C. 500.

After this, Aristagoras sailed to Greece to persuade some of the leading states to espouse his cause. He first went to Sparta, and addressed himself to Cleomenes. At a private interview he brought forth a brass plate, containing a map of the world, according to the most exact notion that had then been formed by the Samian sages of its outlines and its parts. Aristagoras pointed out to the king the situation and wealth of Persia, of which he might make himself master without much difficulty. But when Cleomenes learned the great distance between Sparta and Susa, he was alarmed, broke off the conversation, and bade the stranger quit Sparta without delay. Aristagoras then went as a suppliant to the king's house, and found him with his daughter Gorgo — a child eight or nine years old — by his side. Aristagoras offered to the king a price for his assistance, and gradually raised it to fifty talents; at that moment the child, who had listened unheeded, suddenly exclaimed, "Go away, father, the stranger will do you harm." Cleomenes accepted the omen, and Aristagoras soon afterwards quitted Sparta.

He made his next application to Athens, after Sparta, the most powerful state of Greece; and he had reason to hope for better success there than at Sparta. Athens had already had some transactions with the Persian satrap of Sardis, at the time when Cleomenes threatened to invade Attica*; and the satrap had then consented to protect the Athenians, if they would send the usual signs of submission. The Athenian envoys, either from ignorance of the import of presenting earth and water, or because they thought the danger of their country so pressing that deliverance was cheap at any price, undertook to comply. But on their return to Athens they were sharply censured, and their promise was not sanctioned. About the same time, the exiled Hippias was endeavouring to induce Tissaphernes to take up his quarrel; and when the Athenians heard of his machinations, they sent, as unwisely as before, to deprecate the satrap's interference. The answer they received was, that they should be safe if they would recall their tyrant. This reply at once showed them what they had to expect from Persia, and they prepared themselves to defy its enmity. Such was the state of mind at Athens when Aristagoras arrived. He accordingly found willing hearers when in the assembly of the people he unfolded the tempting prospects which he had spread before Cleomenes. In addition to other motives he urged that it was a religious duty to protect their Ionian kinsmen and colonists. A decree was readily passed to send a squadron of twenty ships for that purpose, under the command of Melanthius.

Aristagoras returned to Asia before the Athenian squadron, which followed soon after him, in B.C. 499, accompanied by five galleys from Eretria. The Eretrians had not, like the Athenians, been provoked to this step by any threats of Persia, but joined in the expedition to discharge a debt of gratitude towards the Milesians, who had once assisted them in a war against Chalcis. After landing near Ephesus, the Athenians were reinforced by a strong body of Ionians, with whom they proceeded without delay against the unguarded capital of Lydia, where Artaphernes then was; he threw himself into the citadel, which was capable of standing a long siege, and gave up the city to be plundered by the invaders. A soldier, in the heat of pillage, set fire to a house; the flames soon spread through the whole city, and reduced it to ashes, as most of the houses were of wicker-work, or were thatched with reeds. The Lydians, however, made a desperate resistance; and the Ionians and Athenians finding their own position dangerous, as they could not hope to force the strong citadel, and might be attacked in their rear, resolved to make a timely retreat

* See above, p. 188.

to Ephesus. The whole force of the province, which had in the mean time been promptly levied, pursued the invaders, and, having overtaken them in the Ephesian territory, defeated them in a battle. Hereupon the Ionians dispersed, and the Athenians and Eretrians sailed home.

When the Persian monarch heard of the burning of Sardis, his rage knew no bounds; but he was more indignant at the obscure strangers who had invaded his dominions, than at the rebellious Ionians; and one of his attendants was charged to recall the name of the Athenians to his thoughts every day. His first care, however, was to quell the Ionian insurrection, which was beginning to spread into other parts. Histiaeus was summoned into his presence, and upbraided with the revolt of his kinsman. But the artful Greek removed all suspicion from himself, and even obtained leave to go to Ionia, pretending that he would suppress the rebellion. Meanwhile, Aristagoras had in vain solicited fresh succours from the Athenians. The Ionians themselves, however, did not remain inactive; their fleet induced Byzantium and the other cities between the Aegean and the Euxine to assert their independence. The greater part of Caria, and the island of Cyprus, also shook off the Persian yoke. Yet all these fair prospects of liberty were soon overclouded; for the generals of Darius, who had routed the Ionians and Athenians, soon reduced the maritime cities to obedience. From the Propontis, where several towns were taken at the first assault, Daurises hastened to suppress the revolt in Caria. After two defeats, the strength of the Carians was broken; but they still held out, and retarded their final subjugation. The revolt of Cyprus lasted for one year, at the end of which the Cyprians being betrayed by one of their own princes, were defeated by a Phoenician fleet. When this was accomplished, Artaphernes and Otanes began vigorously to press the cities of Ionia and Aeolis. After the fall of Clazomenae and Cuma, Aristagoras, who was now as desponding as he had before been sanguine, resolved to take refuge at Myrcinus in Thrace. He was accompanied thither by a large number of his countrymen; but was soon afterwards, while encamped before a Thracian city, cut off with his band by a sally of the besieged.

These things had happened before Histiaeus arrived at Sardis. On Artaphernes hinting to him that he had some connection with the revolt of the Ionians, Histiaeus made his escape from Sardis to Chios. In the latter place he was received with suspicion and anger as the man who had brought Ionia to the verge of ruin. But he appeased the people by telling them a forged story of Darius' intention to transplant all the Ionians to Phoenicia. He also renewed an intrigue which he had commenced at Sardis with some Persians; but the bearer of his letters to them revealed the secret to Artaphernes, who put to death all the Persians concerned in the plot. Histiaeus wished to take the lead in the war which he had kindled, but he was so much distrusted, that he soon found himself a homeless adventurer. Miletus, glad to be rid of Aristagoras, now refused to admit her old tyrant, Histiaeus. He withdrew to Lesbos, where he met with better success, and collected a little squadron of eight triremes, with which he sailed to Byzantium; and there seized the merchant vessels of all the cities which would not acknowledge his authority as sovereign of Ionia. Meantime the insurrection of Ionia was drawing to a crisis. The Persian generals determined to besiege Miletus by land and by sea, being certain that its fall would be speedily followed by the submission of the other cities which looked up to it as their chief. A numerous fleet was collected in the ports of Phoenicia, Egypt, Cilicia, and Cyprus. While this armament was expected, the Ionians assembled at Panionium concerted a plan of defence. It was resolved to leave Miletus to defend itself on the land-side, and to exert all the strength of the confederacy to drive the Persians from the Aegean. The fleet was directed to assemble near the small island of Lade. It consisted of 353 triremes, while the hostile fleet, which was on its way from the East, numbered 600. Notwithstanding their numerical superiority, the Persians were unwilling to encounter the Ionians on the element on which they had the advantage of far greater experience. The tyrants, who at the beginning of the insurrection had been expelled from their cities, and were then serving in the Persian army, were accordingly called upon by the Persian generals each to detach his fellow-citizens from the common cause by offers of pardon and by threats of the most rigorous treatment if they should refuse to submit. The overtures were in every case rejected, because each city imagined that the dishonourable proposal was made to itself alone. During this state of things, Dionysius, a Phocaean, observing that the Ionians at Lade did not display the order and good discipline necessary at such a juncture, prevailed on them to commit themselves to his guidance. He now every day trained his men in military exercises; but, after seven days of this laborious occupation, the Ionians, displeased at his strict discipline, and at the hardships which he imposed upon them, resolved to shake off the intolerable yoke, and again began to neglect every precaution. During the heat of the day, they dispersed over the island, reposing in the most agreeable spots they could find. This folly induced some Samians to send to their banished tyrant Aeaces, the son of Syloson, declaring their readiness to close with his late proposals; and it was agreed, that they should desert during the battle.

When at length the Persian fleet sailed to attack them, the Ionians met them without suspicion of treachery. But at the very beginning of the contest the Samians quitted their post, and bore away to Samos. Their example was followed by the Lesbians, and, as the alarm spread, by the greater part of the fleet. The Chians, who almost alone held out, were at length overpowered by superior numbers, and compelled to flee. Some of them, who had abandoned their ships, while passing by night through the Ephesian territory, where the women were celebrating a festival, were taken for robbers and cut to pieces by the Ephesians. Dionysius of Phocaea had fought to the last, and had taken three of the enemy's ships; when forced to flee he sailed to Phoenicia, sank several merchantmen, and laden with spoil, steered for Sicily, where he carried on an unremitting war against the Tyrrhenians and Carthaginians.

The defeat off Lade, in B.C. 494, was soon followed by the fall of Miletus, which was stormed by the Persians, in the sixth year after the breaking out of the revolt. Those who escaped the sword were carried into captivity with their families, and transplanted to the head of the Persian Gulf, where they were settled in a town called Ampe, near the mouth of the Tigris. The temples of Miletus were despoiled of their treasures, and the city itself became a Persian colony. This catastrophe was felt by the Athenians as a national calamity, and Phrynichus, who ventured to produce it on the stage before his countrymen, was punished by a heavy fine. In the following year the other Ionian cities experienced a similar fate; the islands of Chios, Lesbos, and Tenedos were swept of their inhabitants, and the subjugation of Ionia was complete. The cities on the north of the Aegean were overpowered one after another by the Persian fleet. On the approach of the enemy the inhabitants of Byzantium and Chalcedon left their homes, and established a new one at Mesembria, on the western coast of the Euxine. Miltiades the Athenian, too, thought himself no longer safe in his principality of the Chersonesus, which had been founded by his uncle Miltiades during the reign of Pisistratus, from whose jealous eyes he had withdrawn. Miltiades had been in the undisturbed possession of his principality ever since the return of Darius from his Scythian expedition; but now, when he saw himself threatened with an invasion by the victorious Persians, he sailed away to Athens, having filled five galleys with his treasure. One of his ships conveying his son was intercepted by the Persians, but Miltiades himself reached Athens in safety, and again became one of its citizens.

When the Persians, after the subjugation of Ionia, had satisfied their vengeance, Artaphernes made the conquered country a Persian province: all traces of independence in the cities were effaced; they were compelled to submit all their disputes to arbitration; a survey was taken of the country, and each district had a certain amount of tribute imposed upon it. Order and tranquillity were thus restored at the expense of liberty, and as many who had fled during the insurrection now returned, the cities began to revive. In the year after the close of the war, Artaphernes was succeeded by Mardonius, the king's son-in-law, whose first step was calculated to allay the discontent of the Ionians; this was the deposition of the tyrants who had been set up in the cities by his predecessor, and the restoration of a democratical form of government, a measure which reflects great honour on the understanding of Mardonius, and shows that he had more knowledge of mankind, and larger views, than are commonly possessed by Asiatic princes. He had come with a mighty armament to wreak the vengeance of the king upon Athens and Eretria, and at the same time to spread the terror of his name in Europe. A large fleet was to sweep the Aegean, and to exact obedience from the islands, while Mardonius himself led an army through Thrace into Greece. The fleet first sailed to Thasos, which was well known for its gold mines, and now yielded without a struggle. But the progress of the Persian armament was checked by a violent storm which overtook it off Mount Athos, and was thought to have destroyed no less than 300 ships and 20,000 lives. Mardonius himself was not much more fortunate: on his march through Macedonia, his camp was surprised in the night by the Brygians, an independent Thracian tribe; he lost many of his troops, and was himself wounded. He did not, indeed, leave the country till he had tamed the Brygians, but his forces were so weakened that he thought it prudent to return to Asia. Thus ended the first Persian campaign in Europe, in B.C. 492.

But the resolution of Darius was not shaken by these disasters, and next year he renewed his preparations for invading Greece. In the mean time he sent heralds round to the Greek cities to demand the usual symbols of submission. The arrival of his envoys brought about some changes in the state of Greece, to which we must now direct our attention. The Athenians, as we have seen, had been delivered from the invasion of Cleomenes by the friendship of the Corinthians. Thebes, too weak by itself to revenge its discomfiture by the Athenians, called in the aid of Aegina, between which island and Athens there existed an implacable enmity. The Aeginetans accordingly, confident in the superiority of their naval powers, actively espoused the cause of the Thebans by an invasion of Attica. The Athenians, being otherwise engaged, did not take revenge for this insult, and the quarrel slumbered for a time, until the arrival of the envoys from Darius. Both at Athens and at Sparta they were put to death with cruel mockery; many other cities on the continent of Greece complied with the demand of the Persians, and Aegina with the rest of the islands also submitted to the barbarians. The Athenians immediately sent ambassadors to Sparta, to accuse Aegina of having betrayed the cause of Greece; Cleomenes forthwith repaired to Aegina, and was proceeding to arrest some of the leading citizens, when he was thwarted by his colleague Demaratus, who privately encouraged the Aeginetans to resist the attempt of Cleomenes. The latter now resolved upon freeing himself from his treacherous and troublesome colleague. He revived the old charge against Demaratus, that by his birth he was not entitled to the royal dignity; and Leotychides was instigated to urge his claim to the throne. The Spartans, unwilling to decide so grave a question without the most satisfactory evidence, referred it to the Delphic oracle. The priestess was prevailed on, through the influence of Cleomenes, to declare that Demaratus was not the son of Ariston, to whom the mother of Cleomenes had been transferred by her first husband in a state of pregnancy. Leotychides now succeeded to the throne, and wantonly insulted the deposed Demaratus, who soon afterwards quitted Sparta, and went to the court of Darius, where he was graciously received.

Cleomenes now returned to Aegina in company with Leotychides; and the Aeginetans, afraid of resisting their joint demand, at once surrendered ten of their principal citizens, who were deposited as hostages with the Athenians. Soon afterwards, the fraud committed at Delphi was detected; the priestess was deposed; and Cleomenes, fearing punishment, fled to Thessaly; thence he went to Arcadia, where he formed a plot against his own country, which alarmed the Spartans to such a degree, that they invited him back by promises of impunity. He did not, however, long survive his restoration, for in a fit of madness he died miserably by his own hand. Nor did Leotychides carry his ill-gotten dignity to the grave, for, having many years after this period been convicted of bribery, he was exiled and died at Tegea.

On the death of Cleomenes, the Aeginetans complained at Sparta of the unjust seizure of their fellow-citizens. The Spartans condemned Leotychides to be given up to them in the room of their hostages, but the Aeginetans contented themselves with taking him to Athens to demand the restitution of his deposit. The Athenians, however, refused to release their prisoners, and the Aeginetans retaliated by capturing the sacred ship which was conveying a number of distinguished Athenians to the festival of Apollo at Delos. In consequence of this fresh provocation, a conspiracy, which was formed by some Aeginetans for overthrowing the oligarchical government of the island, was countenanced by the Athenians, but the succours sent by them not arriving in time the plot failed, and the conspirators to the number of 700 were put to death. The Athenians had been delayed by the want of a navy, and had to borrow ships from the Corinthians; but they nevertheless continued the war with varying success, while the Persians were preparing to invade Attica.

In B.C. 490, a new force having been collected in Persia, it was placed under the command of Datis and Artaphernes, and assembled in Cilicia, where a fleet of 600 galleys, together with transports for horses, was ready to take the army on board. The armament first sailed to Samos, and thence crossed over to the Cyclades. The Naxians, who were first attacked, fled into their mountains; those who could not escape were carried off by the Persians, and their city and temples became a prey to the flames. The peaceful inhabitants of the sacred Delos fled to Tenos, leaving their rich temple to the protection of the gods. The Persians, considering Apollo and Artemis, the tutelary deities of Delos, as identical with the sun and moon, which they themselves worshipped, not only spared Delos, but even rendered the greatest honours to its divinities. The fleet then sailed to Euboea, taking in reinforcements and hostages as it proceeded through the islands. Carystus, the first Euboean town before which the Persians appeared, rejected their demands. While it was defending itself, Eretria sent to Athens for succour against the impending danger, and the 4000 Athenians settled on the estates of the wealthy Eretrians were charged to protect that city. But the Eretrians themselves were divided in their opinions, some wishing to imitate the Naxians, others to purchase the favour of the Persians by betraying their country. When the Athenians arrived and were informed of this state of feeling, they returned to Attica; and the event proved the prudence of their retreat. After the fall of Carystus, the Persians laid siege to Eretria. For some days the people made a gallant resistance, but at last the gates were treacherously thrown open by the party which wished to gain the favour of the enemy. The conquerors literally fulfilled the commands of the king; the more rigorously, that the fate of Eretria might strike terror into the Athenians. The city with its temples was plundered, burnt, and razed to the ground. The captives were deposited in a safe place, until they could be conveyed to Persia. The whole armament then steered its course to the coast of Attica.

The aged tyrant Hippias, who had most earnestly urged the expedition, now guided the barbarians against his own country. By his advice the army landed on the plain of Marathon, in the bay of which the fleet lay at anchor. That plain is one of the few level districts in Attica, and is about five miles in length and two in breadth. Near the shore the low grounds at the foot of the hills on either side are swamps, or covered with stagnant pools. On this advantageous ground the Persians encamped, expecting an opportunity of fighting a decisive battle. Had the Athenians shrunk from a conflict, a march of a day or two would have brought the enemy before the walls of Athens; they therefore no sooner heard of the landing of the hostile forces, than they marched out to meet them. At the same time nothing was neglected to strengthen themselves for the contest; they armed not only all the serviceable citizens, but such of their slaves as were willing to earn their liberty with their blood. Phidippides, a man noted for his extraordinary speed, was sent off to request instant succour from Sparta. The Plataeans, as allies and brothers of the Athenians, who were likewise summoned, came and found the Athenians already facing the enemy. Phidippides, on his arrival at Sparta, related the fall of Eretria, and the imminent danger of Athens. The Spartans did not refuse assistance, but they probably did not feel the urgency of the juncture: the moon, moreover, wanted some days of the full, and it was contrary to their religious tenets to set out on an expedition during this interval; they accordingly dismissed the messenger with promises of future succour. On his return to Athens, however, he cheered and encouraged his countrymen by the news that, on his passage through Arcadia, the god Pan had promised to show his good-will towards the Athenians, although they had neglected his worship. Solemn vows were made to Artemis, and their minds being thus strengthened with confidence in the gods, the Athenians crossed the hills which separate Marathon from the rest of Attica.

Their army was commanded as usual by ten generals, Callimachus, the polemarch, being at their head; by law he was entitled to command the right wing, and had a casting vote in all disputes that might arise among his colleagues, one of whom was Miltiades, the late ruler of Chersonesus. On his arrival in Athens, he had been persecuted by persons who represented him as having been a tyrant, and as an unworthy countryman of Harmodius and Aristogeiton; but he had been acquitted, for it could not be denied that, even while in Chersonesus, he had done good service to his country. The islands of Lemnos and Imbros, which were inhabited by a remnant of the Pelasgians, and had greatly annoyed the

Athenians by their piratical expeditions, had been subdued by Miltiades, and subjected, nominally at least, to the dominion of Attica. This achievement, and his conduct on the Danube when Darius was invading Scythia, turned the popular feeling to such a degree, that, on the approach of Datis and Artaphernes, he was elected one of the ten generals.

When the hostile armies were face to face, the opinions of the Ten were equally divided on the question, whether they should give battle to the Persians. Some were for waiting until the arrival of the Lacedaemonians, and hoped that in the mean time their army might accustom itself to the sight of the enemy, whose very name was terrible. But all considerations were outweighed by the representations of Miltiades, who intimated that treachery within the walls or the camp of the Athenians was far more dangerous than the number of the Persians; for Hippias still had some partisans at Athens, and with Persian gold might easily increase their number or purchase traitors. Miltiades also knew how little depended on the inequality of numbers, and how far superior the Athenians were to the barbarians in all that constitutes the real strength of an army. The honest Callimachus saw and felt the force of such arguments, and gave his voice for battle. The generals commanded the army in succession each for one day, and when it came to Miltiades' turn he drew up his little army in order of battle.

The centre of the hostile army was occupied by the Persians themselves, and by the Sacians. Miltiades strengthened his wings at the expense of the centre, although the latter was opposed to the strongest, perhaps the only formidable, part of the enemy's forces. The two armies were separated by an interval of nearly a mile, and the Athenians occupied somewhat higher ground. At the signal of attack they rushed down on the enemy, who awaited them with wonder and scorn, as men who were hurrying into certain destruction. But before the Persians had bethought themselves sufficiently to use their missiles with effect, they found themselves engaged in close combat, in which the Grecian weapons and armour gave the soldier a decided advantage. The Persians and Sacians, however, stood the shock, and soon broke through the opposite centre; but the Athenian wings overpowered the motley hosts which were opposed to them, and drove them towards the shore and the marshes. While they were struggling with the difficulties of the ground, Miltiades drew his men off, and, closing his wings, led them back to meet the enemy, who were returning from the pursuit of the Athenian centre. The defeat of this body decided the battle. The routed army now thought of nothing but reaching their ships; many perished in the marshes, others in their eagerness to embark: Hippias himself is said to have been among the slain.* The victors took seven ships, but Callimachus and one of his colleagues were left on the field. The Persian fleet, instead of shaping its course eastwards, steered towards Sunium, intending to proceed to the southern coast of Attica; but they were foiled by the promptness of the Athenians, who, leaving a detachment to guard the prisoners and the booty, marched to Athens, and arrived there before the Persians appeared off the coast. The Persians, seeing that their plan had failed, set sail for Asia without committing any fresh act of hostility. So ended the day of Marathon.

The battle of Marathon was ever after looked upon by the Athenians as the most brilliant achievement of their history; and they had indeed reason to be proud of it, a small band of patriotic men having on that day gained a complete and decisive victory over a countless host of barbarian invaders, and thus secured the independence of Greece and of Europe generally, which but for this event would probably have become a province of an eastern despot. But the very glory of the achievement so dazzled the Greeks, that they were scarcely able to view it calmly and soberly, so that what they had actually done was increased in their imaginations to something altogether incredible and impossible. This much, however, is certain, that the Athenians, to whom the glory of that victory belonged almost exclusively, then for the first time became aware of their own strength; and thus a state of things was eventually brought about, the consequences of which may be traced even to our own days. The number of Persians who lay dead on the field of battle is said to have amounted to 6400, while the Athenians lost no more than 192, among whom the Plataeans are not reckoned. The Persian army contained the contingents of twenty-six nations. As to the amount of the barbarian host, it is described by some as having consisted of 600,000 men; but if we bear in mind the statement of Herodotus, that the whole army was transported in 600 ships, and another which he makes elsewhere, that each ship carried 200 men, we shall reduce the sum total to 120,000. The Athenian forces, including the Plataean auxiliaries, are uniformly rated at about 10,000, in which, however, no account is taken of the slaves, who served as light-armed troops. This unexampled achievement did not make the Athenians overbearing; they gratefully acknowledged that after all it was mainly owing to the interposition of higher powers, and many a legend was told recording the belief that the gods had taken a

* See, however, Herod. vi. 107.

deep interest in the deliverance of Greece. The place where the battle was fought is still marked by a tumulus, under which the Athenians are said to have been buried; and to this day the field of Marathon is believed to be haunted, as of old, with spectral warriors, and the shepherds are alarmed in the night by their shouts and by the neighing of their steeds.*

The absence of the Spartans on the day of the battle was a momentous event. They came to Attica while the field was strewed with the dead, with no more than 2000 men. But although they were too late to share the glory of the day, they desired to see the field and the formidable barbarians who had been vanquished there; after this they returned home. Their delay in coming to the assistance of their countrymen in the hour of danger could not be wholly justified either by law or by prejudice, and this they themselves appear to have felt.

The new spirit which the victory over the Persians had infused into the conquerors, appeared almost immediately in an occurrence which closed the career of Miltiades. He forthwith demanded of the Athenians a fleet of seventy ships, with which he promised to increase their dominion, and the people granted his request without even knowing towards what object he would direct the expedition. He first attacked Paros, where he had a private enemy, and which was then one of the most flourishing among the Cyclades. But the Parians baffled all his attacks, and, having received a dangerous hurt in his knee or hip, he returned home without fulfilling the promise by which he had induced the people to fit out the fleet. The ill-feeling thus created in the public mind led Xanthippus, the father of Pericles, the chief of the house of the Alcmaeonids, to bring a capital charge against him for having deceived the people. Unable, in consequence of his wound, to defend his cause, which was undertaken by his brother, he was sentenced to pay a fine of fifty talents. As he could not immediately raise this sum, he was cast into prison, where he soon afterwards died of his sore. The principal cause of his condemnation may have been his desire to set himself above the laws of his country, for as he had lived many years like a sovereign in Chersonesus, and had been exalted at Athens by his brilliant victory over the Persians, it is not impossible that he, being a member of an ancient Eupatrid family, may have manifested an inclination to disregard legal restraints; and if so, nothing that

* According to Plutarch (*Camil.* 19.), the battle of Marathon was fought on the 6th of Boëdromion; but according to modern investigations, on the 16th or 17th of Metageitnion, that is, in the month of August.

he had done for his country could justify him in the eyes of the Athenians. We may pity him, indeed, but he assuredly did not fall an innocent victim to popular liberty.

Bas-relief of a Greek Warrior found near Marathon.

(Drawn from the original, by George Scharf, jun.)

The Plain and Tumulus of Marathon.

CHAPTER XIV.

FROM THE BATTLE OF MARATHON TO THE BATTLE OF SALAMIS.

The success of the Persians against the town of Eretria was but a poor compensation for the defeat they had sustained in Attica. When the captive Eretrians were brought before Darius, he was satisfied with planting them in the village of Ardericca, in a part of his own domains. But his anger was doubly inflamed against the Athenians by the event of Marathon, and he now resolved that they should feel the whole weight of his arm. For three years preparations were made throughout his dominions, and every nation that owned his sway had to contribute to the new armament more largely than before. Ships, horses, and provisions in abundance were furnished. In the fourth year his attention was distracted by a quarrel in his family, and by an insurrection in Egypt. In a dispute between his two sons, Artabazanes and Xerxes, about the succession, Darius decided in favour of the latter, the younger, who was his son by Atossa, a daughter of Cyrus. But in the following year, B. C. 485, before he had completed his preparations against Egypt, he died, and Xerxes mounted the throne. Xerxes had all the advantages and all the defects resulting from an education given to a prince at the court of an eastern despot. He was the favourite son of a favourite and influential queen. He himself was not ambitious, but the persons around him urged him to prosecute his father's plans. Mardonius was eager to renew an enterprise in which he had failed through unavoidable mischance, and not through his own incapacity. He was warmly seconded by the Greeks who had flocked to Susa in the hope of accomplishing their selfish ends by the aid of Persia. Among them were members of the Thessalian family of the Aleuadae, and the exiled Pisistratids. They succeeded in inflaming the imagination of Xerxes with the prospect of rivalling, or even surpassing, the achievements of his glorious predecessors. He accordingly resolved on the invasion of Greece; before undertaking which, however, he led an army into Egypt, which he again reduced under the Persian yoke, in the second year of his reign. After this all his thoughts were bent towards the West, and the vast preparations were continued with redoubled activity in order to raise an armament worthy of the king's presence. During four years longer, Asia was kept in restless turmoil to collect the hosts which were to be poured out upon Europe. Magazines filled with stores were formed along the whole line of march as far as the confines of Greece.

In addition to these precautions, two great works were executed which were believed to be necessary for a successful and unimpeded expedition into Greece. The first was the construction of a bridge across the Hellespont, which was to unite the continents of Asia and Europe, and thus form a royal road in defiance of nature: the execution of this bridge was entrusted to Phoenician and Egyptian engineers. The second was the cutting of a canal through the isthmus which connects the peninsula of Mount Athos with the mainland.* The destruction of the fleet under Mardonius, in its attempt to double Mount Athos, had rendered that coast terrible to the Persians. The new canal enabled the fleet in its voyage southwards to avoid that dangerous point. This work employed a multitude of men for three years. When all these preparations were completed, Xerxes set out for Sardis, where he designed to spend the following winter, and to receive the reinforcements which were to join the main army. While he was staying at Sardis, a storm broke to pieces the bridge over the Hellespont; at which Xerxes was so enraged, that he put the architects to death.† New engineers now constructed two firm and broad causeways, stretching from Abydos to the opposite shore, resting each on a row of ships, which were stayed against the current that bore upon them from the north, by anchors, and by cables fastened to both sides of the channel.

* The cutting through of the isthmus of Mount Athos has been regarded, in ancient as well as in modern times, as a mere fiction; but not only have a survey of that coast, and an examination of the localities, shown the advantages of such a canal to the Persians, but the canal itself, though almost filled up with deposits, has been discovered. The only surprising circumstance is, that it should have required so long a time to make the canal, considering that Xerxes had such multitudes at his command. See Long's Essay in the *Classical Museum*, vol. i. p. 83.

† The Greeks sometimes represented the formation of the bridge over the Hellespont as an enslaving or even scourging of those straits (Aesch. *Pers.* 871.; Arrian, *Anab.* vii. 14.); hence arose the story that Xerxes actually chastised the rebellious stream by causing it to be scourged.

When all was in readiness, Xerxes, in the spring of B.C. 480, began his march from Sardis in all the pomp of a royal progress. His mighty host consisted of nations of different colours, costumes, arms, and languages; it moved on towards Abydos, where the king himself, from a lofty throne, surveyed the crowded shores and bosom of the Hellespont. After the performance of certain solemn rites, the army crossed by one bridge, while the baggage went by the other; yet the living tide flowed without intermission for seven days and seven nights before the last man, the king himself, had arrived on the European shore. From Sestos the army marched up the Thracian Chersonesus, and on its arrival at Doriscos the king mustered and numbered his land forces, while scribes recorded the names, and probably also the equipments, of the different races. There also assembled the fleet, consisting of 1207 triremes, and 3000 smaller vessels. The land army is said to have consisted of 1,700,000 foot, and 80,000 horse; but this was not all, for as the armament advanced it received reinforcements which are computed at 300,000 men and 120 triremes. The real military strength of this colossal army, however, was almost lost among the undisciplined herds which could only impede its movements and consume its stores. The Persians themselves were the real core of both the land and the sea force.

From Doriscos the army accompanied by the fleet pursued its march along the coast, through a country which had already been subdued by Megabazus and Mardonius. All the cities near which the army passed, celebrated its arrival with a splendid banquet. There was no scarcity of provisions, as the magazines had been well stored, but the army occasionally suffered from want of water, and it is said that several rivers were drained by the invading hosts. At Acanthos the army parted for the first time from the fleet, and left the coast to strike across Chalcidice to Therma. Here Xerxes indulged his curiosity by sailing to the mouth of the Peneus, and viewing the splendid vale of Tempe through which it flows.

In Greece, those states which had most to fear from the invaders were no doubt greatly disturbed by the mere rumour of what was going on in Asia immediately after the battle of Marathon. Yet their recent victory, and afterwards the revolt of Egypt, retarded their counsels, and prevented them from making an active use of their time. When at length it became manifest that Xerxes was prosecuting the plans of his father, the leading states, and those which breathed the same spirit, saw the necessity of providing against the impending danger. Spies were sent to Sardis, but they were detected, and after the assembled forces had been displayed before them, were sent home again in the hope that the report of what they had seen would crush all spirit of opposition. It was felt in Greece that the safety of the country depended upon the union of its inhabitants. But great was the difficulty of effecting such a union. All the tribes of Greece cherished, indeed, an ardent love of independence; but their unanimity was in many instances suppressed by other passions and interests, which tended to thwart the common cause. The Thessalian family of the Aleuadae had urged Xerxes to invade Greece, in the hope that with Persian aid they might make themselves masters of Greece. The Thessalian people would not have countenanced such treachery, but, being unable to protect themselves, and not knowing what aid they could expect from the other Greeks, they yielded when Xerxes sent ambassadors from Sardis to all the Greeks except Athens and Sparta, to demand earth and water. Their example was followed by all the tribes seated between them and the mountain chain of Oeta, and even by the Locrians, who nevertheless afterwards did not desert the cause of Greece. The Phocians refused to comply with the demands of the barbarians. The Dorians were too weak to offer resistance, and not sufficiently ardent in their patriotism to abandon their towns. Boeotia, which was under the sway of Thebes, yielded to the Persians, with the exception of the Thespians and Plataeans, who were united with Attica by their hatred and dread of Thebes. Thus, in the states north of Peloponnesus, selfish aims and want of patriotism prevented a coalition for the common good.

In Peloponnesus also, causes were at work which hindered its inhabitants from exerting their whole strength. Most of the states of the peninsula were either allies of Sparta, or subject to her influence: but two were led to keep aloof, chiefly by the jealousy and aversion they felt towards her; these were Argos and Achaia, which remained inactive during the war, and acted the part of mere spectators. The Achaeans seem not yet to have become reconciled to the Dorians, who had of old driven them from their homes.

Such a state of things must have been disheartening to those who were ready to stake everything for their liberty and independence. Athens and Sparta, however, prepared for the last extremity, and calmly availed themselves of all the means they had at their command. Athens possessed many great men, but one was now the soul of all her counsels; this was Themistocles, the son of Neocles, connected with the priestly family of the Lycomedae, though his mother was perhaps not of Greek origin. The numerous anecdotes of his youthful wilfulness and waywardness all point the same way, to a soul early bent upon great objects, and formed to pursue them with steady resolution. The end he aimed at was not merely the good of his country, but to make Athens great and powerful, that he himself might move and command in a large sphere. The peculiar faculty of his mind was the quickness with which it seized every object that came in its way, perceived the course of action required by new situations and sudden junctures, and penetrated into remote consequences. Such were the abilities which at this period were most needed for the service of Athens. At the time when Themistocles was beginning to rise into popularity with his countrymen, Aristides already possessed their respect and confidence. Though descended from an ancient and noble family, his fortune was so small that his wealthy relative, Callias, was blamed for allowing his kinsman to be reduced to indigence. He left his family dependent on the public bounty, though the offices he had filled afforded the amplest opportunities of enriching himself. Such disinterested integrity was at all times one of the rarest virtues at Athens, and procured for him the well-deserved surname of the Just or the Disinterested. He, like Themistocles, had the welfare of his country at heart, but simply and singly, not as an instrument, but as an end. Though, therefore, there was no great discordance between him and Themistocles, yet they could not fail to come into frequent collision. But men of the austere character of Aristides are seldom beloved, and many a one must have been vexed at his being distinguished by so honourable a surname as the Just. Without having committed any offence, and even without being charged with any, he was sent by ostracism into honourable exile; and it is said that he assisted an illiterate countryman in writing his own name on one of the sherds that condemned him, B.C. 483.

The removal of Aristides left Themistocles in almost undivided possession of the popular favour. He saw that Athens could not remain in its actual condition, but must either cease to be an independent state, or enter on a new career by taking advantage of its natural position and becoming a maritime power. Soon after the battle of Marathon, Themistocles, with this object in view, persuaded his fellow-citizens to forego the profits derived from the silver mines of Laurion, which till then had been equally shared among them, and to apply the fund to the enlargement of their navy. He carried this object by appealing to their hatred and jealousy of Aegina, which was still at war with them, and mistress of the sea. The Athenians, by building 100 new triremes, increased their navy to 200 ships. At the same time a decree seems to have been passed directing that twenty new triremes should be built every year.* Thus the Athenians became a maritime people, for which, in fact, nature appears to have destined them; and

* Some authors assign this decree to a later period. (Diodor. xi. 43.)

their naval power and skill became the chief source of their glory and influence.

While Xerxes was wintering at Sardis, those Greek states which adhered to the cause of liberty sent envoys to hold a congress on the Isthmus of Corinth. The great object was to bring about union among the Greeks; but it was in vain that an attempt was made at restoring peace between Athens and Aegina. The envoys sent to Argos and Crete met with no better success. The Corcyraeans, who then possessed the most powerful navy in Greece, promised to send a fleet, and actually equipped and manned sixty ships, but their intention seems to have been to keep back, and afterwards to join the successful party whatever might be the issue of the war. Some envoys were also sent to Gelo, the tyrant of Syracuse, the fame of whose power and greatness had spread far and wide. He was quite ready to support the Greeks with a large force, but only on condition that he should be allowed the supreme command of the allied forces. Both the Spartan and the Athenian envoys declared, that the command of the naval force could be entrusted to none but a Spartan. Gelo then answered that they seemed to be better provided with generals than with troops, and bade the ambassadors tell the Greeks that they had lost the spring out of their year; such he deemed his own succour to their cause. The spirit in which the envoys acted in Sicily was wise and prudent; it would have been degrading and perilous to entrust all that was dear to them to the protection of a Sicilian tyrant. That the intentions of Gelo were not of the most honourable kind, is clear from the statement of Herodotus, according to whom he sent a friend to Greece to watch the course of events, and to offer earth and water to the Persians if they should be victorious.

Meantime Themistocles was busied in allaying animosity and silencing disputes among the Greek cities; and he was seconded in this noble task by Cheileos, of Tegea in Arcadia. He also used every expedient for cherishing the ardour and bracing the energy of his fellow-citizens, and the spirit which he infused into them is shown by the circumstance that the assembled Greeks bound themselves by an oath to consecrate to the god of Delphi a tenth of the substance of every Grecian people which, without being compelled by necessity, had surrendered to the Persians.

The next point on which the congress determined was to fix the place where the Greeks should meet the enemy and defend themselves. The Thessalian people, before their surrender to the Persians, had invited the deputies to send a strong body of troops to guard the pass of Tempe. Accordingly, while Xerxes was preparing to cross the channel at Abydos, 10,000 men, under the command of the Spartan Euaenetus and of Themistocles, were sent to take possession of Tempe. But finding that the occupation of that position would be useless, and even dangerous, they took the advice of Alexander of Macedonia, and marched back. The next defensible point appeared to be the pass of Thermopylae; and here it was resolved to make a stand, and at the same time to guard the northern entrance of the Euboean channel, whither nearly the whole naval force proceeded, while a small body of Peloponnesians marched to Thermopylae. The fleet, amounting to 271 triremes, was under the command of the Spartan Eurybiades, although Sparta had sent only ten ships, while Athens furnished 127, and supplied the Chalcidians with twenty others.

While the Persians were still in Pieria, a squadron of ten ships was despatched by their admiral to watch the movements of the Greeks. Off the island of Sciathos they fell in with three Greek vessels, which were overpowered and captured. The alarm which this disaster created in the fleet at Artemisium was so great, that Eurybiades resolved on quitting the station and retiring to Chalcis, where a few ships might defend the Euripus. After the return of the Persian squadron to Therme, the whole fleet began to steer southward. Near Cape Sepias, where they had cast anchor for the night, they were, early in the morning, overtaken by a storm, which burst upon them from the north-east with irresistible fury. The ships were torn from their anchorage, driven against one another, and dashed upon the cliffs. The tempest raged for three days and three nights, and when at length it subsided, the shores for many miles were strewed with wrecks and with corpses. The ships of war destroyed on that occasion were reckoned, on the lowest calculation, at 400; the lives, the transports, the stores, and the treasures which were lost were past counting. The remainder of the fleet then put into the Gulf of Pagasae.

The Greeks naturally attributed this calamity of their enemy to the interference of the gods, and testified their gratitude by offering sacrifices and raising a temple to Boreas. It was believed that nearly the whole armada had perished, and the Greek fleet returned to its station at Artemisium. Fifteen of the enemy's ships, which had been detained at Sepias, were captured at once. But the loss sustained by the Persians, great as it was, was scarcely felt in their vast armament; and they feared the Greeks so little, that their only care seems to have been to prevent them from escaping. The Greeks, on the other hand, were not a little astonished when they perceived the immense force still opposed to them; and Themistocles had great difficulty in restraining them from again turning their backs and seeking shelter in the Euripus. It is even said that he prevailed upon Eurybiades only by giving him a part of the thirty talents which he received from the Euboeans. But, however this may be, the Greeks soon recovered from their first panic, and did not afterwards shrink from facing the enemy. Meantime the Persian fleet stationed at Aphetae did not move, from fear of putting their opponents to flight; soon afterwards, however, the Greeks having ventured towards them, they advanced and drew a circle around their daring foes. The Greeks then began a brave attack, and speedily threw the Persian fleet into disorder. The Persians had already lost thirty ships, when night put an end to the conflict. From this action, the Greeks conceived fresh hopes, for they had gained at least the pledge of victory, and an insight into their enemy's weakness. In the following night another storm came on, and a Persian squadron, attempting to sail round the eastern coast of Euboea, was completely destroyed. The joyful tidings of this event reached the Greeks at Artemisium at the moment when they received a reinforcement of fifty-three ships from Athens. They now boldly sailed out to attack the enemy, who was terror-stricken by what had happened during the night. A squadron of Cilicians, which fell in with the Greeks, was taken and destroyed; while the main body of the Persian fleet remained inactive. But the next day the Persians sailed up to Artemisium to begin the attack. The Greeks advanced, pierced and broke the crescent of the enemy's ships, and the unwieldy armament was thrown into confusion and shattered by its own weight. The contest lasted for a long time, and both parties suffered almost equally. Towards the evening the combatants parted; the Athenians, finding that half their ships were disabled, saw that they could not survive such another day, and resolved to retreat. In this they were confirmed by the news they received of what had just happened at Thermopylae.

At the time when the congress was assembled on the Isthmus, the Olympic festival and that of the Carnean Apollo were at hand; the danger did not seem to be so very pressing as to render it necessary to suspend those sacred games. Accordingly, only a small force was sent to Thermopylae to bar the progress of the enemy until the festivals were over. This little band was commanded by the Spartan king Leonidas, the successor of the wild Cleomenes. It was composed of only 300 Spartans, attended by a body of Helots, 500 men from Tegea, and about 2000 from other Peloponnesian cities. The Phocians, when called upon to join them, came to Thermopylae with 1000 men; 700 Thespians also joined Leonidas as he was passing through Boeotia. In later times it was believed that the Spartan king, when he set out, foresaw the fatal issue of the expedition; but this is only an invention to exalt the glory of the hero; for on his arrival at the pass, he was not aware of the path across the mountain by which he might be attacked in the rear, and there was no reason why he might not, for a few days, withstand the attacks of the enemy in the narrow pass, which is shut in between the eastern promontory of Oeta, called Callidromos, and the shore of the Malian Gulf, and is four or five miles in length. It is narrowest at the two ends, being somewhat wider in the middle. There was, however, a track along the torrent of Asopos on the north side of the mountain, leading to the summit of Callidromos, and descending on the southern side, near the end of the pass. Of this path no one knew anything, until Leonidas on his arrival was informed of its existence; in consequence of which he posted the Phocians, by their own desire, on the summit of the ridge to guard against a surprise.

The first sight of the enemy struck the army of Leonidas with no less terror than the Greeks at Artemisium had felt at the approach of the hostile armada; and the Peloponnesians would have retreated to defend their own Isthmus, had not Leonidas prevailed upon them to stay, and sent messengers to the confederate cities to call for speedy reinforcements. At the northern entrance of the pass the Greeks had built a wall, and Xerxes was not a little astonished when he was informed by his scouts that the Spartans, apparently unaware of their danger, were before the wall, some quietly seated and combing their hair, while others were engaged in gymnastic exercises. He had hoped to scare the enemy by his mere presence, and four days passed away before he was convinced that he would not have so easy a victory. On the fifth day he ordered a body of Median and Cissian troops to fall upon the presumptuous enemy, and to lead them captive into his presence. But their attack on the pass was repulsed, and their repeated onsets on the Greeks were broken like waves upon a rock. The king then sent his ten thousand Immortals, his own body guards, who were led on as to a certain victory, but they too were successfully withstood. During their fruitless assaults, the king, who witnessed the contest seated on a lofty throne, thrice started up in a transport of fear or rage. The slaughter of the barbarians was great, while on the side of the Greeks only a few Spartans are said to have fallen. Next day the attacks were renewed with no better success, and the confidence of Xerxes was changed into despondence and perplexity.

In the mean time the secret of the path, called Anopaea, having been betrayed to the king by a Greek of the name of Ephialtes, Xerxes ordered a detachment of his troops to follow the infamous traitor. They set out at nightfall, and by daybreak reached the spot where the Phocians were stationed. The Phocians retreated to the highest peak of the ridge, and resolved to sell their lives as dearly as they could, but the Persians, without turning aside to pursue them, kept on their way, and descended on the southern side of the mountain. When the Greeks in the pass were apprised of what had happened, there was little time for deliberation, and opinions were divided as to the course which ought to be pursued. Leonidas did not restrain those of his allies who wished to save themselves; but for himself and his Spartans he declared his resolution of maintaining to the last the post which his country had assigned to them. All withdrew except the Thespians and 400 Thebans, who appear to have joined Leonidas only very reluctantly, and who alone survived the battle. The ten thousand, who had been guided by Ephialtes, appeared at the southern entrance of the pass early in the forenoon, and, according to a preconcerted plan, the king began his onset at the same time. Leonidas, now less anxious to save his men than to make havoc among the enemy, sallied forth from the pass, and charged the advancing barbarians, who, according to the Asiatic custom, were driven to the conflict by the lash of their commanders. Many of the barbarians fell, but the Spartans too were thinned, and Leonidas himself died early. Four times the Persians were driven back by the Spartans. When at length the ten thousand had entered the southern end of the pass, the Spartans retreated behind the wall. The Thebans did not follow their example, but threw down their arms and begged for quarter. The Persians now rushed forward without resistance, broke down the wall, and surrounded a hillock on which the Spartans awaited them. They all fell, and where they fell they were afterwards buried. The inscription on the monument raised over the slain stated that 4000 men from Peloponnesus had fought against 300 myriads; and bade the passenger tell their countrymen that they had fallen in obedience to their laws. It is difficult, however, to reconcile the accounts of the numbers engaged in that memorable struggle, which must have taken place in the month of July or August of the year B.C. 480. The Persians are said to have lost 20,000 men, and among them several of royal blood. This hard-won victory taught Xerxes a lesson, which he had refused to receive from the warnings of Demaratus, who now also told him that he would everywhere meet with the same desperate resistance, and advised him to send a detachment of his fleet round Peloponnesus to seize Cythera and infest the coast of Laconia; but this plan was not adopted.

Xerxes was now in possession of the key of northern Greece, and the Thessalians (probably the nobles) endeavoured to direct his course to their own advantage. They sent to the Phocians, demanding a bribe of fifty talents, for which they promised to avert the destruction impending over their country. The Phocians, however, declined the offer, and Xerxes, by the advice of his Thessalian friends, entered Doris, which was spared, having previously submitted to the invaders. Those Phocians who could make their escape took refuge on the high plains under the peaks of Parnassus or at Amphissa; but on all that remained, on the fields, cities, and temples of the devoted land, the fury of the Persians, stimulated by the Thessalians, poured undistinguishing ruin. The sanctuary of Apollo at Abae was sacked and burnt, and fourteen towns shared its fate. The main body of the army then turned off towards the lower vale of the Cephisus, to continue its march through Boeotia to Athens, while a small force was sent round Parnassus with orders to strip the temple of Delphi of its treasures and lay them at the king's feet. The Delphians had quitted the city, leaving it and its sanctuary to the protection of the god himself. On the arrival of the enemy a fearful thunder-storm, it is said, began to rage; huge rocks, broken off from the cliffs overhanging the road, fell upon the enemy, and crushed many; at the same time a war-cry was heard from within the temple of Athene. The Persians, terror-struck, retraced their steps, and were pursued by the Delphians with unresisted slaughter. Thus Delphi was delivered, and the divine power gloriously attested.

When the Grecian fleet quitted its station at Artemisium, the Athenians had hoped that a Peloponnesian army would take up its position in Boeotia to protect Attica; but it soon became evident that the Peloponnesians had no intention of venturing beyond the Isthmus, which they meant to fortify with a wall, and there to collect all their forces for the defence of the Peninsula. The Athenians, therefore, begged their allies to sail on with them to Salamis, that they might provide for the safety of their wives and children, and decide upon the course to be adopted against the approaching invasion. The Athenians had previously asked the advice of the Delphic god; but he had commanded them to fly to the uttermost ends of the earth, as there was no means of saving Athens from the fire and sword of the barbarians. The messengers, in dismay at the prospect of so fearful a calamity, again approached the god as suppliants, praying for a milder decree. This was granted, but in dark and obscure terms: "Zeus," the priestess said, "has been prevailed upon by his daughter Athene to grant that, when all beside is lost, a wooden wall shall still shelter her citizens." The meaning of this oracle was the subject of various conjectures at Athens; the younger men readily believed that the wooden wall was their navy; but the older citizens thought it incredible that Athene would abandon her ancient citadel. The people, in their uncertainty, looked to

Themistocles for advice; and as he himself had probably suggested the oracle, he had no difficulty in interpreting its meaning. He exhorted his fellow-citizens, if all other safeguards should fail them, to commit their safety and their hopes of victory to their newly strengthened navy. This counsel had prevailed; and the time was now come when the resolution founded upon it was to be carried into effect.

After desolating Phocis, the Persian army passed peacefully through Boeotia towards Athens, for all the Boeotian cities, except Thespiae and Plataeae, which were reduced to ashes, had submitted and received Persian garrisons. At Athens, Themistocles moved a decree that the city should be abandoned to the protection of its tutelary goddess, and that the men, after placing their wives and children and the aged and infirm in security, should betake themselves to their ships. This was a severe trial to the feelings of the Athenians, but, yielding to circumstances, they, with the exception of a few who resolved to remain in the citadel, transported their families and movable property, some to Salamis, some to Aegina, and some to Troezen, where the exiles were received with great kindness. The Greek fleet assembled at Salamis was reinforced by a squadron contributed by the same states which had sent their contingents to Artemisium, and by a small number of ships from other quarters. The whole armament thus strengthened amounted to 380 ships. Eurybiades was still the commander-in-chief, and in a council which was held to determine the position in which the enemy's approach should be awaited, the commanders were almost unanimous in their opinion that they ought to leave Salamis and take up a station nearer the Isthmus, where, in case of a defeat, they might join the army and renew the contest. This was certainly opposed to the interest of the Athenians, who had staked their all upon the sea; but although nearly half the fleet had been furnished by them, they had only one vote. Before any decision was come to, it was announced that the Persians had overrun Attica, and that the acropolis of Athens would soon be in their hands. Xerxes had pursued his march without resistance, spreading desolation over the plains of Attica till he came to the Cecropian rock. There the little band assembled in the acropolis baffled every attempt of the monarch and his hosts to take the rock by assault, until at length it was surprised. Some of the small garrison threw themselves down the precipice; others took refuge in the sanctuary of the goddess, but they were hunted out by the Persians and put to the sword. The temples were then plundered, and the whole citadel set on fire. The next day some scruples seem to have disquieted the mind of Xerxes, for he called together the Athenian exiles, who were in his train, and bade them go up the rock and sacrifice according to their rites. They brought back the report of a happy omen for Athens. The sacred olive, which had been consumed by the fire which destroyed the temple near which it grew, had already put forth, from the burnt stump, a fresh shoot a cubit in length.

When the news of these events was brought to the Greeks at Salamis, some of the commanders are said to have made preparations for immediate retreat, and others to have resolved to give battle near the Isthmus. On his return to his ship, Themistocles communicated the result of the conference to his friend Mnesiphilus, a man of a vigorous practical understanding, who at once saw the danger of such a mode of acting. Themistocles, strengthened in his own conviction by the expressions of his friend, hastened to Eurybiades, earnestly entreating him to call together another council and reconsider the fatal resolutions they had formed. This was done, and Themistocles endeavoured to bring the commanders over to his views. Adeimantus, the Corinthian, concerned about the safety of his own city, was his chief opponent. Themistocles pointed out the advantages of their position at Salamis; but finding this of no avail, he at length declared that the Athenians were resolved, if their allies persisted in their design, to take their families and property on board, and sail away to the south of Italy. This threat determined Eurybiades, and his authority or influence decided the resolution of the council.

Six days after the Greeks had left Artemisium, the Persian fleet arrived in the bay of Phalerum. Xerxes immediately went on board one of the ships with Mardonius, and summoned the chief commanders of the fleet into his presence, to determine upon the mode of proceeding. Among the many vassal princes who conducted their contingents in person, there was a woman, Artemisia, queen of Caria. She alone saw the danger of a hasty engagement, and suggested the idea of waiting some time, as the Greeks would be sure to quarrel and disperse. But the king resolved upon attacking the enemy without delay, and forthwith ordered the fleet to sail up towards Salamis and to form in line of battle. As, however, the day was already far advanced, it was determined that the battle should not be commenced until the next morning. The sight of the formidable armada again roused all the fears and apprehensions which Themistocles had been labouring to counteract. The thought of retreating to the Isthmus, where Cleombrotus, the brother of Leonidas, had just arrived with a large force, again arose in most minds. Another meeting was called, in which the voices of the Athenians, Aeginetans, and Megarians were drowned by the rest, who exclaimed against the folly of staying before a country which was already in the enemy's hands. Themistocles, seeing that all his remonstrances would be lost upon the allies, now resolved to save Athens in spite of them, and his allies in spite of themselves. While the commanders were still disputing, he withdrew, and summoning a slave, who spoke the Persian language, sent him to the Persian admiral with the message that the Greeks were panic-struck and bent on flight; and that if the Persians would attack them at once they would insure a complete and easy victory, whereas if they were allowed to disperse the king would have to fight against them one by one. The Persians hastened to follow the advice which was so much in accordance with their own wishes. About midnight they moved from Phalerum to block up the entrance of each of the narrow channels by which Salamis is separated from Attica and Megara. A body of Persians was also stationed in the little island of Psyttaleia. Salamis was thus completely inclosed, while the Greeks were still assembled in council, to which Themistocles had in the mean time returned. Suddenly he was called out of the room to speak to a stranger at the door. It was Aristides, who seems to have been still in exile, and had come över from Aegina under cover of the night, to inform his former rival that the Persians had surrounded the Greeks, and that there was no escape except by cutting a passage through the enemy's fleet. Themistocles told him what he had done, and introduced him into the council-room. When the Greeks were informed of their condition, they would hardly believe it, until a Tenian ship, which came over from the enemy, placed the truth beyond a doubt. Nothing now remained but to brace every nerve for the battle, which was to commence at daybreak.

When the morning dawned, the Persian fleet was seen covering the sea between Psyttaleia and the mouth of the channel, and the army lining the shores of the bay of Eleusis. On one of the heights of Mount Aegaleos, a lofty throne was raised for Xerxes, from which he could view the fight. Before the Greeks embarked at Salamis, Themistocles addressed them in a speech which set before them all that was best and all that was worst in the nature and condition of man, and exhorted them to choose and hold fast the good. They awaited the advance of the Persians in the straits, and when their gigantic fleet was pent up in the narrow channel, an Athenian ship darted forward and struck one of the Persians. This was the signal for a general engagement. The Persians did not yield to the Greeks in courage and perseverance; but the valour of the Greeks, if not directed by superior skill, was cooler and more deliberate, for it had not to struggle with any of the impediments which threw the

Asiatics into confusion. The ships of the latter, taller and larger than those of the Greeks, were turned by the wind, their evolutions were thwarted by their numbers, and their sides exposed to the attacks of the enemy's prows. The ships stationed behind, and pressing forward to signalise themselves in the presence of the king, often fell foul of their friends whom they met retreating. The confusion which thus arose in the Persian fleet was, no doubt, greatly aggravated and rendered more mischievous by the variety of forces that composed it; for the Egyptians, Phoenicians, Cilicians, Cyprians, Ionians, and other nations which served in it, were connected by no other bond than that of having the same master. The following instance of the want of a common feeling among them was probably not the only one which the battle afforded:— The Athenians, indignant at being attacked by a woman, had set a price of 10,000 drachmas on the head of Artemisia. She with many others, was fleeing in the midst of the disorder, chased by the Athenian Ameinias. To make room for herself, she struck and instantly sunk a Persian ship; and Ameinias, thinking that he had been pursuing a friend, now suffered her to escape.

The event of the battle was in reality decided at the first onset, which threw the unwieldy armament into a confusion from which it could never recover, and which so many causes contributed to increase. Yet it was long before the resistance of the mass was finally overcome, and night had begun before the Persian fleet took refuge in Phalerum, whither the Greeks did not attempt to pursue it. An Aeginetan squadron, stationed near the mouth of the channel, completed the defeat of the fugitives. During the battle, Aristides had been watching its course, and when fortune began to turn against the Persians, he landed with a small band at Psyttaleia, where he drove the Persians into a corner, and cut them in pieces to a man; for, though an exile, he longed to share in the glory of the day, and to contribute his mite towards defending the independence of his country.

In this battle, the barbarians are said to have lost 500, or according to others, 200 ships; the Greeks only 40. The number of the dead was proportionately much greater among the barbarians than among the Greeks, and contained many of the highest rank. Xerxes himself began to feel that his situation was dangerous, although he still possessed a force more than sufficient to renew the contest: another such defeat would have utterly ruined his fleet, and left the Greeks in undisputed command of the sea; he himself might be cut off from Asia, and shut up in a foreign country, exposed to famine and incessant attacks from his enemies. He accordingly resolved to retreat. In this resolution he was confirmed by Mardonius, who had reason to dread the king's anger and vengeance, for it was he who had urged the king to an undertaking which had hitherto been nothing but a series of disasters. He now represented to the king that the land army of the Persians was still unconquered; and that although the Greeks had prevailed at sea, which was their own element, they would never be able to resist his land forces. He asked for 300,000 men, with whom he promised to undertake the subjugation of all Greece. Artemisia also supported this advice, and was at once sent to Ephesus with the king's children. Xerxes immediately gave orders to his fleet to make for the Hellespont with all speed, and to guard the bridges till his own arrival. He seems to have been overwhelmed by the thought of his danger, and resolved to make his escape, leaving Mardonius to accomplish the task which he himself gave up so ingloriously.

It was not till about the middle of the following day, that the Greeks were informed of the departure of the hostile fleet. They immediately began to chase it; but on arriving at Andros, without having seen any trace of it, they stopped to hold a council of war. Themistocles and the Athenians wished to sail to the Hellespont, destroy the bridges, and cut off the king's retreat; but Eurybiades thought this a dangerous undertaking, and was of opinion that no obstacle ought to be thrown in the king's way. All approved of this view; even Themistocles yielded, and prevailed upon the Athenians, who were burning to pursue their enemy, to relinquish their design. The fleet now made some stay among the Cyclades to chastise those islanders who had sent succour to the barbarians. There is a tradition that Themistocles, in the spirit of the resolution formed by the Greek commanders at Andros, sent a captive Persian to the king with a message urging him to flee, as the Greeks were contemplating the destruction of the bridges on the Hellespont, and would thus cut off his return. Xerxes, terrified by this warning, hurried with the utmost speed to the Hellespont, accompanied by a body of 60,000 men.*

Mardonius attended his master as far as Thessaly, where he himself meant to take up his winter quarters. The scarcity of provisions during the march, and the consequent sickness among the troops, obliged Xerxes to consign multitudes to the care of the cities that lay on his road, and were already impoverished by his first visit. The passage of the river Strymon is said to have been particularly disastrous, and many perished in its icy waters. On his arrival at the Hellespont he found the bridges destroyed by the

* It is commonly said that Themistocles endeavoured by this advice to secure for himself a welcome reception in the king's dominions if he should ever need it; but such a thought can scarcely have occurred to his mind at that time, when he was at the height of his glory and popularity.

waves, but the fleet was in readiness to carry him and his army over to Abydos. The abundance of provisions which there awaited them, and their excessive indulgence after severe want, were almost as pernicious to the barbarians as the previous famine, so that the band which the king took with him to Sardis was a mere wreck of his huge host.

Many of the Greek cities on the northern coast of the Aegean, when they heard of the results of the battle of Salamis, had shaken off their yoke, and asserted their independence. Olynthus, however, was reconquered by Artabazus, who had accompanied Xerxes, and its whole population was massacred in cold blood. He was less successful at Potidaea, for neither bribes nor open attacks were of any avail, and he had been besieging the place for more than three months, when an extraordinary ebb of the sea left bare the shore of the isthmus under the walls of the city. He accordingly sent a detachment round that part, but in the middle of their march the water returned in an unusually high tide, and the barbarians were either overwhelmed by the waves, or cut to pieces by the garrison. Artabazus, in despair, now raised the siege, and marched back to Thessaly, where Mardonius had taken up his quarters, with an army of 300,000 barbarians, and 50,000 Greeks willing to support them.

While the Greek fleet was engaged among the Cyclades, Themistocles seized the opportunity of enriching himself at their expense. He in vain demanded a contribution from Andros; the town was then besieged, but made so vigorous a resistance, that the Greeks were obliged to abandon the attempt, and returned to Salamis. In several other islands, however, Themistocles was more successful in making the inhabitants purchase impunity for their conduct by large bribes.

All Greece now resounded with the praise of his wisdom and prudence, for the deliverance of Greece was universally ascribed to him, next to the gods. The choicest part of the spoil was sent to Delphi in the shape of a colossal statue; and when the commanders met in the temple of Poseidon, on the Isthmus, to award the palm of individual merit, almost unanimous consent assigned the foremost place to Aegina. When the prize was to be given to individuals, no one was generous enough to resign the first place to another, though most were just enough to award the second to Themistocles. But he was honoured in the highest degree at Sparta, whither he went, according to Plutarch, invited; but as Herodotus relates, wishing to be honoured. The Spartans gave him a chaplet of olive-leaves, which was the reward they had bestowed upon their own admiral, Eurybiades; and 300 Spartan knights escorted him, on his return, as far as Tegea.

At the same time that the glorious battle of Salamis was fought and won by the Greeks, Sicily was delivered from a danger not less threatening. Terillus, tyrant of Himera, had been expelled from his city by Theron, tyrant of Agrigentum, and solicited aid from Carthage. The Carthaginians, glad of an opportunity to gain a footing in the island, sent an army, amounting, we are told, to 300,000 men, under the command of Hamilcar. Himera was besieged; but Gelo of Syracuse, who was married to a daughter of Theron, marched to its relief, and confined the Carthaginians to their camp. By his promptness he succeeded in defeating the enemy, with the loss, it is said, of half their forces; and Hamilcar himself was among the slain. The rest took refuge in a position where the want of water compelled them to surrender. Most of the Carthaginian ships were destroyed by fire, and those which

Persian head-dress.
(From a mosaic at Pompeii.)

Greek woman's head-dress.
(From a bust at Dresden.)

escaped perished in a storm on their way home. This great victory is stated to have been gained on the same day as that of Salamis. The number of prisoners who were sold as slaves was immense; and with their aid the Sicilian towns, especially Agrigentum, adorned themselves with the most magnificent public buildings, the ruins of which still remain as monuments of the great day of Himera.*

* The account of this war in Diodorus, xi. 20. foll., is disfigured by much that seems to have arisen from his national vanity, for he himself was a Sicilian.

Persian Dignitary.
(From the sculptures of Persepolis.)

View of the Islands Salamis and Aegina.*
(Drawn on the spot, by George Scharf, jun.)

CHAPTER XV.

FROM THE BATTLE OF SALAMIS TO THE END OF THE PERSIAN INVASION.

A few days after the battle of Salamis, when the Persians had quitted Attica, the Athenians returned to cultivate their fields and repair their homes, in the hope that their land would not again be visited by the ravages of the same invader, and that, in case of need, the other Greeks would energetically support Athens, which had now twice borne the brunt of the danger which threatened Greece. During the winter the Greeks remained tranquil, but in the spring they displayed all the activity of men who knew that Mardonius was in Thessaly, and a Persian fleet still upon the sea. This fleet was now assembled at Samos, with the intention of acting on the defensive, and was watching the Ionians with great suspicion. It amounted only to 300 ships, including an Ionian squadron. The distrust of the Ionians was not unfounded, for while the Greek fleet of 110 ships was assembled at Aegina, under the command of the Spartan king Leotychides, and the Athenian Xanthippus, some Ionians came over to solicit aid for the purpose of restoring Ionia to independence. But all they could effect was, to induce the commanders to sail eastward as far as Delos, where they stationed themselves in an attitude of defence, but determined not to advance farther east. Every one knew that this time the conflict must be decided by the land forces, and to them all eyes were directed.

Meantime, Mardonius had been making preparations for the approaching contest. He must now have been convinced that the

* The plain of Athens, Porto Piraeus, Munychia, and Phalerum, and the Museum Hill occupy the middle distance. The foreground is a portion of the Acropolis, S.W. angle.

conquest of Greece was not so easy as he had once imagined, and he was looking with no small anxiety towards the opening of the campaign. He sent envoys to all the Greek oracles to gain some insight into the future, and the answers which he received may have suggested the idea of detaching Athens from the cause of Greece, and of gaining her as an ally for Persia. Alexander, king of Macedonia, was chosen to conduct this negotiation.* On his arrival at Athens he laid before the people the proposals of Mardonius, and at the same time added his own advice, urging them to accept the generous offer, as it would be hopeless to engage in a contest with so powerful an enemy. The Spartans, on hearing of the embassy, were alarmed lest the Athenians should allow themselves to be ensnared; they were anxious to retain the alliance of the Athenians, at least until the fortifications of the Isthmus should be completed. Spartan envoys were accordingly sent to Athens to remind her of what she owed to Greece and herself, and to offer liberal support in case Attica should again be called upon to make sacrifices similar to those of the preceding year. The distinct and manly answer of the Athenians at once destroyed the hopes of Mardonius and silenced the fears of the Spartans. "So long as the sun," they said, "held on his course, Athens would never come to terms with Xerxes." The priests were, at the same time, directed to pronounce a solemn curse on every Greek who should negotiate with the barbarian, or abandon the national confederacy.

As soon as Mardonius heard the message, he set out from Thessaly, and marched at full speed towards Athens. The Thessalians were more zealous in his service than ever, and in Boeotia he was heartily welcomed. The Boeotians even advised him to fix his quarters among them, and held out to him the prospect of conquering Greece without a blow, as the Greeks, they said, might easily be induced to turn their arms against one another. But Mardonius wished to make himself master of Athens, in order to restore his credit with Xerxes, who was still at Sardis, and he hoped also to crush the spirit of the Athenians by taking possession of their country and city. He accordingly proceeded: at Athens he found nothing but the deserted walls; for its inhabitants, seeing that no aid was to be expected from the Peloponnesians, had withdrawn to Salamis. This happened in B.C. 479, ten months after the capture of Athens by Xerxes.

Mardonius immediately sent to Salamis to renew the proposals which he had made through Alexander. Only one wretched man was found in the council shameless enough to recommend compliance; but he paid dearly for his audacity, being stoned to death by the populace when he quitted the house in which the commanders were assembled; and when the Athenian women heard of his crime, they vented their fury upon his innocent wife and children. While the Athenians were giving these proofs of inflexible resolution, the Spartans seemed to have wholly forgotten their danger; for, at the news of the approach of Mardonius, instead of hastening to the protection of Athens, they only quickened the completion of the fortification of the Isthmus for their own security. Cleombrotus, the guardian of the young king Pleistarchus, who superintended the work, was instructed not to march against the Persians until Peloponnesus should be quite secured from all fear of a sudden attack. An eclipse of the sun which happened at the time frightened him so much that he returned home, where he soon afterwards died, and was succeeded in the guardianship of Pleistarchus by his son Pausanias. In the meantime Athens, Megara, and Plataeae sent an embassy to Sparta to complain of the indifference and neglect with which their zeal had been requited, and to call for assistance to rid Attica of the barbarians. The ambassadors found the Spartans engaged in celebrating the festival of the Hyacinthia, as if they had no more pressing business to attend to. The envoys held out a threat that they would accept the proposal of Mardonius if no succour was sent, and severely complained of Sparta's backwardness. The celebration of the festival afforded the ephors a welcome pretext for not giving an immediate answer, as they wished to say nothing decisive until the fortifications of the Isthmus should be completed. They, accordingly, preferred keeping the Athenian ambassadors in the dark, and running the risk of losing the alliance of Athens, to disclosing their designs before it was time to carry them into effect. At length, however, when every motive of delay had ceased, the ephors ordered Pausanias to put himself at the head of an army of 5000 Spartans, each attended by seven Helots. But, even now, the army set out at night before the Athenian ambassadors were informed of it; and it was not till the next day, when the threat was renewed that Athens would throw itself into the arms of Persia, that the ephors assured the ambassadors that the Spartan army was already on its march.

Such is the account given by Herodotus of this transaction; but it represents the conduct of the Spartans as so capricious and childish, that we can hardly believe it to be true. The Athenian ambassadors were detained at Sparta for ten days, and it is not improbable that the return of Cleombrotus from the Isthmus, and his death, took place during that period; if so, the time required for appointing a successor, together with that which had elapsed during the illness and death of Cleombrotus, would be sufficient to account for the delay. The army may, at length, have been sent off in haste, and even in secret, perhaps to avoid being waylaid by the Argives, with whom Mardonius seems to have had some influence. These suppositions, if true, would show the conduct of Sparta in a less unfavourable light than it must otherwise appear in.

Mardonius was induced by various reasons not to await the arrival of Pausanias, nor to fight a battle in Attica. He resolved on falling back upon Boeotia, where he would be favoured by the nature of the country, and by the neighbourhood of the city of Thebes. He had, until the last, hoped to induce the Athenians to join him, and had therefore abstained from ravaging their country; but now, before he retreated, he gave the reins to havoc and plunder, ravaged the land, and destroyed all the buildings which had been left standing by Xerxes. On his arrival in Boeotia he pitched his camp in the plain between Erythrae and the river Asopus, expecting that Pausanias would give him battle there, for he longed to have an early opportunity of fighting. But he nevertheless took precautions against the consequences of a defeat. Meantime, Attaginus the Theban entertained Mardonius and fifty of his officers with a splendid banquet, at which some Persian officers are said to have expressed the gloomy forebodings with which they looked forward to the approaching conflict; though the Persians were now supported by nearly all the Greeks north of the Isthmus.

When Pausanias arrived at Corinth, he was joined by the forces of all the Peloponnesian allies, and continued his march into Attica. At Eleusis he met with an Athenian reinforcement under the command of Aristides, and then crossed over into Boeotia. Near Erythrae he halted, and drew up his forces at the foot of Mount Cithaeron. The army, consisting wholly of infantry, amounted to 110,000 men, comprising, it is said, 1800 Thespians who had survived the destruction of their city. The Athenians had furnished 8000 men, but the Plataeans could muster only 600. The number of the Persian army more than tripled that of the Greeks, being composed of 300,000 Asiatics and 50,000 Greeks. Mardonius waited for a time, in expectation that the Greeks would descend from the high ground on which they were stationed and give him battle in the plain. But as this was not done, he ordered his cavalry, commanded by Masistius, to go up and attack them. The Greeks were, on the whole, protected by the rugged ground, but the position of the Megarians was less favourable, and they had to bear the brunt of the charge. Their ranks were rapidly thinned, their spirit began to fail, and when Pausanias called upon the Greeks to hasten to their assistance, there was considerable hesitation, until the Athenian Olympiodorus offered to cover the Megarians with his small detachment. Masistius was thrown from his horse, and the Athenians rushed upon him before he could rise. The Persians making a desperate onset to recover his body, the rest of the Greeks came to the assistance of the Megarians and Athenians. After a sharp conflict, the Persian cavalry was repulsed with some slaughter, and returned to their camp with the sad tidings of the fall of their commander. Although the Greeks had lost many men, they were animated by their final triumph; and the body of Masistius was drawn on a cart along the lines, that every one might gaze upon the gigantic barbarian

This success emboldened Pausanias to seek a position where his army, though more exposed, would be better supplied with water than near Erythrae. With this view he descended into the territory of Plataeae, which still lay in ruins, and posted himself on the banks of one of the tributaries of the Asopus. The Lacedaemonians occupied the post of honour on the right wing, near the spring Gargaphia. The Athenians and Tegeans both claimed the left wing; but in the end the Athenians gave way, on the ground that the juncture was one which did not admit of contention about forms; but the Lacedaemonians, to whom the decision was left, exclaimed, as one man, that the Athenians were the more worthy. Mardonius advanced with all his forces, which he drew up on the opposite bank of the Asopus. The Lacedaemonians were faced by the Persians, the Athenians by the Greek auxiliaries. Amid these preparations the day passed away. On the following morning, the soothsayers tried to discover the issue of the battle from the entrails of the victims. The diviners on both sides read the same answers in their sacrifices: Tisamenus, the Spartan soothsayer, promised victory to the Greeks if they would confine themselves to acting on the defensive, and the Persians were warned by their diviners not to begin the attack. Day after day, accordingly, the armies faced each other, in inactivity. The Greeks were plentifully supplied with provisions, whereas the Persians were daily more and more straitened in their means of subsistence. Eight days thus passed away, during which the Greeks were continually strengthened by the influx of fresh troops, before Mardonius thought of watching the passes through which the Greeks received their supplies and reinforcements. A body of cavalry was now sent out under cover of night, and at once intercepted a convoy of 500 beasts of burden. At length, when after the lapse of ten days the signs continued as unpropitious as before, Mardonius resolved to wait no longer. Notwithstanding the advice of Artabazus, he summoned a council of war, in which he endeavoured to prove that fate was on his side, and that the Persians would be invincible so long as they abstained from spoiling the sanctuary at Delphi. Relying upon this view of the approaching future, he bade his hearers cheerfully prepare for the battle which he had determined to give the next day.

In the dead of the following night, Alexander of Macedonia rode up to the Athenian camp, and informed the outposts that Mardonius was determined to attack them on the morrow; at the same time he exhorted them to keep their ground, as the Persians had only a few days' provisions left, and would soon be compelled to retire. Pausanias, on learning this, ordered the Athenians to exchange their position for that of the Lacedaemonians, since they were familiar with the Persian mode of fighting. In the morning, Mardonius, on hearing of the change, immediately altered his own dispositions, making the Persians again face the Spartans. Pausanias, finding his design thwarted, brought the Spartans back to the right wing, and both armies resumed their original order. Mardonius, mistaking this for a sign of Spartan cowardice, ordered his cavalry to charge them; and their onset was so vehement, that the assailants got possession of the Gargaphian spring. This was a great loss to the Greeks, who were now deprived of their supplies of water; and as provisions from Peloponnesus could no longer reach them, it became evident that the decisive battle could not be long deferred. A war-council was held, at which it was resolved, that if no battle should be fought in the course of the day, they should retire during the following night to a place nearer Plataeae, which was better supplied with water, and that a strong detachment should be sent to clear the pass and open the road for the convoy of the supplies, which were detained on the other side of mount Cithaeron. Mardonius, in the mean time, did not follow up the attack of his cavalry. At nightfall the Greeks moved off, and posted themselves near a temple of Hera, close to Plataeae. A Spartan commander of the name of Amompharetus, who had not been present at the council, and considered this movement as a disgraceful flight, refused to follow with his division. Pausanias and the other commanders in vain endeavoured to persuade the obstinate man; but when at last the other Greeks had gone, and Amompharetus perceived the imminent danger to which he would expose himself and his band by remaining any longer, he reluctantly led them after the main body.

When Mardonius heard that the Greeks had decamped during the night, he too imagined that they had taken flight, and without delay crossed the Asopus to attack them. The Athenians happening to be out of sight, Pausanias sent for them, but they were prevented from obeying the command by the Greek auxiliaries of the Persians. As the signs were still unfavourable, Pausanias ordered his men to wait till the gods should vouchsafe to give the signal for battle. The Persians meantime advanced within bow-shot, and began to ply the Spartans with their arrows. Still no favourable sign appeared, but a loud prayer addressed by Pausanias to Hera changed the aspect of things. The gods sent auspicious tokens, and the next instant the Spartans rushed upon the enemy. The Persians fought bravely, but without method or order. Mardonius himself with 1000 picked horsemen of the royal guard, was foremost in the fight. He was conspicuous by his white charger and by the splendour of his armour; but, while the issue of the conflict was still doubtful, he was mortally wounded by the Spartan Aeimnestus; and his fall decided the fate of the day, which was the 25th of September B.C. 479. The Persians gave way, and their example was immediately followed by all the other barbarians. Artabazus had lingered behind with his division of 40,000 men, and when he came up and found that all was lost, he took the road to Phocis, intending to hasten to the Hellespont. The Greek auxiliaries gladly dispersed without a blow; the Thebans alone maintained for a time a sharp conflict with the Athenians. But at length they were defeated, and sought shelter behind the walls of Thebes. The remainder of the Persian army prepared to defend themselves in their camp as well as they could.

The contest was so quickly decided, that the other Greeks who were posted in the vicinity were too late when, on hearing of the battle, they advanced. It now only remained to storm the camp, and thus to deliver Greece, at one blow, from the presence of the barbarians. The Lacedaemonians, who were foremost in pursuit of the enemy, endeavoured to scale the rampart, but without success. The arrival of the Athenians changed the face of the contest: they were the first to mount the wall, and succeeded in opening a breach by which their allies poured into the camp. The barbarians, who had lost all hope and self-possession, submitted, like sheep crowded in a narrow fold, and were slaughtered without a struggle. The rage of the Greeks could hardly sate itself with blood. Out of the whole multitude, only 3000 are said to have escaped the carnage. The treasure found in the camp was immense, for Xerxes is stated to have left all that was not absolutely necessary for his own use in the possession of Mardonius. Pausanias ordered the Helots to collect the whole of the spoil, that gods and men might receive their due.

A portion of the booty, nominally a tenth, was set apart for the Delphic god, in the shape of a golden tripod supported by a three-headed brazen serpent. Another portion adorned the sanctuary at Olympia with a colossal statue of Zeus, on the base of which were inscribed the names of the cities which had shared in the glory of the contest. A third was consecrated, in a similar form, to Poseidon on the Isthmus; and a sum of eighty talents was set apart to build a temple of Athene at Plataeae. After paying the debt of gratitude to the gods, the valour of the most distinguished champions was rewarded. The first place was, by common consent, assigned to the Lacedaemonians; and a magnificent present was selected for Pausanias, consisting of ten samples of everything that was most valuable in the booty. Three barrows were then raised over the dead, whose number is said to have been very small (91 Spartans and 52 Athenians); one over the officers, a second over the Spartans, and a third over the Helots. Similar barrows marked the graves in which the other cities collected their slain.

Artabazus reached Asia in safety, though a part of his army perished by hunger, and by the attacks of the Thracian tribes during the march. Alexander of Macedonia seems likewise to have fallen upon the fugitives, and was rewarded with the Athenian franchise. According to the general belief, Mardonius was buried at the outlet of the defile near Erythrae.* Greece was now completely and finally delivered from the Persian invader. The issue was decided by the sanguine rashness of Mardonius, and by the firmness and ability displayed by Pausanias at the most critical moment.

Before the army broke up, the Greek commanders, and especially Aristides, were anxious to make some provision for the preservation of union among the allies, and for directing their forces against the common enemy. An altar was erected to Zeus, under the title of the Deliverer (Ἐλευθέριος), and all the fires in the country, as being polluted by the presence of the enemy, were extinguished, and lighted anew from the national hearth at Delphi. It was then decreed, that deputies should be sent from all the states of Greece every year to Plataeae, for the purpose of political consultations, as well as to celebrate the anniversary of the battle with sacred rites; and that every fifth year a festival, called the feast of liberty (Ἐλευθέρια), should be solemnised at Plataeae. The allies were to keep up an army of 10,000 men at arms and 1000 cavalry, besides a fleet of 100 galleys, to prosecute the war against the barbarians. The Plataeans were declared sacred and inviolable so long as they continued to offer the sacrifices now instituted on behalf of Greece; while, in return, they had to perform yearly ceremonies in honour of those who had fallen on their soil in defence of Greece.† The chastisement of the Thebans, who had not only submitted to the barbarian, but had zealously lent their aid to enslave their country, was the next subject of consideration. According to the oath which had been taken the year before on the Isthmus, Thebes should have been compelled to

* Paus. ix. 2. § 1.

† Plut. *Aristid.* 20.; comp. Thucyd. iii. 58.

give up one tenth of all that it possessed to the Delphic god; but, in consideration that the city had been forced into the part it acted by a small faction, it was resolved that the just punishment should fall upon the guilty few. Ten days after the battle, accordingly, the army appeared before the gates of Thebes, and demanded the surrender of the traitors, especially Timagenidas and Attaginus. Their influence, however, was still so great in the city, that compliance with the demand was refused. For twenty days the town was blockaded, and the country ravaged, when at length the offenders consented to be delivered up. Attaginus, however, made his escape. Pausanias spared and dismissed his wife and children; but seeing that his accomplices hoped to bribe their judges, he frustrated their scheme by a measure which is the first indication of his arbitrary and imperious disposition; for, having dismissed the forces of his allies, he carried the prisoners to Corinth, where he put them to death, apparently without any form of trial.

On the same day on which the Persians were defeated at Plataeae, they suffered the first signal blow from the Greeks on their own continent. The fleet under Leotychides was still stationed at Delos, watching the movements of the Persians. During this interval, envoys from Samos appeared before Leotychides, expressing their desire to shake off the Persian yoke, and to put down their tyrant, Theomestor, a zealous supporter of Persia. The Spartan king was strongly inclined to listen to the call, for his former fears seem in a great degree to have subsided during his stay at Delos; and, accordingly, after a brief deliberation, he set sail for Samos. The Persians did not venture to meet him on the sea, and the Phoenician squadron with the remainder of the fleet sailed away towards the mainland to seek the protection of the army which was stationed at the foot of Mount Mycale. It consisted of 60,000 men, and had been left there to keep Ionia in submission. Xerxes himself was still at Sardis. The ships were drawn up on the beach, and enclosed with a hastily constructed wall of stone and timber. The Greeks, after some hesitation, resolved to cross over to Mycale and give battle. Leotychides then issued a proclamation to the Ionians, calling upon them to remember the liberty of their country. This frightened the Persians, for they believed that it was the signal for an outbreak among the Ionians; and, having removed those who were most suspected, they drew up at the foot of the mountain behind a breastwork.

At this moment a report flew through the ranks of the Greeks, that a victory had been gained over Mardonius in Boeotia. This report at once roused the confidence and courage of the Greeks, and, cheered with the assurance that Greece was already delivered, they advanced to combat for the mastery of the islands and the

Hellespont. The Athenians, with the contingents of a few other cities, came up first and began the attack. The Spartans were at some distance from the scene of action, so that before they could reach it the Athenians had forced the breastwork of the Persians, and had driven their antagonists into the enclosure which surrounded their ships. The Athenians entered with them, and the greater part of the barbarians, without attempting to resist their pursuers, betook themselves to the passes of the mountains which they had entrusted to the Milesians. The Persians alone maintained the contest, even after their general Tigranes and one of their admirals had fallen. The arrival of the Spartans at length decided the conflict, and put the enemy to a total rout. The Samians, as soon as it was possible, joined the Greeks, and their example was followed by the other Ionians. The carnage among the Persians was fearful; even those who escaped into the mountains were betrayed by the Milesians, who led them by tracks which brought them upon the enemy, and then joined in destroying them. Only a small remnant escaped to Sardis. The Greeks, after having collected the booty and burnt the enemy's ships, returned to Samos.*

The islands of the Aegean were now safe, and the only remaining difficulty was to devise means for defending the Ionians, who could be permanently protected only by the presence of a Greek force It was at length resolved that they should be left to make the best terms they could with Persia, and that the islands of the Aegean should be solemnly admitted into the Greek confederacy. After this the fleet sailed to the Hellespont for the purpose of destroying the bridges; but when it was found that these no longer existed, Leotychides and the other Peloponnesians proposed to sail home. Xanthippus and the Athenians wished to remain, in order to recover the dominion of Miltiades in the Chersonesus. As no one else had an interest in this matter, the Athenians were left to accomplish their object by themselves. Xanthippus immediately laid siege to Sestos, a strong place, in which many Persians from other parts had taken refuge on the approach of the Greek fleet. The governor of Sestos, Artayctes, who had signalised himself by acts of the most wanton cruelty, was now taken by surprise, having made no preparations for sustaining a siege. The autumn was already far advanced, and, as the fortress was sufficiently strong to resist the attacks of the besiegers, many began to be anxious to return home; but Xanthippus and his colleagues refused to abandon the enterprise, and the blockade was continued during the

* The victory at Mycale is said to have been gained on the evening of the same day on which the battle of Plataeae was fought; but if so it is difficult to comprehend how the report of the latter battle could have reached the Greeks at Mycale.

winter. When the spring of B.C. 478 came, famine began to rage in the town. In this extremity, Artayctes and other Persians of rank attempted to make their escape by night. When, in the morning, their flight was discovered, the Greek inhabitants of the town opened the gates to the besiegers. Many of the fugitive Persians, including Artayctes, were overtaken and brought back. Artayctes tried to save his life by the offer of 300 talents, but such an atonement for his crimes was rejected; he was nailed to a cross, and his son stoned to death before his eyes. After the conquest the Athenian fleet sailed home.

On their return the Athenians found their country a wasted land, and their city, with the exception of a few houses, a heap of ruins. Athens seemed to be reduced to the lowest stage of poverty and weakness; but in reality her strength had never before been so great, and time only was wanting to call it into action and clothe her with beauty and splendour. The restoration of the private dwellings was left to their owners; they were rebuilt without any uniform or regular design, and upon a scale suited to the indigence of the citizens. The streets were narrow and crooked, and the inconvenience thus produced was so great, that the Areopagus was obliged to interfere. But the city never outgrew the defects of this hasty restoration. The rebuilding of the temples was reserved for another season, the thoughts of Themistocles and Aristides being engaged by the care of providing for the immediate security and permanent strength of the city. It was necessary to restore the walls, and to extend them so that they might encompass a larger space. The allies of Athens, however, viewed her proceedings with feelings which the recollection of her noble self-sacrifice ought to have suppressed. What she had suffered was forgotten; and what she had done only awakened jealousy and fear. Aegina and Corinth, her maritime rivals, were perhaps the first to take the alarm; and Sparta was easily persuaded to check the growth of a power which might soon become formidable to herself. Envoys accordingly were sent from Sparta, with a message that sounded like the language of friendship, advising the Athenians to throw down all the walls still standing north of the Isthmus, as they would only serve to shelter the barbarians in any new invasion: Peloponnesus, they said, would always afford a sufficient refuge for all the Greeks. By the advice of Themistocles, the Athenians, not yet able to resist violence, dismissed the envoys with a promise that an embassy should be forthwith sent to Sparta to discuss their proposal. Themistocles himself set out at once, directing that the other ambassadors should not follow him until the walls had been raised to such a height as would sustain an attack. While Themistocles was staying at Sparta, waiting for the arrival of his colleagues, every Athenian capable of labour, without distinction of age or sex, was busily engaged in the work of fortification; no edifice, public or private, sacred or profane, that could supply building materials, was spared. In the mean time Themistocles endeavoured to counteract the reports which were brought to Sparta, and persuaded the ephors to send some trustworthy men to Athens to ascertain the real state of things. At the same time, however, by a secret message he requested his countrymen to detain the envoys until he and his colleagues returned. Aristides and another of the expected ambassadors at last arrived, and informed Themistocles that the walls were high enough to stand a siege. It was now time to drop the mask, and let the Spartans hear the voice of truth. At his next audience Themistocles informed them that the fortification was advanced too far to be stopped, and bade them in future treat the Athenians as reasonable men, who knew what was due to their own safety as well as to Greece. The Spartans with their usual skill dissembled their vexation, and only expressed their regret that what had been meant merely as a friendly suggestion should have been construed as a design of encroaching on the right of the Athenians to do in their own country as they thought fit. So the envoys on both sides returned home, and the city walls were quietly completed.

When this work was finished, Themistocles turned his thoughts to a still more important one, which was to determine the character and prospects of Athens. He had been convinced by recent events that his country, in order to be secure, must be strong, and its position at once pointed out to him the necessity of making Athens a maritime state. He had already made its navy more powerful than that of any of its neighbours; but it was still destitute of a fortified harbour. Hitherto Athens had been satisfied with Phalerum, the smallest of the three harbours near the city; but Themistocles now proposed to fortify the three ports, Phalerum, Munychia, and Piraeus, by a double range of walls; one on the land side, enclosing space for a considerable town; the other following the windings of the shore between the mouth of Phalerum and that of Piraeus. This wall was of a breadth which allowed two waggons to pass each other, and was raised to the height of sixty feet. Piraeus now became a town of great importance; the building of it is said to have been designed and superintended by the Milesian Hippodamus. It soon became the residence of merchants and foreigners, who came to exercise their arts or trades at Athens.

Athens was now prepared for her glorious career, and in the spring of B. C. 477 the allied fleet again put to sea. The thirty ships which Athens sent were commanded by Aristides and Cimon the son of Miltiades; and Pausanias was at the head of the whole armament. It first sailed to Cyprus, wrested the greater part of that island from the Persians, and then having sailed northward laid siege to Byzantium. There the Spartan regent began more fully to unfold a character and views of which he had already given some indications. After the capture of Byzantium, he laid aside the manners of his country, to adopt those of the barbarians, and began to treat his allies as if they were his subjects. His object did not come to light till many years later, but it was quite evident that he no longer felt a pride in being a citizen of Sparta, and, therefore, that his fidelity to the cause of Greece was not to be relied on. His brilliant success at Plataeae seems to have dazzled and bewildered his mind; his ambition was boundless, and he was blind to the dangers which he had to encounter in effecting his designs. He appears to have thought that the condition of a vassal of the great king of Persia was a higher and happier station than that which he occupied, and from which he knew that he must retire in a few years. But it is surprising to find that he was so utterly unable to measure his means with his ends, and that he recklessly neglected the most necessary precautions.

Among the prisoners whom he had taken at Byzantium were some noble Persians connected with the royal family, who afforded him an opportunity of opening a negotiation with Xerxes. He secretly allowed them to escape, and then sent a trusty messenger to Xerxes to claim the merit of this service, and to offer to lay Sparta and the rest of Greece at the king's feet if he would give him his daughter in marriage. Xerxes eagerly caught at the proposal, and sent down Artabazus as governor of the satrapy of Western Asia, enjoining him to keep up an active correspondence with Pausanias, and to supply him with money and every other aid. Pausanias, finding the king ready to enter into the scheme, began to act as if it were no longer necessary to dissemble his intentions; he assumed the state of a Persian satrap, imitated the luxuries and fashions of the barbarians in his table and dress, and travelled through Thrace escorted by a guard of Persians and Egyptians. In his vision of greatness he forgot the ties by which he was still bound, and treated those over whom he held a responsible command with harshness and arrogance. The Ionians, who had only just emancipated themselves, were provoked by treatment worse than they had commonly experienced from the barbarians. The Athenian generals, on the other hand, displayed qualities which were the more winning from their contrast with those of Pausanias, and the allies began to feel how much happier they would be under the command of the just Aristides and the generous and gentle Cimon. This feeling was strengthened by the reflection, that Athens, and not Sparta, was the parent to whom most of them owed their origin. So the wish gradually ripened into a resolution, and all the confederates, with the exception of the Peloponnesian states and Aegina, called upon the Athenians to accept the supremacy, in all the common affairs of the alliance, which had hitherto been enjoyed by Sparta.

It was Aristides who brought about this great revolution, and established his country in this honourable and well-earned pre-eminence. He now undertook, by the general desire, the task of regulating the laws of the union, and its relation to Athens as its head. The object of the confederacy was to protect the Greeks against the barbarians, and to weaken and humble the latter as much as possible. All were to contribute towards this common end, and Athens was to collect and direct their forces as the organ of the public will.

The constitutions and internal administration of the allied states were not to be interfered with. Aristides fixed the assessments of the numerous allied cities so as to satisfy all, and without incurring even a suspicion of attempting to obtain the least benefit for himself. He was acknowledged to be above calumny. The whole amount of the yearly contributions was settled at 460 talents (about 115,000*l.*); Delos was chosen for the treasury of the confederates, and its temple as the place where their deputies were to hold their meeting.

As rumours of the conduct of Pausanias had in the mean time reached Sparta, the ephors immediately recalled him, and sent out other commanders. But it was too late to recover what had been lost, and the new generals found that they must be content with a subordinate rank. Spartan pride was unable to brook this, and they retired from the field of action, leaving their rivals triumphant. Henceforth the strength of Greece was divided between two confederations; for the supremacy of Sparta was still recognised by her Peloponnesian allies, who now rallied round her more closely than ever. Thus Sparta was thrown back into her original sphere, while Athens had risen into an entirely new one. The history of Greece henceforth assumes a wholly different aspect. The supremacy of Athens lasted for a period of 73 years, from B.C. 477 till 404. Before we proceed with the history of the two confederacies, we will briefly notice the later occurrences in the lives of the men who had brought about this great change.

The regulation of the Ionian confederacy was the last great event in the life of Aristides. The changes in the Athenian constitution which are ascribed to him may, however, to some extent, have been the result of the new position to which he had raised his country. He threw down the barrier of privilege which separated the highest of Solon's classes from the lower, by opening the archonship and the council of the Areopagus to the poorest of the citizens; so that the fourth class, the Thetes, were now let into the highest dignities of the state. This change had been gradually prepared by the alteration which had taken place, since the time of Solon, in the value of property, which rendered the archonship accessible to a much more numerous body than the old lawgiver had contemplated. The heroic exertions of all classes at Athens, during and after the Persian invasion, rendered this period particularly fit for placing all citizens upon an equal footing; nay, it may be said that the new state of things rendered such a change in the constitution absolutely necessary.

Aristides lived to see the compact which he had established between Athens and her confederates broken in a material point; but he could not prevent it. He enjoyed to the last the unabated confidence and respect of his countrymen. He died—whether in or out of Athens is uncertain—as he had lived, in poverty. It is even said that he did not leave behind him wherewith to defray the expenses of his funeral. His monument was erected at the public charge, and his posterity for several generations was pensioned by the state.

Pausanias, recalled to Sparta, was subjected to a severe inquiry. On some points he was convicted, and condemned to slight penalties; but no evidence was produced of his correspondence with the barbarians, and the accusation was dropped. Unable to live in the condition to which he was reduced, he cast aside the authority of the ephors, quitted Sparta without their leave, and embarked for Byzantium, which was still in the hands of one of his creatures, whom he had left as his deputy when he was recalled to Sparta. As he renewed his treasonable practices, the Athenians obliged him to leave the place. He then retired to Colonae in Troas, where he carried on his criminal intrigues so openly, that a report of them soon reached Sparta, and he was once more roused from his dream of greatness by a short message from the ephors. He obeyed the command and returned home, for his plans were still far from being ripe, and he could not hope to carry them into effect if he should draw upon himself a sentence of outlawry. He was thrown into prison, but soon obtained his liberty, and demanded a trial. No satisfactory evidence of his treason having been yet obtained, the affair was again dropped; and if he could have remained quiet after this, he might still have lived secure, and died without infamy. But he had gone too far to stop or to recede. He contemplated exciting an insurrection of the Helots, and maintaining himself at the head of the state by the aid of Persia. But the plan was as improvidently concerted as it was recklessly adopted, and was betrayed to the ephors by one of the Helots themselves. But even on this information they, with their usual caution when the reputation of a Spartan was at stake, forbore to act, and patiently waited for more unexceptionable evidence. Pausanias, in the mean time, continued his correspondence with Persia; but he had the prudence to request the satrap to put to death the bearers of his letters. At length the suspicions of Argilius, one of these messengers, were awakened by the remarkable fact that none of those who were sent by Pausanias ever returned. He counterfeited the seal, opened the letter intrusted to him, and found his apprehensions confirmed. His resentment was roused, and he revealed the secret to the ephors. A plan was now devised for the conviction and punishment of the traitor. Argilius took refuge as a suppliant in a temple of Poseidon, near Taenarus, and within the sacred precincts raised a temporary hovel, divided into two compartments by a thin partition, behind which some of the ephors were concealed, in the expectation that Pausanias would soon come to inquire the motive of Argilius' conduct. This anticipation was realised, and the ephors overheard the whole conversation between Pausanias and Argilius, which left no doubt of the traitor's guilt. As Pausanias was returning home, the ephors approached to arrest him, but he escaped into the temple of Athene Chalcioecos. As they could not seize him in the sanctuary, the building was unroofed, its entrance blocked up, and its approaches were carefully guarded. His aged mother is said to have carried the first stone to block up the doorway to immure her son. When he was on the point of expiring, he was carried out of the sacred precincts, in order that the sanctuary might not be polluted, and breathed his last as soon as he had crossed its bounds. But subsequently, the recollection of his past services rendered his fate a subject first of compassion and regret, and at length of religious compunction. By command of the Delphic oracle, his bones were removed to the spot near the temple where he had expired, and two brazen statues of Pausanias were set up in the sanctuary of the goddess. Religious scruples about the death of Pausanias continued for a long time, however, to disturb the minds of some of the Spartans.

The fate of Pausanias involved that of Themistocles. Conscious of the great services he had rendered to Greece, he became proud and indiscreet. After the battle of Salamis his power and influence had reached its height, but his rapaciousness often led him to convert his glory into a source of petty profits, as we have seen in his conduct towards the islanders after the flight of Xerxes. He did not scruple to sell his mediation in the disputes of many of the maritime states to any one who was willing to purchase it, and he thus drew upon himself the well-merited charge of perfidy, avarice, and cruelty. But while he thus made some enemies by his selfishness, he provoked others by his firm and enlightened patriotism. Sparta never forgave him the shame he had brought upon her by thwarting her insidious attempt to crush the independence of Athens. Another blow which he inflicted upon Sparta consisted in his defeating her when she wished to exclude from the Amphictionic council those states which had aided the barbarians; by which measure the influence of Sparta would probably have become predominant in the council. At Athens, however, he was gradually supplanted in popular favour by other men; and his own indiscretions seconded them in their endeavours to persuade the people that he had risen too high to remain a harmless citizen. He was, accordingly, condemned to a temporary exile by ostracism, which he himself had before directed against Aristides. He withdrew to Argos, where he was welcomed as the deliverer of Greece and as the enemy of Sparta. There he was residing in B.C. 471, when Pausanias was convicted of treason. Among the papers of Pausanias were found some traces of a correspondence between him and Themistocles, from which it seemed that he had been implicated in the scheme of the Spartan. Ambassadors were immediately sent to Athens to accuse him, and to insist upon his being punished like his accomplice. No evidence has ever been produced to prove that the charge was well founded; all that can be said with any degree of certainty is, that Pausanias in a letter communicated his designs to the exiled Themistocles, in the hope that he would embrace any opportunity of avenging himself upon his ungrateful country. Themistocles was too prudent not to see at once that the scheme was that of a madman. But, however this may be, his enemies at Athens rejoiced at so good an opportunity for ruining him, and officers were sent out with the Spartans to arrest him. This Themistocles had foreseen, and fled; first to Corcyra, but not feeling sufficiently safe there, he crossed over to Epirus, where he sought shelter in the palace of Admetus, king of the Molossians, who was absent when Themistocles arrived. The queen, with womanly compassion, taught him how he might secure her husband's protection; and when the latter returned, he found Themistocles seated at his hearth, holding the young prince in his hands. Among the Molossians this was the most solemn form of supplication; and when Themistocles disclosed the danger of his situation, the king was touched, and assured him of his protection. When the Spartan and Athenian officers dogged their prey to his house, the king, faithful to his word, refused to surrender his guest.

At the court of Admetus, Themistocles seems to have been

joined by his wife and children; and he might have remained there, but he had already formed the design of seeking his fortune at the court of Persia. Admetus supplied his guest with the means of crossing the Aegean, and Themistocles embarked at Pydna in Macedonia. A storm carried the ship to Naxos, which was then besieged by the Athenians. To avoid being accidentally discovered, Themistocles made himself known to the master of the ship, and, by promises and threats, prevailed upon him to keep his secret, and to prevent any of the crew from going on shore at Naxos. At length the ship landed him safely at Ephesus, where he received the property which his friends had been enabled to rescue for him. Very soon after his arrival in Asia, Xerxes was assassinated, in B.C. 465, and was succeeded by his son Artaxerxes. Themistocles, accompanied by a Persian friend, proceeded to the court. In a letter addressed to the king, he acknowledged the evil which he had inflicted on the royal house, but claimed the merit of having saved Xerxes at Salamis, and of having thwarted the plan of the Greeks to intercept him in his flight. He also intimated, that his present misfortunes were the consequence of his zeal for the interest of the king of Persia, and

Painted Greek Vases.—1 & 2 From Athens. 3. From Corinth. 4. The celebrated Meidias Vase from Magna Graecia. 5. From Etruria.
(From the British Museum.)

desired that a year might be allowed him to acquire the means of disclosing his plans in person. The request was granted, and Themistocles now made himself acquainted with the language and manners of the Persians. He succeeded so well, and won the favour of Artaxerxes to such a degree, that even the courtiers are said to have envied him. At length he was sent down to the maritime provinces, and a pension was conferred upon him in the oriental fashion: three flourishing towns were assigned for his maintenance, of which Magnesia was to provide him with bread, Myus with viands, and Lampsacus with wine. He settled at Magnesia, where he maintained a sort of princely rank. The common story is, that he put an end to his own life, because he saw no possibility of performing his promises; but the disbelief of Thucydides renders this story at least very doubtful. A splendid monument was raised to his memory at Magnesia; but in later times it was believed that his remains were buried within the port of Piraeus.

Primitive mode of pressing the juice out of grapes.
(From a bas relief in the Museum at Naples.)

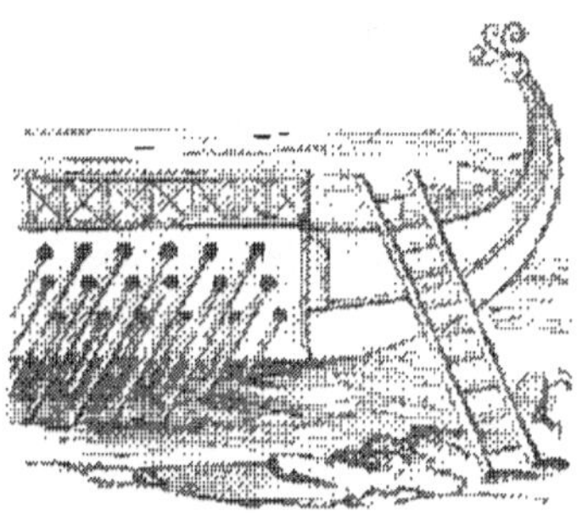

Portion of a Ship.
(From an ancient Fresco painting.)

CHAPTER XVI.

FROM THE COMMENCEMENT OF THE ATHENIAN MARITIME ASCENDENCY TO THE THIRTY YEARS' TRUCE BETWEEN ATHENS AND SPARTA.

As Greece and the islands of the Aegean were now freed from the fear of any further aggression on the part of Persia, most of the states united under the supremacy of Athens would have been satisfied with the security thus afforded to them; but Athens saw a vast field of ambition opened to her in the East, where the situation of the Greek colonies afforded a fair pretext for the continuance of hostilities. Foremost among the men who were active in directing the attention of their countrymen to that quarter, was Cimon the son of Miltiades. In his youth he had given little promise of the talents and the character which he afterwards displayed; and is even said to have neglected the ordinary accomplishments of an Athenian gentleman. As an orator he never distinguished himself, and it is probable that it was his consciousness of this defect which determined him to choose a career away from Athens, and to abandon the popular assembly to his rivals. The penalty of fifty talents, which he had to pay at the death of his father, would probably have ruined him, had not the wealthy Callias undertaken to discharge it in consideration of receiving the hand of Cimon's sister in marriage. He first distinguished himself in the battle of Salamis, and many of his friends saw in him a capacity and a disposition which fitted him for the highest places in the republic. Aristides, in particular, regarded him as fit to be a coadjutor to himself and an antagonist to Themistocles. The readiness with which the allied Greeks, disgusted with the conduct of Pausanias, united themselves with Athens, was in a great measure owing to Cimon's mild temper, and to his frank and gentle manners.

The popularity of Themistocles was already declining, while Cimon, on account of several successful enterprises, was rapidly rising in public favour. The first of these achievements was the conquest of Eion on the Strymon, in B.C. 476. The Persian governor, Boges, finding that he could no longer hold out against the besiegers, set fire to the town, and perished in the flames with his friends, family, and treasures. The acquisition of this place was of great importance to Athens, being the foundation of one of its most flourishing colonies. In the course of the same year, Cimon effected another, and in the eyes of the people no less valuable, conquest. The island of Scyros was inhabited by a mixed race of Pelasgians and Dolopians, who, by their piratical habits, had incurred the ban of the Amphictions; and Cimon seized this opportunity for exterminating the people, and dividing their land among Attic colonists.* The next undertaking was directed against Carystos in Euboea, which had provoked the hostility of the Athenians. It made a long resistance before it was reduced to submission. The conquest of Naxos, which took place in B.C. 466, was an event of far greater moment. That island began to feel its connection with Athens irksome, and the latter was resolved to exact by force that which was no longer cheerfully given. The revolt of Naxos was quelled after a hard siege. Instead of allies, the Naxians now became subjects of Athens, and experienced from their protectors the worst evil which they had to fear from Persia. Their example, however, did not deter others from making similar attempts to throw off the supremacy of Athens. One after another they refused compliance with the demands of the leading state, and were punished with the loss of their independence. Many sought to commute their personal services in the endless expeditions to which they were summoned, for stated payments of money. Cimon, perceiving the advantages of such an arrangement, accepted it wherever it was offered. The effect of it was, that the states which adopted this course ceased to keep up a naval force of their own; and thus became more and more unwarlike, and less able to resist the growing demands of the Athenians.

In B.C. 465, Cimon obtained his most memorable triumph over the Persians. A great sea and land force had been collected at the mouth of the Eurymedon in Pamphylia. The fleet consisted

* Cimon is said to have afterwards discovered in Scyros the remains of Theseus, who was believed to have been buried there. In B.C. 468 they were brought to Athens with great pomp.

of at least 350 sail, which were to be joined by eighty galleys from Cyprus. Cimon, who had gradually strengthened his fleet, as he slowly moved along the south coast of Asia Minor, till it amounted to 250 galleys, provoked the enemy to an engagement before the arrival of the eighty Cyprian vessels; and having defeated them, and sunk or taken 200 ships, sailed up the river to their camp; there he landed his men, flushed with victory, and completely routed the Persian army. On the same day, he is said to have met the squadron coming from Cyprus, and to have utterly destroyed it.

After having gained this double or treble victory, Cimon sailed northwards, where the Persians were still in possession of the Thracian Chersonesus. He dislodged them not only from the territory which had once belonged to Athens, but from perhaps the best part of his own patrimony. It appears to have been in the year B. C. 464 that the Athenians became engaged in a contest with Thasos, which was both able and disposed to make a vigorous resistance. The principal object of the struggle was the gold mines on the continent, which Athens seems to have claimed. The islanders however, were first defeated at sea by Cimon, and then closely besieged. While this siege was going on, the Athenians, who had formed a settlement in Thrace at Enneaodos, suffered a great disaster, being cut off to a man by the Thracians, who viewed the colony as a hostile invasion of their territory. The Thasians, alarmed at the turn which the war had taken, sent an embassy to Sparta, hoping to induce that rival of Athens to make a diversion in their favour by invading Attica. The Spartans readily undertook to do so, and had nearly completed their preparations in secret, when a calamity befell them which forced them to struggle hard for their own existence.

In the year B. C. 464, the whole of Laconia was shaken by an earthquake, which opened great chasms in the ground, and rolled down huge masses of rock from the heights of Taygetus. In Sparta itself, only five houses are said to have been left standing, and more than 20,000 persons were believed to have been killed. Amid the confusion occasioned by this catastrophe, many of the Helots hastened to the city, hoping to take advantage of the helpless condition of their masters. The presence of mind of King Archidamus alone saved Sparta, for he foresaw the danger, and as soon as the first consternation had subsided, gathered all the people in arms around him. The Helots on their arrival, perceiving this, retreated and dispersed. This part of the danger was thus averted; but the Messenians also seized the opportunity of rising against their detested lords, and fortified themselves in their ancient stronghold of Ithome. They were joined not only by numerous Helots, but even by some of the free Laconian towns. The Spartans laid siege to Ithome, but made only very slow progress. In the mean time the Thasians, left to themselves, were compelled to capitulate in the third year of the war, and became subjects of Athens. The Spartans, seeing no prospect of reducing Ithome, called on their allies for aid, and did not blush to ask for help from the Athenians, against whose country they had only just been secretly preparing an expedition. At this time the aristocratic party at Athens was favourably disposed towards Sparta, and was headed by Cimon, who had now reached the height of popularity, and entertained a warm admiration for the character and institutions of the Lacedaemonians. The democratic party opposed the proposal to support Sparta, but Cimon's advice prevailed, and he himself was sent with a large force to assist in the siege of Ithome.

The Spartans had hoped that the Athenians, who were eminently skilled in the art of besieging, would enable them speedily to reduce the place. But as a long time passed away without any impression being made upon the besieged, they began to suspect that the Athenians were unwilling to accomplish that for which they had been invited, and the consciousness of their own guilt made them apprehend a treacherous scheme on the part of their Attic auxiliaries. This feeling gradually became so strong that, while they retained all their other allies, they dismissed the Athenian troops, simply saying that they had no further need of them. The Athenians, perceiving the real motive, were probably more exasperated by the want of confidence thus displayed, than they would have been by a perfidious attack. All connection with Sparta was accordingly broken off, and an alliance was entered into with Argos, Sparta's ancient rival. Meantime the Messenian war was carried on for a number of years, until B.C. 455, when the brave defenders of Ithome obtained honourable terms. They were permitted to quit Peloponnesus with their families, on condition of being detained in slavery if they ever returned. The Athenians gave them the town of Naupactus, of which they had recently become possessed. The site was one full of hope for the unfortunate emigrants, and extremely useful to the Athenians for their operations in the Corinthian gulf.

The abrupt dismissal of the Athenian forces during the siege of Ithome was highly gratifying to the democratic party, and justified the advice they had given at the time when the succour was asked for. There was at that period fast rising in power and renown a young man, whose glory was destined to eclipse that of even the greatest among his countrymen. This was Pericles, the son of Xanthippus, the conqueror of Mycale, by Agariste, a descendant of the famous Cleisthenes. In his youth he had not rested satisfied with the ordinary Greek education, but had applied himself with great ardour to intellectual pursuits, which were then new at Athens, and confined to a very small circle of inquisitive spirits. Pericles entered with deep interest into the abstrusest philosophical speculations, in which pursuits his chief guide was Anaxagoras, with whom he was united in intimate friendship, and who was believed to have exercised a great influence upon his habits of thought, and upon the tone and style of his eloquence All the rare acquirements with which Pericles enriched his mind were considered by him as instruments for the use of the statesman. But although signally gifted and accomplished for political action, yet he entered upon his career with hesitation and apprehension, for his very greatness was calculated to alarm those who were nervously anxious about the maintenance of popular freedom. His personal appearance was graceful and majestic, though his head was somewhat disproportioned in its length; and old men who remembered Pisistratus were struck by the resemblance to him which they discovered in Pericles, not only in his features but in the sweetness of his voice and the volubility of his utterance. After the ostracism of Themistocles and the death of Aristides, while Cimon was engaged in continual expeditions, Pericles began to present himself more and more to the public eye, and was soon the acknowledged chief of the democratic party, which had been headed by Themistocles, and now openly aimed at counteracting Cimon's influence.

After the constitutional changes introduced at Athens by Cleisthenes and Aristides, the aristocracy had no hope of recovering what it had lost; but it became more intent on keeping all that it had, and on stopping any further innovation at home, as the commonalty grew more enterprising. As far as foreign policy was concerned, the aristocratic party wished to preserve the balance of power in Greece, and to direct the Athenian arms against Persia, in the hope of diverting the Greeks from intestine warfare. The democratic party had other interests, and concurred with the views of its opponents only in so far as they tended to enrich and aggrandise the state of Athens. The contest between these two parties seems for a time to have been carried on rather with a noble emulation in the service of the republic than by assaults upon each other. Cimon had enriched both the republic and himself, and he made a munificent use of his wealth. He did much for the security and embellishment of the city; and preparations were now made for joining Athens with its harbours, by walls carried down on the one side to Phalerum and on the other to Piraeus. The greater part of these walls, the construction of which was difficult on account of the marshy nature of the ground, was executed by Cimon, with magnificent solidity, at his own charge. He also adorned the public places of the city with trees, introduced a supply of water, and converted the Academy, a district about two miles north of the city, from an arid waste into a delightful grove, with lawns and courses for the exercises of the young, and shady walks for the thoughtful; a scene of wholesome recreation for all. But besides this noble kind of liberality, Cimon indulged in another which was as degrading to the benefactor as to the benefited: he is said to have opened his gardens and orchards to all who wished to avail themselves of their contents; to have feasted the people at his tables, to which they had access at all times; and to have distributed clothes and money among the poorer citizens. In these points, however, Cimon probably did not stand alone, for the aristocracy, no longer able to oppress the commonalty, must have found it expedient to court the people, and to part with a portion of its wealth for the sake of retaining its power. But though Cimon's munificence no doubt originated in this feeling of the aristocracy, it must have been remarkable not only in its degree, but in its kind; and was not the less that of a demagogue because he sought popularity not merely for his own sake, but for that of his order and his party.

In this light Cimon's liberality was viewed by Pericles, who endeavoured to counteract its influence by several measures. He was not able to rival Cimon's profusion, and even managed his private property with rigid economy, that he might keep his probity, in the management of public affairs, free from temptation and suspicion. His friend Demonides is said to have first suggested to him the idea of rendering Cimon's liberality superfluous by applying the public revenue to a similar purpose. But Pericles perhaps thought, and with justice, that it was safer, and more becoming, that the people should supply their poorer brethren with the means of enjoyment out of its own funds, than that they should depend upon the bounty of wealthy individuals; especially as the fathers of the present generation had willingly resigned the produce of the mines of Laurion to the use of the state, and had thereby raised their country to power and greatness. Pericles thus became the author of a series of measures, all of which tended to provide for the subsistence and gratification of the poorer class at the public expense: but while he was thus engaged in courting the favour of the multitude, he was no less anxious to command its respect; he was unremittingly attentive to business, and never allowed himself to indulge in the convivial entertainments of his friends, confining himself to the society of a very select circle. His speeches were all most studiously and scrupulously prepared, and the impression which they produced was heightened by the calm majesty of his air and carriage, which he maintained under all provocations. He did not appear in the popular assembly except on great occasions, and carried many of his measures through his friends and partisans, the most prominent among whom was Ephialtes, a man distinguished for his rigid integrity as well as for the earnestness and fearlessness with which he bore the brunt of the conflict with the opposite party.

Immediately after the reduction of Thasos, Cimon was expected to accomplish some other conquest, perhaps on the frontiers between Macedonia and Thrace; but he did not attempt it: this forbearance irritated the people, and his adversaries inflamed the popular indignation by ascribing his conduct to the influence of Macedonian gold. This charge was unquestionably unfounded; and Pericles, though called upon by the people to come forward as one of the accusers, declined to do so, at the entreaty, it is said, of Cimon's sister Elpinice; he kept back the thunder of his eloquence, and only rose once, for form's sake, to second the accusation. According to Plutarch, Cimon was acquitted; but from other statements it would seem that he was sentenced to pay a fine of 50 talents.

A more serious struggle between the two parties arose soon afterwards, when Pericles resolved on attacking the aristocracy in its ancient and revered stronghold, the Areopagus, which was composed of the ex-archons, and was at once a council and a court of justice. By the reforms of Aristides, even the poorest Athenian might become a member of it; but the change which these measures produced in its composition was probably as yet hardly perceptible, and had no effect on its maxims and proceedings. Pericles' object was to narrow the range of the functions of the Areopagus, so as to leave it little more than an august name. Ephialtes was his principal coadjutor in this undertaking, and thereby exposed himself to the implacable enmity of the opposite party, which set all its engines in motion to ward off the blow. It was at this juncture that Sparta solicited the aid of Athens against the Messenians; and the treatment which the Athenians received at the hands of the Spartans afforded the party of Pericles a great advantage in the conflict with its adversaries at home, and furnished it with new arms against Cimon, who at once became obnoxious as the avowed friend of Sparta, and as the author of the expedition which had drawn so rude an insult on his countrymen. The attack on the Areopagus, therefore, was now prosecuted with greater vigour, and Cimon could exercise little influence in its behalf. His party, however, put forth all its strength in a last effort to save the stronghold of its power, and was supported in its efforts by the poet Aeschylus, who in his "Eumenides" represented the Areopagus as the most venerable and hallowed institution. This play was probably performed in the year of the rupture with Sparta, and just after the conclusion of the treaty with Argos. But, notwithstanding the surpassing excellence of the drama, the author failed in his political object; and Ephialtes carried a decree, by which the Areopagus was shorn of its authority, and retained only a few branches of its jurisdiction. In what the innovation consisted, is matter for conjecture only; but it is highly probable that the power of the Areopagus as a council was reduced, and that its jurisdiction over the conduct of the citizens was abolished.

This triumph of Pericles and his party over the Areopagus seems to have been immediately followed by the ostracism of Cimon, which took place about two years after the return of the Athenians from Messenia; so that his exile does not appear to have been the effect of popular resentment, but rather a measure to secure tranquillity in the city. Though Athens gained great immediate advantages by its rupture with Sparta, yet it lost the friendship of Corinth, one of its old and most useful allies. Corinth was at war with Megara; the latter, relying on Athens, renounced its alliance with Sparta, and admitted an Athenian garrison. The Athenians then connected Megara with the port of Nisaea and with the sea by a work similar to that which had lately been commenced between Athens and Piraeus.

While these things were going on in Greece, Inarus, king of some Libyan tribes on the west of Egypt, excited, in B.C. 460, an insurrection there against the Persians, and his authority was recognised throughout the greater part of the country. Artaxerxes sent his brother with a large army to suppress the rebellion. An Athenian armament of 200 galleys was lying at the time off Cyprus, and Inarus sent to obtain its assistance. The Athenian commanders at once sailed southward, and having joined the insurgents, enabled them to defeat the Persians, whose general fell in battle by the hand of Inarus. They then sailed up the Nile to Memphis, of one quarter of which a body of Persians was still in possession, and which was now besieged by the Athenians. This siege lasted upwards of five years, at the end of which time the Athenians, being pressed by a far more numerous army, were obliged to abandon Memphis, and were surrounded on an island in the Nile called Prosopitis. Out of their army of 40,000 men, only a few escaped through Libya and Cyrene, and thence returned home. Inarus himself was nailed by the Persians to a cross.

In B.C. 457, while the siege of Memphis was still going on, the

Corinthians, enraged at the occupation of Megara by the Athenians, made war on them, in which they were joined by Aegina and the maritime towns of Argolis. The Athenians, not waiting to be attacked, at once landed a body of troops near Haliae, in Argolis, but were driven back to their ships by the united forces of Corinth and Epidaurus. They soon made up for this check, however, by a victory over the Peloponnesian fleet near Cecryphaleia, in the Saronic gulf; and their admiral, Leocrates, was still more successful in defeating the allies in a great sea-fight near Aegina. He took seventy of their ships, and then, having landed his troops on the island, laid siege to the town. The Corinthians, thinking to effect a diversion, sent only a small force to Aegina, and invaded the territory of Megara. But Athens, though its armies were at this time engaged in Egypt, Cyprus, and Phoenicia, was still indomitable, and animated by as high a spirit as ever. Myronides, a man not inferior to Miltiades or Cimon, assembled all who had been left at home for the defence of the city, and marched out with them against the Corinthians. In the first engagement no decisive victory was gained, but the Corinthians retired from the field of battle. Being reproved at home for yielding so easily, they, twelve days after, came back to the scene of action and challenged the Athenians to another contest. The latter immediately issued from Megara, and completely defeated their enemy. In their flight many of the Corinthians got into a pit, from which they could find no egress. The Athenians surrounded the place, and with their missiles slew every man within.

Some time before this ineffectual attempt of the Corinthians to relieve Aegina, Artaxerxes, in the hope of drawing the Athenians away from Egypt, sent Megabazus to Sparta with a sum of money to bribe the principal Spartans to engage their countrymen in an expedition against Athens. The Spartans were not unwilling to receive the money, but were unable to render the service required for it, for Ithome still held out, and Sparta itself had not yet recovered sufficient strength to venture on the proposed invasion. Pericles, who seems to have received some intelligence of these proceedings, now urged the completion of the long walls. A faction of the aristocratic party, however, who viewed that great work only as a bulwark of the hated commonalty, vehemently opposed its completion. A favourable opportunity for regaining their ascendency seemed to offer itself to that party in the year in which Myronides defeated the Corinthians. The Phocians had invaded Doris, and taken one of its towns. The pious Spartans forthwith assembled an army of 10,000 allied troops, and 1500 of their own, and forced the Phocians to restore their conquest. After accomplishing their objects, the Spartans were informed that the passes of the Isthmus were occupied by the Athenians, who intended to cut off their return. This induced their commander, Nicomedes, to march into Boeotia and to encamp at Tanagra, near the borders of Attica. The oligarchical faction at Athens secretly promised him their cooperation if he would strike a great blow. The better part of the Athenians, suspecting the intrigue, exhorted their fellow-citizens not to wait for an attack. An army of 14,000 men was mustered, and a body of cavalry came to their aid from Thessaly, which was allied with Athens. While the two armies were facing each other near Tanagra, Cimon came to the Athenian camp and requested leave to serve among the men of his tribe. The Athenian generals, suspecting treachery, referred his request to the council of Five Hundred, which rejected it. Cimon, who had only the good of his country at heart, retired, advising his friends to prove by their conduct the falsehood of the suspicion which had been cast upon them. A hard-fought battle then ensued, in which Pericles distinguished himself above all others; but the Athenians were defeated through the treachery of the Thessalians, who in the midst of the action went over to the enemy. The slaughter was great on both sides; and the Peloponnesians, after ravaging the Megarian territory, returned home over the Isthmus, the passes of Geraneia being now open. This battle was fought in B.C. 457.

It is said that the Athenians were so disheartened and discouraged by this defeat, that they recalled Cimon from his exile, in order that by his mediation the war might be concluded. But this seems inconsistent with the facts recorded by Thucydides, and Cimon's recall, moreover, took place a considerable time after the battle of Tanagra, with which it had perhaps no connection at all. Very early in the year B.C. 456, we find the Athenians again in the field, eager to wipe off the disgrace of Tanagra. They had friends in Boeotia, whose influence depended upon the success of the Athenian arms. Under the command of Myronides they met a numerous army of Boeotians at Oenophyta, and gained a brilliant victory, which made their interest in Boeotia and Phocis decidedly predominant. To secure these advantages, Myronides razed the walls of Tanagra, and forced the Locrians of Opus to put into his hands 100 of their citizens as hostages. About this time the Athenians completed their long walls, which gave their city almost the strength of an island. Not long afterwards, in the same year, the Aeginetans capitulated on nearly the same terms as had been granted to the Thasians: demolition of their walls, surrender of their ships, and payment of tribute.

In the following year, B.C. 455, an Athenian armament of 50 galleys and 4000 heavy-armed troops, under Tolmides, sailed round Peloponnesus, burnt the Spartan arsenal at Gythium, took a town called Chalcis belonging to the Corinthians, and defeated the Sicyonians, who attempted to prevent the landing of the troops. But the most important advantage gained in this expedition was the capture of Naupactus, which the Athenians soon afterwards gave up to the exiled Messenians from Ithome.*

The defeat of the Athenians in Egypt took place in B.C. 455, but even after that catastrophe they did not sue for peace, but were bent on extending their power and annoying their enemies. Early in B.C. 454 they availed themselves of an opportunity to increase their influence in the north of Greece. A noble Thessalian, Orestes, had been driven from his country, and applied to the Athenians for aid to effect his restoration. The request was granted, and the forces of Boeotia and Phocis, now at the disposal of Athens, were called out to support the claim of Orestes. This expedition, however, was a failure, for the Thessalian cavalry proved invincible, and forced the invaders to retreat. Pericles endeavoured to soothe the public disappointment, by coasting along the south side of the Corinthian gulf, making a descent on the territory of Sicyon, and routing the Sicyonians who came out to oppose him. Having taken some Achaeans on board, he then sailed over to the coast of Acarnania, and laid siege to the town of Oeniadae. The attempt to take that place, however, was unsuccessful, and the general result of the whole campaign seems to have been neither advantageous nor encouraging.

Such occurrences as these might easily incline the people in favour of Cimon, whose administration had been one unbroken series of victories and conquests; and it is highly probable that he was recalled from exile soon after the above-mentioned expedition of Pericles, about B.C. 453. The decree for that purpose was moved by Pericles himself. Cimon's recall was followed by a cessation of hostilities which lasted for three years before a formal truce was concluded between the belligerents. What motive may have led Pericles to promote the recall of his rival is uncertain, but it is not impossible that he wished to conciliate Cimon and his party on honourable terms, in order that by their united efforts they might counteract the treacherous schemes of the oligarchical faction, which had shown its spirit at the battle of Tanagra, and would willingly have delivered Athens into the hands of a foreign enemy in preference to seeing the democratic party prosperous. Ephialtes, the friend of Pericles, was assassinated, apparently the year before Cimon's recall, and there can be no doubt that the reckless oligarchic faction was guilty of that crime, which showed

* See p. 230.

the spirit by which it was animated, and may have disposed Pericles to strengthen himself by a coalition with Cimon, and to promise his concurrence in Cimon's foreign policy, which happened at this time to fall in with the inclinations of the people.

During the three years which followed Cimon's return, Greece was in the enjoyment of a happy peace; and this pause was followed by a truce of five years, in the course of which Cimon embarked on his last expedition against Persia. The Egyptian pretender, Amyrtaeus, solicited succour from Athens; and as there was not only honour and spoil to be gained, but a stain to be wiped off, Cimon was appointed commander of a fleet of 200 galleys, with which he sailed to Cyprus. Thence he sent a squadron to the assistance of Amyrtaeus, while he himself with the rest laid siege to Citium. Here he was carried off by illness, or by the consequences of a wound, B.C. 449. The armament was soon afterwards compelled by want of provisions to raise the siege. While the Athenians were sailing away with the remains of their commander, they fell in with a great fleet of Phoenician and Cilician galleys, and having completely defeated them, they followed up this victory with another which they gained on shore. After this they were joined by the squadron from Egypt, which returned without having achieved any material object, and all sailed home, in B.C. 449.

In after-times Cimon's military renown was enhanced by the report of a peace which he was said to have compelled the Persian monarch to conclude on the most humiliating terms; for the king was supposed to have agreed to abandon at least the military occupation of Asia Minor to the distance of three days' journey from the coast, or even of the whole peninsula west of the river Halys, and to abstain from passing the mouth of the Bosporus and the Chelidonian islands on the coast of Lycia, or the town of Phaselis, into the western sea. The silence of Thucydides, and the accounts of later writers, which are contradictory in regard both to the date and to the conditions of the treaty, render the whole affair extremely doubtful. From the subsequent history it is quite evident that such a state of things as this alleged peace implies, never existed; and no allusion is made to the peace in any of the later transactions between Greece and Persia. The whole story is a fable, which arose no doubt out of the recollection of Cimon's glorious victories, and seems to have assumed a distinct shape in the rhetorical school of Isocrates.

Cimon's death saved him from the mortification of seeing his exertions for the maintenance of peace in Greece defeated by causes which he could not have controlled. Pericles is said to have carried, about this time, a decree summoning a congress, to be held at Athens, of deputies from various parts of Greece, and even from the islands and Asiatic colonies. The professed objects of this assembly were, the restoration of the temples which had been destroyed in the Persian wars, and to provide for the security of commerce among the Greeks. The real end which Pericles had in view is very doubtful; he may have wished to strengthen the Athenian confederacy, and to gain over some Greeks who were still wavering between Athens and her rival. But whatever may have been the objects of the scheme, it fell to the ground, according to Plutarch, through the counter-machinations of Sparta.

An occasion for hostilities between the two rival states seems to have arisen in B.C. 448, the year after Cimon's death. The Delphians had, from time immemorial, exercised the superintendence of the oracle of Apollo, and the guardianship of the sacred treasures, by ministers of their own choice. The Phocians, perhaps relying on the protection of Athens, wrested this important charge from them. Sparta now stepped forward to assert the claims of her Dorian friends at Delphi, and an army was sent out which restored the possession of the temple to the Delphians. Delphi was, at the same time, induced to renounce the league with the Phocians, and to declare itself an independent state. To Sparta several privileges were granted by the Delphians. But shortly after the withdrawal of the Spartan forces, Pericles appeared at Delphi with an Athenian army, and reinstated the Phocians in the custody of the temple; the privileges which had been bestowed upon the Spartans were now transferred to the Athenians. This, however, was only a prelude to more important movements, which took place in the following year, B.C. 447. Numbers of Boeotian exiles, who had been driven from their homes in consequence of the Athenian ascendancy in Boeotia, took possession of Chaeronea, Orchomenos, and other towns. The danger thus threatening the interests of Athens called for its prompt interference. Tolmides, at the head of a band of 1000 volunteers, set out, against the cautious advice of Pericles, to suppress the insurrection. With this force and some allies he first attacked Chaeronea, and succeeded in reducing it. A garrison was left in the place; but as he was retiring with the rest of his little army, he was surprised in the neighbourhood of Coronea by the appearance of a hostile army; the Athenians were completely defeated, and Tolmides himself was among the slain. The consequence of this disaster was a counter-revolution in Boeotia, which overthrew the Athenian influence throughout that country. To recover their prisoners, the Athenians undertook to withdraw all their troops from Boeotia. The exiles returned everywhere, and the party hostile to Athens gained the ascendancy throughout Boeotia.

In B.C. 445, when the five years' truce expired, the effects of this disaster became more fully manifest. The first was the revolt of Euboea; and when Pericles had crossed over to reduce the island to subjection, he received tidings of a revolution at Megara, where the adverse party had put the greater part of the Athenian garrison to the sword. At the same time he learned that a Peloponnesian army was on its march to Attica; he accordingly returned with the utmost speed to defend Athens. The Peloponnesians soon afterwards entered the country and ravaged the plains on the western frontier. The Spartans were commanded by their young king, Pleistoanax, who was guided by the counsels of Cleandridas. Pericles is said to have prevailed upon the latter by bribes to induce the king to withdraw with his army. On their return home both the king and his adviser were accused of having sold the interests of their country, and both escaped by going into exile. As soon as Pericles saw himself freed from this enemy, he returned, with fifty galleys and an army of 5000 heavy-armed men, to quell the revolt of Euboea. He speedily overpowered all resistance, and many of the wealthy landowners were driven from their estates to make room for Attic colonists of the poorer classes.

Notwithstanding this success, the people of Athens were disposed to make peace; and the Spartans, having been betrayed by their own commanders, were not eager for a fresh expedition; but seeing the state of public feeling at Athens, they exacted conditions which in other circumstances would have been rejected with scorn. They required the complete deliverance of Peloponnesus from Athenian influence. Athens accordingly had to give up Troezen, the ports of Pegae and Nisaea, and its connection with Achaia; on these terms a truce for thirty years was concluded in B.C. 445, between Athens and Sparta, and the confederacies over which each presided. Phocis also seems to have been lost by the Athenians, and the custody of the Delphic temple to have been restored to the Delphians. Pericles may not have considered these concessions so important as they appeared to others, who did not understand the real foundation of the greatness of Athens; for she was still the absolute mistress of the sea, and her maritime empire remained untouched. The majority of the people of Athens appear to have been convinced that their real strength lay in their navy; and backed by this feeling, Pericles bore down all opposition on the part of the aristocracy, which, after Cimon's death, was headed by Thucydides, the son of Melesias, who was sent into exile by ostracism in B.C. 444. This event completely broke the aristocratic faction, and the sway of Pericles in the Athenian councils became more absolute than ever, and lasted with scarcely any interruption to the end of his life.

West Front of the Parthenon restored.

Bust of Pericles.
(From the Vatican Museum.)

CHAPTER XVII.

FROM THE COMMENCEMENT OF THE THIRTY YEARS' TRUCE TO THE RENEWAL OF HOSTILITIES BETWEEN ATHENS AND CORINTH, WITH A GENERAL VIEW OF THE ADMINISTRATION OF PERICLES.

The thirty years' truce afforded to Athens an interval of repose highly favourable to her prosperity; and during this period Pericles was enabled to carry out his views into action with scarcely a breath of opposition to divert him from his purpose. Throughout his public life, Pericles had mainly two objects in view: first, to extend and strengthen the Athenian empire; and secondly, to raise the confidence and self-esteem of the Athenians themselves to a level with the lofty position which they occupied. Nearly all his measures clearly tended to one or the other of these ends.

By this time considerable changes had taken place in the relation between Athens and her allies. Even in the lifetime of Aristides, a proposal was made, nominally by the Samians, to transfer the treasury of the confederacy from Delos to Athens. Aristides, though he saw the unfairness of the measure, admitted its expediency, and it was soon afterwards adopted. The ruling party at Athens, which had probably induced the Samians to make the proposal, thus gained its end without the appearance of open violence. At a somewhat later time, Cimon deprived all the weaker among the allied states of their means of defence; so that when

Pericles came to the head of affairs, there remained little to be done to convert the confederacy into an empire, over which Athens ruled as a despotic sovereign. It seems to have been he who first raised the annual contributions of the allies from 460 talents to 600, and led the Athenians to exercise a direct authority over the states which had lost their independence, and to interfere with the concerns of their internal administration. A democratic form of government, if not always imposed upon the allies at the time of their subjugation, came, in most cases, to be established as a natural consequence of their subjection to Athens. But this was a trifling grievance when compared with the regulation by which all trials for capital offences, and all cases involving property above a certain low amount, were transferred from the cognisance of the local courts to Athenian tribunals. Great as were the advantages which Athens derived from this innovation, the inconveniences and annoyances caused to the allies must have been far greater, for justice was rendered at once expensive, slow, and uncertain.

The interference of the Athenians in the domestic affairs of the allies became the occasion of a war which threatened to put an end to the thirty years' truce; but the issue of which only consolidated the Athenian empire, and afforded Pericles an opportunity of showing his brilliant qualities as a military commander. A quarrel had arisen between Samos and Miletus, and the latter, on being vanquished, sought the protection of Athens. At the same time a party at Samos was endeavouring, with Athenian assistance, to overthrow the oligarchical government which had till then existed in the island; and this effort was favoured at Athens, Pericles gladly availing himself of the opportunity of reducing the island. As the Samians did not at once comply with the request to submit their dispute to an Athenian tribunal, Pericles was sent out with a squadron of forty galleys to enforce obedience, and to regulate the constitution of the island according to the interests of Athens. On his arrival he established a democratic form of government, and secured it against the aristocratic party by taking one hundred hostages, whom he lodged in Lemnos; and having exacted a contribution of eighty talents, he sailed home, leaving a small garrison in Samos. When Pericles was approaching the island, a number of the aristocratic party had quitted their country, and opened a correspondence with the Persian satrap of Sardis; and after the departure of Pericles, they formed a plan for regaining possession of their country: with an army of mercenaries they sailed across, and having entered into an understanding with their friends at home, they succeeded in overpowering the Athenian garrison, and abolishing the newly established form of government. The hostages were secretly removed from Lemnos, and then the Athenian alliance was openly renounced. The Athenian prisoners were handed over to the satrap, and the revolt was complete. This happened in B.C. 440. The Samians tried to make friends in Greece among the enemies of Athens; the allies of Sparta held a congress, but it appears that Corinth prevailed upon her confederates to abandon the Samians to the vengeance of the incensed Athenians. This was a virtual recognition of the supremacy exercised by Athens over her allies.

These deliberations were probably still going on when Pericles and nine colleagues crossed the sea with a fleet of sixty sail to suppress the insurrection. Some ships were detached from this armament to look out for the Phoenician fleet, which was reported to be on its way to assist the Samians, while another squadron was ordered to fetch reinforcements from Chios and Lesbos; but Pericles, even with the forty galleys to which his fleet was thus reduced, did not shrink from engaging with a Samian force of seventy, and gained a victory. Soon afterwards he received reinforcements, and having landed a body of troops on the island, he drove the enemy into the town, and surrounded it with a triple line of entrenchments. After this, however, the Samians gained some advantages at sea, though they must have been very slight. Pericles with sixty galleys sailed out to meet the Phoenician fleet, whose approach was expected every day. The Phoenicians did not make their appearance, but during the absence of Pericles, the Samians surprised the naval encampment of the Athenians, and gained a great victory over their enemies. This success made them masters of the sea, and enabled them to introduce supplies into their town. They remained in the ascendant for about fourteen days, but on the return of Pericles the state of things was reversed, and the Samians were once more closely besieged. Their recent success, however, had created some uneasiness at Athens, and great reinforcements were sent out to Pericles. The Samians, still undaunted, ventured upon another sea-fight. This was soon decided against them, and compelled them to remain on the defensive; until at length, when the war had lasted for nine months, they were reduced by famine to capitulate. The terms which they obtained may be considered mild; they were obliged to dismantle their fortifications, to deliver up their ships, and to pay the cost of the siege by instalments. Byzantium, which had from the first sided with Samos, though it had taken no active part in the war, was reduced very soon afterwards.

On his return to Athens, Pericles was greeted with extraordinary honours. The whole merit of the success was ascribed to him, and he himself compared his conquest with that of Agamemnon. In the funeral obsequies of those Athenians who had fallen in the Samian war, Pericles delivered the customary oration, and at the end of it, was honoured by the women with a shower of diadems and chaplets. The conquest of Samos at once established and consolidated the sovereignty of Athens over her allies: it had been recognised by Chios and Lesbos, which aided in the suppression of the Samian revolt, as well as by Sparta and her allies. The term alliance had now become a mere name, for the allies were in reality the subjects of Athens; and the last remnant of an appearance of independence on their part was effaced by the transfer of the common treasure of the confederacy from Delos to Athens. No account was henceforth rendered to the members of the league of the manner in which the treasure contributed by them was spent, and a great portion of it was generally expended for purposes which benefited none but the Athenians. Every Athenian, therefore, looked upon himself with pride, as one of a people which ruled over a great empire with absolute sway; and upon Athens, not merely as the capital of Attica, but as the metropolis of extensive dominions. This was the object which Pericles had always aimed at; and that class of his measures which provided numerous individuals with the means of subsistence tended to the same end. This was done by the establishment of colonies in places where the new settlers might best promote the interests of Athens: thus 2000 Athenians settled at Oreos, in the north of Euboea, and 500 in Naxos; others formed colonies in Andros, in the Chersonesus, and on the Strymon in Thrace, where they founded the city of Amphipolis, though, owing to the perilous situation of the place, the Athenians themselves never formed a considerable part of its population.

During an expedition of Pericles into the Euxine for the purpose of displaying the power of Athens, and strengthening her influence, he found an opportunity of taking possession of Sinope; and it seems to have been about the same period that Amisos admitted so many Athenians among its citizens that in after-times the whole population was considered as an Attic race.* In the west, the colony of Thurium, or Thurii, was established in B.C. 443, near the site of Sybaris. Among the settlers who joined the Athenian colonists in this settlement were the historian Herodotus and the orator Lysias, for the Athenians invited foreigners from all parts of Greece to share in the risks and advantages of the expedition. The descendants of the ancient Sybarites, who had sent for the Athenians, formed a considerable portion of the population of the

* Appian, *Bell. Mithrid.* 8, 83.

new town, and claimed particular privileges for themselves. This roused the indignation of the other settlers, and led to furious hostilities, in which the ill-fated Sybarites were completely exterminated. Other adventurers from Greece then joined the Thurians on terms of perfect equality, and the new state seems to have framed its constitution upon the model of that of Athens.

For the purpose of raising the value of the Athenian franchise in public estimation, Pericles, about B.C. 444, carried a law enacting that the rights of citizenship should be confined to those persons both whose parents were Athenians. One result of this was, that soon afterwards, when the Libyan prince Psammetichus sent a present of corn to be distributed among the Athenian people, nearly 5000 persons, who had till then acted as citizens, were excluded from a share in the gift, on the plea that they were aliens; and, it is said, suffered the penalty appointed by law for those who usurped the privileges of citizens, being sold as slaves. Those who were found to be really entitled to share in the gift amounted to very little more than 14,000. But small as this number was, and though it was still more reduced by the multitudes that went out as colonists, still Pericles was obliged to make it one of his leading objects to provide for the subsistence of those who were left, and the large expenditure which he directed was devoted mainly to this purpose. Thus a squadron of sixty galleys was sent out every year, and was kept at sea eight months, partly indeed to keep the crews in training, but at the same time with a distinct view to benefiting a large body of citizens by the pay which probably supported them during the remainder of the year. But still more ample employment was provided for the poorer class by the great architectural works which were undertaken, by the advice of Pericles, for the defence and embellishment of the city, and which have rendered his accession to power an epoch no less important in the history of the arts than in that of Attica itself.

In order to secure the communication between Athens and Piraeus, even in case either of the two long walls built by Cimon should be surprised by an enemy, Pericles constructed a third, within the two first, which ran parallel and near to that which joined the city with Piraeus. The temples at Athens and Eleusis, which still bore marks of the ravages caused by the Persians, were restored, and new ones were erected on a scale of magnificence corresponding to the increased wealth and power of the state. The summit of the acropolis was covered with sacred buildings and monuments; among which the Parthenon, dedicated to the tutelary divinity of Athens, rose supreme in majesty and beauty. The Propylaea, an ornamental fortification on the western side, formed a most splendid approach to the temple. A theatre, capable of containing a large portion of the population of Athens, had been begun before the time of Pericles, and he added one designed for the performance of music, thence called the Odeum. In the planning and adorning of these edifices, some of the greatest architects and sculptors Greece ever produced, such as the unrivalled Phidias, found ample exercise for their genius and talents; while multitudes of workmen of an inferior order were employed in a long train of subordinate arts. The colossal image of Athene in the Parthenon was formed of ivory and gold; and the same precious materials were profusely used in the decoration of the sculptures which adorned the exterior of the temple. The groups in the pediments, the work of Phidias, excite, even in their mutilated remains, the admiration of all lovers of the arts. While these works gave employment at home to numerous craftsmen of every description, a great number of persons were actively engaged in procuring from abroad the materials which were required. The rapidity with which the new buildings were completed was no less marvellous than the perfection of art which they exhibited; the Propylaea, the most costly and difficult of all, was finished in five years. During the whole period of this extraordinary activity, there must have been a comparative scarcity of hands at Athens.

But while Pericles thus increased the strength and splendour of the city, he also spent a considerable portion of the public revenue on the spectacles and amusements which ultimately became the all-engrossing objects of Athenian life. He did not, indeed, introduce that passion for amusements, but he increased their number, heightened their attractions, and made them accessible to all the citizens; whereas, until then, they had been reserved for the more affluent. Ever since Athens had had a standing theatre, a small sum had been paid for admission; and Pericles now carried a law which enabled the poorer citizens to receive the amount from the treasury, and thus to enjoy what they had previously been debarred from, or had had to purchase by an inconvenient sacrifice. This measure, though harmless in itself, opened the way for a profuse distribution of money under the pretext of enabling the poor to participate in various festivals, and led to the establishment of a fund *, which diminished the resources of the commonwealth applicable to the public service.

Another innovation of a similar nature seems likewise to have been followed by a train of pernicious consequences, which Pericles himself could not have anticipated: he introduced the practice of

* The name of this fund was τὸ θεωρικόν.

paying the jurors for their attendance in the courts of justice.* This again was in itself no more than fair and equitable; but afterwards, the original pay, which was extremely moderate, was tripled, and became one of the heaviest items of the public expenditure. Another regulation, which is sometimes, though erroneously, attributed to Pericles, was the payment for attendance in the popular assembly †; a regulation which became more and more pernicious as the burden which it laid upon the state was more sensibly felt. In judging of these measures it must not, however, be forgotten that Pericles did not, like a tyrant, bribe the people by largesses; but that the money given to them was, in reality, their own property; that Pericles not only guided, but also followed, the popular inclination; and that, in general, his taste coincided with that of the Athenians. It must be confessed, at all events, that the splendour and magnificence of the age of Pericles was not the work of one mind or genius, but of the Athenian people; and it is this fact which places the age of Pericles far above all similar periods in the history of the world. The public buildings and unrivalled works of art, with which Athens was then adorned, on the one hand tended continually to refine that matchless purity of taste by which the Athenians were long distinguished, and, on the other, exalted and endeared the state in the eyes of its citizens. They were, so to speak, the trophies of the great victories which had been gained over the barbarians, and the fruits of Athenian patience and fortitude. We may, indeed, regret that the treasures spent upon those temples and monuments were not always obtained by fair means, but were in a great measure procured by wrongs and robberies committed upon the subjects of Athens. In this respect, however, the Athenians, after all, were not worse than any other nation, ancient or modern, that has borne sway over others; and whatever wrong was done, did not fail to bring its own punishment; for while it raised the pride and confidence of the ruling city, it called forth in an equal degree the spirit of discontent and resistance among the allies; and both combined hurried on the Athenians to their ruin.

Until the time of the Persian war, Athens had contributed less to the intellectual progress of Greece than many other cities, both in Greece itself—such as Argos, Corinth, Sicyon, Aegina—and in the eastern and western colonies; but her peaceful glories quickly followed and outshone those of her military victories and conquests. In the period between the Persian and Peloponnesian

* This pay was called *μισθὸς δικαστικός*, or *τὸ δικαστικόν*.

† The *μισθὸς ἐκκλησιαστικός*.

wars, both literature and the fine arts tended towards Athens as their most favoured seat; for there genius and talent were encouraged by an ample field of exertion, by public sympathy and applause, as well as by the prospect of other rewards. Accordingly it was at Athens that architecture and sculpture reached the highest degree of perfection, and that Greek poetry was enriched with a new kind of composition, the drama, which united the leading features of every species previously known, and constituted the highest class of poetry. The drama grew out of one of the forms of lyric poetry which had been successfully cultivated before, and which, for the greater part of a century, continued to predominate in the drama. Simonides of Ceos, Bacchylides, and Pindar, were lyric poets, whom the judgment of every succeeding age has considered superior to all others. Of the former two, only fragments have come down to us; but the extant works of Pindar display a grandeur of thought and conception which is beyond dispute, as it is beyond comparison. At the time of his death, in B.C. 438, the Attic drama had just attained its full maturity; and lyric poetry never again rose to the height which it had reached through his genius.

The drama was that branch of poetical literature which peculiarly signalised the age of Pericles. The steps by which it was brought to the form which it exhibits in the earliest remains are involved in great obscurity. Phrynichus, the immediate predecessor of Aeschylus, is mentioned very favourably by the ancients themselves; and the effects which his works are reported to have produced, show that he must have been a poet of great power. Aeschylus looked upon him as a worthy rival, and was in part stimulated by his example to unfold the capabilities of his art by a variety of new inventions. These, however, were so important as to entitle their author to be considered as the father of Attic tragedy. He introduced the dialogue, the story of each drama having previously been told in a series of monologues. This innovation altered the whole character of the drama, inasmuch as the purely dramatic part was raised from a subordinate to the principal rank, while the lyric or choral part became subsidiary. With Aeschylus also arose the usage of exhibiting what was called a trilogy; that is, three tragedies, distinct indeed, but in reality constituting one great drama, so that they were like so many acts of the same piece. According to a long-established custom, he himself bore a part in the representation of his own plays, and not only superintended the evolutions of his choruses, but invented several minute additions to the theatrical wardrobe. Agatharchus is said to have painted for him the first scene which had ever been made according to the rules of linear perspective. Out of seventy tragedies which were ascribed to him, only seven have been preserved; among which there is one complete trilogy, the Oresteia; but they are sufficient to give us an idea of the sublimity and originality of his genius.

His younger contemporary, Sophocles, surpassed Aeschylus in the general harmony of his conceptions, in the equable diffusion of grace and vigour throughout every part, and in the unlimited command over all the power and all the charm of expression which the Greek language supplied; though it cannot be denied that in some respects Sophocles was a genius of a lower order. He gained the highest popularity at Athens, and succeeded in supplanting his elder rival in the estimation of the public. The Athenians were so delighted with his "Antigone," that they appointed him one of the ten generals who accompanied Pericles in the war against Samos, B.C. 440; a reward quite in accordance with the feelings of the Athenians, however strange and unsuitable it may appear to us. He died full of years and glory, but not before he had himself experienced the mutability of the public taste in the growing preference given to Euripides, who died a year sooner, but, in the character of his poetry, belongs entirely to the latest period of the life of Sophocles.

The Attic drama was not merely an entertainment for the idle, or a study of the lovers of literature and art, but was applied to moral, religious, and sometimes even political purposes. Allusions to living persons and occurrences of the day were by no means rare, and were easily introduced; but such things were generally intended more to display the poet's ingenuity than to produce any practical effect on his audience, or to influence the management of public affairs. The sphere of comedy, on the other hand, lay within the walks of daily life, and its main business was with the immediate present; for there was not a class of persons or things, which could engage public attention, that might not be brought within the range of its representations. Another kind of comic drama was called the satiric, and was commonly performed as a farce after a tragedy; in this the chorus consisted of satyrs. It was totally distinct from comedy. All these theatrical performances were connected with the celebration of the festivals of Dionysus, and under that god's protection the comic poets enjoyed unbounded freedom and license; no objects nor persons, not even the gods themselves, were exempt from their unsparing ridicule. With such unlimited power, the comic poets assailed every kind of vice and folly, provided it was sufficiently notorious to render their ridicule intelligible. Of the early Attic comedy we possess no specimens: Aristophanes, the only comic poet of whom complete works have come down to us, belongs to a later period than that of which we are now treating; but there can be no doubt that his predecessors were as unsparing in their assaults, and as unbridled in their censure and animadversion, as Aristophanes himself. The influence which this severe censorship exercised upon public men and measures, however, seems to have been very slight; the exhibition was designed chiefly for amusement, and the time and place of the performance of comedy were not adapted for serious thoughts. The very boldness and impunity of the poets, in fact, rendered them harmless. In B.C. 440, a law was passed to restrain the license of the comic poets, but it did not remain in force more than two or three years, after which it was entirely repealed, and no similar attempt seems to have been made as long as Athens preserved her political independence.

Pericles, in his public life, presented little that could give scope to attacks from the comic poets, except his almost unlimited power, by allusion to which they frequently endeavoured to alarm the people; but his private life offered some vulnerable points, by exposing which his enemies were able to strike more dangerous blows at him, and for a time must have embittered his domestic happiness. His superintendence of the execution of public works, and the large sums of money which for that purpose passed through his hands, could not fail to excite suspicion, and to give a handle for calumny. The first blow was not aimed directly at himself, but was intended to wound him through his friend Phidias, who was accused of having embezzled a part of the gold which he had received from the treasury to use in the colossal statue of Athene already mentioned. This charge, however, fell to the ground, through a contrivance which Pericles had suggested in the composition of the statue, for the golden ornaments had been fixed in such a manner that they could be taken off without doing it any injury. Accordingly, when Pericles challenged the accusers to verify their charge, they shrank from the application of the decisive test. This defeat, however, did not deter them from making another and more successful attempt; they accused Phidias of having carved his own portrait and that of Pericles on the shield of the goddess, which was viewed as an arrogant intrusion among the objects of worship. Phidias was thrown into prison, and died there; and the informer was rewarded with certain immunities and placed under the protection of the ten generals.

This success emboldened the enemies of Pericles to proceed; for they must have seen that, after all, it was not difficult to inspire the people with distrust and jealousy of its powerful leader; and they now began their manoeuvres against Aspasia, in whose safety

Pericles felt as much concern as in his own. She had long attracted public attention, no less by her personal beauty than by her cultivation of the intellectual powers and female graces, in which probably no Athenian woman could compete with her. Her influence over Pericles furnished the comic poets with an inexhaustible fund of ridicule, and his enemies with a ground for serious charges. Another handle was afforded to his enemies by the circumstance that the most independent thinkers of the age, such men as Anaxagoras, Zeno, Protagoras, were ever welcome guests in his house. Their doctrines were certainly very far removed from the vulgar superstitions of the multitude, and this fact gave a plausible pretext for describing the circle in which they moved as a school of impiety. Out of these materials a criminal prosecution was instituted by the poet Hermippus against Aspasia. At the same time a law was passed against persons denying the existence of the gods, which was aimed immediately at Anaxagoras, and indirectly at Pericles. The latter was likewise called upon to give in his accounts to the Prytanes, in order that they might be submitted to a trial; for it was hoped that they would not be able to pass a rigorous scrutiny, and that he would be found guilty of embezzlement, or some other more general offence in the administration of the public funds. But all these machinations failed, at least of reaching their main object. The

Bust of Aspasia.
(From the Vatican Museum.)

issue of those against Anaxagoras is uncertain; according to some he was acquitted; while others state that, by the advice of Pericles, he quitted Athens to escape condemnation. The cause of Aspasia was pleaded by Pericles himself, who is said to have had recourse even to tears and entreaties; and this danger also was averted. Such a proof of his eloquence, and, perhaps still more, of his personal influence, induced his enemies to drop their proceedings against himself, at least for the present, and to wait for a fitter opportunity. After these storms, Pericles recovered his former high and firm position, which to the end of his life was never again endangered, except by one transient gust of popular displeasure. Ancient historians state that he so much dreaded the possibility of being obliged to account for the public money he had expended, that, in order to avert the danger, he kindled the war which put an end to the thirty years' truce; but there are no grounds for this charge beyond the mere assertions of his enemies, which have never been established by proof, and are contradicted most emphatically by Thucydides, the great contemporary historian.

Two Views of the Aspis, or large circular Greek Shield.
(From Vase Paintings.)

Restoration of the West Front of Temple of Athene, at Aegina.

CHAPTER XVIII.

CAUSES AND OCCASIONS OF THE PELOPONNESIAN WAR.

THE peace which terminated the Aeginetan war* had shaken the ascendancy of Athens on the continent of Greece; but the few years of peace down to the outbreak of the Peloponnesian war produced ample compensation by the brilliant administration and the far-reaching policy of Pericles. The completion of the fortifications of Piraeus, the establishment of Thurii in southern Italy, and of Amphipolis in Thrace, the successful war of Pericles against Samos, — all these events tended to increase the long-cherished jealousy of Sparta and the smaller Grecian states; and the hatred and alarm excited by the formidable power of Athens became more and more general. We will not here inquire into the internal causes of the discord which pervades the whole history of the Greek states, and which rendered the outbreak of that unfortunate war unavoidable, but shall at once proceed to consider its immediate forerunners and its beginnings. Thucydides, the most authentic, and at the same time the most intelligent, judge of Greek history, mentions two causes, the Corinthian war, and the revolt of the city of Potidaea.

Epidamnus (the modern Durazzo), a colony founded on the

* Thucydides (i. 87.) calls it the Euboean war.

coast of Illyricum by the Corcyraeans in conjunction with Corinthian and other Doric settlers, had in a short time attained considerable prosperity, but had afterwards been hard pressed and weakened by the Illyrian Taulantians, its eastern neighbours; and shortly before the outbreak of the Peloponnesian war, it was distracted by civil discord. A quarrel between the popular party and the wealthy aristocracy (Dorians) ended in the victory of the former and the expulsion of the latter, who allied themselves with the neighbouring barbarians, and endeavoured to effect their return by force of arms. They ravaged the territory of Epidamnus, and pressed the town so closely, that the Epidamnians applied to Corcyra, their metropolis, to act as mediators between themselves and their exiled fellow-citizens, and to assist them in bringing the war with the barbarians to a close. But the Corcyraeans not listening to this request, the Epidamnians in their distress consulted the oracle of Delphi. The god advised them to surrender their town to the Corinthians, and to choose Corinthians for their commanders. Corinth, the metropolis of Corcyra, which, according to the established custom of the Greeks, had taken part in the foundation of Epidamnus, now promised its assistance the more readily, as an opportunity was thus offered for punishing and curbing Corcyra, which had often disregarded, or wholly neglected, its duties as a colony towards the parent city, and had attained a prosperity and naval power which seemed to be dangerous to Corinth itself. At first, Corinth sent settlers and a garrison consisting of Corinthians, Ambracians, and Leucadians, who, from fear of the Corcyraean fleet, went overland through the territory of Apollonia, which was likewise a Corinthian colony. As soon as the Corcyraeans were informed of this, they appeared with a fleet before Epidamnus, demanding the restoration of the exiles, and the dismissal of the Corinthian garrison. Compliance being refused, the Corcyraeans, joined by the exiles and some Illyrians, laid siege to the town, blockading it both by land and by sea.

The Corinthians, on hearing of these occurrences, began in good earnest to make preparations to relieve their citizens and friends. At their request, new settlers repaired to Epidamnus; many also advanced money and ships, and a considerable fleet was thus raised, consisting, among others, of ships from Megara, from some of the maritime towns of Argolis, from Ambracia, Leucadia, and Cephallenia. Meantime, in order to prevent the fleet from setting sail, the Corcyraeans sent envoys, accompanied by others from Sicyon and Lacedaemon, to Corinth, to propose that the Corinthians should either withdraw their people from Epidamnus, or, if they pretended to any right in the colony, should refer their claims to the decision of some neutral state or of the Delphic oracle. The

Corinthians offered to consent to this proposal, on condition that the Corcyraeans should in the mean time raise the siege. But no decision was come to, and the peaceful solution of the question became impossible; the Corinthian fleet set sail, and a herald was sent out to declare war against Corcyra. The Corcyraeans made one more attempt to deter the Corinthians from waging war against them, but to no purpose. They, too, had in the mean time got ready a fleet of eighty ships, while that of Corinth consisted of only seventy-five. A battle was fought near the promontory of Actium, at the mouth of the Ambracian gulf, in which the Corcyraeans gained a complete victory; fifteen Corinthian ships were destroyed, and the remainder of the fleet hastily returned home. On the same day, Epidamnus surrendered to the besiegers, who, acting mercifully towards the Corinthians alone, kept them in captivity, while they sold all the other inhabitants of the town as slaves, and put to death all the Greeks who had been taken prisoners in the battle, except the Corinthians. This affair took place in B.C. 434.

After this victory the Corcyraeans were for a time in undisputed possession of the sea. They immediately began taking vengeance upon the Corinthian allies, so that Corinth thought it necessary to send a fleet and an army to Actium, and to the coasts of the country of the Thesprotians, for their protection. The Corinthians were at the same time making every effort to provide themselves with new ships for the continuation of the war, and to procure allies, troops, and money. Corcyra, on the other hand, resorted for assistance to Athens. Its envoys there met others who had been sent from Corinth for the purpose of preventing an alliance between Athens and Corcyra, the two most powerful maritime states of Greece. "You must not," said the Corinthian envoy, "interfere in our disputes with our colonies, which have neglected their duties and are ungrateful. It is unlawful for you to enter into an alliance with Corcyra, because you are bound by treaty to Corinth, and it is not in the spirit of that treaty to afford assistance to the states not comprised in it, against those who are, and to become our enemies instead of remaining our friends. Corinth has not deserved this of you; remember our neutrality during the Samian war, and allow us now to reduce to obedience and chastise our rebellious allies in the same manner as we allowed you to act towards yours, preventing even the other Peloponnesians from interfering in your private disputes with the states subject to you."

"The fact that we have been a party neither to that treaty of peace nor to any other," replied the representative of Corcyra, "is the very reason why you should not refuse us your assistance. We desire to be independent, and not to be always subject to a state, which, though it is the founder of our own city, has already been outstripped by us in maritime power. The state which, next to your own, is the most powerful at sea, offers you its alliance: accept it, and consider how conveniently Corcyra is situated for those who sail to Italy or Sicily, how safely we can guide you, and how effectually we can prevent your enemies from opposing your enterprises in the western seas. Examine well the importance of an alliance between the two most powerful maritime states in Greece."

Such were the arguments advanced by the envoys. The Athenians held two assemblies, the first of which was favourably disposed towards the Corinthians; but in the second, the Athenians, though they did not decree war against Corinth, yet concluded a defensive alliance with Corcyra for the mutual protection of their territories, in case either of them should be attacked. The enticing prospect of gaining a footing in distant Sicily, and of extending their maritime dominion, and at the same time the fear lest Corcyra should form alliances with other states, were the chief reasons which led them to take this step, which was in reality a declaration that they did not consider themselves bound by the treaty, for the appearance of neutrality was very soon gone. But, independently of the hopes founded upon an alliance with Corcyra, the war-party at Athens, whose restlessness and insatiable ambition had kept the state almost uninterruptedly engaged in military undertakings ever since the Persian wars, was now anxious to provoke a war the consequences of which could not be foreseen, and which the peaceable portion of the people dreaded as much as, after many years of suffering and distress, it detested it.

In accordance with the defensive alliance thus concluded, the Athenians sent ten galleys to Corcyra, with orders not to engage in any action unless the territory of Corcyra should be attacked. The Corinthians, on the other hand, sailed out with a fleet of 150 ships, including those of their above-mentioned allies, and anchored at Cheimerium, a port and promontory on the Thesprotian coast. The Corcyraean fleet of 110 ships took its station near Sybota, a group of islands between the mainland and the southern point of Corcyra. Their land army and 1000 Zacynthians were encamped on the promontory of Leucimne; and some barbarian forces, allied with the Corinthians, were stationed on the opposite coast of the mainland. Having completed their preparations, the Corinthians sailed by night from Cheimerium towards the north, and at daybreak perceived the Corcyraean fleet approaching. The ships were drawn up in battle-array, and a naval engagement ensued, which, in regard to the number of ships engaged in it, was the greatest in which Greeks had ever been arrayed against Greeks. The ships approached one another very closely, and the heavy-armed troops fought as though it had been a land-fight. The left wing of the Corcyraeans put the right wing of the Corinthians to flight, and pursuing it with twenty ships as far as the coast of the mainland, disembarked, and plundered and burnt the enemy's tents. In the mean time the left wing of the Corinthians was victorious, and the Athenians, who had hitherto taken no part in the contest, were now prevailed upon by the flight of their allies to abandon their neutrality. The Corinthians pursued their enemies as far as the coast, and having secured their wrecks and the slain, were preparing for a fresh attack upon the Corcyraean ships, which had reassembled, when suddenly they observed twenty Athenian ships approaching. These the Athenians had sent as a reinforcement to join the ten which had been previously despatched. The Corinthians, suspecting that there were more galleys than the twenty which they saw, immediately rowed back. The cause of this sudden retreat did not become apparent to the Corcyraeans till afterwards, and as the night was setting in they also withdrew to Leucimne, whither the Athenian ships likewise repaired. On the following morning the thirty Athenian galleys, united with those of the Corcyraeans, sailed to Sybota, to challenge the fleet stationed there to a fresh engagement. The Corinthians, however, felt too weak to accept the challenge; and although they were drawn up in battle-array, yet, after having communicated with the Athenians through a herald and charged them with having violated the peace, they withdrew, and after erecting a trophy on the coast, sailed homewards. On their way, they took Anactorium, a town belonging to them in common with the Corcyraeans, and established Corinthian settlers in it. Eight hundred of the Corcyraean prisoners, who were slaves, were sold; while 250 of the most distinguished and wealthy were kept as captives and treated with great consideration, in the hope that they might use their influence at Corcyra to form a party favourable to Corinth. Although the Corcyraeans had lost 70 ships, and more than 1000 men taken prisoners, yet they likewise erected a trophy, on the ground that they had destroyed 30 of the enemy's ships, and had recovered their wrecks and slain, and that the Corinthians had retreated before the Athenians, and declined a battle on the following day.

This battle, which was fought in B.C. 432, is described by Thucydides as the first occasion of the war between Corinth and Athens. Other circumstances, which gave rise to the general war, and were at the same time a continuation of the hostilities against Corinth, occurred in the peninsula of Chalcidice, immediately after the battle of Sybota. The Athenians were involved in a war with Perdiccas, king of Macedonia, the son of Alexander who during the Persian wars had acted the part of a friend towards Greece. They were supported by the king's brother Philip. Perdiccas negotiated with the Lacedaemonians, allied himself with the Corinthians, and endeavoured in every possible way to induce the towns of Chalcidice and Thrace, which were tributary to, and allied with Athens, to revolt. The Athenians, dreading the revenge of the Corinthians, who were now their avowed enemies, tried to get the start of them, and required the Potidaeans, a Corinthian colony in Pallene, tributary to Athens, to pull down their southern fortifications, to give hostages, to dismiss the Corinthian magistrates, and to receive no more in future. At the same time they instructed the fleet of thirty ships which was then setting out against Macedonia, under the command of Archestratus, to enforce the execution of these orders, the revocation of which the Potidaeans vainly sought to obtain by sending ambassadors to Athens. The Spartans, however, having promised that, if Potidaea should be attacked, a Peloponnesian army would march into Attica, the Potidaeans were emboldened openly to assert their independence before the arrival of the Athenian fleet, in B.C. 432, and their example was followed by many of the Chalcidian and Bottiaean towns. The Chalcidians on the coast were persuaded by Perdiccas to demolish their towns, to transfer their habitation to Olynthus, and there to concentrate their strength so long as the war should last. Meanwhile the Athenian fleet arrived; but finding that the towns had already revolted, and seeing that its force was too small to attempt the reduction of the insurgents, it proceeded to the coast of Macedonia and there commenced hostilities against Perdiccas.

To support Potidaea, the Corinthians sent 1000 men under the command of Aristeus, the son of Adeimantus; and when the Athenians heard of this, they despatched a second fleet of 40 galleys and 2000 heavy-armed men under the command of Callias. They first sailed up the Thermaean Gulf, and found their countrymen engaged in the siege of Pydna; but both armies soon concluded a treaty with Perdiccas, in order to combine their operations against Aristeus. Reinforced by many allies, they now proceeded by land towards Potidaea. Aristeus was waiting for them on the isthmus near Olynthus, and Perdiccas, who had forgotten his treaty with the Athenians directly they had turned their backs, commanded the cavalry. The plan of Aristeus was to place the Athenians between two fires, and to attack them in the rear as soon as they should have commenced the engagement with him. But in order to prevent a sally being made from Olynthus, Callias sent a detachment thither, and with his remaining forces attacked Aristeus. The wing of the army which the latter commanded in person was victorious over the division opposed to it, which he pursued to a great distance; but the rest of his forces were completely routed by the Athenians, and the Peloponnesians and Potidaeans fled into the town. When Aristeus returned from the pursuit and found his army defeated, he thought it best to force his way into Potidaea, and in this he succeeded. In this battle, fought B.C. 432, the Athenians lost 150 men and their general Callias, while the enemy had about 300 slain.

After this victory the Athenians commenced the circumvallation of Potidaea, by carrying a wall across the isthmus on the side of Olynthus; on the southern side, towards Pallene, no similar work was undertaken, until a fresh reinforcement of 1600 heavy-armed men arrived from Athens, under the command of Phormio, who completed the blockade by land and by sea.

The Corinthians now no longer hesitated, seeing that there was little hope of delivering their colony and the Peloponnesians blockaded in it. In their desire to see matters decided, they were supported by the Spartans, who summoned a meeting of the confederates to Sparta, to which all states which thought themselves wronged by the Athenians were invited to send deputies. Most of these deputies brought forward their complaints openly, but some, like the Aeginetans, acted in an underhand way, employing agents who made insinuations rather than straightforward charges. The speeches of all the deputies breathed hatred against Athens and her ambitious proceedings. The Megarians also bitterly complained of their powerful neighbour, saying that their commerce was paralysed, and that Athens, by a formal enactment, had blocked up their ports and markets.*

The Corinthians, being the party most grievously offended, spoke last, and their envoy's words were earnest and impressive. Thucydides puts into the mouth of the Corinthian a masterly description and comparison of the characters of the Spartans and Athenians. The orator strove to stir up the Lacedaemonians to energetic action and incessant watchfulness against a people whose natural disposition was neither to keep peace itself, nor to allow others to enjoy it; which was never reduced to despair by any loss it might sustain, nor satisfied with what it actually possessed, but with restless activity kept hurrying on to its future destinies.

It happened that Athenian envoys, who had been sent on other business, were at this time at Sparta. They obtained permission to represent the interests of Athens in the assembly, where the

* The law here alluded to was passed in B.C. 432, on the proposal of Pericles. (Thucyd. i. 67, 139.; Plut. *Pericl.* 30.)

speaker set forth what Athens had done for the good of all Greece, explained the natural development of the confederacy and supremacy of Athens, and with eloquent arguments urged the necessity of compelling the submission of her refractory subjects and allies; in conclusion, he seriously cautioned Sparta against the passionate demands and instigations of her allies, as well as against any rash breach of the peace.

The assembly then deliberated: most voices were for the instant declaration of war. But Archidamus, king of Sparta, an intelligent and moderate man, dissuaded his countrymen from immediately venturing upon war. As a true Spartan, he advised them to be slow and cautious, and to try to come to an understanding with Athens by means of negotiations; but at the same time he declared that it was due to the position and honour of Sparta to prepare for the eventuality of a war. This moderate counsel was neutralised by the brief but energetic call of the ephor Sthenelaidas to take immediate vengeance upon Athens. At the conclusion of his address, he put the question to the vote*; and war was decreed, B. C. 432. The resolution was at once communicated to the envoys of the confederates, and the assembly broke up.

But although the war had been decreed by the Lacedaemonians, who almost against their own will were driven to take this step in consequence of the power of Athens becoming daily more threatening, yet their preparations were made in the usual cautious way. The Delphic oracle, when consulted, approved of the war, provided that it was carried on with vigour, and promised the aid of the god. A second congress of the allies was then held, and the Spartans again put the question of war and peace to the vote. The majority again declared for war. But it took a long time to complete the preparations both at Sparta and in the other Peloponnesian towns, and a whole year passed away before they were ready for the first invasion of Attica.

Even then the Spartans were anxious to justify the war in the eyes of Athens and of Greece, and for this purpose they despatched envoys to Athens to make demands with which it was extremely difficult, if not impossible, for the Athenians to comply. Thus they demanded atonement for the crime of Cylon†, ostensibly to propitiate the goddess Athene, but in reality to obtain the banishment of Pericles, who by his mother's side was connected with the accursed family of the Alcmaeonids. The Athenians retorted by requiring the Spartans to expiate the pollution with which they had profaned the sanctuary of Taenarus, by dragging from it some

* The Spartans voted βοῇ, not ψήφῳ. (Thucyd. I. 87.)
† Compare above, p. 11

Helots who had taken refuge there, and then putting them to death. The Athenians further demanded that the Spartans should atone for the murder of Pausanias, committed in the temple of Athene Chalcioecus.*

In this manner, things long past and forgotten were brought forward by both parties, in order that they might have on their side, at all events, the appearance of justice and necessity in breaking the thirty years' peace, and recommencing hostilities. The more substantial demands of the Spartans, however, were these: that the Athenians should raise the siege of Potidaea; declare Aegina independent; and abolish the decree against Megara, a point on which they laid particular stress. The last embassy that came from Sparta finally declared, that the Spartans wished for peace, and that it would not be broken if Athens would grant independence to the other Greeks. The Athenians held an assembly for the purpose of giving a final answer. The orators were of different opinions, and no decision was come to, until at length Pericles, in a speech of great persuasive power, showed that the war was unavoidable, and pointed out the manifold advantages of the Athenian navy as contrasted with the poor land forces of Sparta. He accordingly prevailed upon the assembly to declare to the Spartan envoys, that the Athenians were still willing to refer their differences to an impartial judgment, but would hold themselves in readiness to repel any attack. The envoys returned home, and no further negotiations were attempted.

Many of his contemporaries, who ought to have known better, regarded Pericles as the sole, or at least as the main, cause of the war; and the contemptible and impure motives attributed to him by Ephorus (in Diodorus), Plutarch, and others, were certainly not talked of by the idle and gossiping people alone, but were readily assumed by the more enlightened enemies and detractors of the great statesman. All such scandal, however, is more than refuted by the silence of Thucydides, who relates the events of the period critically and with undoubted impartiality, nowhere sparing or concealing the weakness and faults of his fellow-citizens. In his work we find none of the fanciful stories so scandalous anecdotes with which the comic writers and moralising historians regaled their readers.

Even before the general war commenced, and while the preparations for it were yet going on, the Thebans suddenly began hostilities by an attack upon the neighbouring town of Plataeae. This event occurred in the spring of B. C. 431, the first year of the war, the fifteenth after the peace of Pericles, and about six months after

* See above, p. 223.

the battle of Potidaea.* Plataeae, which was allied with Athens, did not belong to the confederacy of the Boeotian towns, and was always at enmity with Thebes. The Thebans, therefore, gladly accepted the invitation of a party at Plataeae, which hoped with their assistance to gain the ascendancy; and in the dead of night, Plataeae was surprised by a body of 300 Thebans. But instead of breaking into the unprotected houses of the citizens, as their Plataean guides advised, and of thus completing the conquest at once, they halted in the market-place, and endeavoured by negotiations to induce the townspeople to surrender. During the first alarm, the Plataeans, not knowing the number of the invaders, were prevailed upon to enter into a parley with them; but as soon as they discovered the fewness of the enemy, they resolved to attack them. They opened passages through the walls of their houses, and thus, unseen by the Thebans, assembled in considerable numbers. Having barricaded the streets and closed the gates, they fell upon the enemy a little before daybreak. The darkness of the night was in their favour; the Thebans at first made a vigorous defence, but as stones and tiles also were showered upon them from the roofs, they began to disperse through the streets, which were unknown to them, and had just been deluged by a heavy shower of rain. The greater part at length rushed through the gate of a large building, which they believed to be a gate of the city, and were there taken prisoners. When the main body of the Thebans, which was on its way to reinforce the 300, received intelligence of their misfortune, it hastened its march; but the river Asopus, which crossed the road, having been swollen by the recent rain, delayed it so long, that when it arrived the struggle at Plataeae was over.† The Thebans now tried to seize as many of the Plataeans as they could find without the walls, intending to keep them as hostages for their own prisoners. The Plataeans, however, threatened to kill the prisoners unless the Thebans quitted their territory. The latter then withdrew; and the Plataeans, having first removed all their moveable property from the country into the town, put to death all the prisoners, amounting to 180, contrary to a promise they had made to the departing Thebans. The Athenians were unable to prevent this catastrophe, although they had received immediate intelligence of

* We may here observe, that in relating the history of the Peloponnesian war, so far as it is contained in Thucydides, we shall adopt his division of the years of the war into summer and winter. Diodorus reckons according to Olympiads and the years of the Athenian archons. The political year of the Athenians began with the change of the archons, which took place at the new moon after the summer solstice. (Comp. Thucyd. v. 20.)

† The distance between Thebes and Plataeae was 70 stadia, not quite 9 English miles.

the attempt upon Plataeae; for the distance between the two cities was so great, that the messengers arrived too late. All that they could do, therefore, was to provide the allied town with a military force and supplies, and transport to Athens all persons who were unfit for service in a siege.

After this event, the preparations for the war were carried on most vigorously, and the allies of both parties were called upon in good earnest to get their contingents ready. All displayed great activity, and were anxiously waiting for the result; but gloomy apprehensions of an approaching period of misfortune were generally entertained. The sympathies of most of the continental Greeks were enlisted in favour of Sparta, for the Spartans from the beginning declared themselves the champions of the independence of all the Greeks who thought themselves injured in any way by the Athenians. But the fear excited by the approaching contest was so general and so great, that all persons paid more than common attention to prophecies, oracles, and natural phenomena, such as earthquakes and eclipses of the sun and moon, and imagined they heard everywhere the voice of the angry gods.

The allies of Sparta included the whole of Peloponnesus, except Argos, which remained neutral; this was the case at first with Achaia also, but the Achaean Pellene, at the commencement of the war, and subsequently the rest of Achaia, sided with Sparta. Beyond the Isthmus, she was supported by Megara, Phocis, Locris, Boeotia, Ambracia, Leucas, and Anactorium. Ships were furnished by Megara, Sicyon, Pellene, Elis, and Leucas; Boeotia, Phocis, and Locris supplied cavalry, and the rest infantry. The Spartans courted the friendship even of barbarian chiefs, especially of the king of Persia, and also called upon their Doric kinsmen in Sicily and Italy, with whose assistance they hoped to increase their fleet to 500 sail. Their land force could be raised to the number of 60,000 men.

The allies of the Athenians were the Chians, Lesbians, Plataeans, the Messenians of Naupactus, the greater part of Acarnania, the Zacynthians, and the Corcyraeans. The following countries were tributary* to them: Caria with its towns on the sea coast, Doris (contiguous to Caria), Ionia, the Hellespont, the coast of Thrace, all the islands between Peloponnesus and Crete, and the Cyclades with the exception of Melos and Thera. To the forces obtained from these must be added Thessalian horsemen from Larissa, Pharsalus, and other towns. The yearly tribute, according to the statement of Pericles, amounted to 600 talents, while the public treasury contained 6000, independently of the treasures of the

* Ὑποτελεῖς, not ξύμμαχοι.

temples. The fleet consisted of 300 triremes manned by at least 50,000 marines and rowers; the land army amounted to 13,000 heavy-armed, besides 16,000 men who were employed in the defence of the fortifications of the city and harbours, exclusive of the garrisons stationed in various fortified places. Ships were furnished by the Chians, Lesbians, and Corcyraeans; the others paid their contingents in troops and money.

The army of the Peloponnesian confederates having assembled on the Isthmus of Corinth, king Archidamus put himself at its head; but before he began his march he sent Melesippus to Athens to see whether the approach of the enemy had produced any change in the minds of the Athenians; but they had long before determined, by the advice of Pericles, not to enter into any negotiations, nor to listen to any herald. Accordingly Melesippus was escorted back to the frontier without having obtained a hearing. On parting from his conductors he exclaimed, "This day will be the beginning of great evils to Greece."

Present State of the Parthenon.
(Drawn on the spot, by George Scharf, Jun.)

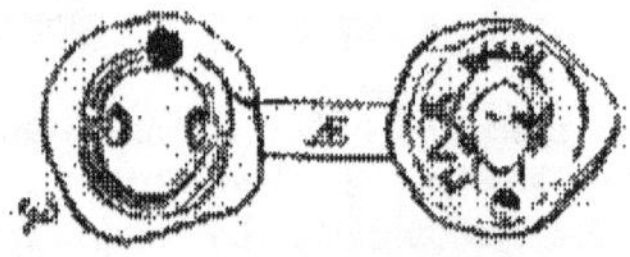

Coins of Plataeae.

CHAPTER XIX.

FROM THE COMMENCEMENT OF THE PELOPONNESIAN WAR TO THE END OF THE THIRD YEAR.

After the return of Melesippus, Archidamus with the united army set forward on his march*; but he advanced slowly, still hoping that the Athenians would avoid coming into conflict with him. Accordingly he did not proceed straight towards Athens, as his army would have wished, but marching through Megaris into the northern districts of Attica, he halted near Oenoë, a frontier fortress, which had been garrisoned. Archidamus laid siege to it, but all his efforts to take it were fruitless. His men began to murmur, and even charged him with partiality and with being bribed; but, in spite of this, he adhered for some time to his plan of action. The Athenians were thus enabled to follow the advice of Pericles to remove with their property from the northern part of Attica to the city. They did so, however, with reluctance; for they had from early times been fond of a country life, and it was only on the most pressing entreaties of Pericles that they made up their minds to abandon their farms, to transport their sheep and beasts of burden to Euboea and the neighbouring islands, and, with their wives, children, and furniture, to protect themselves behind the walls of the city which had scarcely room to receive them all. With the exception of the acropolis and some temples, every place was occupied by the emigrants, many of whom erected habitations for themselves by the sides of the long walls.

At length, finding that his attempts upon Oenoë were useless, Archidamus abandoned the undertaking in the middle of the summer, about eighty days after the attack made upon Plataeae. He turned westward, ravaged Eleusis and the Thriasian plain, and routed the Athenian cavalry. He then proceeded eastward as far as Acharnae, the largest demos of Attica, about seven miles north of Athens, and, having encamped there, made several ra-

* Two thirds of the contingents went with him; the whole army consisted of 60,000 men. Others calculated it at 100,000. (Thucyd. ii. 47.; Plut. *Pericl.* 33.; Schol. on Soph. *Oed. Col.* 697.)

vaging excursions. His object was to draw the Athenians out to a battle in the open field, and for this reason he made no attack upon the city itself. The Athenians, who until then had remained quiet, seeing the Peloponnesian army so near their own city, impatiently demanded to be led out to battle; the 3000 heavy-armed, who formed the contingent of Acharnae, especially burned to take revenge for the devastation of their fields. But Pericles remained immoveable, steadily refusing to risk everything upon the issue of a battle, and heeding neither the clamour of his opponents nor the taunts of the comic poets. He prevented the meeting of the assembly, that the Athenians might not adopt a rash and pernicious resolution, which might compel him against his own will to engage in a decisive struggle. The first object of his care was the safety of the city itself, and the protection of its immediate neighbourhood, by sending out from time to time squadrons of horse. On one occasion, the Thessalian cavalry had a hard fight with the Boeotian horse, but was obliged to retreat with some loss, as a detachment of heavy-armed infantry came to succour the Boeotians.

Archidamus, having waited for a considerable time in the vain hope that the Athenian army would come forth and give battle, at last quitted his encampment, and marched into the north-eastern part of Attica, laying waste the country as he proceeded. He then entered the territory of Oropos, returned home by way of Boeotia, and disbanded his army.

In the mean time an Athenian fleet of 100 galleys, with 1000 men-at-arms and 400 bowmen on board, had set sail to retaliate upon Peloponnesus. They were joined by 50 Corcyraean and some other ships. After ravaging several parts of the coast, they landed at Methone, in Laconia, which was fortified, but had no garrison. There Brasidas achieved his first feat in arms. He happened to be stationed in the neighbourhood, commanding a small body of troops; with only 100 heavy-armed, he cut his way through the besieging army with the loss of a few men, threw himself into the town, and kept possession of it. The Athenian fleet continued its course towards Elis, and captured Pheia; but on the approach of a strong Elean army changed its plan, and after ravaging the country proceeded to other coasts. About the same time the Athenians sent a fleet of 30 galleys into the Euboean channel to protect the island; they devastated the coasts of Locris, took Thronion, and near Alope routed a body of Locrians. While these events were taking place, the Aeginetans with their wives and children were driven from their island, and Aegina was occupied by Athenian settlers. The exiles were kindly received by the Lacedaemonians; and settlements in Thyrea, a border district between Argolis and Laconia, were assigned to them.

While the Athenians were thus actively engaged in several places, their fleet in the western seas continued its course. It took Sollion, a small Corinthian town on the coast of Acarnania, and transferred it to the dominion of its neighbour Palaeros. The Athenians then stormed Astacos, whence they sailed to the island of Cephallenia, which surrendered without resistance. Besides these new acquisitions, which were particularly valued by the Athenians on account of their situation, they gained at the same time the alliance of Sitalces, king of Thrace, a powerful and prudent prince, whose friendship was of great importance to them in the war against Chalcidice and Macedonia. The treaty was concluded through the mediation of Nymphodorus of Abdera, who also prevailed upon Perdiccas of Macedonia to espouse the cause of Athens, in consideration of the restoration to him of the town of Therma.

A considerable time after the departure of the Peloponnesians from Attica, late in the autumn of the same year, the Athenians made another expedition with all their forces, 10,000 heavy-armed citizens, 3000 resident aliens, and a large number of light-armed troops, the greatest army that Athens had ever collected. The object of this expedition was to wreak the popular resentment upon Megara, and Pericles himself undertook the command. But the army confined itself to laying waste the country, and then returned home. As the invasion of Attica by the Peloponnesians was annually repeated, so the devoted land of Megara was henceforth visited twice every year by the unwelcome army of the Athenians, which never advanced farther than the western frontier of that country. The Athenians avoided a battle in the open field, just as the Peloponnesians for a long time did not venture upon a naval engagement; so that during the first years the war consisted of a series of predatory expeditions only, without any serious intention on either side of bringing the contest to an issue by a decisive battle. At Athens, at least, it was generally believed that the war would be very protracted: it was therefore resolved to put aside 1000 talents of the public treasure in the acropolis, as a fund not to be touched except in an extreme case; and, in like manner, to keep always ready 100 of the best galleys for the protection of the city, and not to employ them for any other purpose. Permanent sentinels also were stationed in certain places in the neighbourhood, as a security for Athens on any sudden emergency.

During the winter after the first year of the war, the Athenians, according to the custom of their ancestors, honoured with a solemn burial those who had fallen. Pericles was chosen to deliver the funeral oration, the substance of which has been preserved by Thucydides, who was probably one of the bystanders. This speech is full of a noble consciousness of the dignity and greatness of Athens, and is a splendid panegyric of its glories.*

The immediately succeeding years of the war very much resemble the first; the struggle is going on in several places at once, in the west and in the east, but nothing is decided. The internal strength and vigour of Athens, however, were remarkably displayed under the heavy visitation of the fearful plague, whose ravages in Attica were greater than any which the armies of the Peloponnesians were able to inflict upon the country.

Scarcely had Archidamus, early in the summer of B. C. 430, again entered Attica with his army and commenced his devastations, when a pestilential disease, which with few interruptions continued to rage for two years and carried off numerous victims, made its appearance at Athens.† By the advice of Pericles, the country people had again taken refuge within the city, the crowded state of which increased the virulence of the malady to a most alarming extent. Thucydides himself was attacked by it, but was one of the few who recovered from it; he had also many opportunities of observing the disease in others, and has left to posterity a most complete and lucid account of all the symptoms, so far as they could be described by one who was not a medical man. We shall pass over his description, which has ever been regarded as unsurpassed, and only mention the unfortunate moral consequences of the disease. The plague, which, in the opinion of the historian and his contemporaries, originated in the most distant south, had spread over Egypt, Libya, the Persian empire, and the islands of the Aegean, and at Athens first broke out in Piraeus; for some time it was commonly believed that the Peloponnesians had poisoned the wells.‡ From the port it spread into the over-crowded city. As men died in the temples in which they had taken up their abode, as well as elsewhere, the profanation of sacred places soon ceased to be regarded as a violation of religion, and the corpses of the dead were left unheeded even in the sanctuaries of the gods. The religious rites of burial were likewise

* The fact that Plato (*Menex.* p. 236.) ascribes this oration of Pericles to Aspasia, must be regarded as a piece of irony perfectly in accordance with the object and tenor of that dialogue.

† Thucyd. ii. 87.; Diod. xii. 58. This plague proved fatal to 4400 heavy-armed, and to upwards of 10,000 slaves. To restore the reduced population, Pericles repealed the law which withheld the franchise from all whose fathers and mothers were not Athenian citizens.

‡ The same belief is frequently met with in history at the outbreak of great epidemics. In our own times, the country people in various parts of Europe entertained similar opinions on the first appearance of the cholera.

neglected amid this fearful distress; many did not think of burying their dead at all, but threw them into the streets. The wells were crowded with the bodies of those who had thronged to them to quench their burning thirst; in short, all that had hitherto been considered sacred and inviolable in the pious customs of the people was disregarded during the calamities of that time. As the plague carried off indiscriminately men of all classes, rich and poor, high and low, the feeling of insecurity produced in many persons a perfect indifference to all the obligations of law and morality, leading them to indulge in debaucheries as long as they could, in order that they might enjoy to the utmost the probably brief remaining period of life; no one felt inclined to make any sacrifice for what was good and noble; no one ventured to think of the consequences of his actions; and no one believed in retribution for excesses and offences which were committed without scruple, in the belief that death would snatch the offender from the hands of avenging justice.

During this period of calamity the army of the Peloponnesians, not deterred by the news of the frightful ravages of the plague, laid waste the northern districts of Attica, and then marched past the city towards the south. Having devastated the country about Laurion and the lands on the southern coast, they quitted Attica after a stay of about forty days. In the mean time, however, Pericles had prepared a fleet of 100 galleys, and embarked 4000 heavy-armed Athenians and 300 horse in transports formed out of old ships; the whole force being destined for an expedition against Peloponnesus. The armament was joined by fifty ships from Chios and Lesbos, and having made a descent upon the coasts of Argos and Laconia, and ravaged the territories of Epidaurus, Troezen, Haliae, and Hermione, advanced as far as the small Laconian town of Prasiae, after the destruction of which the Athenians returned home: but the fleet, under the command of Hagnon and Cleopompus, immediately proceeded northward to assist in the siege of Potidaea. There, however, no important result was gained; for the disease, which had been brought from home in the fleet, spread through the rest of the besieging army, which had hitherto been free from it. As, within forty days, it carried off 1050 men out of 4000, Hagnon, with the remainder, returned to Athens. The siege of Potidaea, however, was continued as before, and the Potidaeans held out till towards the end of the second year of the war.* At length the want of provisions reached such a height, that the besieged were forced to live upon human flesh; they were in the end

* According to Plato (*Sympos.* p. 219.), Socrates and Alcibiades took part in the expedition against Potidaea.

compelled to enter into negotiations with the Athenian commanders, Xenophon, Hestiodorus, and Phanomachus, for the surrender of the town. The besiegers, desirous of bringing their difficult operations in a cold climate to a close, and at the same time considering the enormous expense of the siege, granted to all a free departure. The Athenians were not satisfied indeed with this form of the surrender, and would have preferred one at discretion; but they acquiesced, and during the same winter sent new settlers to Potidaea.

The other military operations of this year were less successful. A naval expedition of the Lacedaemonians, the first they had fitted out in this war, was directed against the island of Zacynthos, but produced little or no effect, and Zacynthos remained allied with Athens. Equally unsuccessful was an undertaking of the Ambraciots against the Amphilochian Argos, another ally of Athens. During this winter, the Athenians displayed their activity in several quarters. Phormio sailed with twenty galleys round Peloponnesus, and establishing himself at Naupactus, blockaded the Corinthian and Crissaean gulfs. At the same time Melesander sailed with six galleys to Caria and Lycia, partly to raise money, partly to protect the Athenian merchant ships against Peloponnesian pirates. But on an expedition into the interior of Lycia with his small force and some allies, he was killed. The shameful manner in which the hostile parties acted towards each other, violating even the common laws of nations, is shown by the murder of some ambassadors which occurred in the course of this year. Aristeus of Corinth, with other Peloponnesian envoys, had set out for Asia to request the king of Persia to support the cause of the Peloponnesians, and take part in the war. On their way they went to the court of Sitalces, whom they endeavoured to draw away from the alliance with Athens. There they met Athenian envoys, who contrived to get them seized while crossing over into Asia, and delivered up to the Athenians: they were carried to Athens, and put to death without a trial; the Athenians alleging that this was only an act of retaliation for the outrages committed by the Lacedaemonians on Athenian and allied merchants, who had been captured and put to death. The Lacedaemonians actually killed every one, without distinction, who did not espouse their cause.

Before proceeding to relate the events of the following year, we must mention the close of the career of the great statesman Pericles. Cast down and discouraged by the double calamity of their unfortunate country and city, the people of Athens had already become weary of the war; and whatever might have been their hopes when, under the auspices of Pericles, they entered upon the contest, they were now inclined for peace, and even sent envoys to Sparta. As this proved fruitless, all, rich as well as poor, murmured against Pericles as the chief cause of their misfortunes; and being no longer able to live in peace and luxury, they seemed inclined to call to a severe account the very man by whose labours they had risen to their power and influence. Perceiving that the people acted, as he had anticipated, with reluctance, pusillanimity, ingratitude, and disregard of duty, Pericles convened an assembly to soothe their anger, encourage their faint hearts, and lead them to form a more correct estimate of their own position. His speech, full of the grandest thoughts, the truth of which must ever be recognised, exhibited him as the real ruler of the people, whose sovereignty was virtually limited to occasional expressions of discontent, and whose indignation found vent in slanderous reports: such a master was in fact necessary for the Athenians, and they were intelligent enough to acknowledge his surpassing excellence. It almost sounds like irony when he says, "It is you that have decreed the war, not I alone;" for he only had been the spiritual lever of the popular will. His description of the power and invincibility of Athens was listened to by the people with gratification; they obeyed their leader; made more energetic preparations for war than before, and gave up all thoughts of peace. But the grudge against Pericles, nevertheless, remained unabated, because there was none more powerful on whom the popular indignation could vent itself; and he was sentenced to pay a fine, and deprived of his office as general. Soon afterwards, however, he was re-elected, and all his former power was restored to him; the people having meanwhile changed their mind. Everything was committed to his care and discretion, because most other men had become indifferent to public affairs owing to domestic afflictions; and because, after all, it was well known that there was no one more capable than he of conducting the business of the state. In this manner, he continued to exert himself for the good of Athens till about the middle of the third year of the war; that is, till the autumn of B.C. 429. He was then seized by the plague, which had previously bereft him of his children, his relations, and friends. Plutarch relates that at the deathbed of his last son, Paralus, he burst into tears; and that this was the only time in his life that he was overwhelmed by grief, and lost his self-possession. When he himself lay at the point of death, and his friends around him were speaking to one another of his power and of his many victories, Pericles, who was believed to be insensible, interrupted them by saying, "I wish you would rather remember the fact, that no Athenian has ever through me put on mourning." The Athenians soon found out what they had lost in him; how moderate and how zealous for the greatness of Athens he had been in times of peace; and how cautious and calculating in war. The preservation and careful increase of their navy, and unremitting vigilance for the safety of Athens, on the one hand; and, on the other, abstinence from attempting distant conquests, and moderation in the management of the war;—these were the conditions on which alone they could look forward to certain victory. But the successors of Pericles were under the influence of ambition, avarice, and envy; and the star of Athens soon began to sink. His authority was unquestioned; the people confided in his wisdom, and allowed itself to be guided and restrained by him, for the power of his eloquence was irresistible. Thus the government, while nominally a democracy, was in reality in the hands of the first man in the state. How different were his successors! Jealous of one another, they courted popular favour, and the people was at times more arbitrary and fickle than ever. Hence the unfortunate occurrences during the latter period of the war, in contemplating which we can only wonder how the state could for so many years with such indomitable perseverance and energy sustain the greatest exertions and reverses.

The year B.C. 429, the third of the war, is remarkable also for the heroic and almost miraculous defence of Plataeae against the united power of the Peloponnesians. In the beginning of the summer, king Archidamus with his Peloponnesian army again passed the Isthmus. But instead of marching into Attica, he directed his course against Plataeae, whose fidelity to the Athenians made her as odious to the Peloponnesians as to the Boeotians. On his arrival in the territory of Plataeae, and when he was on the point of beginning his usual ravages, the Plataeans sent envoys to remonstrate with him, and appealed to their acknowledged bravery and self-sacrifice in the Persian war for the good of all Greece. They reminded him that, after the glorious battle of Plataeae, Pausanias had guaranteed to their state its independence as a reward for its services. But Archidamus announcing himself as the deliverer of Greece from the tyranny of the Athenians, proposed that they should remain neutral during the war, and admit both parties alike to amicable intercourse without aiding either. But the Plataeans could not act independently, for their wives and children, together with all those who were unfit for service, were at Athens. They accordingly sent envoys to consult the Athenians, who advised them to persevere and rely upon the assistance of Athens; the ambassadors therefore returned, and the negotiations with Archidamus were broken off. The wonderful fact is, that 400 Plataeans, 80 Athenians, and 110 women who had remained behind to prepare the food of the besieged, were able to resist the united efforts of a large army. Archidamus was engaged for seventy days and nights in raising a strong mound in front of the city. In order to prevent this mound from rising above the level of the wall, the besieged, with incredible exertions and rapidity, surmounted the latter with a superstructure of brick; and to render the conquest of their town as difficult as possible, they built a second wall within the old one. By undermining the ground they caused the fortifications of the enemy to break down, and by various contrivances rendered the military engines of the besiegers useless. In short, they defended themselves so energetically, that Archidamus was obliged to complete his fortifications all around the town, and to leave them in the custody of the Boeotians and their allies. He himself returned home with the rest of his army about the middle of September.

The heroism of the besieged deserved a better fate than that which befell them; but Plataeae, in general, performs a tragic part in Greek history. Its faithful attachment to Athens drew upon it the hatred of its parent city, Thebes; which, during the flourishing period of Greece, always acted equivocally, and, being unable to check the growing power of Athens, tried to injure it by a mean and jealous policy, which even sacrificed or risked the independence of all Greece. The siege of Plataeae continued two years longer, and it was not till the summer of the year B.C. 427 that the besieged, who had been reduced by one half, surrendered to the Lacedaemonians. In the winter of the fourth year of the war, B.C. 428, they were hard pressed by want of provisions, and determined to make a sally; but half their number, fearing failure, did not join in the enterprise. The others chose a dark and rainy night for their bold adventure; the roaring wind was a protection to them, and while those who remained behind contrived to engage the attention of the enemy, the daring Plataeans, with incredible difficulty, succeeded in reaching their goal. Only one was taken prisoner, but several had remained behind, so that only 212 reached Athens by roundabout ways. Those who had been left in Plataeae continued to defend themselves for a considerable time, until the Lacedaemonian commander himself saw that they were reduced to the last extremity, and were no longer able to defend or even to man their walls. He therefore proposed to them that they should surrender themselves and their town, and leave their fate to the judicial decision of Sparta. The Plataeans submitted, and soon afterwards five judges appointed by Sparta arrived. They asked the Plataeans this question only; whether, during this war, they had done any service to the Lacedaemonians or their allies? The question at once revealed to the unfortunate men the fate in store for them. Their spokesman tried by the most moving words to excite the compassion of the Spartans; he eloquently described the claims of his countrymen to the gratitude of all Greece, and especially of Sparta, on account of their prompt assistance in the war with the Helots*, and ended with an urgent entreaty that they might not be handed over to the Thebans, their most inveterate enemies, but be allowed to return to their own town, and left to their fate; for, he added, they would rather die the most fearful of all deaths, the death of hunger, than fall into the hands of the Thebans. But the Thebans, who were present during this address, endeavoured to efface the impression which it had produced. They exculpated themselves as well as they could, from the charge of having supported the Persians, and accused the Plataeans of partiality for Athens, which was more dangerous to the independence of Greece than hosts of barbarians. They bitterly reproached the Plataeans with having been guilty of a breach of promise a few years before, when, after the nocturnal surprise of their town, they had faithlessly murdered the most distinguished Thebans; and for this offence they now demanded that instant and bloody vengeance should be taken. What they wished was done. The prisoners were brought forward one by one; the above question was put to each, and as soon as he answered in the negative, he was led to death: not one was spared. Thus died 200 Plataeans and 29 Athenians; the women were all made slaves. The town of Plataeae was given up for one year to Megarian exiles, and to such Plataeans as were favourably disposed towards Thebes; afterwards it was razed to the ground. This was the end of a town which had for 93 years been a faithful ally of Athens. As Thucydides does not mention the sending of any succour from Athens during the long period of the siege, we must suppose that the Athenians, distracted by other military undertakings, and perhaps also by the plague, forgot to relieve their allies. We are not informed what became of the Plataean women and children who had taken refuge at Athens, or of those who made their escape before the final catastrophe. The want of active sympathy displayed by the Athenians on that occasion enables us to form some idea of the distracted state of their affairs, and of the light in which connections between states were viewed. It is not impossible, however, that irresolution, or the maxim laid down by Pericles not to venture upon a decisive battle by land, may have influenced the conduct of the Athenians.

Let us now return to the military enterprises of the third year of the war. The Athenians continued the struggle in two places,

* This refers to the third Messenian war, from B. C. 464 to 455. See above, p. 230.

Chalcidice and the Gulf of Corinth. The expedition sent against Chalcidice advanced to lay siege to the Bottiaean town of Spartolos; but a sally of the inhabitants, and repeated attacks, compelled the Athenians to throw themselves into Potidaea, whence they soon afterwards returned to Athens.

They were more successful, however, at sea. The Ambracians, in conjunction with the barbarous tribe of the Chaonians, formed the design of conquering Acarnania. They secured the aid of the Lacedaemonians by entreaties, and by holding out to them the prospect of becoming masters of Zacynthos, Leucas, Cephallenia, and Acarnania: some ships, with 1000 heavy-armed soldiers, were accordingly sent under the command of Cnemus; and these, being joined by a numerous army concentrated in those parts, marched against Stratos, the principal city of Acarnania. The Stratians were prepared to receive their enemies; they rushed from an ambuscade upon the Chaonians, who were advancing most impetuously, and put them to flight. This deterred Cnemus from venturing upon another engagement; he withdrew with his army to Oeniadae, which had sent some troops to join him, and there disbanded it. It had been arranged that the fleet of Corinthians and Sicyonians should set out from the Crissaean gulf to join the army of Cnemus; but Phormio, with his twenty galleys, was still maintaining his post at Naupactus, and when the Peloponnesian fleet, amounting to forty-seven sail, was on the point of crossing over from Patrae to the coast of Acarnania, he compelled them to fight a battle in the open sea. His skill and naval experience were of great advantage, and he cunningly availed himself of the moment when a fresh morning-breeze was forcing the enemy's ships against one another. In the battle which ensued he gained a complete victory, and having captured twelve ships, he sailed into the harbour of Molycrion, on the coast of Aetolia. Having raised a trophy on Rhion, at the entrance of the Corinthian gulf, and dedicated one of the captured vessels to Poseidon, he returned to his station at Naupactus. The Peloponnesians hastened towards the southern coast, and on their arrival at Cyllene met Cnemus returning from the Acarnanian expedition. In order to retrieve their double defeat, the Spartans sent three of their citizens, and among them Brasidas, to act as counsellors or colleagues of Cnemus. In a short time they had collected a fleet of seventy-seven galleys. Phormio also had asked for reinforcements, but they came too late. He was stationed with his twenty ships outside the gulf in the open sea, determined to accept battle there only. The Lacedaemonians, on the other hand, wished to fight in the straits. Thus the fleets faced each other for several days, until the Lacedaemonians by a stratagem compelled Phormio to abandon his position, and then attacked him in the straits. He lost nine of his ships, but the remaining eleven, which escaped to Naupactus, there threw themselves upon their pursuers with such spirit, that they captured six ships and recovered their own. The Messenian army of Naupactus, which followed the movements of the fleet along the coast, did good service by recovering some of the captured ships from the Peloponnesians. Both parties claimed the victory, and the Peloponnesians also set up on the Achaean Rhion a ship which they had taken, as a trophy. In the following night, however, they retreated to Corinth, from fear of the reinforcements expected by Phormio. The twenty ships which had been engaged about Crete soon arrived and joined those of Phormio at Naupactus. During the winter of the same year, this fleet undertook an expedition to the coast of Astacos in Acarnania, in order to strengthen the authority and dominion of Athens. Against the hostile Oeniadae, however, no attempt was made, because it was protected all round by marshes. At the beginning of spring the fleet returned from Naupactus to Athens laden with booty and prisoners, who, according to an established custom, were exchanged in case of their being freemen.

But before the dispersion of the Peloponnesian fleet for the winter, the Megarians suggested to the Spartan commanders that a sudden attack should be made upon Piraeus. Accordingly, providing themselves with all necessaries, they went across the Isthmus, and embarked at Nisaea in forty ships; but instead of at once proceeding to Piraeus, they first bent their course to Salamis, where they took three ships, and overran the island, laying waste the country wherever they went. No sooner were the Athenians informed by signals of what was going on in the island, than they hastened down to Piraeus and sailed across. But they came too late, for the Peloponnesians, laden with booty, had already departed, and were on their way to Corinth. In consequence of this alarm, the Athenians were afterwards more careful in guarding their harbours.

At the beginning of the winter a new champion, who, according to the custom of barbarians, announced himself in a most pompous manner, appeared to support the cause of the Athenians, but after all did nothing. This was Sitalces, who promised to conquer Chalcidice for the Athenians with an army of 150,000 men, to drive king Perdiccas from his kingdom, and place his brother Philip on the throne. The Athenians were to assist in the conquest of Chalcidice with their fleet and army, but they sent only envoys and money. The winter, moreover, was very severe, so that the expedition of the Thracian prince ended in his merely laying waste

Chalcidice and a large portion of Macedonia, after which he returned into his kingdom, having been absent only thirty days.

Thus terminated the third year of the war, during which the efforts of the Athenians appear insignificant, especially in comparison with what they did in the following years. We may suppose the cause of this to have been the melancholy condition of the city, and especially the loss of Pericles, which may have prevented their sending to Sitalces the aid they had promised. Afterwards they displayed greater vigour, but also greater passion, in the management of the war.

Group of the Fates.
(From the eastern pediment of the Parthenon.)

Seated youth.
(From a vase painting.)

Tombs on the Plains of Plataeae.

CHAPTER XX.

FOURTH AND FIFTH YEARS OF THE PELOPONNESIAN WAR.

The fourth year began with the usual invasion of Attica by the Spartan king Archidamus. The Athenians also followed their former tactics, and employed their cavalry only to prevent the enemy from approaching too near the city. At the same time, the island of Lesbos, distinguished for its wealth and its navy, renounced the alliance with Athens. Even before the outbreak of the war, the Lesbians had entertained thoughts of joining the Lacedaemonians, but had been rejected by them. They had, however, made all possible preparations, having fortified their capital of Mytilene, and increased their army and navy; yet the revolt broke out sooner than they themselves wished, in consequence of the inhabitants of Methymna, some of the neighbouring islanders, and even Mytilenaeans, who wished to keep up the connection with Athens, having informed the Athenians of the design. The Athenians still suffering from the epidemic, and pressed by the invasion of the Peloponnesians, at first endeavoured, by envoys, to induce the Mytilenaeans to remain faithful to their ancient treaty, and to prevent their continuing their hostile preparations. But failing in this, they despatched a fleet of forty galleys, which had been originally destined to operate against Peloponnesus, under the command of Cleïppides, with orders to make a sudden attack upon the Mytilenaeans at a festival of Apollo, which was approaching, and during which the people used to assemble at some distance from the city. He was also to compel them to pull down their fortifications and surrender their ships. The ten galleys which formed the Lesbian contingent in the Athenian fleet were seized, and their crews imprisoned. The Lesbians, however, were informed of the approach of the Athenian fleet, and, postponing the festival, protected themselves behind their fortifications. The Mytilenaeans having rejected the proposals of the Athenians, the latter commenced hostilities; but the Mytilenaeans feeling themselves too weak to make a successful resistance without the aid of allies, and also with a view to gain time, concluded a truce with the admirals, and sent envoys to Athens to negotiate for peace and the withdrawal of the fleet. But at the same time they secretly despatched ambassadors to Sparta to solicit the support of the Lacedaemonians. The envoys sent to Athens returned without having effected anything, and hostilities were recommenced. After a sally and an indecisive engagement, the Mytilenaeans remained quiet within their fortifications, and the Athenians blockaded the city on the sea side, while the Mytilenaeans, supported by the other Lesbians, except Methymna, continued masters of the island. Meanwhile, the ambassadors, who had gone to Sparta, had proceeded, by the advice of the Spartans, to Olympia, where the great games happened to be then going on, and where they might explain their case to the assembled allies. There they brought forward the oft-repeated complaints about the domineering spirit of the Athenians, who had deprived their allies, with the exception of Lesbos and Chios, of their independence, and reduced them to the condition of subjects. The same fate, they said, was now preparing for them; the original understanding of the alliance, that Athens should deliver the Greeks from the barbarians, had been forgotten, and for a long time Athens had been, not the liberator of the Greeks, but the destroyer of their freedom. Their proposals were readily listened to, and they were admitted into the Peloponnesian league. But both parties were mistaken in believing that the Athenians were now too weak to offer a vigorous resistance, and in imagining that the time had come when they might be completely annihilated. For in the face of the growing dangers, the Athenians during this year displayed a military power such as they had never displayed before, and as they rarely did afterwards; the cause of this was, either that they had recovered from the calamities of the preceding years, or, as is more probable, that they now wisely made the greatest efforts, in order not to appear to be really weakened or to have lost any part of their power. Attica, Salamis, and Euboea, were guarded by 100 ships; 100 others were cruising about Peloponnesus; many also were engaged at Potidaea and in other quarters; so that during this summer not fewer than 250 excellently equipped galleys were in active service. The rapidity with which they were got ready furnished evidence of the unimpaired resources of Athens.

When the Peloponnesians had concluded their treaty with Lesbos, they immediately summoned two thirds of the contingents of their allies to assemble on the Isthmus, and caused engines to be constructed for the purpose of transporting their fleet across into the Saronic gulf, in order to attack Athens at once by land and by sea. But the Athenians quickly and unexpectedly appeared with a fleet of 100 galleys on the coasts of Peloponnesus, and even advanced to the neighbourhood of Sparta. Hence the Peloponnesians who on account of the harvest had assembled but slowly, found themselves compelled to give up their expedition. The Lacedaemonians, however, sent a fleet of forty sail, under the command of Alcidas, to assist the Lesbians. Meanwhile the Mytilenaeans had made an unsuccessful attack upon Methymna, which remained faithful to Athens; and an attempt of the Antissaeans upon the same town was likewise repulsed. But the Mytilenaeans still remained in possession of the rest of the island, until in the autumn the Athenians sent an army of 1000 heavy-armed, under the command of Paches, who carried a single wall round the land-side of the city, which was thus in a short time completely invested both by land and by sea. The expense of the warlike operations, which had suddenly been conducted on so large a scale, had completely drained the public treasury of Athens, on which heavy demands had previously been made, especially on account of the siege of Potidaea; and the Athenians now, for the first time, imposed upon themselves a property-tax, which produced 200 talents. They also sent out Lysicles with twelve galleys to levy contributions from friends and foes. On his arrival in Caria, he proceeded inland as far as the vale of the Maeander, where he perished in a battle with the Carians and Anaeans.

The fleet of the Lacedaemonians did not make its appearance at Lesbos in the course of this year; but towards the end of the winter they despatched Salaethus, who actually made his way through the blockading fleet into the city, to inform the Mytilenaeans that the fleet would soon follow, and that the allies would at the same time invade Attica: the besieged were thus encouraged to continue their resistance. In accordance with this promise the Peloponnesians, in the summer of B.C. 427, the fifth year of the war, invaded Attica, under the command of Cleomenes, the uncle and guardian of the young king Pausanias. They ravaged not only the districts which had been cultivated again, but those also which had been spared in former invasions; so that the Athenians were now more severely pressed than ever. As in B.C. 430, the Peloponnesians, expecting to receive good news from Lesbos, made a long stay, and left the country only when they began to suffer from want of provisions. Their fleet had been detained on its course towards Lesbos, and the Mytilenaeans had surrendered to the Athenians before its arrival. Salaethus, despairing of any succour from Sparta, had entrusted the commonalty with the arms of the regular infantry, which had hitherto been reserved for the privileged class; but the people, instead of sallying out against the enemy, became clamorous for bread, and declared that unless the wealthy citizens would distribute their hidden stores of corn among the famishing people, they would make their own terms with the Athenians. The ruling body, dreading a capitulation from which they would be excluded, thus found themselves compelled to surrender the city to Paches, stipulating only for their personal liberty, until the return of the envoys who were to be sent to Athens for further orders. Although Paches accepted the proposal, the Mytilenaeans crowded as suppliants round the altars. Paches allayed their fears, and for the present sent them to Tenedos. He then subdued Antissa, and thereby became master of all the island.

At length the Lacedaemonian fleet, under the command of Alcidas, approached; but on receiving intelligence of the fall of Mytilene, it made for the south, landed at Embaton, in the territory of Erythrae, and there tried to obtain accurate information about the state of affairs. Alcidas then held a council of war, in which Teutiaplus, a brave Elean, suggested an immediate attack upon the Athenians, who were probably intoxicated with their victory. Others were of opinion that they should take possession of the Ionian and Aeolian cities, and enter into negotiations with Pissuthnes, the satrap at Sardis. But Alcidas thought it most advisable to return to Peloponnesus as soon as possible. He accordingly sailed southward along the coast, and landed at Myonnesus, where he ordered most of his prisoners to be put to death, and thereby offended the Ionians. Thence he proceeded to Ephesus, where, at the request of the Samians, he set free some Chian prisoners. He then hastily directed his course homewards, perceiving that the Athenians in Lesbos had been informed of his presence, and that Paches, in order to protect the defenceless Ionian towns, had set out in pursuit of him. His fleet, however, was overtaken by a storm, and dispersed before it reached the coast of Peloponnesus. This was the first Lacedaemonian fleet that had ventured as far as the coasts of Asia Minor; it was, in fact, such an unexpected phenomenon, that the inhabitants of the coast-towns believed it to be an Athenian fleet, and, coming out peaceably to meet it, fell into the hands of Alcidas, who afterwards cruelly put them to death as above mentioned.

Before Paches returned from the pursuit, he conquered Notion the port-town of Colophon; and restored the dominion over it to the Colophonians; but subsequently an Athenian colony was established there. After his return to Lesbos, Salaethus was taken and sent to Athens along with the Mytilenaeans kept in Tenedos, and many others who were believed to have stirred up the revolt. At the same time he sent back the greater part of his army, while he himself remained behind for the purpose of settling the affairs of the island.

The Athenians ordered Salaethus to be put to death as soon as he arrived. The fate of the Mytilenaeans was discussed, and in the first heat of their exasperation it was resolved that all the men should be put to death, and the women and children sold as slaves. With these bloody orders a ship was sent to Paches. But on the following day, the Athenians repented of their hasty anger: another assembly was immediately convened for the purpose of reconsidering their resolution. Among the orators who spoke on that occasion was Cleon, the son of Cleaenetus, who on the previous day had supported the cruel decree; he was generally known among his fellow-citizens as a person fond of violent measures, but he enjoyed the greatest popularity with the multitude. This popular leader is known to us less from Thucydides, who gives a brief but pregnant description of him, than from the comedies of Aristophanes, his bitterest and most implacable enemy. There is no one else among his contemporaries against whom that great poet displays such profound hatred and deep moral indignation as against Cleon; and no other public man had so incessantly to experience the fearful earnestness of his comic muse. Cleon is treated by him as the very essence of all human vulgarity and brutality; as characterised by an insolence and vanity bordering upon madness, by a supernatural and inhuman thirst of blood, and, lastly, by a degree of cowardice such as is found only in the most cruel natures.

Allowing for the poetical exaggerations of Aristophanes, who blames or brands with honest truth and undisguised anger that which the delicate-minded historian only alludes to, the two descriptions completely supplement each other; and Thucydides, well understood, judges of Cleon as severely and with the same indignation as Aristophanes. The people of Athens had become very unlike what they were during the great period of the Persian wars; the last years of "the Olympian," as the Athenians called Pericles in their admiration of his power and wisdom, were troubled and embittered by the obstinacy, fickleness, and pusillanimity of the people, whose bad qualities were praised and fostered by their leaders, among whom Cleon had been busy in undermining the authority of Pericles, and in exciting the people against him and his measures. It was Cleon who stirred the popular passion at the time when Pericles restrained it, and would not allow the people to engage in an open contest with Archidamus; he is also mentioned as the person who proposed the fine which Pericles was sentenced to pay. In the accusations of Anaxagoras, Phidias, and Aspasia, Cleon is said to have acted the part of an informer. Yet Cleon did not at once, after the death of Pericles, obtain his influential position. Aristophanes mentions as the immediate successor of Pericles, Eucrates, a dealer in flour, who may have been animated by the moderation of Pericles. His influence was only of short duration, and he must have been thrown into the shade by Cleon. Eucrates was succeeded by Lysicles, a cattle dealer, who married Aspasia, and perhaps intended to act in the spirit of Pericles; but we have already seen that he perished in Caria. After him Cleon, the leather merchant, was decidedly the most influential demagogue. In such hands was the fate of Athens, and such were the men who flattered and guided the sovereign people. They strove to outdo one another, and undertook to manage the affairs of a state, which they were utterly incapable of conducting, not to say governing. They all stood on the same level, and lacked the qualities which Pericles was conscious of possessing, and which are indispensable to form a perfect statesman,—a correct judgment of the wants of the state, ability to give a sound exposition of them, patriotism, and disinterestedness. Cleon had no qualification but the second,—some oratorical power.* Nicias, who stood infinitely higher in all other respects, did not possess this talent, and was therefore unable to acquire a great influence with the people. Alcibiades, lastly, was intelligent and eloquent in the highest degree, but neither disinterested nor truly patriotic, and hence his brilliant natural talents brought the greatest misery upon Athens. Under such guides, who were too powerless, selfish, or dishonest to guard the people against mistakes, who even hoped to establish their personal power upon the ruins of the state, the Peloponnesian war could not but become an abyss into which the victorious party itself must sooner or later sink.

But of all the men who prepared the downfall of Athens, none was, in the opinion of Aristophanes, more impure and brutal than Cleon; and Thucydides, in the speech on the fate of the Mytilenaeans put into his mouth, places him in a no less unfavourable light. His energy there appears as thoughtless rashness, and his courage as a mixture of narrow-mindedness and brutality; in it he shows himself calumniating, insolent, jealous of the merits

* Ἑρμηνεῦσαι.

and talents of others, fond of scandal, crouching before the people, corruptible, and boastful. But Thucydides in the same speech describes a people which was worthy of such a guide: credulous, vain, fond of innovation, cruel, and unjust.

Cleon, however, did not carry his bloody proposals: the moderate speech of Diodotus, who wished only the most conspicuous among the rebels to be put to death, was supported by a small majority; and this fact characterises the altered disposition of the people. In consequence of this defeat, Cleon's influence with the people must for a time have been weakened, and during some years men of moderate principles were at the head of affairs. The arguments of Diodotus having prevailed upon the assembly to reverse their previous decision, a second galley was quickly despatched with orders to spare the city. By the great exertions of the rowers, supported by a favourable wind, it arrived in time, Paches having just read the fatal decree, and being engaged in making preparations to carry it into effect. Thus the city was saved by a mere chance, but the ringleaders who had been sent to Athens, 1000 in number, were put to death. Mytilene lost its ships and walls. The remainder of the island was divided into 3000 lots, 300 of which were consecrated to the gods, the rest being assigned to Attic colonists, to whom the Lesbians, who were allowed to cultivate the land, paid a fixed rent of two minae for each lot. The possessions of Mytilene on the continent likewise fell into the hands of the Athenians, and Lesbos lost its independence.

We may observe in general that this year is particularly remarkable for cruel and bloody occurrences. We have already related the fearful fate of the Plataeans; but the civil war which broke out in Corcyra was characterised by an exasperation and cruelty which surpassed everything previously known. Corinth had sent back the Corcyraean prisoners for the purpose of gaining over the island through their influence, and of withdrawing it from the alliance with Athens. The returned prisoners, joined by the wealthy and aristocratic citizens, succeeded in overpowering the democratic party. But in a few days the latter, supported by the majority of liberated slaves, and even by women, gained the upper hand, and the defeated party in self-defence set fire to the houses round the market-place, and did incalculable damage. On the following day, Nicostratus arrived from Naupactus with twelve ships and 500 heavy-armed Messenians. As an Athenian general he supported the popular side, and endeavoured to put an end to the civil contest by a fair and moderate arrangement; but party animosity burst forth again when the Peloponnesian fleet, amounting to fifty-three galleys, under Alcidas and Brasidas, arrived. The Corcyraean ships, which were got ready in great haste, were unable to withstand those of the Peloponnesians; and the Athenian squadron, though it fought bravely and skilfully, was too weak for a serious contest. Thus the Peloponnesians gained the day, and captured thirteen Corcyraean galleys. But Alcidas, notwithstanding the prudent advice of Brasidas, made little use of his victory; and when, in the second night after the battle, fire-signals conveyed intelligence of the approach of an Athenian armament, the Peloponnesian fleet hastily retreated under cover of the night. On the arrival of the Athenian fleet of sixty galleys, commanded by Eurymedon, and the withdrawal of the hostile armament, the Corcyraeans proceeded to take revenge, with unprecedented cruelty, upon the vanquished party; and, as is commonly the case in civil wars, personal enmity, jealousy, avarice, and all other evil passions, suggested means for denouncing and murdering private foes on the ground of their being enemies to the popular cause. No sanctuary afforded protection, no ties of blood or kindred were regarded. Eurymedon departed without having done anything towards the pacification of the town. The exiled nobles, however, fortified themselves on the hill Istone, and made themselves masters of the open country, harassing their adversaries by interrupting their commerce, and cutting off their necessary supplies.

To the description of these scenes of horror Thucydides subjoins a reflection on the subsequent history of the war, in which such fearful occurrences were no longer unusual; "for afterwards," says he, "all Greece was in commotion, there being everywhere two parties, and the leaders of the popular party calling in the aid of the Athenians, while the minority of nobles invited the Lacedaemonians." Every one was obliged to side with one of the two parties; those who wished to remain neutral were persecuted by both; and party spirit destroyed even the most sacred family ties. The honest simplicity of the good old times was gone for ever: what had formerly been regarded as a human weakness, now became a virtue; what used to be censured, now became an object of praise and imitation. The prudent were outwitted, and the uneducated, who rushed into action without reflecting, were generally victorious.

Besides Lesbos, the Athenians made in this year another conquest which was important in a different way. In order to protect Salamis and Attica against such attacks as that which had nearly proved successful in the third year of the war, and to render the coast of Attica still more secure, Nicias, having taken possession of the small island of Minoa, on the coast of Megaris, south of the port of Nisaea, fortified it by a wall facing the mainland, and made use of it as a permanent outpost.

It was in this year that the Athenians began to interfere in the affairs of Sicily. There, too, the Dorians were hostile to the Ionians, and Syracuse was at war with Leontini. All the Doric cities, except Camarina, sided with Syracuse, and had joined the Peloponnesian confederacy; the Locrians of Italy took the same side. The Chalcidian towns, Camarina and Rhegium in Italy, supported the Leontines. They sent envoys to Athens, and Gorgias the Leontine, by his brilliant and persuasive eloquence, induced the thoughtless Athenians to promise succours. Twenty ships under the command of Laches and Charoeades, were sent out, partly to prevent provisions being carried from Sicily to Peloponnesus, partly to see whether it might not be possible to reduce Sicily to a condition of dependence upon Athens. The forces conveyed by the squadron landed at Rhegium, and, conjointly with the Athenian allies, made preparations for war. In the same winter they made an expedition with the Rhegines against the Aeolian islands, to the north of Sicily, which were allied with Syracuse, and having ravaged them, they returned to Rhegium.

Meanwhile the plague, after a short cessation, had broken out at Athens a second time, and continued for one year longer the most formidable enemy that the Athenians had to dread; for hitherto they had generally defeated the Peloponnesians, and in the following years their military success was still greater.

Mytilene.

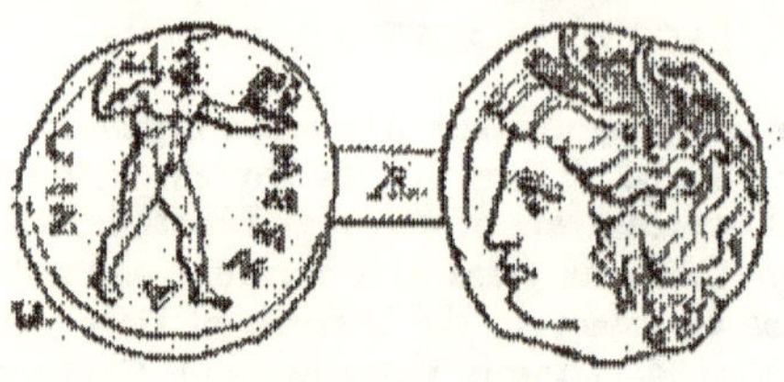

Coin of Messene.

CHAPTER XXI.

FROM THE BEGINNING OF THE SIXTH YEAR OF THE PELOPONNESIAN WAR TO THE GENERAL PACIFICATION OF SICILY.

For some years the Athenians obtained decided advantages over their opponents, and, elated by the tide of momentary good fortune, they became more haughty and domineering than ever. Believing that their arms were invincible, they several times rejected proposals of peace, and punished the generals who had needlessly, in their opinion, entered into negotiations, or had, as it was said, accepted bribes from the enemy.

But the war assumed a different character, chiefly because the Athenians began to venture more and more upon carrying on their operations by land. At the commencement of the sixth year, when the Lacedaemonians, under Agis, the son of Archidamus, were preparing again to invade Attica, and had already advanced as far as the Isthmus, earthquakes occurred in various parts of Greece, which filled the minds of the Greeks with terror, and prevented the Spartan army from entering Attica; while the Athenians, thus left at liberty for other enterprises, were successful in Boeotia, Locris, and Aetolia. Sixty galleys, with 2000 heavy-armed on board, under the command of Nicias, sailed against the island of Melos, with the view of compelling it to join the confederacy of Athens. Although they laid waste the island, they could not accomplish their principal object, and Nicias, quitting Melos, sailed to Oropus, where he disembarked his troops and immediately marched against Tanagra, in Boeotia. At the same time, the whole force of Athens, under Hipponicus and Eurymedon, arrived, and on the following day the Tanagraeans with their Theban auxiliaries were defeated. The two Athenian armies then separated, and after Nicias had ravaged the coasts of Locris he returned to Athens.

Meanwhile Demosthenes had sailed round Peloponnesus with thirty galleys, and being joined by all the Acarnanians, by forces from Zacynthos and Cephallenia, and by fifteen Corcyraean ships, he proceeded to attack Leucas. The Acarnanians wished him to lay siege to the town, but Demosthenes yielded to the prayer of the Messenians of Naupactus to make war upon the Aetolians; an additional inducement to do this being the prospect of opening a road through Aetolia, the country of the Ozolian Locrians, and Phocis, into Boeotia. The Acarnanians, vexed at the siege of Leucas being given up, did not accompany him on this expedition, and the fifteen Corcyraean galleys likewise sailed home. From Oeneon, on the Locrian coast, Demosthenes advanced into the interior of the country, and made himself master of several towns. But the Aetolians had in the mean time collected their forces; and when the Athenian general had taken the town of Aegition, situated about ten miles from the coast among the hills, the Aetolians, guided by the fugitive inhabitants, descended upon the invaders from the heights. The latter held out for a long time, but at length, when the commander of the bowmen had been slain, when their arrows were spent, and when they were completely exhausted, they sought safety in flight, and the greater part perished in the unknown country, their Locrian guide also having fallen. A few only escaped to Oeneon. The majority of the slain were allies; but the Athenians lost 120 of their best warriors, and Procles, the colleague of Demosthenes. The latter himself returned to Naupactus, and remained there from fear of his fellow-citizens. The Aetolians, on the other hand, immediately solicited the aid of the Lacedaemonians against Naupactus, and towards autumn the desired succour, consisting of 3000 heavy-armed, arrived, under the command of Eurylochus. He marched from Delphi through the country of the Ozolian Locrians, who, though allied with Athens, consented to give hostages to him; thence he proceeded towards Naupactus, where he made himself master of an unfortified suburb. By many entreaties, Demosthenes had at length prevailed upon the Acarnanians to send him a force of 1000 heavy-armed. With these and his own troops he now defended Naupactus, which, under these circumstances, Eurylochus thought it impossible to take. He accordingly proceeded westward, and, at the request of the Ambracians, directed his course against the Amphilochian Argos, after having waited in the neighbourhood of Calydon and Pleuron until the Ambracians had commenced hostilities. He succeeded in joining them, while Demosthenes and the Acarnanians hastened to the assistance of the Argives. By a skilfully laid ambuscade, Demosthenes forced the far more numerous army of the Peloponnesians to retreat, and the rest of the allied forces also were put to flight, although the Ambracians, who were stationed on the right wing, had at first been victorious. The loss of the enemy was great. The Peloponnesians now entered into negotiations with Demosthenes, and were allowed to retreat under the command of Menedaeus, for Eurylochus and Macarius had both fallen in the battle. Soon afterwards the Ambracians suffered a still greater defeat. In entire ignorance of what had taken place, they hastened to the scene of action and encamped on an eminence, where they were attacked by Demosthenes at daybreak. The carnage which ensued is almost incredible, considering the extent and power of their state. "This calamity," says Thucydides, "was the greatest that befel a Hellenic city in this war within so short a space of time." The Acarnanians and Amphilochians, however, fearing the growing power of Athens, prevented the destruction of Ambracia, with which, after Demosthenes' return to Athens, they concluded a treaty of alliance for the period of 100 years, the principal terms of which were neutrality and mutual protection.

In Sicily, too, the Athenians made some progress in the course of this year. Laches, who, after the death of Charoeades, was the sole commander of the fleet, proceeded with his allies to besiege the Messenian town of Mylae, the inhabitants of which were compelled to surrender and accompany him in his expedition against Messene. This town, likewise, soon afterwards surrendered on certain conditions, and gave hostages. The Athenians also made a successful naval attack upon the Epizephyrian Locrians in southern Italy, and gained possession of a fortified place on the river Halex. During the winter, they and their allies undertook an expedition against Inessa, the citadel of which was in the hands of the Syracusans. This enterprise failed; and as the invaders were retreating, the Syracusans attacked their rear, and slew many. Laches, however, made some successful descents on the coast of Locri, Himera, and the Aeolian islands. He was then superseded in the command by Pythodorus, who had arrived with a few ships, forming part of the reinforcements which the Athenians, at the instance of their Sicilian allies, who wished to see the war brought to a speedy termination, had resolved to send: the main body of the auxiliary squadron followed under the command of Sophocles and Eurymedon. Pythodorus, in the mean time, made an expedition against the Locrians, which, however, proved a failure.

This was the last event of the sixth year of the war.* In the following year the contest between the Syracusans and the allies

* To this year also belongs the purification of Delos, and an eruption of Mount Aetna, which occurred in the spring of B. C. 426, and was the third within the recollection of the Greeks in Sicily. (Thucyd. iii. 116.)

of the Athenians was continued, without the Athenians themselves taking any active part in it; for they were engaged nearer home with more important affairs in Greece itself, and in Peloponnesus. At the beginning of the summer B.C. 425, the Syracusans, in conjunction with the Locrians, took Messene, whose inhabitants themselves, weary of the alliance with Athens, had in fact invited them. At the same time Rhegium, which was distracted and weakened by party feuds, was hard pressed by the Locrians. Messene was made the centre of all future undertakings. After some insignificant skirmishes on the coast of Messene between the Syracusans and Athenians, in which the latter lost a few ships, the Messenians advanced against the Chalcidian town of Naxos, but were repulsed with the loss of 1000 men. Immediately after this, the Leontines and Athenians again attacked Messene; but the land army of the Leontines was defeated by a sally of the Messenians and Locrians; the naval force of the Athenians, however, immediately effected a landing, and drove the Messenians back into their town. But the Athenians now withdrew to Rhegium, and took no further part in the struggles of the islanders, which in the course of the following year were terminated throughout Sicily by a general peace. But, before we give an account of this, we must cast a glance at the affairs of Greece itself.

The Lacedaemonians commenced the hostilities of the seventh year with an invasion of Attica under Agis. They arrived earlier than usual, and did not find such ample supplies of provisions as on former occasions; and as bad tidings also were brought from Peloponnesus, the army, after a stay of only fifteen days, broke up again. This invasion, the fifth, was the last. The subsequent war in Attica, commonly called the Decelean, was of a different nature.

The unfavourable tidings from Peloponnesus were that the Athenians had gained a firm footing in the peninsula. Demosthenes, the conqueror of Ambracia, though not invested with any command, had sailed in the fleet commanded by Sophocles and Eurymedon, with permission to land on the coasts of Peloponnesus and to make conquests. The commander of the fleet, indeed, wished to sail at once against Corcyra, whither 60 Peloponnesian galleys had proceeded to support the aristocrats who had fortified themselves on Mount Istone; but Demosthenes advised them to land at Pylos on the coast of Messenia; and they were forced to comply by a storm which rendered it necessary for the fleet to put into that very harbour. His plan was to fortify the town, which appeared to him to be a position of great importance for the future operations of the war. The continuance of the storm was favourable to his scheme, which the generals Sophocles and Eurymedon thought fanciful and of small advantage. The soldiers, finding the time heavy on their hands, set about the work proposed by Demosthenes, and displayed such ardour, that within six days Pylos was provided with fortifications on those sides where it had been weak and vulnerable. As soon as the work was completed, the fleet under Eurymedon and Sophocles sailed away, but Demosthenes remained behind with five ships and a small force. At first the Spartans were not much concerned about this new fortress, which in fact they believed to be too weak to offer any resistance. Yet as soon as the news of it reached Attica, the Peloponnesian army hastily withdrew from that country, and the Spartans themselves marched against Pylos. The fleet stationed at Corcyra was likewise called back, and, in order to avoid the Athenians, was transported across the Leucadian isthmus. Not long afterwards the land army also arrived from Attica. Demosthenes, on the other hand, quickly despatched two galleys to Zacynthos to inform Eurymedon of his danger, and request him to return with the fleet. The Lacedaemonians designed to block up the harbour, and to render it impossible for the Athenians to effect an entrance into it. The island of Sphacteria, situated in front of the harbour of Pylos, was fifteen stadia in length; it was uninhabited, covered with wood, and occupied by a body of heavy-armed troops, who at first relieved one another, but those ultimately left on the island were 420 Spartans with their retinue of Helots, commanded by Epitadas. Demosthenes made a very prudent use of the small force under his command. The greater part of it he posted in the best fortified places on the land side, while he himself with sixty heavy-armed men and a few bowmen marched down to the water's edge to prevent the Lacedaemonians from disembarking. He found it scarcely necessary to encourage his men, whose spirits were raised by the very boldness and danger of the enterprise. The Lacedaemonians commenced a simultaneous attack by land and by sea. Forty-three ships had run into the harbour, under the command of Thrasymelides. They advanced in small squadrons, relieving one another, and displaying the utmost ardour. Brasidas, the greatest Spartan hero during this period of the war, was most conspicuous in urging on the commanders of the galleys not to spare the ships, if with their loss they could but effect a landing; in his eagerness to accomplish this object, he drove his own ships ashore and was on the point of landing, when the Athenians fell upon him, so that he was covered with wounds and at length sank backwards into his ship, while his shield fell into the sea. All similar attempts were repelled with undaunted courage and perseverance. The most skilful sailors of Greece were here fighting on land against the ships of the Lacedaemonians, the most renowned warriors in land battles! The Athenians, on Lacedaemonian ground, withstood the Spartans on the sea, the real element of the Athenians! After a struggle which lasted for nearly two days, the contest was discontinued, while the Spartans sent to procure timber from Asina for constructing engines. But in the meanwhile the Athenian fleet arrived from Zacynthos, augmented to the number of 50. They awaited the attack of the Spartan fleet in the open sea, but the latter remained in the harbour, which, however, was not closed as had been intended. The Athenians accordingly entered it, to attack their foes. In the battle which ensued, the Lacedaemonians fought with desperation. From the shore they defended their ships with the greatest obstinacy; but the Athenians ultimately prevailed, and the result of the victory was, that Sphacteria with its garrison was closely blockaded. The Peloponnesians maintained only their position on the main land. The consequences of this battle were as unexpected as they were overwhelming; the most illustrious Spartans were shut up in Sphacteria, and there was little chance of rescuing them by a fresh contest. The Spartans, therefore, were all at once seized by a desire for a truce and peace. An armistice was immediately concluded with the Athenians, on condition that the Spartan fleet should remain in the hands of the Athenians until the return of the envoys who were to be sent to Athens, and that the captives in Sphacteria should be supplied with a certain quantity of provisions under the superintendence of the Athenians. Hostilities of course ceased, and everything remained unchanged until the return of the envoys. An Athenian ship conveyed them to Athens. They offered peace and alliance, on the one condition that their fellow-citizens in Sphacteria should be set free, and they hoped to obtain it, as the Athenians had sued for peace a few years before. The Spartans imagined that it would now be accepted as an equivalent for the object of their own desires. But the Athenians, that is, those who had the popular ear, aimed at more than this. By the advice of Cleon, they made quite different proposals, claiming the restitution of possessions which had been lost in former wars, such as Nisaea and Pegae in Megaris, Troezen, and Achaia. The envoys proposed to discuss these claims with a few chosen individuals, but this was successfully opposed by Cleon, who asserted that the question was one to be decided by the whole people. Hereupon the envoys thought it necessary, for the honour of Sparta, to break off the negotiations and return. After an absence of twenty days they again arrived at Pylos, and the truce was forthwith put an end to. But the Athenians, alleging that the truce had been infringed, refused to restore the sixty ships, and the struggle was recommenced with unexampled efforts on both sides. The island was watched in the daytime by two Athenian galleys, which were continually cruising round in opposite directions, and at night the whole fleet, now increased to seventy sail, was moored round the coast. The Peloponnesians, on the other hand, made repeated attacks upon the fortress.

The siege was protracted in both places. The Athenians began to suffer from want of provisions, and especially of water; the prisoners in the island received their regular supplies, chiefly from the sea and by means of Helots, who were rewarded with money and liberty. All devices and artifices were resorted to; even divers approached the island and carried provisions into it. The Athenians at length were growing weary of the siege, which they were apprehensive it might be necessary to continue even during the winter; in which case matters might, after all, take an unfavourable turn. They almost regretted not having accepted the proposals of peace. As usual, their dissatisfaction now vented itself upon those who had been opposed to the peace, and especially upon Cleon. At first the people wished to send him to Pylos, in order to ascertain the situation of the Athenians, and to convince himself of the truth of the alarming reports which he had denied. Such a mission was not to Cleon's mind; he advised the people to despatch reinforcements, and thus to bring the matter to a speedy and glorious termination; at the same time he pointed out Nicias, his personal enemy, as the man best qualified to undertake the task, which, he added, was in his opinion by no means difficult. Nicias eagerly caught at this, and declared himself ready to resign his office of general to Cleon for this undertaking. Cleon, believing the proposal to be only a joke, accepted it with equal readiness. But finding that Nicias was in earnest, and called the people to witness that he laid down his office, Cleon endeavoured to evade the dangerous honour by various excuses. The more he drew back, however, the greater was the amusement of the multitude, who would not let him escape, but formally appointed him general, and laughingly called upon him to embark at once. Seeing that there was no alternative, he at length consented to accept the post, and again assumed his vaunting tone, boastfully declaring that with the small additional force which he was to take along with him, and the soldiers already at Pylos, he would within twenty days either bring the Spartans alive to Athens, or cut them to pieces on the spot. The people laughed at his bravado, but the more rational among them entertained a hope either that they would now get rid of Cleon for ever, or else that he would really succeed in the important object entrusted to him.

What Cleon had rashly asserted, accident verified. He artfully caused the cautious Demosthenes to be appointed his second in command *, because he knew that he had already formed the plan of putting an end to the siege by an attack upon the island. Demosthenes had deferred this step chiefly because the thick wood covering the island rendered a regular attack impossible. But now, just at the right time, a great part of the forest was accidentally destroyed by fire, and Demosthenes discovered that the enemy were far more numerous than he had until then believed. When Cleon arrived, the armies united, and at the dawn of day landed on the island. Demosthenes had made his dispositions in such a manner, that the whole island was attacked at once. Epitadas and his men made a long and valiant resistance. At first the Athenian soldiers ventured to attack their enemies only from a distance, so firmly rooted was their respect for Spartan warriors; but they soon became accustomed to face them, and poured down upon them with a simultaneous charge and a deafening shout. The Lacedaemonians were almost blinded and choked by clouds of dust which rose from the ashes of the burnt trees; all orders were drowned by the enemy's clamour; and at length, yielding to the superior numbers of their assailants, they retreated to a fort at the north end of the island. There they held out for a long time, and the struggle remained undecided, until the commander of the Messenians, unobserved, ascended the heights in the rear of the Lacedaemonians, who were thus hemmed in on every side. That they might not be all cut to pieces, Cleon and Demosthenes stopped the fight, and sent a herald to ask whether they would surrender to the Athenians at discretion. The Spartans, of whom 290 were left alive, seeing that further resistance was hopeless, submitted, and were carried as prisoners to Athens. The siege had lasted for seventy-two days, and Cleon had made good his promise.

The Athenians and Messenians of Naupactus garrisoned Pylos, and many Helots deserted to them. The fields of the Lacedaemonians were laid waste, and the presence of the enemy in their immediate neighbourhood became so troublesome and harassing, that the Spartans repeatedly endeavoured by negotiations to recover Pylos and their captive countrymen. But in vain; the haughty demands of the Athenians being always of such a nature that they could not be accepted by the Lacedaemonians. The prisoners remained in the hands of the Athenians, who declared that, if the Peloponnesians should again invade Attica, they would put them to death.

In their other undertakings also during this year, the Athenians

* The more intelligent of the Athenians, and among them Aristophanes (*Equit.* 55.), considered Demosthenes as the real conqueror.

were generally successful. Nicias was sent against Corinth with a fleet of eighty galleys, 2000 heavy-armed Athenians, and horse-transports with 200 cavalry. He landed at Solygeia, about sixty stadia south-east of Corinth, and fought a successful battle against the Corinthians, who had hastily assembled to meet him, and lost 200 men, while only fifty of the Athenians were slain. He then sailed towards Crommyon, which he plundered, and thence proceeded to the coast of Argolis, where he took possession of Methone, and ravaged the territories of Troezen, Haliae, and Epidaurus; after which he returned to Athens.

After the victory of Pylos, Eurymedon and Sophocles, on their way to Sicily, arrived at Corcyra, and supported the Corcyraeans against those who had fortified themselves on Mount Istone. The latter were obliged to come to terms, and submit to the arbitration of Athens. But by a stratagem the people of Corcyra inveigled the prisoners into an infraction of the agreement, and then acted with unparalleled and most atrocious cruelty towards the unfortunate men. They were led out of the temple in which they were shut up, in troops of twenty, between two rows of armed men, who aimed their blows each at the object of his personal hatred as he passed. When sixty had been executed in this manner, the others, seeing their fearful fate, refused to leave the building. The murderers then ascended the roof, and through an opening attacked their victims with arrows; but most of them made away with themselves. The nobles were thus completely annihilated; the popular party became the unopposed masters of the city, and the bloody civil war which had raged so long was now terminated.

Towards the end of the year the Chians were ordered by the Athenians to break down their fortifications, but were promised that they should retain their constitution; for the example of Lesbos had taught the Athenians to distrust the islanders.

In the following year, B.C. 424, the eighth of the war, the Athenians still continued victorious, and made new conquests. They now reached the highest point of their good fortune; but the continuance of the war, which they might have terminated on the most favourable terms, soon restored the equilibrium of power between the two contending parties. For the Athenians left nothing untried; no success satisfied them, or prevented them from immediately aiming at a still greater one. They were so enterprising and ambitious, that they regarded everything which they had not attempted as a real loss.

They now established themselves on the eastern coast of Peloponnesus, as they had done before on the western. Under the command of Nicias, with two colleagues, a fleet of sixty galleys, with 2000 heavy-armed, some cavalry, and many Milesian and other allied troops, sailed against the island of Cythera, which, being of great importance to the Lacedaemonians as a station for the transports from Egypt and Libya, and as a bulwark against any attacks from the sea, had always been strongly garrisoned by them. The Athenians landed on two points, and with their main force advanced against the town of the Cytheraeans, who at first offered some resistance, but afterwards surrendered to the aggressors, on condition that they should not be put to death; with this one exception, the Athenians were to dispose of them according to their pleasure. Nicias left them in possession of their island, and only garrisoned the towns of Cythera and Scandeia. The fleet then proceeded to Laconia, the Athenians everywhere ravaging the towns and fields on the coast, and meeting with no resistance; for the Lacedaemonians, after so many disasters, and especially after the loss of Pylos and Cythera, had scarcely courage to continue the war with any vigour. They had, from the beginning, embarked in maritime warfare with reluctance, and the Athenians had now decided advantages even on land. In this desponding mood, the Spartans confined themselves to defending the most important points, allowing the Athenians to continue their landings and ravagings. The latter, after having visited Epidaurus and Limera, took Thyrea, which was occupied by Aeginetans, and having plundered and burned everything, they carried the surviving Aeginetans with them as prisoners to Attica. The people of Athens resolved to transport the Cytheraean prisoners to other islands, but to leave the rest of the inhabitants to cultivate their ancient possessions, subject to the payment of a tribute of four talents. The Aeginetans were sentenced to death; and the Lacedaemonian governor of Thyrea was added to those who had been taken prisoners in Sphacteria.

While the Athenians were thus elated with their good fortune and victories, they were extremely annoyed at the intelligence that the commanders of their fleet in Sicily, without having gained a victory or effected a conquest, had concluded a peace with the Sicilians. Weary of their long-protracted quarrels, and justly arguing that their internal wars would render them defenceless against foreign enemies, the Sicilian towns began, at first one by one, to make peace with each other; they then all met in a peace congress at Gela, where, by the urgent advice of the Syracusan Hermocrates, who cautioned them against the powerful Athenians, as aiming at nothing less than the possession of their fair and wealthy island, they concluded a general peace. The allies of Athens gave notice of this peace to the Athenians, intimating that they no longer required their assistance. The commanders of the fleet, Pythodorus, Eurymedon, and Sophocles, forthwith returned to Athens; but the people received them with murmurs, because they came without having gained any victories, and without booty: two of them were sent into exile, and Eurymedon was sentenced to pay a fine, on the alleged ground that they had been induced by bribes to quit Sicily. The people was so elated with its recent good fortune, that as no enterprise was too great for its ambition, so it neglected all proportion between its means and its ends, and would not hear of any obstacles which nature or man could oppose to its success.

View of Navarino, the ancient Pylos.

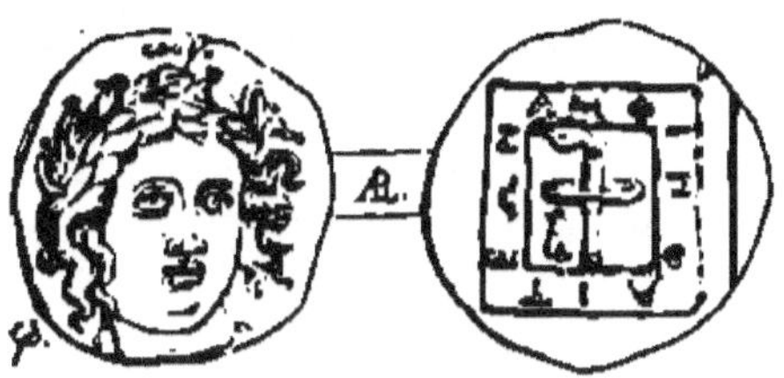

Coin of Amphipolis.

CHAPTER XXII.

FROM THE GENERAL PACIFICATION OF SICILY TO THE PEACE OF NICIAS.

During the latter years of the first half of the Peloponnesian war, there appeared among the Spartans a hero such as Sparta never again produced in the course of the war. Lysander, the conqueror of Aegospotami, was brave and successful, indeed, but his character is much censured by the ancients; whereas Brasidas, with whom we have already become acquainted, is praised by Thucydides unconditionally, though that author is generally sparing and scrupulous in his commendations. Independently of his undoubted bravery, Thucydides praises especially his kindness and affability, which gained for him more hearts and towns, and did more injury to the Athenians, than his courage and success in arms. He restored the confidence of his countrymen, and by his bold but cautious undertakings rendered it possible to conclude a peace on equal terms. Nicias and Cleon, on the side of the Athenians, could not stand a comparison with him; for the former had none of his quickness and boldness, while the latter possessed neither his valour, his caution, nor his humanity.

Brasidas first checked the undertakings of the Athenians against Megara. The Athenians, as we have already noticed, had made themselves masters of the small island of Minoa. In the present year they led a great force against Nisaea, and being supported and guided by treachery among the Megarians themselves, they obtained possession of the port town and the long walls connecting it with Megara; the capital itself was in imminent danger, for there, too, traitors were ready to open the gates to the Athenians. At this time Brasidas was in the territory of Corinth, collecting an army against Thrace. On being informed of the peril of Megara, he hastened thither with a considerable force, while Boeotians came to its assistance from the other side. The armies for a long time faced each other without engaging: the Athenians, knowing the advantage of the enemy in point of numbers, and carefully weighing the circumstances of the case, were unwilling to stake their military glory on the issue of a battle; they contented themselves, therefore, with occupying Nisaea, and returned to Attica. The Megarians then selected 100 of the most guilty among the popular party, and compelled the commonalty itself to condemn them to death. After this an extremely narrow oligarchical form of government was instituted at Megara, and remained in power for a long time.

This undertaking, which was far from answering the expectations which the Athenians had founded on it, was followed by a great calamity,—the first after a long series of victories. A vast scheme devised against Boeotia, and especially against Thebes, failed. A number of men, exiles, emigrants, and others, dissatisfied with the political condition of the Boeotian towns, were negotiating with the Athenian general, Hippocrates, and with Demosthenes, the commander of the fleet at Naupactus, with a view to overturn the existing oligarchical constitutions of the towns, and to establish a popular government on the model of that existing at Athens. Some of them intended to betray the port of Siphae, on the Corinthian gulf, into the hands of Athens; while others were to deliver up to her Chaeronea, on the borders of Phocis, which was tributary to Orchomenos. In the east, the Athenians were to take possession of Delium, a place sacred to Apollo. All this was to be done in one day, and it was arranged that Hippocrates should at the same time invade Boeotia from the south. It was intended by this plan to divide the military forces of the Boeotians, and thus the more easily to compel the towns to change their constitutions. Besides his forty galleys, Demosthenes was accompanied on this expedition by all his Acarnanian allies. But, neglecting the appointed time at the beginning of winter, he arrived too early at Siphae; and his design had also been betrayed. Accordingly, he found Siphae and Chaeronea guarded by all the forces of the Boeotians. Hippocrates arrived afterwards, but the men who had carried on the negotiations did not now venture to cause the towns to rise. He did not take possession of Delium until the Boeotians had already withdrawn from Siphae. In less than three days he surrounded the sacred place with a wall and ditch, and after leaving a garrison in it, he began to retreat with the rest of the army. The heavy-armed forming the rear had already reached the territory of Oropos, in Attica, when the whole of the Boeotian army came in sight. Ten out of the eleven Boeotarchs were against giving battle, but Pagondas, the eleventh, who was at the same time their military commander, prevailed upon them to adopt his advice, by reminding them that the Athenians, without provocation, had crossed the frontier, and that it was the duty of the

Boeotians to put an end for ever to such encroachments by boldly repelling and chastising the aggressors. Pagondas then drew up the army for battle; and the Athenians, joined by the division of Hippocrates from Delium, did the same. The extreme wings of the two armies were not engaged, being separated by two rapid brooks. On their left wing the Thebans were defeated, although the Thespians, at all times renowned for their valour, distinguished themselves particularly against the Athenians, most of whom were cut to pieces. On their right wing the Boeotians were victorious, and, by surrounding their opponents with brigades of cavalry, completed the confusion and defeat of the Athenians, who dispersed in all directions towards the coast and frontier. The pursuit and massacre lasted till the darkness of the night put an end to them. The garrison of Delium alone remained in Boeotia; the rest of the army fled by land to Attica, or took refuge in the ships on the coast of Oropos. On the following day, the Boeotians made preparations to take Delium by storm. They refused to give up the dead unless that place was surrendered, alleging that the sanctuary of the god had been profaned and polluted by the Athenians.* After a siege of seventeen days Delium was taken; a part of its garrison was put to the sword, 200 were made prisoners, and the rest escaped. The loss of the Athenians in this war was very considerable; 1000 heavy-armed Athenians, with their commander Hippocrates, had fallen, besides a large number of light troops and others.† The Boeotians lost about 500.

This defeat was the most important and bloody during the first half of the Peloponnesian war, but it was only the beginning of still greater disasters, which destroyed the proud confidence of the Athenians in their good fortune, and soon inclined them to accept the peace for which Greece was longing. The unsuccessful landing of Demosthenes with his allies on the coast of Sicyon, which took place soon after the battle of Delium, was of less importance; nor had the loss, in the winter of the same year (B. C. 423), of the long walls of Megara, which the Megarians afterwards entirely destroyed, much influence upon the events of the war. But the undertakings of the bold Brasidas against the Athenian possessions in Chalcidice and Thrace were of the greatest consequence. As in former years the Athenians had made ravaging expeditions

* It was not customary for the victors to make any stipulations or conditions on delivering up the dead to the vanquished party for burial; but in this case the Boeotians probably considered that the seizure by the Athenians of a sacred place had deprived them of any claim to the ordinary courtesies.

† According to Plato (*Sympos.* p. 221.), Socrates and Alcibiades were together during the battle and in the flight. Xenophon is mentioned also by Strabo (ix. p. 403.). Laches, too, served on that occasion in the infantry.

against the coasts of Peloponnesus, in order to force the Lacedaemonian armies to quit Attica, so now the Lacedaemonians commenced a war against the transmarine possessions of Athens, hoping that thus they might be enabled to recover Pylos and Cythera.

The Lacedaemonians were called upon to support and encourage the revolt of the Chalcidian towns, not only by their inhabitants, who wished to have Brasidas for their deliverer and protector, but also by Perdiccas of Macedonia, who had secretly become untrue to his treaty with Athens. The Lacedaemonians accordingly sent Brasidas from Peloponnesus with 1700 heavy-armed and a number of mercenaries. He went by land, and, without encountering any great resistance on the part of the towns allied with Athens, reached Thessaly, whence with an escort of Thessalians he entered Macedonia. Perdiccas immediately joined him, in consequence of which the Athenians thenceforth regarded the king as their enemy. Brasidas, thus reinforced, proceeded first against Arrhibaeus, king of the Lyncestian Macedonians, whom it was intended to subdue. But Brasidas, before having recourse to arms, wished to try negotiations, and proposed an amicable arrangement, especially as Arrhibaeus himself had appealed to his decision. Although Perdiccas was opposed to this, yet Brasidas had an interview with Arrhibaeus, and was prevailed upon to withdraw his forces from Lyncestis. The immediate consequence of this was, that Perdiccas, to show his displeasure, reduced the amount of pay and supplies which he furnished to the Lacedaemonians from one-half to a third.

But Brasidas had not gone to the north, to waste his time in interfering in quarrels with which he had no concern; the Athenian possessions in Chalcidice and on the coast of Thrace were the chief objects of his enterprise; he proclaimed himself the deliverer of the Greek towns from the dominion of Athens. In this mission he showed himself so brave, prudent, and kind, that for many years afterwards his name was honoured throughout those regions; the name of the Lacedaemonians through him became popular among the Athenian allies, and many began to wish to connect themselves with Sparta.*

Brasidas first advanced against Acanthos, a colony of Andros, on the eastern coast of Chalcidice; he made his appearance about the time of the vintage, and by the promise that he would maintain their independence,—fear for their fields may likewise have had some influence on their determination,—he induced the Acan-

* Respecting the great influence of Brasidas, compare, besides Thucydides, Aristophanes (*Vesp.* 474. &c., 640.). Thucydides describes him as a model for all his Athenian contemporaries; and throughout his whole work he bestows unconditional praise on two men only, Pericles and Brasidas.

thians to revolt from Athens, and to admit the Lacedaemonians within their walls. Soon afterwards Stagiros also, another colony of the Andrians, embraced the cause of the Lacedaemonians.

During this winter Brasidas proceeded northwards against Amphipolis, an important colony of Athens, on the Strymon, in the territory of the Edonians. Eion was situated farther south, near the mouth of the river, and likewise belonged to the Athenians. Quick marches, the severity of the season, and the ready assistance of those who sided with Sparta, enabled Brasidas unexpectedly to appear before the walls of Amphipolis. He immediately took possession of the country round the city; but as he delayed attacking the place itself, the party at Amphipolis which was in favour of Athens, and for the moment was still the more powerful, looked round for assistance, and sent for Thucydides *, the celebrated historian of the Peloponnesian war. He happened to be on the coast of Thrace, about half a day's journey from Amphipolis, and hastened with seven ships to save at least Eion, which he succeeded in occupying; but Brasidas, in order to avoid being encamped too long before one place, sent a herald to offer to the Amphipolitans the mildest possible terms, and thus speedily induced the town to surrender. He was, however, unable to make himself master of Eion and the mouth of the river; and for this the Athenians were indebted to their countryman, Thucydides. The taking of Amphipolis was followed in rapid succession by the conquest of less important towns; but it was above all things the prudent and kind conduct of Brasidas that inclined the towns allied with, or subject to, Athens to revolt. They had heard of the defeat of Delium, of the effectual defence of Megara by Brasidas; accordingly the Athenians appeared to them to be weaker than before, and a revolt as so much the less dangerous. During this winter the Athenians actually did nothing beyond here and there strengthening the garrisons of the towns; while the Spartans, either from fear for the safety of their captive countrymen at Athens, or from envy of Brasidas, left their glorious general without support. But he nevertheless continued his operations. He proceeded southwards towards Acte, the eastern peninsula of Chalcidice, which the canal of Xerxes had changed into an island. The small towns there were easily won over, with the exception of Sane and Dion, for whose surrender he could not wait, being

* It is possible that Thucydides was condemned (προδοσίας), perhaps at the instigation of Cleon, for not having saved Amphipolis. The legal punishment of death was either commuted into that of exile, or he escaped from it by flight. The latter is more probable, because he remained in exile for twenty years (Aristoph. *Vesp.* 288. &c.; Pausan. i. 23. § 11.), partly in Thrace, and perhaps also in Sicily; but generally near the scene of the war, as he himself (v. 26.) states.

called away by some of the inhabitants of Torone, on the coast of the peninsula west of Athos, who promised to give up their town to him. On his arrival in the neighbourhood at night, he found his friends waiting for him, and ready to admit him secretly into the town. The plan succeeded: the partisans of the Lacedaemonians immediately joined the invaders, and the others were pacified by a mild proclamation, in which Brasidas assured them that they might trust to the faithfulness and honourable conduct of the Lacedaemonians, and that they, like the people of the other towns, would find in him their deliverer from the yoke of the Athenians. The few Athenians who were in the place fled to the fort of Lecythos, situated north of Torone, and there prepared to defend themselves. An unfortunate accident, however, enabled Brasidas to take the place by storm, and he put all the prisoners to the sword. A few only succeeded by means of boats in crossing over to Pallene. After this, Brasidas was engaged in making arrangements in the newly conquered towns, and in planning new expeditions: and while he was thus occupied, the winter of the eighth year of the war came to a close.

The victorious progress of Brasidas in Chalcidice did not, indeed, neutralise the advantages which the Athenians had gained in Peloponnesus; but the balance of power was sufficiently restored. The Athenians, seriously alarmed about their dominion in Chalcidice and Thrace, were anxious to check the rapid advance of Brasidas, and at the same time to make their preparations with the necessary circumspection. The Lacedaemonians, on the other hand, thought that the proper moment had now come for recovering their prisoners, about whose safety they had all along been deeply concerned. Hence both parties seem to have been equally desirous of peace; and thus a truce was agreed upon at the very beginning of the ninth year of the war.* It was concluded for one year, and its terms were to be the preliminaries of a definite peace. The proposals of the Lacedaemonians, that everything should remain *in statu quo*, and that the negotiations for peace should be forthwith commenced, were accepted by the people of Athens on the advice of Laches. But while the treaty was being ratified by the envoys of both parties, an event took place in Chalcidice which rendered compliance with its stipulations impossible. This was the revolt of Scione from the Athenians to Brasidas. The latter, by his insinuating conduct, had quickly won the affections of the people of that town, who were at first disinclined to join him; and the Scionaeans were now so much delighted with him, that they honoured him, as the deliverer of Greece, with

* On the 14th of Elaphebolion (March), B.C. 423.

a crown of gold, and presented him with fillets, as if he were a victor at the Olympian games. Just at the moment when he was preparing to advance against Mende and Potidaea, Athenian and Spartan commissioners arrived to inform him of the truce which had been concluded. Brasidas immediately returned to Torone, and the treaty was everywhere approved of. But now it was discovered that Scione had revolted from Athens two days after the conclusion of the treaty, and the Athenian commissioner accordingly demanded that the town should be restored to its former masters. Brasidas would not listen to this, and maintained that Athens had no right to make such a claim. When the Athenians were informed of these events they immediately prepared to send an expedition against Scione. The Lacedaemonians, on the other hand, proposed to submit the matter to a judicial decision, and declared that any other mode of acting would be a breach of the treaty. But the Athenians, seeing one town lost after another, thought they ought no longer to act the part of mere lookers on. Cleon did his best to stir up the people, and it was resolved that Scione should be taken and every man in it put to death.

In the mean while, Mende also joined Brasidas, who, as it had come over of its own accord, did not hesitate to accept its inhabitants as his allies. Both towns now made vigorous preparations to defend themselves against the Athenians. But before the latter appeared, Brasidas, in conjunction with Perdiccas, made a second expedition against Arrhibaeus. The Lyncestians were defeated, and Perdiccas was only waiting for the arrival of the Illyrians, in order to complete the conquest with their assistance. Brasidas, apprehending some danger for his Chalcidian towns, and unwilling to remain any longer at a distance from them, was preparing to return, when on a sudden a report was spread that the Illyrians had declared for Arrhibaeus. The barbarian troops of Perdiccas were seized with a panic, and dispersed in the greatest disorder. Brasidas alone remained behind; he determined upon a well-organised retreat, and encouraged his men to hold out and show themselves worthy of their country. The barbarians soon observed that his was not the retreat of a conquered or routed enemy. They accordingly set out in pursuit of the fleeing Macedonians, and occupied a defile through which Brasidas had to pass on his march into Macedonia. But there, too, the prudence of the Spartan outwitted his enemies, and he soon arrived in Macedonia with his army in safety. Indignant at the faithless flight of Perdiccas, the Lacedaemonians treated his country like that of an enemy, and carried off everything that came in their way. The enmity which thus arose between Brasidas and the king induced the latter again to ally himself with the Athenians.

On the arrival of Brasidas at Torone, the Athenians were already in possession of Mende. In point of fact the truce was broken; but still throughout this year the war was carried on only in those distant countries, while in Greece itself the two leading states, either by accident, or actuated by an irresistible desire for peace, seemed to observe the truce. Nicias and Nicostratus who had arrived in Chalcidice with an armament of 50 galleys and a considerable number of troops, began to carry on their operations against Mende from Potidaea. They made an unsuccessful attack upon the garrison of Mende, which they found encamped in a strong position before the town. On the following day, the Lacedaemonians having gone to Scione, the Peloponnesian and Athenian parties in the town began to quarrel and fight, in the midst of which the gates were thrown open to the Athenians. The town was plundered, and the citadel closely invested; but the garrison succeeded in forcing their way to Scione. In the latter place, too, the garrison occupied a strong position outside the town, which had to be conquered before the siege could be begun. As it was clear that this would be a tedious undertaking, the Athenians were satisfied for the present with completely investing the town.

While this siege was in progress, Perdiccas concluded a treaty with the Athenians, and, to give them a proof of his new friendship, he prevented the reinforcements, which were approaching by a road pointed out by Brasidas, from joining the Lacedaemonians. Towards the end of the winter, Brasidas made another attempt to surprise Potidaea by night; but was baffled by the Athenian garrison. At the beginning of the tenth year of the war, the truce expired, and, on the part of the Athenians, Cleon undertook the command. Entrusted with a force of 30 galleys, 1200 heavy-armed, 300 horse, and a large number of allies, he proceeded to Scione, which was still besieged. Taking along with him a part of the besieging army, he landed in the port of the Colophonians, not far south from Torone. On learning there that the garrison of Torone was weak and that Brasidas was absent, he attacked it both by land and by sea, and was fortunate enough to take the place before Brasidas, though he was not far off, could come to its assistance. The men were sent to Athens, and the women and children reduced to slavery. This happened in the spring of B.C. 422. Leaving a garrison in Torone, Cleon sailed round Mount Athos towards Amphipolis. From Eion, he first made an unsuccessful expedition against Stagiros, but took Galepsos from the Macedonians. In the mean time, Brasidas had received succours which increased his army to 2000 heavy-armed and 300 Greek horsemen; his light-armed troops were still more numerous, for he was joined by all the forces of the Edonians, Myrcinians, and Chalcidians. With 1500 of these troops he encamped on an eminence called Cerdylion, not far from Amphipolis, whence he could watch the movements of the enemy. The other troops took up their position at Amphipolis, under the command of Clearidas. Brasidas calculated that Cleon, underestimating the strength of his enemy, would soon advance against Amphipolis; his expectation was realised, not because Cleon was impelled by his courage, but because his army began to show signs of discontent, and gave him to understand that it was only his ignorance and cowardice which prevented him from advancing. He was thus compelled to march up the country. In the vain hope that he would not have to encounter any enemy, and that all would proceed very smoothly, he pitched his camp upon an eminence before Amphipolis. Seeing no troops on the walls, and the gates closed, he imagined that he might take the town at one blow. While Cleon was approaching, Brasidas had withdrawn into Amphipolis. He did not, however, consider it advisable to make an open attack upon the superior forces of the enemy, but determined to take them by surprise, before Cleon departed or received reinforcements. He accordingly selected 150 heavy-armed, and, in an inspiriting speech, cheered them on in their bold undertaking.

The Athenians had observed that Brasidas had entered the town, and Cleon was informed that the enemy was preparing to carry some plan into execution. No sooner had Cleon convinced himself of the truth of the report, than he gave the signal for a retreat, having no desire whatever to engage in a battle. But not being able to wheel the left wing quickly enough, his awkward tactics exposed the whole army, and Brasidas, seizing the opportunity, with his men fell upon the retreating ranks of the Athenians. At the same time, Clearidas attacked the enemy on another side, and the whole army was soon routed. Brasidas himself, while rushing against the right wing, received a mortal wound; but the Athenians did not observe his fall: he was taken up and carried away by those who stood nearest to him. Cleon, who had from the first thought of nothing but flight, was overtaken by a Myrcinian targeteer, and slain. The heavy-armed, who were all Athenian citizens, made a long and brave resistance, but in the end they also were put to flight. Brasidas, having been conveyed to Amphipolis, was there informed of the victory of his men, and died soon afterwards. Six hundred Athenians fell on that day, while the victors lost only seven men, for there had been no regular engagement,—only a pursuit of fugitives. Those who escaped immediately returned with the fleet to Athens. At Amphipolis, great honours were paid to the memory of Brasidas; he was buried in the market-place, his tomb was surrounded with a fence, sacrifices were offered to him as a hero, and annual games were celebrated in his honour. The Amphipolitans, having formed a close alliance with the Lacedaemonians, henceforth regarded Brasidas as the real founder of their city, and destroyed everything which might remind them of Hagnon and the Athenians.

In the mean while, an auxiliary force which had been sent from Sparta had tarried too long at Heracleia, and had, moreover, been refused a passage through Thessaly. Thus the plans of Brasidas were not prosecuted, and the Lacedaemonians thought only of making peace. The advantages gained by the belligerents might be considered equal. The recent defeat at Amphipolis made the Athenians apprehensive about their allies, and their pride and arrogance were considerably lowered. The Spartans still thought of the fate of the prisoners of Sphacteria, of the disgraceful loss of Pylos and Cythera, and of the danger of an insurrection among the Helots.* In addition to all this, the thirty years' peace with Argos had expired, and Sparta did not feel herself strong enough to carry on a war with it and Athens at the same time. Moreover, Brasidas and Cleon, who had hitherto been the chief obstacles in the way of peace — the former, because war afforded him opportunities of displaying his military talents, and of gaining glory; the latter, that he might amid the din of arms conceal his evil designs, his calumnies of others, and his own faithlessness — both these men had been removed by death from the scene of action. Nicias, who loved a quiet and undisturbed life, though he was brave and possessed of warlike ability, and Pleistoanax, king of Sparta, were engaged in bringing about a peace, the negotiations for which were continued during the winter. With a view to accelerate its conclusion, the Peloponnesians, about the beginning of spring, even commenced new preparations for war. But after many conferences, the basis of a treaty was at length settled in the spring of B.C. 421, on the footing of a mutual restitution of conquests made during the war; and as the Thebans would not admit that Plataeae belonged to this class, on the ground that it had been freely surrendered, it was stipulated that Athens should keep Nisaea, which she had acquired by a similar transaction. With the exception of the Boeotians, Corinthians, Eleans, and Megarians, who did not agree to this treaty, all the confederates accepted it, and mutually ratified it with sacrifices and oaths. Among the stipulations, of which Thucydides has

* An instance of unexampled cruelty against the Helots is recorded by Thucyd. iv. 80.

preserved the original document, we may mention, that the Athenians restored to the Lacedaemonians, Pylos, Cythera, Methone, and Atalanta; that the Chalcidian and Thracian towns conquered by Brasidas became neutral; that Amphipolis was restored to the Athenians, as also Scione, which, together with Torone and some other towns, was left entirely at the mercy of the Athenians. The neutral towns were to pay only the tribute fixed by Aristides, and in other respects to be independent. All Athenian and Lacedaemonian prisoners were to be returned without ransom. This peace was ratified at Athens on the 25th of the month of Elaphebolion (the 4th of April), B.C. 421, the eleventh year of the war. This peace, commonly called the peace of Nicias, was concluded for the period of fifty years.

The question, which of the two states was first to comply with the stipulations of the peace, was decided by lot, which fell upon Sparta. She forthwith liberated the prisoners, and sent envoys to Clearidas, with orders at once to surrender Amphipolis to the Athenians. He at first showed some hesitation, being actuated in some degree by a desire to please the Chalcidians, who were hostile to the Athenians; but he was ultimately obliged to comply

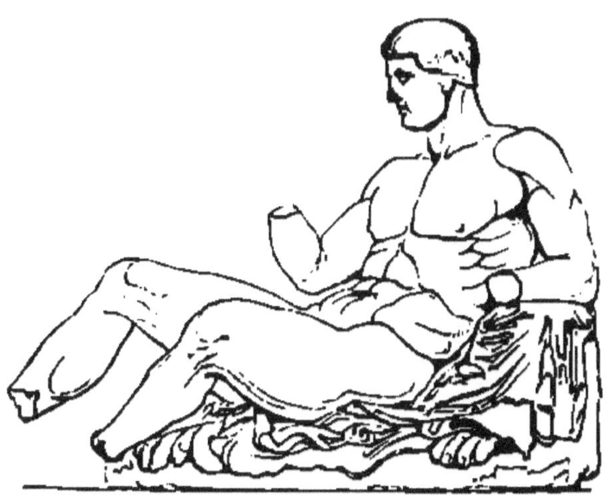

Statue of Theseus.
(From the eastern pediment of the Parthenon.)

with the commands of Sparta, or at least to withdraw the Lacedaemonian garrison from the town. But as the confederates who were dissatisfied with the peace evinced no intention, notwithstanding the urgent entreaties of Sparta, to give in their adhesion, the Lacedaemonians, in order to be well prepared for any contingency, especially in case of a war with Argos, concluded, in April of the same year, an offensive and defensive alliance with Athens, which contained the stipulation, that each of the contracting parties should be entitled at its discretion to increase or diminish the number of its allies or subjects. This at once roused the fear and opposition of all the second-rate states; and numerous elements were at work which might lead to a speedy violation and termination of the peace.

Caryatid Portico forming the Cecropium of the Erechtheum at Athens.

Group from the Western Frieze of the Parthenon.

CHAPTER XXIII.

FROM THE PEACE OF NICIAS TO THE CONQUEST OF MELOS.

For a period of nearly seven years, the two leading states, Athens and Sparta, observed the treaty so far as not to invade each other's territory, but otherwise Greece was by no means in the enjoyment of peace. From the very beginning, the contracting parties did not strictly adhere to the conditions they had nominally agreed to; each endeavoured to injure its dreaded and hated rival by forming new connections, and the states of inferior rank continued to stir the fire of war until it burst forth into a fierce and ruinous blaze. Thucydides, considering the contest to have been carried on uninterruptedly for twenty-seven years, treats even this intermediate period as belonging to the war; and we shall adopt the same method, so long as we have him for our guide.

The Corinthians began the movement; they themselves, indeed, did not at once renounce the Peloponnesian alliance, but they induced the Argives to put themselves without delay at the head of a new confederacy, which was to be joined by all the Greek states except Athens and Sparta. The Mantineans, who had of late enlarged their dominions, were the first to join the new league, in order to secure their new acquisitions. Their example was immediately followed by the Eleans, who concluded an alliance, first with Corinth, and then with Argos, because they thought they had been treated unjustly by Sparta; this new alliance, therefore, was a sort of demonstration against Sparta. The Corinthians themselves next went over, ostensibly in order to fulfil the terms of ancient treaties and vows which bound them not to abandon their Chalcidian allies, but in reality because they considered themselves wronged by the Athenians, who retained possession of Solion and Anactorion. With them, the Chalcidians also joined the rising confederacy. The Boeotians and Megarians were, for the present, prevented from becoming members of it, by the circumstance that Argos had a democratic form of government, while they themselves were ruled by oligarchies. Thus no further allies were gained at this time. The Tegeatans were decidedly opposed to the new confederacy, and the Boeotians too, in spite of Corinthian machinations, maintained their separate armistice with Athens.

In the face of these hostile manifestations, Sparta and Athens were engaged during the summer in negotiations and controversies respecting the carrying into effect of the peace; but no satisfactory results were come to. What both wanted was the honest will, for Sparta, which had shown itself so ready at the beginning, now hesitated, and owned that it was not strong enough to restore Amphipolis to Athens against its will, or to compel the Boeotians and Corinthians to accept the terms of the peace. The Athenians replied, that under these circumstances they could not give up Pylos, and only after long negotiations consented to assign other settlements in Cephallenia to the Messenians and Helots who were living at Pylos.

Matters became still more complicated, when, in the following winter, at the election of the ephors, men of the party in favour of war were placed at the head of affairs at Sparta. Assisted by the Boeotians, they endeavoured to enter into the alliance with Argos; the negotiations, however, were carried on slowly and without energy, and, for the present, nothing was effected. But the Lacedaemonians, interested above all things in the recovery of Pylos, concluded, about the end of the winter, a separate treaty with the Boeotians; this act was contrary to the treaty with Athens, according to which such connections could be entered into only by both states in common. By this treaty, the Boeotians agreed to surrender to the Lacedaemonians Panacton, which had been taken in the tenth year of the war from Athens, and the Athenian prisoners who were kept at Thebes. This was to enable the Spartans to obtain from the Athenians the restoration of Pylos. But when, in the spring of 420, Spartan commissioners came to take possession of Panacton, they found that it had been dismantled by order of the Boeotian government, on the plea of an ancient compact between Boeotia and Athens. When the Argives were informed of this alliance, they imagined that it had been entered into with the consent of Athens; and fearing lest they might be involved in a war at once with Sparta, Tegea, and Athens, they sent envoys to Sparta, in the beginning of B.C. 420, to negotiate for a treaty and alliance. The Spartans were willing to accept the proposal, but suddenly the Argives broke off the negotiations and embraced the cause of Athens.

The Athenians, dissatisfied with the alliance between Sparta and Boeotia, indignant at the destruction of Panacton, and remembering the many terms of their own peace with Sparta which had not been carried into effect, dismissed the Spartan envoys with a somewhat stern answer. Alcibiades, the son of Cleinias, above all others, urged his countrymen to violate the peace. "In comparison with the statesmen of other republics, he was yet young, but he was honoured by the people on account of the fame of his ancestors." In reading this statement of Thucydides, we might be inclined to believe that he intentionally passed over or undervalued the circumstances which, at the first appearance of so extraordinary a man in public life, would certainly have been touched upon by other historians. But in Thucydides everything is well considered and in accordance with the artistic rules of historical composition. The transition from the accounts of public matters to the description of a man's personal character is everywhere kept within strict limits, and carried out with wonderful moderation and impartiality. Hence, we also shall abstain from saying in this place more of that perfect image of the Athenian character and genius than Thucydides himself thought it right to state. The events in the life of Alcibiades, down to his coming forward against Nicias, appeared comparatively unimportant to the calm and thoughtful mind of Thucydides, although his name had long been in every one's mouth, and his manners and conduct gave the tone to the fashionable circles at Athens. We may pass over the various stories about his youth, as relating to the results merely of his birth and education. Everything belonging to him was marked by dazzling splendour and possessed wonderful fascination: his birth, his wealth, his beauty, and his virtues, not more than his vices. In him, Nature seems to have tried to combine her most varied productions. The consciousness of his powers and a restless ambition impelled him on all occasions to claim the foremost place, and his calculating subtlety was always a more powerful incentive than strict justice or a regard for the interests of his country. He was so reckless about his intellectual endowments, his personal beauty, and his wealth, that the rapid changes in his favour with the people were only the reflex, as it were, of his own fickleness. He was naturally of an aristocratic temperament, which was confirmed by the circumstances amid which he was brought up, and his more than oligarchic sentiments were displayed in decisive moments most unequivocally. Whenever he assumed the appearance of a popular leader, it was always for the purpose of gaining some personal object.*

The history of the period of the war which now follows, down to its termination, is at the same time the history of the life of Alcibiades. He exerted himself to prevent the conclusion of the intended alliance with Sparta, because he considered a treaty with Argos to be more advantageous and lasting, but still more, because he had from the first been opposed to the peace which was brought about by the mediation of Nicias and Laches, and in the conclusion of which he himself, who was then at the utmost only twenty-eight years of age, had been taken no notice of. For although he had done good service to the prisoners of Sphacteria, and had renewed the connection of public hospitality which had existed between his family and Sparta, yet the Spartans seem to have preferred transacting business with the sober and intelligent Nicias. For this slight, Alcibiades now took revenge. He invited the Argives to come to Athens, accompanied by envoys from Elis and Mantinea, in order to conclude an alliance against Thebes and Sparta. The Argives willingly sent their envoys, but at the same time there arrived others from Sparta, who were commissioned to demand the restoration of Pylos in exchange for Panacton, to justify the treaty concluded with Thebes, but, above all, to prevent the conclusion of an alliance with Argos. Alcibiades contrived to thwart the designs of Sparta, while an insult offered to the ambassadors† rendered a peaceful settlement almost impossible; and thus the alliance between Athens, Argos, Elis, and Mantinea, was actually concluded. It was both offensive and defensive, and was to last for 100 years. The peace between Athens and Sparta still continued, but the immediate consequence of these proceedings was, that Corinth, which had only accepted the previous treaty with Argos, but had not sworn to it, again inclined towards the Lacedaemonians, and afterwards, when the celebration of the Olympic games was over, could not be induced to return to its former allies. The Eleans, feeling secure under the protection of the new confederacy, excluded the Lacedaemonians from the Olympic games of this year, because they had occupied Lepreon during the religious truce; nay, they even fined the Lacedaemonians, who, as no understanding could be come to, were actually obliged to perform the customary sacrifices in their own country.

In the following year, B.C. 419, the thirteenth of the war, there appeared in Peloponnesus symptoms of a greater and more gene-

* This seems to be the meaning of Thucyd. viii. 48.
† Thucyd. v. 45.

ral struggle. A war had arisen between the Argives and the Epidaurians in consequence of a dispute about some sacrifice, and the Athenians actively assisted the Argives. Alcibiades, who was then one of the Athenian generals, had entered Peloponnesus with some troops, evidently with a view to make himself acquainted with the scene of his future operations. At the same time, he gained over the town of Patrae in Achaia to the alliance with Athens, and persuaded its inhabitants to extend their walls as far as the sea-coast. But his plan of fortifying the Achaean Rhion, and of thereby obtaining the command of the entrance to the Corinthian gulf, was thwarted by the Corinthians and Sicyonians. The Lacedaemonians were prevented by unfavourable sacrifices from supporting the Epidaurians, but even their approach was enough to induce the Athenian forces to retreat; and throughout this year, although the ravaging inroads were continued, nothing decisive was effected. It was only towards the end of the year that the Spartans sent 300 men by sea to Epidaurus, upon which the Argives immediately applied to the Athenians, reminding them of the terms of their alliance; and on the proposal of Alcibiades, the Athenians inscribed on the pillar containing the treaty with Sparta the words, "the Lacedaemonians have not observed their oath:" Helots also were sent to Pylos to harass Laconia. But, notwithstanding all this, the peace was formally still maintained. As the Epidaurians, however, continued to be distressed, and symptoms of discontent and hostility became here and there visible, the Lacedaemonians thought that they ought to hesitate no longer, and in the latter part of the summer of B.C. 418, they assembled an unusually large army of allies, which they themselves joined with all their forces, and invaded the Argive territory in three divisions. Yet no decisive battle was fought, for king Agis allowed himself to be persuaded by two Argives to conclude an armistice, in the hope that it would lead to a final and peaceful settlement; accordingly, to the great annoyance of the Spartans and their allies, he departed with his splendid army without having struck a blow. The Argives, too, were so eager to fight, that they severely punished those who had, without orders, acted the part of mediators. The Athenians had come too late with their auxiliary force of 1000 heavy-armed men and 400 horse, under the command of Laches and Nicostratus.

Although, after the truce just concluded, the Argives no longer needed these auxiliary forces, yet they remained in their territory, and, by the advice of Alcibiades, it was resolved to commence hostilities, on the ground that the truce had been concluded by Argos alone, and was, therefore, invalid. All the allies, who were soon joined by the Argives, now set out against Orchomenos in Arcadia, and compelled the town to surrender. Thence they proceeded to Tegea, which was to be delivered up to them by treachery. This danger roused the Spartans, who were greatly exasperated at the truce concluded by their king, and they not only assembled their own military forces, but commanded their Arcadian and other allies to furnish their contingents as speedily as possible. On the frontier of Laconia, they dismissed the sixth part of their army, consisting of the oldest and youngest men, to protect their homes, and with the rest entered the territory of Mantinea, ravaging the country and pitching their camp near a sanctuary of Heracles. The Argive allies chose a position, strong and difficult of access, for drawing up their forces in battle array; and Agis, taking the counsel of an experienced warrior, did not venture to attack them on that day. On the morrow, when he again advanced, he found the enemy already drawn up in the plain, and the Lacedaemonians, in the greatest haste and alarm, prepared for battle. But in the conflict, they fought with calmness and undaunted courage, and gained a decisive victory. Of the Argives 1100 fell, while the Lacedaemonians lost only 300. This battle of Mantinea was one of the most important in the whole war; and for the Spartans it was doubly advantageous, because it restored their ancient military glory, which had been impaired by the defeats of Pylos and Sphacteria.

At the time of this battle, which occurred in the month of August, just before the festival of the Carneia, the Epidaurians had made a ravaging expedition into the territory of Argos, which was feebly protected, but were themselves closely invested by the Eleans and Athenians. Soon after the Carneian festival, about the beginning of winter, the Lacedaemonians again advanced as far as Tegea, but this time they made proposals of accommodation to Argos, where a faction, hostile to the democratic government and favourably disposed to Sparta, was inclined to make peace. These negotiations, which Alcibiades in vain endeavoured to frustrate, were brought to a satisfactory termination. The Argives accepted the proposals, the principal stipulation of which was that they were to leave the Epidaurians in peace, and oblige the Athenians to depart from their territory. Soon afterwards another treaty of alliance was concluded for 50 years between Argos and Sparta, whereby Argos renounced its former allies. The new confederates immediately exerted themselves to extend the league: they renewed the ancient treaties with the Chalcidians, and called upon king Perdiccas of Macedonia to join the confederacy, a request with which he who traced his own origin to Argos, was not unwilling to comply. The Athenians now withdrew their besieging forces from Epidaurus, and towards the end of the winter the

Mantineans found themselves constrained to join the alliance between Sparta and Argos. At Sicyon an oligarchical government was established, and the same change was effected at Argos with the aid of Sparta. Such were the immediate consequences of the new confederacy, which, however, did not last long.

While the Lacedaemonians were engaged in setting up oligarchical governments in the towns of Achaia, the popular party at Argos again raised its head, B.C. 417. The struggle commenced at a time when Sparta was celebrating a festival, and the democratic party gained the victory. The aid sent by Sparta to support the minority came too late, and was altogether too slow; the victorious party hastened to form connections with Athens, and built strong and long walls from Argos to the sea-coast, by which they were enabled to receive support and supplies by sea in case of their city being besieged. It was not till the following winter, that the Spartans with their allies arrived before Argos; they succeeded in making themselves masters of, and in breaking down, the walls which had been erected with enormous exertions; the Argive town of Hyriae was taken; its free-born inhabitants were put to death, and then the Lacedaemonians withdrew from Argos. After this, the Argives attempted to make a ravaging expedition into the territory of the Phliasians, who had given shelter to their exiles. In order to strengthen their league, and to prevent the re-establishment of an oligarchical government, Alcibiades in the following summer, B.C. 416, sailed with a squadron of 20 galleys to Argos, took 300 of the oligarchs on board, and carried them to the neighbouring islands, where they were kept under the superintendence of Athens.

Soon afterwards the Athenians undertook an expedition against the island of Melos. The Melians, who were a Doric colony, boasted of having been in the undisturbed possession of their island for 700 years, that is, ever since the Doric migration; and they were the only islanders who did not belong to the Athenian confederacy. Some years previously, B.C. 420, Nicias had in vain attempted to conquer the island, and the Melians, who had before been neutral, then became open enemies of the Athenians. The inactivity of Sparta now tempted the latter to make another attempt to subdue the island. Thirty-eight ships, most of which were Athenian, and about 3000 heavy-armed, partly Athenians and partly allies, approached the coast of Melos under the command of Cleomedes. At first, negotiations were tried between Athenian envoys and the Melian oligarchs; they did not lead to any result, but are characteristic and remarkable for the pride and confidence of the Athenians in their own power, as contrasted with the courageous hope and undaunted bearing of the Melians, who considered it a disgrace to surrender without fighting for their independence. In spite of the threatening language of the Athenians, the Melians would only consent to become the friends of Athens, and insisted on preserving their neutrality as before. The Athenians, adhering with equal obstinacy to their demand that the Melians should become either allies or tributary, and treating with contempt the assistance which they expected from Sparta, began to lay siege to the town. The siege was continued till the following winter, being protracted by the bold defence and successful sallies of the Melians, until the Athenians sent reinforcements, and traitors among the besieged themselves rendered further resistance impossible. The Melians surrendered at discretion, and experienced the same fate as had been inflicted upon the people of Scione. Some time afterwards, the conquerors sent 500 settlers to occupy the desolate island. The Lacedaemonians had not sent to their kinsmen the expected assistance, and on the whole showed no hostility towards Athens, but acted in accordance with the existing treaties. For while the Athenians made predatory excursions from Pylos into Laconia, the Spartans merely proclaimed that whoever wished, might in his private capacity retaliate upon the Athenians. Once only, the Athenians meditated another expedition against Argos, which however was thwarted by unfavourable signs in the victims; so that the only result of their preparations was to induce the Argives to deprive those oligarchs who were suspected of favouring Sparta of any power to do mischief, and to establish the democratic government still more firmly. The Lacedaemonians assigned to the Argive exiles Orneae, a town on the Arcadian frontier, and made a ravaging excursion into the territory of Argos; but after their departure, an Athenian armament joined by the Argives took Orneae and destroyed it.

About this time, numerous trifling occurrences and disputes seemed to forebode more important events, and even the winter of this year saw the beginning of the great Sicilian war.

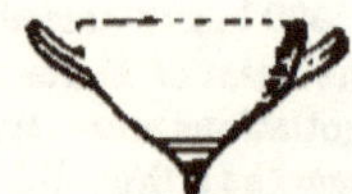

Ancient drinking-vessel called Mastus.

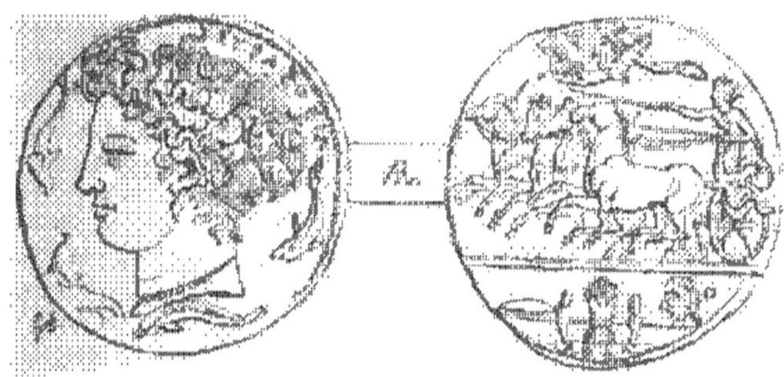

Coin of Syracuse.

CHAPTER XXIV.

THE SICILIAN EXPEDITION BEFORE THE ARRIVAL OF GYLIPPUS IN SICILY.

We have now reached, if not the most interesting, at least the most important period — the turning point — of the bloody drama of the Peloponnesian war. At the beginning of the expedition against Syracuse, Athens was at the height of her power and pride; but after the termination of the Sicilian war, we find her entering upon the gloomy path of gradual decline, which is marked by only a few glorious events, and those connected with particular persons, especially with Alcibiades; confidence in themselves and in their good fortune forsook the Athenian people, and their authority among their allies and tributaries was evidently gone. The ship of the state, which had so long maintained its course under the management of reckless as well as bold and skilful pilots, was now overpowered by the billows beating against it on all sides, and was fast hurried to destruction.

The expedition to Sicily was one of the fruits of the Athenian democracy, such as it had been developed after the time of Pericles. All the conservatives, or men of the moderate party, were opposed to it; and the crime committed against the Hermae, of which we shall have to speak hereafter, may be regarded as a desperate attempt of those wishing for peace to prevent the sailing of the fleet, and to put an end to the war by any means, however violent.

The desire of the Athenian people and its leaders to establish themselves in the western seas, in Sicily, and even beyond it, had been awakened long before this time, but became manifest more especially after the death of Pericles, when the people and the demagogues obtained the uncontrolled management of public affairs, and with few interruptions retained it until the downfal of Athens. Her participation in the Leontine war, which lasted from the fifth until the eighth year of the Peloponnesian war, and ended without any important results, has already been noticed. The peace of Gela, which was brought about by the wise counsel of the Syracusan Hermocrates, checked for a time the designs of the Athenians who had not yet come forward with the energy which might have been expected from their power. That peace united all the Siceliots * against Athens, their common enemy. The embassy of Phaeax, in B.C. 422, the object of which was to protect the popular party of the Leontines, which had been expelled by the nobles and the Syracusans, and to gain allies for Athens and the people of Leontini against the powerful state of Syracuse, had not been very successful; but the delight of the Athenians in extensive and adventurous undertakings had become so influential a feeling, that men like Alcibiades knew how to make the excitable people adopt their own bold and ambitious schemes, which it thenceforth regarded with almost parental fondness. An additional incentive to action in Sicily was the fact that the undertakings of the Athenians in Peloponnesus were not carried on with ardour or on a grand scale, on account of the peace which had never yet been formally abrogated; nor were they particularly successful. The people wished for war, and yet were loth to be the first to break the peace, to which Sparta clung with obstinacy as long as it possibly could. Alcibiades moreover was not satisfied with the manner in which the war had hitherto been carried on; his mind was full of some brilliant expedition, worthy of the maritime power of Athens; his and the people's thoughts rose even to the idea of establishing a universal empire. Lastly, the majority of the people did not know the extent and population of Sicily, nor take into consideration the fearful consequences of the failure of such an undertaking. The causes and the beginning of the Sicilian war were as follow.

In the winter of the sixteenth year of the Peloponnesian war, ambassadors of the Egestaeans came to Athens, soliciting aid against the Selinuntians, their neighbours, who, supported by the Syracusans, were harassing Egesta by land and by sea. Their description of the dangerous and increasing power of Syracuse, and their promise to support the Athenians with money, induced the people to send envoys to Sicily, to ascertain the state of affairs and what means the Egestaeans had at their disposal. In the spring of B.C. 415 the envoys returned with the Egestaeans,

* *Siceliotae* is the name of the Greek inhabitants of Sicily; while the original inhabitants of the island and the settlers from Italy were called *Siculi*, and *Sicani*.

who brought with them sixty talents of uncoined silver, as a month's pay for sixty galleys, and repeatedly and urgently implored the Athenians to assist them. The Athenian envoys also gave rapturous descriptions of the wealth of the town, and it was at once decreed to send a fleet under the command of Alcibiades, Nicias, and Lamachus, who were invested with unlimited powers Alcibiades thus saw the realisation of his most ardent wish, in being placed at the head of so important an undertaking. Lamachus also was delighted, because he would now have opportunities of displaying his valour. Nicias, who was cautious and a lover of peace, did not much like his new office; and having a presentiment of the evils that might be occasioned by the projected enterprise, he endeavoured at a meeting of the people, which was held five days after the first assembly, to dissuade them from their plan. He advised them not to expose the state, which had scarcely recovered from the effects of the plague and the miseries of the war, to fresh dangers and sufferings; he cautioned them not to make new enemies in addition to the old ones, who were ever ready to seize the first favourable moment for recommencing the contest; he warned them against the dangers to be apprehended from the existence at Athens itself of factions, which in the event of an unfortunate issue of the undertaking, would make common cause with the Lacedaemonians; he entreated them above all things not to allow themselves to be cajoled into a war by the ambitious and inexperienced Alcibiades, and that too in behalf of a powerless state, which in case of need would be unable to render any service in return. His advice met with little support; the majority was for war. Alcibiades, who had been personally attacked by Nicias, flattered the people by talking of the greatness of Athens, and declared that this war was a necessary consequence of the national character, and of the policy which Athens had hitherto pursued. A sudden halt was, in his opinion, more dangerous than an unsuccessful contest. By the brilliant prospects which he held out to the people, he filled them with enthusiasm for the expedition, and Nicias saw that it could not be prevented. He therefore advised his countrymen to send a large force to Sicily, in order that they might with certainty calculate upon success, and in consideration of the great distance, to provide all the needful supplies on a most liberal scale. He hoped thus to make the people reflect upon what they were doing; but they interpreted his remarks as implying an approval of the war, and as such warmly applauded them; so that the desire to enter upon the undertaking became only more ardent and more general. It was decreed that the generals should have full power to determine the force of the armament necessary for the expedition. Extensive preparations accordingly were made; and as the state was actually in a flourishing condition, everything went on rapidly, and with perfect confidence in the success of the undertaking.

But the warlike youths and the restless party with Alcibiades at their head were disappointed in their expectations. All those who had been silent in the assemblies from fear of being considered ill-disposed citizens, or who from the most different motives and from a regard to their own interests wished for peace, but especially both the secret and the avowed enemies of the sovereign people—all these exerted themselves to prevent the decree of the people from being carried into effect, and more particularly to injure Alcibiades, who was the soul of the whole undertaking. The intriguing selfishness and jealousy of the peace party ruined the common cause and effectually prevented the successful execution of the Sicilian expedition, the plan of which was by no means ill conceived. The fear that Alcibiades, returning at the head of a victorious fleet, might attempt to set himself up as tyrant, united the different parties in a scheme to ruin him who alone was capable of carrying out the undertaking; and by this means they soon afterwards brought the greatest calamity upon their own country.

When all the preparations for the expedition were completed, it happened that one morning nearly all the numerous busts of Hermes, with which the piety of private citizens and of public bodies had adorned the streets of Athens, were found mutilated by unknown hands. Such mutilations of the Hermae had occurred at Athens before this time, but on a smaller scale; they had been the work of drunken rioters at night, and in that age of scepticism and unbelief such things did not excite much attention. But the great number of the images mutilated in the same night gave to the deed unusual importance, and filled the minds of the citizens with alarm. The crime was considered as a bad omen for the fleet, which was ready to sail; it was believed to be the work of a wide-spread conspiracy, whose object was to overthrow the popular form of government. Great rewards were publicly promised to any one who could give information about the perpetrators of the crime; nay, accomplices in it received assurances of impunity, if they would denounce the other offenders; and all persons were called upon to come forward with evidence not only about the sacrilegious crime committed on the Hermae, but also about other offences against religion, particularly the violation of the mysteries of Eleusis. Informers immediately presented themselves, especially resident aliens and slaves; who were soon followed by others of the higher classes, such as Andocides, who had himself been thrown into prison on suspicion of having been one of the criminals. Those who were thus denounced generally took to flight, either because they were really guilty, or because they saw that the excited people would not listen to any defence. Nearly all who were apprehended were put to death; those who had escaped were condemned, and their property was confiscated. Thucydides himself was unable to give the secret history of this trial of the Hermocopidae, as they were called; though he is the only impartial and unbiassed authority; for Andocides, one of the accused, who defended himself fifteen years later, was a thorough party-man and bent only upon exculpating himself. If we take Thucydides as our guide, we shall be led to the following conclusions.

The affair was not, at the outset, aimed against Alcibiades, nor was he among those denounced for the mutilation of the Hermae. The accused were all men belonging to the higher classes of society, avowed oligarchs and enemies of the democratic government, but at the same time enemies or rivals of Alcibiades, whose popularity and influence with the people seemed to be employed by him only for attaining higher objects, perhaps the tyrannis itself. Now as Alcibiades, though not named among the Hermocopidae, was among those who were charged with having violated the mysteries, all his enemies came forward against him, because he was an obstacle in their way, preventing them from acquiring lasting influence with the people, and because they hoped that after his removal they might occupy the first place in the republic. In these words, Thucydides may be describing either the demagogues or the oligarchs; but it is also possible and even probable that the demagogues and leaders of the oligarchy had made common cause on this occasion with a view to attain the same object, both regarding Alcibiades as their enemy. Thus we can understand that the informers, such as Cleonymus and Androcles, were democrats, while the judges, like Charicles and Pisander, were oligarchs. Both parties thus zealously exerted themselves in the eyes of the excited and frightened people to prevent the overthrow of the popular sovereignty; and both were in the first instance satisfied with the removal of Alcibiades. What they wished took place. For Alcibiades, who felt himself strong enough, and perhaps also innocent enough, to defy all charges of being concerned in the profanation of the mysteries — none of the informers had stated that he was an accomplice of the Hermocopidae — demanded to be immediately tried in a court of justice, declaring himself ready to submit to any punishment if he should be found guilty. His desire was not to enter on his office as commander of the fleet until he should be perfectly cleared from suspicion, and to have the whole affair settled before his departure. But his enemies were afraid lest he should be acquitted, for the soldiers were attached to him, and he still possessed the favour of the great body of the people. Hence they induced the Athenians to pass a decree, that the investigation should be deferred till the termination of the Sicilian war. Their secret intention was to devise new charges during his absence, and then to get him recalled and condemned.

About the middle of summer the fleet was ready to sail. The whole population of Athens accompanied the warriors down to Piraeus. Their minds were agitated by hope and fear, for Athens was now committing to the perils of a long voyage and a distant war a large portion of her wealth and strength: the citizens had rivalled one another in equipping the ships as splendidly as possible; the warriors wore their best armour, and the whole resembled a triumphant military spectacle rather than an expedition against an enemy. The greatness of the armament was nearly what Nicias had declared to be necessary: 100 Athenian galleys and 34 of the allies, with 5100 heavy-armed (2200 of them Athenians), 480 bowmen, 700 Rhodian slingers, 120 light-armed Megarians, and 30 horse. The fleet was accompanied by 30 transports and 100 boats. After general prayers, in which the soldiers were joined by the people on shore, and libations to the gods, the fleet, on which Athens rested her boldest hopes, set sail. It first made for Aegina, and thence proceeded to Corcyra, the place of rendezvous for the other allies.

Before the fleet left Corcyra, the news of the expedition had reached Syracuse, but it was far from being universally believed. Hermocrates, who had brought about the peace at the congress of Gela, gave, indeed, the most positive assurance that the Athenians were approaching, and urged his countrymen to prepare themselves without delay for a resolute resistance. At the same time he advised them not to wait for the enemy's arrival at Syracuse, but to sail towards the coast of Tarentum to meet them, and thus, perhaps, to thwart the whole expedition. Athenagoras, on the other hand, who was a great favourite with the people, acted a part like that once played by Cleon at Athens, accusing Hermocrates and the nobles of intentionally frightening the people, in order, during the general consternation, to further their own oligarchical schemes. At last one of the generals declared that they ought at least to prepare themselves for all emergencies. Thus ended the first debates, in which the wise counsel of Hermocrates, to go to meet the enemy, was overruled.

Meanwhile the Athenian fleet, divided into three squadrons, for the better maintenance of order, sailed from Corcyra. Three ships were sent ahead to reconnoitre and ascertain the sentiments of the Sicilian and Italian towns, before an attempt was made to land. The fleet itself sailed round the Iapygian foreland along the coast. The towns of Italy showed a hostile spirit, and allowed the Athenians only to cast anchor and take in water. At Rhegium the fleet halted; the Rhegines did not, indeed, admit the Athenians into their town, declaring in general that they would remain neutral, and follow the example of the other Italian towns, but they supplied them with a market. Soon afterwards the three ships arrived from Egesta with the discouraging news that there was no trace of the wealth of Egesta, about which the first envoys had said so much; thirty talents was all that could be found. This piece of news surprised the generals not a little, for it proved that the whole expense of the expedition would in the end have to be borne by Athens alone. Nicias, therefore, was of opinion that they should straightway proceed against Selinus, in order to put an end to the war between that town and Egesta, either by force or by persuasion, and should induce the Egestans at least to maintain the sixty galleys which they had asked for. After such a display of their power, he advised his colleagues to return, and not to enter into a tedious and costly war with Syracuse in behalf of Leontini. Alcibiades, whose prospects of glory and power would have been destroyed by this course, maintained that they ought first to try to gain as many allies as possible in Sicily, and then, united with them, advance against Selinus and

View of Syracuse.
(Drawn on the spot, by George Scharf, Jun.)

Syracuse, unless these towns should previously yield to their demands. Lamachus, ever ready to fight, thought that they ought at once to attack Syracuse, which he hoped to take at the first assault. His advice was no doubt the best according to our notions, but the manner in which the Greeks carried on war must be judged of by a different standard. Never throughout the Peloponnesian war do we find a direct aiming at a great object; and decisive battles, such as those of Delium and Amphipolis, appear to have been the results of some accidental necessity. The Greeks displayed bravery when they had to fight their way out of difficulties, but they do not seem to have known how to carry out a bold attack, sword in hand, and an appearance of weakness is everywhere manifest. We must not, however, forget the difficulties with which they had to contend in war, especially in sieges.

The opinion of Alcibiades was adopted, just because it presented a middle course between those proposed by his colleagues; and preparations were forthwith made to gain allies among the Sicilian towns. Messana refused to admit the Athenians, and only consented to offer them a market outside the walls. Naxos was taken; Catana was seized by surprise and forced into the alliance;

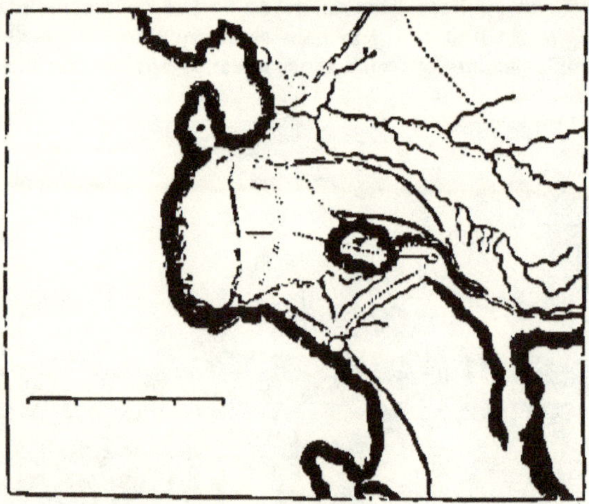

Plan of Syracuse.

but Camarina clung to the treaty of Gela. During this expedition, the fleet appeared before Syracuse also, partly to reconnoitre, partly to announce the Athenians as the deliverers of the exiled Leontines. No attack, however, was made upon Syracuse, which was engaged in active preparations, but was not yet ready to venture on an open contest. An attempt to land in the territory of Syracuse and carry off plunder was prevented by a detachment of Syracusan horse, who killed some of the scattered light-armed troops of the Athenians.

Hostilities had thus scarcely commenced, when the Salaminia, the Athenian state-vessel for conveying heralds, arrived, to recall Alcibiades from the command of the army, and to take him back to Athens to answer the charges brought against him. For after his departure, his enemies had been busy at work: the people had been systematically excited into an almost feverish state of mind; an inquiry was set on foot and continued without interruption; everything was believed without scrupulous examination, and the most honourable citizens fell victims to the denunciations of wicked hirelings. The exasperation of the people, which was fostered artificially, was increased to raging madness by the suggestion that the real malefactors had after all not yet been detected. At length, one of those already imprisoned, the orator Andocides, was prevailed upon by the promise of impunity for himself to give a complete account of the sacrilege committed on the Hermae, in which he confessed himself to be an accomplice. The people rejoiced at this; and as he confessed his own guilt, they had no hesitation in believing his statements. Of the men thus denounced all who could be apprehended were put to death; those who had escaped were sentenced to receive the same punishment, and rewards were promised for their heads.

Peace was thus, to some extent, restored to the heated and excited minds of the people. But Alcibiades, whose violation of the mysteries had been interpreted as an act no less hostile to the people, had not yet been punished. His enemies had succeeded so far, that the people now regarded their former favourite in the light of an odious tyrant, and some accidental circumstances increased their exasperation against him. While the Lacedaemonians were on the Isthmus of Corinth, making preparations for some undertaking against the Boeotians, a rumour was spread at Athens, that by the advice and with the consent of Alcibiades, they were to invade Attica, and overthrow the popular government. Oligarchical movements were at the same time observed in Argos, and it was supposed that Alcibiades was concerned in them also. Under these circumstances, the Salaminia was ordered to bring Alcibiades and some others who had likewise been accused to Athens. The proceeding was to be conducted with as little noise as possible, because it was well known that the army was attached to him. Alcibiades embarked in his own galley and departed from Sicily, accompanied by the Salaminia. Near Thurii, in southern Italy, however, he and the other accused landed and made their escape; the Salaminia, after having for some time in vain searched for him, continued her voyage homeward. Soon afterwards Alcibiades crossed over to Peloponnesus; but the Athenians condemned him and the other fugitives to death; his property was confiscated, and the curse pronounced against him by the Eumolpids was engraved upon pillars.

When Alcibiades was gone, the soul of the Sicilian expedition was lost; whatever was undertaken was now carried on in a slow and tedious manner, and the Syracusans soon overcame their fears, seeing that the Athenians attempted nothing against their city, but proceeded to distant districts of the island; nay, their feeling of security increased so much, that they began to treat the Athenians with insolence and contempt. Nicias had not given up his old plan, and Lamachus does not seem to have had sufficient influence to oppose him. The army, moreover, was divided into two parts, each of which could probably carry on its own operations. Thus Lamachus proceeded with the fleet along the northern coast towards Egesta, made himself master of the town of Hyccara, and carried away its population into slavery. Into Himera he had not been able to gain admittance. At Egesta, only thirty talents were obtained, and then the fleet sailed back to Catana, whither the army had in the mean time proceeded by land.

At length, when the winter had already set in, it was resolved to lay siege to Syracuse. Some Syracusans who had joined the enemy, had directed the attention of the Athenians to an excellent place for pitching their camp, near the Olympieum, at little more than a mile to the southwest of the city. In order to effect a landing there without being harassed by the hostile cavalry, the Athenians by a stratagem drew the Syracusan forces to Catana; while they themselves sailed by night past Syracuse towards the Olympieum, and had time enough to pitch their camp in a very convenient place, which was inaccessible to cavalry; for on the one side they were protected by walls, houses, and a marsh, and on the other by precipitous heights. At the same time they inclosed their ships with a palisade, and near a point called Dascon, threw up a hasty work, because on that side they were most open to attack. The bridge over the Anapos was broken down. The Syracusans did not interfere with the Athenians, but pitched their camp on the road to Heloros, between the Anapos and Syracuse. On the very next day a battle was fought, which the Syracusans had not expected so soon. The excellent tactics and skill of the Athenians gained the victory over their enemies, who fought with the greatest courage; and a complete defeat was averted only by their cavalry. Such a defeat might have been followed at once by the fall of Syracuse, which had lost 250 men, while the Athenians had only 50 killed. But, as it was winter, the latter thought it advisable to withdraw towards Catana, to provide themselves with money, provisions, and horses. Hermocrates made a prudent use of this defeat; he encouraged the army, and by his advice the number of military commanders, which had hitherto been fifteen, was reduced to five, of whom he was one. During the winter, the army was well drilled, and envoys were despatched to their kinsmen of Corinth and Sparta, to solicit succours. The Athenians in the mean time endeavoured to gain over Messana to their alliance, but in vain. They then formed a fortified camp in the neighbourhood of Naxos, and while wintering there waited for supplies of money and horses from Athens.

By enclosing the quarter called Temenites within the wall running along the western side towards Epipolae, the Syracusans increased the extent of the city, and thereby rendered it more difficult for the enemy to invest. They also strengthened the fort Megara, and the one situated near the Olympieum, and by fixing poles in the ground on all points of the coast where the enemy might attempt to land, they endeavoured to render that operation as troublesome as possible. But above all things, they tried to increase the number of their allies, and especially to gain over to their side the town of Camarina, whose inhabitants had concluded a treaty with Laches, during the first Sicilian war, and were still suspected of favouring the Athenians. Hermocrates cautioned them against the ambitious schemes of the Athenians, the natural enemies of all the Sicilians, and especially of the Dorian population. He put to them the alternative, either to become the subjects of Athens, if the Athenians should succeed, or to draw upon themselves the vengeance of Syracuse, if Syracuse should be victorious. The Athenian Euphemus, on the other hand, defended the conduct of Athens towards her allies and subjects, and excused the severity of her measures and rule, by adducing the extent of her dominion. The Camarinaeans, who were anxious to avoid offending either party, declared that they wished to remain neutral during the war.

The Athenians also now began to bestir themselves again: they left Naxos, and pitched their camp at Catana; they sent envoys round Sicily, to Carthage, and to the Tyrrhenian towns of Italy to gain allies or subsidies for the war, and were busily engaged in preparing the materials for the siege, which was to commence at the beginning of spring. The less the Syracusans could rely upon the assistance of the rest of the Sicilians, who were restrained by their fear of the all-engrossing power of Syracuse, the more actively were they supported by a state from which they had least expected it.

Alcibiades had sailed over to Cyllene in Elis, and thence proceeded to Sparta, where he was received with marks of friendship. Not long afterwards, Syracusan ambassadors accompanied by others from Corinth arrived at Sparta, for Corinth had at once declared itself ready to assist its kinsmen in the west. They were joined by Alcibiades, and what their representations were unable to effect, was brought about by the cunning speech of the exile. He plainly told the Spartans what were the plans of Athens, the fanciful vastness of which had probably no other origin than his own imagination,—that after the conquest of Sicily, of Italy, nay of Carthage, Athens would exert all her power to conquer Peloponnesus. In order to check her victorious progress, the Spartans, he said, ought to send troops to Syracuse, and more especially an able commander, who could discipline and control their untrained and reluctant troops; they ought to divide the power of Athens by establishing themselves in Attica, making themselves masters of Decelea, and thus carrying into effect what had long been dreaded, and would be most painfully felt by the Athenians.

The Spartans trusting Alcibiades, for his advice was plausible, at once resolved to act according to his suggestions. They sent Gylippus with a small force to the Syracusans, and made preparations for supplying them with further assistance. The plan of fortifying Decelea, and establishing themselves in the heart of the enemy's country, was taken up immediately. Thus ended the seventeenth year of the war.

At the beginning of the spring of B.C. 414, the Athenians broke up from Catana to lay siege to Syracuse; but a considerable time yet passed away, before the city could be completely invested. They proceeded to lay waste the country north of Syracuse, for the reinforcements of cavalry from Segesta and their other allies, with what were brought from Athens, increased their cavalry to 650 men.

The first conflict occurred on the heights of Epipolae; for as the western part of the city was most open to attack, the Syracusans had resolved to occupy the heights, which commanded the city on that side, with a body of picked troops, under the command of Diomilus. But at the same hour, the Athenians had landed near Leon, had disembarked their land-army, and withdrawn their fleet to Thapsos, where the naval troops remained in a fortified camp. The land-army immediately mounted Epipolae at full speed, and reached the top called Eryelos, before Diomilus with his force could arrive from the south. The Syracusans, notwithstanding this, advanced in haste and disorder, the Athenians having the advantage of the rising ground. The Syracusans were defeated, and Diomilus himself was among the slain. After this victory, the Athenians erected a fort on a height called Labdalon, west of Epipolae, for the security of their baggage and treasure. They then advanced against the northwestern quarter of the city called Syke or Tyche, and began actively to carry on the work of circumvallation. The besieged, struck with alarm at the rapid progress of the enemy, endeavoured to interrupt the work by force; but they were defeated a second time, and now turned all their thoughts to erecting a counterwork across the line of the intended circumvallation. This too was destroyed by the Athenians, who in the meantime continued their wall southward through the marshy plain towards the great harbour. The besieged, not yet wholly disheartened, carried a new counterwork, south of the first, across the plain. This again was taken and pulled down by the Athenians. Lamachus, who commanded the right wing, and wished to cut off the flight of the enemy's left wing across the Anapus, was slain. The Syracusans, encouraged by this event, even attempted to surprise the Athenian lines on Epipolae; but Nicias, quickly hastening with his men to the spot, prevented it: the Athenian fleet had at the same time sailed from Thapsus round Achradina and Ortygia, and had entered the great harbour. At this moment the whole army of the besieged threw itself into the city, and the circumvallation was completed. This success gained over many of the Sicilians as allies of Athens, and even some Tyrrhenians were induced to join them. Provisions arrived from all parts, and the army, now under the sole command of Nicias, was animated by the hope of certain victory. The spirits of the besieged, on the other hand, were so depressed that they began to think of peace, and in their despondency they became unjust, for Hermocrates and two of his colleagues were deposed, and three new men, Heracleides, Eucles, and Tellias, were appointed their successors.

Such was the state of affairs when Gylippus, the Lacedaemonian, was on the point of sailing with a few ships from Leucas to Syracuse. On receiving intelligence of the condition of that city, he gave up all hope of saving Sicily, and only thought of reaching Italy. A storm, which considerably injured his ships, delayed his voyage. At Locri, however, he learnt that it was still possible to reach Syracuse, and he accordingly determined to fulfil his mission. He escaped from the four ships which Nicias had sent out against him, and landed near Himera, on the north coast of Sicily. Great numbers soon gathered around him; his very arrival excited the hope of a vigorous support from Sparta, and Dorians as well as Sicels flocked to his standard. Having gathered an army of about 3000 men from Himera, Selinus, and other Sicilian towns, he marched towards Syracuse. His arrival had already been announced by Gongylus, a Corinthian commander, who had hastened to Syracuse from Leucas, where the Corinthian fleet was assembled. His representations had changed the minds of the Syracusans, and put aside all thoughts of peace. The Syracusans boldly went out to meet Gylippus, who succeeded in gaining the heights of Epipolae, and having effected a junction with the Syracusans, marched against the fortifications of the Athenians. Towards the great harbour the works were nearly completed, and in the north, towards the port of Trogilus, all the necessary materials were in readiness for use.

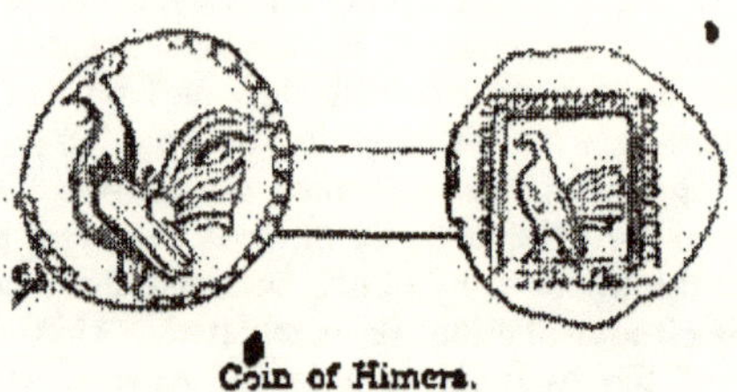

Coin of Himera.

Part of bronze statue of a Satyr.
(In the Museum at Naples.)

Metopes from the South Side of the Parthenon.

CHAPTER XXV.

THE SICILIAN EXPEDITION, FROM THE ARRIVAL OF GYLIPPUS TO ITS CLOSE.

At the time when Gylippus arrived before Syracuse, hostilities had also commenced between Sparta and Athens in Greece. The Lacedaemonians made a predatory expedition into the territory of Argos, and the Athenians assisting the Argives with thirty ships, ravaged Epidaurus Limera, and Prasiae—the most manifest breach of the peace that had yet been committed. The Lacedaemonians no longer hesitated; Decelea was soon afterwards in their hands, and fortune began to favour them decidedly.

The arrival of Gylippus changed the aspect of affairs in Sicily no less decisively, to the disadvantage of the Athenians. They were not only interrupted in completing their walls, but lost their stores at Labdalon, and Nicias soon discovered that the war carried on by land would not lead to the desired issue, and that the decision must depend upon the fleet. The part of the wall extending towards the great harbour, which was already completed was raised higher, and occupied by a number of troops sufficient to defend it. But Nicias also fortified the headland of Plemmyrion, and there assembled his army, his fleet, and his stores. By this operation he entirely gave up the land side of Syracuse. The Syracusan cavalry commanded the whole district, and did much mischief to the Athenian sailors whenever they went on shore to provide themselves with water or wood, the third part of the cavalry being stationed near Polichne, south of the Olympieum, for the purpose of preventing the enemy's predatory excursions. Gylippus, in the meantime, vigorously prosecuted the building of a counterwork, which was to be carried across Epipolae, and to cut off the double wall of the Athenians. In addition to this he trained his troops and drew them up every day in battle array. In the first battle which the Athenians accepted, they gained a victory, because the Syracusan cavalry could not operate in the narrow space between the walls. But in the second engagement, the Athenians were driven back into the fortifications of Plemmyrion, in consequence of which the counter-wall of the Syracusans was completed without further interruption; so that it now became impossible for the Athenians wholly to invest the city.

The successes of the Syracusans since the arrival of Gylippus induced the Sicels and Siceliots, who had previously been hesitating, or even hostile, to embrace the cause of Syracuse. The allies of the Athenians were almost limited to Naxos and Catana, which were too weak to afford any active assistance. Moreover, thirty galleys from Corinth, Leucas, and Ambracia, arrived unmolested and safely in the harbour of Syracuse. The Syracusans themselves also manned their ships for the approaching and decisive contest, and again sent to Sparta and Corinth to solicit reinforcements.

All these events had placed Nicias in a most dangerous position. His ships being obliged to be constantly out at sea, became leaky; a number of his soldiers and marines deserted, and the naval service had to some extent to be entrusted to inexperienced slaves. Nicias felt that he and his army which had come to lay siege to Syracuse, were themselves besieged. In this distress he wrote to the people of Athens, requiring them to send him reinforcements at the beginning of spring. He himself desired to be recalled, because the state of his health rendered him unfit to discharge the duties of a commander. The latter request was refused by the people, but they appointed Demosthenes and Eurymedon as his colleagues, and immediately despatched the latter with ten galleys and twenty talents of silver to Sicily, while the former began to raise a larger army for the spring. The report of the fresh preparations of Athens at length determined the Lacedaemonians to act, and having got everything ready during the winter, they invaded Attica in the beginning of B.C. 413, under the command of their king Agis. They first laid waste the fields in the neighbourhood, and then established themselves at Decelea, so that their fortifications could be seen from Athens. This was a second great blow for Athens, and a more troublesome one than even the defeat at Syracuse, which was soon to be added to their misfortunes. Athens was, as it were, in a constant state of siege, and the Athenians were obliged to be continually in arms to guard the walls. The incessant ravages of the country produced a dearth of provisions, and the supplies which had formerly been brought from Euboea by Oropos and Decelea, became more expensive, in consequence of being conveyed round Sunion. The double war increased the expenditure enormously, while the revenues were diminished. In short, Athens was soon reduced to a sad condition, and the influence of its outward misfortunes was manifested in discontent with the internal affairs of the state, which ultimately ended in the overthrow of the existing constitution.

For the purpose of making some reprisals, Charicles sailed with thirty galleys to the coast of Laconia, where he was soon joined by the army of Demosthenes, which was destined to proceed to Sicily. They succeeded in establishing themselves in a place opposite to the island of Cythera, and in raising a fort like that still maintained at Pylos. After this Demosthenes sailed to Corcyra to collect reinforcements, but before he arrived at Syracuse, Nicias had suffered another severe loss.

Gylippus, who during a visit to the interior of Sicily had found new resources for Syracuse, was joined by Hermocrates in urging upon the Syracusans the necessity of venturing upon a naval engagement. They yielded to these representations and made the attempt, sailing with thirty-five galleys out of the great harbour, while forty-five others were ordered to come round from the lesser harbour, north of Ortygia. The Athenians quickly manned sixty galleys, and sailed out with twenty-five to meet the thirty-five Syracusan ships, while the rest were to operate against those which were coming round Ortygia. The battle was fought at the entrance of the great harbour; the Athenians gained the victory, and sunk eleven ships; but when the conquerors sailed back to their station near Plemmyrion, they found Plemmyrion itself in the hands of Gylippus, who had set his army in motion at the same time as the fleet sailed out, and had surprised the Athenian land forces, which were anxiously intent upon the issue of the naval engagement. Large quantities of provisions and military stores fell into the hands of the conquerors; but the worst result of these events was, that the obtaining of provisions by sea now became extremely difficult, and was not to be accomplished without fighting. The Syracusans, notwithstanding their first defeat, had become emboldened at sea, and did serious injury to the besiegers by successful predatory excursions. The Athenians, indeed, succeeded in destroying the palisades made by the Syracusans for their own protection, but new ones were forthwith constructed; nay, the zeal and eagerness of the besieged to encounter the naval power of their enemies had become so ardent, that soon afterwards, but before the arrival of Demosthenes, they fought a second naval battle, which lasted several days, and at last obliged the Athenians to retreat behind their fortifications. The loss of the latter, and the injury done to their fleet, were not inconsiderable, but the worst result of the engagement was that they had lost the reputation of being invincible at sea, for the Syracusans now felt certain that their fleet would soon be a match for that of the Athenians; and there was good reason for hoping to overcome them by land also. The Athenians, indeed, still maintained their fortifications south of Temenites, but the vigorous attacks of Gylippus, who carried on his operations not only during the sea-fights, but at all other times, rendered their situation extremely difficult and dangerous. The influx of reinforcements also to Syracuse from all parts of Sicily increased daily and became very formidable.

At this critical moment Demosthenes and Eurymedon arrived with a fleet of 73 galleys and 5000 heavy-armed, about 1200 of whom were Athenians, many light-armed troops, and a sufficient quantity of supplies. The alarm of the Syracusans was great, as they had not thought it possible for Athens, involved as she was in two wars, to send out such a force. The hopes of the Athenians revived; Demosthenes resolved to attack the enemy at once, in order to avoid falling into the condition of Nicias, who, he thought, had ruined the reputation of Athens. Still some days passed away, during which the valley of the Anapos was laid waste; an unsuccessful attack was then made upon the cross wall of the Syracusans, and Demosthenes at length determined to recover Epipolae, which Gylippus had taken from Nicias. He began the attack shortly before midnight, and the army victoriously mounted the height, no great resistance being offered by the enemy, who were surprised and stupified by the suddenness of the assault. A portion of the wall was already pulled down, and the victory seemed decided; but the army advanced in too much disorder, imagining that all might be gained by one bold stroke. Some Boeotians among the Syracusan forces were the first to make a stand and repel the advancing enemy; fortune now turned, and the joyous hope of victory was destroyed. The darkness of the night, the wild shouting of the combatants, the betrayed watchword of the Athenians, the same war-cry (for Dorians were fighting on both sides), and especially the restoration of order among the forces of Gylippus, produced incredible confusion in the army of the Athenians, who injured and hindered one another more than the swords of their opponents. Thus this nocturnal battle ended in the complete defeat of the auxiliary army of the Athenians;

those who did not know their way were cut down by the scattered horsemen, but the older soldiers escaped to the camp. The loss of arms was even greater than that of men, because the fugitives were obliged to throw themselves down the heights of Epipolae.

This new and unexpected piece of good fortune increased the courage of the Syracusans to such a degree, that they even began to think of making conquests in Sicily. The Athenian generals, on the other hand, were disheartened, and diseases among the troops added to the hopelessness of their condition. Demosthenes, therefore, was of opinion that it was expedient to raise the siege, and return home before it was too late, and to assist in driving the enemy from Attica. Nicias, too, would have been glad to adopt this plan, but he did not conceal from his colleagues that it was dangerous to allow the army to see their despondency, or to appear before the people at Athens without having achieved something brilliant; he added that their men, however ready to return home, would be sure afterwards to come forward as their accusers. He also knew and said, that the finances of Syracuse were in a bad condition, and that it could not possibly sustain the siege much longer; that a party of the Syracusans, favourable to the cause of Athens, wished the Athenians to remain; and lastly, that reliance might still be placed on the fleet. Although his colleagues yielded to these arguments, yet Demosthenes, with the concurrence of Eurymedon, recommended that they should quit their narrow and unfavourable position, and continue the siege from the north, where it would be easier to obtain supplies of provisions; but neither did this plan meet with the approval of Nicias. The discussion lasted for some time, and the army and fleet remained where certain destruction awaited them.

Soon afterwards, however, Nicias changed his mind, for Gylippus had obtained new and important reinforcements from Sicily; from Peloponnesus, too, heavy-armed men had arrived, and the Syracusans at once prepared for a fresh attack. The signal was given for departure, which was to take place without the knowledge of the enemy, when an eclipse of the moon occurred, and superstition prevented that which all desired. Moreover, the Syracusans had received information of the design of the Athenians, and they were now so confident of their own superiority, that they determined not to allow the enemy to escape. They actively drilled their sailors and soldiers, and then advanced with seventy-six galleys towards the place where the Athenians were stationed, whilst the land-army marched against their fortifications. The Athenian fleet, amounting to eighty-seven ships, was completely defeated. Eurymedon, who commanded the left wing, endeavouring to evade the enemies' ships, approached too near the coast, his retreat was cut off, and he himself was slain. The other ships fled in confusion towards their protected naval camp. In order to destroy these also, Gylippus sailed along the coast, but the Tyrrhenians, who kept watch there, offered a brave resistance, until the Athenians, hastening to the spot, defeated and routed the army, and succeeded in protecting the remnant of their fleet, and rendering a fireship, which was sent against it, harmless.

But their loss was, nevertheless, great; eighteen ships had been taken, and all their crews put to death: the army was nearly in despair. The state of things had been so much changed, that the besieged now aimed at nothing short of annihilating the army of the besiegers. They conceived the bold hope of liberating the Athenian allies and subjects, of overthrowing the most powerful state, and of gaining for themselves that glory and power which would raise them to the rank of a state of the first order.

Immediately after their naval victory they determined to close the entrance to their great harbour by a line of galleys, transports, and small boats, and made active preparations for another sea-fight. The Athenian commanders held a consultation; they knew that the approaching struggle would determine their fate, and made their arrangements accordingly. The fortifications which they had erected farther inland were given up; all the implements, and those who were unable to take part in the battle, were conveyed to a place as near as possible to the ships. A great part of the land-army was ordered to embark in the fleet; for it was Nicias' plan to change the sea-fight into a land-fight. With this view he took precautions against the dangerous battering poles of the enemies' ships, and provided his own galleys with grappling irons, or iron hands, to detain the adversaries' vessels till they should be boarded and taken. When all the fleet, amounting to 110 galleys, was manned and ready for the contest, Nicias exhorted his troops to do their best, since everything, both there and in Attica, was at stake.

Gylippus had been informed of all these arrangements, and also knew that it was the plan of the land-army, in case of a defeat, to take refuge in some town that might be favourably disposed towards Athens. He furnished his ships with hides to render the grappling irons useless; and before the beginning of the battle he cheered his men on to the last contest with an army which had already lost its courage and confidence in itself, which deserved no mercy, but only vengeance and punishment, and which, owing to the great number of ships, would probably work its own ruin in the limited space it had for its operations.

After Nicias, in his fear and alarm, had once more addressed each officer separately, the battle commenced. He himself remained with the land-army, which was drawn up in a long line on the coast. Gylippus, with his Syracusans, was stationed near the harbour, and the exhortations and threats of the hostile commanders could be distinctly heard. The contest, which was carried on with the greatest exasperation on both sides, was for a long time undecided; at length, the Athenian ships retreated towards the coast. The marines were here and there seen leaping from the ships, and hastening towards the camp. The land-army broke up in utter confusion; some amid wailing and lamentation hurried to assist the ships, others sought shelter behind the remnants of the fortifications, but most of the men fled at random. Never before had an Athenian army been in such a state of dissolution. Nearly half the fleet was destroyed; and the Athenians even forgot to ask for the surrender of their dead and their wrecks; all they wished was to depart as speedily as possible. As the Syracusan fleet of eighty sail had been reduced to fifty, Demosthenes urged the expediency of attempting to force their way out to sea with the remaining ships; but the crews refused to return on board, and thus in the end all agreed to retreat by land.

Hermocrates, by a stratagem, induced the Athenians not to commence their retreat that same night. By this means, the Syracusans gained time to occupy all the roads and passes through which the enemy had to march. At the same time they took possession of the fleet, of which the Athenians in their hurry had burnt only a small part. It was not till the third day after the sea-fight, that the Athenian army broke up: what a contrast between its first starting from Piraeus and this last and desperate attempt to escape with their lives! Even the dead remained unburied—a thing unprecedented in Greek history—and the wounded, who were left behind, envied the dead. This was the most fearful reverse ever sustained by a Greek army. Nothing was so heart-rending as the parting from the wounded and the sick, whose cries and lamentations filled the air. But the army still amounted to 40,000.

Nicias comforted and encouraged his men, and restored order as well as he could; the army marched in the form of a hollow square, Nicias commanding the van, and Demosthenes the rear, the baggage being in the centre. They forced the passage of the Anapos, and marched that day about five miles to the west; during the night they encamped on an eminence. On the following day they advanced only half as far as on the first, but in the same direction, and pitched their camp in a cultivated plain, for the sake of collecting provisions and laying in a supply of water.

The Syracusans, who throughout the march had greatly harassed them, now occupied a hill which the Athenians had to pass. On the next day, the latter suffered much from the Syracusan cavalry, and were obliged to retreat to the place where they had encamped during the preceding night. The cavalry also cut off their supplies. For two days they endeavoured to storm the hill and the enemy's fortifications, but were always repulsed. Nicias and Demosthenes then resolved to lead the army by another road towards the coast. In the night after the last engagement, they kindled many fires, and departed in a south-eastern direction. During this retreat more than half of Demosthenes' troops dispersed; Nicias and the rest reaching the coast about daybreak, took the road of Heloros, with the view of afterwards proceeding up the river Erineus into the interior of the country. At the dawn of day, the Syracusans, discovering that the enemy had escaped, hastily broke up, and before noon overtook the division of Demosthenes. He was forced to draw up his troops in order of battle; the pursuers had shut him up in a narrow district, and attacked him incessantly on all sides. When the Syracusans perceived that the enemy was sufficiently weakened, they, by a proclamation, invited all the Sicilians to come over to them, promising that they should retain their liberty. Few, however, accepted the offer. Demosthenes and the other troops were then summoned to surrender their arms, on condition that none of them should suffer a violent death. All, 6000 in number, accepted these terms, and laid down their arms. Nicias, who was somewhat in advance of Demosthenes, crossed the Erineus on the same day, and encamped on an eminence. On the following day, he was overtaken by Gylippus, and learnt the fate of Demosthenes. At first he did not believe the report, and made another proposal; but the Syracusans, refusing to listen to it, attacked his army on all sides, and continued doing so throughout the day. In the night, the Athenians endeavoured to proceed on their march, but the enemy watched their movements, and only 300 succeeded in leaving the camp; and even they were afterwards captured with the rest. Next day, Nicias continued his march, and hastened towards the river Assinaros, partly to escape from the pursuing enemy, but more especially to quench the burning thirst of the soldiers. In their eagerness to drink, they rushed into the river in the greatest disorder; the wildest confusion arose; the men fought for the water and crushed one another, while the enemy on the banks attacked them with showers of missiles.

At length, Nicias also surrendered to Gylippus at discretion. The army had by this time become greatly reduced; for during the last few days incredible losses had been sustained, and many had deserted. The captive Athenians and their allies were sent into the quarries at Achradina and Epipolae; their treatment was most cruel: they lived crowded together in a pestilential atmosphere (for the dead were not removed), and the scanty food they received only increased their torments. After seventy days, the survivors, except the Athenians and the Sicilian and Italian Greeks, were sold as slaves. The whole number of prisoners had amounted to about 7000. The generals, Nicias and Demosthenes, notwithstanding the efforts of Gylippus to save them, were put to death. Both, especially Demosthenes, were men worthy of a better fate.

Thus ended an undertaking, which, in the opinion of Thucydides, was the greatest, not only in the Peloponnesian war, but in any war that had ever been carried on. The defeat of the Athenians was fearful and far beyond all precedent.

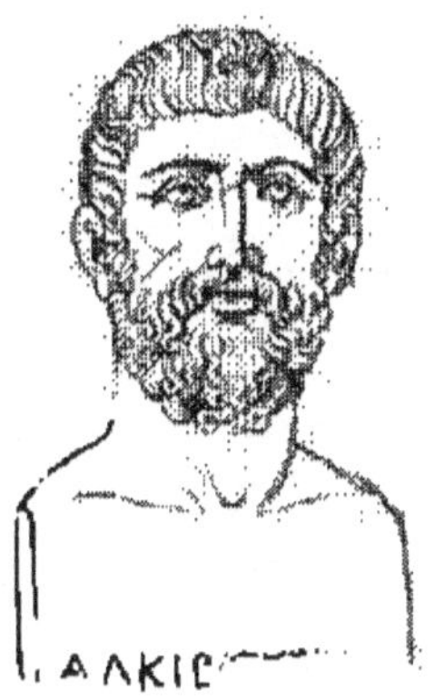

Bust of Alcibiades.
(From the Vatican.)

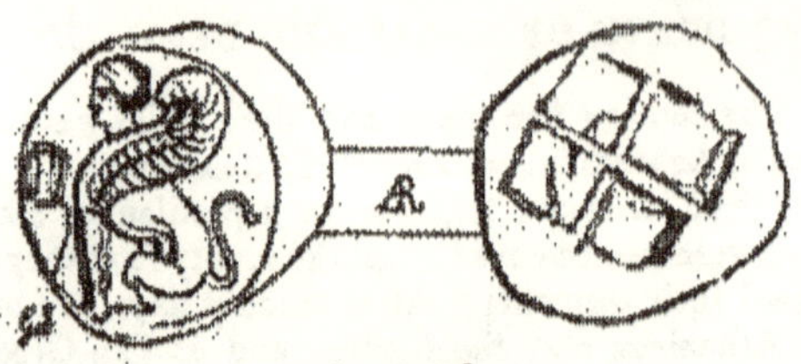

Coin of Chios.

CHAPTER XXVI.

FROM THE CLOSE OF THE SICILIAN EXPEDITION TO THE RESTORATION OF ALCIBIADES.

When the news of this irreparable loss reached Athens, it was at first disbelieved. Plutarch relates that the matter was first mentioned by a stranger in a barber's shop in Piraeus. The barber hastened to the archons, and repeated before them and the assembled people what he had just heard. The archons ordered him to be tortured as an impostor who could not state his authority; but at length the soldiers, who had escaped from Sicily, brought full and accurate information. When the Athenians were thus forced to believe that all was lost, they became desponding and disheartened, and the orators who had recommended the expedition, the priests and soothsayers who had inaugurated it, were the first that were made to feel the indignation of the people. It was the most critical moment in the whole history of Athens. A few months before, she had been at the height of her power and hopes; but now she felt powerless and unable to resist a direct and bold attack of any foe. Her enemies, however, were the slow and cautious Dorians, while the Athenians were easily comforted and roused to cherish new hopes and plans. Thus it happened that Athens, although in a most deplorable condition, yet thought of continuing the war, and preserving the power she still possessed. The people showed themselves great and moderate; in all that had to be immediately done they trusted to the counsel of older men, and consented to make several economising arrangements in the administration, in order to supply the place of the lost fleet and army. The tribute was raised to one-twentieth *; but even this did not suffice. and at last the 1000 talents, which Pericles had laid aside as a reserve-fund, were appropriated.

Thus the war which Sparta did not venture to bring to a close

* Εἰκοστή. The εἰκοστολόγοι were the collectors of this tax.

by a bold stroke, was continued, with varying success, for nine years longer. This last act of the great drama is commonly called the Decelean war, from the uninterrupted occupation of Decelea by the Lacedaemonians. The principal scenes of the war, however, were the sea and the coasts of Asia Minor, for through the Sicilian war Sparta had become a maritime power, and henceforth her intention was to destroy the naval resources of Athens, and above all things to deprive her of her allies and her fleet. Under the command of Lysander, who soon began to act a prominent part, Sparta quickly reached the height of her maritime power.

The influence of the Sicilian calamity upon the relation between Athens and her allies, very soon became manifest. The latter felt themselves relieved from the threatening danger of being reduced to the condition of subjects; and believing Athens to be too weak and too near her own downfal to present much resistance to their wishes, they were ready to revolt. While the two leading states were preparing for the renewal and energetic continuation of the war, and the active king Agis directed his attention particularly to the formation of a great fleet, several of the most powerful allies of Athens were negotiating with him during the winter about their revolt. Agis was applied to especially by the Euboeans, whose fidelity to Athens was a matter of the highest importance, and by Lesbos. The Spartans gladly promised and prepared to support them. Chios and Erythrae on the opposite coast referred their case at once to the government of Sparta. With them there also appeared envoys from Tissaphernes, the Persian satrap of the maritime provinces (Ionia, Lydia, and Caria), and from Pharnabazus, satrap on the Hellespont. Both proposed to deprive Athens of the towns tributary to her, and to gain over the Spartans to the interest of the king of Persia, hoping to be thereby enabled to pay to the king the arrears of their tribute. The Lacedaemonians resolved to send succours first to the Chians and to Tissaphernes; but the execution of the decree was delayed till the following year, B.C. 412, and would perhaps not have been carried into effect at all, had not Alcibiades urged them to quick and resolute action; for as the Athenians had in the meantime defeated the Corinthian fleet, and Gylippus on returning from Syracuse had a severe encounter off Sunium, and reached Corinth with great difficulty, the Spartans had again lost their confidence. Alcibiades sailed with five ships under the command of Chalcideus to Chios, where the oligarchical party had made all the necessary preparations. By the promise that a larger fleet would follow, the small force of the Spartans succeeded in inducing the people to renounce their alliance with Athens. Their example was soon followed by Erythrae and Clazomenae, which forthwith commenced military preparations. The news of the revolt of Chios, one of their most important allies, roused the Athenians, though at first they were somewhat cast down, to take active measures. Yet neither Strombichides, who pursued Chalcideus with eight ships, nor Thrasycles, who came up with a reinforcement of twelve galleys, was able to check the progress of the skilful Alcibiades. Teos surrendered to Erythraean and Clazomenian troops, and lost its walls; before the Athenian fleet could approach, Miletus was in the hands of Alcibiades, who in his unbounded ambition endeavoured to gain over all, or most of the allies of Athens, before the arrival of the great Peloponnesian fleet. Immediately after these events the first treaty between the Persian king and Sparta was concluded by Tissaphernes and Chalcideus; it was directed against Athens, and restored to the king the tributary towns of Asia Minor. So far had Sparta forgotten the Persian wars and their object.

A new reinforcement of sixteen galleys, commanded by Diomedon, arrived from Athens. Although a Chian fleet was put to flight by them, yet the Chians did not cool in their zeal, but tried to secure as many associates as possible in their revolt from Athens. They first gained over Lebedos and Erae, two coast-towns north of Samos, and soon afterwards Lesbos also joined them. Meanwhile, the Peloponnesian fleet had successfully fought its way through the surrounding ships of the Athenians off Piraeon, and under the command of Astyochus had sailed to Chios. But the Athenians, too, were active; they had gradually sent a considerable fleet and army into those quarters, and by a series of rapid attacks compelled most of the revolted towns to return to their allegiance. In this manner they first recovered Lesbos, and Teos was forced to observe at least a sort of neutrality. Clazomenae surrendered after its citadel, Polichna, had been taken by the Athenians. Chalcideus, the Lacedaemonian commander, also was defeated and slain by them near Panormos, in the territory of Miletus; the wealthy and flourishing island of Chios was laid waste, and the Chians themselves were beaten in several engagements. Late in the summer a large force arrived in Samos from Athens, under the command of Phrynichus, Onomacles, and Scironides, who forthwith proceeded to attack Miletus. A battle ensued, in which Tissaphernes and Alcibiades took part; each party claimed the victory, for the Athenians routed the Peloponnesian auxiliaries, while the Milesians and Alcibiades defeated the Argives, the allies of the Athenians. The Athenians were already preparing for a siege and blockade of the city, when an auxiliary fleet arrived from Syracuse. Phrynichus now thought it advisable not to venture on a decisive contest, and retreated to Samos, a step which, in the opinion of Thucydides, was wise. The Argives, however, mortified by their recent defeat, returned home.

On the continent of Asia, the Spartans and their allies remained in possession of Miletus, and at the instigation of Tissaphernes made themselves masters of Iasos, a coast-town south of Miletus. Afterwards they succeeded in gaining over Rhodes also. Tissaphernes gave the pay which he had promised, and a new treaty was concluded between him and the Spartans, in which the supplies in money to be provided by the king were expressly mentioned, but which in other respects was the same as the first. At sea, the Athenians had, on the whole, the ascendancy; they prevented a second revolt of Lesbos, and established themselves in Delphinion, not far from the city of Chios, which they reduced to a state of extreme distress. Another part of the fleet appeared several times before Miletus, without gaining any particular advantage. But their superiority at sea was somewhat checked by the arrival of a new fleet from Sparta, which brought eleven commissioners to examine the treaties, and at the same time to watch the conduct of Astyochus. They found the two treaties concluded with Tissaphernes unsatisfactory, and considered it impossible to carry them into effect; Lichas, one of the eleven, urged the conclusion of a fresh treaty, which should secure the independence of the Greek towns. A third agreement was soon afterwards actually concluded; in it Asia alone was described as the property of the king, who promised his allies provisions, and the support of a Phoenician fleet. But although the new Lacedaemonian fleet, commanded by Antisthenes, seemed to commence a victorious career by defeating Charminus and conquering Rhodes, yet the state of things soon assumed a different aspect. Even Tissaphernes had become dissatisfied, because the commissioners refused to ratify the treaty which had been concluded; but presently a still more powerful friend deserted the Spartans and went over to the Athenians. This was Alcibiades. Hated by Agis on account of a personal injury, and suspected by the Peloponnesians ever since the battle of Miletus, he made his escape, fled to Tissaphernes, and easily persuaded him to diminish the support and subsidies which he had hitherto given to the Spartans. He convinced him that it was not to his own and the king's interest to allow the Spartans to gain the upper hand, but that it would be much more advantageous to allow them and the Athenians to weaken each other by a protracted war. Tissaphernes followed the counsel of his prudent adviser, and the rising naval power of Sparta received a severe check from the equivocal conduct of the Persian satrap.

Alcibiades, however, in giving this advice to the barbarian, had been thinking chiefly of himself and of his return to Athens. His object was to see his own country so far weakened and humbled as to consider it necessary and useful to recal him from exile. With this view he had taken care to let the Athenians at Samos see on what intimate terms he was with Tissaphernes, and had proposed to them to gain the satrap over to their side, and to return to Athens if an oligarchical government were instituted, under which he himself could take a part in the management of affairs. These overtures were not displeasing to the Athenian nobles at Samos: many already fancied themselves at the head of an oligarchy, and even the men of the popular party, who were present, were tempted by the prospect of Persian gold to sacrifice the sovereignty of the people. Phrynichus, the commander-in-chief, was alone against the scheme, for he saw through the selfish designs of Alcibiades, who in reality cared nothing about any particular form of government, but only about his own return; and it was clear to Phrynichus that by such a change Athens would undermine her power and influence with her remaining allies, while those who had already revolted could hardly be recovered by such an event.

But when Phrynichus saw that his opinion was overruled, and that Pisander was already fixed upon to proceed to Athens and make the necessary preparations, he endeavoured to render Alcibiades suspected in the eyes of Astyochus and Tissaphernes. But in this, too, he failed, and plunged himself into great difficulties, while Alcibiades contrived to win over Tissaphernes entirely to the side of Athens, for it was just at this time that the satrap felt annoyed at the proceedings of Lichas.

Pisander now went to Athens to communicate the terms proposed by Alcibiades. The people were somewhat surprised and reluctant indeed; the nobles too, and especially the priestly families of the Eumolpidae and Ceryces, were vehemently opposed to the return of the man who had violated the mysteries. But Pisander persevered, trying to persuade every one individually that the prosperity of Athens depended solely upon Alcibiades, and on the assistance of the king of Persia, the support of both being entirely contingent on the adoption of the oligarchical form of government. The people yielded, though not without a lurking hope that a change might soon occur. Pisander and ten other envoys were sent to Tissaphernes and Alcibiades. Phrynichus, who had been slandered by Pisander, was deposed, Diomedon and Leon being appointed his successors. Immediately on their arrival they made an attack upon Rhodes, and then fixed their head-quarters in the island of Cos. But Alcibiades, acting on behalf of the king of Persia, made such extravagant demands, that the Athenian commissioners indignantly put an end to the negotiation, and returned to Samos. It was, in fact, the intention of Alcibiades to prevent the actual conclusion of the treaty, but at the same time he did not wish Tissaphernes to enter into a new arrangement with the Lacedaemonians. Tissaphernes had taken particular notice of that portion of Alcibiades' advice which recommended him to maintain the balance between the contending parties. Amid these transactions the twentieth year of the war came to its close, towards which Oropos in Attica was taken by the Boeotians.

At the very beginning of the following year, B.C. 411, the oligarchical government was established at Athens. The revolution proceeded very rapidly, and on the whole without bloodshed; for the leaders of the movement were men of acknowledged energy and eminent talent. Pisander and his party wished to set up the oligarchy, not only at Athens, but also in the allied states. In many places the revolution was accomplished, but the consequence was, that those towns became estranged from Athens, and openly strove to gain entire independence. Pisander, according to an understanding with the oligarchs at Samos, went to Athens itself, accompanied by five other envoys. They no longer reckoned upon Alcibiades, who, in the negotiations with Tissaphernes, had acted so equivocal a part; and he, as we shall see hereafter, had already formed different plans.

Meanwhile, those who were of the same mind, had made all the necessary preparations at Athens. Although their measures were not marked by any particular violence, they put to death several opponents and popular leaders, who openly counteracted their designs, or contrived to get rid of them in other ways. The people were intimidated and discouraged, especially because they believed the conspirators to be more powerful and numerous than they actually were. The latter accordingly found it very easy to spread and increase the distrust and fear that prevailed among the people. All being thus ready, and every hostile demonstration kept down, Pisander, as soon as he arrived, came forward with his proposals; ten men with unlimited power were elected, who were to submit a series of new laws to the assembled people. They summoned the people to meet at Colonos, and decreed first of all, that any one should be entitled to suggest, with impunity, any change in the constitution. Pisander then proposed to appoint five presidents, who were to select ninety-five men, and each of the one hundred thus chosen was again to nominate three. The four hundred thus elected were to take possession of the senate-house, to rule with unlimited power, and to convene the five thousand citizens, to whom the franchise was limited, whenever they should think fit. Pisander, the celebrated orator Antiphon, and Theramenes, were the chief promoters of this oligarchical scheme, which was imposed upon the free people of Athens exactly 100 years after the expulsion of the Pisistratids. The Four Hundred, meeting with no resistance, took possession of the senate-house, paying to the five hundred ancient senators their full salary for the remaining period of their office, divided themselves into prytanies, observed the customary religious ceremonies, and carried on the government with great energy. All their thoughts and efforts were directed towards a speedy conclusion of peace with Sparta. King Agis, to whom they applied first, had no confidence in the new political arrangements; he even made an expedition against the city, but was repulsed, and found out that, after all, the new government was well organised.

At the same time, the oligarchs deputed ten of their number to Samos to gain over the army to the new order of things; but it was there that the first impulse was given to the measures for the restoration of democracy. The oligarchical party at Samos, three hundred in number, harboured the design of overthrowing the popular government. They were supported in this scheme by Charminus, the Athenian commander, and some others. But the popular party applied to the generals of the Athenian army, Leon and Diomedon (the successors of Phrynichus and Scironides): who, in conjunction with Thrasybulus, then commanding a galley, and Thrasyllus, an officer in the army, both decided friends of the popular cause, prevailed upon the army, especially the crew of the Paralos, to defend the cause of the Samian as well as of the Athenian people. When, therefore, the Three Hundred made the contemplated attack, they were overcome by the Samians and Athenians: thirty were killed, three only were exiled, the rest submitted to the popular government. A galley despatched to Athens with the news of these events, did not arrive there until the Four Hundred were already installed. The crew of the galley were apprehended, some were thrown into prison, and the others were sent to a fort in Euboea. Chaereas, the commander of the galley, however, escaped to Samos, and there gave a fearful description of the bloodthirsty conduct of the Four Hundred; he thus led the fleet and the army to bind themselves by a solemn oath to remain faithful to the old constitution: they moreover resolved, that, as they were strong enough by themselves, they would, if necessary, renounce Athens and conquer a new home. At the same time, Thrasybulus and Thrasyllus, who were the soul of the whole democratic movement, were appointed generals; great hopes were also placed in the support of Alcibiades. As matters had thus assumed a serious aspect, the envoys of the

Four Hundred remained at Delos, instead of proceeding to Samos.

When the Peloponnesian army at Miletus heard of the political disturbances at Athens and Samos, it was greatly inclined to come to close quarters with the enemy; and Astyochus, being obliged to yield to the loud murmurs of the soldiers, advanced with his fleet towards Mycale. The Athenians, however, retreated to Samos; and did not accept battle till Strombichides had returned from Abydos with his squadron, which increased their fleet to 108 sail. The Peloponnesians in their turn now withdrew to Miletus, without striking a blow. In this manner they wasted their time, and neither the subsidies nor the Phoenician fleet promised by Tissaphernes came to their support. But, although the Peloponnesians on the whole undertook very little, still the Athenians sustained many losses during the period preceding the recall of Alcibiades by the army in Samos. Abydos and Lampsacos had revolted some time before; their example was followed by Thasos, as soon as it had received an oligarchical government, by Byzantium, and many other cities. Even Euboea, respecting which Athens was most apprehensive, and the defection of which was felt most painfully, was lost in the same year. But Alcibiades was now placed at the head of the Athenian army assembled in Samos, and this one event and its consequences were an ample compensation for all those losses.

Thrasybulus had at length so far prevailed upon the army, that the majority of the soldiers demanded the recall of Alcibiades, and he himself brought him over from Tissaphernes. The cunning exile contrived to display his patriotism before the soldiers, by bitterly lamenting the misfortune of his banishment, and was particularly eloquent respecting his unlimited influence with Tissaphernes. The soldiers elected him their commander, along with Thrasybulus and Thrasyllus; intrusted him with the management of everything, and entreated him to sail without delay with them to Piraeus. But this did not suit the plans of the ambitious man, who wished to appear at Athens, not as a usurper, but as a general crowned with victory, and invited by the people. When, therefore, he was invested with his new dignity, he returned to Tissaphernes, and succeeded in inspiring him with the highest opinion of his present position.

The Peloponnesians were now completely at variance with Tissaphernes; and the army, enraged at the inactivity of Astyochus, openly charged him with being bribed. Soon after this, Mindarus arrived from Sparta to take the place of Astyochus as commander of the fleet. Matters, however, had not yet come to an open rupture, nor did Tissaphernes intend undisguisedly, and at once, to give his support to the Athenians; he only wanted to gain time, and by delay to weaken both the Athenians and the Peloponnesians.

In the meantime the envoys of the Four Hundred had, after all, arrived in Samos; where they endeavoured to justify the new form of government in the eyes of the exasperated army, and to prove its moderation and mildness in opposition to the exaggerations of Chaereas. But they were not listened to, and the army tumultuously demanded to be led against Athens. Alcibiades, however, restrained their impetuosity, and that wisely; for, if the Athenians had returned home, they would evidently have lost Ionia and the Hellespont: his eloquence encouraged all to continue the war with energy.

It was not, however, the well-meant advice of Alcibiades, nor the prospect of a reconciliation with the Samian army, but quarrels among the leaders of the oligarchy and new reverses, that put an end to the short-lived government of the Four Hundred. Theramenes in particular changed his views, and placed himself at the head of a counter-revolution; while Phrynichus, Pisander, Antiphon, and Aristarchus, zealously adhered to their own system. The building of the fortress of Eetioneia at the entrance of Piraeus, and the appearance of a Lacedaemonian fleet in the Attic Sea, drew great suspicion upon them, and they lost many of their partisans. Heavy-armed Athenian citizens themselves pulled down the fortifications. Phrynichus was murdered; and it was not without great difficulty that the Four Hundred, by making concessions, succeeded in rendering the people more tractable. But it suddenly became known that Agesandridas had sailed with his fleet round Sunium towards Euboea; the internal strife was immediately forgotten, and the people hastened to their ships. Fortune, however, did not favour them: the Athenians lost twenty-two ships off Eretria, and Euboea was wrested from them. This threw the people into despair, and again a moment had arrived when a quick and resolute attack by the Lacedaemonians might have crushed Athens. But the people speedily regained courage; they hastened to the pnyx, deposed the Four Hundred, and restored power to the Five Thousand, who included all the heavy-armed Athenians. No officer was in future to have any salary; legislators were appointed, and many salutary regulations were made. It was resolved to recall Alcibiades and others, and commissioners were forthwith sent to Samos. This moderate mixture of oligarchy and democracy is praised by Thucydides, and was beneficial to the state. Pisander, and some others, sought refuge among the Lacedaemonians at Decelea; and Aristarchus, by an act of treachery, put the small frontier fortress of Oenoë into the hands of the Boeotians.

Alcibiades had, in the meantime, continued his ambiguous policy towards Tissaphernes; he had followed him to Aspendos with thirteen ships, hoping thereby to alienate the Lacedaemonians still more from him; and the latter becoming at length tired of waiting for the arrival of the Phoenician fleet, Mindarus at once proceeded to Pharnabazus on the Hellespont; but he was detained by a storm, and anchored at Chios. Thrasyllus, following him, landed at Lesbos, in order to prevent the enemy from continuing his voyage, and to recover the revolted Eressos. But while Thrasyllus was engaged in Lesbos, Mindarus sailed along the coast of the continent, and reached the Hellespont in safety. The Athenians, who perceived too late that the enemy had passed by, arrived in the Hellespont one day later; anchored near Elaeos, and prepared for battle, which, after the lapse of five days, was fought near Cynossema. The fleet of the Peloponnesians, amounting to eighty-eight galleys, had at first an advantage over the enemy's armament, which consisted of only seventy-six ships; but the confidence of success, and the cautious management of Thrasybulus, gained the victory for the Athenians, though it was dearly purchased. The Athenians, however, derived fresh courage from the success, and the belief in their own superiority at sea was revived.

A few days later, the Athenians recovered the revolted city of Cyzicos; but Antandros, which was severely oppressed by one of the lieutenants of Tissaphernes, surrendered to a Peloponnesian force which had been invited from Abydos. Tissaphernes now thought that he had lost the friendship of the Peloponnesians, and, in his jealousy of Pharnabazus, proceeded through Ionia to the Spartan fleet to complain of their conduct, and at the same time to justify himself, for Cnidos and Miletus also had expelled the Persian garrisons.*

Meanwhile, Mindarus sent Epicles to Euboea for the ships which were stationed there. A squadron of fifty galleys was soon assembled; but it was utterly destroyed by a storm near Mount Athos, and only twelve men were saved. After some insignificant engagements of separate detachments of ships, in which the Lacedaemonians were successful, a second great naval battle was fought off Abydos. The struggle had lasted till the evening without any decided result, when Alcibiades appeared with eighteen galleys, and the Peloponnesians fled to Abydos. Pharnabazus, indeed, came to their assistance from the shore, and they succeeded in getting the remaining ships safely into port, but

* We here lose the guidance of Thucydides, for these are the last events mentioned in his great work.

their loss was great. Tissaphernes, also, now arrived on the Hellespont, and Alcibiades sailed to meet him for the purpose of endeavouring to gain him over by presents; but Tissaphernes seized him, on the pretext that the king of Persia wished to continue the war against Athens, and Alcibiades was conveyed a prisoner to Sardis. After a detention of thirty days, however, he made his escape. From Clazomenae he again joined the fleet, which had retreated before Mindarus to Cardia. He accordingly waited at Sestos until the ships came round, and until Theramenes and Thrasybulus had returned, the former from Macedonia, the latter from Thasos, with fresh treasures. He then sailed with a fleet of eighty-six galleys to Parion, at the entrance of the Propontis, and thence to the island of Proconnesus. He there learned that Mindarus had already been joined at Cyzicos by the land-army of Pharnabazus. He determined upon giving battle for various reasons; one of which was that want of supplies urged him to bring matters to a decision. Intending to take the enemy by surprise, he carefully concealed his design, and his object was favoured by a heavy rain and a thick mist, in which he set sail for Cyzicos. As he approached the harbour, the sun suddenly broke through the clouds, and he perceived 60 Spartan galleys engaged in manoeuvring so far out at sea that the Athenians were enabled to intercept their retreat to Cyzicos. They were immediately attacked, and fled toward the shore. But Alcibiades sailed around their flank with twenty ships, and effected a landing. Mindarus also landed, and an engagement ensued on shore. Mindarus fell, and his men were put to flight; the entire fleet becoming the prize of the victors. The Syracusans alone prevented their ships from falling into the enemy's hands, by setting fire to them; those of the Peloponnesians were taken to Proconnesus.

This occurred in the twenty-second year of the war, B.C. 410. How completely the Peloponnesians were defeated, and how hopeless their situation was, is evident from a laconic letter of Hippocrates, a lieutenant of Mindarus:—"Our good luck is gone; Mindarus is dead; the men are starving, and we know not what to do."

The consequences of the battle were brilliant. Cyzicos and Perinthos were recovered; Selymbria was obliged to pay subsidies, and a custom-house was built for ships coming from the Euxine at Chrysopolis, where Theramenes and Eubulus stationed themselves with thirty ships to exact the duties. The Peloponnesians indeed had in Pharnabazus an active friend, for he gave to the fugitives money and timber from Mount Ida, to build new ships; but even he was unable to check the victorious career of Alcibiades, and the Athenians soon became masters in that region of the sea and its coasts. The sudden change in the state of affairs made such a discouraging impression upon the Spartans, that a proposal of peace from them, which is mentioned by Diodorus, is not at all improbable. But it is no less probable that the Athenian people, being again flushed with victory and insolent, yielded to the counsels of their warlike leader Cleophon, and rejected all such proposals *; for in Attica, also, an attack made by Agis from Decelea, had been successfully repelled by Thrasyllus, who, happening to be at Athens, whither he had brought intelligence of the victory of Cyzicos, placed himself at the head of the men capable of bearing arms. The loss of Agis was not very great; but he began to see that the siege of Athens, in the manner in which it had hitherto been conducted, was useless, unless Piraeus also was blockaded; and as this could not be done, he sent the ships stationed upon the Attic coast to the scene of the war in the Propontis.

But Thrasyllus, who had risen in popular favour, easily obtained a new fleet of fifty (according to Diodorus, thirty,) ships, with 1000 heavy-armed, 100 horse, and 5000 peltasts. He first sailed to Samos, thence proceeded to the coast of the continent, effected several successful landings, and invaded Lydia; but during an attack upon Ephesus, he was defeated by Tissaphernes and his allies, among whom were the brave Syracusans, who had distinguished themselves in the battle of Abydos. At length he joined the fleet at Sestos with his army. From Sestos, the whole force sailed over to Lampsacos, and besieged it during the winter. Pharnabazus was defeated by Alcibiades in an engagement of the cavalry near Abydos; and in the course of the winter, the Athenians made several ravaging incursions into the interior of the country.

In the beginning of the spring, B.C. 409, the Athenians sailed to Proconnesus, and thence to Chalcedon, around which they formed a circumvallation; and Alcibiades, having got possession of all the property which the inhabitants had carried into Bithynia, defeated its garrison while making a sally. As Pharnabazus was unable to relieve the town, it surrendered. Byzantium on the opposite shore was delivered up to the Athenians by traitors, and a treaty was concluded with Pharnabazus, in which he promised to pay to the Athenians 20 talents, and to provide a safe passage for an embassy, consisting of Athenians and Argives, to the king of Persia. The envoys did indeed set out on their mission, but never reached the king. They were detained in Phrygia, and under all manner of pretexts, were kept almost as prisoners for a period of three years, and then dismissed. For the king had

* Diodor. xiii. 52, &c.

promised the Peloponnesian envoys to assist the Spartans, and had appointed Cyrus, his younger son, governor and commander of his forces in Asia Minor. Cyrus displayed great zeal in the cause of the Peloponnesians, as we shall see hereafter.

The time had now come when Alcibiades could return to his country as the victorious and admired conqueror of its enemies. This was the year B.C. 408. He had restored the dominion of Athens in the islands, on the Hellespont, and on the coast of Thrace; he had enriched the army with booty, and completely

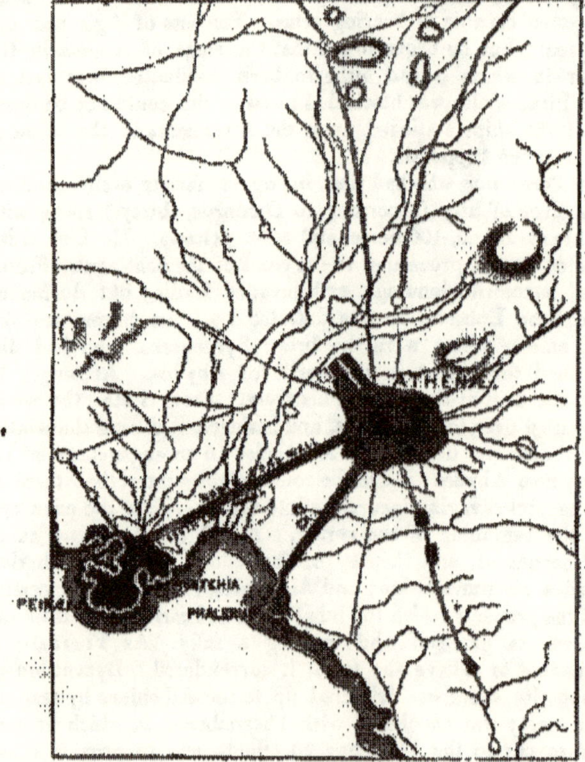

Harbours of Athens.

reconciled the people to himself. His reception was enthusiastic. He had been appointed commander with unlimited power, his colleagues being Thrasybulus and Conon. When he landed in Piraeus loaded with booty and money, and with 200 captured ships, he was met by the whole population. Every one in the crowd was anxious to catch a sight of him, as if he were returning alone, as if he alone had achieved those exploits, although his colleagues, and especially Thrasybulus, had no small share in them. The exulting multitude showered wreaths of flowers upon him, and accompanied him in triumph to the city. Everything that had been laid to his charge was forgotten. And if the recollection of the unfortunate expedition to Sicily called forth tears amid the general rejoicings, the Athenians shed them with sorrow for their own blindness in having deprived themselves of such a commander. Alcibiades knew how to turn these emotions of the excitable people to good account; he spoke in the popular assembly in such a manner, that there was no one who did not weep, or did not feel indignation against those who had caused his exile. So quickly had the people changed its mind; but with the same rapidity it soon afterwards allowed itself to be led by the enemies of Alcibiades to rash measures against its own favourite.

Cupids making Wreaths and Garlands.
(From a painting at Pompeii.)

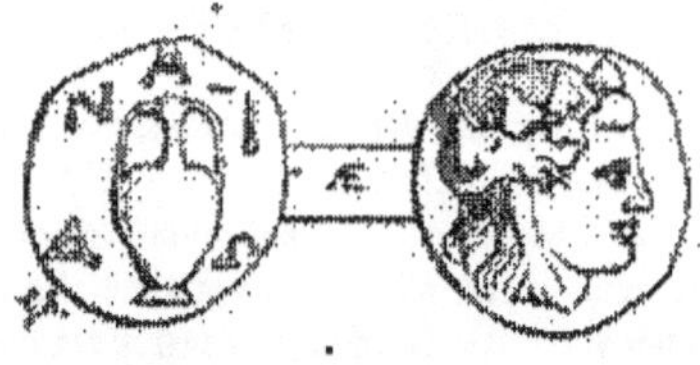

Coin of Andros.

CHAPTER XXVII.

FROM THE RETURN OF ALCIBIADES TO ATHENS TO THE END OF THE PELOPONNESIAN WAR.

Soon after his return, Alcibiades conferred upon the people a benefit which furnished his enemies with fresh means of attack, and brought about his second exile. Ever since the fortification and occupation of Decelea by the Spartans, it had been found necessary to discontinue the processions from Athens along the sacred road to Eleusis, in celebrating the Eleusinian mysteries. Alcibiades now accompanied his fellow-citizens with an armed force to Eleusis, and thus enabled them once more to perform the ancient and sacred rites. The enemy did not stir; and this brilliant act of piety inspired the army and people with such enthusiasm, that, as Plutarch states, they offered Alcibiades the tyrannis itself. Whether this was what he wanted, is uncertain; but the oligarchs thought it advisable to get him speedily removed from the city. He had been at Athens scarcely three months, when he was appointed to command a fleet of 100 galleys. He first sailed against Andros, which had revolted from Athens. After a victory over the Andrians, he blockaded their town, but did not succeed in reducing the island. This furnished his enemies with the first handle against him, for the people believed that he could succeed in whatever he really wished, and every failure was ascribed to his want of will. From Andros he sailed to Samos, where he intended to continue the war.

Sparta, too, had now found the hero who was destined to bring the last act of the great drama to a close. This was Lysander, a man who can be compared with Brasidas and Gylippus, the true Spartan heroes of the first and second periods of the war, only in regard to his valour and success; for the fundamental features of his character were faithlessness, cunning, and falsehood. He was, moreover, proud, domineering, cruel, and ready to risk anything to promote the greatness of Sparta;—a worthy adversary of Alcibiades, though he was less talented. He equalled him at least in the desire to rule his country. As the successor of Mindarus in the office of navarchus, he proceeded to the late scene of the war with a fleet of seventy ships. He landed in Cos and at Miletus, and waited at Ephesus for the arrival of Cyrus. The latter was favourably disposed towards Sparta, if for no other cause than his hatred of Tissaphernes; besides which, he thought that the Spartan land-army would be of greater service to him than the Athenian navy. Lysander did his best to strengthen this feeling, and contrived in particular to obtain from Cyrus high pay for his soldiers.

While Lysander was staying at Ephesus with his fleet, which had now been increased to ninety ships, Alcibiades joined Thrasybulus, who had come from the Hellespont to lay siege to Phocaea, B.C. 407. Alcibiades left the fleet at Notion under the command of his lieutenant, Antiochus, with orders to undertake nothing against Lysander. But notwithstanding his instructions, Antiochus with a few ships sailed from his station into the harbour of Ephesus, challenging the fleet of Lysander. This occasioned an engagement, in which all the Athenian galleys ultimately took part. The Athenians lost fifteen ships and some prisoners, Antiochus himself being slain or drowned; the remainder of their fleet sailed to Samos. On his return to assume the command, Alcibiades endeavoured to repair the loss which had been sustained, but Lysander did not accept the battle which was offered, and Alcibiades was obliged to return to Samos. The Athenians were indignant against him, ascribing their defeat to his carelessness; he was accordingly deposed, and ten generals named in his stead. He now left the army a second time, and went to Chersonesus, where he had property. Among his successors, Conon, who was appointed by the people to the supreme command, was no doubt the ablest. The present exile of Alcibiades was voluntary; he dreaded the inconstancy and cruelty of the people, and never saw his ungrateful country again. His patriotism, however, remained undiminished, as he proved by his conduct before the unfortunate battle of Aegospotami. After that catastrophe, not feeling himself safe in Thrace, he went to Pharnabazus in Phrygia; but the hatred of the Spartans pursued him thither, and Pharnabazus abandoned him to his enemies, who murdered him.* This happened soon after the downfal of Athens, which was the unavoidable consequence of his second deposition; for it showed the influence of the fearful party-spirit to which everything, and in the end the state itself with all its power and glory, was sacrificed.

Conon and his colleagues remained throughout the year in the

* The manner of his death is variously related. See Plut. *Alcib.* 38. foll.; Diodor. xxiv. 11.; Corn. Nep. *Alcib.* 10.

sea about Samos, making several predatory expeditions. In the following year, B.C. 406, Lysander, whose period of office had expired, was succeeded as admiral of the Peloponnesian fleet by Callicratidas, a youthful hero, of the same kind as Brasidas; he was noble-minded, humane, winning, and unquestionably brave. He was indignant at being obliged to pay court to barbarians for the sake of obtaining pay, and would rather have made peace with the Athenians at once. After having received subsidies from Miletus, and increased his fleet to 130 sail (afterwards it amounted even to 170), he took Methymna in Lesbos by storm, and showed great humanity on that occasion. Conon, who wished to relieve Lesbos, was obliged to flee, but as Callicratidas cut off his retreat to Samos, he with Leon and Erasinides took refuge in the port of Mytilene. Thither he was followed by Callicratidas, who compelled him to fight, and took thirty ships; the others were blockaded while the Spartan obtained reinforcements from Methymna and Chios. Diomedon, who came to the assistance of Conon with twelve ships, was defeated, and escaped with only two galleys. In this desperate situation Conon sent out two ships, one of which succeeded in reaching Athens. The Athenians with all possible haste equipped a fleet of 110 sail, armed slaves as well as freemen, and in thirty days everything was ready. On its way, at Samos, the armament was reinforced, so that the number of galleys amounted to 150. Callicratidas, being informed of the arrival of the fleet at Samos, left fifty ships before Mytilene, for the Athenians had already reached the Arginusae, a cluster of islands between Cape Malea, the southernmost headland of Lesbos, and the mainland. Callicratidas with his remaining 120 ships sailed from Malea to attack the enemy. The Athenians accepted the battle; Callicratidas fell in the course of the engagement, soon after which event victory declared for the Athenians. The Peloponnesians lost upwards of seventy ships, but the conquerors, too, lost twenty-five. Eteonicus, Callicratidas' lieutenant, concealing the defeat, immediately ordered the fleet stationed at Mytilene to sail to Chios, and led the land-army to Methymna. Conon, on the other hand, joined his colleagues.

Soon after this battle, the other generals were recalled to Athens: Conon and Philocles alone remained, and were soon joined by Adeimantus, who had been newly appointed their colleague. Protomachus and Aristogenes did not return to Athens; but the other six obeyed the summons, and went to their destruction. A violent storm, which occurred immediately after the battle of Arginusae, had rendered it impossible to collect the wrecks, the shipwrecked, and the corpses of the dead, although the generals had given orders that it should be done. Accusers now came forward at Athens charging them with various crimes, and especially with that of not having collected and buried the dead after the battle. Among the accusers was Theramenes, who had himself fought in the battle as commander of a galley, and ought to have executed the command of the generals. The trial was put off in consequence of an intervening festival. This delay gave the enemies of the unfortunate men, who may perhaps have been suspected by the democratic leaders of favouring oligarchical schemes, time to mature their plans, and to make all the necessary preparations. Callixenus and Euryptolemus, especially, urged the necessity of putting the generals to death, and false witnesses were hired to establish and aggravate their guilt. The people, thus deceived, demanded vengeance, and was determined once more to see its will carried into execution. It was in vain that the better men, such as Socrates, exerted themselves to shake the resolution of the people. The six were condemned to death. Repentance followed immediately after the act, and the reckless advisers of the people had to pay for their evil counsel with their lives. In this manner, the people raged against its own vitals. The ochlocracy, or government of the populace, was at its height. It is possible that the Spartans may again have turned their thoughts towards peace, but under the circumstances it is quite natural that their proposals were not listened to.*

After the death of Callicratidas, the Peloponnesian fleet demanded the appointment of Lysander as admiral, and their demand was supported by Cyrus. This, however, being contrary to law, Lysander obtained only the office of lieutenant (ἐπιστολεύς) of the admiral Aracus, but by secret orders of the government he was invested with supreme authority. In the following year, B.C. 405, he proceeded to the fleet at Ephesus, joined Eteonicus, and reinforced himself in other ways. He went in person to Cyrus to obtain money. Cyrus, who was evidently anxious to win the friendship of the Spartans, readily granted the request, for just at this time he was summoned to attend his dying father, and foresaw the consequences of his death.

Lysander soon left Caria and the coasts of Asia Minor, and sailed to the Hellespont. From Abydos he made an attack upon Lampsacos, which was allied with Athens. The town was taken, and his army obtained rich booty. Immediately afterwards, the Athenian fleet, amounting to 180 sail, arrived. It touched at Sestos, and having taken in provisions there, proceeded about fifteen stadia farther to Aegospotami, opposite Lampsacos, at some distance from any harbour or town, so that in order to obtain pro-

* Proposals of peace on the part of Sparta are mentioned by Aristoph. *Ran.* 1532.

visions the men were obliged to leave their ships. Alcibiades, who was living in the neighbourhood, observed this; he directed the attention of the commanders to their unfavourable position, and advised them to go to Sestos, it being unsafe to quit the ships for ever so short a time. This advice was scorned; but what he had predicted, came to pass. For four days Lysander had refused a battle, which was daily offered by the enemy, who in consequence began to despise him. At length on the fifth day, when they had left their ships, he suddenly gave the signal of attack. Conon saw the enemy approaching, but it was impossible to gather his scattered troops with sufficient quickness. He himself fled with eight ships and the state galley, Paralos, which alone were fully manned. All the rest fell into the hands of Lysander, and their crews were cut to pieces on shore or taken prisoners. Conon, seeing that all was lost, fled with his eight galleys to Evagoras in Cyprus, while the Paralos carried the melancholy tidings to Athens. Lysander sent to Sparta a despatch, giving an account of his victory. Two of the Athenian generals, Philocles and Adeimantus, were among the prisoners. Their fate was discussed, and all the Athenians, with the exception of Adeimantus, were put to death at Lampsacos.

After this great victory, Lysander destroyed the power of Athens by subduing her allies one after another. Byzantium and Chalcedon were the first that surrendered; their garrisons were sent to Athens, for it was Lysander's intention to produce want and famine in the city, by crowding the people together. He then sailed to Lesbos, which likewise surrendered. Eteonicus gained over the towns of Thrace, and thus, within a very short time, all renounced the alliance of Athens, except Samos, where the people maintained their ascendancy. Lysander now sent information to Agis, that he was approaching with a fleet of 200 sail. By the command of king Pausanias all the forces of Peloponnesus, except the Argives, assembled in Attica and encamped in the Academy, before the city. At Athens itself preparations had been made with all possible speed; the worst was apprehended, and the people dreaded a fate like that which they themselves had so often inflicted upon revolted towns. As he approached, Lysander restored to the Melians and Aeginetans their islands; Salamis was ravaged, and with a fleet of 150 sail he appeared before Piraeus.

Athens was invested by land and by sea; she was without ships, without allies, without provisions. Still her people did not surrender immediately; their fear of a cruel fate deterred them from such a course. The two parties in the state agreed to recall the exiled, and to set free those who were undergoing punishment.

Many died of hunger, but the city held out to the last extremity. At length, when the famine had reached its height, they sent to Agis and offered to treat with him, if he would promise that the city and the long walls should be preserved. Agis referred them to the ephors at Sparta. But even before the envoys reached the Laconian frontier, they were received at Sellasia by Spartan messengers, bidding them return home and come back with better proposals. They now learnt their fate; one of the terms of peace was that the long walls should be pulled down, those walls which they had built with such joy, with which the most glorious recollections were connected, and which were viewed as the bulwarks of democracy. This thought was not to be endured, and it was expressly forbidden to be mentioned in the assembly. At last, Theramenes offered to go to Lysander, hoping at least to discover why the enemy laid most stress upon this one condition. Having obtained permission, he went, and remained with Lysander for more than three months, until Athens, completely exhausted, was obliged to comply with any demand that might be made. This faithless act, the consequence of his effeminate heart, afterwards received its reward under Critias. On his return in the fourth month, he asserted that Lysander had detained him all that time, and at length referred him to the ephors. Ten envoys now were sent to Sparta with unlimited powers, and one of them was Theramenes. When the negotiations commenced, the Corinthians and Thebans, the sworn enemies of Athens, and the deputies of many other states, proposed the destruction of the city. The Lacedaemonians opposed this plan; they wished only to humble their enemy, whose services in the common cause of Greece they still acknowledged, but not to reduce them to slavery. Peace was accordingly to be concluded on the following terms: the long walls and those round Piraeus were to be pulled down; all ships, with the exception of twelve, were to be given up; the exiles, mostly oligarchs, were to be recalled; henceforth the Athenians and Spartans were to have the same friends and the same enemies; lastly, Athens was to recognise the supreme command of Sparta by land and by sea. The allies, moreover, who had not yet revolted, were to become independent.

With these terms the envoys returned to Athens. The exhausted people were ready to submit to anything; all they had been afraid of was, lest this last embassy also should be sent home without an answer. On the following day the hungry multitude was informed of the offered terms, which Theramenes advised it to accept. Some still refused to yield, but the majority had at length become submissive, and all the demands were complied with.

Lysander now entered Piraeus, the exiles returned, and a great part of the walls was pulled down, while flute players, brought from the camp and the city, accompanied the work of destruction with their music; for this day was said to be the beginning of the liberty of Greece. What a delusion! the self-styled deliverers were far more unfeeling and selfish tyrants than the Athenians had ever been. These events occurred on the 18th of Munychion, B.C. 404, a few days before the end of the twenty-seventh year of the war, on the very day on which the glorious battle of Salamis had been fought.

View of Eleusis.
(From an original sketch by Sir William Gell.)

Eros.
(From a Pompeian painting.)

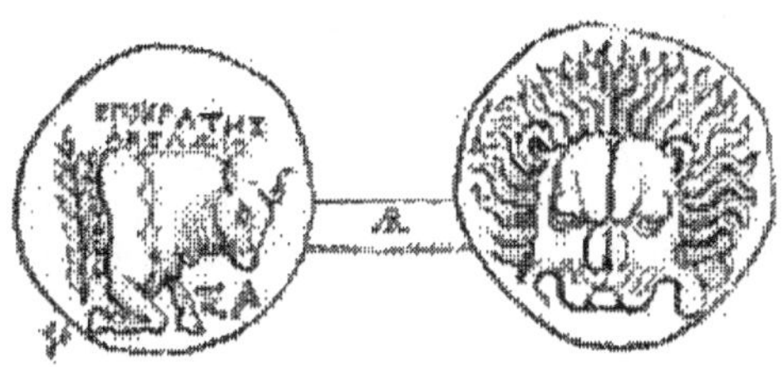

Coin of Samos.

CHAPTER XXVIII.

FROM THE END OF THE PELOPONNESIAN WAR TO THE RE-ESTABLISHMENT OF DEMOCRACY AT ATHENS.

As soon as the walls were destroyed, the Athenian people, as Xenophon says, but in reality Lysander, elected thirty men, who were to govern the state in accordance with the revised laws.* Among these Thirty, the most notorious were Critias, the degenerate disciple of Socrates, though a man of talent, Melobius, Peison, Theognis, and Eratosthenes. Diodorus relates that the people elected Theramenes, in order that he might counteract the cruel measures of his colleagues; but Lysias, who seems to be better entitled to belief, describes the mildness of Theramenes as cowardice and simulation. When the election of the Thirty was completed, Agis at length disbanded his army; while Lysander went with his fleet to Samos. This island was soon compelled to surrender; its free citizens obtained permission to quit their native land, but were obliged to leave their property behind. The old citizens, who had been exiled by the Athenians, returned, and a body of ten men was appointed to undertake the government. After this, Lysander disbanded his allies, and towards the end of the summer he himself returned to Sparta with immense booty, the Athenian galleys, and 470 talents, the remainder of the tribute which he had collected, and which had formerly flowed into the state treasury of Athens.

The Thirty, who had proclaimed themselves the restorers of order, soon began to act in such an arbitrary, insolent, and cruel manner, that they became the most violent of tyrants.† At first, indeed, their rigour was directed against those only who were notoriously bad, but this rule of procedure was soon forgotten, or

* A real revision of the laws was not undertaken till after the expulsion of the Thirty. (Andoc. *De Myst.* p. 89.)

† This year in the history of Attica is not marked by the name of the archon, but is styled "the year of anarchy." (Xenoph. *Hellen.* II. 3. § 1.)

made a mere pretext, and the noblest men, such as Niceratus, the son of the celebrated Nicias, Leon, who had been a commander in the war, and Polemarchus, the philosopher and brother of the orator Lysias, were put to death to gratify the ambition and cupidity of the tyrants; for it was especially the wealthy whom they picked out for their victims. The number of exiles was still greater, and their property was confiscated. Among these was the noble Thrasybulus; the orator Lysias fled to Megara, and lost the whole of his property, which was considerable. The brutality of the tyrants went so far, that they did not spare even women; Melobius, for example, while plundering the house of Polemarchus, tore the gold rings from the ears of his wife. We still possess a most eloquent description of all these horrors in the speeches of Lysias against Eratosthenes and Agoratus.

As a means of enabling them to manage public affairs in their own way, and without difficulty, the Thirty requested Lysander to send them a band of mercenaries, and the harmost Callibius, who was commissioned to command these troops at Athens, supported the tyrants in their doings. The council and all public officers were merely their creatures; from among the citizens they selected 3000, who alone were to enjoy the franchise, and be permitted to bear arms. All the rest were disarmed, and placed beyond the protection of the law, for the Thirty assumed the right of putting any of them to death, without a judicial verdict. They were also assisted in their bloody executions by a body of cavalry formed of young nobles. Nearly 1400 Athenians fell victims during this fearful period, and 5000 emigrated, leaving behind all that they possessed. Even the cities hostile to Athens, such as Thebes and Megara, took pity, like Argos, upon the unhappy exiles, although the Spartans threatened to exact a fine of five talents from any one who should not hand the fugitives over to the Thirty. In order to destroy the very foundations of Attic democracy and power, the noble embankments and fortifications of Piraeus, which had cost the state 11,000 talents, were sold for three talents to be demolished; instruction in oratory was forbidden, and the hustings for the orators in the Pnyx was turned inland, in order that the sight of the sea might not awaken a longing for the lost palladium of democracy.

Theramenes, who at first walked in the same path as his colleagues, and whose cruelty was branded by his contemporaries no less than that of the others, at length abandoned his bloody career, either from a feeling of humanity, or from jealousy and hatred of Critias, who seemed to possess more power and influence; for such, according to Thucydides, is always the case in oligarchies. Theramenes came forward especially against Critias, advising him to act with moderation. In return for this, Critias did not scruple to destroy him. He kept ready an armed band; a meeting of the council was convened, and Critias openly charged Theramenes with treason against the established constitution. It was in vain that Theramenes attempted to defend himself, and when he described the unjust and inhuman conduct of his colleagues, he only made things worse. Critias at once effaced his name from the list of citizens, and thereby declared him an outlaw. Theramenes fled to the altar, but none of his colleagues or of the senators attempted to protect him. The ministers of penal justice, headed by Satyrus, the most shameless among the satellites of the tyrants, dragged him from the altar, and hurried him across to a prison. There he drank the hemlock in a cheerful spirit, which might have been the crowning grace of a nobler life.

After this the recklessness of the Thirty became still greater; but their days were already numbered. Thrasybulus, one of the heroes of the Peloponnesian war, had quitted his place of refuge in Thebes, and being supported by the noble Theban Ismenias, he and 70 companions in exile had taken possession of the small border fortress of Phyle. On being informed of this, the Thirty with their 3000 and their cavalry made an attack upon Phyle; but they were driven back, and as a heavy fall of snow prevented them from laying siege to it, they were obliged to content themselves with posting a corps of observation in the neighbourhood. Meanwhile, the 70 had increased to 700; with these Thrasybulus fell upon the enemy at daybreak, and put them to flight. The Thirty now began to feel unsafe at Athens, and resolved to establish themselves at Eleusis. Three hundred horsemen, whom they suspected, were murdered. Thrasybulus, whose band continued to increase, proceeded to Piraeus; but as he did not think he could maintain himself there, and as his opponents had advanced from the city, he first occupied Munychia. A battle took place in the streets of Piraeus. The exiles fought for their lost property, their country, and their freedom; and animated by these powerful motives, they gained the day. Critias fell fighting bravely, and with him Hippomachus, one of the Thirty, besides seventy of their followers. The conquerors took only the arms, and abstained from injuring the property of their fellow-citizens who had been forced to fight against them. The vanquished retreated into the city, and on the following day the tyrants, with the exception of Pheidon and Eratosthenes, fled to Eleusis. The 3000 were not agreed among themselves: many, whose consciences were not clear, dreaded those in Piraeus, and accordingly refused to admit them into the city at once. They chose ten men, one from every phyle, to form a government, which was equally opposed to the fugitives at Eleusis and to Thrasybulus. But as the army of Thrasybulus was ever increasing, the oligarchs, both of Eleusis and of Athens, sent envoys to Sparta for succour. Lysander immediately led an army against the city, while his brother Libys blockaded Piraeus with a fleet. The cause of the patriots was thus in a most precarious condition, when the Spartan king Pausanias, jealous of Lysander, and wishing to prevent his conquering Athens a second time, obtained another army from the ephors, and advanced to Piraeus. He did indeed attack the Athenians, and several engagements took place; but he wished the city to be saved, and peace to be restored. He, accordingly, caused the hostile parties to send deputies to him; and as the two ephors, who were with him, likewise favoured the restoration of peace, an understanding was come to. The Thirty, their ministers (the Eleven), and the ten archons in Piraeus, were the only persons exempted from the general reconciliation, which was secured by a complete amnesty. Pausanias then disbanded his army, and Thrasybulus, with his forces, marched in arms from Piraeus to the city, and offered sacrifices in the acropolis to Athene. Thrasybulus advised his countrymen to maintain peace and unity, and return to their ancient constitution. The people followed his

Phyle.
(From an original sketch by Sir William Gell.)

advice; but when they heard that the Thirty at Eleusis were preparing for a renewal of the civil war, they marched out in a body, and the oligarchical leaders were put to death; the other seceders were prevailed upon to return to the city and accept the offer of reconciliation. At length a new and general amnesty, which was extended even to the children of the Thirty, reconciled all minds. Democracy was re-established, and to this day, says Xenophon, they continue to live under it, and remain faithful to their oaths. A law was passed, that any attempt to overthrow it should be punished with death. Thus ended the tyranny of the Thirty and the year of anarchy, B.C. 403.

This year is that of the archonship of Eucleides. His name marks an epoch in the political history of Athens, for the Solonian constitution, which was restored and extended under him, henceforth remained unimpugned, until long after the time when Athens had lost her political influence. A commission of 500 nomothetae or lawgivers was entrusted with the revision of the laws, and Nicomachus, who however discharged his duties carelessly, was commissioned to draw up a new transcript of the laws. This event is remarkable also from the fact, that what is called the Ionic alphabet was first used on that occasion; that is, all those letters of the Greek alphabet which are still in use, were then employed at Athens for the first time.

Athenian Horseman wearing the Petasus and Chlamys.
(From the frieze of the Parthenon.)

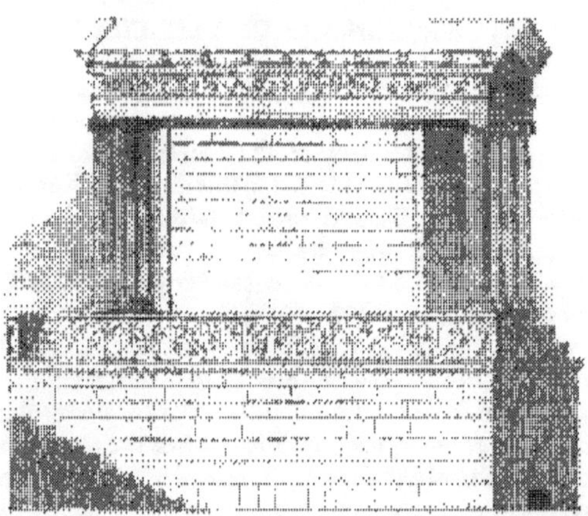

The Temple of Nike Apteros at Athens, restored.

CHAPTER XXIX.

RETROSPECTIVE SURVEY OF THE INTERNAL CONDITION OF GREECE DURING THE PELOPONNESIAN WAR.

It is difficult to give a fair and satisfactory estimate of this great and stirring period, for the ancient authors themselves are diametrically opposed in the views they take of it. If we consult modern historians, we shall find in most of them a sort of preconceived opinion or conviction, that the Peloponnesian war forms the conclusion of the bright portion of Greek history. All, however, are agreed, that throughout this period Athens is the centre of interest, and that the other parts of the Greek world only contribute to complete the history of that one state, the type of the intellectual culture of all the rest. Every one must feel himself constrained to recognise the undisputed pre-eminence of that wonderful city, and to share in the admiration which is so cheerfully bestowed upon it; and this will be done more readily by those who judge of the greatness of a state, not from the mere display of physical strength, but from the spiritual and intellectual influence which always subdues and outlives the mere physical strength of man and his institutions. In the following pages, accordingly, we shall have mainly to speak of Athens.

The speeches which Thucydides puts into the mouth of Pericles, give us a fresh and glowing picture of the greatness of Athens, and after the death of that distinguished statesman the historian pictures in dark colours the forlorn condition of an ill-advised people, which became more and more reckless and demoralised. Further on, when describing the scenes of horror which occurred at Corcyra, he speaks in still sadder strains of the demoralisation that broke in upon all Greece in consequence of the war. From numerous allusions we must conclude, that he considered the Peloponnesian war as a malady, the inevitable result of which would be the ruin of Athens. His great contemporary, Aristophanes, was of the same opinion; in the luxuriant playfulness of his imagination, he uttered many a wise and serious admonition to the men of peace and to the admirers of the great times of old, who in vain laboured to withstand, not to say, to check the rolling torrent of unbridled democracy. All the great minds of Athens, who still speak to us in their works, bear witness that the real greatness and the golden age of Athens had then departed. This mode of viewing things is as old as the human race itself; but we, to whom the Peloponnesian war appears only as an integral part in the development of Greece, must confess, that although after that time Athens did not advance in her victorious career of conquest, yet her political greatness was as yet by no means undermined; while on the other hand, her spiritual and intellectual vigour not only did not suffer through her unfavourable external circumstances, but on the contrary, was to all appearance as steadily progressing and flourishing as if the political consequences of her long-continued struggles had passed by without producing any effect whatever upon the freshness and productive powers of the Athenian mind. As, therefore, we estimate the life and prosperity of a nation by the results of its mental activity, we must extend the flourishing period of Greek history down to the time when Macedonia exercised its influence and power in the affairs of Greece. For the period from the end of the Peloponnesian war down to the breaking up of the vast Macedonian empire is so rich in products of art and literature, that in variety and universality it undoubtedly surpasses the earlier and happier times. There is only one characteristic difference, though that is certainly an important one, between the two centuries: fancy, imagination, and poetical emotion now give place to the powers of thought and reflection, and poetry is supplanted by learning.

It has often been said, that the struggle between the two leading states of Greece not only affected their external power, but brought about a thorough change in their character and nature. But if we consider that, in the case of Athens, the loss of her supremacy was only transitory, and that the momentary change of her constitution cannot be taken into account at all, we must avow that Sparta underwent far greater changes both in her internal and in her external relations, and that her very victory was the cause of her decay.

The Peloponnesian war made Sparta a maritime power, and this one fact alone was subversive of the constitution of Lycurgus and of the Spartan character. But the course of events had rendered it necessary to combat the enemy with her own weapons and on her own ground; yet how slowly and with what difficulties had Sparta entered on her new career! When, after the glorious struggle with Persia, the power of Athens was ever increasing, Sparta was kept back, not by wars with the neighbouring states of Peloponnesus or with revolted subjects, such as the Messenians, but by her natural caution and slowness, which made her wait passively until the contests in Boeotia drew attention to the relation between Athens and Sparta, and the thirty years' peace of Pericles guaranteed their mutual supremacy. But while Sparta adhered to the basis of the treaty, and was content with the supremacy of Peloponnesus, the ever-active spirit of the Athenians soon set the terms of the peace at defiance, and their power, which assumed a more and more threatening aspect, their arrogance and love of conquest, at last forced the Lacedaemonians to take up arms. The war was commenced for the purpose of delivering the weaker Greek states from the dominion and oppression of Athens; but towards the end of it, Sparta aimed at nothing short of the annihilation of the power of Athens, and the establishment of her own supremacy over all Greece.

The want of decision displayed in the beginning of the war is remarkable. It was not till the Sicilian expedition, or rather after it, that Sparta made any serious efforts to establish her power at sea. This was quite natural; for the Spartans had neither revenues nor other resources, so long as they maintained the ancient constitution of their state. When, at length, they aimed in good earnest at the destruction of the naval power of Athens, they concluded a treaty with the natural enemy of Greece, and paid their marines with Persian money. It is not surprising, therefore, that foreign manners, luxuries, and effeminacy, of the injurious effects of which we read so many complaints, easily found their way into Sparta. How little, in fact, the severity of laws can do in strengthening or establishing virtue, is clear from the fact that the Spartan kings, even in the good old times, were so accessible to bribes that their weakness became proverbial. We mention this, because in a state of rigid principles, such things lead to the worst possible consequences; since any transgression of the narrow limits fixed by law can rarely be remedied by openly retracing one's steps, and therefore leads to hypocrisy. Throughout this period the external forms of the old constitution were, generally speaking, strictly observed, but the power of the ephors, in their relation to the kings, had been immensely increased. They were more powerful and influential then the Roman tribunes of the plebs; and during the Peloponnesian war the executive appears to have been chiefly in their hands. They convened and conducted the popular assemblies, gave audiences to foreign ambassadors, and sent embassies to foreign states; they arranged the campaigns, appointed the commanders, and were furnished with constant reports of the proceedings in the camp and in the field. Formerly, the king who went out at the head of his army, had been absolute commander; in B. C. 418 the ephors gave him ten assessors as his councillors, and toward the end of the war, two ephors accompanied the king during the campaign. In addition to this it must be observed, that the two royal families, instead of uniting to resist the influence of the ephors, endeavoured, in their perpetual disputes, to injure each other, and were thus obliged to court the favour of the ephors. The ephoralty had thus entirely lost its original democratic character, for which it is praised by Plato, Aristotle, and others, who have held up the constitution of Sparta as the model of a wise mixture of all forms of government; it had become a despotic power, which could not always aim at the public good in its efforts to preserve its own importance.

The magnitude of the war rendered the creation of new offices indispensable; harmosts (ἁρμοσταί) were appointed to govern conquered towns, admirals (ναύαρχοι) and vice-admirals (ἐπιστολεῖς) were chosen to command the fleet, the former originally for one year, and only once; but we have seen how, in the case of Lysander, this law was evaded.* A far greater change, however, was brought about by the introduction of coined money. Plutarch and others mention Lysander as the first who introduced this custom at Sparta. This much at least is certain, that before the war the state had no public treasure, although the weakness of the Spartan kings in reference to bribery may have made the people familiar with money long before this time. But now, as Plato says, Sparta soon became the richest state in Greece. Private citizens naturally imitated the example of the state; for the equality of property established by Lycurgus among the citizens of Sparta had been set aside. The perpetual wars had reduced the number of Spartans, and the accumulation of several estates in one family had created disproportionate wealth. This tendency was promoted by a law passed soon after the war by Epitadeus, which forbade the transfer of property by sale indeed, but allowed every one to dispose of it by gift or will in any way he pleased. It began to be customary to give large dowries, which was likewise contrary to the laws of Lycurgus; and the wealthy intermarried and left

* See above, p. 359.

their property to one another, which gave rise to distinctions of rank according to the amount of property. The poorer citizens soon found themselves excluded from the active exercise of their civic rights, as they were no longer able to defray the expenses of the syssitia, and in general could not compete with the rich in their mode of living, nor fulfil the indispensable conditions which had been imposed by Lycurgus upon every Spartan citizen. Thus it came to pass that instead of the 9000 Spartans mentioned in the legislation of Lycurgus, the number had been reduced to 700, and of these only 100 were in the full enjoyment of all civic rights.

One consequence of these irregularities on the one hand, and of the obstinate clinging to the ancient forms on the other, was, that even as early as the time of Aristotle, two-fifths of all the landed property were in the hands of heiresses; and considering their Spartan education, the ascendancy thus conferred upon women could not possibly work for the public good. The small number of Spartan citizens produced other evil effects also. It naturally increased the fear entertained of the Helots, and rendered necessary greater harshness and severity towards them. During the war, Helots had been employed in the armies, for which purpose they were emancipated. Brasidas made his successful expedition to the distant Chalcidice with such an army. Subsequently, perioeci and neodamadeis only were sent out to remote countries, as in the case of Gylippus' expedition to Sicily. Spartans generally had the command, though perioeci also are mentioned as commanders of galleys. When a king took the field he was accompanied by thirty Spartans, who formed a sort of honorary body-guard. Notwithstanding all this, however, the few Spartan families remained in proud and strict seclusion from the rest of the population, and thereby endangered the safety of the state itself; the conspiracy of Cinadon, for example, whose object was to overthrow the existing constitution, was frustrated only by the prudent caution of Agesilaus.

This conflict between external circumstances and the inflexibility of the ancient institutions, does not exhibit Sparta, successful as she had been in the war, in a very brilliant or enviable light. The fact that notwithstanding all this, the state maintained its supremacy for several years, and its independence even for centuries, arose from circumstances, respecting which we shall have occasion to speak hereafter.

Athens had come forth from the long contest outwardly humbled, but not internally broken. Its constitution, the very opposite of the stiff and inflexible institutions of Sparta, capable of any development and reforms for good as well as for evil, had passed through several crises, and had finally returned to its Solonian type. It cannot be denied that the state sustained momentary injuries from its many political convulsions; for it is certain that the banishment of Alcibiades, and the deplorable infatuation of the Athenians after the battle of Arginusae, were followed by the most melancholy consequences for the thoughtless people; but with all its errors and faults, Athens displays extraordinary vitality, and a high degree of skill in accommodating itself to new circumstances, or returning, if required, to its ancient institutions. The most important element in maintaining this state of things through all the phases of political change, was no doubt the fact that the number of Athenian citizens was never allowed to decrease, but was constantly filled up. If we suppose with Boeckh, that the number of citizens was, on an average, 20,000 (for according to Thucydides, they amounted at the beginning of the Peloponnesian war to nearly 30,000), the admission to the Attic franchise must have been liberally granted in those times, when war and pestilence carried off so many, and when the cleruchiae, or assignments of land in conquered districts, drew away considerable numbers from Athens. It is true, the cleruchi (persons who received assignments of land), who were generally of the poorer classes, might let their lot to farm and remain at Athens; but there can be no doubt that many settled in the districts thus distributed, and remained there to protect their new acquisitions as the real lords of the land. We are not informed of the exact manner in which the number of citizens was kept up; some allusions, however, justify the supposition that the Athenians were not very scrupulous in conferring the franchise, and that they admitted to the enjoyment of it citizens of allied states as well as resident aliens at Athens, and even slaves. Thus in the first years of the war, the Plataeans, driven from their homes, were admitted in a body; and although such things were not done without considerable formalities, still such admissions must have been so numerous and so irrespective of the previous circumstances of those receiving the favour, that Andocides was probably right in saying, "I see you give the franchise to slaves and all kinds of foreigners." This custom of raising strangers to the rank of citizens was unknown at Sparta, and Athens, in this respect, had an unquestionable advantage over her rival.

The property-classes of the Athenian citizens, as established in the Solonian constitution, had ceased to mark civil distinctions and privileges; but the natural distinction between the rich and the poor had, if possible, become greater, and was now injurious to the public weal. Generous and wise statesmen, like Cimon and Pericles, had endeavoured to remedy the evil by personal liberality or legal enactments; but the demagogues stirred up the masses, who possessed no property, to acts of injustice and insolence against the rich, who formed the minority, and naturally entertained almost exclusively oligarchical, or at least anti-democratical sentiments. Largesses of corn and money to the poorer classes occur even in earlier times; we need only remember the distribution of the produce of the silver mines of Laurion, before the time of Themistocles; nor had the cleruchiae any object except the relief of the poorer citizens. But Pericles went still farther, for the introduction of the theoricon or theatre-money is ascribed to him. Boeckh thinks it probable that even previously to Olymp. 70, B.C. 500, when the building of the great stone theatre was commenced, money was paid for admission to the theatre, and that Pericles introduced only its payment by the public treasury, at first for the poorer citizens alone. The theoricon amounted to two oboli, but was subsequently raised by Agyrrhius to three; it was distributed in an assembly of the people, held in the theatre before the beginning of the festival. In the time of Demosthenes the wealthier classes also availed themselves of it. The lessee of the theatre, of course, paid back to the treasury only a small portion of his receipts. It became customary to give the same sums under the name of theoricon on other festive occasions also, when there were no performances in the theatre; and if, according to Boeckh's calculation, the expenditure for every holiday is estimated at one talent (supposing there were 18,000 recipients), it is quite clear that the theoricon must have swallowed up all the money destined for war and the civil administration; for the holidays were very numerous, and Pericles increased the popular taste for them. His personal character and influence, indeed, exercised a salutary check, but in a few years everything was altered. The sovereign people paid itself also for several other things. Thus we may mention the pay for attending the popular assembly (*μισθὸς ἐκκλησιαστικός*) which was introduced in the time of Pericles, but not by him. It consisted at first of one obolus, but in B.C. 360 it was increased to three by Agyrrhius, who generally squandered the public revenue in an unpardonable manner. His object was to indemnify the citizens for the losses occasioned by the interruption of their occupations, caused by attending the popular assemblies. In like manner, the pay for attending the courts of justice (*μισθὸς δικαστικός*), the introduction of which is ascribed to Pericles, and which at first amounted to one obolus, and afterwards to three, was intended as a compensation. Idleness, pettifogging, and public speaking, gradually became the characteristic features of the Athenian people, for which, even during the first period of the Peloponnesian war, it was chastised by the muse of Aristophanes. A complete enumeration of all the arrangements made for the pleasure and comfort of the people, in and after the time of Pericles, would lead us beyond the limits of the present history. But we may remark, that Pericles neglected no lawful means by which he might maintain his supreme influence over the people. His successors were in every respect unlike him: they flattered and crouched before the people, whom he had guided according to his own will; and the factions which he had kept down assailed one another with more openness and bitterness than they had ventured to display during his lifetime. The unfortunate events of the war had a direct influence upon the relative position of these factions. The oligarchs were gainers, whenever the fleets or armies of their country perished; and the ascendancy of the people at home went hand in hand with the victories abroad. Real political operations and intrigues were carried on by the oligarchs alone, who through their clubs * kept up connections with kindred spirits, even far beyond the boundaries of their own country, and whose reckless tendencies are manifest from their oath preserved in Aristotle, "to hurt and injure the people as much as possible." The conquerors in this intestine strife were invariably cruel, but the oligarchs, though belonging to the higher classes, were always more so than the victorious people.

The violent changes that were made in the Athenian constitution during the war have been already mentioned. The moderate democracy which succeeded the oligarchy of the Four Hundred, began with such strict principles that it cannot possibly have existed until the downfal of Athens. Those who then restored democracy abolished all salaries, which may refer especially to the pay for attending the assemblies and courts of justice. The clubs continued to be as busy as before, and Alcibiades, who returned about that time, soon fell a victim to their machinations. But the people acquired a new leader in Cleophon, a worthy successor to Cleon and Hyperbolus. It was he and Theramenes, who managed the disgraceful accusation of the conquerors in the battle of Arginusae. The government of Athens seems to have now become a perfect ochlocracy; but the more infatuated the people, the more confident were the oligarchs, and the defeat of Aegospotami brought the oligarchs and friends of Sparta into power. The abolition of the rule of the Thirty by Thrasybulus, and the restoration of democracy under the archon Eucleides, seem to have been followed by a radical change in the policy of the

* Ἑταιρεῖαι or συνωμοσίαι. They were originally intended only for mutual support at elections and in the courts of justice.

oligarchs. The people were so much in earnest in returning to the Solonian constitution, that they again placed it under the superintendence of the Areopagus.

Thus at the end of the Peloponnesian war, Athens appears weak in her foreign relations indeed, but internally the party struggles had brought her to a better and purer condition, and we may take it for granted that during the next generation the Athenians continued to act with a certain degree of moderation. The party feuds began again, when Philip of Macedonia interfered in the affairs of Greece, or, as Justin remarks, "with the death of Epaminondas the virtue of the Athenians disappeared."

It is a wonderful phenomenon that during this period of misfortune and internal distraction, there flourished at Athens the greatest minds that ever graced the history of any nation with the highest productions of poetry, art, and philosophy. This shows the extraordinary vitality and imperishable vigour which so remarkably distinguished Athens from all other states. The golden age of Attic art and literature extends from the beginning of the Persian wars down to the time of the successors of Alexander, that is, to the end of the fourth century before Christ, and consequently lasted nearly 200 years. No other nation has ever presented a similar spectacle. During the former of these two centuries, poetry and art were fostered with a loving care, and Pericles raised the drama, the crown of all poetry, to the highest degree of popularity. The richness and perfection displayed in sculpture and architecture during the Periclean and the subsequent age, awakened and developed a general sense of the beautiful, which no doubt distinguished even an ordinary Athenian, when abroad, as the son of a classic land. During the second century of this golden age, the drama, tragedy as well as comedy, maintained its influence, although the productive power disappeared, or at least did not meet with that sympathy and appreciation which are necessary for its preservation. The public taste seems, on the whole, to have inclined more towards comedy, as we may infer from the extraordinary fertility of Menander, Diphilus, and the numerous other comic writers. The extant fragments of Menander are specimens of the unrivalled refinement of the Attic dialect. But it is more especially the perfect development of Attic prose, in oratory and philosophy, that characterises the latter century.

The period of the Peloponnesian war, to which we must here more particularly direct our attention, may without hesitation be called the most flourishing season of that long-continued golden age. For to it belong Sophocles and Euripides, two of the triad of great tragic poets; of the comic poets, above and besides many others, Aristophanes; of the historians, Thucydides, whose pre-eminence over those of both earlier and later ages no one has ever disputed; lastly, of the philosophers, Socrates, the wisest of all the Greeks, whose merits have been immortalised in the works of his great disciples Plato and Xenophon.

According to a tradition founded on late authorities, Euripides was born on the day of the battle of Salamis, in which Aeschylus, the eldest of the three tragic poets, fought for his country's independence among the foremost and the bravest; and around the trophies gained in the battle Sophocles danced in the chorus of boys.

Whatever opinion we may entertain as to the truth of this story, we cannot deny that it expresses a proud consciousness of the excellence of the Attic poets, who are here brought into connection with the most glorious event in the history of Greece. Both Sophocles and Euripides lived till the end of the Peloponnesian war. The aged Aeschylus died in the year preceding that in which Euripides, at the age of twenty-five or twenty-six, came forward with his first production, B.C. 455. Thirteen years previously, in B.C. 468, Sophocles had gained the victory with his first play. Each of the three was the offspring of his own time, and their productions reflect their respective ages as faithfully as the comedies of Aristophanes do. Aeschylus, a hero of the Persian war, was the favourite at once of Ares and of the Muses: rough warriors, heaven-storming giants, and beings of superhuman characters, are his chief dramatis personae. "Their very sight," he himself is made to say, "inspired the spectators for war and victory." The early youth of Sophocles belongs to the period through which Aeschylus passed as a man, and as one of the most distinguished citizens; but he was more under the influence of the subsequent age, during which Athens was in the ascendant, and enjoyed the fruits of the noble efforts she had made against the barbarians. His dramas are the reflex of a glorious and peaceful time, which was not yet distracted and undermined by evil passions. His characters are human, but noble and pure, so that he himself could say of them, "I describe men as they should be."

Euripides, his younger contemporary, shows the enormous progress which the Athenian people had made in intellectual culture within a short period; and how this culture at once brought forth all the dark features of human nature. The subjects of his tragedies are taken from the same mythical and heroic cycles; but we see neither the Titan-like figures of Aeschylus, nor the lofty and pure characters of Sophocles: we hear the ancient heroes speak like ordinary mortals; we see in them all the little sufferings of human frailty, and all the passions and sophistries which every educated Athenian knew but too well from his own experience. If we were to adopt the judgment of Aristophanes, a most able though not impartial critic, we should at once condemn Euripides; but a fairer opinion, probably, is that of Aristotle, who regards him as at least the most pathetic tragic poet. Euripides described men as they were in his days; and it is a noble proof of the good taste of the Athenians, that although he composed about ninety dramas, he was only five times honoured with the prize. In comedy, the Athenians delighted to see men represented in their actual characters and circumstances; but, in tragedy they looked for the ideal men of an age which they were accustomed to regard with veneration.

While we must thus acknowledge that the moral condition of the age exercised an unmistakeable influence upon the development and changes of the drama, we can ascribe only a very slight and insignificant influence to the passing political occurrences of the time. The few political allusions met with in the extant tragedies scarcely justify the attempt to discover more; nay, it would be unfair towards tragedy, even that of Euripides, thus to degrade it by connecting it with the petty events of the day. If we examine such tragedies as the *Oedipus in Colonus* or *Philoctetes*, and remember when they were composed and performed, we must own, that the drama remained faithful to its principles and dignity, which required it to be superior to party feelings, and free from their perverting influence.

Comedy, on the other hand, performed the office of a free press at Athens, sometimes giving a faithful image of the period, sometimes a caricature. Even before the first appearance of Aristophanes, comedy, notwithstanding the liberty of the democratic institutions, had been confined within the bounds of moderation. These restrictions, however, appear to have fallen into disuse, at least at the beginning of the Peloponnesian war; for the youthful poet came forward at once with the greatest boldness and bitterness against the most influential persons, until, about the middle of the war, a law of Syracosius forbade the practice of ridiculing any one by representing him on the stage under his real name. This liberty, however, did not cease during the period of what is called the ancient comedy, of which Aristophanes was the great Coryphaeus, and which continued to flourish even for some time after the Peloponnesian war; but the persons attacked were less powerful than Cleon or Alcibiades had been. The eleven plays of Aristophanes which have come down to us, and are the only complete specimens of Greek comedy extant, contain a somewhat caricatured representation of Athenian life; and in them the leading men of the period are ridiculed along with, and on account of, the men of an inferior order. We may safely assert, that there was at that time no poet, statesman, or public character of any kind at Athens, who was not obliged to submit to the exhibition of his great or small foibles in some of the plays of Aristophanes. The noble and pure greatness of Sophocles alone is always mentioned by him with admiration, because he knew nothing respecting him that he could censure. With Aeschylus he finds fault for his uncouthness and inflexibility; at least, he puts this criticism into the mouth of Euripides. But Euripides, Cleon, and Socrates were regarded by him as the incarnations of all the sins committed in poetry, politics, and philosophy. Besides Euripides, a vast multitude of smaller minds received severe rebukes from the dramatic satirist. Among the politicians, men who were otherwise very respectable, such as the brave Lamachus, were often lashed by Aristophanes, because they advocated the continuance of the war. As he regarded Euripides and his followers as spoilers of tragedy, Cleon and the other members of the war-party as preparing the ruin of their country, so he saw in Socrates and his doctrines the destruction of religion, and of the faith of the ancient Athenians. Aristophanes everywhere condemns the degenerate state of his country; everywhere manifests his attachment to the good old times of proud simplicity and noble enthusiasm; everywhere exhibits the heroes of Marathon as models of virtue and valour. He does not hesitate to attack the leading propensities of the whole people, such as their fondness for sitting in judgment upon others, while they neglected their own domestic affairs.

His treatment of philosophy and Socrates is most surprising, and has been the subject of much discussion; for we must observe, in the outset, that he himself treated the ancient religious dogmas very unceremoniously, and tried the dangerous experiment of endeavouring to cure unbelief by unbelief. In the *Clouds*, which was performed about twenty-four years before the death of Socrates, he attacks the great philosopher very unsparingly, but is evidently more concerned about his doctrines than about his person. It seems sufficiently clear from Plato's *Symposium*, that Aristophanes was not a personal enemy of Socrates, and Xenophon makes no allusion to any such hostility. The examination of the question, whether Socrates was justly condemned to death, would lead us too far. He had to pay the penalty for propagating the new ideas, which, in the advanced state of Athenian culture, were struggling into life. He disregarded the sensuous character of the popular religion, and aimed at a true and spiritual knowledge of the divine Being. He led his disciples to self-knowledge and self-culture above all things, leaving untouched their religious feeling and their natural faith. But as he inculcated upon them the necessity of trying to comprehend the essence of all things, and the nature and destiny of man, he naturally led them to reflect upon the nature of the Deity and to doubt the correctness of the faith of their ancestors. The scepticism which thus sprung up cannot be laid to the charge of Socrates; it was the unavoidable consequence of the thoughts which he had awakened, and he himself outwardly, complied with established customs. Being of a pious disposition, and adhering to the ancient worship, he always performed the customary sacrifices and holy rites, and advised his disciples also to do the same. His accusation belongs to the time of the restoration, immediately after the Peloponnesian war, when the Athenians seem to have been most anxiously endeavouring to give new stability to the commonwealth by reviving their old institutions. This attempt and the belief that, by restoring the ancient forms they could resuscitate the ancient spirit, were probably the chief causes of the condemnation of Socrates. He did not withdraw from its consequences, for he had always lived in obedience to the law, and regarded any attempt to evade it as inconsistent with his teachings. The charge brought against him was threefold; that he did not worship the gods recognised by the

Bust of Socrates.
(From the Vatican.)

state, that he introduced new divinities, and that he corrupted the young. He spent the short period between his condemnation and execution in prison, surrounded by his friends and disciples, and drank the hemlock with the greatest calmness and cheerfulness of mind. This happened in B.C. 399, when Socrates had attained the age of seventy. No sooner was the deed done, than the Athenians, as after their condemnation of the victors of Arginusae, began to repent of their rashness. Melitus, one of the accusers, was put to death, and the two others, Anytus and Lycon, were sent into exile.

These few observations are sufficient to give some idea of the moral and intellectual condition of Athens. We must bear in mind that the master-works of men, like Sophocles and Aristophanes, were thoroughly understood, enjoyed, and appreciated by the Athenian public; a fact which indicates the possession by it of an extraordinary degree of mental culture, and of a vast amount of knowledge.

Funeral Feast.
(From a marble bas-relief.)

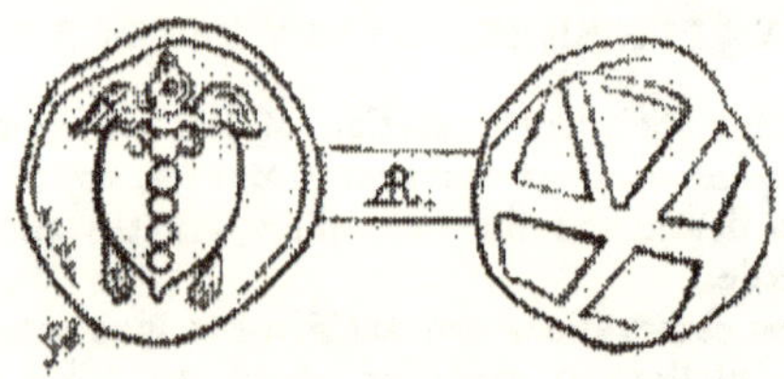

Coin of Aegina.

CHAPTER XXX.

FROM THE EXPEDITION OF CYRUS THE YOUNGER TO THE PEACE OF ANTALCIDAS.

THE most important of the events preceding the appearance of the great Spartan king Agesilaus, and what is called the Corinthian war, was the adventurous expedition of the Greeks under the command of Cyrus the younger against his brother Artaxerxes, king of Persia. This enterprise shows the sad and deplorable condition of the affairs of Greece itself, for we here see malcontents and exiles from all parts of Greece enlisting in the service of a barbarian and an avowed enemy of Greece. The long war had demoralised thousands of men, who now found it unbearable to live in peace and support themselves by honest labour, and therefore looked to war and booty for the means of subsistence.

Cyrus was a son of Darius II., and governor of the maritime districts of Asia Minor. His eminent qualities as a man and a ruler endeared him so much to his mother Parysatis, that she preferred him to his elder brother Artaxerxes, the legitimate heir to the throne, who was now king of Persia. Parysatis, wishing to raise Cyrus to the throne, urged him to rebel against his brother. Cyrus resolved to follow her advice, and his knowledge of the Greek cities in Asia, his connections, especially with Lysander and the Spartans, but above all, his money, enabled him to assemble a considerable number of Greeks from Asia Minor, Chersonesus, Thessaly, and various other parts of Greece. His most intimate friends alone knew of his great scheme, while all the rest were made to believe that he was merely preparing an expedition against the rebellious Pisidians. From the account given by Xenophon of a review held by Cyrus, we learn that there were assembled 10,400 heavy-armed Greeks, and 2500 peltasts, who, together with 100,000 barbarians and 20 scythe-chariots, marched against the army of Artaxerxes, amounting to 1,200,000 men and 200 scythe-chariots. In the summer of B. C. 401, Cyrus set out from Sardis, and it was not till the army reached Thapsacus that he informed the Greeks of what they had long suspected, that they were marching against the king of Persia. Their reluctance to proceed any farther was overcome by liberal pay and still more liberal promises. The army then crossed the Euphrates and advanced, meeting with no resistance, until in the neighbourhood of Cunaxa they encountered all the forces of the king. In the ensuing battle, the Greeks, who occupied the right wing, gained the victory. Cyrus, after having for some time observed the enemy's movements, vehemently attacked the centre, where Artaxerxes stood, but fell in the first onset after a short struggle. Artaxerxes himself was wounded. The death of Cyrus decided the defeat of the barbarians, and this one battle put an end to the whole insurrection. But the Greeks were still unconquered, and had not lost a single man in the engagement. When they learnt the death of Cyrus, they offered the command to his companion and friend Ariaeus, who afterwards faithlessly deserted them; and they were so much encouraged by their victory, that when the Persian king required them to lay down their arms, they refused to give this mark of submission. Their heroism, however, had to pass through severer trials. Under the pretence of friendship, and the promise to lead them back into Ionia, Tissaphernes and the king drew them still farther into the interior, as far as the river Tigris; their commanders were ensnared and put to death, in the hope that the army might thus be overcome more easily. But fortune did not forsake the Greeks; it was Xenophon, the disciple of Socrates, and the historian of this extraordinary expedition, who was chiefly instrumental in restoring their sinking courage, and exhorted them to persevere and return home under all circumstances. Cheirisophus, a Spartan, began the memorable retreat, he commanding the van, and Xenophon the rear. They did not take the known road by which they had come, for they could not force the passage over the Euphrates; and moreover, the districts through which the immense army had passed, had been too much drained and exhausted to furnish them again with necessaries, and they therefore went northwards, through unknown mountainous countries. After encountering unspeakable difficulties, being pursued by the forces of Tissaphernes as far as the country of the Carduchi, where they were attacked by the warlike mountaineers, and underwent all the hardships of a severe winter in Armenia, they at length reached a height from which they saw the sea. With indescribable joy they hastened down to it, and when they entered Trapezus, the first Greek town they came to, forgetting all their sufferings, and again feeling as Greeks, they indemnified themselves by festive games for all the hardships of their retreat: 8000 were still surviving; they marched along the coast, while the sick and infirm embarked in ships. They had still to encounter many dangers, but they were trifling compared with those they had escaped from. No sooner, however, had they reached the countries in which they felt confident and safe, than disputes and quarrels arose among the leaders as well as among the men. It was with difficulty that Xenophon kept the army together, and succeeded in bringing them to the western coast of the Euxine; 5000 of them then entered the service of Seuthes, a Thracian prince, the successor of Sitalces; but they were soon afterwards summoned back into Asia by two Spartan commissioners, fresh hostilities having a short time previously broken out between Sparta and Tissaphernes.

The whole expedition lasted fifteen months, from the summer of B.C. 401, till the autumn of B.C. 400. We are fortunate enough to possess an excellent and detailed account of the march into the interior of Asia and of the retreat, written by the brave and able Xenophon himself.*

The remainder of the 10,000 Greeks were incorporated with the troops of Thimbron, the Spartan harmost, who had been appointed to conduct the war against Tissaphernes. By the death of Cyrus the relation subsisting between Sparta and Persia had become altered. Tissaphernes had obtained from Artaxerxes the satrapy of Cyrus as a reward for his fidelity; and on his return from the interior of Asia, he was immediately involved in quarrels with the Greek towns, which refused to submit to his authority. The situation of the Greeks in Asia had been rather unfavourable during the late wars; the fruits of the ancient successes over the Persians, and especially of Cimon's victories, had in a measure been lost during the unfortunate contests in the mother country. The undertakings of Tissaphernes and Pharnabazus during the latter years of the Peloponnesian war, against the freedom of the Greek cities in Asia, show that the power of Persia was reviving, at least relatively to the Greeks, for in the interior it may have been weak enough. We have no accurate information about the condition of the Asiatic colonies, and from Xenophon's description we can only infer that the majority of them, especially the less important towns, had been reduced to subjection by the Persian

* For having taken part in the expedition, Xenophon was exiled from Athens, which was then on terms of friendship with Persia. He went to Sparta, accompanied Agesilaus on his Asiatic expeditions, and afterwards lived on an estate in Elis, which the Spartans had given him. The decree of his exile was repealed in B.C. 399, but he was not recalled till B.C. 371. He remained at Corinth, however, and died there, in B.C. 355, at the advanced age of 90. His partiality towards Sparta has been severely censured; but all Greece honoured him at Olympia as the deliverer of the 10,000 Greeks.

satraps, and that the larger cities, from fear of a similar fate, invoked the assistance of Sparta. Thimbron accordingly went into Asia with 4000 Peloponnesians, 1000 Neodamodeis (freed men), and 300 Athenian horse. The Greek cities in Asia also furnished their contingents, for all had now to obey the commands of Sparta. Thimbron's success was not very great, and being soon afterwards succeeded by the cunning Dercyllidas, he was banished, because he had neglected the discipline of his army, and had not spared the countries of the friends of Sparta. The war now at once assumed a different aspect. Dercyllidas, wishing to direct all his forces against his personal enemy, Pharnabazus, entered into negotiations with Tissaphernes. Within eight days he took or obtained the adhesion of nine towns of Aeolis, which belonged to the satrapy of Pharnabazus, and then concluded a truce with the barbarians, as he intended to spend the winter in Bithynia, so as not to be a burden on the friendly towns. In the spring of the following year, B. C. 398, he went to Lampsacos, and after having renewed the truce with Pharnabazus, proceeded to Chersonesus, at the request of the towns of that peninsula, whose application had been forwarded to him from Sparta. There he caused a wall to be built across the isthmus, to protect the country against the inroads and ravages of the Thracians. He completed the structure during the summer, then returned to Asia, and laid siege to Atarneus, opposite to Lesbos, which was in the hands of Lesbian exiles, and served them as head-quarters during their piratical expeditions. After a siege of eight months he took the place, and proceeded thence to Ephesus. There he received orders from Sparta to attack the possessions of Tissaphernes in Caria, and thus to accelerate the liberation of the Greek colonies. Meantime Tissaphernes and Pharnabazus had become reconciled; they had made all necessary preparations in Caria, and crossed the Maeander. The hostile armies faced each other for some time, and then a truce was concluded until the terms of peace should be ratified on both sides; for Dercyllidas demanded the independence of the Greek towns, the evacuation of which the satraps promised only on condition that the Greek armies and harmosts should be withdrawn from them. This happened in B. C. 397.

During these operations of Thimbron and Dercyllidas, Sparta had been engaged in a war with her north-western neighbours of Elis, which lasted for two years, B.C. 399 and 398. During the summer, Agis invaded the enemy's country twice. The first campaign was frustrated by an earthquake, but in the second his success was complete. The Eleans had joined the alliance between Athens and Argos, and had even excluded the Spartans from participation in the Olympic games and sacrifices. In accordance with the mission Sparta had undertaken, but which she often abused, she now required the Eleans to restore the towns within their territory to independence, and as the Eleans did not comply with this demand, Agis ravaged their territory up to the very walls of their capital, and compelled them to accept a humiliating peace. They were obliged to demolish their fortifications, to recognize the independence of the towns in Triphylia, and to form an alliance with Sparta. They retained, however, the superintendence of the Olympic games and of the temple of the Olympian Zeus.

The aged king Agis died soon after the conclusion of peace with Elis, and was succeeded by his brother Agesilaus.* In his personal appearance he had no advantages, for he was of small stature, and lame in one foot; but his mind was all the greater, and Sparta never had a more intelligent ruler. He possessed an intellectual culture which enabled him to look far beyond the narrow views of the earlier Spartans, and which was the result of the civilisation recently introduced at Sparta. Xenophon, in his eulogy on Agesilaus, mentions, as occurring in the first year of his reign, the conspiracy of Cinadon, or of the poor against the few wealthy Spartans. This conspiracy is an unmistakeable symptom of the decay of the ancient Lycurgian institutions. Its discovery, and the punishment of Cinadon, could not heal the disease from which the state was suffering. It was not till information was brought to Sparta of fresh preparations being made by the Persians, and of the approach of a large Phoenician fleet, that, by the advice and according to the plans of Lysander, Agesilaus undertook an expedition with 2000 Neodamodeis and 6000 allies. He was accompanied by Lysander himself and 30 Spartans. He wished to set out from Aulis, like Agamemnon; but the Boeotarchs showed so much hostility towards him, that he went to Geraestos, in Euboea, and after having ordered the army and fleet to assemble there, sailed across to Ephesus. Tissaphernes, not thinking himself strong enough to oppose the Spartans openly, induced the unsuspecting Agesilaus, who announced himself as the deliverer of the Greeks, to conclude a truce, under the pretext that he would in the meantime endeavour to obtain the king's sanction of the independence of the cities. The truth, however, was that he sent out messengers to collect an auxiliary force.

Meanwhile, Lysander and Agesilaus quarrelled. The former had perhaps hoped to domineer over the king whom he had assisted in raising to the throne. His acquaintance with the cities, ob-

* Leotychides, the son of Agis, was excluded from the succession, because his parentage was doubted. (Plut. *Alcib.* 23.)

tained in former campaigns, made him appear in the eyes of the multitude as the more influential of the two. Agesilaus, however, contrived with so much prudence and vigour to put things in their true light, that Lysander, feeling himself crushed, desired to be discharged, and was sent by the king to the Hellespont, where he soon found fresh opportunities of showing his skill. When at length Tissaphernes, trusting to his reinforcements, openly threatened Agesilaus with war unless he withdrew from Asia, the latter also began seriously to prepare for the contest, and drew reinforcements from the cities of Asia Minor. He announced to all that he contemplated an expedition into Caria, and thereby deceived the satrap; for he marched into Phrygia, and ravaged a portion of it. Yet this first undertaking was not followed by any great results, because he was deficient in cavalry; and the army returned to Ephesus, where the men were kept in constant exercise and fully armed. He then marched again into Phrygia, and even into the very neighbourhood of Sardis, while Tissaphernes, being again deceived, was protecting Caria with his infantry. On the river Pactolus a battle was fought with the Persian cavalry, in which Agesilaus gained a complete victory. This loss the Persians ascribed entirely to Tissaphernes, who remained at Sardis during the battle. In consequence of this, he fell into disgrace and was deposed, and his successor, Tithraustes, ordered him to be put to death. The new satrap immediately concluded a truce with the Spartan, and by a bribe of thirty talents induced him to continue the war against the neighbouring satrap, Pharnabazus. So strange and so perilous was the relation of the satraps to one another, and to their sovereign! While Agesilaus was on his march, he received news from Sparta, that he had been appointed admiral also, in order that he might be able to carry on his operations more vigorously with both the army and the fleet. The fleet, however, did not yet exist. At his command the Asiatic cities willingly fitted out an armament of 120 sail, and Agesilaus appointed the courageous but inexperienced Pisander, his wife's brother, admiral of the fleet, B.C. 395. He then advanced farther into the province of Pharnabazus: he was victorious everywhere, ravaged the greater part of the satrapy, and soon made himself master of the whole; so that he was enabled to spend the winter there, and to make preparations for penetrating, in the beginning of the following spring, B.C. 394, into the interior of the Persian empire.

His great plan, however, was not executed, for in the midst of his victorious career he was obliged to quit the scenes of his glory. At the commencement of spring, when he was on the point of setting out, he was called back to his distressed country. For while he had been gathering laurels in the satrapy of Pharnabazus, the circumstances of Greece underwent a change much to the disadvantage of Sparta.

Tithraustes, the new satrap, contrived by Persian gold to stir up a general war in Greece against Sparta; he hoped thus to stop the successful progress of the Spartan king, and to remove him from Asia as soon as possible. For this purpose he sent Timocrates (or Hermocrates), of Rhodes, with fifty talents to Greece. Thebes, Corinth, and Argos accepted the money, for they had good reasons to be indignant with Sparta; but the Athenians joined the league against her, unsolicited and unbribed. The Spartans had rendered themselves odious to all the Greek states; for during the Peloponnesian war they had proclaimed themselves the deliverers of Greece, and now acted as its tyrants by the agency of their harmosts.

As the Lacedaemonians at first took no notice of the new alliance, the contest, at the instigation of the Thebans, began between the Locrians and the Phocians. The Thebans supported the former, and the Phocians called upon Sparta for assistance. The Spartans granted the request the more readily because they were displeased with the Thebans, who were least inclined to acknowledge their supremacy. Lysander was sent out to assemble the tribes of Mount Oeta for the ensuing struggle, and succeeded in drawing the powerful Orchomenians over to the side of Sparta. King Pausanias, who was assembling the allies at Tegea, was to follow him. Lysander, however, did not wait for his arrival, but with the army he had just raised, made an attack upon Haliartos, B.C. 395, after having in vain tried to induce it to revolt from Thebes. The Thebans hastened to its assistance, and Lysander fell under the walls of the town. In him Sparta lost a man who in heroism equalled the best of her sons, but in intrigue and faithlessness surpassed even Alcibiades, to whom he was not inferior in his love of dominion. The period of Sparta's greatest power was his work, but the means he employed to strengthen that power were calculated only to bring about its speedy downfal.

The victorious Boeotians, being too eager in the pursuit, suffered a great loss, but still their enemies acknowledged themselves vanquished, and retreated. This was the first conflict in that unhappy war, which is commonly called the Boeotian or Corinthian, and the consequence of which was the ascendancy of Persia in Asia Minor. After these occurrences, king Pausanias arrived; but when he heard what had happened, thinking a fresh conflict would be perilous, he contented himself with demanding the surrender of the dead; nay, he even consented to evacuate Boeotia, if the slain were given up to him. This retreat, which the insolence of the Boeotians rendered still more disgraceful to the Spartans, brought a capital charge upon the king; but he withdrew from punishment, and died at Tegea in exile. He was succeeded by his son Agesipolis, who was yet under age.

After this victory, the enemies of Sparta displayed still greater zeal. The Corinthians, Argives, Boeotians, and Athenians held a congress at Corinth, in which the continuance of the war was discussed, and new allies were gained, the league being joined by the Euboeans, Leucadians, Acarnanians, Ambracians, and Chalcidians. Medius, tyrant of the Thessalian Larissa, with their assistance took Pharsalus from the Lacedaemonians. The Boeotians and Argives took Heracleia, and restored it to the Trachinians. Ismenias, the Theban, who distinguished himself above the others, induced some of the Oetaean tribes to revolt; in a bloody battle near the Locrian town of Naryx, he defeated the Phocians, who were commanded by a Spartan, and then retreated to Corinth, where an army of 15,000 men and 500 horse assembled, and was soon afterwards increased by the arrival of additional forces.

The king of Persia too had made an acquisition dangerous to Sparta, in the person of Conon, the celebrated Athenian admiral, who, by the advice of Pharnabazus, had been appointed by the king commander of the Persian fleet, as early as the time when Agesilaus went over to Asia; and he was now entrusted with unlimited power to equip a fleet against the Spartans.

Amid these unfavourable circumstances, Agesilaus received orders to return home. He had spent the winter at Dascylion, and had just evacuated the satrapy of Pharnabazus in accordance with an amicable agreement. He obeyed the orders with a heavy heart, and, followed by a splendidly equipped army, took the road which Xerxes had once occupied six months in traversing, and by quick marches reached Greece in thirty days. Before he arrived in Boeotia, the war had broken out afresh. Aristodemus, the guardian of Agesipolis, had undertaken the command of the army. The Corinthians and their allies were at Nemea, intending to commence hostilities as soon as possible, in order to prevent the Spartans from assembling a greater number of allies. Thus a battle ensued near Nemea, the two armies being of almost equal strength. The Lacedaemonians gained the victory, but their success was due to the 600 Spartans who were in the army. They fought with such good fortune, that only eight of them were slain. The first news of this battle, commonly called the battle of Corinth, reached Agesilaus while he was at Amphipolis; he immediately sent Dercyllidas, the bearer of it, to the Asiatic Greeks, to inform them of the victory, and continued his march.

The Thessalian towns harassed Agesilaus greatly as he marched past them, but he boldly and successfully forced his way, and on the fourteenth of August, B.C. 394, a day marked by an eclipse of the sun, he reached the borders of Boeotia. There he received intelligence of the defeat of the Spartan fleet and of the death of Pisander. The Graeco-Persian fleet, under Pharnabazus and Conon, had gained a victory off Cnidos, and this destruction of the Spartan navy produced consequences of incalculable advantage to Athens. Agesilaus concealed the sad news from his men, and in order to keep up their courage, told them that the Spartan fleet was victorious although Pisander had been killed. Some days later, a battle took place on the banks of the Cephissus, between Agesilaus and the confederates, who had been joined by the Locrians and Aenianians, and whose forces extended along the foot of Mount Helicon. In the plain of Coroneia, Greeks arrayed against Greeks fought with rage and hatred, animated by a real desire to destroy one another. Agesilaus was wounded several times; finally, he gained the victory, but could not make use of it to pursue the enemy. Immediately after the battle he visited Delphi, and there dedicated to the god the tenth part of his Asiatic booty, 100 talents. He then went to Sparta by sea, and his army was disbanded, the soldiers returning to their homes.

The war, which now ceased for a time, was continued for the most part in the territory of Corinth, the Lacedaemonians and their allies infesting Corinth from Sicyon. Many Corinthians, the best, as Xenophon says, desirous of putting an end to the war, sought to bring about a peace with Sparta. But the war-party at Corinth took fearful and unprecedented revenge upon them. A festival was chosen as the day for the massacre of the men of peace, and suppliants were murdered even at the altars of the gods whose protection they implored. But those who escaped, being anxious to bring this insupportable state of things to a speedy termination, negotiated with the Lacedaemonians, and opened to them the gates of the port-town of Lechaeon. On the following day the Argives hastened to the place, but were repelled after a murderous fight, and the Lacedaemonians remained in possession of the port. Praxitas, the conqueror, ordered part of the walls to be demolished, then led his army towards Megara, and having taken the towns of Sidos and Crommyon, in which garrisons were placed, he disbanded his army, as the time of the campaign had expired. This occurred in B.C. 393. The struggle in the Corinthian and neighbouring territories, however, did not cease. Both parties engaged mercenaries, and the Athenian general Iphicrates, by a change in the armour of the peltasts, enabled them to fight successfully, even against heavy-armed men. In the following summer

Agesilaus made another (his last) expedition against Corinth, which was protected by Iphicrates; but this time he was repelled with great slaughter, and was forced to quit the Corinthian territory. All the places that had been lost in the preceding year, with the exception of Lechaeon, were recovered through the skill of Iphicrates.

While Sparta was thus engaged in Peloponnesus, Athens was reaping the fruits of her naval victory off Cnidos. First of all, the Greek cities in Asia were delivered from their harmosts, and by the promise of independence were gained over to Pharnabazus and Conon. Pharnabazus then proceeded by land to Abydos, which Dercyllidas had kept faithful to the cause of Sparta; and Conon appeared with his fleet before Sestos. The attempt to take Abydos failed. Conon, however, assembled a fleet in the Hellespont, and in the spring of the following year, B.C. 393, he sailed with Pharnabazus to Melos, one of the Cyclades, and thence across to the coast of Laconia. After having landed in several places, ravaged the coasts, and made himself master of Cythera, he sailed to the Isthmus, while Pharnabazus exhorted the Greeks to persevere in the war against Sparta, and supplied them with money. He readily consented to Conon's plan of restoring the walls of Athens, and thus to inflict a wound which Sparta would feel most severely. For this purpose too he gave money. Conon now went to Athens, and the walls were restored with Persian gold. All heartily assisted in the rebuilding; even the crews of the fleets lent a helping hand. The influence of Athens in the towns and islands which had been so quickly recovered, and the no less rapid restoration of the walls — for at the beginning of the following year, B.C. 392, the work was completed — at once convinced Sparta, that her short-lived maritime supremacy was at an end, and that Athens was on the point of recovering her former position. The Spartans immediately directed their policy against Conon, endeavouring to get rid of him by intrigues, and with the aid of the natural enemy of Greece, whom selfish interests had long since ceased to regard in that light. The cunning Spartan Antalcidas went to Tiribazus with proposals of peace; Conon also was sent thither from Athens, and they were joined by other envoys from Thebes, Corinth, and Argos. The terms of the peace proposed by Antalcidas, and which were afterwards actually adopted, sacrificed the Asiatic towns to the king of Persia, but for the other towns and the islands independence was demanded. Tiribazus was, of course, pleased with this plan, but all the envoys except Antalcidas opposed it; for no one was willing to give up what he possessed; and thus the negotiations were, for the present, broken off. The Lacedaemonians, however, obtained from

Tiribazus money to build a fleet, it being hoped that this would make the Athenians more willing to yield; but Conon, who had spoken against the peace, and consequently against the king, was taken prisoner. He soon succeeded, indeed, in making his escape from captivity, but took no further part in the war, and died in Cyprus. While Tiribazus was laying the disgraceful proposals of Antalcidas before the king, Struthas, who filled his place in his absence, inclined towards the Athenians, and accordingly, the Lacedaemonians, under the command of Thimbron, continued the war against Struthas. The war, originally confined to Corinth, had become a general one, which was now carried on simultaneously in Greece and on the coasts of Asia Minor.

One year after the last-mentioned expedition against Corinth, Agesilaus, in conjunction with the Achaeans, whose possession of Calydon was in danger, set out against the Acarnanians, who were allied with the Athenians and Boeotians. By a successful campaign, and the threat of a fresh invasion, he induced the Acarnanians to conclude peace with the Achaeans, and form an alliance with Sparta, B.C. 390.

In the same year Agesipolis made a predatory incursion into the territory of Argos, and committed great havoc, but while he was besieging Argos he was induced to retreat by unfavourable signs in the victims offered up as sacrifices.

The events which followed the renewal of the maritime war were of much greater importance, and were connected in the first instance with a revolution in Rhodes. The popular party having gained the upper hand in that island, the Spartans endeavoured to deprive the Athenians of the advantages which they might derive from that change. The Spartan Teleutias had at length collected a fleet of twenty-seven sail, and having met Philocrates, who was hastening with ten ships from Athens to the assistance of Evagoras, captured or destroyed all the Athenian ships. "Both parties," says Xenophon, "were doing the very opposite of what they should have done; for the Athenians, the allies of the king of Persia, sent assistance to Evagoras of Cyprus, the king's enemy, and Teleutias, although Sparta was at war with the king, destroyed the ships which were going to fight against him." So completely had the political relations of Greece been perverted by jealousy and hatred, that Sparta would rather aid her natural enemy than allow Athens to gain an advantage.

Teleutias was successful in Rhodes, and the Athenians, dreading the growing maritime power of Sparta, sent out the aged hero Thrasybulus to check it. Leaving Teleutias unmolested in Rhodes, he sailed with forty ships to the Hellespont, reconciled Seuthes and Amadocus, two princes of the Odrysians, and concluded an alliance with them; he then made himself master of the towns on the coast, and restored to Byzantium its democratic form of government; he also re-established the impost of a tenth on vessels coming out of the Euxine. After this he expelled the Laconian garrisons from Lesbos, and levied contributions at Aspendos, intending thence to proceed to Rhodes. But the Aspendians fell upon his camp in the night, and killed him in his tent, B.C. 390.

Thrasybulus was succeeded by Agyrius, or Agyrrhius, the effeminate and reckless squanderer of the public treasures, who increased the pay for attending the popular assembly to three oboli. The Spartans now sent Anaxibius to the Hellespont, where he was successful, until the arrival of Iphicrates, by whom he was defeated at Abydos in B.C. 389.

In the following year the Spartans succeeded in establishing themselves in the island of Aegina, and attacked the fort still occupied by the Athenians so vigorously, that the latter withdrew their garrison from it. The Spartan commanders harassed the Attic territory from Aegina in various ways; they were sometimes beaten, as Gorgopas was by Chabrias, but sometimes they succeeded, as, for example, when Teleutias, the idol of the soldiers, boldly surprised Piraeus, and, loaded with booty, returned to Aegina before the very eyes of the astonished Athenians. While these events were going on, Antalcidas had again gone to Tiribazus, determined to conclude a treaty with the king, if the opponents of Sparta would not consent to his terms of peace. At the same time he was active as a commander near Abydos, and by reinforcements from the Ionian cities and Syracuse, increased the Spartan fleet to upwards of eighty ships, which gave him so much power at sea, that he prevented the ships coming from the Euxine from sailing to Athens. The Athenians, seeing that their enemy was thus gaining the ascendancy, now began to think of peace. The other states, too, the Corinthians as well as the Argives, were tired of the war, and all the belligerents were present by their envoys when Tiribazus proclaimed the peace in terms dictated by the king himself. This peace ran as follows: — "King Artaxerxes thinks it right that the Greek cities in Asia, and the islands of Clazomenae and Cyprus, should belong to himself; but that all the other Greek cities, both small and great, should be left independent, with the exception of Lemnos, Imbros, and Scyros, and that these should, as of old, belong to the Athenians. If any state refuse to accept this peace, I will make war against it." The Thebans and Argives were little pleased with these terms, for the former were unwilling to give up their supremacy over the Boeotian towns, and the Argives refused to withdraw their garrison from Corinth The Thebans wanted to swear to the treaty in the name of all the Boeotian towns, but when Agesilaus threatened them with war, they yielded. In like manner the Argives were compelled to retire from Corinth, and the exiles returned.

The peace of Antalcidas was concluded in B.C. 387. The Spartans, who had to carry it into effect, derived the greatest advantages from it; they gained the Corinthians as their allies, they humbled the Argives, and, what they had desired most, they destroyed the supremacy of Thebes in Boeotia. Sparta itself, on the other hand, retained its sovereignty over the Laconian towns and Messenia. This disgraceful peace, the work of Sparta, completely

Horologium of Andronicus at Athens.

destroyed the fruits of the noble efforts of the Greeks during the Persian war, and sacrificed the freedom of the Greek cities in Asia. At this time we find only isolated traces of that great national feeling which breathes in the works of Herodotus and Aeschylus, and which inspired the whole nation to fight for its independence. But this too was one of the consequences of high intellectual culture; for the comparatively narrow feeling of nationality becomes weakened as the mind of an individual or of a nation rises to more comprehensive views, and recognises the universality of the laws of human existence; and it would seem that martial bravery decreases in the same proportion.

Plan of Stadium at Cibyra in Asia Minor.

Grove, Altar, and Statue of Diana.
(From the Arch of Constantine at Rome.)

Female Centaur, playing the double flute.
(From a bronze bas-relief in the Museum at Naples.)

CHAPTER XXXI.

FROM THE PEACE OF ANTALCIDAS TO THE DEATH OF EPAMINONDAS.

The division of all Greece into a number of small independent states, which had been the object of the peace of Antalcidas, was never completely realised; for the Lacedaemonians themselves, who were appointed to see the terms of the treaty carried into effect, not only tacitly retained their supremacy in Peloponnesus, but manifested a desire to extend their dominion over the whole of Greece, and the more openly, the more the sad condition of the different states favoured the realisation of such selfish schemes. The only pleasing event of this period was the restoration of Plataeae in B. C. 386, forty years after its destruction by the Lacedaemonians. Those states the capitals of which had exercised the right of supremacy with any degree of harshness, such as Boeotia and Elis, were now most divided, in consequence of the general desire of independence on the part of the separate towns. The notorious weakness of such isolated towns naturally led to their speedy subjugation by their more powerful neighbours.

Sparta herself was least inclined to comply with the terms of the peace; she fostered disputes within the smaller towns and states, then took a part in them, and having subdued the weaker states, at length attempted to do the same with the more powerful ones. The Spartans first commanded the Mantineans to demolish their walls, in order that in future they might have the less to fear from them. They alleged as a pretext the understanding which existed between Mantinea and Argos, the imperfect manner in which the Mantineans had discharged their duties as allies, the expiration of the thirty years' truce, which had been concluded in B. C. 418, after the battle of Mantinea, and lastly, the hostile disposition manifested by Mantinea towards Sparta. The Mantineans having refused to comply with this demand, Agesipolis (for Agesilaus from a private feeling declined to conduct the operations) advanced with an army, and at length compelled the town to surrender by diverting the stream Ophis into it, and thus laying it under water. Those of its citizens who were favourably disposed towards Argos, as well as the leaders of the popular party, obtained a free departure, through the mediation of Pausanias, who was living at Tegea; but Mantinea lost its political existence; its inhabitants were distributed among the four villages out of which they had been collected into the capital; "and in the course of time," says Xenophon, "the aristocratical Mantineans were quite satisfied to live near their estates, and to have got rid of the troublesome popular leaders, so that they cheerfully contributed their contingents to the Spartan levies." In B. C. 384, Phlius was compelled in a no less cruel manner to recall the exiled oligarchs, who had applied to Sparta for assistance.

Thus Sparta established, by violent means, her supremacy in Peloponnesus, of which Argos alone kept independent. Athens allowed her to act as she pleased, and did not even send succour to the Mantineans, who implored it. But Sparta's love of dominion soon went beyond the limits of Peloponnesus; other states also were commanded to yield the same ready obedience as the Peloponnesians. The Spartans, well known and dreaded as arbitrators, soon interfered in disputes in the most distant parts of Greece. Envoys from Acanthos and Apollonia appeared at Sparta to solicit aid against Olynthos, which had become overbearing. It had united the Greek towns of Chalcidice into an alliance which was directed against Amyntas of Macedonia, and was endeavouring to compel the two above-mentioned towns to take part in the alliance and in the expedition against Macedonia. A report that the Athenians and Boeotians would likewise join the confederacy, was the principal cause that induced the Spartans to act with quick determination. The allies, to please Sparta, displayed great zeal, and Eudamidas, having set out at once with a force of 2000 men, occupied Potidaea, from which he prepared to make war upon Olynthos. This was the beginning of what is called the Olynthian war, which lasted about five years, from B. C. 383 till 379. The great army of the Peloponnesian allies having assembled, set out under the command of Phoebidas. On its march through Greece, it arrived at Thebes at a time when that city was agitated by factious feuds, in which the democratic party under Ismenias had gained a victory over the oligarchs, and had resolved to take no part in the war against Olynthos. Leontiades, the leader of the oligarchs, now proposed to betray Thebes into the hands of the Spartans, and Phoebidas accepted his offers. In broad daylight, while the women were celebrating the Thesmophoria in the Cadmea, and the council was assembled in the market-place, Leontiades conducted him to the Cadmea, and delivered to him the keys of the gates. He then hastened to the market-place, and having informed the council of what had happened, ordered his opponent Ismenias to be arrested. He afterwards hastened to Sparta, and excusing Phoebidas' violation of the peace of Antalcidas, induced the Spartans to sanction the occupation of the Cadmea. At the same time he caused Ismenias to be tried and condemned to death by a packed court of the allies, as an old friend of Persia, and as a seditious citizen. Thus fell Ismenias, whose generosity and great talents were much esteemed; but about three hundred of his followers escaped to Athens, and among them was Pelopidas, the future deliverer of Thebes. His intimate friend, the still more celebrated Epaminondas, was allowed to remain at Thebes, as, not being possessed of property, it was believed that he would not be dangerous.

The Spartans now displayed still greater zeal in the Olynthian war. Teleutias, the harmost and brother of Agesilaus, assembled a large army by acting with the prudence and humanity of a Brasidas. Derdas, Prince of Elymia, also joined him. In the spring of the following year, B. C. 382, the Lacedaemonians were not successful; they were first defeated in an engagement of the cavalry, and soon afterwards the brave Teleutias fell, his army again sustaining a severe reverse. Notwithstanding these misfortunes, however, the Spartans still maintained their ground. The year after, B.C. 381, Agesipolis, with a newly-formed army, and accompanied by thirty Spartans, marched against Olynthos, and the old allies, Amyntas, Derdas, and the Thessalian horse, took part in the campaign, so that the Olynthians, no longer venturing upon battle in the open field, confined themselves to little sallies and the defence of their walls. While matters were in this state, Agesipolis was attacked by a violent fever, the consequence of excessive heat. He caused himself to be carried to the shady grove of Dionysus near Aphytos in Pallene, and died there in B.C. 380. He was succeeded by Cleombrotus, but the conduct of the war was entrusted to the harmost Polybiades, who at length, when all provisions in the town were consumed, compelled the Olynthians to sue for peace. Their envoys concluded a treaty with the conqueror, and recognised the supremacy of Sparta in B.C. 379.

At the same time Agesilaus had humbled Phlius also. The exiles who had been restored a few years before through the mediation of Sparta, felt themselves aggrieved by their fellow-citizens, and again solicited her protection. Agesilaus, in spite of the disapproval of many, and especially of his brother-king Agesipolis, marched against Phlius, demanded as a security for its fidelity the surrender of the citadel, and forthwith began to lay siege to the town. His anger was increased by the fact, that when the Phliasians began to suffer from famine, they entered into direct communication with the government of Sparta. He contrived to obtain the grant of unlimited power, and when at length the town surrendered, he formed a court-martial of fifty exiles and fifty citizens, to bring the guilty individuals to trial. New laws were to be introduced, and until all should be completed, a garrison remained in possession of the citadel. The operations against this insignificant town had lasted one year and eight months, from B.C. 381 to 380.

After the termination of the Olynthian war, the Spartans exercised undisputed supremacy in Greece, and the year B.C. 379 marks the highest pinnacle of their power. The rebellious and reluctant allies had been compelled to yield obedience, Thebes and Boeotia were subject to their will, the Athenians remained quiet, the Corinthians and Argives had suffered too severely in the preceding war to venture to oppose her; in short, Sparta ruled throughout Greece, and her power seemed everywhere to be firmly established. But the year of her greatest prosperity was at the same time the beginning of her downfal.

The deliverance of Thebes came from Athens. In concert with a certain Phyllidas, Pelopidas *, Mellon, and some other Theban exiles, went from Phyle to Thebes. It was late in the autumn, and under cover of night, and in the disguise of huntsmen, the exiles succeeded in reaching the house of Charon, one of their most resolute partisans. Thence the conspirators proceeded to the mansion of Phyllidas, who enjoyed the confidence of the oligarchs, and was at that moment, according to a plan previously arranged with the exiles, entertaining Archias and Philippus, two of the polemarchs, at a banquet. Phyllidas introduced them in the disguise of hetaerae, and the polemarchs were murdered. Thence the conspirators hastened to the house of Leontiades, another of the polemarchs, who was likewise put to death. The prisoners were set at liberty, and the citizens of Thebes called upon to assert their freedom. As soon as the day dawned, all who were capable of bearing arms assembled, and the Athenians, 5000 foot and 500 horse, who had been waiting on the frontier, hurried to Thebes by quick marches, to assist Pelopidas and his party. The Spartan harmost, who was in the acropolis, first sent to Thespiae and Plataeae for assistance; but an armed band of Plataeans, which came at his summons, was defeated, and the garrison of the Cadmea was soon obliged to capitulate. It obtained leave to depart un-

* Xenoph. (*Hellen.* v. 4. § 2.), in his partiality, does not mention Pelopidas, but assigns the chief share in this transaction to Phyllidas.

molested, but those Thebans who had made themselves most odious to their countrymen, were put to death, and even their children were not spared.

When the news of these events reached Sparta, the harmost was condemned to death, and an army was sent against Thebes. This was the beginning of the Theban war, which lasted upwards of sixteen years, from B.C. 378 to 362, in which all Greece took part more or less, and which greatly contributed to increase its weakness against foreign enemies. Thebes, in the first instance, contended for the supremacy in Boeotia only; its attempt to obtain the same position in reference to all Greece, was the result of subsequent victories, and the work of Epaminondas. But Athens, in the mean time, recovered her supremacy at sea.

The war was commenced by Cleombrotus in the beginning of the year B.C. 378. Chabrias, the Athenian general, obliged him to take the road into Boeotia by Plataeae and Thespiae, and Cleombrotus so studiously abstained from doing any damage during the short time he remained in the Theban territory, that his men were at a loss to understand whether they had been at war or at peace with Thebes. But notwithstanding this, the Athenians, from fear of the Lacedaemonians, were on the point of giving up the alliance which they had concluded with Thebes. In order to prevent this, the Thebans bribed Sphodrias, whom Cleombrotus had appointed harmost of Thespiae, to invade Attica. He did not indeed get beyond the Thriasian plain, and the Athenians even had the satisfaction of seeing him condemned to death for his act of wanton aggression; but still this circumstance inclined them to remain faithful to their treaty with Thebes, and the more so, as Agesilaus obtained pardon for Sphodrias; accordingly, they now zealously prepared for war. They completed the fortifications of Piraeus, built ships, and formed a close alliance with the Boeotians. They went still further; concluded alliances with the most powerful maritime towns against Sparta, and thereby re-established their own supremacy at sea. They were joined first by Chios and Byzantium, whose example was followed by seventy other towns, among which were Rhodes and Mytilene. Euboea, with the exception of the northern part and Histiaea, likewise joined them. The seat of the council of this new confederacy was at Athens, every state had a separate vote, and Athens had the supreme command in war. The Thebans also were admitted, but Aegina remained faithful to the Lacedaemonians. The Athenians endeavoured to win confidence by wise moderation; two of their measures which had this object in view, were the restoration of the cleruchiae to their former owners, and the decree that no Athenian should acquire landed property out of Attica. Their navy, as in the period of their greatest prosperity, was again increased to 300 galleys.

In the meantime Agesilaus made two predatory expeditions against Thebes; in the first he advanced up to the very walls of the city; then, having appointed Phoebidas harmost of Thespiae, he returned to Sparta. His second inroad in the spring of B.C. 377, before which time Phoebidas fell in a battle against the Theban Gorgidas, was without any great result, the Thebans keeping for the most part behind their fortifications, and on one occasion, when a battle had been fought, each party claimed the victory.

In the following spring, as Agesilaus was ill, Cleombrotus led an army from Peloponnesus into Boeotia, but was unable to force his way through the passes of Cithaeron, which were occupied by the Athenians and Boeotians, and was obliged to return without having effected anything.

Although these invasions distressed Thebes so much that provisions began to be scarce, yet in other respects, it was benefited, and, under the exemplary management of Pelopidas, an excellently trained army was raised. The most illustrious among these warriors formed what was called the "sacred band" (ἱερὸς λόχος), which had been founded by Gorgidas, and consisted of noble-minded youths, united by patriotism and friendship. With this band are connected the greatness and glory of Thebes down to the battle of Chaeronea.

After so many useless campaigns, the Lacedaemonians began to feel the necessity of employing a fleet against the maritime power of Athens, and also for the purpose of transporting their army in case of need to Boeotia. But in this attempt, too, they were unsuccessful; their fleet of sixty sail was defeated off Naxos by the Athenians under Chabrias, and the latter were again the undisputed masters of the sea, B.C. 376. Soon afterwards the scenes of the Peloponnesian war were renewed, for at the request of the Boeotians, the Athenians sent the bold and fortunate Timotheus with a fleet of sixty ships to the coasts of Peloponnesus, one of their objects being to prevent the Spartans from venturing upon an expedition against Thebes. Timotheus gained over Corcyra, and induced Cephallenia, Acarnania, and several Epirot tribes, to join the Athenian confederacy. He defeated the Spartan fleet under Nicolochus near Alyzia, and even Xenophon owns that Timotheus far surpassed his enemies at sea.

While Athens was recovering her maritime power, the Thebans also gained their immediate object, and established their supremacy in Boeotia. When no longer harassed by the invasions of the Lacedaemonians, they proceeded without hesitation against the neighbouring states, and compelled them to recognise their sovereignty. They had made an attack upon Thespiae as early as B.C. 378, but until about B.C. 375, the Boeotian towns remained under the sway of Sparta; in that year, however, Sparta's influence was broken by a battle near Orchomenos, in which the valour of the sacred band of the 300 gained the victory for Thebes.

But the growing power of Thebes alarmed the Athenians, and made them inclined to conclude peace. The Persian king, in the hope of obtaining a Greek army for an expedition against Egypt, advised the Greeks to renew the peace of Antalcidas, the terms of which had in reality never been entirely carried into effect. The Thebans alone refused to become a party to this arrangement. Guided and supported by their great generals, Pelopidas, Epaminondas, and Gorgidas, they were irresistibly advancing towards supremacy in Boeotia. Plataeae which, as before, sympathised with Athens, and had formed a new alliance with her, was taken by surprise and changed into a heap of ruins, after having scarcely been completely rebuilt. Its exiled citizens again took refuge at Athens, and there obtained the franchise. Thespiae, which until then had sided with Sparta, had to suffer the same fate; and Orchomenos, the last refuge of the oligarchs, was given up as a prey to the flames, the men being put to the sword, and the women and children sold as slaves.

The peace between Sparta and Athens was not of long duration; but in the war which ensued, Athens acted independently, and thus Sparta, which would not have been able to resist the combined efforts of Thebes and Athens, succeeded in maintaining the contest on something like equal terms. The rest of Greece, however, did not by any means act the part of a mere spectator in the war between the three most powerful states. The ever-renewed contests between oligarchy and democracy had only received fresh fuel from the recent peace. It was especially in Peloponnesus and in the islands that the intestine struggles immediately recommenced. In most instances, the oligarchical party, being no longer supported by Sparta, had to submit, and the people, on recovering their ascendancy, exercised their power with all possible harshness and cruelty. But the renewal of the war between Athens and Sparta was occasioned by the former. Timotheus, on returning from his victorious expedition, restored the exiles of the popular party at Zacynthos. The favourers of oligarchy immediately solicited and obtained succours from Sparta, which at the same time supported its partisans in Corcyra. This war, called by Demosthenes ὁ ὕστερος πόλεμος, ended unfortunately for the Spartans. While their general Mnasippus was closely besieging Corcyra, and levying contributions in the island, the Athenians sent against him Stesicles, who with his peltasts succeeded in getting into the town. Timotheus was also ordered to equip a fleet of sixty ships; but as he seemed to be rather slow in carrying this command into effect, he was deposed, and Iphicrates received the commission. The latter had, in the meantime, B.C. 374, made an expedition with the satrap Pharnabazus against the rebellious Nectanebus in Egypt, and had commanded a force of 20,000 Greek mercenaries; but as the army of the satrap, amounting to 200,000 men, was very inefficient, and he himself was thwarted in his undertakings by the satrap's jealousy, he had secretly disbanded his army and returned to Athens. He now quickly assembled the fleet, and with Callistratus and Chabrias sailed to Corcyra. Meanwhile Mnasippus had been defeated and killed in a desperate sally of the Corcyraeans, and the Spartan fleet, from fear of that of the Athenians, had retreated to Leucas, B.C. 373. On his voyage to Corcyra Iphicrates, whose great talents as a general are acknowledged by Xenophon, subdued the island of Cephallenia, captured a fleet of ten ships, which had been sent by Dionysius, the tyrant of Syracuse, to assist the Spartans, and reinforced his own fleet with ninety Corcyraean galleys.

But before Iphicrates could continue this glorious campaign, and begin his operations against Peloponnesus itself, negotiations for peace were again commenced. On this occasion, too, the king of Persia proposed the terms of the peace of Antalcidas, and they were accepted by both Sparta and Athens; whereas Thebes was excluded, because it would not give up its claims to supremacy over Boeotia. Thus ended another act of this long war, which was accompanied, to the horror of the superstitious, by extraordinary phenomena in the heavens as well as on the earth. An earthquake and an inundation of the sea swallowed up two towns on the coast of Achaia, and in the following year a great comet made its appearance. But the widely-spreading custom of employing mercenaries, which began to supply even the place of the Spartan symmachy, was a still more extraordinary phenomenon. The allies now paid money in order to be exempt from serving in campaigns beyond the sea.

Thebes was to be punished immediately after the conclusion of the peace, and accordingly king Cleombrotus received orders from the ephors to leave his position in Phocis, and march into Boeotia. On the 15th of Hecatombaeon (the 8th of July), B.C. 371, the Thebans, who were now entirely without allies, accepted a battle against far more numerous forces, in the neighbourhood of Leuctra. They formed an army of 6000 men, commanded by the Boeotarch Epaminondas, the sacred band being headed by Pelopidas. Epaminondas endeavoured to bring his mass of infantry to bear upon the enemy's right wing, where Cleombrotus with the Spartans was posted. But when Cleombrotus also began to change his position, Pelopidas with his band broke into his lines, which were already thrown into disorder by the defeated cavalry, and amid a fearful carnage put them to flight. Cleombrotus fell in the battle, and with him 400 out of the 700 Spartans. The Lacedaemonians lost 4000 men altogether; the Thebans only 300. When this fearful catastrophe was announced at Sparta, the people happened to be celebrating the last day of the festival of the Gymnopaedia. The ephors did not allow the solemnity to be interrupted, and the news of the irreparable loss was received, as Xenophon says, with great composure.

This battle, one of the most remarkable and important in the history of Greek warfare, was the first great exploit of Epaminondas, whose merits are concealed by Xenophon, who does not mention even his name. But other authorities place his prudence and personal courage beyond all doubt. When the fight had continued for a long time without any decisive result, his encouraging word, "Only one step forward!" led his men on to victory. How vehement and hot the contest was, is clear from the statement that the Spartans, contrary to their ancient custom, ordered their flute-players to be silent during the fight. The Thebans were so proud of this victory, that they commemorated it by an annual festival at Lebadeia; and as Epaminondas had decided the issue of the battle with the left wing, the commander-in-chief henceforth always conducted that wing. Whether Archidamus, the son of the second Spartan king, took part in the battle of Leuctra is uncertain. Diodorus speaks of a meeting of the two kings before the battle; while Xenophon is silent on this point. At any rate, it would have been an irregularity to send both kings into the field. The question whether Jason, the tyrant of Pherae in Thessaly, was present, is likewise somewhat doubtful. According to Diodorus, he joined the Thebans before the battle; but Xenophon states, that he came immediately after it, at the request of the Thebans, and that through his interference the fresh army of Archidamus, which was approaching, returned, and a treaty was concluded.

At Athens, the intelligence of this victory was received very coldly. Xenophon says that the Athenians were greatly vexed at it, and would not listen to any proposal to lend their assistance against Sparta. But neither did they feel any sympathy with Sparta; and in order to show to the belligerents their independence, they thought it best to call upon the other states to comply with the terms of the peace of Antalcidas. This summons was obeyed, and the peace was again sworn to. The Eleans alone refused to give up their supremacy over the small towns in their neighbourhood.

In the battle of Leuctra Sparta had lost her military glory and her power. The supremacy in Peloponnesus which Sparta had possessed for 500 years, and which, in spite of the peace of Antalcidas, she had claimed and retained, was now gone. The Arcadians were the first people of Peloponnesus that began to stir. The Mantineans again united in one city; the Arcadians assisted them in building their walls, and even the Eleans aided them with a present of three talents. In B. C. 371 all the Arcadian districts united into one state, though this was not effected without violent party struggles, which were particularly bloody at Tegea. The building of a capital of the Arcadian union was resolved upon, and forthwith commenced. Ten thousand representatives of the members of the confederacy were to reside in the new city, which was called Megalopolis. Lycomedes, of Mantinea, was particularly active in calling this confederation into existence. The Spartans endeavoured to prevent its growth, and check its proceedings; but the expedition of king Agesilaus, in B. C. 370, produced no effect; the Arcadians remained quiet, looking forward to the powerful assistance of the Thebans.

Thebes had in the meantime strengthened herself by the acquisition of new allies; she had become mistress of Orchomenos, and been joined by Phocis, Aetolia, and Locris; and in B. C. 369 the Thebans, being now at the head of a confederacy embracing the Boeotians, Phocians, Euboeans, Locrians, Acarnanians, Heracleans, and Malians, invaded Peloponnesus under the command of Epaminondas and Pelopidas. Here they were joined by Arcadians, Argives, and Eleans. An army of 7000 men advanced against Sparta; which was allied only with the remaining cities of Peloponnesus, Corinth, Epidaurus, Troezen, Hermione, Haliae, Sicyon, and Pellene. The magnitude and urgency of the danger induced the Spartans to enlist the Helots in their army, under the promise that they should be freed if they deserved well of their country. But as this prospect induced more than 6000 to come forward, the Spartans themselves began to be afraid of them. From Sellasia, in Arcadia, where the armies had assembled, the Thebans penetrated into Laconia, and advanced to the immediate vicinity of Sparta, which had never seen an enemy so near. The attack upon the city, which was preceded by a very difficult passage of the rapid river Eurotas, made no impression. Epaminondas accordingly proceeded southward as far as the coast-towns Helos and Gythion, which he set on fire. Great numbers of perioeci and Helots deserted to him, and this circumstance was felt most painfully by Sparta. But the restoration of Messenia was the main blow aimed at the enemy Epaminondas invited the Messenians scattered over all parts of Greece to return to their country, and the new capital Messene, of which the ruins still exist, was built on the site of the ancient Ithome, which had so bravely stood out in the second and third Messenian wars. Epaminondas accomplished all this within the space of eighty days, and having left a garrison in Messenia, and arranged the affairs of Arcadia, he returned with the allied army to Boeotia, B. C. 369.

Sparta being cast down, especially by the revolt of her subjects, now applied to Athens for assistance. The Athenians, forgetting their eternal enmity against Sparta, their national antipathy, and the manner in which they had been treated at the end of the Peloponnesian war, generously sent Iphicrates into Peloponnesus. But before he went, a treaty was concluded between Athens and Sparta, which provided that the supreme command should belong to them alternately. In the following year, the almost impracticable clause was added that the command should alternate every five days. Iphicrates, however, was unable to cut off the return of Epaminondas' army from Peloponnesus. For this he is severely censured by Xenophon, on the ground that it would have been easy to stop the passage by the Isthmus.

In the following year, B. C. 368, Epaminondas undertook a second expedition against Sparta. The Arcadian union had already had opportunities of trying its strength. Lycomedes, the commander of the confederates, with 5000 chosen men, had laid waste the Laconian town of Pallene, before the Spartans could come to its assistance. In accordance with the treaty between Athens and Sparta, Athenians under Chabrias occupied the Isthmus conjointly with Peloponnesians. Epaminondas forced his way into the peninsula by a victory over the Athenians and Spartans, and then, being joined by the Arcadians, Argives, and Eleans, attacked Sicyon, Pellene, Epidauros, and Troezen, ravaging their territories. Sicyon, Phlius, and other towns, overpowered by the sudden attack, were forced to surrender. An attempt upon Corinth failed; the Corinthians gained a victory, and the allies of Sparta took fresh courage. About the same time there arrived to the assistance of the Spartans, from Dionysius of Syracuse, upwards of twenty triremes, and the fifty horsemen, who had come with them, greatly harassed the Thebans. Soon after this the belligerents withdrew from the Isthmus. Another circumstance improved the position of Sparta. The successful efforts of the Arcadians under the command of the bold Lycomedes, and their aiming at an independent position, or rather at the supremacy over Peloponnesus, alienated from them the Thebans as well as their Peloponnesian allies. Every one now desired to be independent. At Sicyon, Euphron established even a tyrannis. But notwithstanding all this, the proposals of peace which just then arrived from the court of Persia were not listened to, and the Thebans insisted upon maintaining their supremacy in Boeotia. The war continued, and the Thebans had now to combat a second enemy in the north, who was not less powerful than their southern foe.

A movement had commenced in the fertile plains of Thessaly, similar to that in the heart of Peloponnesus. Jason the tyrant of Pherae, powerful and experienced in war, had already subdued many Thessalian towns, and being Tagus (commander-in-chief of the Thessalian towns), he even aimed at the supremacy over the rest of Greece. In B.C. 374, he thought the time had come for carrying his ambitious schemes into effect, for Sparta was weakened, Athens desired only maritime supremacy, Thebes seemed to be unworthy of being at the head of Greece, and Argos was distracted by internal disputes. With these views he interfered in the contest between Thebes and Sparta, and seems to have taken part in the battle of Leuctra. But just after that battle, when the most favourable moment for the realisation of his plans seemed to have arrived, he was assassinated while reviewing his cavalry, B.C. 370, and his murderers were honoured as the deliverers of the Greeks. He was succeeded by Polydorus and Polyphron, both of whom were murdered in rapid succession. They were succeeded by the fratricide Alexander, who thus became both Tagus of Thessaly, and tyrant of Pherae, and distinguished himself by his cruelty and love of dominion. He, too, after ruling eleven years, was assassinated by his brother-in-law, at the instigation of his own wife. Alexander's undertakings were successful; he took the town of Larissa, and marching into Macedonia, concluded an alliance with king Alexander, who had succeeded Amyntas in B.C. 370, and whose brother Philip he received as a hostage. In the year B.C. 368, Pelopidas entered Thessaly a second time, but both he and his brave friend Ismenias were made prisoners by the tyrant of Pherae. In order to obtain his liberation, a powerful army was sent into Thessaly, which compelled Alexander to solicit the speedy assistance of Athens. Thirty ships were sent to his aid, and this time the Thebans effected nothing. But in a second campaign, conducted by Epaminondas, the Thebans succeeded in liberating Pelopidas. The design of overthrowing the tyrannis of Alexander was not, however, given up. Some years later, Pelopidas, being again implored by the towns struggling for their liberty, made his last expedition. He ended his heroic career in the bloody battle of Cynoscephalae;

but the Thebans gained the victory, and its fruits were not lost, for Alexander, after being defeated a second time, was obliged to recognise the independence of the Thessalian towns. Phthiotis and Magnesia allied themselves with the Boeotians, and the tyrant himself, being confined to Pherae, was compelled to enter into an alliance with Thebes, in B.C. 364. How much the Thebans appreciated Pelopidas, the worthy friend of Epaminondas, is clear from the fact, that they elected him every year for their commander, and that they regarded the victory of Cynoscephalae as a defeat, because it had been purchased by the death of their hero.

Meanwhile, the brilliant period of the Arcadian union had come to an untimely end. The Arcadians already felt strong enough to carry on the war without the aid of the Thebans. But Archidamus, supported by the troops of Dionysius of Syracuse, defeated them, B.C. 367, near Midea, in what is called "The Tearless Battle," because upwards of 10,000 Arcadians and Argives fell in it, while not a single Lacedaemonian is said to have been killed. This was the first successful event for Sparta since the battle of Leuctra, and Xenophon thinks that the allies of the Arcadians, the Thebans and Eleans, who had long looked with envy upon their growing power, rejoiced at their defeat. So completely was Greece distracted by party-spirit and selfishness! The same party-spirit also led the Greeks again to the throne of the Persian king, who was to act as mediator in bringing about a peace. Pelopidas contrived to win the king's favour for Thebes, and the clauses of the peace ratified by Pelopidas, the object of which was the independence of Messenia, and the destruction of the Athenian navy, or in other words, the establishment of the supremacy of Thebes, were laid before the other envoys to be accepted and sworn to. All of course refused, and the war was continued.

In the following year, B.C. 366, Epaminondas made his third expedition into Peloponnesus, where he gained over Achaia, and restored some towns to independence. But this new acquisition was soon lost, because the Thebans, without the knowledge of Epaminondas, sent harmosts into the Achaean towns. The Achaeans now allied themselves with the Lacedaemonians, and pressed upon Arcadia from the north.

Next year the Arcadians formed a new alliance with Athens, which had become estranged more and more from Thebes, one of the principal causes of offence being that the Thebans had refused to restore to the Athenians the town of Oropos, which had been committed to their keeping by the usurper Themison, the tyrant of Eretria in Euboea. At the suggestion of Lycomedes, the Arcadians now concluded an alliance against Thebes with the Athenians, who otherwise stood isolated. This changed the position of the minor states; Phlius, which had hitherto remained faithful to its alliance with Sparta, and had also received active assistance from the Athenians under Chares, now felt itself constrained to conclude peace with Thebes. The Corinthians did the same, and Sparta herself advised them to keep aloof from the war, which she had still to carry on. The Argives also felt inclined to put an end to the war.

These peaceful prospects, however, were soon overcast by a war which broke out between Arcadia and Elis. The quarrel began in B.C. 365 about Lasion, a strong town of Triphylia, which had originally belonged to Elis, but was now tributary to Arcadia. The Arcadians victoriously penetrated into Elis, which they traversed and plundered, leaving garrisons in all places, except the capital, which was protected by the Achaeans. The Lacedaemonians immediately allied themselves with the Eleans, and in the following year, when the Arcadians renewed their predatory incursions, and had already defeated their weak opponents between Elis and Cyllene, Archidamus appeared with an auxiliary force. But in the neighbourhood of Cromnos he was defeated by the superior numbers of the Arcadians, and he himself was wounded. The inhabitants of Pisatis availed themselves of the presence of the victorious Arcadians for the purpose of recovering the superintendence of the Olympian games which had lawfully belonged to them from early times.

In B.C. 364, the Arcadians occupied Olympia and allowed the games to commence. The Eleans, disregarding the religious peace which was always observed during the festival, made a vigorous attack and put the Arcadians and Argives to flight, but still were in the end obliged to succumb. In consequence of this, they effaced the festival of that year from the list of the Olympiads.

Soon afterwards, Olympia and the treasures of its temple became the cause of dispute and hostility among the Arcadian towns. The party favourable to Sparta, with Mantinea at its head, opposed the employment of the treasures taken from the temple in paying the army of the allies; and in the end, all who were interested in the future prosperity of Peloponnesus, saw that it was the evident desire of the Thebans to make the peninsula as weak as possible in order to gain the mastery over it the more easily. The partisans of Thebes, on the other hand, headed by Tegea, were unwilling, like the Mantineans, to give up the treasures, and called in the aid of the Thebans. Still the parties apparently came to an understanding, and most of the Arcadians made a peace, which was sworn to by those Thebans also who were present. But during the celebration at Tegea of the solemnities attending the conclusion of the peace, the Theban harmost suddenly ordered the envoys and the most distinguished persons to be arrested. Most of the Mantineans, at whom this blow was principally aimed, made their escape. The Mantineans now called all their countrymen to arms, demanding reparation and the liberation of the prisoners. But Epaminondas, who approved of the harmost's conduct, was already approaching.

Epaminondas, steadily pursuing the object of his life, the establishment of the supremacy of Thebes, had, throughout these struggles in Peloponnesus, endeavoured to make Thebes a maritime power. By his advice the Thebans resolved to build 100 galleys, and he himself took the maritime towns and the islands of Rhodes, Chios, and Byzantium from the Athenian commander Laches. His premature death, however, prevented the further development of the naval power of Thebes.

When fully prepared for war, he entered Peloponnesus for the fourth and last time; but fear had induced many to abandon the cause of Thebes. The only Greeks that accompanied him were the Euboeans and Thessalians; the Phocians refused to do so. In Peloponnesus he was joined by the Argives and Messenians, as well as by the Tegeatans, Megalopolitans, Pallantians, and the inhabitants of a few other less important Arcadian towns. The Lacedaemonians were supported by the other Arcadians, the Athenians, Achaeans, and Eleans. Epaminondas chose Tegea as the head-quarters of his operations; the army of his allied enemies being encamped at Mantinea. An attempt to take Sparta by surprise failed by a mere accident. For king Agesilaus had already reached Pellen, on his march to Mantinea with his whole army, when he was informed by a Cretan that Epaminondas was approaching Sparta. He immediately returned, and repelled the attack of the Thebans.

After this, Epaminondas sent his cavalry on a predatory excursion to Mantinea, but it was put to flight by the cavalry of the Athenians, which had just arrived. After these failures, he resolved to venture upon a decisive battle, for the time of his command had nearly expired, and he could not quit Peloponnesus without a victory. The men learned his determination with joy; all prepared and adorned themselves, burnishing their armour as for a festival. The army halted at the foot of the hills near Mantinea. It was just about harvest time (the 8th of July, B. C. 362). The enemy was not prepared to meet him, for they imagined that he intended merely to encamp there. On being suddenly attacked, they hurried to their arms and horses, while Epaminondas, at the head of his best troops, made so vehement an onset, that all resistance was overpowered, and a general flight ensued. But the hero of the day fell, and the conquerors were so terrified by this disaster as to be unable to follow up their victory; some troops were cut to pieces by the Athenian cavalry. A spear had pierced the breast of Epaminondas, and the shaft was broken off. It is said that he would not allow the fragment of the weapon to be extracted from the wound until he was assured that the Thebans had gained the victory; on being informed of which, he almost immediately expired. After the battle each party claimed the victory. Fifty thousand Greeks had fought against one another! So great a battle had never before been fought, nor had so many renowned generals ever met on the same field of battle. And what was the result? Xenophon says, that everything remained as it had been before; while Diodorus asserts, that through this battle the Spartans lost their supremacy. The truth is, that the death of her great general caused Thebes to sink from the height on which she had stood; but at the same time Sparta's power was broken. Both parties, weakened by their mutual efforts, remained inactive for a short while; but this did not pave the way for peace and tranquillity, but rather led to confusion and fresh struggles, which, in fact, became more alarming after the battle than they had been before.

This is the last event related by Xenophon in his Greek History, the only contemporary authority that has come down to us. His undisguised partiality for Sparta and Agesilaus, and his equally open aversion to Epaminondas and Pelopidas, cannot but make his readers mistrustful, especially as Diodorus, who followed other authorities, and Plutarch, speak with enthusiasm of the Theban heroes. Nay, the ancients believed that Epaminondas fell by the hand of Gryllus, the son of Xenophon, who fought among the Lacedaemonians at Mantinea. The orator Aeschines also fought on that day in the Athenian cavalry.

In the following year, B.C. 361, a general peace was concluded, by which independence was secured to the Messenians. Sparta alone refused to join in it, that she might not be obliged to recognise the independence of a state over which she had for centuries exercised absolute power. Thus Sparta alone, of all the Greek states, cherished her implacable hatred, and remained in the attitude of war.

This year also was the last of the great Spartan hero, Agesilaus, the worthy opponent of Epaminondas. At the age of eighty he went out with an army of 10,000 mercenaries, to support the rebels Tachus and Nectanebus in Egypt, and at the same time to weaken Persia. Chabrias, the Athenian admiral, commanded the fleet of Tachus. On his return home in the winter, with a treasure of 230 talents, Agesilaus landed at a port on the Libyan coast, and there died, after a reign of thirty-eight years. He had raised the power of his country to the highest point, and had at the same time seen its deepest humiliation. He was succeeded by his valiant son, Archidamus III.

Greek Warrior.

View of Chaeronea.

CHAPTER XXXII.

FROM THE DEATH OF EPAMINONDAS TO THE BATTLE OF CHAERONEIA.

Justin appears to express a well-founded opinion, when he says that "with the death of Epaminondas the virtue of the Athenians also perished. For after the loss of him in whom for a time they had had a rival, the Athenians sank into idleness and a state of insensibility; and began to spend their revenue, not as formerly, upon their fleets and armies, but upon the celebration of festivals and public games. Having the most distinguished actors and poets, they visited the theatre more frequently than the camp, and prized verse makers higher than generals. The public revenues with which formerly soldiers and rowers had been paid, now began to be distributed among the population of the city."* What is here said of Athens is more or less applicable to the minor states also, nay to the whole of Greece. It cannot be asserted that the valour of the Greeks was lost, or that their love of war had decreased; it was only the mode of warfare that had undergone a change. While the Athenians at home led a luxurious life, and frequented the theatres and law-courts, bands of mercenaries were engaged in fighting for the honour of Athens, and for the preservation of its power. Mercenaries, it is true, had been employed even in the Peloponnesian war, partly as rowers in the galleys, partly both as hoplites and as light-armed men, in the land armies; but it was not till about the time of the death of

* Justin, vi. 9.

Epaminondas, that it became a regular custom to hire men, who, as Isocrates observes, would readily have marched against Athens, if any one had offered them higher pay. And this custom became prevalent at a period when the revenue of the republic was reduced, and the treasury exhausted by a variety of other circumstances. It moreover often happened, that when the people had voted money for fresh troops, the commanders cheated either the soldiers or the state, by receiving payment for forces which were not raised, and afterwards bribing the public examiners of their accounts and reports. Ten or twenty thousand mercenaries were often believed to have been enlisted, while they existed only on paper, though the people had to pay for them. Of all the higher officers appointed to command the armies, one only used to set out; the others remaining at home, and amusing themselves with sacrifices and games. Under such circumstances, it is not surprising to find that capital charges of embezzlement, treachery, and bribery, were of frequent occurrence. In addition to all this, the old custom of engaging an army for only one campaign, then disbanding it, was still observed. Even Demosthenes proposed to his countrymen to keep a standing army, the fourth part of which should consist of Athenian citizens, in order that greater reliance might be placed in it.

But notwithstanding all these symptoms of internal decay, our authorities mention efforts and displays of power, such as occur only during the most flourishing period of Athenian history. Demosthenes calculates, that as late as B.C. 355, Athens had at her disposal 300 triremes, 1000 horsemen, and hoplites to any amount. The orator Lycurgus induced his countrymen even to equip 400 galleys, and that at a time when Athens was assisting Byzantium with a fleet of 120 sail; and shortly before the battle of Chaeroneia, 200 galleys were ordered to be fitted out.

All these proofs, however, of the extraordinary vitality of Athens cannot conceal the fact, that there, as well as in the other Grecian states, the active consciousness of national honour, and of the intellectual superiority of Greece, gradually died away. How different was the state of things when a Macedonian king coveted the honour of being called a Greek! At that time Greek nationality was still definable and clearly contrasted with everything foreign. Philip of Macedonia not only became a Greek himself, but it was one of the objects of his life to give to his Macedonians a Greek culture, which newly-acquired civilisation his great son Alexander carried to the far distant east and south. But the old external political power of Greece was lost amid this diffusion of Hellenism; and it almost seems as if the mother country had exhausted herself in the effort to elevate other less civilised nations.

The absence of a feeling of national honour displays itself most conspicuously in the relation that sprang up between Athens and Philip of Macedonia. We do not mean to say that because Cleon or Hyperbolus did not actually sell their country, they were any better as guides of the people; but the fundamental ideas of the position and importance of Athens had become so completely altered, that the demagogues here mentioned can scarcely be compared to such men as Eubulus and Demades. The latter and the other contemporary leaders were fully conscious that they were working the ruin of Athens; they betrayed their country to Philip, after having previously well weighed and calculated the consequences of their measures. The people looked on with indifference, delighting only in festivals, spectacles, and largesses, which the impudent Demades used to call the cement of democracy. The money, however, was furnished by Philip; who well knew what use to make of that powerful demagogue, and how to increase his influence in all directions. The Pythia at Delphi was as venal, and as suspected of favouring Philip, as the demagogues of Athens and the leaders of parties in other states.

When, at times, the people's eyes were opened, and in the face of the most threatening danger, they willingly buckled on their armour, and risked their lives and all that they possessed, for the defence of their country's liberty, we again see the imperishable power of true intellectual culture, which, though it suffered the people to become effeminate in preferring festive solemnity and pomp to the hardships of the camp, yet roused them to manly energy when the hour of need arrived.

We have first to give an account of three wars,—the Social War, and the two so-called Sacred Wars. In the first, Athens lost her allies, the best support she had; and by the two last Philip succeeded in securing his influence in the affairs of Greece. The towns on the Thracian coast were the cause of the first conflict between Philip and the Athenians. The latter had taken many steps to maintain or increase their maritime power; but the good fortune of earlier times seemed to be gone. A fleet which was sent, under Leosthenes, to assist the island of Peparethos, was defeated by Alexander, the tyrant of Pherae; and even Timotheus was no longer successful, for he was unable to save Amphipolis, the ancient colony of Athens, from falling into the hands of the Olynthians. It was there that Philip commenced his operations against Greece. The power of Athens on the coast of Thrace had been increased by the acquisition of the Thracian Chersonesus, which Cersobleptes, a prince of the Odrysians, had given to the Athenians, to reward them for the assistance they had afforded him in a contest with two other pretenders. According to Diodorus, the Athenians did not take possession of that peninsula until B.C. 353. At the same time, Perdiccas of Macedonia, fell in a war against the Illyrians, in consequence of which event Philip, the son of Amyntas, who was living as a hostage at Thebes, escaped to Macedonia to establish his claims to the throne. The kingdom was in a most dangerous condition; it was threatened by the victorious Illyrians, who had destroyed a great part of the Macedonian army, and also by the Paeonians. In addition to this, Philip was opposed by two pretenders, Pausanias and Argaeus; the former being supported by the Thracians, the latter by the Athenians. Pausanias was induced by presents to withdraw his claim; and Argaeus with his allies was defeated near Methone. Immediately after this, Philip, whose most anxious desire was to prevent the Athenians from gaining possession of Amphipolis, sent envoys to Athens: a peace and an alliance were concluded, and the independence of Amphipolis was guaranteed, or rather the town was left in the hands of the Olynthians, B.C. 359. With the Paeonians, too, peace was made by means of bribery and persuasion; but soon afterwards, on the death of their king, Philip violated the peace and subdued the country. He was equally successful against the Illyrians, his western neighbours, and in B.C. 358 he conquered all the country as far as Lake Lychnitis.

After these brilliant successes, Philip, disregarding the peace which he had just concluded, directed his arms against Amphipolis, and after a short siege made himself master of the town, which may be regarded as the key to the Thracian coast. With a view to indemnify the powerful Olynthians, with whom for the present he wished to remain on good terms, he assigned to them Potidaea and Anthemos, which had been taken from the Athenians. Pydna, which until then had likewise belonged to Athens, he retained for himself. Notwithstanding all this, he treated the Athenians very politely, and sent their garrisons home in the most friendly manner. He then marched against the town of Crenidae, at the foot of Mount Pangaeos, the gold mines of which had been neglected by the Thracians, whose king was obliged to cede that district to him. The insignificant town of Crenidae afterwards became the populous city of Philippi, and the mines were worked so vigorously, that they yielded a yearly produce of 1000 talents. With the gold thus obtained, Philip paid not only his armies, but also the traitors in various parts of Greece; with it he opened the gates of towns, broke the power of rival kings, and undermined the freedom of Greece.

How did Athens act towards this cunning prince, who left no means untried to accomplish his ambitious objects? Demosthenes in his speeches describes with pain and bitterness the want of decision and the fickleness of the Athenians, who, unconcerned about the future, thought only of their present enjoyments; and is not less severe on the deplorable influence of bribed popular orators. His glowing orations on behalf of Athens and Greece, and his vigorous efforts to rouse the people from their lethargic indolence were unavailing, his influence being paralysed by Aeschines. To the struggle between these two men we are indebted for the most splendid monuments of Attic eloquence, which make the downfal of such a people all the more tragic.

But Athens could not effectually oppose the victorious commencement of the career of Philip, for it was already involved in an unfortunate war. Scarcely had Timotheus prevented the revolt of Euboea to Thebes, by a quick and skilfully managed expedition, and concluded an alliance with the Euboeans, when the powerful island of Chios, supported by Byzantium, Rhodes, Cos, and Mausolus of Caria, revolted from Athens. The war which hence arose, is commonly called the Social War, and lasted three years, from B. C. 357 to 355. A fleet and an army, under Chares and Chabrias, were first sent against Chios, and while the former with his army besieged the town, Chabrias fought a naval battle, in which he was unsuccessful, and lost his life, as he refused to save it by retreating or abandoning his vessel. The war, however, continued without any decisive result, though both parties made great efforts. The allies had collected a fleet of 100 galleys, with which they ravaged and plundered Imbros, Lemnos, and Samos. The Athenians, on the other hand, increased the fleet of Chares to 120 sail, and appointed Iphicrates and Timotheus his colleagues in the command. As the Athenian fleet sailed to Byzantium, the siege of Samos was given up, and the two fleets met in the Hellespont. Chares wished to offer battle, although a violent storm had begun to rage; but as the more cautious Iphicrates and Timotheus refused to do so, nothing was done. In consequence of this Chares charged his colleagues with treachery, and they were deposed and fined; Timotheus ended his life in exile at Chalcis, but Iphicrates was afterwards declared innocent. Athens thus deprived herself of her best generals. Chares, the most incapable of all, being now sole commander, formed connections with the satrap Artabazus, who had revolted against his master. But when Artaxerxes III. threatened to support the allies with a fleet of 300 ships, Chares received orders to suspend hostilities, and a peace was concluded, by which Athens lost her most powerful allies, and with them the greatest part of her revenue. The tribute of the remaining allies henceforth amounted to only forty-five talents. But the revolted allies did not long enjoy their independence, for they soon became the subjects of the Carian prince. Imbros,

Lemnos, and Scyros, remained in their ancient relation to Athens. Although the islanders had suffered very severely in this war, yet Chares extorted from them sixty talents. Demosthenes soon afterwards devised wiser measures to increase the revenue of his country.

In the meantime Philip had interfered in the internal affairs of Thessaly. Lycophron of Pherae, the murderer of the tyrant Alexander, had succeeded him, and become involved in a dispute with the powerful family of the Aleuadae at Larissa. They called in the aid of Philip, for whom nothing could have happened more opportunely. He acted with such energy as to procure freedom and independence for all the Thessalian towns. They were obliged, indeed, to pay him tribute for this service, but still for a long time they sided with him. He allowed the tyrannis at Pherae to continue, and was thus the protector of freedom and of tyranny, as it suited his interest. His connection with Pherae opened to him the road to the south, as Pherae supported the Phocians in the struggle in which they were soon afterwards engaged, and which was a continuation of the Theban war. It is commonly called the Sacred War, and was carried on with unparalleled exasperation for ten years, from B. C. 355 to 346, and nearly all the states of Greece took a part in it.

The first occasion to it was given by the Thebans, who attacked at the same time the neighbouring Phocians and the Lacedaemonians; the former from a love of conquest, the latter from hatred and disappointment, because they had not been able to obtain the supremacy over all Greece. The council of the Amphictions, which had so long been dormant, was found a convenient instrument for conferring upon the demands of the Thebans at least the appearance of justice. Even at an earlier period they had caused Sparta to be fined by that court for the manner in which Phoebidas had taken possession of the Cadmea, and as Sparta disobeyed the verdict, the fine was increased from year to year until it amounted to an enormous sum. The Thebans now made a similar use of that court against the Phocians, who had exasperated them by refusing to accompany Epaminondas on his last expedition; besides which, the Thebans hoped to indemnify themselves by the conquest of Phocis for the loss of Peloponnesus, and imagined that they would have easy work with that small country. The Phocians accordingly were charged with having robbed the temple of Delphi, because they had taken into cultivation a tract of land between the Cephissus and Mount Thurion, which had until then been a barren district. They were condemned and required to pay an enormous fine, as well as to destroy the work of their own industry.

The Phocians had long discovered the plans of the Boeotians for the subjugation of their country, with the assistance of the Thessalians, and for the renewal of the war against Sparta. Foreseeing the fate which awaited them, the Phocians, as early as B. C. 357, had taken possession of Delphi; for they were aware that Thebes felt a strong inclination to seize the treasures of the temple. When the Amphictions had pronounced their verdict, and the Thebans, Thessalians, Locrians, and the tribes about Mount Oeta, as members of the Amphictionic league, began to execute the sentence, the Phocians took up arms, and soon gained Athens and Sparta as their allies, B. C. 354. It is not impossible that from the very beginning they were secretly supported by king Archidamus, who was bribed by the Phocian Philomelus. The latter, a bold and eloquent man, was the soul of the contest. He had at first endeavoured, but in vain, to bring about a peaceful settlement of the dispute, and excused the seizure of the treasures of the temple, by referring the Thebans to the very ancient right of the Phocians to watch over the temple. The Locrians and Thebans conjointly began the war for Apollo. In the first conflict, near Delphi, the Locrians were defeated, and Philomelus, who now could not retrace his steps, ordered the bronze tables containing the condemnations of the Phocians and Spartans to be destroyed, and loudly proclaimed that he only wished to protect the integrity of Phocis against the unjust verdict of the Amphictions, but did not intend to rob the god of any part of his property. However, as he was but feebly supported by his allies, he soon found himself obliged to make use of the sacred treasures for raising and maintaining an army of 10,000 mercenaries, and in addition, to levy a war contribution upon the wealthy Delphians. As a justification of his doings, he ordered the Pythia to declare that the conqueror of Delphi might do anything he pleased.

The war was carried on with unexampled cruelty, for even the surrender of the dead was refused, contrary to the universal practice of the Greeks; and as all Phocian captives were put to death, as being guilty of sacrilege, Philomelus naturally retaliated. During the long continuance of the war, the treasures of the temple gradually disappeared, the Phocians having coined the enormous sum of 10,000 talents to defray the expenses of the contest.

After Philomelus had been successful for a time, and had severely chastised the Locrians, he was defeated in a bloody battle near Neon, by the overwhelming numbers of his enemies. As the mountainous country rendered a retreat impossible, Philomelus, who was severely wounded, threw himself down a rock, in order to escape from his pursuers and from an ignominious death. His brother Onomarchus now undertook the command, for the Phocians were determined to fight to the last. He was as courageous and skilful as his brother, but in order to gain the object of the war, he spared nothing and squandered the treasures of the temple, not only in paying his mercenaries, but also in distributing bribes at Thebes and in Thessaly. He also acted violently and cruelly towards those Phocians who were inclined to make peace. He subdued Thronion in Locris, reduced the Amphissians to a state of dependence, and then entered Boeotia, where he conquered Orchomenos; but, being afterwards defeated by the Boeotians, he was obliged to retreat into Phocis. He soon marched out again, however, and this time his operations were directed against Philip in Thessaly.

While this war was going on, Philip had continued his conquests. He had subdued Pagasae, and destroyed Methone. During the siege of the latter place he had lost one eye. The Thessalian towns then called upon him for assistance against Lycophron of Pherae, who had been gained over by the bribes of Onomarchus; which circumstance had induced the other Thessalians also to remain quiet for a time. Phayllus, the brother of Onomarchus, came with a force of 7000 men to the support of Lycophron, but was defeated by Philip. Soon afterwards Onomarchus followed with his whole army, and routed Philip and the Thessalians in two battles. Philip returned to Macedonia, intending soon to come back to the scene of the war with fresh forces. Onomarchus, in the meantime, was victorious in Boeotia and took Coroneia. When Philip reappeared in Thessaly, and Lycophron again requested succours, Onomarchus for the second time hastened northward with an army of 25,000 men. Philip had called all the Thessalians to arms, and had assembled a force of 23,000 men, among whom there were 3000 horsemen. A bloody battle was fought near Magnesia: the Macedonians, who, as the champions of Apollo, were adorned with laurel wreaths, gained the victory through their Thessalian cavalry. Six thousand Phocian mercenaries were slain, and Onomarchus, who, along with others, had endeavoured to swim to the Athenian fleet stationed near Thermopylae, under the command of Chares, was among the dead. Three thousand Phocian prisoners were put to death. Philip immediately directed his attention to the best mode of turning this victory to his own advantage, but he succeeded only partially. Lycophron gave up Pherae to him, on condition of obtaining a free departure; and with 2000 mercenaries he joined the army of Phayllus, who succeeded his brother Onomarchus as commander-in-chief of the Phocians. Philip was unable this time to penetrate any farther into Greece; he attempted indeed to force his way through the pass of Thermopylae, but the Athenian fleet prevented him, and he returned to Macedonia in rather an ill humour. He had, however, gained much by his victory, especially the right to take part in the war against the enemies of the god, and consequently to interfere in the internal affairs of Greece, whose period of decline had now commenced. In this year, B. C. 352, Demosthenes delivered his first Philippic, in which for the first time he directed the attention of the Athenians to the designs of their most dangerous enemy.

Phayllus continued the war with renewed vigour. He had been joined by 1000 Lacedaemonians, 2000 Achaeans, and 5000 Athenians, and the Delphic treasures were not yet exhausted. He penetrated into Boeotia, but was thrice defeated, at Orchomenos, on the Cephissus, and near Coroneia; and after he had gained some advantages over the Epicnemidian Locrians, the Boeotians defeated him a fourth time near Abae; soon after which an illness terminated his life, B. C. 351. He was succeeded by Phalaecus, who at first was likewise unsuccessful. The war raged for many years longer, and Boeotia suffered so much from the invasions and ravages of the Phocians, that the Thebans were obliged to look about for new allies and fresh resources. They received 300 talents from the Persian king, and thereby estranged Philip from their cause. In the end, the Phocians gained the upper hand; the Boeotians were defeated at Coroneia, and many Boeotian towns, such as Orchomenos and Coroneia, fell into the hands of the enemy, B. C. 346. Philip's aid was now again called in, and he was not slow in giving it.

He had in the meantime greatly increased his power. Euboea was now the scene of his operations against Athens; there he established tyrants in all the towns; but two of them Plutarchus of Eretria, and Callias of Chalcis, having rebelled against him and joined Athens, the incorruptible Phocion was sent over by the Athenians to support them against Philip. But on the eve of the battle which was to decide the issue, he was faithlessly abandoned by them, and saved his army only with great difficulty. Philip maintained his power over Euboea, nay, he even encroached upon Attic ground, and having landed at Marathon in B. C. 350, carried off the sacred galley. It was Olynthos, however, that occasioned the open outbreak of the war between him and Athens.

Olynthos, alarmed at the progress of Philip, had concluded an alliance with Athens as early as B. C. 353, and the other Chalcidian towns had likewise joined it against their common enemy. After his return from Thermopylae, Philip for a time remained quiet, and was apparently inactive at Pella. But when the Athenians, thus lulled into security, again began to give themselves up to their usual occupations, he suddenly set out with a great army against Olynthos. The terrified Olynthians sent three successive embassies to Athens, and the three Olynthian orations of Demosthenes induced the Athenians, who began to see through the king's designs, to send to Olynthos three auxiliary armies under the command of Chares, Charidemus, and again under Chares. The last contained 2000 Athenian citizens. Nay, Athens now endeavoured to form a league of all the states of Greece against Macedonia. Neither the voluptuous Chares, nor Charidemus, however, was able to check the king's progress. He first restored his authority in Thessaly, which had manifested a spirit of revolt, and then conquered, one after another, the Chalcidian towns of Mecyberne, and Torone; Olynthos also was soon afterwards delivered up to him by the traitors Euthycrates and Lasthenes, and, together with upwards of thirty other Thracian and Chalcidian towns, was razed to the ground, B.C. 347. Philip now advanced irresistibly as far as the Thracian Chersonesus, of which the Athenians had lately taken possession. Even while negotiations for a peace were being carried on, he continued his conquests. It was in vain that Athens called upon the other Greek states to make common cause against the enemy; so great was the power of gold, says Diodorus, that no one moved; it was in vain that Demosthenes cautioned his fellow-citizens against Philip, and tried to inflame their courage; he himself was in the end deceived, for the king kept assuring the Athenians of his friendly disposition towards them.

Accordingly, when Philip was invited by the Thebans to bring the war to a close, the Athenians also availed themselves of the opportunity to conclude peace with him, for they were tired of the war, which had exhausted their patience and resources; the siege of Olynthos had cost them no less than 1500 talents, their commerce in the Euxine was completely destroyed, and many Athenians were pining in Macedonian captivity. While Philip's envoys were negotiating a peaceful settlement of affairs, the Athenians, by the advice of Demosthenes and Philocrates (from whom the peace was named), sent ten ambassadors to Macedonia, in B.C. 346. Among them were the two men who had recommended the embassy, and Aeschines.* The king refused, indeed, to give up Amphipolis, and also excluded the Phocians from the treaty of peace, in order not to offend the Thebans, his old allies; but he feigned friendship for the Phocians, and the

* This embassy is the subject of discussion in the orations of Aeschines and Demosthenes Περὶ Παραπρεσβείας and Περὶ Στεφάνου.

bribed envoys were unconcerned about the matter. Accompanied by the king's ambassadors, they returned to Athens with the terms of the peace, which the people swore to observe. A second embassy, headed by the traitor Aeschines, now went to Pella, to receive Philip's oath, but he was still engaged in his conquests on the Thracian coast. On his return he immediately made fresh military preparations; the ambassadors, who were purposely detained, were obliged to accompany him to Thessaly, and at Pherae he at length swore to the peace. But it soon became manifest why he had dragged the ambassadors with him to Pherae; he wanted to be as near to Boeotia as possible, for as soon as the ambassadors had left him, he passed through Thermopylae with his army unopposed. Phalaecus did not trust the decision of the contest to a battle, but betraying his country, concluded a treaty with Philip at Nicaea, near Thermopylae; and having obtained free departure, he immediately went to Peloponnesus. The humbled Phocians now surrendered. But Aeschines quieted the alarmed Athenians with the assurance, that Philip entertained no designs but to humble Thebes, to restore Thespiae and Plataeae, and to give back Euboea to the Athenians. The traitor was believed, notwithstanding the efforts of Demosthenes to unmask the base hireling. The Phocians, too, who had willingly admitted the king, because he had promised to interfere on their behalf with the Amphictions, were bitterly disappointed. The Amphictionic council, which was hurriedly convened, consisted only of the most exasperated enemies of the Phocians, that is, of the Locrians, Thebans, and Thessalians, and their verdict accordingly was of the most merciless severity. The Phocians were for ever excluded from the league, their arms and horses were to be delivered up, their towns to be destroyed, the people were thenceforth to live in small villages, and to pay annually sixty talents to the temple of Delphi, until the god should be completely indemnified. Macedonian and Theban troops carried the judgment into execution; twenty-two towns disappeared from the face of the earth, and the fertile banks of the Cephissus remained for many years a wilderness; 10,000 captive Phocians were transported to the Thracian colonies of Philip, Philippopolis and Cabyla. The rest of the people were compelled to cultivate their devastated country for the purpose of raising the fine imposed upon them. This happened in B.C. 346.

On this occasion Corinth lost its presidency at the Pythian games, because it had latterly assisted the Phocians; and the Boeotian towns which were hostile to Thebes, such as Orchomenus, Coroneia, Thespiae, and Plataeae, were given up to the vengeance of the Thebans. They lost their walls, and their citizens were sold as slaves. The Thebans thus carried into effect the intentions with which they had commenced the war.

Philip now stepped into the place of the Phocians in the Amphictionic league, and had two votes. At the same time he obtained the superintendence of the Delphic temple, with the presidency at the Pythian games, and thus already held in his hands the fate of a large portion of Greece.

The king's breach of faith, and the terrible fate of the Phocians, created the greatest exasperation and alarm among the Athenians; but they were unable to oppose force by force. Demosthenes himself advised them to keep the peace and to be cautious; at his suggestion they at length resolved to recognise the decrees of the Amphictions. They showed their feelings, however, by kindly receiving the fugitive Phocians, and by abstaining from sending deputies to the Pythian games.

In Peloponnesus, too, war had been raging throughout the period of the Phocian struggle, and continued even after the close of the latter. Sparta had maintained the contest in the hope of thereby recovering her supremacy in Peloponnesus. Accordingly, in B. C. 353, the Spartans invaded the territory of Megalopolis, the capital of the Arcadian confederacy. The Megalopolitans called upon the Argives, Sicyonians, and Messenians, for assistance. Ambassadors were also sent to Athens, where they met Spartan envoys who had come with the same intention. Demosthenes advised his fellow-citizens to conclude an alliance with Megalopolis, pointing out to them how necessary it was for Athens to keep Sparta in a state of weakness, and to reduce Thebes to the same condition. The Spartans at the same time marched against the Argives who were routed near Orneae, and that town itself was taken; the Lacedaemonians however retreated when the Thebans came to the assistance of Argolis. Soon afterwards, the allies were successful in several engagements, but the Spartans in the end gained the victory in a decisive battle. This was followed by a cessation of hostilities, which lasted for several years; at the expiration of which the war was renewed, and continued until after the close of the Sacred war, when Philip began to interfere in the affairs of Peloponnesus, B. C. 344. His gold had found its way into the peninsula also, and Sparta apprehended an invasion as early as B. C. 346, for she well knew that the Argives and Messenians were willing to join the Macedonians, and that her enemies were already supported with money and mercenaries. In order to deprive Philip of every pretext for intervention, Athens hastened by an embassy to bring about a peace, Demosthenes himself being one of the ambassadors. About the same time, he delivered at Athens his second Philippic (B. C. 344); his thundering eloquence roused the people from their indolence, which he said was as fatal as the existence of traitors within their walls, or the lurking policy of Philip abroad, the first object of which was the overthrow of the Athenian democracy. He at length succeeded in opening their eyes to the fact, that Philip had never honestly wished for peace, and that he did not intend to keep any of its terms.

While Philip kept all Greece in inactivity, and fostered internal discord by a complete system of bribery, which spread over the whole country like a net, he enjoyed for a time the fruits of the peace. He was engaged in establishing colonies, increasing the productiveness of the mines, and embellishing his capital of Pella; he borrowed the money necessary for these purposes from Greek capitalists, who were thus drawn into his interest. He then undertook a successful expedition into Illyricum, and annexed to his kingdom the country from lake Lychnitis to the Ionian Sea. Thence he proceeded to Thessaly, putting an end to the tyrannis of Pherae, and placing a garrison in the town; and in order to secure the possession of Thessaly, he divided it into four districts or tetrarchies, over each of which an archon or governor was set. As he had no pretext for invading Greece from that quarter, he tried to do it from the extreme west, from Illyricum and Epirus. His arms were in the first instance, directed against Ambracia, but it was not difficult to see what ulterior object he had in view. The Athenians were on their guard; they prepared themselves, and at the same time sent an embassy headed by Demosthenes, whose eloquence succeeded in preventing the king from advancing any farther. Philip, however, continued his conquests on the coast of Thrace, where he was master of every place as far as the Chersonesus, for Cersobleptes had been subdued by him. But there he again came in contact with the Athenians, and Demosthenes once more exerted himself to rouse his countrymen to an energetic war against the king, who had never yet observed the terms of any peace, and now came forward more openly and in a more threatening manner than ever. It was manifest that Philip wished to stir up war: he attempted to remove the garrison of the small island of Halonesus, which belonged to the Athenians; and he desired them to recall Diopeithes, whom they had sent out with colonists (κληροῦχοι) to protect the Chersonesus. In B. C. 342 he remained for about ten months in those districts, in order to be always within reach of the Chersonesus. But Demosthenes was unable to rouse the Athenians to act with decision and vigour. Worse things were yet to come before they would move.

About this period, Phocion of Athens, who, though aristocratic in his views, deserved the praise, great and rare in those times, of being incorruptible, had overthrown the tyrants set up and supported by Philip in Euboea, and had recovered the island for Athens. In Megara, also, he succeeded in breaking the power of the party favourable to Macedonia, which until then had maintained the upper hand. Meanwhile Philip pursued his conquests, acting with undisguised hostility against Athens. Selymbria was compelled to surrender to him, and the ships of the Athenians, which were to fetch grain from the Hellespont, were captured. When at length, in B.C. 340, he laid siege to Perinthos and Byzantium, the latter a place of extreme importance to the Athenians in their commerce with the corn-growing countries on the Euxine; when even the king of Persia himself began to be alarmed; then at length the Athenians bestirred themselves. They now made every possible effort: they prevailed upon Cos, Rhodes, and Chios to support Byzantium, and at their request the king of Persia sent an auxiliary force thither. All the states of Greece, especially the Peloponnesians, Euboeans, and Acarnanians, were called upon, though to no purpose, to form a general coalition against Macedonia. Chares was despatched first, but of course could effect nothing; Phocion, who succeeded him, however, compelled Philip to retreat. In point of fact the war was thus begun by the Athenians, who were now resolved to prosecute it with vigour. In the spring of B.C. 339, the pillar on which the terms of the peace of B.C. 346 were engraved, was thrown down in accordance with a law proposed and carried by Demosthenes; the burden of the trierarchy was more fairly and equitably distributed; and the people resolutely set to work to equip a fleet.

In the autumn of the same year, Philip proceeded from Byzantium to the mouths of the Danube, to make war upon a Scythian prince. On his return he lost, in an engagement with the Triballians, all his booty, consisting of 20,000 prisoners, and a still greater number of noble horses, which he had destined to improve the Macedonian breed. He himself was lamed by a wound in the thigh; but the valour of his son Alexander, who was then seventeen years old, saved him and his army. While yet on his march homeward, he was met by ambassadors from the Amphictions, who informed him that he was appointed commander-in-chief of their forces, and requested him to return to Greece without loss of time.

A fresh war had broken out; a fact which did not surprise Philip, for he himself had a hand in it, and Aeschines, the Athenian, was his agent. The latter was present, in the spring of this year, at the meeting of Amphictions at Delphi, in the capacity of pylagoras. He there became involved in a quarrel with a Locrian of

Amphissa, and in order to take revenge, and at the same time to promote the designs of Philip, he charged the Locrians of Amphissa before the assembly with having taken into cultivation the plain of Cirrha, which 300 years before had been consecrated by the Amphictions to Apollo. His eloquent speech led the assembly to adopt the rash resolution to destroy all the houses and plantations of the Amphissians on the sacred ground. The decree was immediately carried into execution by the Delphians, but as they were returning from their work of destruction, they were attacked by Amphissians, who waylaid them, and cut them to pieces. The Amphictions now outlawed the Amphissians, and at an extraordinary meeting, the Thessalian Collyphus obtained the command of an army to invade the territory of Amphissa. But as he had no success, king Philip was appointed commander-in-chief at the next meeting, which was held in the autumn. The Athenians, by the advice of Demosthenes, had sent no deputies to the meeting at which this resolution was adopted. Philip readily accepted the new dignity, for the whole war had been stirred up to further his interests, and he advanced with an army far larger than was necessary to wage war against Amphissa. The Athenians sent an auxiliary force to the Locrians, but Proxenus, the commander of the mercenaries, turned traitor. Philip heard of the efforts which Athens was making to bring about a league against him, and before going any further, he contrived for the present to prevent an alliance being concluded between Athens and Thebes, and to stir up the old mutual antipathy of the two states. He promised the Athenians a truce if they would deliver up to him his personal enemies; and with Thebes he actually succeeded in renewing his alliance. During these negotiations Philip fulfilled his mission, but he nevertheless remained during the following winter in Locris, and by his sudden occupation of Elateia and Cytinion in the spring, he at once revealed to the astonished Greeks his object in remaining. The alarm was particularly great at Athens, and for the moment no one knew what to do. Demosthenes alone was undaunted; he exhorted his countrymen to hasten the conclusion of an alliance with Thebes, and with inspiring eloquence called upon them again to make a resolute stand for the freedom and honour of Athens and of Greece. He himself with others was sent as ambassador to Thebes, and although the Boeotarchs were favourably disposed to Macedonia, although the Macedonian orators had made many promises, and endeavoured in various ways to rekindle the old animosity, yet the impressive words of the great orator and the urgency of the moment prevailed, and the alliance was concluded; the Athenians indeed were ready to make any sacrifice; they consented to bear two-thirds of the expenses of the war, and satisfied the ambition of the Thebans by guaranteeing to them the supremacy over Boeotia. Chares and Lysicles were elected commanders of the army, which was reinforced by a considerable number of troops from Corinth, Leucas, Achaia, Euboea, Megara, and Corcyra. Other states, though favourable to Macedonia, refused to serve under Philip, in order that they might not be obliged to fight against their own countrymen. The two hostile armies were of about equal strength, for that of the Greeks, independently of the citizens serving in it, amounted to 15,000 mercenaries and 2000 horsemen; while Philip had assembled upwards of 30,000 men. At first the Greeks were successful; they advanced as far as Phocis, and succeeded in restoring some of the towns. Philip was defeated in two battles, and already began to be apprehensive of the issue of the war, when at length, in the autumn of B.C. 338, a decisive battle was fought on the plain of Chaeroneia. The Athenian commanders were either men of no ability, as Chares and Lysicles, or they were bribed. The Macedonians, on the other hand, had most excellent commanders in Philip, his heroic son, the young Alexander, and the experienced Antipater. For a long time the issue was uncertain; at first the Athenians under Lysicles, who faced the king, gained the upper hand, and in their joy advanced too far. But the vehement attack of Alexander and the Thessalian horse upon the Thebans, and the charge of the Macedonian phalanx, decided the day. The Athenians lost 1000 slain, and 2000 prisoners. Many of the Thebans also fell, and the sacred band was cut to pieces to a man. Philip honoured the dead, the bodies of the sacred band being treated by him with special respect. On the whole, it must be owned that he showed great moderation and prudence after his victory. He abandoned himself indeed to his joy so unrestrainedly, and with such ridicule of the former boasts and threats of the Athenians, that the notorious orator, Demades, who was among the captives, though a partisan of Philip, asked him why he acted the part of Thersites, while fate had assigned to him that of Agamemnon. But he treated his prisoners with humanity, restored them without ransom, and even left them their baggage. He refused to listen to those advisers who tried to persuade him to inflict severe punishment upon the Athenians. On the contrary, he offered them peace, on condition that next spring they should send deputies to a general congress of the Greeks at Corinth, that they should give up the island of Samos, the main stay of their maritime power, that they should receive as a compensation the town of Oropos, and that Athens should retain her political constitution. The people of Athens, indeed, after recovering from the first consternation, were ready to defend themselves and continue the war, and Demosthenes and Hyperides zealously encouraged their warlike spirit; Demosthenes, moreover, in his capacity of superintendent of the fortifications, caused the walls to be repaired at his own expense; and Lycurgus, the orator, by his accusation of Lysicles, roused the excitable people to such a pitch, that they dragged the wretched man to death. But the actual state of things obliged them to accept the terms of the peace; their warlike disposition and their patriotic hatred of Philip were of no avail. On the proposal of the Areopagus, Phocion was placed at the head of affairs, and an embassy, headed by the straightforward Demochares, was sent to Philip to ratify the peace. The people now again showed their amiable character, for Demosthenes, the implacable enemy of Macedonia, was commissioned by the relatives of the slain whom he had urged on to the unfortunate war, to deliver the funeral oration over the dead. In these sad times Athens, as formerly on similar occasions, had the happiness to possess men of true greatness of character and noble sentiments at the head of the administration; men like Phocion, Demosthenes, and Lycurgus, preserved the state from instantaneous ruin, in spite of all the forces which dragged it downwards. Athens remained, without a rival, the first among the Greek states, although the kings of Macedonia were the real and acknowledged masters of Greece; and the wise financial administration of Lycurgus, from B.C. 338 to 326, restored Athens, comparatively speaking, to a high degree of prosperity.

Thebes was not treated so mildly as Athens, because it had faithlessly renounced the alliance with Philip. The Thebans were obliged to ransom both the dead and the living with money, to give up Oropos to the Athenians, surrender the authors of the revolt to be put to death, and restore the exiles, 300 of whom were appointed by the king as judges and rulers of the state. The Cadmea, moreover, was occupied by a Macedonian garrison, and Thebes, of course, lost her supremacy over Boeotia. Orchomenos and Plataeae rose again from their ruins as free towns. Philip also interfered in the affairs of Peloponnesus, as if he had been absolute ruler; the Corinthians, Achaeans, Eleans, and the towns of Argolis submitted to him; he defined the boundaries between Argos, Messenia, Tegea, and Megalopolis on the one hand, and Sparta on the other. Sparta was weak, and with suppressed indignation yielded to the power of the conqueror. But its lot was more fortunate than that of any other state except Athens, for all the rest had lost even the appearance of freedom. The beautiful epitaph on those who had fallen at Chaeroneia *, and the opinions expressed by orators and historians, show that the Greeks themselves knew quite well that the day of Chaeroneia was the end of Greek liberty.

In the spring of the following year the deputies of all the Greek states — Sparta alone sent none — met on the Isthmus of Corinth, by the command of Philip. There the king announced that the true and final object of his undertakings was the subjugation of Persia. The Ephesian Dius, by an enthusiastic speech, induced the Greeks to elect Philip commander-in-chief, with unlimited power, and to entrust to him the management of the great national war. The Arcadians alone refused to sanction this election. The contingents to be furnished by all the Greeks for this war was fixed at 200,000 foot, and 15,000 horse. Philip himself made preparations on the largest scale. Attalus and Parmenio were sent on before; and without effecting anything of importance, they awaited in Aeolis the arrival of the main body of the army. But a war in Illyricum, and domestic disturbances, prevented Philip himself for the present from following his two generals. His son Alexander, seeing his mother Olympias treated with disrespect, had quarrelled with his father. When a reconciliation had been brought about, and the king's son and wife had returned to court, Philip, in order to strengthen the reconciliation by a new family tie, gave his favourite daughter Cleopatra in marriage to king Alexander of Epirus, the brother of Olympias. In the autumn of the year B. C. 336, the most brilliant festivals were celebrated at Aegeae. The Greek states vied with one another in honouring the kings with presents and distinctions; but the splendour and pomp were disgraced by insolence on the one hand, and by adulation on the other. In the midst of these festivities a sudden end was put to the life of the king, to whom a mysterious oracle of the Pythia had already foretold the approaching termination of his career. Having gone to the theatre without an escort, to show the Greeks how safe he felt among them, he was murdered at the entrance by Pausanias, one of his own body-guards. This man had been grievously wronged, and had been unable to induce the king to punish the offender. For this he took vengeance on the king; but it is also possible that he was bribed by the Persians. Philip died in his forty-seventh year, the twenty-third of his reign. The people and the army demanded the succession of Alexander, who was then twenty years old, and ascended the throne with the energy and intelligence of mature manhood. The circumstances of the time required just such a ruler as he was; for the sudden

* See Demosth. *De Cor.* 322.

death of Philip seemed to undo all that had hitherto been gained. Greece was in commotion, Athens showed its pleasure without disguise, and Demosthenes did everything he could to stir up all the states to cast off the yoke of Macedonia. The barbarous tribes in Macedonia which had been recently subdued, likewise began to stir, and at the court there were conspirators against the throne and life of Alexander. But the young prince overcame all difficulties.

From an ancient wall painting preserved in the Vatican Library.

Bronze Statue of Alexander on Bucephalus.
(Found at Herculaneum.)

CHAPTER XXXIII.

FROM THE BATTLE OF CHAERONEIA TO THE DEATH OF ALEXANDER.

WHAT would have become of Greek civilisation, if Darius had succeeded in subduing Athens and Greece? Like all historical inquiries to which no certain answer can be given, this question is useless, and we here put it only to point out the wonderful ways of a benevolent Providence. An admirer of Hellenic culture reaches the summit of political power, and his son, the grateful disciple of the most universal genius that Greece ever produced, becomes himself a perfect Greek, and carries the civilisation of his spiritual fatherland to the most distant countries in the East and South; and by this extension renders it imperishable for all time to come. When the physical power of Greece began to sink, her intellectual conquest commenced. Her conquerors in battle became her mental subjects; the empire of Greek civilisation survived for many centuries, and Greek culture became the connecting link between Pagan antiquity and Christianity.

During the period from the end of the Peloponnesian war down to the accession of Alexander the Great, Greek culture gradually rose to the character of universality. Conscious speculation was superadded to the productions of unconscious genius and pure inspiration. The ever varying political condition of that period produced the artistic perfection of oratory, and the uncertainty of religious belief led to philosophical speculation. In the earlier and happier days of victorious greatness, the dramatists and historians of Athens reached an unrivalled perfection, and now again, in the same city, oratory and philosophy attained the highest point probably which the human mind is capable of reaching. In the speeches of Pericles and others reported in Thucydides, we find the first specimens of an eloquence regulated by the principles of art. His and Socrates' contemporaries, the sophists, were the teachers of the artistic form of eloquence, without regard to its substance. Hence the greatest orators, from Antiphon down to Demosthenes and Hyperides, were either the greatest friends or the most obnoxious enemies of their country. It would lead us too far to characterise the individual orators. There are but very few among them whom history represents as true friends of their country, and we cannot mention one who was its real saviour. Who could resist the power of circumstances? or who could do so in all emergencies? Although Demosthenes, when compared with any of the others, stands forth as a great, noble, and pure character, can we altogether clear him from the charge of having accepted bribes, which his enemies Dinarchus and Aeschines brought against him? He who wishes to exculpate Aeschines, who openly betrayed his country to Macedonia, must believe that in Aeschines' opinion the only means of saving Athens lay in her joining Macedonia, and that he was wiser than Demosthenes, who in his noble enthusiasm overvalued the power of his country, and in his indignation at the encroachments of the Macedonian, overlooked the weakness and apathy of his countrymen. For the Athenian people had arrived at that stage of intellectual culture, in which the conscious enjoyment of life was of greater importance to them than all political questions. Once during this period, when the voting of money for the building of a fleet was discussed in the assembly, the orator Demades, who had the administration of the Theoricon, said, that there was no money to spare for such purposes, because if a fleet were built nothing would be left to expend upon festivals and games—and no fleet was built. The art of acting on the stage had at that time reached the highest perfection. Painting and sculpture displayed their powers, not in the production of grand and sublime works like those of Phidias, but in exhibiting the charming beauty of the noblest human forms. All learning and knowledge were concentrated in Aristotle, whose influence on the fate of mankind was increased by the circumstance of his being the teacher of Alexander, and thus indirectly contributing towards the diffusion and preservation of Greek civilisation. In consequence of this extraordinary diffusion, we shall be obliged in the remaining part of this work to confine our attention to the history of Greece proper, for otherwise we should have to write almost a universal history.

When the news of Philip's death reached Athens, Demosthenes and Charidemus exerted themselves energetically to stir up the people, who immediately passed a decree to honour his murderer with a crown, and not to allow Alexander to assume the supremacy over Greece. The people were once more in a state of intoxicating joy, and thought that they would have easy work with "the boy of Pella." They knew not how soon they were to feel his rapid and energetic mode of action. He first settled his domestic affairs. Attalus, who was in Asia, was not disinclined to usurp the regal dignity, which he claimed for his nephew, the son of his niece Cleopatra, Philip's second wife, for he did not consider Alexander to be a son of Philip. In consequence of this scheme, he was condemned as guilty of high treason; and as he neither submitted to punishment, nor sued for pardon, he was despatched by an assassin. After this, the young king went to Thessaly in order to assert his right to the supremacy over Greece sword in hand. He found the pass of Callipeuce occupied by the Thessalians, and accordingly had to force his way over the rocky heights of Olympus into the plain of Thessaly, by which movement he turned the enemy's rear. The Thessalians offered no further resistance, and recognising his supremacy promised to send their contingent whenever he should require it. He found the passes of Mount Oeta unguarded, for the Greeks, and especially the Athenians lulled into security by Demosthenes, had not expected that Alexander would act with such rapidity. At Thermopylae, the Amphictions acknowledged his supremacy, but the votes of Thebes, Sparta, and Athens, were wanting. In order to obtain them also, he proceeded farther south, traversing Boeotia, without meeting any resistance, and encamped before the walls of Thebes. This at once induced the Athenians to change their minds, and they sent ambassadors to beg his pardon. Demosthenes himself was one of the ambassadors, but while on his road to Thebes, he secretly returned, for he dreaded the anger of Alexander, which he had provoked by his hostile conduct. His motive perhaps was the generous desire not to damage the cause of Athens by appearing before the king. Alexander complied with the prayer of the Athenians, demanding only that they should send deputies to the congress of Corinth, whither he himself now proceeded for the purpose of regulating the affairs of Greece. Sparta alone sent no deputies, while all the other Greek states accepted the king's terms of what was emphatically called "a general peace and alliance." Henceforth a permanent congress of deputies from the different states of Greece was to have its seat at Corinth, where all the common affairs of the country were to be decided. Alexander was appointed commander-in-chief to continue the war against Persia, for which the states had to furnish their contingents according to the king's orders. No change, however, was to be made in their constitutions, nor was their independence to be impaired. The congress had to watch over the preservation of peace; without its sanction no exiles could be recalled, no one could be banished, no distribution of land could be made, and no slaves could be publicly emancipated. Thus, in spite of the guarantee of independence, the treaty aimed at suppressing the free life and intercourse of the states of Greece. Until the death of Alexander this congress actually continued to exercise its functions.

After pacifying the Greek states in this manner and giving them proofs of his energy, the king, in the spring of the following year, B.C. 335, undertook an expedition against the northern and western neighbours of Macedonia. These expeditions into distant countries were made with the most astonishing rapidity and energy. Directing his march from Amphipolis across Mount Haemus, he humbled the Triballi, dwelling between that mountain and the Danube; and having crossed the river he terrified the Getae who dwelt on its left bank. There, we are told by Arrian, he received embassies from the most distant nations, even from the Celts, who offered him friendship and gold. He then returned, directing his armies westwards against the rebellious Illyrians, and by his extraordinary quickness and personal bravery, he not only rescued his army from a most perilous position amid the Illyrian mountains, but compelled the conquered princes to do homage to him, and send contingents for his expedition against Persia.

Alexander's difficult situation in Illyricum gave rise to various reports of defeats, and even of his death. This caused great commotion in Greece, and the party hostile to Macedonia was particularly active. Ten thousand darics also, which the Athenian Ephialtes brought from Persia, were not without effect. The Aetolians and Eleans rose in arms, and the army of the Arcadians had already advanced as far as the Isthmus of Corinth. But Thebes and Athens distinguished themselves above all by their eagerness to cast off the Macedonian yoke. In the latter city Demosthenes and Lycurgus were the foremost in calling upon Greece and Athens to assert their liberty, since by the king's death the treaties were annulled, and the king of Persia would support the Greeks with troops and money. War was decreed, but first of all the revolt of Thebes had to be secured. Thither the exiles returned, the Macedonian garrison was blockaded in the Cadmea, and two of its captains were put to death. The Athenians sent arms and promised succours; but the troops did not leave Attica, as they prudently wished first to see the result of the struggle at Thebes. Suddenly, even before the Cadmea had surrendered, the king, whom all believed to be dead, appeared at Onchestos in Boeotia with an army of 23,000 men. On receiving the news of the revolt of Thebes, he had marched in the incredibly short period of twelve days from the Illyrian town of Pelion through the valley of the Haliacmon and the Perrhaebian passes into Thessaly, and through the pass of Thermopylae towards Onchestos. On the following day, he was at the gates of Thebes, before any of the Greek allies had arrived. Alexander first proposed an amicable arrangement, and a return to the terms of the peace of the preceding year; but as the Boeotarchs and the exiles rejected every offer, he took the city by storm, after an heroic defence by its citizens. He penetrated into it by the southern gate along with the fugitive Thebans who had been defeated in front of their fortifications. The massacre which now ensued was caused not so much by the Macedonians as by the old enemies of Thebes, who were serving in Alexander's army: the Phocians, Orchomenians, Thespians, and Plataeans took fearful vengeance upon the unfortunate city. On the following day the king left it to his allies to decide upon the fate of Thebes. The Greeks determined to keep possession of the Cadmea, but to raze the city to the ground, to distribute its territory, except that which belonged to temples, among the allies, and to sell for slaves all its inhabitants, without distinction of sex or age, excepting only the priests, priestesses, and those who were connected with the king by ties of hospitality. This decree was literally and mercilessly executed by the Greeks. The temples and the house of the Theban poet Pindar alone were spared, the latter by the express command of the king: 20,000 men were made slaves, 6000 had fallen in the battle, and many had saved themselves by flight. The ancient Cadmea stood alone amid a heap of ruins. This was a fearful retaliation for the merciless destruction of Plataeae in the time of the Peloponnesian war, and for the faithless conduct of Thebes during the Persian invasion. Had Alexander been allowed to follow his own inclinations he would no doubt have acted more mildly. Plutarch relates that he restored to freedom Timocleia, the sister of Theagenes, who had fallen at Chaeroneia, together with her children, on learning that she had thrown into a well and stoned to death a brutal Thracian captain who had attempted to violate her honour. At a subsequent period, when Alexander found Thebans among the captive mercenaries of the king of Persia, he treated them kindly.

The news of the fall of Thebes made a deep impression upon all the Greeks, and the Athenians were the first to alter their plans. It was during the celebration of the great mysteries that they were informed of the fearful catastrophe, and they forthwith determined to send ten ambassadors to implore the king's mercy, and permission to show to their unhappy brethren of Thebes the kind offices of hospitality. The king granted this request, but demanded that they should first deliver up to him ten of the leading orators who were hostile to him, among whom Demosthenes and Lycurgus were especially mentioned. Owing to the mediation of Demades, however, who had received from Demosthenes a bribe of five talents, the king was satisfied with the surrender of Charidemus alone; but he escaped to Asia. Alexander was evidently anxious to win the goodwill of the Athenians by every means in his power; nay he even condescended to flatter a city which would not have been able to offer greater resistance than Thebes. His object in general was, by benevolence and kindness, to keep the Greeks quiet and faithful during his absence in Asia; but, at the same time, he felt a natural reverence for the unrivalled greatness of Athens in past times, which prevented him, as it did all subsequent conquerors, from approaching the sacred buildings of the acropolis with a destructive hand.

Thespiae and, for the third time, Plataeae, now rose from their ruins, in accordance with a decree of the congress at Corinth; but in the autumn of B.C. 335 Alexander quitted Greece, which he had apparently quieted by fearful severity, as well as by mildness. During the winter, he was occupied in Macedonia with preparations for the war against Persia, and in the spring of the following year his army, amounting to about 30,000 foot and 5000 horse, was on its march. From Aegeae he proceeded along the high road, which Philip had so often traversed, to Amphipolis, and thence to Sestos on the Hellespont. The fleet there transported the army to the coast of Asia; for the expedition was accompanied by 160 triremes, 20 of which had been furnished by Athens. With such a comparatively small army, he confidently set out against the myriads of the Great King, knowing from the history of Greece the real value of those myriads, which were driven to battle with scourges. He set out like a true conqueror, feeling certain of victory. He took with him scarcely seventy talents in money, having distributed his treasures among his friends before his departure. When he was asked what he meant to keep for himself, he answered "hope."

We can accompany the youthful hero, who never returned, only thus far, although as the commander-in-chief of the united Macedonians and Greeks, he may to some extent be regarded as a successor of Themistocles, Cimon, and Agesilaus. Upon the history of Macedonia we can enter only where it comes in contact with that of Greece itself. The share of the Greeks in the Asiatic expedition, moreover, was a very small one. From the contradictory statements of the ancients we may gather this much, that the total number of Greeks serving in Alexander's army was about 7000, of whom 2000 were horsemen, including 1500 Thessalians. Among the Persians, on the other hand, we find many Greeks serving as mercenaries against Alexander; for in order to thwart their nearest and most dangerous foe the enemies of Macedonia had recourse to any means, and even went so far as to assist the natural enemy of Greece, the Persians, who during the last century had ceased to be looked upon in that light. Demosthenes too had accepted money from Persia, to employ it against Macedonia. Accordingly, hosts of Greeks now went into the service of the Persians, in order to fight in their ranks against Alexander, totally disregarding the decrees of the Corinthian congress, which continued to exert itself for the interests of Macedonia. The connection with Persia was kept up by constant embassies also, so that Alexander had good reasons for fearing a fresh revolt during his absence. In the first decisive battle on the river Granicus, a Greek of great military fame, the Rhodian Memnon, was at the head of the whole Persian army, in which there were no less than 20,000 Greek mercenaries, a circumstance which rendered Alexander's victory all the more bloody. Alexander, however, still remained faithful to his mission as commander-in-chief of the Greeks, for the result of that battle was the liberation of the Ionian cities in Asia, in which he restored the democratic form of government. Memnon, his most dangerous enemy, who, as commander of the Persian fleet and governor of the coast of Asia, conquered the islands and formed connections with the Greeks on the continent, especially with the Lacedaemonians, died in the following year, B.C. 333; and his successors Pharnabazus and Autophradates, who endeavoured to carry out his plans and made preparations for an expedition into Greece, were defeated the year after. Nothing now checked the king's victorious career.

While Alexander was subduing Asia, Agis III., king of Sparta, who in B.C. 338 had succeeded Archidamus III., put himself at the head of a Peloponnesian confederacy, the object of which was to cast off the Macedonian yoke. Accordingly, the Arcadians, with the exception of Megalopolis, the Eleans, and the Achaeans, took up arms; they were joined by homeless Thebans, and connections were formed with the above-mentioned satraps, Pharna-

To face page [illegible]

Mosaic representing a battle between Alexander and Darius, discovered at Pompeii.

Restored by George Scharf, Jun.

NOTE.—The thick lines mark the most important [illegible] in the original.

bazus and Autophradates, whose fleet had already advanced as far as the island of Siphnos, and who furnished the Greeks with money and ships. Agis had sent his brother to Crete to maintain the influence of Sparta there. The Athenians, also, were soon prevailed upon to support the insurrection with a hundred galleys. But Demades, the frivolous and voluptuous manager of the Theoricon, declared that by such military preparations the people would be deprived of the money required for the games and festivals; and the Athenians, more concerned about their amusements than about their liberty, cancelled the decree; so that Athens, which Alexander had captivated by his insinuating civilities, remained quiet. In consequence of this, after the battle on the Granicus, he sent a report of his victory to the Greeks, and especially to the Athenians, to whom he also made a present of 300 suits of Persian armour, as an ornament for the temple of Athene; and from Susa he sent back the statues of Harmodius and Aristogeiton, which had formerly been carried off by the Persians. But in B.C. 331, Agis having assembled an army of 20,000 foot and 2000 horse, laid siege to Megalopolis, and a victory which he gained there increased the courage and the hopes of the Greeks. Antipater, who had been entrusted with the administration of the kingdom of Macedonia during the absence of Alexander, was at this time engaged against a rebellious governor of Thrace. But soon after this, he received from Asia a sum of 3000 talents with orders to quell the insurrection in Peloponnesus. He now quickly arranged matters in the north, and with an army of 40,000 men invaded Peloponnesus. In the neighbourhood of Aegae, not far from Megalopolis, a decisive battle was fought, in which the Lacedaemonians behaved in a manner worthy of their ancient renown, but were unsuccessful. They were overpowered by the numbers of their enemies, and lost 5300 men, among whom their king fell fighting bravely, and covered with many wounds. This new blow completely disheartened the Greeks. Eudamidas, the successor of Agis, gave up all thoughts of further resistance, and the Spartans sent ambassadors to Alexander to implore his pardon. Antipater referred the case of the conquered to the congress at Corinth, where it was decreed that Sparta should join the Greek confederacy, and pay 120 talents as an indemnification to the faithful city of Megalopolis.

Greece, thus again humbled, remained quiet for a time. But the death of Alexander was the signal for fresh struggles, not only in the other parts of his vast empire, but also in Greece, which again began to long for freedom and independence. The immediate consequences of his death render that event one of the most important in the history of the world. His mighty arm had united under one sway countries and nations of the most different characters and dispositions; but his early death prevented him from binding them firmly together as parts of one great empire; he was carried off in the midst of new and vast schemes, as well as in the midst of oriental luxuries, to which he had abandoned himself. After his successful campaign in the Pentapotamia (the Punjaub), he had scarcely begun making plans and arrangements for establishing his power in the newly conquered countries, when he died of a fever at Babylon, in June B.C. 323, at the youthful age of thirty-two years. Until the very last days of his life he made the most extraordinary efforts, never giving the reins of government out of his own hands. Death itself had no power over him; for Curtius relates the extraordinary fact, that his body lay for seven days exposed to the burning sun, before the Egyptians and Chaldaeans commenced embalming it, without presenting any indications of decomposition. The detailed reports of his death, the rumour of his having been poisoned, his last regulation that the worthiest should be his successor, the giving of his ring to Perdiccas:—all these circumstances are so unauthenticated, and some of them show such manifest traces of being inventions of later or even contemporary writers, that we may here pass them over in silence.

Alexander had been the idol of his army, but among the higher officers many had been ill-disposed towards him, and thought that he had too great a disposition and inclination to become an eastern despot. Conspiracies were discovered and punished with inexorable severity; the chief offenders being Greeks in his own army. That he was of a passionate nature and inflicted punishment on the spur of the moment, will not excite our surprise, if we recollect his position, which demanded quick decision and energy at every step. We cannot refrain from directing attention to one thing, which became of greater importance in the history of civilisation than even his conquest of the Persian empire and his colonies in the distant East. We allude to the foundation of Alexandria in Egypt, in B.C. 332; there the treasures of Greek literature were afterwards collected and carefully preserved and cherished; there grammatical studies, the beginnings of which appear in Greece itself about a century earlier, were cultivated with the greatest success; and there, under the mild sceptre of the first Lagidae, art and literature found an asylum, while in Greece they would, perhaps, have been neglected and become extinct. We of modern times must feel the more grateful for the foundation of that city, because the Museum of Alexandria and its celebrated library were among the principal means of preserving and multiplying the copies of the Greek classics that have come down to us.

Alexander's body was conveyed with regal pomp to that city, which preserved his memory longest and most beneficially, and which down to this day bears his name. As his empire broke to pieces during the violent struggles of his ambitious generals, so also all the members of his own family died a violent death. In B.C. 317 his mother Olympias killed his immediate successor, his half-brother Arrhidaeus, together with his wife Eurydice, a step-sister of Alexander. Two years later, Olympias was made prisoner by Cassander at Pydna, and put to death. The same person also killed, in B.C. 311, Alexander's posthumous son Alexander, and his mother Roxana; lastly, in the year B.C. 309, Polysperchon killed Heracles, a son of Alexander by Barsine. We pass over the various motives for these and other acts of violence, but we may remark that they all arose from the ambition of the generals, and from the desire of each to establish himself in the possession of regal power. Scarcely a trace is found of affection or attachment to the family of Alexander, or of reverence for his name and memory.

Bas-relief from the Villa Albani, showing the position of votive tripods in the public street.

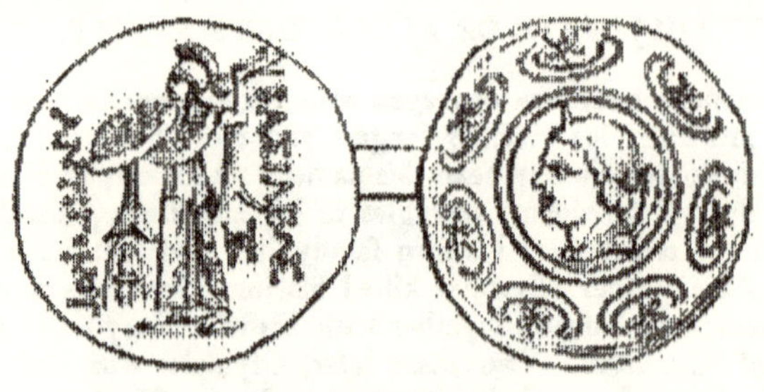

Coin of Antigonus.

CHAPTER XXXIV

FROM THE DEATH OF ALEXANDER TO THE TIME OF THE ACHAEAN LEAGUE.

Of the three principal kingdoms, Macedonia, Syria, and Egypt, which were formed by the successors of Alexander, the first from its geographical position naturally came into frequent, and for the most part hostile, contact with Greece. Alexander himself had shortly before his death been the cause of a fresh war. At the celebration of the Olympic games in B.C. 324, which was attended by a great number of exiles and oligarchs favourably disposed towards Macedonia, Nicanor, a commissioner sent by Alexander, read the following message of his master to the exiles from the Greek cities. "We were not the author of your exile, but we will restore you to your homes,—all except those who are under a curse. And we have written to Antipater on the subject, that he may compel those cities which are unwilling to receive you." The Thebans alone were excluded from this dictatorial amnesty, the object of which evidently was to strengthen the Macedonian party in those Greek cities whose fidelity and peaceful disposition were always doubtful. There were present at the festival about 20,000 exiles from all parts of Greece. Their property had long been in the hands of others; Athens, for example, had distributed the land in the island of Samos among cleruchi; and Aetolians had again taken possession of the town of Oeniadae. This message, accordingly, caused exasperation and opposition. The Athenians and Aetolians refused to comply with it, and, together with other Greeks, sent an embassy to Babylon, which, however, did not gain its end with Alexander. The thought of open resistance was fostered by other circumstances. Harpalus, Alexander's treasurer, had some time before, in B.C. 324, secretly quitted Asia with 30 ships, 6000 mercenaries, and 5000 talents, the greater part of which he deposited at Taenaron in Laconia, and then came to Athens. He succeeded in forming a party among the most influential demagogues and leaders, and even Demosthenes was charged by his enemies with having received bribes from Harpalus, though it is probable that this charge against him, as well as that against Phocion, was unfounded. But Antipater having demanded that Harpalus should be given up, and Demosthenes, in consequence, as he said, of a sore throat, being unable to speak, the people of Athens resolved to arrest Harpalus, who, however, escaped, and taking with him his treasures from Taenaron, went to Crete, where he ended his life in a miserable manner, being slain by a Lacedaemonian who fled with his money across the sea to Cyrene. His book-keeper, however, was taken with the books containing accounts of the manner in which the money had been spent and the names of those who had received it, and he was delivered up to the king's treasurer Philoxenus. The Athenians, from fear of Antipater, now determined to institute a strict inquiry to ascertain who had accepted bribes from Harpalus, and thus began the famous Harpalian inquisition. Demosthenes was unable to give a satisfactory account of a sum of money which he had received from Harpalus, nominally to take care of it; and he was sentenced to pay a fine of fifty talents. Not being able to raise that sum, he fled to escape imprisonment, going first to Aegina and thence to Troezen. Many other most distinguished citizens were exiled on similar grounds. Demosthenes, however, even in his exile continued to exert himself for the freedom of Athens, and when, after Alexander's death, Greece rose to engage in a fresh struggle for its independence, he spoke in the assembly of the Arcadians. When the war was at its height and seemed to promise a favourable termination for Athens, his fellow-citizens recalled him in the most honourable manner, and paid the fine of fifty talents for him.

When the news of Alexander's death reached Greece, the Athenians especially were overjoyed, and ready to take up arms at once without listening to the warnings of Phocion, who, although an aristocrat, was a patriotic man. Persons of property, in general, were favourable to Macedonia, and dissuaded their fellow-citizens from war; but the people, believing that their policy was founded on selfishness, sent many of them into exile. The above-mentioned decree of Alexander had exasperated the Greeks and prepared their minds for war. Leosthenes, a man of great military experience, had just returned from Asia with 8000 mercenaries, and had landed at Taenaron. The Athenians now sent to him desiring him to retain those troops under some pretext or other, until after the arrival of the official news of Alexander's death, when preparations would be carried on openly. This request was complied with. The orator Hyperides and some others, enthusiastic in the cause of freedom, undertook the administration of affairs after the removal of the friends of Macedonia. The people resolved to equip a fleet of 240 ships; all the Greeks were called upon to assert their independence, and most states obeyed the summons. In Peloponnesus, the Achaeans, Arcadians, and Spartans refused to co-operate with the rest, the latter, from jealousy of Athens; in central Greece, the Boeotians declined taking part in the general rising, chiefly because they dreaded the restoration of Thebes, the territory of which had fallen into their hands. An army of 30,000 men, however, was raised, to which the Aetolians and Athenians furnished the largest contingents, the Aetolians sending into the field 7000 men, Athens 5000 hoplites, 500 horse, and 2000 mercenaries. The fleet amounted to 200 sail. Leosthenes, the commander-in-chief of the allies, after having defeated the Boeotians who refused to allow his army a passage through their country, took possession of the pass of Thermopylae. The Illyrians and Thracians also rose against the detested rule of Macedonia. Antipater, who, after the death of Alexander, acted as supreme military commander in Macedonia, in place of the weak-minded Arrhidaeus, quickly invaded Thessaly with a considerable army, sending at the same time demands for reinforcements to Craterus, who was returning from Asia with an army of 10,000 men, and to Leonnatus, the governor of Phrygia on the Hellespont. The hostile armies met in the neighbourhood of the Trachinian Heracleia. The Thessalian horse went over to Leosthenes, and Antipater was obliged to retreat. It seems that he was cut off from returning to Macedonia, for he threw himself into the town of Lamia on the Malian gulf, and there waited for the arrival of reinforcements. But Leosthenes having invested the town with circumvallations, Antipater at length made overtures of peace.

These successful undertakings created such enthusiasm at Athens, and the Athenians became so elated, that, flushed with victory, they demanded the unconditional surrender of Antipater. Phocion alone did not partake of the general enthusiasm. But Antipater refused to surrender; and fortune now forsook the arms of the Greeks. The first misfortune which occurred was, that the Aetolians left the confederate army, under the pretext that they must look to the affairs of their own country. A still greater loss was the death of Leosthenes, who had been wounded during a sally from Lamia. The Athenians honoured him as they had honoured their great heroes in former times. Hyperides delivered the funeral oration over him and his companions in arms who had fallen, and all were buried near the road leading to the Academy, by the side of Pericles, Conon, and Chabrias. Leosthenes was succeeded by the youthful Antiphilus, for Phocion was at the advanced age of eighty.

Meanwhile, Leonnatus had entered Thessaly with 20,000 foot and 2500 horse; while the army of the confederates had been reduced to 22,000 foot and 3500 horse. Thus threatened in rear as well as in front, Antiphilus raised the siege of Lamia, and in the neighbourhood of the town defeated in a bloody battle the troops of Leonnatus, who was himself killed. But still Antipater was relieved, and having joined the remainder of the conquered army and the forces of Craterus who had just arrived, he took up a strong position in the north of Thessaly. There a decisive battle was fought near Crannon, in the autumn of B. C. 322. Antipater's army had been increased to 48,000 men, and the Macedonian phalanx gained the day. The Thessalian cavalry fought in a manner worthy of its great reputation, but unsuccessfully. The Athenian fleet of 170 galleys, commanded by Eetion, was likewise defeated twice by that of the Macedonians under Cleitus. Micion even effected a landing near Rhamnus in Attica, but Phocion overpowered him, and the invader was slain Thus the war suddenly took a turn unfavourable to Greece, and especially to the liberty of Athens. The towns of Thessaly surrendered immediately, the confederate army dispersed, and the smaller towns hastened to accept the not very severe terms offered by Antipater. The Aetolians and Athenians alone were resolved to continue the war. Antipater quickly advanced against Athens, and having encamped in the Cadmea, he first demanded of Athens the surrender of the enemies of Macedonia: whereupon Demosthenes, Hyperides, and many other patriots fled from the city. The impudent Demades, who had been branded with infamy in consequence of having been found guilty of receiving bribes in the inquisition about the proceedings of Harpalus, was now released from the punishment of his crime, and actively supported the cause of Macedonia. He and Phocion were sent to Antipater to obtain favourable terms; a second embassy headed by the aged philosopher Xenocrates, also made earnest representations, but it was all in vain; Antipater insisted upon their surrendering at discretion, delivering up the enemies of Macedonia, paying the expenses of the war and an additional sum of money, receiving a Macedonian garrison into the port of Munychia, and establishing a timocratic oligarchy in the place of democracy. Athens at last yielded on every point. At the festival of the great Eleusinian mysteries in September or October, B. C. 322, a Macedonian garrison took possession of Munychia. The franchise was retained only by those citizens whose property amounted to 2000 drachmas; the rest, 12,000 in number, quitted the city. Although the census was very low, yet the number of those who remained did not amount to more than 9000. Some of the exiles were transported as colonists to Thrace. The patriots and enemies of Macedonia were to be surrendered, as Antipater obstinately persisted in his demand. On the proposal of Demades, they were summoned to appear in court, and, as they did not come, they were sentenced to death. Hyperides and some others were seized in Aegina by one Archias, an actor, and sent to Antipater, who was at Cleonae, and ordered them to be tortured and put to death. Demosthenes had taken refuge in the temple of Poseidon in Calaureia, near the coast of Argolis; when he learned the intentions of Archias, who had come to entrap him, he took poison, which he carried about with him in a reed; for he well knew that his asylum would be no protection against the band of barbarians by whom Archias was assisted in his hunt.

This war, which is commonly called the Lamian, thus deprived Athens, for the second time within a century, of her freedom and her constitution: with them she also lost her noblest citizens, the indefatigable champions of freedom. When a few years later she recovered her ancient free constitution, she had at least no longer to dread a Demades; that vile traitor, after having for a time enslaved his country, in conjunction with other friends of Macedonia, among whom Phocion was the only noble character, was sent in B.C. 318 to Antipater, to effect the removal of the Macedonian garrison from Munychia. But Antipater, knowing that he had been engaged in secret negotiations with Perdiccas to bring about his own downfal, ordered him and his son to be seized and put to death. About the same time the contemptible Archias also died in poverty and disgrace, B.C. 319.

After having humbled Athens, Antipater and Craterus marched against the Aetolians, but before they were able to effect anything decisive, they were obliged to give up the war in consequence of disturbances in Asia.

The other generals and satraps were allied against the insolent Perdiccas, the first guardian of young Alexander. After the murder of Perdiccas at Memphis, in B.C. 321, Antipater became guardian, and at Trisparadeisos in Syria a new distribution of the conquered countries was made among the generals of Alexander, who had already become, to some extent, independent sovereigns. While the armies of Antigonus were fighting in Asia against Eumenes, Antipater died at the age of eighty, in B.C. 318, and in his place Polysperchon was appointed guardian. But Cassander, Antipater's son, took up arms to oppose the new regent, and to obtain for himself possession of Macedonia; during this struggle the family of Alexander the Great was extirpated. After this Cassander took part in the general war against Antigonus, which ended in B.C. 311, when a peace was made, by which the empire of Alexander was divided among four rulers. Cassander having obtained the government of Macedonia only temporarily, and in the character of the guardian of young Alexander, soon caused his dangerous rival to be despatched; and in B.C. 300, the governors of the provinces had made such progress, that Antigonus, Demetrius, Cassander, Ptolemaeus, and Lysimachus could assume the title of king. In the peace concluded after the battle of Ipsus, B.C. 301, in which Antigonus lost his throne and his life, the countries of Macedonia, Thrace, Syria, and Egypt, were recognised as four independent kingdoms. During these wars among the successors of Alexander, which lasted till B.C. 301, Athens suffered much; it experienced several times a change of masters, and was even obliged to alter its constitution.

When Polysperchon, who was advanced in years and experienced in war, but possessed little energy, had been appointed by Antipater guardian of the royal family, Cassander immediately formed the plan of overthrowing him, but as the war called him into Asia, he sent for the present his friend Nicanor to take the command of the garrison at Munychia. He was received at Athens before Antipater's death was known there. Polysperchon, on the other hand, in order to increase his power by attaching Greece to himself, proclaimed, in the name of the kings, the freedom of the Greek states, the restoration of the democratic form of government, and the recall of the exiles. Samos was to be given back to the Athenians, and the Macedonian garrisons were to be withdrawn from all the towns. The aristocrats, who were in favour of Macedonia, were naturally dissatisfied with this measure; they were, however, obliged to yield. But Nicanor, in spite of the commands of Polysperchon, did not evacuate Munychia, and Phocion intentionally remained inactive, though he had received orders to dislodge Nicanor by force. Nay, the latter, probably with the knowledge of Phocion, even took possession of Piraeus, cutting off the communication between Athens and the sea. A command from Olympias, who had been recalled by Polysperchon from Epirus, was as ineffectual as an expedition commanded by Alexander, the son of Polysperchon. Alexander himself formed the design of establishing himself as tyrant at Athens, and it is not improbable that Phocion may have promised to assist him. But the people thwarted this scheme. The orator Agnonides accused Phocion and his partisans of high treason; they fled to Polysperchon, who, however, delivered them up to the Athenians to be tried. Phocion did not deny the charge brought against him, and the Athenians, though many no doubt pitied the old man, condemned him to death. In the spring of B.C. 317, Phocion, with a composure and cheerfulness worthy of his whole life, drank the hemlock. His policy, which saw no safety except in joining Macedonia, was unfortunate, but he carried it out honourably and consistently till the very hour of his death.

Soon afterwards Cassander, a brave but revengeful man, appeared before the gates of Athens. His father Antipater had raised him only to the rank of chiliarch. Dissatisfied with this, he had fled to the powerful Antigonus in Asia, from whom he obtained thirty-five galleys and 4000 mercenaries. With this force he now entered Piraeus; Aegina fell into his hands, and Salamis was threatened. At the same time Polysperchon appeared before Athens, but did not himself venture upon anything decisive; leaving his son Alexander to carry on the siege of the port towns, he marched into Peloponnesus with an army of 20,000 men and 65 elephants. The peninsula, with the exception of Megalopolis, was subdued. In order to deliver themselves from two hostile armies, the Athenians concluded a peace on tolerable terms with Cassander; their territory and their independence were restored. The census previously established was reduced one-half, that is, to 1000 drachmae, and Demetrius of Phaleron, celebrated both as an orator and as an author, and popular on account of his affability, was appointed administrator or governor * of Athens. Under his administration Athens visibly revived. A census of the people, which was held either at the beginning or at the end of his administration, which lasted for ten years (from B.C. 318 till 307), showed that there were at Athens 21,000 citizens, 10,000 resident aliens, and 400,000 slaves. Demetrius knew so well how to win the affections of the excitable people, that on one day 360 statues were erected to him, to make up which number the artists had in some instances to alter previously-made statues; a proof of the flourishing condition of the arts. Subsequently the Athenians may have repented of their excessive admiration, for his extravagance rendered Demetrius more odious to the people than any tyrant had ever been. Greece was always the bone of contention among the successors of Alexander. In order to make friends for himself during the great war against the other generals, Antigonus had proclaimed the freedom of Greece, and he generally appeared to act as if he had undertaken the war in the interest of the royal family and of Greek liberty. At the same time, in B.C. 314, his enemy Ptolemy also declared the Greeks to be free. But of course neither he nor Antigonus did anything to realise his promises.

* Ἐπιμελητής.

Cassander gained more than either of them by his command, in B.C. 315, to rebuild Thebes, which caused great delight among all the Greeks, and especially among the Athenians. That city had now lain in ruins for twenty years, and the Athenians distinguished themselves above all others by their active assistance in restoring the city of their ancient enemies. Cassander had to engage in various struggles for the purpose of maintaining the union of Greece with Macedonia; first with Polysperchon and his son Alexander; then, when the latter had died, and Cassander had gained over the aged Polysperchon by giving up to him the supreme military command in Peloponnesus, with the troops of Antigonus, whose generals destroyed the Macedonian power in all parts of the peninsula, with the exception of Corinth and Sicyon, which remained faithful to Polysperchon. In addition to this, Ptolemy, in B.C. 312, took Euboea, Boeotia (where he was immediately joined by the Boeotians, who were indignant at the rebuilding of Thebes), Phocis, and Locris from Cassander, who for the present was obliged to abandon Greece, Antigonus having threatened to attack Macedonia. It is true that in the peace of B.C. 311, which first sanctioned the division of the vast Macedonian empire, the freedom and independence of Greece were expressly guaranteed; but the terms of the peace were adhered to only while each contracting party felt it his interest to do so. Cassander, the ruler of Macedonia, possessed a predominant influence until the year B.C. 307; he contrived to keep Polysperchon in a dependent position as military commander in Peloponnesus, and in B.C. 308 he came to an arrangement with the powerful Ptolemy of Egypt, who again strove to make himself master of Greece, and had already conquered Corinth and Sicyon; according to this agreement both parties to it were to retain what they had conquered.

Meanwhile a new hero had appeared on the scene, who was more dangerous to his enemies, especially to Cassander, than all who had preceded them. This was Demetrius, the son of Antigonus, who afterwards obtained the surname of Poliorcetes, "the besieger of cities." During the war of Antigonus against the other generals, he had, for the first time, been entrusted with the command of a detachment, being then only twelve years old. Having been left to protect Syria, he allowed himself to be tempted to undertake an expedition against Ptolemy of Egypt, but was defeated near Gaza in Phoenicia, B.C. 312. Six years later he completely wiped off this disgrace by a victory off Cyprus. When Demetrius of Phaleron had governed Athens for about ten years in the name of Cassander, and had by his reckless extravagance become as detested by the Athenians as he had at first been admired for his affability and his great talents, Demetrius, the son of Antigonus, suddenly appeared at the entrance of Piraeus with a fleet of 250 galleys, announcing to the Athenians that he had come to restore their freedom and their democratic government. The people received its deliverer with immense enthusiasm. The Phalerean negotiated with the conqueror, and obtained free departure and safe conduct to Thebes, whence he afterwards went to Ptolemy in Egypt. Munychia was not taken till after a siege, and its commander, Dionysius, was made prisoner. At the same sime Megara fell into the hands of the conqueror, and now the youthful hero entered Athens, where he was received with the greatest joy. He restored to the people its ancient freedom and constitution, which had been lost after the unfortunate Lamian war, and Antigonus, his father, gave to the people 150,000 bushels of corn, timber for 100 galleys, and restored to them the island of Imbros. The grateful people overwhelmed both father and son with honours: they presented them with golden crowns; erected statues and altars to them as to their deliverers; ordered their names to be annually woven, by the side of those of Zeus and Athene, into the garment (peplos) of Athene; sent to them, as to gods, not ambassadors, but theori (θεωροί, deputies sent to the gods); and lastly, to make them entirely their own, they added two new phylae to the ten instituted by Cleisthenes, calling them Antigonis and Demetrias. In accordance with this, the number of senators also was increased from 500 to 600. This joyous enthusiasm, however, did not last long; for when Antigonus was dead, and Demetrius fell from the height of his power, these honours and the names of the two phylae disappeared, the names Ptolemais and Attalis being substituted for them. Demetrius, who was as handsome as Alcibiades, was no doubt the most extraordinary character of his time, for he possessed in an unusual degree all the virtues and vices of the age. The Athenians loved him, and his affability and regal dignity made them forget his vanity and love of pleasure. With him they spent a short but delightful dream, and the year B.C. 307 is perhaps the most happy in the whole history of Athens. Demetrius soon quitted the scene of his purest triumph: he hurried from one enterprise to another, and at the end of his career had gained nothing, although Macedonia, the object of his ambition, was for a time in his hands. He died in the end as a captive exile in Syria.

Being called away by Antigonus before he had expelled the garrisons of Ptolemy from Corinth and Sicyon, and the Macedonian ones from other towns, he was obliged to give up the work of delivering Greece, and engage in war against Ptolemy. The latter, having advanced to protect Cyprus, was defeated in B.C. 306 in a naval engagement, and the island was conquered by Demetrius. Antigonus now assumed the diadem, and taking the title of king, allowed his son to do the same. The other generals not wishing to be inferior to them, Ptolemy, Seleucus, Lysimachus, and Cassander, likewise assumed the regal title.

When Athens recovered the appearance of her democratic freedom, political parties also began to raise their heads again, and the friends of Macedonia and the patriots or democratic party renewed their mutual attacks. The most conspicuous among their leaders were Stratocles, impudent and false, a cringing flatterer of those who happened to have power in their hands; and Demochares, a son of the sister of Demosthenes, surnamed Parrhesiastes, that is, the frank and open-hearted, a sincere lover of his country and its constitution. Along with the orators, the comic poets, as of old, exercised a decided influence upon parties, for at Athens comedy always exerted the same power as in modern times belongs to a free press. Thus the poet Philippides sided with Demochares, and Archedicus with Stratocles. Political strife extended over all the spheres of life, as we see from a law passed by Demochares, enacting that no one should be allowed to keep a philosophical school without the sanction of the council and assembly. Most of the philosophers then residing at Athens were strangers and friends of Macedonia; and some of them, it must be confessed, were men of loose moral principles. By such means of coercion, Athens endeavoured to protect her constitution against hostile elements; but bygone times could not be recalled by measures of this kind.

The dream of freedom soon vanished: in B.C. 304, Demetrius besieged Rhodes, which was allied with Ptolemy; and notwithstanding a most obstinate resistance, at length compelled it to conclude a peace, which secured to the Rhodians freedom and independence, and required them only to send their contingent to the army of Antigonus (though not against Ptolemy). But while Demetrius was thus engaged, the Macedonians recovered the ascendancy in Greece. Polysperchon conquered the greater part of Peloponnesus, and Cassander invading Attica laid siege to Athens. Demochares saved the city, and Olympiodorus, a distinguished general, hastened to Aetolia to fetch reinforcements. But at this moment Demetrius concluded peace with the Rhodians, and with a fleet of 330 galleys sailed to Greece. He landed at Aulis, and succeeded, in a short time, and by the most brilliant and victorious expeditions, in putting an end to the government of Cassander in Greece. The delivered towns received him with the greatest enthusiasm. Sicyon for a short time changed its name into Demetrias, and Athens even went beyond the honours she had already conferred upon him: Athene was called his sister, and her temple was assigned to him as his residence. At a congress held at Corinth he was entrusted with the supreme command over all Greece as far as Thermopylae, which had been liberated by him. But Demetrius was no longer what he had been: he had become an insolent and voluptuous tyrant, and the hearts of the Athenians soon became estranged from him. He did not, indeed, interfere with their constitution, but with the assistance of Stratocles he sent the noble and gallant Demochares into exile. His short stay at Athens was not calculated to regain for him the affection of the excitable people.

He was already on the point of penetrating into Thessaly, in B.C. 301, when Antigonus again recalled him. Cassander, being hard pressed, had concluded a fresh alliance with Ptolemy, Seleucus, and Lysimachus. Demetrius having sailed to Ephesus, joined Antigonus, and at Ipsus in Phrygia a decisive battle was fought. King Antigonus, who, notwithstanding his advanced age of eighty-one, had all along displayed the greatest activity, lost his throne and his life; and his kingdom was divided between Lysimachus and Seleucus. After this defeat, Demetrius wanted to return to Athens, where he had left his wife, his treasures, and his ships, and intended to indemnify himself for the loss of Asia Minor by establishing for himself a kingdom in Greece. But the Athenians were already estranged from him: when he reached the Cyclades, ambassadors brought to him a decree of the people, declaring that they would not admit a king within their walls. Severely hurt by the ingratitude and inconstancy of the Athenians, he sailed towards the Isthmus to maintain his Peloponnesian conquests; but these too had, for the most part, embraced the cause of Cassander. Demetrius accordingly quitted Greece: he conquered the Thracian Chersonesus from Lysimachus, allied himself with the powerful Seleucus of Syria, who became his son-in-law, and took Cilicia from Pleistarchus, the brother of Cassander, who had obtained possession of that country after the battle of Ipsus. While he was thus successful in Asia, Lachares supported by Cassander, who had again acquired power and even invaded Attica, had set himself up as tyrant, and had established a reign of terror in the unhappy city; for he surpassed every one in blood-thirstiness and wickedness. Being informed of this, Demetrius quickly appeared before Athens, and stormed the city, which was suffering from famine. The tyrant, however, had escaped with his plunder into Boeotia, where he was murdered by the people of Coroneia. Ptolemy, who had come to his assistance with 150 ships, was obliged by the superior force of Demetrius to retreat. The Athenians were at first determined to resist to the last, but after a time their powers of endurance were exhausted; they surrendered to Demetrius, and awaited their fate, B.C. 295. Demetrius having ordered the people to assemble in the theatre, to their great astonishment, pardoned their offence, reproached them in a friendly manner for their conduct, and made the famished people a present of 100,000 bushels of corn. However, he occupied the port-towns of Munychia and Piræus with garrisons, and fortified the Museum, which was situated on an eminence at Athens, in order to prevent a fresh revolt, and to check the democratic spirit of the people. After this, he proceeded into Peloponnesus, and having gained a victory over king Archidamus, he appeared, like Epaminondas, at the gates of Sparta, when he was again obliged to stop short in his victorious career and quit Greece. It was not the loss of his Asiatic possessions which Lysimachus took from him, nor that of Cyprus, which was conquered by Ptolemy, that led him to engage in new enterprises, but the affairs of Macedonia.

After the death of Cassander in B.C. 296, Philip IV. had ascended the throne of Macedonia; but he died the year after, and the succession was disputed between his brothers, Antipater and Alexander. Antipater had killed his mother, and fled to Lysimachus in Thrace for assistance; Alexander allied himself with Pyrrhus of Epirus and with Demetrius. The latter arrived when affairs were already settled, and his appearance therefore was inconvenient. Alexander tried to get rid of his powerful and dangerous guest, but was anticipated by Demetrius, who killed him and mounted the throne of Macedonia, in B.C. 294. He maintained himself in this kingdom for seven years, during which nearly all Greece paid homage to him, and submitted to the commands of his son Antigonus. His haughtiness and domineering spirit, however, alienated the minds of the Macedonians from him, and the Athenians also revolted. He formed the reckless plan of waging war at one time against Lysimachus, Seleucus, and Ptolemy, and for that purpose had assembled an army of ten myriads, and 500 galleys. But before he set out he was obliged to employ his army against Pyrrhus, who had been induced by the threatened kings to take up arms against Macedonia. When the hostile forces met, the troops of Demetrius went over to Pyrrhus, who had become very popular among the Macedonians on account of the simplicity of his manners and his bravery. He now took possession of the throne without opposition, but after the lapse of seven months he too was expelled by Lysimachus, B.C. 286. Demetrius, however, never recovered his former power; after various adventures and misfortunes he died, B.C. 283, in Syria, a prisoner of Seleucus, his own son-in-law. In the same year Demetrius of Phaleron ended his life as a prisoner in Egypt.

When Demetrius Poliorcetes was defeated by Pyrrhus, Athens

again rose to assert her freedom; young and old took up arms, and commanded by the brave Olympiodorus stormed the Museum, which was occupied by Macedonians; the port-towns were recovered, and the Macedonians were conquered near Eleusis. Pyrrhus assisted the Athenians, who once more enjoyed their ancient freedom; the people honoured those who had fallen, like the heroes of the Persian war, and buried them on the road leading to the Academy. Demochares returned from exile, and during his administration, which lasted till about B.C. 280, he promoted in every possible way the good of the state, which had been so severely tried and was in a condition of great exhaustion. The re-establishment of law and order, a sensible administration of the finances, treaties of friendship with the liberal kings Lysimachus and Ptolemy, and the restoration of the Eleusinian mysteries, allowed the Athenians for a short period to enjoy the happiness of former and better times.

The dominion of Greece and the throne of Macedonia were now contested by Antigonus Gonatas, the son of Demetrius, and by Ptolemy Ceraunus, the eldest son of Ptolemy Soter. Within the space of one year, Macedonia had three pretenders or kings. After a reign of five years, Lysimachus, at the age of seventy-four, was defeated and killed by Seleucus at Cyrupedion, in the neighbourhood of Sardis, B.C. 281; this was the last struggle among the generals and companions of Alexander the Great. Seleucus, however, was soon afterwards assassinated by Ptolemy Ceraunus, whose father also died about this time. After a short reign Ptolemy Ceraunus himself was attacked, and lost his kingdom and his life. Macedonia now fell into a state of anarchy and desolation, which lasted during a considerable period.

About the time when some Celtic tribes were inundating the plains of Lombardy, others proceeded farther east to the countries about the Danube, and southward into the peninsula of Mount Haemus. In B.C. 280, a Celtic host, under Belgius, invaded Macedonia, where king Ptolemy was conquered by them and lost his life; but the noble-minded Sosthenes repelled the victorious enemy, whose successes had made them careless. Another army of 150,000 foot and 15,000 horse (each of the latter being attended by two mounted followers), commanded by Brennus and other chiefs, then marched southward with the view of plundering the temple of Delphi, while another host of the barbarians turned westward against Aetolia. Even now the Greeks were resolved to defend themselves, and collected all their forces.

Megaris, Phocis, Locris, Boeotia, Aetolia, Thessaly, and more particularly Attica, raised an army of 23,000 foot and several thousand horse. The Athenian Callippus had the supreme command in this war, and Athens, for the last time, enjoyed her supremacy. In B.C. 279, the Celts crossed the Spercheios, intending to march southwards through Thermopylae. But finding the pass occupied and defended, they advanced across the mountain as far as the neighbourhood of Delphi. There a brave band of Delphians, trusting to the aid of the God, fought against the barbarians. Justin states that huge blocks of stone rolling down Parnassus and a fearful thunderstorm terrified the barbarians and made them take to flight. Brennus himself fell, and his routed army suffered immensely. One portion of the Celts settled in the country between the Danube and the Save, another established a kingdom in Thrace, and a third crossing the Hellespont formed settlements in the eastern part of Phrygia, which from them received the name of Galatia.

Antigonus Gonatas now ascended the throne of Macedonia, and maintained possession of it until his death in B.C. 239, with the exception of a period of two years (B.C. 274—272), during which Pyrrhus, after his return from Italy, was again king of Macedonia. As soon as peace and order were restored, Antigonus undertook a war against Athens, which through the victory of Olympiodorus had recovered its independence. The occasion of this war, which broke out in B.C. 269, seems to have been the refusal on the part of Athens to admit a Macedonian garrison. The Athenians were supported by king Areus of Sparta, and Ptolemy Philadelphus, a great admirer of the Greeks, also sent a considerable fleet under the command of Patroclus, while in the north Macedonia was again threatened by the Celts. But it was all in vain. For seven years the Athenians held out against the besieging Macedonians, but in B.C. 262, they were compelled by famine and complete exhaustion to surrender. Munychia, Piraeus, and the Museum again received Macedonian garrisons. Those who had encouraged and guided the people in their defence, were sent into exile. Among them was Chremonides, who afterwards entered the service of Ptolemy Philadelphus. Athenaeus * speaks of a Chremonidean war, and Niebuhr has shown that in all probability this war is meant. It was the last great effort of Athens, which had now become utterly powerless. Antigonus acted more mildly than his father Demetrius; he may have been influenced by the glorious recollections connected with the city, as well as by the prayers of the philosopher Zeno, who was highly esteemed by him. Accordingly, the garrison was soon removed from the Museum, and the constitution remained democratic. But still Athens continued to be dependent on Macedonia, and the garrisons of

* vi. p. 250.

Munychia and Piraeus daily reminded her of her real position. This state of affairs lasted until the year B. C. 229, when by a bribe of 150 talents Aratus prevailed upon the Macedonian commander, Diogenes, to depart with his men. Then Athens again began to feel free, but it had become politically so weak, that it could not show its gratitude to Aratus by joining the Achaean league of which he was the head.

Throughout this whole period of decay, Athens yet continued to be the centre of intelligence, and the arts still flourished in Greece, especially at Corinth and Sicyon. Much indeed of what had made the Greeks so great, had already disappeared, for there were no more tragic poets, and what is called the "new comedy" was fast coming to a close. But the scenic art was far from being extinct, and the dramas of the great masters were still highly esteemed. Demetrius of Phaleron and Demochares were the last great orators; but the models of eloquence which Athens had produced, have served as patterns to all succeeding generations. The philosophical schools, which were flourishing during the time of Alexander the Great, likewise declined both in zeal and celebrity; but the seeds which they had sown were not lost, for Athens became the training school of other towns and of whole nations. The fact that during this period literature and philosophy began a new and

View of Corinth, showing the remains of the ancient temple immediately below the Acrocorinthus.

active life in Egypt and Asia Minor, and also at Rhodes and Apollonia, was owing in a great measure to the influence of Athens, which had given the first impulse to all that was great, good, and noble. Greek art and literature owed it only to their own unrivalled excellence, that they were fostered and cherished at the courts of Alexandria, Antioch, and Pergamus. The extravagances of the plastic art, which manifested themselves on the one hand in such colossal works as the Apollo of Rhodes, and on the other in the miniature smallness of many productions, may be compared to the luxuriant weeds of an over-fertile soil. What subsequent times and even the Romans produced, is sufficient to show that those extravagances did not render it impossible to return to the classical simplicity and noble forms of an earlier period. With what pride must the friend of Greece have looked upon Egypt, Syria, and Asia Minor, which countries, renouncing their own civilisation, became entirely Hellenised! and with what still greater pride must he have observed that even the Romans considered it necessary to ennoble their minds by means of Greek culture, literature, and art! Yet notwithstanding all the assistance they derived from this source, the Romans never could outstrip the Greeks, or rise to a higher degree of perfection than that which had been reached by the Greeks. Such is the reward which Athens then gained and still enjoys.

Figure of Youth dressed in the Chiton and Chlamys.
(From a vase painting.)

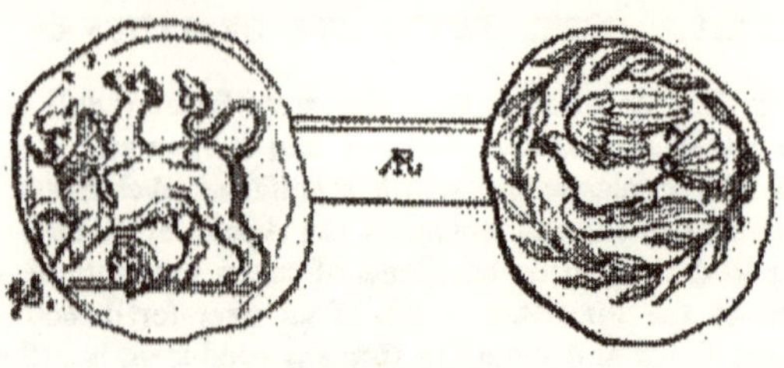

Coin of Sicyon.

CHAPTER XXXV.

THE ACHAEAN AND AETOLIAN LEAGUES DOWN TO THE BATTLE OF SELLASIA.

When Athens had already withdrawn from the scene of great historical events, and in her weak retirement presented the appearance of profound peace, Sparta had yet to pass through a series of violent revolutions and convulsions. Her fate shows the danger of a stern and inflexible constitution, which cannot be reformed so as to harmonise with the altered circumstances of a nation. That state which, according to the varying interests of its polity, was sometimes the avowed enemy of the tyrannis, and at other times supported it, but had always favoured oligarchical tendencies and opposed democratical forms of government, was itself destined to try all these, and end as a tyrannis and a democracy.

The constitution of Lycurgus with its fundamental principles, equality of property and a careful preservation of the national character, had now degenerated into a mere matter of form. The kings were simply the representatives of two families; for after the time of the great Agesilaus, the ephorate had, without opposition, become the highest authority in the state. In earlier and better times, the kings took the field only in defence of Sparta and her national honour; but afterwards, and that even as early as the time of Alexander the Great, they went out at the head of bands of adventurers, and sold their services to foreign rulers. They also indulged themselves in various ways at foreign courts; whereas formerly, a king was not allowed to quit Sparta except in times of war. The number of Spartans had become so much reduced, that immense and illegal wealth existed by the side of unlawful poverty, and destroyed the ancient ideas of simplicity and equality. Since the time of Philip, the external power of Sparta had sunk so low that it could do nothing for the deliverance of Greece from the usurpation of the Macedonians; nor did it take any part in the war against the hosts of Celtic invaders. It made no opposition of any kind to the aggressions of Cassander, Polysperchon, and Demetrius; and it was owing to a mere accident that it did not fall into the hands of the latter. The fact that Sparta was then fortified is a proof that the warlike spirit and the courage of its citizens were no longer what they had been. But during the invasion of Pyrrhus, who was called into Laconia through family disputes, the Spartans, supported by the heroic courage of the women, once more showed themselves worthy of their ancient renown, and Pyrrhus was obliged to retreat after sustaining severe losses.

The distressing internal condition of the state induced king Agis IV., the noble son of Eudamidas, to endeavour to bring about better times by a thorough reform of the constitution. He was supported by the younger generation of Spartans; the elder men and the women, on the other hand, headed by his colleague, Leonidas II., were hostile to his innovations. In conjunction with the ephor Lycurgus, a man of congenial mind, he carried laws enacting that the debts, under the weight of which the poor people were suffering, should be cancelled; that a fresh division of Laconia should be made; that 4500 lots (κλῆροι) should be assigned to the Spartans, whose number was to be supplemented by perioeci, and 15,000 to the perioeci. With great generosity, the king gave up to the state all his own property (600 talents, independently of his landed estates). His colleague and opponent Leonidas was declared by the ephors to be the son of a foreign mother, and incapable of holding the regal dignity; he was, therefore, deposed, and Agis escorted him safely to Tegea. All obstacles thus seemed removed; but during the king's absence on an expedition to the Isthmus against the Achaeans, the selfishness of the ephor Agesilaus, who had been entrusted with the distribution of the land, spoiled everything. When he returned home, Agis learnt that Leonidas had come back, on hearing which he fled into the temple of Athene Chalcioecos; but when he left the asylum, he was treacherously seized, and the new ephors ordered him, together with his mother and grandmother, to be put to death, B.C. 241. This crime was more revolting than even that formerly committed against Pausanias in the same place. It was a strange circumstance that the son of the murderer Leonidas, Cleomenes III., the last Heracleid king, having been married by his father to Agiatis, the beautiful and rich widow of Agis, who had exercised considerable influence upon the high-minded plans of her husband, now completed, by force, the reforms which had been commenced by Agis. Warned by the fate of Agis and his betrayal by the ephor Agesilaus, Cleomenes began his reforms in the year B.C. 226 with the overthrow and murder of the ephors, whose arbitrary and excessive powers justly appeared to him as the cause of all the misfortunes of Sparta. After this, he undertook the cancelling of debts and the distribution of land, without any opposition. The ancient discipline was restored, the Macedonian mode of warfare was adopted, and Sparta was on the point of seeing the good old times return, and of recovering her supremacy over Peloponnesus, when a war with the Achaean league brought about the speedy downfal of Cleomenes and of Sparta.

This leads us to give some account of the leagues formed by the Achaeans and Aetolians. It cannot be stated with certainty when these confederacies were first entered into; they resemble each other in their tendency, but not in their character. Community in religious matters had existed in Achaia, and perhaps also in Aetolia, for a long period; and it is probable that at the time of the Macedonian domination, the loose bond between the several towns was drawn tighter; for in B.C. 280 four Achaean towns united for the common purpose of expelling the Macedonians from Peloponnesus, and of securing their liberty and ancient constitutions. In B.C. 275 other towns, as Aegion, Bura, and Ceryneia, whose tyrants were expelled or abdicated, joined the league; but its flourishing period and its political importance began in B.C. 251, when the Sicyonian Aratus became strategus of the league. Its central point was Aegion with the temples of Zeus Homagyrios and Demeter Panachaia. There the assemblies, which lasted for three days each, were held every year in spring and autumn; extraordinary meetings might be summoned to any other of the confederate towns. The officers of the league were elected at the meeting in spring. The league was originally headed by two strategi; but subsequently to B.C. 255 by one only, who was assisted by another officer bearing the title of hipparchus; to them was added a secretary (γραμματεύς). We also find mention of an hypostrategus. The strategus had the right of convening extraordinary meetings, had the supreme command in war, called in the contingents and contributions in money, carried on all negotiations with foreign states, and kept the public seal of the confederacy. The functions of the hipparchus seem to have resembled those of a Roman master of the horse; the hypostrategus was perhaps the same officer as the hipparchus. A senate was entrusted with the supreme management of all the affairs of the league; its members were called demiurgi (δημιουργοί), and together with the two highest officers formed a college of twelve, the representatives, as it were, of the twelve free towns of Achaia. They prepared all measures to be brought before the general assembly, in which every Achaean who had attained the age of thirty had a right to sit and vote The senators were at the same time the coadjutors of the strategus, with whom they decided on any sudden emergency and on matters of small import. The towns composing the league formed a political union, possessing the right of coining money, and of determining weights and measures; its representatives could confer the franchise, and decided upon disputes among the states which were members of the confederacy, as well as upon those with foreign powers; for which purpose, however, special judges were appointed. No confederate state was permitted to accept presents from a foreign power, nor allowed to withdraw from the league, to which he was bound for ever. The confederation thus constituted in every respect a single indivisible state; in this spirit it acted, and the excellence of its strategi contributed to secure for it the esteem of the Greeks and a comparatively long duration.

The object of the Aetolian league was not so much the promotion of the common good of Greece, as to further the interests of Aetolia itself; hence we find the Aetolians forming alliances with the avowed enemies of Greece; and they never could conceal the fact that, in point of intellectual culture and moral principles, they were semi-barbarians. After the death of Alexander, they distinguished themselves among the Greeks by their bravery and energy. The strength and influence of their confederacy are manifest from the active part they took in the Lamian war; from their brave resistance amid their own mountains, after its unfortunate termination; from their subsequent mode of acting against Cassander by occupying Thermopylae; and lastly, from their victory over king Areus of Sparta, in what is called the last Amphictionic war. At the time of this victory, the Aetolians were in possession of Phocis and the Ozolian Locris, and had compelled Heracleia at the foot of Mount Oeta to join their league. They also took part in the war against the Celts, and gained great credit in the defence of Thermopylae. The constitution of their confederacy resembled that of the Achaeans, and was, perhaps, an imitation of it; both were essentially democratic. The meetings of the Aetolians were held regularly in the autumn near the temple of Apollo at Thermon; there the office-bearers of the confederacy were chosen, consisting of a strategus, an hipparchus, and a secretary. A commission called the Apocleti (ἀπόκλητοι) formed the council of the league; the administration in each town was in the hands of a Polemarchus. Extraordinary meetings of the Aetolians (Panaetolia) also assembled at Naupactos, Lamia, and Hypata, and at a later period usually at Thermopylae. The confederacy had reached its highest power and prosperity at the time when it came into conflict with Macedonia and the Achaean league; for Boeotia was humbled, and the Cephallenian islands were in its possession as well as a portion of Acarnania, whose hostile inhabitants had long checked the progress of the confederacy; a great part of Thessaly and Peloponnesus likewise belonged to it, and Elis was on terms of friendship with the Aetolians. But notwithstanding this great extent, the league, on the whole, cannot be said to have had a Greek character; it possessed neither taste for nor susceptibility of Greek culture, although it fought for the freedom of Greece and against foreign influence. In comparison with the Achaean league, it appears rude and strong, fond of plunder and quarrelsome, treacherous even against what was sacred; the conduct of the Aetolians towards the Romans was obstinate and impolitic, frank even to recklessness, and unsparing in unmasking secret plans and intrigues.

The Achaean league possessed in Aratus of Sicyon a leader who was excellent in every respect. He is one of the noblest characters in Greek history, and worthy to be placed by the side of Pericles. His father Cleinias had liberated Sicyon, his native city, from a tyrannis, but had been slain by the hand of the tyrant Abantidas. Aratus, then seven years old, was taken to Argos, where some friends kindly received him and procured for him an excellent education. At the age of twenty, fired by love of liberty and hatred of tyranny, he in conjunction with exiled Sicyonians delivered his native city from the tyrant Nicocles, and induced it to join the Achaean confederacy, B. C. 251. He was twelve times appointed to the office of strategus, and even when nominally not in power, he was virtually always at the head of affairs; the object which he restlessly struggled for until the day of his death was to destroy the power of tyrants, and to unite all the states of Peloponnesus under one free constitution. His most striking virtues were a disinterestedness rarely to be met with in those times, love of justice, and great powers of eloquence and persuasion. Through this talent he effected more than by force of arms, for as a general he was wanting, as Plutarch says, in resolution, nor had he much personal courage. When once at the head of the league, he quickly increased both its power and extent. In B. C. 243 he expelled the Macedonian garrison from the citadel of Corinth, and persuaded the Corinthians, and soon afterwards the Megarians also, to join the Achaean confederacy. The Aetolians showed themselves hostile even at that time, and had already concluded a treaty with Antigonus Gonatas about a division of Achaia. The example of Corinth was soon followed by Troezen and Epidauros. The eloquence of Aratus prevailed upon Lydiadas, the tyrant of Megalopolis, to lay down his power; the tyrants of Phlius, Hermione, and Argos, likewise abdicated, when Aratus was strategus for the eleventh time, and all these towns joined the Achaean league about B. C. 226. In B. C. 229 Athens got rid of Diogenes, the commander of the Macedonian garrison, who was bribed by Aratus, but, as we have already observed, the city did not join the confederacy.

But now the Lacedaemonians, together with the Messenians, the Eleans, and those Arcadians who favoured the Aetolians, made preparations to oppose the powerful league and check its extension. King Cleomenes, partly of his own accord, and partly commissioned by the ephors, who began to fear for the integrity of Sparta, made himself master in B. C. 226 of the fort Athenaeon, situated in the territory of Megalopolis, near Belmina, and compelled the towns of Tegea, Mantinea, and Orchomenos, which were members of the Aetolian league, to form an alliance with Sparta. The Aetolians, from hatred of the Achaeans, not only gave those towns up to Cleomenes, but themselves concluded a treaty with him. In the following year B. C. 225, when Aristomachus was strategus of the Achaeans, Cleomenes took Methydrion in Arcadia, and although the Achaeans met him with a far superior force near Pallantion, yet by the advice of Aratus they did not commence hostilities, but retreated. This induced Lydiadas to bring forward an accusation against Aratus, who, notwithstanding this, was elected strategus for the following year. But when Cleomenes rejected the terms proposed by Aratus at a meeting in Argos, for a peaceful settlement and for forming a union of all the states of Peloponnesus, the Achaeans at last, in B. C. 224, resolved upon war. Aratus had even before been in negotiation with Antigonus Doson, who was king of Macedonia from B. C. 229 till 220, and the Macedonian had promised his assistance. But Aratus wished to try what the Achaeans alone could effect against Sparta; the brilliant success of Cleomenes, however, soon compelled the Achaeans to avail themselves of Macedonian aid. Cleomenes defeated them in three battles in the neighbourhood of Megalopolis, near the Lycaeon, in the Laodician plain, and near the Hecatombaeon; the towns of Caphyae, Rheneios, Pellene, Phlius, Cleonae, Argos, Epidauros, Hermione, Troezen, and the city of Corinth fell into his hands, and he laid siege to Acrocorinthos. Immediately after his victories he commenced negotiations with the Achaeans; peace was nearly concluded, and Cleomenes would have obtained the supremacy, but a change took place in the state of affairs. In his distress, Aratus called in the assistance of Antigonus Doson, and surrendered to him the citadel of Corinth, which the king had demanded as a pledge and as a point from which he could carry on his military operations. This request was complied with the more readily, as the Achaeans were already despairing of being able to maintain Acrocorinthus. Aratus had thus been led to take a step which was totally opposed to his efforts for the liberty and unity of Greece; he had been driven to it by his fear of the progress of the Spartan king, who was on the point of gaining the supremacy in Peloponnesus, and would then certainly have brought about the dissolution of the league. Aratus' confidence in the personal character of the Macedonian king had also made him overlook the dangerous nature of this measure. Antigonus came towards the Isthmus with an army of 20,000 foot and 1400 horse from Thessaly by way of Euboea. The Aetolians by occupying Thermopylae, had compelled him to take this roundabout way. His arrival changed the fortune of the war. Cleomenes, indeed, offered a brave resistance on the Isthmus, but Argos again joined the Achaeans, and a portion of Arcadia was reconquered. In the meantime Cleomenes was obliged to return to Sparta, where the death of his wife Agiatis caused him much deeper grief than the loss of his conquests.

Antigonus, after having wintered at Corinth and Sicyon, set out for Arcadia in the spring of B.C. 223; at Tegea he joined the Achaeans and occupied Tegea, Orchomenos, Mantinea, and Heraea, Cleomenes not being able to prevent it. Antigonus spent the following winter among the Achaeans at Aegion and Argos, having sent his Macedonians home, and keeping with him only his mercenaries. But Cleomenes did not let this winter pass without profiting by it; he unexpectedly attacked and conquered Megalopolis, and Mantinea, which was occupied by Achaeans, surrendered to him of its own accord. Thence, in the spring of B.C. 222, he made an incursion into Argolis, and ravaging the country advanced as far as the walls of Argos. Antigonus, who had not yet assembled his army, could not, to the great vexation of the Argives, undertake anything against his bold opponent. But soon afterwards he invaded Laconia with an army of 30,000 men. Cleomenes, having foreseen this, had pitched his camp near Sellasia, north of Sparta, where the river Oenus flows through a valley between the mountains, and had occupied the heights of Evas and Olympus. The other passes leading into the interior of Laconia were protected by outposts, ditches, and abatisses, so that Antigonus was obliged to take the road through the valley of the Oenus. The first attack was made upon the eastern hill, which was occupied by Eucleidas. The victory was undecided, and the assailants were attacked in their rear, and hard pressed by the light-armed troops of Cleomenes. At length the bold assault of the cavalry under young Philopoemen of Megalopolis, who, however, was not a commander on that day, decided the victory; and while he with the Achaean cavalry defeated the Laconians in the valley, Antigonus with his phalanx took Olympus by storm. Cleomenes, who was stationed there himself, fled with a few horsemen to Sparta, and despairing of his safety, proceeded in the same night to Gythion on the coast, embarked, and sailed to his friend Ptolemy III. in Alexandria, from whom he hoped to receive support in continuing the war. But Ptolemy died soon after, and his successor, Ptolemy Philopator, was unlike his father in every respect; he was a voluptuous man, unconcerned about the affairs of his state, and entirely dependent on his courtesans and favourites. Cleomenes, who was not only disappointed in his hopes, but was kept like a prisoner, excited an insurrection against the debauched king; but he was deserted by the people, and in order to escape a still more miserable fate, he and his friends made away with themselves. Polybius and Plutarch relate marvellous events which occurred at his death. When Ptolemy ordered the king's body to be suspended on the gallows, a snake wound itself round his head and covered his face; Ptolemy was frightened at the prodigy, and the people of Alexandria, who crowded round the scene, called Cleomenes a hero and the son of a god. The mother and children of Cleomenes, who had come to Alexandria as hostages, were, by the command of Ptolemy, put to death together with other Laconian women, and died with true Laconian heroism. Thus ended the life of the last king of Sparta, a worthy descendant of the Heracleids.

After the battle of Sellasia, Antigonus took Sparta without any resistance; he treated the heroic city very mildly, restored the ancient constitution by reviving the ephorate, and established a Macedonian garrison in the place. A few days after this, he broke up and quitted Peloponnesus, for he had received intelligence of an inroad of the Illyrians into Macedonia.

The defeat of Sellasia had broken the power of Sparta; but the victorious Achaeans too had lost their independence; they were henceforth obliged to admit and keep Macedonian garrisons. Acrocorinthos and Orchomenos remained in the hands of the Macedonian, the former being one of "the three fetters of Greece." The Achaean league could undertake nothing without the consent of Antigonus; and Aratus, whose influence had once been so paramount, now had no power, except that of his own personal vote. But still, a happier time was yet to come for the confederacy of the Achaeans.

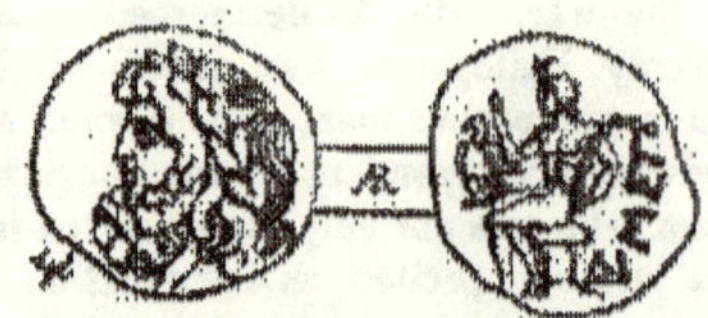

Coin of Megalopolis.

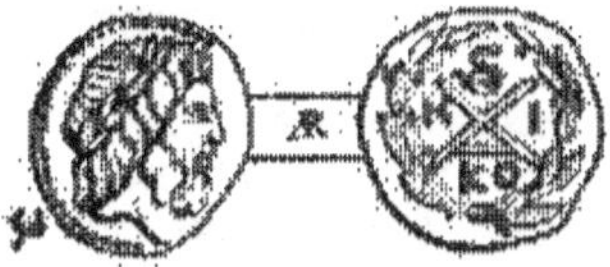

Coin of Epidauros, with the Monogram of the Achaean Confederacy on the reverse.

CHAPTER XXXVI.

FROM THE BATTLE OF SELLASIA TO THE DESTRUCTION OF CORINTH.

IMMEDIATELY after the death of Cleomenes and of king Antigonus Doson, who was succeeded by Philip V., the son of Demetrius II., a youth of seventeen years, Greece was shaken by a fresh convulsion, known by the name of the Social War. Its consequences were ruinous to the independence of Greece, inasmuch as they enabled the Romans, who had shortly before reduced Sicily to the condition of a Roman province, to interfere in the internal affairs and disputes of Greece. The occasion to this war was given by Sparta. After the death of king Cleomenes the last descendant of the Eurysthenids, Agesipolis III., who was yet under age, had ascended the throne under the guardianship of his uncle Cleomenes. Lycurgus, who was not a Heracleid, purchased from the ephors the place of second king, and then expelled his young colleague, who was afterwards killed by robbers. In this manner, Lycurgus made himself sole king of Sparta. The ephors, from hatred of the Achaeans and Macedonians, had even before commenced secret negotiations with the Aetolians; but they now openly concluded an alliance with them, although the Aetolians had already violated the general peace, having invaded Messenia from Phigalea, a confederate town in Arcadia, and trespassed even upon the territory of the Achaeans. For this reason, Aratus in B.C. 220 entered upon the office of strategus five days earlier than the legal period, and attacked the Aetolians near Caphyae, in the territory of the Arcadian Orchomenos; but as he was not favoured by fortune, and did not possess great talents as a general, he was defeated. The Aetolians now met with no further opposition, and plundering the country returned across the Isthmus.

This was the beginning of the Social War, for the Achaeans immediately followed up the event by a declaration of war, which was forthwith accepted by the Aetolians, to whom war and plunder were always welcome, and who hated the Achaeans on account of their having availed themselves of the assistance of Macedonia. Supported by Philip, the Achaeans, Boeotians, Phocians, Epirots,

Acarnanians, and Messenians fought against the Aetolians, Spartans and Eleans. In b.c. 219, Philip himself marched with 10,000 heavy-armed phalangites, 5000 peltasts and 800 horse, through Thessaly and Epirus into Aetolia. He ravaged and traversed the country as far as Oeniadae, at the mouth of the Achelous, which, together with other towns, he captured. In the following winter he invaded Elis, and destroyed Psophis in Arcadia, the stronghold of the plundering Aetolians. Meantime, the Aetolians made predatory incursions into Epirus, and from Elis into Achaia. In the spring of b.c. 218 Philip renewed his invasion of Aetolia, and having taken its capital Thermon, entered Peloponnesus and traversed Laconia to its southernmost point. Lycurgus made a stand against him in the neighbourhood of Sparta, but was beaten. At the same time the king had ordered a fleet to be equipped to attack Cephallenia, which likewise belonged to the Aetolian confederacy. But when Philip quitted Peloponnesus, the Achaeans were thrown into sad distress. The Aetolians suddenly fell upon them from Elis, and occupied the Panachaicon near Patrae. Eparetus, the strategus of the Achaeans in b.c. 217, was unable to offer them any effectual resistance; for he was a man without ability, and under him the Achaeans were without discipline or power. Aratus indeed restored discipline and good fortune, but a change took place in the relation of the Achaeans to Macedonia.

Philip had heard of the success of the great Carthaginian Hannibal against the Romans; he was now forming more extensive schemes, and endeavoured to get rid of the war in Greece. In the beginning of the summer, b.c. 217, he concluded a peace with the Aetolians, through the mediation of the Rhodians, Chians, Byzantians, and of the ambassadors of king Ptolemy. The terms were that the Aetolians should surrender Acarnania to him; in all other respects each party retained what they had. The Achaeans, who stood alone, for no great reliance could be placed upon the other allies, were naturally dissatisfied with this peace, and Aratus in particular opposed the arbitrary proceedings of the king The consequence was that Philip soon afterwards caused his noble friend and excellent adviser to be poisoned, in order to get rid of a troublesome monitor.

Prince Demetrius of Pharos, who had been driven from his country in consequence of a war between the Romans and Illyrians, and had gone to the court of Macedonia, was instilling his hatred of the Romans into the heart of the young king. Philip first undertook a war against the Illyrians, in order not to leave an enemy in his rear, and thus to pave the way into Italy. He also prepared a fleet of 100 Illyrian ships called *lembi* (λέμβοι). The reports of Hannibal's victories in Italy made him more and more warlike, and soon after the battle of Cannae a regular treaty was concluded between him and Hannibal, in which all the possessions of Rome east of the Adriatic were given up to Macedonia. The commencement of hostilities, however, was delayed by the circumstance of Philip's ambassadors to Hannibal being twice intercepted. The Romans set apart a fleet of fifty ships for the war against him; and this fleet was stationed in B.C. 215 at Tarentum, to prevent the king from crossing over into Italy. In the following year, the praetor, M. Valerius Laevinus, sailed with a portion of it to Illyricum, took the towns of Oricon and Apollonia, which latter was besieged by Philip, and compelled the king to flee. The Macedonians, however, continued to keep possession of Illyricum until B.C. 212; for the Romans, being wholly occupied with the war in Italy, operated against him with only a small force. But to make up for this, they concluded a treaty with the Aetolians, for the purpose of keeping Philip occupied through them, and thereby they involved all Greece in a fresh contest, which was in reality only a continuation of the Social War; for the new alliance with Rome was joined by the Eleans, Messenians, Lacedaemonians, and also by the kings of Pergamus, Thrace, and Illyricum. Philip, on the other hand, was supported by the Achaeans, Boeotians, Thessalians, Acarnanians, Epirots, Euboeans, Phocians, and Locrians, and by king Prusias of Bithynia. Thus Greeks were fighting for the most part against Greeks, and for the interests of foreigners. Plunder and pillage were indulged in throughout Greece, the scenes of the war being Acarnania, Thessaly, Euboea, and Elis. Philip and the Romans, according to their pleasure, took part in the war or retired from it, making the Greeks fight for them. In B.C. 211 M. Valerius Laevinus conquered for the Aetolians, his allies, the towns of Oeniadae and Zacynthos, and in B.C. 210 Anticyra; Acarnania saved itself by a desperate resistance. Laevinus was succeeded by the praetor P. Sulpicius Galba, who had the command till B.C. 206. In B.C. 208 Philip twice defeated the Aetolians, near Lamia, under their strategus Pyrrhias, but was afterwards himself routed in Elis. It was in vain that about this time Ptolemy, the Rhodians, Athenians, and Chians endeavoured to bring about a peace; the Aetolians were urged to continue the war by the Romans, and by the report that king Attalus of Pergamus was approaching. During the year B.C. 207 Attalus did take part in the war, but nothing of any importance was effected; for although Sulpicius Galba attacked the towns of Oreos, Chalcis, Opus, and others, yet he was obliged to retreat. Even before the end of the year Attalus was called back to his kingdom, which was threatened by Prusias of Bithynia. From B.C. 206, the Romans themselves no longer took any part in the war.

During this period, the Social War had been continued in Peloponnesus also. In B.C. 208 Philopoemen, whose first exploit in the battle of Sellasia has been noticed above, became strategus of the Achaean league. He is one of the noblest characters in the whole history of Greece, and by his brilliant qualities as a statesman and general, by his prudence, moderation, valour, love of truth, and generous and enthusiastic efforts for the good of his country, he acquired the most animating influence upon the Achaeans, who had become weary and indifferent. He restored military discipline, improved the armour, and neglected no honourable means to revive the warlike spirit of his countrymen. Within eight months, the reorganisation was completed, and the first expedition was undertaken against Sparta. After the death of Lycurgus, about B.C. 211, Machanidas had assumed the sovereignty, and had become the first tyrant of Sparta. To take revenge for his hostilities against the weakened Achaeans, Philopoemen in B.C. 207 marched against him, and defeated him near Mantinea after a long struggle, in which the Achaean mercenaries were routed. Sparta however was not delivered from the tyrannis, for in the course of the same year Nabis, an unnatural, bloodthirsty monster, usurped the sovereignty, and with the most senseless rage and cruelty caused the noblest citizens to be put to death, and changed Sparta into a den of robbers.

When the Romans ceased to take part in the war, the Aetolians at length found themselves obliged to conclude peace with Philip, and to allow him to dictate his terms. After this settlement, the proconsul Sempronius arrived with 10,000 men and 35 ships, but the war was not renewed. The Epirots also mediated a peace between the Romans and Philip, and between the two confederacies, according to which the Parthinians, an Illyrian people, and some Illyrian towns were given up to the Romans, and the country of Atintania to Macedonia. It was further agreed that neither party should attack the allies of the other. This peace was concluded in B.C. 204.

Philip from the beginning did not observe its terms; for among the Carthaginian prisoners taken in the battle of Zama (B.C. 202) there were Macedonians, who had served against the Romans. In addition to this, there were other causes which led to the renewal of the war. In conjunction with the king of Syria, Philip took from young Ptolemy Epiphanes the Thracian coast-districts with their important maritime towns, a portion of Asia Minor, and the Cyclades. This Ptolemy was allied with Rome, in the same manner as the Rhodians and Attalus, who, when attacked by Philip, successfully repelled him. They and the Athenians, who were besieged by Philip, sent ambassadors to Rome to complain of his conduct. The Athenians had suffered severely for an act of rashness which they had committed. Two Acarnanian youths, who from ignorance had taken part in the celebration of the mysteries of Demeter at Athens, had been murdered by the Athenians in the excitement of religious zeal. The Acarnanians, exasperated at this, and supported by Macedonia, ravaged Attica with fire and sword. Upon this the Athenians, being allied with Attalus and the Rhodians, resolved to make war against Philip, who was then besieging Abydos. Philip sent an army against Athens, and blockaded it, but a Roman fleet of twenty ships came to its assistance. Soon afterwards the king himself appeared; but his attack was likewise repelled by the Athenians. To revenge himself for this, Philip, before his departure, in a truly barbarian spirit, destroyed the buildings and plantations outside the city, the grove and temple of the Cynosarges, the Lyceum, and even the tombs of the heroes. Thence he went to Corinth, but immediately returned, and being reinforced by 2000 Thracians and Macedonians, again ravaged Attica with such fury, that he even ordered the marble blocks and the statues of the gods to be broken to pieces. Punishment for these crimes did not at once overtake him, for the allies of Athens were, for the moment, too weak to assist her effectually. The Romans and Rhodians indeed took possession of the fortified town of Chalcis, destroyed the Macedonian garrison and its stores, but were unable to maintain themselves, and retreated to Piraeus. The king's punishment came from the west. In B. C. 200, the consul Sulpicius Galba commenced the second Macedonian war on the river Apsos, between Apollonia and Dyrrhachium. The belligerent powers had the same allies as before, and Greece was again involved in a civil war for the interest of foreign states. The victories of Sulpicius did not bring the matter to a decision, nor was his successor, the consul P. Villius Tappulus, able to carry out his plan of invading Macedonia. But T. Quinctius Flamininus, the consul of B. C. 198, seriously and successfully attacked the Macedonians. He at once changed the position of the Greeks who took part in the war. The Achaeans, who had been allied with Macedonia since the former wars, were gained over by the consul; the strategus, Aristaenus (Philopoemen being absent in Crete), was the more easily prevailed upon to join the Romans, as Philip refused to give up Corinth. By this circumstance, and because Nabis was always hostile to the Achaeans, the Spartans, who in the first Macedonian war had been allied with the Romans, were now induced to conclude a treaty with Philip. Thus both the Achaean and the Aetolian confederacy for a time fought on the same side, for Philip had shortly before, B. C. 201, again provoked the Aetolians by attacking their allies on the Hellespont and in Asia Minor. But we shall see how soon this union between the two leagues was dissolved.

Flamininus drove the Macedonians from their position on the river Aous in Epirus, and being joined by the Aetolians and Athamanians, advanced into Thessaly. Philip retreated into Macedonia, and Flamininus, having taken possession of Elateia, concluded a truce with the king, and spent the winter in Phocis and Locris. Negotiations were commenced, but they led to no result. Accordingly, in the following year, B. C. 197, Flamininus, as proconsul, broke up with his new allies, and set out for Thessaly. Philip, as well as the Roman, tried to occupy Scotussa, and this circumstance quickly and unexpectedly led to a decisive battle. The detachments which preceded the main body of the hostile armies became involved in an engagement on the line of hills called Cynoscephalae. The armies, coming up soon afterwards, continued the fight, which ended in the total defeat of Philip. He lost 8000 slain and 5000 prisoners. The Aetolians had particularly distinguished themselves during the battle. The king, in an interview with the proconsul in Tempe, obtained a truce, and ambassadors were sent to Rome with the terms of peace proposed by the conqueror. It was not till the following year, however, that ten commissioners arrived from Rome with the ratification of the peace. The first condition was, the abolition of the Macedonian supremacy in Greece, and Philip was obliged to withdraw his garrisons from all the Greek towns, while the Romans reserved to themselves the right of occupying the most important fortresses, Acrocorinthos, Demetrias, and Chalcis. The Athenians, who were treated with special favour, obtained the islands Paros, Imbros, Delos, and Scyros, while Aegina was given up to Attalus. The Aetolians, who were as blunt and frank as they were brave, openly showed their dissatisfaction with the arrangements of Flamininus and with the mock freedom which he established: they required him first of all to break the three fetters of Greece, as Philip used to call the three fortresses mentioned above. Flamininus himself declared to those who brought the ratification of the peace, that all Greece must be restored to freedom, if the bitter reproaches of the Aetolians were to be silenced, and if the Roman name was to be cherished with true affection among all nations; he urged the necessity of showing that the Romans had come across the sea really to liberate Greece, and not to assume that dominion which had hitherto been exercised by Philip. But notwithstanding these fine words, the fetters of Greece remained in the hands of the Romans.

In B. C. 196, Flamininus proceeded from Elateia to Corinth to be present at the Isthmian games. There he solemnly proclaimed through a herald, and in the name of the Roman people, the freedom of all the Greeks. The joy and enthusiasm of the people were so extravagant, that he was almost crushed under the weight of the garlands and flowers which were showered upon him. The deliverers of Greece, however, remained in the country for a considerable time longer; for king Antiochus of Syria, in concert with Hannibal, was engaged in vigorous preparations against Rome; and Nabis, the tyrant of Sparta, refused to give up Argos, though he was required to do so by the terms of the peace. It was also feared that he would ally himself with the king of Syria. Flamininus, therefore, conjointly with the Achaeans, liberated Argos by force. He then attacked Sparta itself, which appears now to have been fortified with walls; another detachment of Romans, with the help of a Rhodian and Pergamenian fleet, under the command of Eumenes of Pergamus, occupied the maritime towns of Laconia, and obtained possession of a considerable quantity of military stores in the fortified town of Gythion. These circumstances obliged Nabis to accept the terms proposed by Flamininus. His dominion was confined to Laconia, he was compelled to renounce his claims to Argos, and was cut off from communication with the sea. He had, therefore, to cede the maritime towns to the conquerors, and to surrender all ships except two; he was, moreover, not allowed to conclude a treaty with any one nor to make war; he was obliged to pay down 100 talents of silver at once, and 400 more by eight annual instalments; and lastly, he had to give hostages as a security for his observing the peace. But notwithstanding these hard terms, Nabis remained tyrant, and under the protection of the Romans, who meant by this means to keep the Achaeans in check; but the latter felt the injustice of this arrangement keenly, especially as they had assisted in conquering Nabis. The Aetolians also openly and strongly expressed their disapproval of the conduct of the Romans. It cannot be denied, that although in B.C. 194 the garrisons were withdrawn from Corinth, Demetrias, and Chalcis, yet Rome did not allow Greece to enjoy peace; and civil war soon broke out afresh. Filled with hatred of the Romans, the Aetolians stimulated Nabis to reconquer the maritime towns which he had ceded to the Romans and Achaeans, and thus occasioned a war between the tyrant and the Achaeans. While the latter sent succours to Gythion, which was besieged by Nabis, the tyrant made a predatory inroad into their territory. Near Pleiae, in the territory of Gythion, Philopoemen, who was now again strategus of the league, attacked Nabis with Cretan mercenaries and Tarentine horsemen, and after having gained a victory over him, blockaded him in Sparta. Meantime, Alexamenus arrived with Aetolian auxiliaries, not with a view to assist the tyrant, but to kill him, and to take possession of his treasures and city. After the murder was committed, Alexamenus retreated into the citadel; but the Spartans took it by storm, and he, together with nearly all the Aetolians, was cut to pieces; the survivors were sold as slaves. The fruits of this deed, however, were not reaped by the Spartans but by Philopoemen, for during the confusion he seized upon the city, and added it as well as Laconia to the Achaean confederacy, which now embraced the whole of Peloponnesus, B.C. 192.

About this time the war with Antiochus of Syria broke out. The Aetolians, ever dissatisfied with the Romans, concluded a treaty with him, and in B.C. 192 he arrived at Demetrias. His arrival was the signal for a fresh rising; the Eleans, Boeotians, Messenians, and Demetrias joined him, and the distant Epirots testified, by an embassy, their sympathy with him. But instead of availing himself of this favourable disposition of the Greeks, and of quickly advancing through Thessaly into Epirus, Antiochus took up his winter-quarters in Chalcis, and there with great pomp and solemnity celebrated his marriage with a Greek beauty. In the spring of B.C. 191, the consul M'. Acilius Glabrio invaded Thessaly, and gained a victory at Thermopylae over the Syrians and Aetolians. The defeated king did not rally his forces till he reached Elateia; with only 500 men he escaped to Chalcis, and thence immediately crossed over to Ephesus. We here omit the sequel of his history and the victory of the Scipios. The Aetolians, his allies in Greece, shared his fate. Acilius Glabrio, on his return from Chalcis, whither he had pursued the king, went to Thermopylae, and stormed Heracleia, which was still in the hands of the Aetolians. This loss broke their obstinate courage; they sued for peace, and after long deliberations obtained, in B.C. 190, a truce for six months. But during this interval they seem to have changed their mind, for after the expiration of the truce, hostilities recommenced; the consul M. Fulvius Nobilior, however, put an end to them in B.C. 189, and in his camp at Ambracia dictated to the Aetolians the terms of peace. They were obliged to recognise the majesty and supremacy of the Roman people; to have the same friends and enemies as the Romans; to allow no army a passage through their country against any ally of Rome; to dismiss from their confederacy all the towns which had been conquered by the Romans, or had joined them of their own accord, together with the island of Cephallenia; and to pay 500 talents, 200 at once, and 300 in six yearly instalments. The power of the Aetolian confederacy and its influence upon the affairs of Greece were thus for ever annihilated, and internal party feuds soon completed the destruction of the league; for the Romans availed themselves of every opportunity of giving weight to their authority in Greece. The war with Perseus of Macedonia enabled them to lead the most illustrious of the Aetolians as hostages to Rome. When Augustus, after his great victory of Actium, founded the town of Nicopolis in commemoration of it, he collected the remnants of the Aetolian nation into that place; but a kind of Aetolian league still continued to exist, and to it Amphissa belonged in the days of Pausanias, about A.D. 150.

Let us now return to the Achaean confederacy. Some years after the humiliation of Sparta by Philopoemen, the war between the two states broke out afresh. The Lacedaemonians, contrary to the treaty, had taken by storm the town of Las, on the coast south of Gythion, and as they refused to deliver up the instigators to the Achaeans, the latter, by the advice of Philopoemen, declared war in B.C. 188. It was the interest, and also the intention of Rome, to foster this civil war rather than to suppress it. The ambassadors of both parties at Rome received equivocal answers, so that the Achaeans imagined they had received full power over Laconia, while the Lacedaemonians refused to concede this. At length Philopoemen having prevailed, led back to Sparta those who had been exiled by Nabis, and who had not been recalled in compliance with the treaty. On that occasion the most distinguished of the opposite party, sixty-three in number, were put to death, and the city and state had to pass through a bloody process of reforms. Philopoemen ordered the walls of the city to be demolished, and the mercenaries to be dismissed; by his command many of the citizens recently admitted by Nabis to the franchise (emancipated Helots) were put to death, and others were removed from the city to the villages in the country. He lastly compelled the Spartans to abolish the constitution of Lycurgus, under which they had lived for 700 years, and to adopt the manners and constitution of the Achaeans, that is, to establish a democracy. Sparta, thus deprived of its lost power, obeyed the commands of Philopoemen with angry reluctance, and its urgent appeals to the Roman senate produced nothing but vague answers and delay, as the Romans were only waiting for a favourable opportunity to interfere in a dictatorial manner and destroy both parties. Thus, although they did not approve of the conduct of Philopoemen, they expressed an opinion that nothing should be done contrary to his proceedings; afterwards they expressly wrote that the demands of Sparta were granted. During these intricate negotiations, which were intentionally protracted, Sparta was not again formally incorporated with the Achaean league until B.C. 181. The year before, Messenia, probably not without the connivance of Rome, revolted, under Deinocrates, from the Achaean confederacy; it had been compelled by Flamininus, scarcely ten years before, to join it, and had all along been a very reluctant member of the league. Philopoemen forthwith set out against Deinocrates with his Thracian and Cretan mercenaries and a detachment of cavalry, composed of the noblest of the Achaeans, but death overtook him. In a valley near Corone he was surprised by some Messenian horsemen, and after a brave resistance was overpowered. His horse fell, and Philopoemen, now at the age of seventy, and having scarcely recovered from an illness, was conveyed in a dying state to Messene. There Deinocrates quickly withdrew him from the sight of the admiring and sympathising people, and locked him up for the night in a treasure vault (thesaurus). On the following day he was brought to trial, at which the bloodthirsty party prevailed. Philopoemen emptied the poisonous cup with calmness and intrepidity, for he received at the moment the cheerful news that Lycortas and the select band of cavalry were safe. Under his successor Lycortas, the brave father of the historian Polybius, the Achaeans took revenge; Messene was conquered, and those who had voted for the execution of Philopoemen were put to death. The remains of Philopoemen were conveyed to Megalopolis, and buried there with due honours. But the disputes continued until the mighty hand of Rome crushed the rival states, and suppressed all quarrels by force of arms.

The influence of Rome had already become so powerful in Greece, that when Perseus, the successor of Philip (B.C. 179), and a bitter enemy of the Romans, employed the last resources of his kingdom for a final struggle with the all-absorbing republic, and formed connections with the kings of Illyricum, Thrace, Syria, Bithynia, with the princes and towns of Epirus and Thessaly, nay even with Carthage and the Celtic tribes on the Danube, the Boeotian towns alone could be prevailed upon to conclude an alliance with Macedonia. Even from this there were some dissentients, who, when a Roman ambassador appeared at the Boeotian congress at Thebes, cancelled the treaty, and delivered up those who were favourably disposed towards Macedonia. The Boeotian confederacy was dissolved, and each separate town was declared an independent state. But Haliartos and Coroneia, which alone remained faithful to the treaty with Perseus, were razed to the ground, and their inhabitants sold as slaves. The Roman senate afterwards, indeed, caused the dispersed inhabitants to be recalled, and restored their property to them; but the territory of Haliartos was already in the hands of the Athenians, who had received it from the Romans, and the restoration of that ancient town was impossible.

During the third Macedonian war, in which Perseus lost his kingdom in the battle of Pydna, B. C. 168, the Achaeans, though not without great reluctance, had fought on the side of the Romans. This induced the hired traitors, Callicrates and Andronidas, who were taunted with their base conduct by the very boys in the streets, to traduce the noblest men, who were animated by the love of freedom and by patriotism, as disaffected and seditious persons. Callicrates had been busily at work to destroy the league ever since the year B. C. 179, and with the help of the Romans had stirred up factions within it, to the party spirit of which the most eminent men fell victims. After the close of the Macedonian war, regular inquisitions were instituted in the towns, and upwards of 1000 Achaeans, among whom was Polybius, were sent to Rome to answer for their conduct, the strategus Xenon having insisted upon being permitted to plead his cause in person before the Roman senate. But when they arrived in Rome, no opportunity was given them to defend their conduct, and they were distributed as hostages among the Italian municipia. After what may be termed a free custody of seventeen years, from B. C. 167 to 150, the survivors, 300 in number, mostly old men, were allowed, by the advice of Cato and the younger Scipio, to return to their country. These men were among the first who then roused their countrymen to engage in their last struggle with Rome.

The Aetolians, who were suspected of favouring Macedonia, experienced a still harder fate, for they were carried to Rome with their wives and children, and 550 of the most distinguished were put to death; few only saw their country again after a long imprisonment. Such was the cruelty of the Romans towards a country from which they derived the best part of their mental culture.

The final decision of the fate of Greece, after so many and such severe trials, was brought about by the Athenians. During the Macedonian wars, they had been so much reduced, that, as Pausanias relates, from mere want and poverty, they plundered their own town of Oropos. The Oropians brought a complaint respecting this strange deed before the Roman senate, and the Sicyonians were commissioned to inquire into the matter. As the Athenians did not obey the summons to appear before the commissioners, they were sentenced to pay a fine of 500 talents. In consequence of this, they sent, in B. C. 155, three ambassadors to Rome; they were the philosophers Carneades, Critolaus, and Diogenes, and their object was to induce the senate to cancel the severe verdict of the Sicyonians. Their wisdom and oratorical powers were greatly admired at Rome, and they succeeded in getting the fine reduced to 100 talents. They remained at Rome for a time, but were at length ordered to quit the city, because it was thought that they exercised a bad influence upon the young.

Soon after this, Athens again committed an act of injustice against Oropos, and the injured solicited the protection of the Achaeans. The latter at first refused their assistance out of regard for Athens; but at last Callicrates, who had been bribed with five talents, caused a threatening decree to be passed against Athens; in consequence of which the Athenians ceased from molesting Oropos. A fresh feud also arose between the Achaeans and Lacedaemonians about the possession of Belmina, which was claimed by the latter. The Spartans were hard pressed, and escaped only through the treachery of the strategus Democritus, who being afterwards sentenced to pay a fine of fifty talents, fled from Peloponnesus because he was unable to raise the money. He was succeeded by Diaeus, an infuriated enemy of the Romans, who now interfered in the new disputes. The consul Metellus, who in B.C. 148 was engaged in a war against the Pseudo-Philip of Macedonia, ordered the Greeks to desist from their hostilities, which were to be decided by a Roman commission. But when the ambassadors, Orestes and Junius, called upon the Achaeans assembled at Corinth to exclude Corinth, Argos, Heracleia, at the foot of Mount Oeta, and Orchomenos in Arcadia from their confederacy, their demand was treated with scorn and indignation. Other envoys sent by Metellus were even ill-used, and the Achaeans declared war against Rome.

Thebes and Chalcis immediately joined the Achaeans. Metellus, who had just concluded the war against the Pseudo-Philip, compelled Macedonia and Thessaly to acknowledge the sovereignty of Rome, and in B.C. 147 marched with his army into Boeotia. The strategus Critolaus, who had intended to occupy the pass of Thermopylae, came too late, and was put to flight in the neighbourhood of Heracleia. He fled, but being overtaken by Metellus near Scarpheia in Locris, was defeated a second time. He himself perished while endeavouring to effect his escape. The progress of the Romans was as great as the despair of the Achaeans. In the meantime a Roman fleet landed a force in Peloponnesus, which laid waste the country; 1000 Arcadians were cut to pieces. Diaeus now drew together the last forces of the confederacy; he armed 12,000 slaves, and assembling all men capable of bearing arms in the neighbourhood of Corinth, he had at his command an army of 14,000 foot and 600 horse. Metellus, before advancing any farther, punished the Thebans, who had taken part in the war, and from fear had fled into the mountains; he destroyed Thebes, leaving only the Cadmea uninjured. He then occupied Megara, and even now offered terms of peace to the Achaeans. But

Diaeus, who was thoroughly infatuated, rejected all proposals, and even ordered the bearers, three Achaeans, to be seized and put to death. At length in B.C. 146, the consul L. Mummius, the successor of Metellus, occupied the Isthmus with an army of 23,000 foot and 3500 horse, and in the ensuing battle of Leucopetra, not far from Corinth, decided the fate of Greece. Diaeus, who had fought like another Leonidas, with a band of 614 brave men, fled in despair to his native city of Megalopolis. He killed his wife that she might not become the slave of a Roman, and having himself taken poison, he set fire to his house.

Three days after the battle, Mummius entered the defenceless city of Corinth, and ordered it to be plundered and destroyed by fire; all the male inhabitants were put to the sword, and all the women and children as well as the remaining slaves were sold. Many of the numerous works of art collected in that wealthy commercial city were destroyed, and others were carried to Rome, or were given to king Attalus of Pergamus, to reward him for the assistance he had rendered in the war. The ten commissioners of the Roman senate now declared the Achaean league and all other confederacies of towns in Greece to be dissolved, everywhere established an oligarchical government, forbade the wealthy to acquire landed property in any part of Greece, except that in which they resided; the Corinthian territory became domain land (*ager publicus*), and the country had to pay to Rome a heavy tribute. It does not, however, appear that Greece was at once constituted as a Roman province under the name of Achaia, as is commonly believed; for there are no distinct traces of such a state of affairs until the time of the dictator Sulla. Many of the severe measures, adopted after the fall of Corinth, were subsequently withdrawn, such as the imposition of fines which some of the towns were condemned to pay, and the prohibition respecting landed property. Nay, even the ancient constitutions were revived, and the confederacies among several towns were restored under Roman supremacy. Perfect freedom was enjoyed by Athens, Delphi, Thespiae, Tanagra, and the country of Laconia (Ἐλευθερολάκωνες), to which Augustus added Nicopolis. Amphissa and the Ozolian Locrians were exempted from taxes; Corinth, Patrae, Dyme, and Megara subsequently became Roman colonies.

In the distribution of the provinces under Augustus, Achaia became a senatorial province, but in the early part of the reign of Tiberius it was transferred to the emperor, until Claudius again changed the *legatus Augusti* into a proconsul. The absurd fancy of Nero in once more proclaiming the freedom of Greece at the Isthmian games, was followed by such sad consequences, that

Vespasian wisely withdrew the untimely gift. Hadrian's favours to the country of art and literature were much more substantial; but the sunbeam of his goodwill shone on nothing but ruins, and no festival of the Panhellenia could restore the national feeling, which existed only in the mouths of philosophers and orators. The wars among the Greeks themselves, and still more so those with the Romans, had almost changed the country into a wilderness; vast districts were desolate, and infested by bands of robbers; the whole of Greece could scarcely raise an armed force of 3000 men. No wonder, therefore, that even as early as A.D. 265, Athens was the only Greek city which, owing to the strength of its position, was able to resist the invasion of the Goths; 130 years later, the treachery and cowardice of its Byzantine rulers entirely abandoned it to the destructive fury of Alaric, leaving to the proconsul of eastern Rome the command over nothing but the wrecks of bygone greatness.*

Athens enjoyed many advantages over the other states of Greece, until its participation in the Mithridatic war, into which it had been seduced by Aristion, brought upon it all the horrors of the siege and conquest by Sulla in B.C. 86. But it still retained its freedom, almost without interruption or change, throughout the whole imperial period, except that its constitution assumed an aristocratic character through the increasing authority of the strategi, and the exalted position of the Areopagus. Even its imprudent policy and participation in the civil wars of Rome produced no evil consequences beyond the fact that Augustus took away Eretria and Aegina, which Antony had given to it. It need not surprise us that the political life of the Athenians became a mere empty form consisting in trifles, and that the people became the flatterers of the great and powerful; as, for instance, when they conferred almost divine honours upon their great benefactor Hadrian, as in former times they had done in the case of Demetrius and Antigonus. The emperor Severus is said to have limited the privileges of Athens, but we do not know what privileges are alluded to. The outward forms continued, unchanged on the whole, to exist for a long time; and the names of the free institutions do not seem to have become extinct until the time of the Byzantine empire.

Sparta, too, enjoyed as much freedom as a Greek city could have under the dominion of Rome. The coast districts of Laconia, however, appear to have remained independent of it. The emperor Augustus fixed the number of free townships in Laconia (Eleutherolacones) at twenty-four, and their magistrates bore

* Hermann, *Lehrb. der griech. Staatsalterth.* § 190.

the title of ephors. At Sparta itself, the office of the patronomi, which had been instituted by Cleomenes, continued to exist along with the ephors and the senate.

Greece, though conquered by the arms of the Romans, subdued them by its vast superiority in the arts and in literature; the Romans themselves owned that they were the humble disciples of Greece; and that country in which we first meet in its full development with all that is noble and beautiful in man, is still the perennial spring at which we and all future generations may refresh our minds and drink intellectual inspiration.

Temple Ruin at Corinth.
(From an original drawing by Sir W. Gell

A kind of Flute, played at Bacchic Festivals.
(From a bas-relief in the Vatican.)

SUPPLEMENTARY CHAPTERS

ON THE

RELIGION, LITERATURE, AND ART OF THE GREEKS.

CHAPTER I.

GENERAL CHARACTERISTICS OF HELLENIC CIVILISATION.

THE political history of Greece has now been conducted to a close. It seems only natural that we should ask ourselves, as we cast a backward glance on the ground we have traversed, what was the destiny or mission which the Greeks fulfilled in furthering the cause of civilisation, what the social state and habits of thought which are displayed in the progress of their history. In offering a few suggestions towards an answer to this inquiry, it will be our object to arrive at some general principles in the light of which that history may with advantage be read, and which may give a meaning and a key to those details of the social usages of the Greeks which the student meets with in the pages of Hermann, Becker, and Wachsmuth.

A glance at the topography of Greece has been thought sufficient to indicate *à priori* that it was destined to be the theatre of a civilisation widely different from that of the Eastern world. Girt by a triple sea; studded with countless islands which wooed the enterprise of the mariner and the colonist; indented throughout its long line of coast with deep and narrow creeks and bays, which fostered a kind of amphibious disposition in its inhabitants; intersected throughout its surface by the physical barriers of mountain, valley, and ravine, high enough to break the sameness of a material uniformity, and low enough to admit the permeation of a moral and intellectual unity; furnished with a vegetation which, though breathed on by the balmiest of heaven's airs, and shone upon by the brightest of heaven's suns, was not, on the one hand, as in the East, sufficiently exuberant to dispense with the labours of man, nor on the other hand, so penurious as to cramp his leisure; inhabited by populations, divers and diverse indeed in origin and aptitudes, tastes and institutions, but by that very diversity ministering to the life and vigour, the energy and emulation, of the whole nation, and so contributing each one of them an arch to that bridge by which civilisation strode onward from East to West,—all the features here enumerated so intertwine the history with the geography of Greece, that it is impossible not to see how providentially the outward circumstances of the country were mated to the inward character and social condition of its inhabitants. This social condition, which we now proceed to consider, assumes different aspects at different periods in the history of Greece. They may fitly be divided into three groups, terminated respectively by the Persian war, the Peloponnesian war, and the Macedonian monarchy.

With regard to the social state of the primitive and prehistoric populations of what was afterwards called Hellas, our information is exceedingly fragmentary. Comparative philology indeed gives us some glimpse into the amount of civilisation, if we may so speak, which the Pelasgic offshoot of the Arian race brought with them into Europe. But the data thus afforded, though most reliable in kind, are limited in number and narrow in extent. A comparison of the Sanscrit words paçu, gaûs, açva (Zend, açpa) van, çavis, urana, aya, hansa, with the corresponding Greek words (which again have their counterpart in the Latin tongue) πῶυ, βοῦς, ἵππος, κύων, ὖις, ἀρνός, αἴξ, χήν, warrants the conclusion, in the estimation of the best writers, not only that the terms in use among a nomade race are the same in the two cases, but also that the animals which we find domesticated among the Greeks were likewise known to the primitive populations of pre-Hellenic times. In like manner we may infer the use of chariots drawn by horses and oxen, and the knowledge of metals, such as iron, gold, and silver. More important, perhaps, is the familiarity betrayed with fixed habitations (as distinguished from the tent or Scythian chariot) in the identity of the Sanscrit words dama, dvara, veça, puri, with the Greek δόμος, θύρα, οἶκος, πόλις. Although these primitive populations may not have been unacquainted with the first elements of agriculture, their knowledge of the plough, of various vegetables, of vines and olives, seems to have been acquired subsequently to their arrival in Europe; the Greek terms for such objects not having any equivalents in Sanscrit. Again, although the Greek ναῦς, πλοῖον, and ἐρετμός are obviously identical with the Sanscrit words naûs, plava, and aritram, the analogy does not extend either to sails, or masts, or rigging generally. When we add the existence of a lunar division of the year, and of a decimal notation, we have exhausted the principal evidence which is here furnished to us on the social state of the Pelasgic populations of Greece. The civilisation portrayed in the Homeric poems has already been treated so fully in an earlier part of this volume, that we feel ourselves enabled to pass on at once from the poetical to the historical period. Of course it is beside our purpose to go over again the ground which has already been traversed; but if we were asked briefly to comprehend in a few words the various phases through which the social state and civilisation of the Greeks thenceforth passed till they fell into subjection to the power of Rome, we should select the words of Plato: τὸ μὲν κοινὸν ξυνδεῖ, τὸ δὲ ἴδιον διασπᾷ τὰς πόλεις. They seem to embody that idea of *civicism*, that complete absorption of the man in the citizen, which is the best explanation we can offer of the peculiar characteristics of Hellenic civilisation. With axiomatic terseness this passage conveys implicitly what is more explicitly set forth in numerous other passages both of the *Laws* and the *Republic*. It tells us that in the opinion of one who was Greek to the heart's core (far more so than his master), the assertion of a personal individuality, and of private rights and interests, wrenched asunder the bonds by which states were made to cohere. Müller has wisely remarked that in antiquity a state was not, as in modern times, an institution for protecting the persons and property of the individuals contained in it. We shall approach nearer to the ancient notion, if we consider the essence of a state to be that by a recognition of the same opinions and principles, and the direction of actions to the same ends, the whole body becomes, as it were, one moral agent.* It was the refusal to subscribe to this recognition, and to submit to this common direction, on the part of individuals, which elicited from Plato the provisions of his utopian Republic (nowhere so entirely Greek as where it seems to us most visionary), which made Aristophanes rail at his contemporaries and extol the "men of Marathon," and which finally handed over Greece into the arms of Philip of Macedon.

Before we examine the higher purposes which this march of events was intended to subserve, let us pause to consider some of the influences which this fusion of the individual into the body

* *Dorians*, iii. 1.

corporate of the state must have exercised on the social condition of the inhabitants. In the first place, we realise very forcibly the truth which has often been remarked, that the civilisation of antiquity was the civilisation of towns. When every citizen was expected to consider that the greatest of all freedom was to be a vital active member of the body of the state, and to abstain from any infringement, by his individual acts, of the authority of the whole, we can understand, on the one hand, the startling assertion in Aristotle, that the man was made for the state, not the state for the man, and, on the other hand, the cautious proviso of the same philosopher, that in order to compass a healthy political action, the number of citizens in a state should be so restricted as to render it difficult for them to escape surveillance. To the like effect are the injunctions in Aristotle's Politics on the necessity of every citizen having ample leisure at his command, and on the consequent exclusion of artisans from the privileges of citizenship; a feature in the political philosophy of the Greeks which finds its practical illustration, on the one hand, in the institution of slavery as a machinery for relieving citizens proper from the occupations of a *βάναυσος*, and, on the other hand, in the narrow development which trade and the industrial arts obtained in antiquity as compared with modern times. But this is not all. The manner in which Aristotle deprecates the idea of each man's making unto himself a state out of his own family, as incompatible with the very existence of all polity, is but one of many facts and indications which throw a flood of light upon the position occupied by the family in Hellenic civilisation. Apprehensive lest the bonds and affections of family relationship should weaken the allegiance of the citizen towards his *πόλις*, the Greek legislator did all in his power to denude the wife and the mother of everything which could confer upon her higher functions than the half servile offices of *ταμιεία* and *παιδοτροφία*. She was regarded as a kind of necessary evil (*ἀναγκὴ γάρ*, says Menander, *γυναῖκ' εἶναι κακόν*), only to be tolerated for the sake of keeping up the breed of citizens. Accordingly, she was relegated to a distinct portion of the dwelling, called on that account the *γυναικωνῖτις*, from which she was rarely permitted to emerge, except at certain religious festivals. She was not allowed to show herself at the domestic meals, if any man other than her husband was present. So that in addition to the meagre instruction which cramped and impoverished her mental faculties, she was likewise denied that powerful aliment of female education which is supplied by intercourse with men. When the tidings of the battle of Chaeronea reached Athens, numbers of terror-stricken women peered before the doors of their houses to inquire after the fortunes of fathers, husbands, and brothers. The old fashioned notions of the Attic orator Lycurgus were scandalised at this breach of female propriety, which he pronounces to be equally disgraceful to the culprits and to the city. This story shows that the almost cloistral seclusion of the respectable portion of the female community was no mere sham. But a still more painful aspect of Hellenic society has yet to be examined. It was not sufficient to reduce the matron and maiden to comparative insignificance; they had formidable rivals outside the *γυναικωνῖτις*, who fed the passions, and beguiled the leisure, but were unable to command the esteem of the husband. There is something extremely graphic in the following passage of Demosthenes, which gives, as it were, a classification of every phase of Athenian female society. In the oration, *κατὰ Νεαίρας*, he observes, with singular *naïveté*: *τὰς γὰρ ἑταίρας ἡδονῆς ἕνεκ' ἔχομεν· τὰς δὲ παλλακὰς, τῆς καθ' ἡμέραν θεραπείας τοῦ σώματος· τὰς δὲ γυναῖκας, τοῦ παιδοποιεῖσθαι γνησίως καὶ τῶν ἔνδον φύλακα πιστὴν ἔχειν.* We have no desire to arrest the attention of the student on the putrefying sores and plague spots of Athenian society; but the influence exerted by these Hetaerae, the kind of *ἡδονή* which they were expected to furnish to their admirers, assigned them a position and a prominence so different from what the same class of persons obtain in modern Europe, that any view of Hellenic civilisation would be singularly incomplete which gave them altogether the go-by. Our main object, however, in alluding to them now, is to remark that if the state not only tolerated but protected them, and allowed them to play a part in society which was denied to the wife, the reason probably was that the absence of any closer tie beyond the caprice of the hour, precluded the danger of the Hetaera becoming, as in the case of the matron-wife, a kind of personal centre around which a sort of *imperium in imperio* might be set up, which, by dividing, might weaken the allegiance which each citizen owed to the state.

Domestic architecture, one of the strongest evidences of the social state of a people, tends to corroborate the view here insisted on as to the supremacy of *τὸ κοινὸν* over *τὸ ἴδιον*. When the framework of Hellenic society was in full vigour, the plainness, not to say meanness of the private houses of the Athenians, when contrasted with the gorgeous magnificence of their public buildings, told a tale as to the principles on which that society was founded, the meaning of which no one could mistake. The evidence of Demosthenes on this point is exceedingly strong. He lived at a time when that framework was hastening to decay, when those principles had ceased to actuate the heart and conduct of his fellow citizens; and in two of his orations he bitterly bewails the change which in this respect had come over the domestic architecture of the Athenians since the days of Themistocles and Miltiades. The passage here following is repeated almost verbatim in another speech, and the subject is made the butt of his sarcasm in a third.* "In those days," says the orator, "everything connected with the state was opulent and magnificent at the public expense; but in private life (ἰδίᾳ δὲ) no man thought of being a cut above his neighbour. I can prove it. If any of you know the style of dwellings which were inhabited by Themistocles or Miltiades, or any of the worthies of that time, he finds that they were not a whit finer than the common run of houses. Whereas their public buildings and establishments, yon Propylaea, docks, porticoes, Peiraeus, or any other edifices with which you see the city is provided, left their descendants nothing to improve upon either in quantity or quality. Now-a-days, however, so affluent are the private means of those who manage public affairs, that some of them have got them private dwellings far finer than many public buildings, while others have bought up more land than all of you in this court put together. And as to your public edifices, I am ashamed to mention them, so mean and shabby are all your building and whitewashing." †

In keeping with the above are the reproaches and obloquy which Alcibiades drew upon himself for making Agatharchus paint the walls of his rooms; the innovation being held to involve too strong an assertion of individual importance, and to be one of the indications of a τρυφῶσα πόλις.

The history of Hellenic art furnishes another illustration of the fusion of all personal individuality in the absorbing action of the state; witness the narrow development which portrait painting attained. It is not till a comparatively late period that we meet with any traces at all of this branch of art. It is true that in the 58th Olympiad statues began to be erected in commemoration of victorious athletes, but we are expressly told that they did not profess to be *likenesses*, except in the case of those who had thrice won the conqueror's crown. If we turn from sculpture to the sister art, it is not till the Macedonian period that portrait painting can with any truth be looked upon as a recognised branch of Hellenic art.

We have endeavoured to call attention to a few of the most suggestive of those social aspects which make up the idea of Hellenic civilisation. More than a few, the narrowness of our limits

* This remark, however, must be qualified by the circumstance that Wolf and Schäfer pronounce one of the orations in question to be spurious.

† *Aristocr.* 689.

prevents us from attempting. The student will do well to apply the views here insisted on to other phases and details of the social usages of the Greeks. It only remains to see if we can discover to what point all these usages may be said to converge, and how far they may be said to reveal the peculiar characteristics of Hellenic civilisation, and the part which the Greeks were called upon to play in the drama of the world's history.

It may perhaps seem hazardous to attempt to compress the lessons which we gather from the history of the most enlightened people that ever lived, into a formula of a few words. But the attempt, however pedantic, will not be thrown away if it should furnish the student of Greek history with the conditions of thought under which he should approach it. With this view, we venture to suggest (agreeing in substance with the profoundest writers on the philosophy of history) that the history of Greece *embodies* the evolution of the idea of *humanity*, of man, as man, out of the husk and shell of the mere πολίτης of a finite nationality. All the steps, it must be remembered, by which the heathen rose to that notion of a universal human society which finds its fullest heathen embodiment in the familiar line,

"Homo sum: humani nihil a me alienum puto,"

were hewn and fashioned by the hand of Hellas. In this respect, the civilisation of antiquity was widely different from our own. It required no ordinary effort and no narrow period of time for the Greek or the Roman to rise to the idea of man, as man. The Greek was confessedly a man; but over and above all he was a Greek. This was an artificial state of society. However brilliant may have been the prowess and virtues it produced at Marathon and Salamis, it could not resist the turmoil of the Peloponnesian war, or parry the subtle questionings of the Sophists. Socrates was the first to point to a new and a better way. He bade them look within for that strength and support which the shattered framework of effete traditions no longer afforded; and while Plato strove to revive the spirit of the past in schemes which, however Utopian they may seem to us, had more or less of historical foundation in the various forms of polity then or previously current in Greece, Socrates made it his business to persuade his countrymen, in the language of one of his later disciples, "ut id suâ sponte facerent quod cogerentur facere legibus." If Alexander be one of the most illustrious representatives and types of Hellenic civilisation, and such he assuredly is, it is only because he was the instrument by which that civilisation advanced more and more on that ὁδὸς ἄνω which it cost Socrates his life to open out. Greece might now depart from the world's stage: her spirit survived at Alexandria and Antioch. The Greek and the Barbarian had met together on the holy ground of their common humanity. Greece might now depart: she had done all that in her lay to promote the social transformation which it was her mission to impart to the civilisation of antiquity; she had brought out all the excellences of which unassisted humanity was capable; and had whispered tidings of a universal society, of which all the associations of earthly citizenship and nationality were but faint and faithless images.

From a Greek vase.

Bust of Aristotle.
(From the Spada Palace at Rome.)

CHAPTER II.

RELIGION OF THE HELLENES.

Is there a God? Is there remission of sins? If a man die, shall he live again? Such appear to be the principal questions which all religions, covenanted and uncovenanted, have alike attempted to answer. Accordingly, it should seem that the best mode of ascertaining the religious condition of any particular people, would be to ascertain, as far as may be, the nature of the answers thus returned, and the general character of those notions which prevailed among the wise and simple alike, respecting those fundamental elements of religious life which the above inquiries seem to embody. Now when we have to do with worshippers of gods many and lords many, a consideration presents itself *in limine* on which it is of importance to insist. All forms of Polytheism owe their origin to the yearning after some mode of mediating between God and man. The metaphysician indeed in his closet might by searching find out the existence of a Being Infinite, Perfect, and Immutable. But amid these icy abstractions of cold, hard Reason, Religion cannot so much as breathe. In the presence of this impassive creation of Pure Thought, the heart finds all its desires, hopes, fears do but throb with yet greater violence than before. It instinctively demands some other god; it turns chilled and dissatisfied from the Being to whom Reason would fain extort its allegiance. This invincible yearning after a god who should take upon him the nature, so as to be within the reach of the infirmities of man, lies at the bottom of all the religions of antiquity, constitutes the reasonableness of Polytheism, and is one of the strongest witnesses to the truth of Christianity. To speak of the Hellenic mythology as an apotheosis of the powers of nature and the passions of man is a statement which may not be substantially false, but which fails to convey an adequate or accurate idea of the genesis of that as of all mythology. Rather should we style it the idea of the Deity, as seen through the gross medium of the senses, clothed in the garb of nature, and proportioned to the corruptions and weaknesses of the human heart. It is this idea to which we shall endeavour to penetrate in showing how the Greek answered the question—Is there a God? It is in this light we shall regard the Religion as distinguished from the Mythology of Hellas, and shall fix our attention on the *numen divinum* rather than on the individual *dii* in whom it was vested by the fancy of the poets and the feeling of the people.

First, then, as regards the personality of the Deity, the conflict which we have represented as existing between the aspirations of the heart and the abstractions of reason, ended, in the case of Greece, in the complete ascendency of the former. A walk through the British Museum, it has been observed, is sufficient to show us that in this respect a wide gulf separates the Egyptian from the Hellenic faith. "The oppression of huge animal forms, the perplexity of grotesque devices, has passed away." The notion that the gods of Hellas were, as Herodotus and Aristotle term it, *ἀνθρωποφυεῖς* and *ἀνθρωποειδεῖς*, was one which showed itself as palpably in the Homeric poems—the Bible of the Greeks—as in the sculptures which adorned the exterior of their temples, or the *ἄγαλμα* which looked down upon the worshipper within. We meet with repeated evidence at every period of Greek literature and fable, that this association of a divine nature with a human form was often felt to be at variance with the first principles of a superhuman existence. It was left for revealed religion to show how the two could be made to harmonise. But to the Greek the ironical address of the Hebrew seer to the worshippers of Baal would have sounded as sober earnest. The popular view never wholly exempted the Deity from the animal wants and weaknesses of the man. But a way of escape from this difficulty was provided. That last and greatest infirmity of man, the gods of Hellas knew not. Made, created, and begotten they might be, but they were exempt from death—"The Immortals" was their familiar name. It was this which formed the sap and marrow of the divine essence, just as the want of this made so cold and rayless the destiny of man. It was this which in Homeric language made them *πολὺ φέρτεροι* than the "race of mortal men." For along with the immortality came omniscience (*θεοὶ δέ τε πάντα ἴσασιν*) and omnipotence (*θεοὶ δέ τε πάντα δύνανται*), qualities which, however imperfectly adhered to in the facts of legendary lore, were always asserted in theory. But did this omnipotence, in the eyes of the Greek, rise to the height of an orderly moral government of the world? In other words, was the idea which we attach to God's Providence familiar to him? To this inquiry an answer must be returned in the negative. It is of the essence of Providence to be holy, just, and good. These qualities the god of the Greek did not unite. Just indeed he uniformly was, more so than can be predicated of any other attribute which the Greek attached to the idea of the Deity. The human conscience, it should seem, helped to maintain unimpaired the doctrine that the Deity must needs be a punisher of the wrongdoer and the rewarder of them that do well. But it was not thus with holiness and goodness. Malice, envy, and deceit are operating motives which perpetually actuate the conduct of the dwellers on the Homeric Olympus, from which they were never wholly emancipated at a later age; and as regards the goodness or love of God manward, it is of importance to note that while particular individuals may become the objects of that love, and succeed in propitiating the favour of God, man as man is not justified in postulating its existence: such expressions as the love or grace of God, which are familiar to our ears as household words, had nothing correlative to them in the religion of the Greeks. Stray statements in the writings of Philosophers must not mislead us on this head. In the popular apprehension there was nothing spontaneous or initial in the love felt towards man by the Deity. It had to be extorted by supplication: it could not be relied on as an ever present help.

Any general scheme of orderly providential care being thus frustrated in the religion of the Greek by the imperfect notions entertained of divine holiness and the feeble reliance placed on divine goodness, the sense in which the Deity was held to govern the order of nature and the affairs of men was proportionately circumscribed and incapable of being reduced to any general law. Even the fundamental idea of a Creator, that is, of a Being who, by the act of his free will, brought the world and all that is therein into existence, is wholly foreign to the mythology of the Greek. On the other hand, the ordinary phenomena of the natural world were held to reveal a marked personal intervention on the part of the gods to an extent in our eyes as excessive as their influence in the moral world was defective and obscure. For there the conceptions afloat as to the divine agency were extremely confused. That the gods influenced the counsels and conduct of man was admitted: but this influence was in a great measure haphazard, that is, governed by no fixed moral laws, and subservient to no definite moral aim; nay, at times exerted on behalf of unrighteous ends.

Such were the delusions into which the Greek was betrayed by his endeavour to bring down the sublimity of the Divine Being to a level with the infirmities of human nature and a kinship with the waywardness of the human heart.

It should here be observed that the identification already alluded to of the powers and phenomena of nature with divine personalities was alike favourable to the growth of the Hellenic mythology and fatal to that unity of action and of purpose by which monotheism fosters the notion of a Divine Providence. It is beside our purpose to enter into any details as to the names and functions of the particular deities of that mythology. Multitudinous and intricate as these confessedly are, it must not be forgotten that even in the popular mind a visible effort may at times be discerned to lay hold of some monotheistic principle, which is soon, however, abandoned amid the ever present seductions with which their sculptures fed and sustained the polytheistic traditions of the national faith. This groping after some supreme mysterious Μοῖρα ultimately dwindled down, in the decline of all moral and religious life, into the recognition of a blind chance, or Τύχη, as the capricious disposer of events.

Such being the notions entertained by the Greek respecting the nature of the *numen divinum* as a being omnipotent, omniscient, and just, but not, as of necessity, supremely holy or good, we shall not be surprised at finding that his own life should bear visible traces of the deficiencies in his faith. This brings us to consider the aspect in which sin was regarded by the Greek, and the means and hopes of remission which were within his reach. As will readily be inferred from what has been said as to the attributes of the Hellenic god, one of the most powerful incentives to virtue —love to God and love to his fellow man—was lacking to the Greek. The whole life of man, says Plato, needs some harmony and adjustment; and in accordance with this thoroughly Greek sentiment, the whole duty of man, the sum of all human virtues, was comprised in a quality which, when viewed absolutely, was called *σωφροσύνη*, and relatively, *δικαιοσύνη*. In this was embodied all that was good in the moral life of the Greek. It was the bond of all virtues, and, as such, occupied a place analogous to that of Charity in the Christian scheme. It is in the opposite of this *σωφροσύνη* that we must look for the essential characteristic of sin. This the Greek designated as ὕβρις, that foolhardy casting off of all the restraints imposed by the unwritten laws of God, which makes each man a law unto himself (*αὐτὸς αὑτῷ νομοθετεῖ*). That to this ὕβρις human nature was continually exposed, is the almost universal language of the poet and the philosopher alike. Lusts of every kind wooed to transgression. It would be a mistake to suppose that the Greek religion regarded this general proneness to sin as the fruit of any such primeval violation of law as that which we know by the name of the Fall. All traces of such a notion, which have been pointed out in their myths (as in that of Prometheus, for example), are purely fanciful, and unworthy of any serious attention. More important is it to note that the gods themselves were not unfrequently held to instigate men to sin. The overt implications of the Deity in human guilt, which we meet with in Homer, were veiled in later times under the notion that this θεοβλάβεια was intended to work out the punishment of sins already committed. Kindred to this were the functions assigned to the ἀλάστωρ. But whatever was the source from which man was tempted to transgress, on him alone rested the guilt of the transgression. This the Greek forcibly illustrated by projecting, as it were, the inward pangs of conscience into an outward objective personality, chasing and persecuting the sinner as an avenger of wrong. The doctrine of punishment, as embodied in the maxim δράσαντι παθεῖν, witnessed to the same full imputation of personal guilt on the transgressor. Such being the nature of sin, what assurance did the Greek possess of its remission? Sacrifice, indeed, and peace offerings were at his disposal to appease the wrath of heaven; but how far could they avail? In answering this question, we must in the first place put aside the notion peculiar to covenanted religions, that such sacrifices were vicarious. It was only in cases where *one* was made to die in the place of *many*, as in the case of Iphigenia, or where an animal supplied the place of the human victim, that such a conception of sacrifice obtained. And further, when the sacrifice was offered up, and the transgressor purified by washing with blood or water, no assurance of remission was conveyed to his mind — all his acts of worship, all his feelings of contrition, might prove but lost labour: the only thing on which it was not given him to doubt was the determination of the gods to punish; nothing but doubt was left to him as to their willingness to pardon. Thus was the Greek left to misgivings in a matter on which above all things a sure and certain hope must have been the fondest desire of his heart. It was here that the rites of the so-called Orphic mysteries seem to have intervened to supply the kind and degree of satisfaction and peace which the more popular and exoteric forms of faith and worship in the national religion failed to afford. Whatever may have been the character of the lustrations which formed the main ingredient in those rites, their object seems to have been to convey to the initiated a consciousness of being cleansed from the impurities of sin to an extent which could leave no reasonable doubt of their having secured to them the pardon of the gods. It would be idle to speculate on the more or less disingenuous character of these rites, or to deny that they ultimately sank into a vile machinery of religious quackery for the extortion of money from the superstitious. It is sufficient for our purpose to have insisted on the fact that in their original institution (which dates from the first rise of philosophical speculation in Greece) they were intended to supply, and so corroborate, the existence of a void in the religious appliances of the national faith. We shall presently have occasion to remark how other mysteries played a like part in the religious life of the Greeks.

We now come to the concluding inquiry which seems to complete the cycle of ideas by which that religious life was sustained. Is there a Hereafter?

The Greek had a hard fight for it when exposed to the attacks of tribulation and sorrow. Thoroughly sensual, joyous, and light-hearted as he was by temperament, his bark may have glided smoothly enough over the sea of life in the hours of prosperity. But when the winds of adversity lashed that sea into fury, he had no haven for which to steer. That kind of resignation which we are taught to foster, and which is grounded on the assurance that all such inflictions are intended for our good, can have had but little place or influence in the breast of a man who was wont, under such circumstances, to consider himself the victim of a malignant and vindictive deity. The resignation of the Greek was the fruit and expression of his sense of utter helplessness, rather than of a quiet confidence and acquiescence in a Wisdom and Love which human understanding could not fathom.

φέρει μέν, ἀλγεῖ δ' αὐχέν' ἐντιθεὶς ζυγῷ.

We cannot now pause to inquire how far the mysteries of Dionysus and of Samothrace were calculated to rouse their worshippers from the dogged dejection which was inspired by the prevalent notions on the condition of suffering humanity. Those who either failed or never attempted to find in them the means of chasing away their gloom which they were supposed to afford, had only one refuge left; they looked to death as the end of all their woe. But here arose the great question of questions — If a man die, shall he live again? It was this cloud of uncertainty which lowered over the tomb that filled the heart of the Greek with perplexity and dismay. To quote the language of one of his own poets, was he "to quit the darling light of the sun, that he might lie beneath the ground like a voiceless stone?" Such there can be no doubt, in substance and effect, was the joyless nature of the Hereafter which the popular religion of the Greeks held out to its worshippers. Such was the teaching of that great storehouse of popular theology among the Greeks, the Homeric poems. It was only in a narrow and cheerless sense that the condition of the εἴδωλον in the mansions of Hades could be called another (much less a better) life, robbed as it was of everything which gave consciousness, feeling, intelligence, and volition to the first life. Was there no quarter to which the Greek could apply for some more comforting assurance as to his condition hereafter? It is very generally agreed that the Eleusinian mysteries helped to supply the want. The evidence on this point is so cogent that it seems impossible to resist it. In no measured language Pindar and Sophocles vaunt the blessedness of those who have been partakers or spectators of the Eleusinian rites. "To them it is given to know the end of their existence: they only can be said to live when they get to Hades; all others are encompassed with all manner of ills." And if it should be objected that this is the language of poets (an objection thoroughly futile, for among the Greeks the poet held, as it were, the office of a teacher and preacher), the language of prose writers is equally precise. Isocrates, for example, declares that those who partake in the Eleusinian τελετῇ "have more comfortable hopes about the end of life and the whole cycle of their existence." Passages equally strong might be quoted to the same effect. We have not space to inquire, nor perhaps are we provided with sufficient data fully to determine, by what means and artifices these impressions may have been made on the minds of the initiated. The principal point which the student should keep before him seems to be that the Eleusinian as well as the other mysteries already mentioned, were probably indebted for their institution to those ardent yearnings which must have goaded the mind of the Greek to a state bordering on despair when he reflected on those questions to which the voice of the popular religion gave forth answers of uncertain sound—Is there remission of sins? If a man die, shall he live again?

It is needless to observe that in the above sketch of the religious notions which prevailed among the Greeks we have studiously avoided attempting anything more than a sketch of the *popular* religion. To what extent, and after what fashion, the foremost among her thinkers may have raised themselves on the springtide of lofty speculations above the average water line of the popular theology, would be an inquiry which would only throw a false light on the religious state of the Greeks *as a people*. This last it is impossible to consider attentively without recognising its propaedeutic character as a forerunner of Christianity. The long, loud cry for a Deliverer which runs through that religion, the palpable failure which accompanied the efforts of the most enlightened people of heathen antiquity to make man *at one* with his god or with himself, the despair which came over them as they saw what seemed to them the impossibility of that *at-onement* being wrought, —all these may surely be reckoned among the negative evidences of Christianity, and give to classical studies a place and an importance in Christian education of which nothing but narrowness and ignorance could wish to see them deprived.

Group of Physicians and Astronomers.

(From a Mosaic discovered at Sarnus, and now in the Villa Albani. An example of the decline of Art.)

Bust of Homer.

CHAPTER III.

HELLENIC LITERATURE.—POETRY; EPIC, DIDACTIC, LYRIC.

LITERARY history is at one with psychology in showing that in the infancy of society the imagination is the dominant faculty, that at a subsequent stage it is combined with reflection or observation, which in turn take precedence of imagination in the years of declining age. The literature of Greece furnishes a striking illustration of this organic development of the faculties which govern the production of literary works, the rather on account of its undoubted and paramount originality. No extraneous elements worthy of note arrested or diverted its progress. By right of primogeniture, as it were, it is preeminently *the* literature,—a literature which fulfilled all beauty, and laid the stepping-stones by which succeeding eras rose to yet higher things. In tracing the phases through which this literature passed, it will be our object not to lose sight of this organic feature in its development.

The first literary monument we meet with is the Homeric poems. We do not, however, need either the internal evidence of those poems, or the external and traditionary indications given elsewhere, to show us that as there were "many mighty men" before Agamemnon, so were there poets many before Homer, all of whom

> "Ingenio superavit, et omneis
> Restinxit, stellas exortus uti aetherius sol."

If we submit all the evidence, internal and external, to the action of those laws which we are warranted in assuming respecting the early rise of poetical literature in general, and of that of

Greece in particular, it appears to us that the names which figure as types of ante-Homeric minstrelsy may be associated with some such order of ideas as the following.

Poetry is the source or root of all national culture. No people is so utterly sunk in barbarity but what it possesses some vestiges of a popular minstrelsy. Song in some shape or other is heard by the cradle of every people. The infancy of poetry is as the poetry of infancy; it is instinctive, spontaneous, as instinctive as the song of birds; called to life by the first sentiment of admiration, joy, fear, love. The voice of one, echoed by all.

Not a trace of this impulsive poetry is left to us in the literature of Greece. That it existed we cannot doubt. Sacerdotal poetry is the earliest of which the record has been preserved—a class of production which is as much removed above the region of pure art, as popular poetry sinks below it. It traverses the beautiful at a bound, to perch itself on the summit of the sublime. The sacred poetry of the Hebrews, the Vedas of India, and the Zend Avesta of Persia are the most famous extant monuments of this order of poetry. Greece, indeed, has left us no Vedas as specimens of the poetry which prevailed anterior to her Ramâyâna and Mahâbhârata, but the legends which hang about the names of Orpheus and Linus, Musaeus and Eumolpus, are more than sufficient evidence as to its existence. Wherever this sacerdotal poetry is wanting, the art never rises above the first stage of what we have styled the impulsive poetry; witness the Tartar races of northern and central Asia: wherever it reigns in undisputed ascendancy, the progress of literature as an art, as with the Hebrews, is of stunted growth. It is in the equilibrium of these two primeval elements, as in India and Greece, that art and literature attain their normal development.

We are thus landed at the threshold, as it were, of a third period in the life of Poetry, in which the *vox populi* and the *vox Dei* combine to form the voice of the poet proper. A sense of national life and unity strikes root in the heart of the people. They come, as it were, into the fuller and calmer enjoyment of that patrimony of usages, laws, traditions, language, faith, which the more isolated efforts of previous generations had in a long tract of time hoarded up. But great is the effort demanded jealously to keep what has with so much jeopardy been won. The triumph of order over chaos, of good over evil, of mind over matter, has both to be achieved and preserved. To compass this triumph is a sacred mission. The age of mighty men has come. The priest and the prophet must give way to the hero. In his person are combined, to his charge are committed, the twofold elements of the divine and the national life. He goes forth conquering and to conquer. A beneficent vanquisher of baleful foes, he puts hydras and dragons beneath his feet, and wrestles with every form of disorder and of ill. In the track of the hero follows the ἀοιδός, who disseminates on wings of words the memory of valiant deeds. To the jejune minstrelsy of the primitive epoch, to the mystic hymn of the sanctuary, has now succeeded a third phase of poetry more richly endowed with elements of human culture. The ἔπος gathers up in its ample folds every variety of custom and manner which merges into the unity of the national life. Clothed in the same form, animated by the same spirit, and converging towards the same end, these multitudinous indeed, but homogeneous ἔπη fall, as it were, into wholes, swell into Epopees, and glide as tributary streams into the deep bed of song from which ages of heroes quench their thirst. The epic ἀοιδός has thus supplanted the sacerdotal ἀοιδός. What had formerly been recounted of the gods by way of symbol is now taken in its literal acceptation and converted into a myth. With myths is the whole religious life of the Greek in this fashion overspread. In this sense were Homer and Hesiod declared by Herodotus to be "the makers of the Greek Theogony."

It is of great importance that the student should keep steadily in view these successive phases of the primitive poetry of Greece, and the peculiar genesis of the Epic proper, before he proceeds to entangle himself in the question of the authorship and history of the Homeric poems. Any amount of conviction at which he may arrive by acquiescence in the arguments of those who maintain, in opposition to Wolf's *Prolegomena* (1795), the unity of authorship of the Iliad and Odyssey by a man called Homer, will be dearly bought if it should involve the obliteration from his mind of those peculiar features which distinguish the two great Epopees of Greece from those of modern Europe. If the Iliad and Odyssey are the creations of the man Homer, Homer himself is the creation of his age. It is so difficult for us to divest ourselves of the notions which attach to a *written* literature, that we are apt to bring them with us to the consideration of a literature which did not, till a late age, cast off the characteristics which marked its early prime—when it addressed itself to the ear, not to the eye; was said or sung, not conned or read. We may not perhaps go so far as the quaint old biographer, who accounted for Homer's reputed blindness by the labour it must have cost him to write out his poems; but on the other hand we do not adequately realise the power of the living ἔπος or word, leaping from lip to lip, giving utterance to all the feelings, fancies, and fictions which lived quivering in the hearts and imagination of a whole people, making the past present, and the distant nigh, touching everything in its passage, and adorning everything it touched. That the Homeric poems (independently of any question of authorship) were not originally committed to writing, seems to be the only fair conclusion: (1.) from the internal evidence afforded by the poems; (2.) from the traditions of antiquity; and (3.) from the history of Greek writing. That some kind of figurative signs were in use as a rude method of thought-picturing, seems evident from the well-known affair of Bellerophon, and from the lots drawn by the Achaean warriors as to who should pit himself against Hector. But, on the other hand, the absence of any allusion to written truce, treaty, or transaction, or to any inscription on tomb or temple (the memory of the dead being preserved by a block or an oar placed over the grave); the curious designation or eulogy affixed to a navigator in the Odyssey as *φόρτου μνήμων* *, and which a scholiast interprets as significative of the absence in those days of *any* means of keeping a written invoice; all these, to mention but a few, have been considered serious stumbling-blocks in the way of the Homeric poems having been originally committed to writing.

Secondly, the tradition which Josephus speaks of as having been the generally received opinion in his time, that these poems were first promulgated orally, is corroborated by the story which associates the name of Peisistratus with the first collection of those poems into their present shape. It is not, indeed, now very generally believed that they were first committed to writing, integrally, by the orders of the Athenian ruler: written copies of particular portions may have existed in different parts of Greece; but it is justly contended that the nature of the task, and the amount of glory which tradition assigns to him, are incompatible with the fact of the poems having been otherwise than orally transmitted from the first. The question has therefore been fairly urged, "If in the sixth century before our era there were to be found none but rude and fragmentary copies of the Iliad and Odyssey, is it credible that three centuries earlier (the date ordinarily assigned to Homer) there should have been even these?

Thirdly, the study of Greek palaeography confirms us in the impressions which internal evidence and external traditions produce on our minds. When we look at the characters on the oldest known inscriptions, which range between the fortieth and forty-eighth Olympiads, it is impossible to believe that more than a century earlier they could have been used to indite thousands of verses.

Again, it is a remark as old as Athenaeus that the Homeric poems, in their metrical structure, bear evident marks of having been originally intended for oral recitation. Examples will readily suggest themselves to the most superficial reader of the Iliad and Odyssey.

* viii. 163.

The views which have here been insisted on, as to the characteristics of the primitive Greek epic, are confirmed and illustrated by the great mass of similar poems which fall under the head of the Epic Cycle, so called from the endeavour of their authors to connect their poems with those of Homer, so that the whole should form one great cycle. In fact, the bond of connection thus established with the Homeric poems, as a central point, led to the practice of confounding the whole mass under the name of Homer. Each of these Cyclic poems, however, is assigned, in more accurate accounts, to particular authors who lived considerably later than Homer. First among these may be mentioned Stasinus, whose "Cyprian Songs" were a long prologue to the Iliad. For this purpose he went back to the birth of Helen; and it is not improbable that Horace, in a well-known passage *, alludes to Stasinus. Arctinus continued the Iliad, in the *Sack of Troy* and the *Aethiopis*. The latter commenced with the arrival of the Amazons at Troy, immediately after Hector's death. Among other events related was the death of Penthesilea, a scene repeatedly portrayed in Greek sculpture. Among other Cyclic poems may be mentioned the *Little Iliad* of Lesches, the *Nosti* of Agias, the *Telegonia* of Eugamon, together with others only indirectly connected with the Trojan war, such as the *Thebaid*, *Epigoni*, *Heracleid*, *Capture of Oechalia*, and others. They are chiefly important, for our present purpose, as witnessing to the strong hold which epic poetry had on the life of the Greeks, and as furnishing a huge body of mythical story which in a later age fed the drama of Hellas. The whole subject is one which Welcker has exhausted in his *Epischer Cyclus*, to which we cannot do better than refer the student.

Just as the name of Homer may in a sense be regarded both as personal and as eponymous, and Homer himself as the type of that phase of epic poetry which found its development in Asiatic Greece, so is Hesiod, in the second of the two poles of early epic poetry, at once the chief and representative of the Epopee of European Greece. The northern provinces of Greece, more especially Boeotia and Euboea, formed the theatre on which the school of Hesiod flourished. We shall assign it a date either anterior or posterior to that of Homer, according as we happen at the time to have the *Theogony* or the *Works and Days* before us. In the one, Hesiod may be considered as having caught his inspiration from the half-spent echoes of the sacred poetry which marked, as we have said, the second phase in the literary development of Hellas. In this sense he is undoubtedly anterior to Homer. In the other, he is the poet

* Ad Pis. p. 147.

of a social state of riper growth than that which is presented to us in the Iliad and Odyssey. He is evidently much further removed from the age of the Hero, much nearer to the normal status of civil life. We see at a glance that the quasi-feudal monarchies have passed away, that the heroic age is henceforth a thing of the past. Hesiod, it has been well remarked, was a poet of the people and peasantry rather than of the ruling nobles. The strongest indication of his belonging to a later age than Homer, resides in the visible increase of subjectivity observable in the poems which bear his name. And along with this increased subjectivity, we find, as might be expected, a didactic tone, which makes the *Works and Days* a type of the didactic poetry of Greece. Both these poems, in the opinion of the best scholars, are much interpolated. Other poems passed current among some of the ancients as genuine Hesiodic productions. Such are the *Eoiae*, the *Shield of Heracles*, and others. The doubts which rest over the authenticity of portions at least of the two larger poems, apply with still greater force to the whole of the other so-called Hesiodic productions.

This sketch of the epic poetry of Greece would be yet more incomplete than it now confessedly is, if we did not take note of the attempted revival of the epic spirit in the decline, or Alexandrian age, of Greek literature. Equally destitute of imagination, invention, or taste, the poets of that era seem to have thought that, by reviving the obsolete forms of early epic poetry, they could at the same time recall the spirit by which that poetry had been animated. The works of Lycophron, Apollonius Rhodius, and we may add Callimachus, are equally destitute of sap and savour when compared with their great prototypes. These coryphaei of Alexandrian poetry do but enable us to span the gulf which separates the pedant from the poet, art from artifice, the man of letters from the man of genius.

Epic poetry is the utterance of the infancy of a nation. It always looks out of itself; is marked by an absence of self-consciousness; is objective, not subjective. In Hesiod we have already had occasion to note a visible declension from those peculiar characteristics which distinguish the Epopee proper; a gradual assumption of those features which are peculiar to the poetry of a nation's youth. For it is of the essence of youth to abound in self-consciousness, to turn its gaze within, to ponder on the mysteries of its being; in a word, to be subjective. So that if epic poetry belongs to the infancy, lyric poetry belongs to the youth of a nation. The two centuries which elapse between the Homeric and the Hesiodic age, and the first appearance of lyric poetry, constitute a void in the history of Greek literature. It was an age of transition in which political convulsions were working out a complete change in the social state of the nation. Out of the ferment of these popular turmoils (which again find their analogy in the development of youthful passions) arose the new cast of thought and order of feeling which found their expression in lyric poetry. This poetry takes different forms of utterance according to the difference which prevails among the multitudinous feelings by which it is inspired. At one time it was a hymn in honour of a god, at another a lampoon in abuse of a foe; at one time it was attuned to martial strains, at another it whispered notes of sorrow, of wisdom, or of love.

But this character of introversion or subjectivity is not the only principle which separates lyric from epic song. The latter buried itself in the past; the former busies itself with the present: that present it reflects in the mirror of its innermost thoughts, and the impressions thus conveyed are either poured forth in the easy flow of elegiac distich, or the angry tide of strophic metre. The origin of this lyric poetry is so closely connected with the organization of republican institutions throughout Greece, that it may be regarded in nearly equal portions as their source and their fruit. The incessant vicissitudes through which Hellenic constitutions passed, kept alive a flame of animosity and a passion for liberty, which formed the principal aliment of lyric song. At one time the poet gave himself up to the passion of the hour, at another he exhorted to constancy and endurance; at one time he launched his lampoons against crimes which had been gilded by success; in another and more frolicsome mood he urged mankind to pluck the roses of life ere they withered. And as amid these public disasters were mingled private griefs, more plaintive notes were heard amid the martial and civic strains. All these causes, which thus fostered the development of lyric poetry, received fresh impulse from the accompaniments of music and song which among the Greeks beguiled all public solemnities, and games, and private festivals; and this close and constant union of music and of song imparted a peculiar character to the various branches of lyric poetry which we meet with under the denominations of iambic, elegiac, melic, and dithyrambic poetry.

This sketch of the general character and origin of lyric poetry must now be followed by a brief enumeration of the principal individuals who exercised the craft.

The Homer of lyric poetry is Archilochus, who flourished about B.C. 700. In the bitterness of satiric iambic poetry he reigned supreme.

"Archilochum proprio rabies armavit iambo."

To the license of the democratic spirit which was then spreading through Greece, was added a sense of private resentment at having been refused the hand of a daughter of one Lycambes. So ferocious was the malignity his verses displayed, that the girl and her sisters are said to have been goaded to suicide; so that the ancients spoke of Archilochus as having been the first to put arms in the hands of the Muses, and to stain Helicon with blood. Powers of the highest order seem, however, to have accompanied this excessive bitterness; and it may safely be asserted that the loss of his poems is one of the most severe which the literature of Greece has sustained. Just as the Homeric poems are the highest embodiment of objective song, so may we believe that the verses of Archilochus constituted an outburst of acutely intense subjective personal feeling, the like of which no other monument of Greek literature can supply. As in the case of Lord Byron, the whole man seems to have unbosomed himself in his verse. This estimate of the great merits of Archilochus is fully borne out by the verdict of the ancients. An epigram ascribed to Theocritus speaks of his "countless glory spreading from east to west;" another, of the Emperor Hadrian's, relates how the Muses, fearful for Homer's renown, inspired Archilochus with the idea of iambic in lieu of heroic verse; while Cicero places him on a level with Homer, Sophocles, and Pindar, and Horace boasts of having reproduced in his epodes the "numeros animosque" of Archilochus. The efforts of this poet, however, were not confined to iambic verse. Elegiac and trochaic metre enter largely into the fragments which have come down to us. Martial, plaintive, and amorous songs seem to have been handled by him with equal success. He shares with Alcaeus and Horace the questionable moiety of valour, in the fact of his having in a battle thrown away his shield to run for his life, and the still more questionable candour of parading his shame in self-complacent triumph.

Along with Archilochus may be mentioned his contemporary, Simonides, called by turns Simonides of Amorgos, or Simonides the Iambographer, to distinguish him from his more famous successor in melic poetry, Simonides of Ceos. As Archilochus led a colony from Paros to Thasos, so did Simonides from Samos to Amorgos. As Archilochus had his Lycambes, so had Simonides his Orodecides. A considerable fragment of his satiric poetry has come down to us under the title of Περὶ Γυναικῶν. Women are there ranged, according to their characters, under certain fontal types from which they are severally assumed to derive their origin. These types are as follows:—the swine, the fox, the dog, clay, the sea, the ass, the weasel, the mare, the ape, the bee. This poem is one of the most remarkable manifestations of that deplorable estimate of the female sex which was one of the vilest features of Greek civilisation.

Hipponax, who flourished about B.C. 540, and who was compelled to quit his native city Ephesus for Clazomenae, forms the third of those poets whose fame is chiefly built on their iambic verse. This metre underwent a modification in his hands — the substitution of a spondee for a pure iambus in the last foot — which gave rise to the so-called choliambic or scazon trimetre. Bupalus and Athenis, two Chian sculptors, became the objects of his bitterest invectives, for having caricatured his person. He also spent his fury with indomitable energy against the depraved and frivolous tastes of the Greeks of Asia Minor. He so excelled in parody as to acquire the title of its inventor. Theocritus wrote on him the following epigram: "Here lies Hipponax, bard to the Muses dear. If thou art a vile knave, come not nigh his tomb. But if thou art a good man and a true, be not faint of heart, but sit thee down, and, if it so please thee, go sound asleep." Leonidas, of Tarentum, on the other hand, bids men beware lest they awake the slumbering wasp; and another epigrammatist says that his very ashes keep *iambizing* against Bupalus.

The ancients were in the habit of attributing to Callinus, of Ephesus, a somewhat elder contemporary of Archilochus, the invention of elegiac verse. The martial sentiments which pervade his remains have led to the conjecture that this metre was originally confined to war-songs, and only took the name of elegy when used as a vehicle for sentiments of a plaintive character. It seems, however, that the elegiac distich was originally designed as an adaptation of the old dactylic metre to epigrammatic purposes, such as epitaphs and the like*, and was subsequently used indiscriminately either for martial, patriotic, or mournful strains, as occasion required. The fragments of Callinus are exclusively of the former character. The "dulce et decorum est pro patria mori" of Horace (which is almost a literal rendering of the Greek τιμῆέν τε γάρ ἐστι καὶ ἀγλαὸν ἀνδρὶ μάχεσθαι γῆς πέρι κ. τ. λ.) is, throughout, the burden of the poet's song. The particular aggression against which Callinus thus sounds the note of alarm was that of the Cimmerians and Treres.

The elegies of Tyrtaeus, who flourished B. C. 680—660, are of a like tenor with those of Callinus. During the second Messenian war (B. C. 685) the Spartans applied to the Athenians — so runs the legend — for a leader. In derision the Athenians sent a lame schoolmaster, Tyrtaeus by name. Not only did his spirited verse lead the Spartans to victory, but his wise counsels saved them from internal social disorders. He thenceforth became Sparta's adopted son. Three of his war-elegies have come down to us, as well as a few anapaestic verses of a war-march. The pomp and circum-

* Mure's *History of Greek Literature*, vol. III. p. 16.

stance of war are set forth with great power; the baseness of a craven nature is denounced with spirit-stirring vehemence. The perusal of these elegies, or fragments of elegies, seems to justify the fame which Tyrtaeus enjoyed among the ancients. We have also a fragment of a social or political elegy, called *Εὐνομία*, in which the Spartan constitution appears to have been extolled with a view to arrest the designs of agrarian agitators.

The name of Mimnermus is associated with elegiac poetry of a half-voluptuous, half-plaintive, character. A native of Smyrna at the close of the seventh century, he was deprived, along with his independence, of everything which could feed noble thoughts and sustain manly purposes. To grovel in the pursuit of sensual pleasures, or to look back with impotent sighs at the past, was all that was left him to do. Such was the position of Mimnermus, and such is the character of his verse. The fragments which remain betray a mind zealous for nothing, and a body wasted with indolence and debauchery. In passing from Tyrtaeus to Mimnermus, we abandon the invigorating breeze of the downs for the fetid, sickening atmosphere of a hot-house.

The great renown of Solon as a legislator seems to have operated prejudicially on his fame as a poet, which might otherwise have placed him abreast of an Archilochus or a Tyrtaeus. Such, at least, appears to have been the merit of his famous Salaminian elegy, in which he roused the Athenians not to submit to the annexation of Salamis by the Megarians. His other poetical achievements were of that mixed moral and political character which belongs to the so-called Gnomic poetry. Of this class, in particular, were the elegies of Theognis of Megara, who flourished in the last half of the sixth century. He had been the victim of the revolutionary anarchy which followed the overthrow of Theagenes at Megara. Thus deprived of his ancestral acres, the exiled Theognis delivers himself of querulous invectives against the democratic party. *Ἀγαθοί* and *ἐσθλοί* become in his hands convertible terms for "nobles," *κακοί* and *δειλοί* for "the commons." Alongside of these atrabilious political verses we meet with passages of a moral and others, again, of a convivial tenor. The order and authenticity of the fragments of Theognis (consisting of nearly 1400 verses) was one of the most vexed questions in Greek literature, till Welcker set himself to its solution with his wonted acumen and erudition.

The two branches of poetry — iambic and elegiac — we have hitherto passed under review, since we quitted the epic, may be called Epico-lyric, as distinguished from purely *melic* poetry. This we now proceed to consider. And here the intimate connection which existed in Greece between music and song induces us, *in limine*, to place the name of Terpander, the father of Greek music, inasmuch as he reduced to a system the musical "styles" prevalent in his day (B.C. 676), and substituted the *heptachord*, or seven-stringed cithara, for the older *tetrachord*. It is beside our purpose to enter either into the details of the musical improvements of Terpander, or into those of his successors Olympus and Thaletas: we merely make use of his name as a symbol of that close bond between music and lyric poetry, which the student should keep stedfastly in view.

Lyric poetry proper divides itself into two schools, the Aeolic and the Doric. Chief among the former stand Alcaeus and Sappho, whose names are connected together in literature, just as we see them represented together on a terracotta in the British Museum, where we may conceive Alcaeus to be addressing Sappho in the words extant among his fragments, "Something would I fain say, but shame prevents." Alcaeus belonged to a noble family of Mitylene, in Lesbos. He took an active, not to say a bitter, part in the revolutions and counter-revolutions of his native city; and in his conduct and vituperations towards Pittacus, a clement and patriotic ruler, proved himself destitute alike of good sense and good feeling. His erotic and convivial poetry betray as complete an absence of all moral earnestness as his public career and political pasquinades. He was the inventor of the metre which bears his name. Horace was notoriously under the greatest obligations to Alcaeus both for the form and matter of a considerable number of his odes, such as Carm. i. 9. 10. 14. 18. 37. Alcaeus flourished about 611 B.C.

To the same period belongs his fellow-citizen, "the burning Sappho." Considerable interest attaches to the works of this illustrious poetess, from the circumstance of her having been the victim of certain gross calumnies at the hands of the Attic comic poets, who were either unable or unwilling to give to the ardent language of her poems a construction different from what their own coarse natures and debauched lives would *primâ facie* attach to it. For the subversion of these calumnies the world is indebted to Professor Welcker, whose arguments have met with the assent of the most eminent scholars. The kind of poetry in which Sappho particularly excelled was the nuptial ode, or Epithalamium. All the fragments that have come down to us fully justify the fervid enthusiasm which was lavished upon this extraordinary woman both by Greeks and Romans. Among the latter, Horace and Catullus have borrowed largely from her poems.

Plato's description of a poet, as a "light and winged thing," applies with peculiar force to Anacreon. This poet was born at Teos, in Asia Minor, about the year 560 B.C., but spent the greater part of his life at Samos under the patronage of Polycrates, and at Athens under that of the Peisistratidae, returning at its close to his native city. A few fragments only have been preserved — all the so-called Anacreontic odes being spurious productions of the Alexandrian or yet later ages. As fugitive pieces, both the genuine and the spurious poems have a considerable amount of prettiness, which scarcely redeems the rank voluptuousness which must have festered in the bosoms of their composers.

We now come to the more strictly choral lyric poetry of the Greeks. Alcman was a younger contemporary of Terpander, and seems to have contributed largely to the maturity of the Doric choral song. Most of his odes were adapted for choruses of young girls (Parthenia), and had both an erotic and a religious tendency, as occasion required. One of his fragments contains a fine description of night: "Now sleep the mountain crests, the gorges sleep, ravines and headlands; sleep too the leaves and all the footed things who get them nurture from the sable earth; the beasts that range the hills, the race of bees, monsters that make sea's purple depths their lair, and all the feathered tribes with drooping wings."

Arion is spoken of as a pupil of Alcman's. It is difficult to discern fact from fable in the stories which hang about his name. This much seems certain, that he introduced great improvements in the arrangement, composition, and execution of the dithyramb, and may thus be said to have hastened the development of those germs which ultimately bore fruit in the Greek drama.

The strongly marked choral character of the lyric poetry now under consideration is forcibly illustrated in the person of Tisias, more generally known as Stesichorus, or "leader of choruses." He broke the monotonous alternation of strophe and antistrophe by the introduction of the epode. His poetry dealt with the past more than with the present, and with outward events more than with inward feelings. It is on this ground that Quintilian speaks of him as "epici carminis onera lyra sustinentem." He was born at Himera about the year 640 B.C. Plato relates that Stesichorus was punished with blindness for his strictures on the character of Helen. The wrath of the deified heroine was appeased, and the poet's sight regained, by the famous Palinode in which Stesichorus made out that the Helen who had gazed from the walls of Troy at the battle below was a mere phantom or εἴδωλον.

We are anxious to hasten on to Pindar, the only great lyric poet whose extant works are other than fragments. We cannot, however, pass over in silence the names of Simonides of Ceos, and his nephew Bacchylides. The most considerable fragment of Simonides (B.C. 556—468) is interwoven in the *Protagoras* of Plato, where it furnishes a theme for a somewhat intricate discussion on the communicability of virtue. Simonides was the first to give a definite form to the Epinician ode, in which his rival Pindar so greatly excelled. With Simonides the particular victory celebrated was in a stricter sense the text, with Pindar it was more the pretext, of his song. No lyric poet seems to have been as prolific as Simonides. He gained fifty-six oxen and tripods in the poetical contests at public festivals. These poems on state occasions formed but a small item in his entire works. Among his fragments we possess an exquisite ode in which Danaë bewails the fortunes of herself and child as they float at the mercy of the waves. Bacchylides, who lived with his uncle at the court of Hiero (where the favour enjoyed by both seems to have given great umbrage to Pindar), supplied by elaborate finish the absence of that lyric spontaneity which gave so much brilliancy to the productions of Simonides. Many of his poems seem to have been of a lighter cast than the Epinician odes or pathetic threnes of his uncle. He lacked that close moral observation with which Simonides penetrated below the surface of life.

The sensual character of Ionian lyric poetry, the pathos of the Aeolic, formed a marked contrast with the calmness and gravity of the Doric style, which finds its highest development in the poems of Pindar. The most conspicuous feature of Doric lyric poetry is the prominence given to the choral element. This of itself implies that the subjective feature, characteristic of lyric poetry, is here kept somewhat in the background. Pindar was born in the vicinity of Thebes in the year 522 B.C. Of all the poems enumerated by Horace in a famous ode (iv. 2.), of all the Hymns, Paeans, Dithyrambs, Prosodia, Parthenia, Hyporchemata, Scolia, and Threni, nothing but shreds and fragments remain. But to compensate in some sort for this loss we have his Epinician, or triumphal odes, which have come down to us entire. They celebrate the glory of victors at the four great public games of Hellas, festivals which fostered by the arts of peace that sense of unity and nationality which in war had found its strongest expressions beneath the walls of Troy and on the plain of Marathon. It is impossible duly to understand these odes without being thoroughly possessed with the important part which these games played in the life of the Greeks, how they shaped their habits of thought, and moulded their forms of faith. They were essentially religious rites; and to this must be attributed not merely the lavish admixture of mythological elements and episodes in the Pindaric Epinicia, but also the grave sublimity and earnestness of tone which is preserved throughout. No monument of Greek literature is so strongly impressed with sober religious awe. Never were so many daring efforts of imagination, so much passionate feeling, put forth in a form so calm, simple, and subdued. A very common idea of a so-called Pindaric ode is that which represents the poet as riding a kind of steeplechase upon Pegasus, and so scampering to the end of the ode with all possible despatch and confusion. Nothing could give a falser notion of the Odes of Pindar. The rich variety of the topics embraced and the thoughts enunciated in any particular ode, is only to be matched by the unity which underlies them all, and the cunning texture with which they are woven together. More important than all is the twofold relation the odes of Pindar bear to the epopee and the drama respectively: to the one, by their intermixture of mythology and history; to the other, by the alternations of chorus and dance which accompanied their recital. We shall find this consideration of value in the history of the dramatic literature of Greece.

Female swinging.

(From a painted vase: The death of Phaedra was poetically expressed in this manner)

Scene from a Greek Comedy.

CHAPTER IV.

LITERATURE.—DRAMATIC POETRY.

The literature of Greece has hitherto been, as it were, sporadic. In lyric and epic poetry her islands and colonies bore a large part in the literary culture of the mother country. We now arrive at a period and a phase in the history of literature which brings to a focus the scattered rays of intellectual light. For just as Athens, in the exercise of her political supremacy, united the energies both of the mother country and of the colonies, of the Doric and of the Ionic elements, so in the Drama (essentially the literature of Athens) she fused into one the two classes of poetry — epic and lyric — which have been considered in the previous chapter. In no respect is the organic development of Greek literature more strongly manifested than in this origin of the Greek drama. For that branch of poetry seems to have assimilated all the characteristics of every previous phase of song. By virtue of its origin it was essentially a religious rite, and so manifested a kinship with the poetry of the sacerdotal age. The themes it embraced were notoriously gathered from the time-honoured traditions of the age of heroes which were embodied in the great cycle of epic poetry. In its form and structure, on the other hand, it is needless to insist on its vast obligations to lyric song. Nor is this all. Every reader of Homer will have remarked that whenever that poet indulges in a comic vein it is principally, if not exclusively, at the expense of the dwellers of Olympus. This side, as it were, of epic poetry was seized hold of by the Greek comedy. So that the epopee may be said to have fallen into two parts, each of which, with the aid of the lyric art, gave rise to tragedy and comedy. These we shall now proceed to consider in order.

The worship of the Greeks, whether in the mysteries or in its more exoteric character, abounded in dramatic elements. That, however, which was paid to Dionysus was pre-eminently calculated to give birth to the drama, and particularly to tragedy. The *ecstasy* manifested by the worshipper in his almost frantic sympathy with the "sorrows of Dionysus," contributed, as its name implies, to strengthen that desire to get out of self which lies at the bottom of the drama. The word tragedy, or goat song, originally referred to the choral performances of the Dionysiac worshippers, as they danced in a ring round an altar on which a goat was being sacrificed. This choral performance, or dithyramb, was the germ from which the drama arose; and the lyric element thus formed, in times of the fullest maturity, an essential feature of the best productions of the art. It was only at Athens, however, that this germ attained development—so that, although the invention of tragedy belongs confessedly to the Dorians, its perfection was the work of the Athenians. It is easy to understand how the choral performers of the dithyramb, in recounting the sorrows of Dionysus, should arrive, by the excess of their sympathy, at a degree of impersonation closely bordering on a scenic representation. The first step, however, into the regions of tragedy proper was effected by an innovation of Thespis (a contemporary of Solon), who introduced an actor who, by way of episode, interrupted the choral song by monologues, either in answer (ὑποκρίτης) to the remarks of the chorus, or for expressing his own reflections, or to provoke the chorus to fresh bursts of song. Some conception of the Thespian tragedy, as far as form is concerned, may be gathered from the Ἱκέτιδες of Aeschylus, where, with the exception of one dialogue, there is never more than one actor at a time with the daughters of Danaus who compose the Chorus. Thespis was succeeded by Phrynichus, the first who introduced female characters upon the stage. A story is related concerning him by Herodotus, which throws a strong light upon the ideal character which only abandoned the Greek drama in time of decay. He brought upon the stage the capture of Miletus (B. C. 498), an ally and colony of Athens, by the Persians; the drama moved the spectators to tears, but the poet was sentenced by the people to a heavy fine for having reminded them of their own misfortunes (ὡς ἀναμνήσαντα οἰκήϊα κακά). The Greeks never forgot that the "chief end," as of all art, so of poetry, the art of arts, was "to raise the thoughts and soothe the cares of man"—to take men out of themselves, to mould the heart to its own high purposes by placing it amid the associations of an ideal humanity.

So that, just as in their plastic art strictly historical battles were never represented as such, but were symbolised under the type or figure of some event in the legendary age which was thus supposed to cast its shadow before, and prefigure the particular battle with which the sculptor was engaged, so also, in their drama, the few occasions in which the plot of their tragedies was taken from contemporary history (and yet what a mine of such plots is given us in the third book of Thucydides!) do but constitute exceptions which confirm the stringency of the rule. Cleon, indeed, might reproach the Athenians with their incurious disregard of what was going on before their eyes (*ζητοῦντές τι ἄλλο τι, ὡς εἰπεῖν, ἢ ἐν οἷς ζῶμεν, φρονοῦντές τε οὐδὲ περὶ τῶν παρόντων ἱκανῶς*); but to this aptitude for living in a world without and above, we are indebted for all those treasures of ideal beauty which are the pride and joy of the whole earth. As tragedy came to be occupied with fables distinct from those of Dionysus, these last continued to be cultivated in a distinct form, under the title of the Satyric drama, which was thus separated from tragedy. This separation is associated with the names of Choerilus and Pratinas, the latter of whom Aeschylus found in possession of public favour, while the former extended his poetical career down to the time of Sophocles. The satyric drama was not a comedy, but a *παίζουσα τραγῳδία*; "and for the most part three tragedies and one satyric drama at the conclusion were represented together, forming a connected whole." The *Cyclops* of Euripides is the only extant specimen of the satyric drama.

Mask, with wig and bonnet.

(From a tragic scene at Pompeii.)

Under the auspices of Aeschylus (B.C. 525—456) tragedy throve apace, and passed from a feeble infancy to a vigorous youth. "He it was," says Aristotle, "who first raised the number of actors to two, abridged the functions of the chorus, and instituted the part of Protagonist,"—that is, introduced a central personage, towards whom all the sympathies of the audience and the sufferings of the plot may be said to converge.* The abridgment of the functions of the chorus, spoken of by Aristotle, must not be taken as implying that the chorus was a mere windfall of the Dionysiac worship, retained from an obsequious compliance with the traditions of the drama, but having no essential connection with the organic structure of the Greek tragedy. This is a notion which modern associations with the idea of a play are apt to foster, but which is utterly at variance with the idea of the classical drama. The chorus is the characteristic of an age in which the moral law is not yet reduced to a fixed code, or fenced around with the higher barriers of religious ordinances. In those struggles and collisions between the moral liberty of man and the necessities imposed by an overruling destiny, about which, as on a pivot, the classical drama may be said to revolve, it was the part of the chorus to execute the functions of arbiter, and to vindicate the workings of the moral law apart from the passions and interests by which individuals might be animated. The chorus, as Schlegel well expresses it, was the idealised spectators; that is, it conveyed to the actual spectator a lyrical and musical expression of his own emotions. Or, as Hegel still more beautifully expresses it, it was a kind of moral and spiritual scenery which brought out into due relief and colour the words, thoughts, and actions of the *dramatis personae*. So essentially, in fact, was the chorus a vital element of the Greek drama, that the decline of tragedy was then most plainly visible, when it ceased to form an integral part of the whole, and sunk into a mere adventitious ornament or accompaniment of the more strictly dramatic element of the play.

Out of the seventy plays and upwards composed by Aeschylus, only seven have come down to us. Of these the *Oresteia*, or trilogy, consisting of the Agamemnon, Choephorae, and Eumenides, is, along with the Homeric poems, the greatest monument of poetry which Greece has handed down to us. When Sophocles declared "that Aeschylus did right without knowing it," he did but witness to the unconsciousness of genius with which that φρενοτέκτων ἀνήρ, as Aristophanes styles him, wrought out his sublime creations. His compact and serried diction (ῥήματα γομφοπαγῆ), not plucked in very wantonness from the flowery surface, but torn up root and all (λόγοι αὐτόπρεμνοι) from the deep-dug soil of thought, is an evidence—so at least declared Aristophanes—of the facile power with which Aeschylus clothed in burning words the majestic conceptions of his mind. "Sublimis et gravis

* Müller's *Greek Literature*, p. 306.

et grandiloquus saepe usque ad vitium"* Aeschylus towers so high above the low level of everyday life, that it is difficult to feel at home in that atmosphere of thought which to him seems as natural and as normal as the outer air. As we behold him unfolding, in the Prometheus, the Titanic mysteries of primeval worlds, or in the Oresteia following the track of that *protarchal* curse which defiled the hearth and bed of a kingly race, we feel that this morning star of the Greek drama is as yet encompassed with the clouds and darkness of Night.

These were dispelled at the approach of Sophocles (495—406 B.C.), of whom Schlegel has well remarked, that any man who is thoroughly imbued with the beauties of Sophocles, may rest assured that he has mastered the spirit of Hellenic art. Whether in the coordination of details, or the general effect of the whole,—whether in the moral dignity of the thoughts, or the suavity of the diction,—this Attic bee, as the ancients styled him, approaches as nearly to perfection as it is possible for man to conceive. In audacity of conception, and the intrinsic grandeur of the themes embraced, he does not, like Aeschylus, dazzle and bewilder; but his matchless grace and moral loveliness cast a charm over his verse which Aeschylus would not stoop to conquer. His heroes have not, so to speak, the saurian dimensions of the Titan world in which the lofty cothurn of Aeschylus paces sublime; but it is precisely because we feel that they are not far from any one of us, that we are prepared to yield to them our fuller, deeper sympathies. There is nothing which affords a better illustration of the relative position of the Greek dramatists, than the parallel march of Greek sculpture. The personages in Sophocles are to those of Aeschylus what the sculptures of Pheidias and Polycleitus are to the Aeginetan marbles. In fact, familiarity with the purest productions of Greek sculpture is one of the best clues to the right appreciation of the genius of Sophocles. And just as sculpture occupies in plastic art the same place that the epic holds in poetry, the plastic forms of the Sophoclean characters led the ancients to remark that Homer was an epic Sophocles, and Sophocles the tragic Homer. In nothing does Sophocles more strongly exhibit the extreme fecundity of his resources, than in the great simplicity of his plots. In the alternations of thought and purpose by which a man is swayed to and fro when placed in circumstances of tragical moment, in the development of character which these successive fluctuations work out, Sophocles found elements of interest for which the intricate combinations of dramatic incidents are but feeble makeweights. With regard to the

* Quint. x. 1. 66.

diction of Sophocles, Müller has shrewdly remarked, that much of the obscurity and pregnancy of his expressions arises from the fact that he uses words according to their derivation rather than according to their actual use, and so makes them imply something which people in general would not expect to find in them. With regard to the outward improvements which he introduced into the drama, must be mentioned the addition of a third actor, the fixing of the number of *Choreutae* at fifteen, and the abandonment of the trilogy, so far as that term implied the development of one and the same plot throughout the three plays. Those of the Sophoclean trilogy were each of them complete in itself. Out of 130 plays which he is said to have composed, seven remain, which were brought out in the following order: *Antigone*, *Electra*, *Trachiniae*, *Oedipus Tyrannus*, *Ajax*, *Philoctetes*, *Oedipus at Colonus*.

The name of Euripides (486—406) ushers in the decline of the Greek drama. There appear to have been circumstances in his private life and social status which were calculated to foster the more unfavourable tendencies of his art. He was not, like Aeschylus, the hero of Marathon and Salamis, who beguiled his leisure with dramatic composition; he was not, like Sophocles, the high-born Eupatride, fitted by position to take the lead in the religious rites of the Dionysiac festivals: he was a man of low origin, not always scrupulous in the arts by which he enlisted on his side the passions of the public, and of whom it might be said, in the language of Seneca, "ad famam ingenii confitentibus magis hominibus quam volentibus pervenerat." Nor is this all. The period at which he flourished coincided with the loosening asunder of those traditionary bonds of an uncodified σωφροσύνη, by which Hellenic civilisation had been held together; and although Aristophanes was no doubt justified in attributing to Euripides a large part in this depravation of society, due account should be taken of the general influences of the age by which the poet was surrounded. Aeschylus had awed by the portraiture of superhuman grandeur; Sophocles had charmed by the healthy development of moral beauty in the creation of character; it was left for Euripides—in this sense τραγικώτατος τῶν ποιητῶν—to find the aliment of his art in the coarser working of uncontrolled emotions and disordered passions. In proportion as men are strangers to Greek habits of thought, and insensible to the ideal beauty of Greek art, they will be liable to what Lucian quizzes as Euripidomania, and disposed to place him, as many moderns have done, above Aeschylus and Sophocles. There is profound truth in the saying attributed to Sophocles, that whereas he represented men as they ought to be, Euripides represented them as they are. For with Euripides began that system of photographing the coarse realities of life, which, under the high-sounding name of copying nature, does but mask the abandonment of art. By straining after effect, by heaping up incident on incident, by the unsightly display of overwrought feelings, Euripides appeals to the lower appetites of our nature, and seeks to compass emotional excitement rather than elevation of soul. Doubtless, in any detailed criticism of the plays of Euripides (especially of the *Medea*, the *Bacchae*, and the *Iphigenia in Aulide*), it would be easy to point to passages of unexampled beauty, pathos, and truth. It is not, however, by isolated bits, however exquisite, that a dramatist must vindicate his claims to the position of a truly great poet. Taken, therefore, as a whole, Euripides must be convicted of having precipitated the decline of the Greek drama. Among the more outward signs of this decline, may be mentioned the manner in which Euripides perverted the proper functions of the chorus, and his nauseous abuse of the expository prologue at the commencement, and of the *Deus ex machina* at the close of the play. The number of tragedies he composed is variously stated at seventy-five and ninety-two. Of these eighteen remain, exclusive of the *Cyclops*, the only extant satyric drama.

The three great dramatists who have now been passed under review seem to have entirely eclipsed their rivals, and to have left little to glean for their successors. In the Alexandrine Canon, or list of classical authors drawn up by Aristarchus and Aristophanes of Byzantium, two names indeed—Ion and Achaeus—are thought worthy to figure along with the great dramatists. To them we might add the name of Agathon (a contemporary and friend of Euripides), in whose hands the dramatic chorus sunk to a mere musical interlude. At a later date, Chaeremon (B. C. 380) is placed by Aristotle among dramatists whose works are "to be read." Tragedy was now defunct, and the crazy efforts of Alexandrian literati could not so much as evoke its ghost.

As tragedy sprung out of the choral performances at the *Lenaea* or winter Dionysia, so did comedy or the "Comus-song" arise from the festal procession and its choral accompaniment at the *Lesser* or *country* Dionysia. Susarion of Megara occupies in comedy a place analogous to that of Thespis in tragedy, as having been the first to reduce the wild effusions of the Bacchanalian revellers to something more in conformity with the laws of an artistic representation. In the colony of Megara, in Sicily, there flourished a school of comedy, which is identified with the name of Epicharmus, and which seems to have approximated more nearly to the New Attic comedy of Menander, as a comedy of manners, than to the Old Attic comedy of Aristophanes. This idea is in keeping with Horace's statement that Plautus formed himself on the model of Epicharmus. Sicily, it may be observed in passing, seems to have possessed in an eminent degree the faculty of Invention. The bucolic poetry of Theocritus, who flourished at the close of the third century before our era, some of which partakes of a mimetic character, is, along with the comedy of Epicharmus, a proof of the aptitude of the Dorian race for jocose sallies. Theocritus, it may be observed, has left us an epigram in which he styles his countryman ὁ τὰν κωμῳδίαν εὑρών. Epicharmus died about the year 450 B.C. A long time elapsed before we hear of any poets of eminence in Attica cultivating the art of which Susarion had there sown the germ. The license which accompanied it needed the shelter of democratic institutions. Chionides, Magnes, and Ecphantides, who flourished about the time of the Persian war, were among the first masters of the Attic comedy. These were succeeded, just before and during the Peloponnesian war, by Cratinus, Crates, Eupolis, and Aristophanes. For details respecting those representatives of the so-called Attic comedy, whose works have not come down to us, the student is referred to Müller's History of Greek Literature. Our limits compel us to confine our remarks on this head to Aristophanes.

The colossal political caricatures of Aristophanes constitute a stupendous phenomenon in the history not only of Greek but of all literatures, which had never been witnessed before, and will probably never be repeated again. If anything were needed to corroborate the views put forth in a previous chapter regarding the social features of Hellenic civilisation as embodying the absorption of the man in the citizen, and out of the citizen the gradual development of the man, the comedies of the Old Attic Comedy would abundantly supply that need. In common with Plato (whose sympathies with Aristophanes are manifested not only in the *Symposium*, but in the well-known epigram where he speaks of the Graces having got them a sure abiding place in the breast of that poet), Aristophanes made it his object to shore up and underpin the tottering framework of the old Hellenic fabric of society, and to arrest the progress of that subjective spirit which the Sophists did their utmost to poison, and Socrates to purify. It is this which lies at the bottom of all his lavish praise of the days of Marathon, and of Aeschylus, in whose verse lived and breathed the spirit of the olden time; it is this which points his epigrams against Euripides and the Sophists, and makes him beside himself with fury when he comes across Cleon and the Ochlocracy. It is obvious that such an aspect of comedy can have few or no essential features in common with that which we find in the plays of Menander or of Molière. In fact the newspaper press is the only analogue of the comedies of Aristophanes which is to be found in modern literature. Like a newspaper, Aristophanes occupies himself with every phase of public life which the passing hour brings to view. His plays are a mine of dramatic and aesthetic criticism, which Aristotle's Poetics cannot rival in depth or richness. Like a newspaper, he was the organ of a party, the reactionary party of the old Hellenic spirit, and, as such, extreme in his views, illiberal in his prejudices, and recklessly vehement in his abuse. If we regard the encyclopaedic range of subjects embraced (as in a newspaper) in the comedies of Aristophanes, we are amazed at the high state of culture at which his audience (no select few) must have arrived in order to comprehend discussions, and to take in subtle allusions, which go far to baffle the understanding of the most educated modern reader. The caricatures of Aristophanes are framed in arabesques of the most capricious design. His versatility is wholly without a parallel. The most intoxicated sallies of wanton mirth are followed by accents of the gravest moral earnestness. Not Sophocles in all his glory can reach the heights of beauty to which Aristophanes sometimes soars. What La Bruyère said of Rabelais, that he was at once "le charme de la canaille" and "le mets des plus délicats," may be applied to Aristophanes. But only at Athens could a canaille be found capable of appreciating the *Clouds* and the *Frogs*. The literary life of Aristophanes terminated about the year 390 B.C., having commenced B.C. 427. The eleven plays which have come down to us, out of fifty-four, may be classed as follows: Political satires — *Acharnians*, *Knights*, *Peace*, *Lysistrata*. Philosophical satires — *Clouds*, *Wasps*, *Ecclesiazusae*, *Plutus*. The *Birds*, a play of the wildest fancy, will not fall into any of these divisions.

The Middle Comedy is the comedy of a state of transition. Alarmed at the wild license of the Old Attic comedy, the thirty tyrants forbade personal satire. This law was a kind of censorship of the press. The *Plutus* and *Ecclesiazusae* of Aristophanes foreshadow the changes which were to supervene with the Middle Comedy. Antiphanes, one of the writers of this comedy, complains sadly of the dearth of subjects for his craft. Tragedy had them made to hand in the popular mythology; but Comedy had to cast about and invent everything. The problem which thus embarrassed the writers of the Middle Comedy (who flourished between B.C. 380 and the time of Alexander the Great) was solved by the writers of the New. The Middle Comedy was nothing but the Old Comedy gutted. Menander, on the other hand (B.C. 342—290), and his younger contemporary Philemon, are the types and organs of a wholly new state of society, which they further felt and admitted to be so. Private life had now supplanted public life—the man had asserted his supremacy over the citizen. The New Comedy became what the Old never had been,—what the Middle, with all its gropings, never knew how to be,—Comedy proper, that portraiture of men and manners, that "imitatio vitae, speculum consuetudinis et imago veritatis," as Cicero defines it, which we associate with the names of Menander and Terence, Plautus, Shakespeare, and Molière.

Masks.

An agricultural instrument.
(From an ancient MS. of Terence in the Vatican Library.)

Bust of Demosthenes. (From the Vatican.)

CHAPTER V.

PROSE COMPOSITION.

HISTORY AND ELOQUENCE.

ONE of the French philosophers of the eighteenth century was so impressed with the incalculable results which flowed from the invention of printing, that he divided the history, and especially the literary history, of the world into two portions, respectively anterior and posterior to that great discovery, which seemed to him the *fiat lux* of modern civilisation. We have been reminded of this curious paradox by meeting with an event, in our passage from the poetical to the prose composition of Hellas, scarcely less important in its bearings on Hellenic culture than the invention of printing on that of modern Europe. For, just as, in the fifteenth century of the Christian era, the wealth of Byzantine lore and the quickened wits of Italy would have been nothing more than a parenthesis in the lethargy of the middle ages, if Guttenberg had not lent a helping hand to cast off their wrinkled skin, and to compass the renaissance or new birth of letters and of art, so, in the sixth century before our era, it was assuredly a coincidence little short of providential, that at the very time when the reflective powers of the Hellenic mind were awakening to life, and the poetical or imaginative epoch was clearing away as the mists before the morning sun, the increased intercourse with Egypt, which history associates with the name of Psammetichus and the emporium of Naucratis, placed at the disposal of the Greeks an unlimited supply of the papyrus or writing material indigenous to Egypt, for which skins, stone, and metal had hitherto been but an imperfect substitute, and in the use of which Pliny finely vests the safeguard of civilisation and of history: "cum chartae usu maximè humanitas vitae constet et memoria." Concurrently with that transformation of Hellenic culture which we designate as the rise of prose composition, there came from the marshes of Egypt appliances for giving permanence to a class of literary productions which, without the aid of metrical structure, had but a lax hold on the memory, as superior, both in quantity and quality, to the ruder materials which had hitherto prevailed, as was the introduction of movable types to the costly vellum and scanty paper on which the monks of the middle ages had exercised their skill. The student's attention once directed to the parallel here instituted, with respect to the adaptation of material aids to mental requirements, it is of importance he should note where the analogy ends. For, unlike the literature of Europe posterior to the invention of printing, the literature of Greece posterior to the sixth century ever bewrayed its origin. The oral characteristics which marked the promulgation and transmission of the living Word, the Epos, never wholly abandoned the prose literature of a later age. Where a modern author addresses his *readers*, a writer as accomplished as Thucydides cannot shake off the association that he has before him a *hearing*, not a reading public. The ear was still regarded as the vestibule of the mind. The language of one of the best of ancient critics, on a passage in Herodotus,—κρεῖττον γέγονεν ἀκουσθῆναι λεγόμενον ἢ ὀφθῆναι γινόμενον*—when taken in connection with the whole treatise in which it occurs, is significative of the peculiar aspect under which prose composition was regarded by the Greeks. To the same effect is the curious retort which Plato puts into the mouth of the Egyptian king Thamus, when the god Theuth recommends that monarch to introduce the art of writing among the Egyptians.† Behind the light banter which abounds throughout the whole of the *Phaedrus*, there lurked, we may believe, in Plato's mind a consciousness of the change which had come over his own country, in consequence of the usurpation which writing had exercised on the once undivided rule of oral culture.

These remarks are intended to furnish the student with the conditions of thought under which he should approach the consideration of Greek prose, as such. We now proceed to give a brief sketch of the first efforts to which that branch of literary composition was applied.

At the threshold of the historical literature of Greece we meet with productions, of which the authors are generally known by the name of logographers. Cadmus of Miletus (probably a mythical personage); Acusilaus of Argos, of whom, as well as of Eumelus, another logographer, Clemens Alexandrinus says, τὰ δὲ Ἡσιόδου μετήλλαξαν εἰς πεζὸν λόγον καὶ ὡς ἴδια ἐξήνεγκαν; Hecataeus of

* Dionys. Halicarn. *De Comp. Verb.* tom. v. p. 18. ed. Tauchnitz.

† Plato, *Phaedr.* p. 275.

Miletus, a writer of far higher calibre, and a man of great consideration among his countrymen, whose *Travels round the Earth* and *Genealogies* were greatly in advance of the jejune efforts of his predecessors; Pherecydes of Leros, who flourished about the time of the Persian war, and busied himself with collecting myths and genealogies; Charon of Lampsacus, a contemporary of Pherecydes, who continued the speculations of Hecataeus on ethnography, and wrote separate treatises on Persia, Libya, Ethiopia, &c., as well as the *Annals* or ὧροι of his own country; Hellanicus of Mitylene, almost a contemporary of Herodotus, who, along with genealogical and such like registers (of which the most important was a catalogue of the Priestesses of Hera at Agos), composed a narrative of some of the events between the Persian and Peloponnesian wars, which, Thucydides tells us, was executed βραχέως τε καὶ τοῖς χρόνοις οὐκ ἀκριβῶς; Xanthus, the Lydian, ἱστορίας παλαιᾶς εἰ καί τις ἄλλος ἔμπειρος ὤν, as Dionysius of Halicarnassus writes, with special reference to that author's *Lydiaca*;—such were the principal logographers who in the latter half of the sixth century preluded to those more finished efforts in prose composition which were reserved for the succeeding generation. The general character of these works, of which nothing but fragments remain, is thus described by Dionysius of Halicarnassus: "These writers resembled each other in the choice of their subjects, and in point of ability presented no very striking disparity. Some wrote histories of Greece, others those of foreign nations, but none of these joined on to each other, but were divided by cities and peoples: and though their authors wrote independently, they all had one and the same aim in view, namely, to publish to the world, just as they found them stored up in religious or civil archives, without either addition, or omission, all local traditions, arranged by peoples and cities. Among these were certain myths, of which the antiquity disarmed scepticism, and sundry theatrical adventures which now-a-days seem silly enough. All of those who chose the same dialects, were alike in their style: it was clear, simple, unadulterated, concise, adapted to the subjects in hand, and free from all manner of artificial trickery. A certain amount of freshness lies scattered over their works, and more or less of grace. Accordingly, their works have survived to the present day." *

We pass on from the imperfect essays thus characterised by the Greek critic (who had before him complete works, of which we have nothing but scanty fragments) to one who has been called with justice the Father of History. He may with equal propriety

* Dionys. Halic. *Op.* tom. vi. p. 66.

be called its Homer, — not only because he stands in the same relation to the logographers who preceded him that Homer bore to the ante-Homeric ἀοιδοί, but also because his work has in plan and execution an Homeric cast, which enables us to call it the Epopee of History. While his uncle the poet Panyasis was vainly endeavouring to recall the departed spirit of the Homeric era, Herodotus breathed into the jejune art of the logographer the breath of life, and created a new kind of epic, commensurate with the wants of an age in which sober reflection and a yearning for inquiry (ἱστορία) were rapidly supplanting the naive credulity of that legendary Foretime in which the imagination reigned supreme. In the struggle between the Greek and the Barbarian, which was but a particular case of that momentous antagonism between the West and the East, of which Englishmen assuredly will not be disposed to speak with indifference or disdain, Herodotus found him a theme, around which, as around an epic centre, he might group, in due sort, the history of all peoples to the uttermost parts of the then known world, and so reduce to harmonious unity of execution a complicated variety of details, to which his predecessors had given the dryness of a register and the confusion of a bazaar. Born at Halicarnassus (B. C. 484), the capital of a small hereditary kingdom under the suzerainty of the "Great King," Herodotus spent the early years of his manhood in acquiring, by travels on land and sea, those materials for his history which no other sources of information could in those times supply. At this, and probably still later periods of his life, he appears to have visited every part of Greece and its dependencies, island and continent, explored the Propontis and the Euxine, the eastern shore of Scythia, Colchis, the coasts and islands of Asia Minor, the interior of Persia, Tyre, and parts of Palestine, Egypt from the Delta to Elephantine, Libya and the "parts about Cyrene." Six hundred years after the time of Herodotus, a story finds its way into the pages of Lucian, of the historian having recited, at the great Olympian festival, those nine books, on which were thenceforth conferred the names of the Nine Muses. Another account relates that Thucydides, then a boy, was present at the festival, and shed tears at the recital of the prose rhapsodist. Belief in this legend involves the absurdity that Herodotus had completed his history before his thirtieth year. Similar statements have been put forth respecting recitals at Corinth, Thebes, and Athens. To the latter tradition (of which the date is given as 446 B C.) Colonel Mure does not consider himself precluded from giving credit by the suspicions he justly casts on Lucian's interesting romance. But whatever may be the amount of fact contained in any of these stories, all of them, however *unreal*, are in this respect *true*, that they witness to the aspect in which the ἱστορίαι were regarded by antiquity as a great national prose epic, setting forth the glories of Hellenic Foretime. Would not those glories wax brighter and brighter as the hearer was reminded, in the silvery flow of the Ionic historian's language,—"sine ullis salebris quasi sedatus amnis fluit,"—how those Persians, the conquerors of the East, who had vanquished Lydia and Babylon, Media and Egypt, Thrace and Macedon, and forced their way through Libyan sands and Scythian snows, shrivelled up as a scroll at Marathon and Salamis, Mycale and Plataeae, and left intact the independence of Hellas? And in and through all the moving incidents and countless episodes with which the narrative is interspersed, one leading idea makes itself heard and felt, namely, that no human power or might can withstand a power and a might divine, and that every proud thought which lifts itself against Heaven will unsparingly be crushed. That kind of halting between the ideas of fatalism and an overruling Providence which forms so salient a feature of the Greek mind, from Homer to Sophocles, gives a somewhat sombre cast to the thoughtful reflections with which Herodotus frequently takes occasion to point the moral of his tale. To this an ancient critic seems to refer when he declares: *ἐν μέντοι τοῖς ἠθικοῖς κρατεῖ Ἡρόδοτος, ἐν δὲ τοῖς παθητικοῖς ὁ Θουκυδίδης.* To the same effect is the "remissis affectibus melior" of Quintilian. With regard to style and diction, it seems safest to conform to the opinions expressed and the words used on this head by native writers. Aristotle speaks of the λέξις of Herodotus as *εἰρομένη* or "jointed," as indicating the absence of that symmetry and artificial connection which marked the periodic structure of later Greek prose. The fullest criticism, however, on the style of Herodotus is to be found in a passage of Dionysius of Halicarnassus: Οὗτος δὲ (Herodotus) *κατὰ τὴν ἐκλογὴν τῶν ὀνομάτων, καὶ κατὰ τὴν σύνθεσιν, καὶ κατὰ τὴν τῶν σχηματισμῶν ποικιλίαν, μακρῷ δή τινι τοὺς ἄλλους ὑπερεβάλετο, καὶ παρεσκεύασε τῇ κρατίστῃ ποιήσει τὴν πεζὴν φράσιν ὁμοίαν γενέσθαι, πειθοῦς τε, καὶ χαρίτων καὶ τῆς εἰς ἄκρον ἡκούσης ἡδονῆς ἕνεκα· ἀρετάς τε τὰς μεγίστας καὶ λαμπροτάτας ἔξω τῶν ἐναγωνίων οὐδὲν ἐν ταύταις ἐνέλιπεν εἴτ' οὐκ εὖ πεφυκὼς πρὸς αὐτάς, εἴτε κατὰ λογισμόν τινα ἑκουσίως ὑπεριδών, ὡς οὐχ ἁρμοττουσῶν ἱστορίαις· οὐδὲ γὰρ δημηγορίαις πολλαῖς ὁ ἀνήρ, οὐδ' ἐναγωνίοις κέχρηται λόγοις, οὐδ' ἐν τῷ παθαίνειν καὶ δεινοποιεῖν τὰ πράγματα, τὴν ἀλκὴν ἔχει.** These words are but an amplification of the *unperiodic* or *jointed* style attributed to Herodotus by Aristotle. "Of all varieties of prose," says Müller, "it is the furthest removed from a written style." Herodotus

* Dionys Halic. *Op.* tom. vi. p. 92.

wrote as he talked, or as he might have talked (τῆς φράσεως τῶν ὀνομάτων τὸ κατὰ φύσιν Ἡρόδοτος ἐζήλωσε *): hence his frequent repetitions of words and phrases, in order to catch up again the dropped thread of the discourse: hence, too, that ἀφέλεια, or naive simplicity, for which he is so famous, and which has more than once suggested a parallel with the quaint and easy flow of Froissart.

In addition to the nine books of history, we possess a *Life of Homer*, erroneously attributed to Herodotus. Like the history, it is written in the Ionic dialect, and was probably a literary pastime by some grammarian of far later date.

Very different from the "dulcis et candidus et fusus Herodotus" is the "densus et brevis et semper instans sibi Thucydides." We cannot do better than quote a very beautiful passage from the writings of Fr. Jacobs on the general characteristics which distinguish these two historians. "The Attic history of Thucydides bears the same relation to the Ionic history of Herodotus as Attic tragedy to the Ionic Epos. Like tragedy, the Attic history abstains from the freedom of episodic narrative: to beguile the passing hour is not its aim; it seeks to inculcate wisdom for all coming time. If the Ionic history may be compared to the smooth mirror of a still lake, in whose bosom is seen transfigured the serenity of the heavens and all the varieties of nature which lie clustering round its smiling shore, Attic history is as a mighty stream, which keeps a steady course between its solid banks, crushes every obstacle, never swerves from its path, preserves the even tenor of its way through banks gay with blossom and sad with gloom, and finally, after a long and joyless course, mixes its waters with the world's wide main. If history proper does not begin till the reign of the legend is at an end, and the boundaries between history and poetry can be rigidly defined, if its very conception is inseparable from that critical spirit which searches out the truth, and from that profound sagacity, sharpened by experience, which ferrets out the connection of events, then are we justified in affirming that Attica is history's true home, and that Thucydides is the first founder of this branch of literature."

Thucydides, the son of Olorus, was born in the vicinity of Athens, about the year 471 B.C., and died about 395 B.C. In the eighth year of the Peloponnesian war he commanded an Athenian fleet in the Aegean sea, and, having failed in preventing Brasidas from making himself master of Amphipolis, was sent into exile by the Athenians. This exile lasted from 423 to 403 B.C.; and

* Dionys. Halic. *Op.* tom. vi. p. 40.

during that period Thucydides employed himself in collecting materials for one of the most majestic monuments of historical literature which the world possesses. The eighth or last book brings down the history of the Peloponnesian war — the dramatic theme of the whole — to the middle of its twenty-first year. The work was therefore left in an unfinished state, for Thucydides contemplated carrying it on to the demolition of the Peiraeeus and the Long Walls. Had we not known this intention, we might have inferred, from the perceptible falling off and inferiority in execution of the eighth book, that Thucydides had been prevented by circumstances from bringing his design to completion. The plan of this history does not call for any analysis. Events succeed each other with the same regularity as the seasons. The historian's reckoning is by summers and winters,— a point for which he is severely handled by Dionysius of Halicarnassus — and from this order nothing can induce him to depart. The *συγγραφὴ περὶ τοῦ πολέμου τῶν Πελοποννησίων καὶ Ἀθηναίων* is no epic poem, like the *Musae* of Herodotus, gathering up within its ample folds the traditions, customs, and geography of a world,—everything which would impair the unity of action, or distract the reader's attention from the great contest for the Hegemony is rigorously excluded. But while the theatre is thus narrowed to adapt itself to the proportions of the great historical drama which Thucydides brings upon the stage, the spectators have all the more opportunity for studying to advantage the action, character, and physiognomy, of the *dramatis personae*. Nor is this all; in the speeches—forming nearly a fifth of the whole work—and moral reflections with which the history of the Peloponnesian war is interspersed, Thucydides may be conceived as performing in history and in prose that part which the chorus performed in the poetical dramas of an Aeschylus or a Sophocles. It is observable that in the magnificent monodies of which these harangues may be said to consist, we find the same difference (when compared with the body of the history), if not in diction and dialect, yet in style and strain, as that which obtains in the lyric portions of the Greek drama, when compared with the regular or iambic verse. As regards the accuracy and trustworthiness of Thucydides, none of the ancients, with all their love of sifting such matters, has raised a dissentient voice. For knowledge of character and terse vigour in expressing what he knew,— not so much by saying *what* men thought, did, spoke, as by making them think, do, speak, before our own eyes,—Thucydides well deserves the epithet of *δεινὸς ἠθογραφῆσαι* applied to him by his biographer. It requires very great familiarity with the style of this historian in order to overcome the sensation of harshness and obscurity with which the reader is oppressed on a first acquaintance. Dionysius of

Halicarnassus, and—to a less degree—Cicero, were both of them unfavourably impressed in this particular with the style of Thucydides, and especially with that of the harangues. But all labour, however severe, in overcoming these obstacles which meet the student at the threshold, is amply repaid when he once gains access to the inner penetralia of the historian's meaning. He then admires, for energy, pregnancy, and precision, what he at first had taxed with uncouth ruggedness and obscurity. He feels that the rapid changes and other irregularities of structure, the inversion of words, the frequent use of the so-called σχῆμα πρὸς τὸ σημαινόμενον and other peculiarities of style and diction are but the result of those serried masses of thought which ruthlessly crush down all the pretty flower-beds, bordered with rules of grammar, in which less vigorous thinkers lay out, as it were, their sentences. On the whole, of all ancient historians, Thucydides approaches nearest to the requirements which Milton demands of an historian: "Ego vero sic existimo; qui gestas res dignas dignè scripserit, eum animo non minus magno rerumque usu praeditum scribere oportet quam is qui eas gesserit: ut vel maximas pari animo comprehendere atque metiri possit, et comprehensas sermone puro atque casto distinctè graviterque narrare."*

Xenophon appears before us under a triple aspect, that of a commander, a philosopher, and an historian. It is with the latter that we are now more immediately concerned; though it is obviously impossible that his discharge of any one of these functions should not take some tone and direction from the spirit which animated the remaining two. The main particulars of his life have been laid before the reader in earlier portions of this volume; we are therefore at liberty to confine ourselves to a literary estimate of his worth as an historian. Thucydides, we have seen, left his history incomplete. Xenophon, in his *Hellenica*, not only completed the history of the Peloponnesian war, but carried down the history of Greece to the battle of Mantinea. The opening words of that work—μετὰ δὲ ταῦτα οὐ πολλαῖς ἡμέραις ὕστερον—take up the narrative after the naval engagement at Sestos (August B. C. 411), with which the eighth book of Thucydides terminates. The *Hellenica*, as we now possess them, are divided into seven books; a division posterior, it should seem, to Xenophon. They reflect better than any other work which has come down to us the political ferment, and, with the ferment, the scum of the times. With dishonesty we are scarcely justified in taxing their author; for there is such a total absence of disguise or artifice in the way in which he exalts his hero Agesilaus at the

* Milton's Works, vii. p. 402.

expense of other and greater actors, such as Epaminondas, Pelopidas, and Conon, that we must acquit him of any intention wilfully to deceive or to mislead. Acquit him, however, we cannot, of fainthearted attachment to the cause of freedom, of weak rather than base detraction of his country, of revolting servility to Sparta, and of sour dissatisfaction with evils against which he doubtless found it easier to grumble than to provide a remedy. Pericles and Demosthenes, we may observe in passing, were the only public men who faltered not in their attachment to liberal principles, clung to them through evil report and good report, and in the worst of times put manfully to the wheel the shoulder which Xenophon was content to shrug. Good, humane, amiable, and religious, Xenophon would have passed muster in less turbulent times: but his character wanted bone and muscle: his principles were too flabby, lacked that great and noble spirit, that unflinching faith in a righteous cause, which alone could carry an Athenian with honour through the trials of his age. It would be a crying injustice to condemn him as flagitious; the height of partiality not to deplore his infatuation and weakness. We have thought it the more necessary to enter this protest against Xenophon's conduct and character as a man, in order to place the student on his guard against the very great seductions which he exercises as a writer. For, however flat and dull the *Hellenica* may appear to a man who has just laid down his Thucydides, it cannot be denied that the *Anabasis* is one of the most fascinating works ever penned. That "jucunditas inaffectata, quam nulla potest affectatio consequi," which Quintilian attributes to this Attic bee, imparts a charm to the narrative that almost makes one forget that it has no higher claims to our regard. His words are sweeter than honey, says Cicero; by his mouth the Graces and the Muses found utterance. Such is the tone in which antiquity speaks of the style of Xenophon. Qualities of this mellifluous character are apt to pall, and to beget a somewhat tedious monotony. But from such defects, which are of the essence of such a style, the *Anabasis* is freer than any other of Xenophon's compositions. The incidents of the narrative, and the part played by the narrator, give an animation to the work which carries the reader along. Strange to say, in consequence of a passage in the *Hellenica* (iii. 1. 2), some doubts have been thrown on the authorship of the *Anabasis*; but whatever hypothesis be resorted to, to explain the allusion to Themistogenes, we must not let go the fact, that Xenophon, and not another, wrote the *Anabasis*. We almost hesitate whether to class the *Cyropaedeia* as an historical composition. It has long ago been observed by Cicero, that "Cyrus ille non ad historiae fidem scriptus est, sed ad effigiem justi imperii;" and every subsequent investigation tends to show that Xenophon's object here was to write a kind of romance, in which he put forth his peculiar views on political theories and ideal governments. "As a history, it has no authority at all." This view of the *Cyropaedeia*, which is undoubtedly correct, renders it all the more a curious phenomenon in the literature of Greece. Apart from its historical worthlessness, it may be called, in point of style, Xenophon's masterpiece.

Of the historians who flourished during the fourth century before our era, Xenophon is the only one whose works have not come down to us in a purely fragmentary state. Though it is as difficult to judge of a work from a fragment as of a house from a brick, it may be conjectured that the writers whom time has visited thus severely were but feeble rhetorical imitators of the great high-priests of historiography who have here been passed under review. The contemptuous epithet of "paenè pusillus Thucydides," which Cicero applies to one of their number, Philistus of Syracuse, might probably be extended to the remainder, of whom the least inconsiderable were Ephorus, Theopompus, Hecataeus of Abdera,—the first Greek probably who wrote on the history of the Jews,—and Megasthenes, who wrote on India.*

The historians who flourished in the third century have been still less fortunate in shooting the cataracts of time; for not one of them has reached us entire. Of the losses thus sustained, the most severe is that of the Sicilian Timaeus. Though roughly handled by Polybius for his malignity and superstition, his chronological investigations were reckoned by the ancients as peculiarly valuable. His works are thus characterised by the great critic Longinus: *θατέρου δὲ ὧν εἴπομεν, λέγω δὲ τοῦ ψυχροῦ, πλήρης ὁ Τίμαιος, ἀνὴρ τὰ μὲν ἄλλα ἱκανὸς, καὶ πρὸς λόγων ἐνίοτε μέγεθος οὐκ ἄφορος, πολυίστωρ, ἐπινοητικός· πλὴν ἀλλοτρίων μὲν ἐλεγκτικώτατος ἁμαρτημάτων, ἀνεπαίσθητος δὲ ἰδίων, ὑπὸ δὲ ἔρωτος τοῦ ξένας νοήσεις ἀεὶ κινεῖν πολλάκις ἐκπίπτων εἰς τὸ παιδαριωδέστατον* (iv. 1.). This judgment may be compared with the eulogy passed on Timaeus by Cicero: "Timaeus longè eruditissimus," &c. (*De Orat.* ii. 14.) To sum up, it may be stated, on the one hand, that between Xenophon and Polybius—a period of nearly a century and a half—there flourished upwards of a hundred writers, who have more or less claim to the title of historian; and on the other hand, that, out of this number, not one has come down to us entire, though the contents of their works have been largely made use of by Diodorus Siculus, Strabo, and others. To

* For details as to their lives and the nature of their works the student is referred to Westermann's excellent edition of Vossius, *De Historicis Graecis.*

Polybius, therefore, we now pass on, he being the last writer whom the limits of this history warrant us in including in this sketch of the historical literature of Hellas. Polybius — who boasts that he was the only man of that name—was born at Megalopolis about B.C. 212—204. His father was one of the chiefs of the Achaean league, and he himself, as the reader has seen, played no inconsiderable part in the catastrophe which handed over Greece to the power of Rome. His *ἱστορία καθολική*, or "universal history," consisted of forty books, of which five entire, and considerable extracts of the remainder, have come down to us. It was intended to relate all that had occurred from the second Punic war down to the fall of Carthage and Corinth (B.C. 218—146): the first books, however, contain an introductory summary of events anterior to B.C. 218. For profound and sifting analysis of the causes, occasions, and issues of events, Polybius is without a rival among all the historians of antiquity, Greek or Roman. It is in this sense that he calls his work a pragmatical history, implying that scientific evolution of causes and effects by which Polybius has given us both a history and a philosophy of history in one. He is not content with setting before us what statesmen and commanders did; he is at pains to show what they left undone. It is not perhaps surprising, that a man whose whole heart and soul — *τὸν οὕτως ἐσπουδασμένον ἄνδρα*, as Strabo has it — was so wrapt up in the subject-matter of his work, the *τὸ ἔμπρακτον καὶ τὸ ἀληθὲς τῶν ἐννοιῶν*, should have been unduly inattentive to its form, style, and diction. With these last, modern critics agree with antiquity in expressing their dissatisfaction. Seldom has so large an amount of instruction and information been conveyed in so unpalatable a shape. His style is without colour, and his diction without elegance. No imagination fires, no grace adorns, no energy quickens the cold monotony of his austere reasoning and dry narration. The beauties which we meet with in his work are all moral; and accordingly, though compelled to give him a lower place than either Herodotus, Thucydides, or even Xenophon, we cannot withhold a large measure of esteem from a man who was ever animated by the noblest instincts of patriotism and probity.

We purpose to conclude this chapter with a brief sketch of the oratorical literature of Greece. We are sometimes told that eloquence was an exotic, planted in Sicily by one Corax, about the middle of the fifth century before our era, and transplanted to Athens by another Sicilian, Gorgias, and watered by his pupil Polus. The fact is, however, that the history of Greek eloquence is as old as the history of Greece itself; and must not be confounded with that of its base counterfeit, the quibbling rhetoric of a sophistical age, of which the highest triumph was to make the worse appear the better cause, and to produce a showy display of hollow words, with a minimum expenditure of sense. Themistocles, Aristeides and Pericles were orators as great as, and even greater, than any or all of the "Oratores Attici" who have won themselves a place in the canon of Alexandrian literati. For the sake of keeping within convenient limits, it is to these ten orators that we shall confine the brief sketch here attempted of Greek eloquence. Taking them in their accustomed order, we begin with Antiphon of Rhamnus, the friend of Socrates and Thucydides. The latter speaks in the highest terms of his integrity and eloquence.* The comic poets, on the other hand, treat him with severity, as having been the first to receive money for speeches, which he wrote to be delivered by others in criminal causes. The fifteen orations which have come down to us — of which twelve are only show-exercises of rhetorical skill — are sometimes referred to as *λόγοι φονικοί*, being all of them connected with the commission of a murder. The three actually delivered by the parties for whom Antiphon composed them are valuable for the light they throw on criminal procedure. We have some difficulty in raising the merits of these orations to a level with the praise pronounced on Antiphon by ancient writers. They savour strongly of the Sicilian drug which Gorgias, we have seen, brought into the Athenian market.

Andocides has already appeared in a somewhat unfavourable light in an earlier part of this history, in the matter of the Hermocopidae. Of the four orations which bear his name, one (*κατὰ Ἀλκιβιάδου*) is probably spurious. The remaining three are very valuable for contemporary history. The exordium of the oration *περὶ τῶν Μυστηρίων* is exceedingly ingenious, and the pathos with which he describes what passed when he was in prison, and the art with which he traces the portraits of his enemies, show that Andocides was as clever as he was flagitious.

To Lysias (born 458 B.C.) the ancients attributed as many as 230 genuine orations. Of this number only thirty-five have come down to us, and only one of these was delivered by Lysias himself, on the accusation he brought against Eratosthenes for the judicial murder of his brother Polemarchus. This speech gives an interesting picture of the political history of the time. One of the most admirable features of the remaining thirty-four speeches is the art with which Lysias adapts his style, in each case, to the position and character of the particular individual for whom the oration was penned. To this the ancients probably referred in praising his *ἠθοποιΐα*, *ἐνάργεια*, and *διατύπωσις*. The diction of Lysias is the purest specimen of the Attic idiom. The excessive gracefulness of his style, however, occasionally lapses into feebleness and

* viii. 68.

insipidity. This general want of animation and of power induced Quintilian to say that Lysias was more like a clear fountain than a rolling river. Dionysius of Halicarnassus has furnished us with some very elaborate criticism on this orator.

We now come to Isocrates (B. C. 436—338). Brought up himself in the sophistical school of a Prodicus, a Gorgias, and a Tisias, it is only surprising that his orations are not more deeply tainted than they confessedly are with the flaunting meretricious graces of the vicious style of rhetoric there taught. Prevented, as he himself tells us, by natural modesty—we certainly should not have guessed this from his works — and a feeble voice from taking any part himself in public assemblies, he opened a school of rhetoric, first at Chios, and subsequently at Athens, to which pupils flocked in large numbers, and through which he exercised a potent influence on the development of public oratory. Greedy of gain, of pleasure and applause, Isocrates is entitled to little esteem as a man, and as an orator all his skill in the cooking up irreproachable periods and harmonious cadences cannot disguise the absence of even a particle of true eloquence or noble thought. Many of what he considered his most finished speeches, when stripped of the idle gewgaws and rhetorical millinery in which he so complacently decks them out, are nothing but sheer rhodomontade, great swelling words, which shrink at the prick of the critic's pin into their true inanity. For a man who thought little and felt less, it cannot be denied that he is a consummate master in the art of word-veneering. But the very praise thus awarded precludes all claim to any more substantial merits. Of the twenty-one orations which have come down to us, the majority are pre-eminently show-speeches. He tells us that he spent fifteen years in polishing up his famous *Panegyric*: he has forgotten to add that he failed after all in making it a masterpiece. With unconscious irony, his speech against the Sophists launches out invectives against the very blemishes with which his works abound. Müller has wisely remarked that it is very doubtful whether Plato would have accorded to Isocrates in his maturer age those high praises which he has bestowed upon him in the earlier years of his life. The student may rest assured that, in proportion as he admires the orations of this wordy rhetorician, he has yet a long way to go before his taste can be pronounced pure or his judgment sound. The declamation of Isocrates is as far removed from true eloquence as fencing is from fighting. No amount of grace in the attitude should blind us to the feebleness of the thrust.

The eleven orations left us by Isaeus (B.C. 393) are a perfect mine of information on the Athenian laws of succession, the theme of them all. An orator we can scarcely call him: he is rather a first-rate barrister. Vigorous in attack, prompt in reply, clear in his statements, cogent in argument, his diction has all the simplicity, and his style all the energy, of a man who knew thoroughly well what he had to say and was right earnest in saying it. We have omitted naming his master-work, to wit, his pupil Demosthenes.

We would willingly dispose of every line that Isocrates has written in exchange for the fifteen orations of Lycurgus. Of this number only one has come down to us; and its masculine vigour, somewhat uncouth though it be, leads us to infer that he must have been one of the idlest of Isocrates' pupils. He certainly exhibits no traces of his master's teaching The noble spirit and unflinching severity with which Lycurgus carried on the administration of Athens, is matter of history. The extant speech is directed against Leocrates, a rich citizen of Athens, whom the orator accuses of treason for having fled from the city after the disaster at Chaeronea. Critics find fault with its shortcomings as a work of art. It possesses, however, a bluff and healthy order of eloquence, which stirs men's blood, and is worth more than all the *ἀντίθετα*, and *ἰσόκωλα*, and *ὁμοιοτέλευτα* with which Isocrates racked his brains and sickens his readers.

Up to the year 1847, Hyperides had been the only orator of the chosen "Ten," of whom nothing had been preserved. This loss was the more to be regretted, as ancient critics had pronounced him second only to Demosthenes and Aeschines. In the year above-named, however, two Englishmen, Harris and Arden, purchased some fragments of papyrus rolls, which, to some extent, repair the loss. They were found to contain (1) portions of the oration against Demosthenes for having received money from Harpalus, the Macedonian emissary; (2) fragments of a speech in defence of Lycophron, and another, entire, in defence of Euxenippus. These orations, all that as yet have been discovered out of fifty-two, are said to confirm the reputation which Hyperides previously enjoyed for easy grace, dexterity, and raillery. The fragments of the Harpalic oration leave the question of Demosthenes' innocence where they found it.

The three extant orations of Deinarchus also refer to the question of Harpalus, and are directed against Demosthenes, Aristogeiton, and Philocles. The chief impression which the first of these orations leaves on the mind is a feeling of regret that the reply of Demosthenes has not come down to us. As an orator, Deinarchus was a mere imitator, and, what is worse, an unsuccessful imitator, of the great models of Attic eloquence, especially Demosthenes. Hence his sobriquet of *Δημοσθένης ὁ κρίθινος*.

We now come, in conclusion, to the two greatest names in the canon, Aeschines and Demosthenes. Of the former, we possess entire all the speeches he ever made,—namely, (1) the *κατὰ Κτησιφῶντος*, eminent, if for nothing else (which we are very far from implying), yet for this, that it called forth his rival's ever famous speech on the Crown; (2) the *κατὰ Τιμάρχου*, one of the richest additions ever made to the glossary of abuse; and, lastly, (3) the *περὶ παραπρεσβείας*, or his defence on the charge of having misconducted his mission to Philip. These orations were known in antiquity by the name of the Three Graces. Quintilian complains that Aeschines has more flesh than muscle. He might have added to this defect a marked inferiority to his great antagonist in the art of arranging and digesting the course of an argument. Or, as we should rather put it, the component elements of his argument are not sufficiently condensed to leave on the mind a unity of effect. For passion, animation, and felicitous expression, he is second to none.

A Frenchman, a German, and an Englishman, Chateaubriand, Niebuhr, and Henry Brougham, agree in declaring that Demosthenes was the greatest statesman that Greece ever possessed at any period of her history. However much this verdict may be liable to be traversed by those who consider that his zeal consumed and his foresight abandoned him, judges at once so severe and so unjust are not to be met with when his supremacy as the prince of orators is discussed. Genius such as his defies at once criticism and praise. Any one who is even superficially acquainted with the history of Greece is aware of the courage and perseverance with which Demosthenes overcame the obstacles which nature had opposed to his triumphs as an orator. This caution never abandoned him. The sedulous discipline with which he acquired the principles of his art accompanied him in its practice; for his speeches were carefully prepared, improvisation carefully eschewed. The strongest evidence of this is furnished by the frequent repetitions of the same passages in different orations. At the bottom of all his orations, firing every word, prompting every thought, lies a passionate love of Athens, her liberties within, her power without. The facility with which he bends his argument — and such argument! so compassed about with vigour, solidity, and taste!—to every conceivable exigency in which retort or obloquy might imperil its safety, is one of the most striking features of his works; the very greatest of his triumphs being most conspicuous for the absence of all effort. To admire the genius of Demosthenes, we have nothing to do but to read his orations; but to penetrate into the secrets of his art, and see unveiled the elegancies and subtleties of his actions, the student should study the tract of Dionysius of Halicarnassus περὶ τῆς λεκτικῆς Δημοσθένους δεινότητος. After mentioning the three styles of Thucydides (whose works Demosthenes is reported to have copied out eight times,— an example followed in later times by Alphonso V. of Spain), Lysias, and Isocrates, the Greek critic remarks: "Demosthenes, who came after these great men, formed so high an idea of the oratorical style, that he took no one of them in particular for his model, either as a man or as an orator; for all of them appeared to him to fall short of his ideal: but taking from each what was best and most useful, he wove it up, and out of these many styles brought his own to perfection, being at once grandiloquent and homely, subtle and simple, *recherché* and familiar, pompous and true, austere and lively, earnest and easy, tender and acrimonious, sober and vehement, altogether the image of that Proteus fabled by ancient poets." * The sixty orations of Demosthenes which have come down to us—though some are of more than doubtful authenticity—may be classed as follows:—eleven political speeches; forty-seven judicial; and two epideictic: these last, however, are considered apocryphal.

We cannot but feel, after passing under review this particular branch of Hellenic literature, how high must have been the intellectual culture of that populace, to whom the orations of such orators were addressed, and by whom they were thoroughly understood and relished. "It is not classical authors," said Goethe, "but classical readers, that are scarce." If the student reflects for a moment on the kind of literary diet on which the Athenians were fed, he will feel that no such scarcity could have existed in that great capital of the intellectual world, "mother of arts and eloquence," and will readily acknowledge, with Lord Macaulay, that, "in general intelligence, the Athenian populace far surpassed the lower orders of any community that has ever existed."

* Dionys. Halic. *Op.* tom. vi. p. 167.

Coin of Hadrian with statue of seated Jupiter holding a victory.
Taken from a chryselephantine statue which he erected in the Temple of Jupiter Olympus at Athens, A. D. [illegible])

Bust of Thucydides. (From the Vatican.)

CHAPTER VI.

PHILOSOPHY.

At the threshold of Hellenic philosophy we are met by an inquiry, on which it is necessary that the student should arrive at some satisfactory solution before he makes any further way into the inner penetralia of Hellenic thought. Was that philosophy the indigenous production of the Hellenic mind? or was it derived from foreign, to wit, Oriental sources? In the case of isolated tenets and doctrines the Greeks, themselves, in their palmiest days, always exhibited a tendency to seek for points of contact in the wisdom of the East: but such affiliations were not only themselves open to discussion, but were also widely different from what took place when their philosophy was at its last gasp, when its degenerate exponents vied with Alexandrine Jews and Egyptian priests in looking without for those elements of vitality and vigour which it no longer possessed within. In one sense indeed the philosophy of Hellas was assuredly Oriental. Like every other branch of the Indo-Germanic family, the Greeks must needs have brought with them from the Aryan cradle of their race habits of thought and elements of speech which may have given shape and hue to that development of their speculative inquiry which was brought to maturity in a subsequent age and under a different clime. But it may be doubted whether the Oriental extraction of Hellenic philosophy, in any sense less narrow than this, be not one of those crude theories set up in an age of which an uncritical syncretism was one of the predominant features, but incapable of producing on its behalf any solid ground of fact, or any plausible appeal to probability. The incoherent statements and random assertions advanced in support of such a theory by the later disciples of Pythagoras and Plato are shown to be utterly worthless when we go for their corroboration to the pages of earlier writers. That Pythagoras sojourned in Egypt, few would deny; but that he borrowed all his system, as a system, from Egyptian priests, is an assertion which is first made by Isocrates, an orator ever more solicitous about sounding a flourish than about sifting a fact. That Plato sojourned in Egypt, may be equally true; but assuredly it is not from Plato we learn of his obligations to Egyptian lore,—from Plato, who enlarges indeed on the antiquity of their traditions*, their skill in writing, arithmetic and mensuration, and other technical appliances †, but who also fastens upon a sordid love of gain (τὸ φιλοχρήματον) as the distinguishing feature of their national character, in the very same passage in which he speaks of a thirst for knowledge (τὸ φιλομαθές) as the no less peculiar portion of his own countrymen. But waiving the discussion of particular instances, into which our limits will not allow us to enter, we may observe that the whole character of early Hellenic philosophy, and the nature of the successive stages which marked its subsequent development, are alike unfavourable to this Oriental hypothesis. The tenets of the first Hellenic sages, or, as we should rather call them, physiologists, have pre-eminently the character of *first efforts*, of independent guesses at truth. While diving into the mysteries of nature—for they had scarcely begun to grapple with the destinies of man—they never exhibit a vestige of any collision with foreign elements of speculation, or of any of those attempts to adapt existing formulas to new bodies of thought, or of those appeals to results antecedently arrived at, which are so marked a feature of mediaeval philosophy. We find them at work making their own tools, before they begin to build. Nor is this all. The Greeks were but sorry adepts at foreign languages; and it has yet to be shown through what channels they were to be put into communication with eastern systems and tenets, always assuming—for it is nothing more than an assumption—that of such philosophical tenets, as distinguished from theogonical and cosmogonical dogmas, Egypt had anything to expound. Again, the advocates of the Oriental ancestry of Hellenic philosophy have never, so far as we are aware, offered any explanation of a fact which, apart from all other considerations, would be fatal to their views. The countries from which the alleged importation was effected, were all of them subject to the dogmatic teaching of a priestly caste. Utter emancipation from any such trammels was of the very essence of Hellenic philosophy and religion alike. Herein is that philosophy emphatically distinguished from all the

* *Tim.* p. 21, E., a passage, we should add, not untinged with that banter so common in the Platonic dialogues.

† *Phaedr.* p. 274, *Phileb.* p. 18, *Epinom.* p. 986, *Leg.* vii. p. 819.

philosophies of the ancient world. The office of the Hellenic priest, as defined by Aeschines and Plato*, and corroborated by the concurrent testimony of all ancient writers, was simply to offer up gifts and sacrifice, and to pour forth prayers on behalf of the people. It has yet to be shown by what process bodies of doctrine indissolubly intertwined, down to their lowest roots, with the jealously guarded dogmas of a hierarchical sacerdotal caste, could be transplanted to a soil so alien to their nature, without bringing along with them some vestige at least of that intricate machinery which alone had given them significance and vitality in their native home.

Such are some of the considerations which should make the student hesitate ere he relinquish the autochthony, if we may so speak, of Hellenic philosophy, as indeed of every other form of Hellenic culture.† The internal evidence of Hellenic philosophy, that consent of parts and organic development which it betrays, are sufficient, to our apprehension, to withstand the assault of a whole host of limping facts and casual coincidences which may be brought against it from without.

One of the most illustrious philosophers and historians of philosophy of the present day, M. Cousin,—from whose pages we shall borrow largely in this chapter, believing that on such a subject we shall give most of what is true by giving least of what is our own,—has traced the march of all philosophical inquiry in antiquity, eastern and classical, and, in recent times, mediaeval and modern, through the four phases of sensualism, rationalism, scepticism, and mysticism. The rival tendencies of the two forms of dogmatism first named are founded on the opposition between body and soul, sense and reason, matter and spirit. Their influence is visibly marked in the first period of Hellenic philosophy which extends to B. C. 400, and in the four schools — Ionic, Italic, Atomic, Eleatic—which, during that period, held the reins of philosophical speculation. In both cases, however, that is, both in the empirical and in the rationalist tendency, it should be remarked that the movement is thoroughly objective, so that if we couple them both under the head of dogmatism we have the same successive phases of (1) Objective, (2) Objective-subjective, and (3) Subjective, which we have pointed out in the general civilisation, in the literature, and which has yet to be shown in the arts of Hellas. The remark will not have been superfluous if it shall have enabled the student to seize the spirit, and trace the organic

* *Ctesiph.* 66; *Politic.* p. 290.

† Those who wish to hear what can be said on the opposite side are referred to Röth's *Abendländische Philosophie.*

development of every department of Hellenic life. When we state that the movement is thoroughly objective, we mean that the Greek began by inquiring into the world without, before he turned his gaze into that inner microcosm, his own nature; that he constructed his theory of Being before he bethought him of the theory of Knowing; that he strove to determine what really *is*, before he had found out what is really *known*. But in this outer world two aspects may be chosen for examination — the phenomena themselves, and the relations by which those phenomena are governed; — hence we meet the two schools, Ionic and Italic, of which the one was a sensuous school of physicists, the other a rationalist school of mathematicians, and which were founded by Thales and Pythagoras respectively. The Ionic physiologists fall into two categories, according as they refer the origin of the universe — the great problem they endeavoured to solve — to a determinate or an indeterminate number of principles. Thales, Anaximenes, Heracleitus, Diogenes of Apollonia, and Archelaus belong to the former, and Anaximander and Anaxagoras to the latter; — Anaximander seeking for the origin of all things, for the primitive material element in the τὸ ἄπειρον, or "unbounded in pure space;" and Anaxagoras having recourse to an infinite number of elementary principles which he called ὁμοιομέρειαι, or "similar parts." The physiologists in the first category — with the exception of Archelaus, who admitted a determinate plurality, to wit a duality*, of material elements, namely, fire and water, or heat and cold — confined themselves to one element. With Thales this was moisture; with Anaximenes and Diogenes, air; with Heracleitus, the more subtle but still material element of fire. "Now fire," says Cousin, "animates and destroys all things; it is essentially the emblem of motion; motion is variety: hence the theory that everything is in a perpetual flux or change, and that the common character of all the phenomena of the universe is a perpetual contradiction, ἐναντιότης, a warring, but a warring on regular principles; for it has its laws, the same laws as the universe, laws which are necessary and irresistible." But these are not the only divisions into which the Ionic physiologists may be parted. Those of them who admitted either a determinate or an indeterminate plurality of primordial elements, grounded their theory of the constitution of the universe on the *mechanical* action of those elements on each other. Those, on the other hand, who postulated a single element, conceived the idea of a vital

* δύο αἰτίας γενέσεως, Diog. Laert. ii. 16.

active force, manifesting itself under forms divers and diverse, and may be called the *dynamical* physiologists.

The Atomistic school may be considered a kind of appendix of the Ionic, the doctrines of Leucippus and Democritus being little else than a more scientific development of those which were held by the mechanical section of the Ionic physiologists, and more especially by the promulgator of the *homoiomeriae*, Anaxagoras. The elementary atoms which give the name to the school, were supposed to combine with each other according to certain inherent laws, and to form all the bodies of the universe. The soul was held to be a collection of round igneous atoms which generate motion and thought. The atoms perpetually emitted from bodies constitute their εἴδωλα or images: these images, by contact with the organs of sense, produce αἴσθησις, or sensation, which in turn produces νόησις, or thought. The plague-spot of materialism, pantheism, and atheism on the forehead of this school was but a legitimate consequence of the Ionic doctrines, when pushed to extremes.

The tenets of the Italic and Eleatic schools we shall state, as nearly as possible, in the language of M. Cousin. Almost contemporary with Thales and Anaximander, Pythagoras passed on from the phenomena of the universe themselves to the law of relation which existed between; that relation is an abstraction only cognisable by thought. Hence we find a tendency totally the reverse of that which we have observed in the Ionic school. The peculiar characteristic of the Italic school is to be mathematical and astronomical, and at the same time idealist; a combination we might expect, *à priori*, from the abstruse nature of mathematical inquiries. Accordingly we find in the list of the Pythagoreans the names of some of the greatest mathematicians of antiquity. First, Archytas and Philolaus, and, at a later period, Hipparchus and Ptolemy. Arithmetic, geometry, astronomy, music, all of them studies which raise the mind above the level of sensuous objects, were the familiar pursuits of the disciples of Pythagoras. The Ionic physiology, setting out from facts to arrive at principles, considered the relations between the different phenomena of the universe as simple modifications of those phenomena. The Italic physiology set out from principles to arrive at facts, and on the ideal groundwork of a relation, expressed under the form of Number, built up the phenomena of the world, which they considered, as Aristotle expresses it, to be "mimetic of numbers," their active principles or causes. The first numerical decade was symbolical of ten spheres rolling round a centre which itself was unity That centre in the sensuous system of the Ionic school was the earth, with the speculative Italic school the sun. Now as the sun represents unity, and as unity, though an active principle, is without motion, motionless is the sun. The laws by which the decade of bodies revolve around the sun constitute the music of the spheres; the entire universe is an harmonious whole, to wit, a κόσμος. We have here a purely mathematical physiology. The like may be said of the Pythagorean psychology. The soul was held to be a self-moving number; ἀριθμόν εἶναι τὴν ψυχήν, κινοῦν δὲ ἑαυτόν, is Aristotle's account of the matter. As a number, it is evolved from unity, that is, God. As unity, God is the perfect one. Imperfection is measured by its distance from unity. Accordingly, perfection consists in going on, step by step, from variety to unity. In unity, therefore is the good; in diversity the evil. The return to good is the return, (ἄνοδος) to unity. And consequently the rule of all "holy living" is the resemblançe of man to God, that is, the return of number to its fontal principium, unity, and virtue is nothing more than harmony. From the same source flows the political philosophy of the Pythagoreans. It is founded on a relation of equality, and justice is a square number.

What the Atomistic school is to the Ionic the Eleatic school is to the Italic. Xenophanes, its founder, is so impressed with the idea of the harmony of the Kosmos brought out by Pythagoras, that he exalts unity at the expense of variety in the constitution of the universe; Parmenides goes still further by a total neglect of that variety, and Zeno furthest of all by an explicit denial of its existence. Everything that was variable, multiple, divisible, everything that was susceptible of change, modification, birth, growth, decay, was declared to be a contradiction and a sham. This was the rankest rationalism—idealism run mad; and thus we have two schools confronting each other, and both of them founded on an exclusive principle, fraught with error and delusion. So true is the remark of Leibnitz that philosophy errs more frequently in what she denies than in what she affirms. Thales and his successors were struck with the varied phenomena of the universe, as displayed to their view in the changing glory of seedtime and harvest, in the blue depths of the unquiet sea, in the ruby flush of dawn, and the starlit majesty of night. But the purely sensuous attempt to solve the mysteries of nature could only end in a half-fledged pantheism, barren of all lasting results on the march of philosophical speculation. Equally unsound, one-sided, and dangerous in an opposite direction, was the arbitrary and illegitimate repudiation on the part of the Eleatic school of all evidence and data furnished by the senses.

Philosophy, or the science of real existence, could ill be promoted by a system which reduced all reality to a shadowy abstraction. The subtle dialectic of the Eleatics had small difficulty in confuting the empirical tenets of the Ionic, just as on the other hand the Ionic gained an easy triumph over the vaunted unity of the Pythagoreans and Eleatics. Empedocles and Anaxagoras endeavoured to effect a compromise between the two. The latter complemented the Ionic physiology with the Pythagorean notion of a ruling mind, independent of the universe, a *νοῦς αὐτοκράτης*, and which, in connection with that universe, is the cause of all motion, *ἀρχὴ τῆς κινήσεως*. The former introduced some Ionic elements into the tenets of Pythagoras and Xenophanes, and encouraged a taste for physical researches.

The whole tendency, however, of the exclusive dogmatism which characterised the speculations of physicists and rationalists alike, was to bring about a sceptical and destructive movement, impugning man's ability to *know*,—a movement frivolous in its origin, impotent in its conclusions, and fallacious in its aim, but still the herald of a better state of things, the groundwork of a more solid and lasting superstructure. Such a movement was consummated by the *Sophists* of whom Gorgias and Protagoras were the most famous champions. The former exaggerated the tenets of the Eleatics by maintaining that nothing really existed, and that, if anything did exist, it would be beyond the cognisance of human ken: the latter carried to its legitimate consequences the materialist teaching of the Ionic and Atomic schools by asserting that all thought resolved itself into sensation; that, apart from those sensations, confessedly fugitive and fluctuating, we know nothing; and that consequently man is the measure of all things; that is true which each man troweth; and thus good may be evil, and evil good. Doctrines so execrable as these were purely negative and destructive, but along with them might be observed one positive and constructive tendency. To the pure objectivity of the four schools we have been considering was added a subjective element. Philosophy, it was now seen, could not live by bread alone, could not exist on the coarse fare of the materialist, any more than on the impalpable abstractions of the idealist. The cycle of nature had run its course; a higher cycle was now to be entered on. The proper study of mankind was man. Some surer ground of consciousness was yearned for. The demand was met by Socrates.

The name of this great reformer stands at the head of the second period of Hellenic philosophy. Some of his most conspicuous characteristics are modesty, prudence, and sobriety. He does not, like the founders of preceding schools, pretend that he has won his way into all the mysteries of the universe, or set himself up, like the Sophists, as the possessor of all knowledge. That he knew nothing was the sum total of all he knew; such was his familiar language. Three things in particular have to be considered in the work he achieved. The way in which he convicted of imposture the crude sophistry of his adversaries; the new method he introduced into philosophy; and, lastly, the doctrines that he taught. With regard to the first, the ingenuity with which he made his antagonists confess that they were fully as ignorant as he was himself, was so conspicuous that it has become identified with his name under the head of "Socratic irony." His method might be summed up in the familiar maxim, *γνῶθι σεαυτόν*, "Know thyself." For in lieu of the baseless fabrics and adventurous hypotheses which earlier schools had constructed on a superficial examination of the world without, Socrates desired that man should first look within, and determine what were his tools, before he began to build, what the limits of his reason and the nature of his consciousness. This principle of self-reference, this analysis of the powers, forms, and processes of the human mind, might well create a new era in the history of Hellenic philosophy. Wholly differing from the dogmatists of either sort who preceded him, Socrates had what they wanted, a true conception of philosophy, and wanted what they had, arbitrary and shallow assertions on the nature of things. Among the more detailed features of the Socratic method singled out for special commendation by Aristotle, are induction and definition. *Δύο γάρ ἐστιν, ἅ τις ἂν ἀποδοίη Σωκράτει δικαίως, τούς τ' ἐπακτικοὺς λόγους, καὶ τὸ ὁρίζεσθαι καθόλου.* We see here, as inchoate and in the germ, those processes which in a more exact and scientific form furnished Plato with the machinery of his Dialectic. As to the doctrines put forth by Socrates, it would be a mistake to suppose that they were only of a moral order. He wished indeed that philosophy should no longer weave her cobwebs in the corners and by-ways of a speculative dreamer's brain, but should thenceforth descend into the market-place, and be as a loadstar, guiding man through the every-day walk of social and private life; but the principle of his reform reached to the very roots of every department of science and of truth, and was not confined to those particular tenets of which he was the apostle and martyr, which he adorned in his life and ratified by his death.

This narrow view of the Socratic philosophy was embodied in the exclusively moral schools which are known as the Cynic and the Cyrenaic, founded by Antisthenes and Aristippus: the morality, however, there taught was but a cloak for maliciousness, an art of indulging in vices on philosophical principles. To these we may add the Megaric school of Euclides, a kind of cross between the Socratic and the Eleatic, which soon degenerated into scepticism. In order, however, to form a correct idea of the influence exerted by Socrates, we must turn from these minor schools to that fuller development wrought out by Plato and Aristotle.

The corner-stone of the Platonic Philosophy is the observation of Facts; its object, the searching out of Ideas, Universals, Laws; its method, Dialectic.

The hidden treasure, after which true wisdom is ever seeking, if haply she may find, is not that which *seems* but that which verily *is*. Beneath the fleeting phenomena which surround us, philosophy demands if there be not something which passes not away. For amid the manifold and conflicting variety of those phenomena, the mind discovers relations, analogies, resemblances, and sees dimly, indeed, but still sees, a reality which is in them, without being of them, a type which they imitate and recall. This reality, this essential and universal element, Plato calls the Idea. Of that idea sensuous things contain but the image. From that image the mind rises as on wings to the direct contemplation of the idea. We have here a marked distinction drawn between sense and reason: but Plato does not stop here; he endeavours to search out the nature of that reason, and, to do this, starts the hypothesis of the soul's existence in an anterior state, when the idea was seen, not as through a glass darkly, not as through the medium of the image, but face to face. Reason is thus nothing more than reminiscence; and when the dialectic arrives at unfolding the universal in the phenomena of the world, it does but revive the reminiscence, and bring out a clear conception of truths of which we formerly had the full fruition.

The sequel of the Platonic doctrines is in keeping with the grandeur of this beginning. Plato, in explaining the nature and origin of the visible world, teaches us to compare it with the ideal world, as a copy with the model. But how was that copy wrought and fashioned? If we need to find out the cause of the phenomena which meet the senses, we no less need a cause of the ideas which invite the homage of the reason. And thus, from step to step, the Platonic dialectic leads us on to the sovereign reason, to absolute unity and perfection, to a self-existing Being, by whom and in whom all being, motion, life, come into existence, to a First Cause, a perfect Intelligence, a God. The world of ideas, and the world of sense form a vast system, of which God is the centre, and build up a universal harmony of which it is man's truest and highest province to discern the laws.

In man, as in the world, as in the state, Plato was at no loss to discover a ruling principle, call it Mind or Reason, which gives to human nature its fellowship with the divine, and enables it in the conduct of life to be conformable to the order and harmony to which the entire universe is in bondage. Intermediate to the mind and the body was the soul, which consists of two parts or members: the one has been lodged by the gods in the breast, the seat of all noble and generous emotions; the other imbedded between the diaphragm and the navel, and full of violent and disastrous passions and affections. To conform to the will of deity, to make divine perfection the guide of life, to love good, eschew evil, quell passion, and rob the senses of their power to lure, such is Plato's idea of man's proper function. In his political philosophy he advocated the unity of the state, as resulting from unity of will and vested in a sovereign power based on justice and exercised with righteousness. Here as everywhere the reins of order are to be entrusted to the keeping of the "best,"—not according to an aristocracy of birth or wealth, but from superiority in intelligence and virtue. As long as philosophers are not kings, as long as kings do not become philosophers, no effectual remedy, thought Plato, could be found against the evils by which states are encompassed. The whole object of the political philosophy of Plato was to bring about a general harmony and consent of parts among the different component members of a state, just as in his moral philosophy he strove to hush that jarring music by which disordered passions and earth-bound affections bring confusion and discord in the place of order and of law. To sum up this most feeble account of the Platonic tenets, it should be observed that in every department Plato made it his endeavour to measure all things by the standard of the ideal. It is this which gives to his inestimable dialogues an influence that at once soothes and elevates the mind. The good, the beautiful, and the true, are there conterminous; we pass from one to the other without being scarcely conscious that we have changed our ground. His philosophy is an organic whole, root, leaf, and branch; and so far from being lost in the clouds, it has its foundation in the innermost depths of human nature.

Plato and Aristotle are generally represented as the respective heads of the ideal and the experimental philosophy. This is a true statement, if construed with considerable latitude; but if pushed to its literal meaning would involve a gross misapprehension of both philosophers. The theory of Ideas being the cardinal tenet, the sap and marrow of the Platonic system, and Aristotle's writings teeming with attacks on that theory, it was not unnatural, on a hasty view, that the one should be regarded not as polar and complemental, but as diagonally opposed to and subversive of the other. This narrow and exclusive view, both of Plato and Aristotle, had a marked and mischievous effect on the subsequent development of their doctrines by their respective disciples. The fact is that Aristotle is an idealist and an experimentalist in one; he assigns a twofold origin to man's knowledge, particular truths being derived from sensuous perception, and general truths from the understanding through the channel of induction. To the former he assigns a psychological anteriority, to the latter a logical anteriority and superiority. While both these classes of truths form the matter of science, logic is its form: it is indeed the instrument, or organum, common to all science. His theory of the syllogism is a masterpiece of ingenuity and analysis. It is important to note, however, as a connecting link between Plato and Aristotle, that the Stagyrite seems to have been led to his conception of the syllogism by the Platonic dialectic. That dialectic, it should be remembered, has an ascending and a descending portion. It is with the first of these aspects that we are most familiar; we rise with Plato to the contemplation of the idea, but with him rarely descend from the idea to the realities which are its types. This descent is effected by two special processes; Definition, which finds the one in the many, and Division, which finds the many in the one. If the student will turn to three important passages in the *Analytics* (*Prior.* i. 31., *Post.* ii. 5, 13), he will find that Aristotle considered the dialectic division into genera and species an important element of the syllogistic method; that syllogisms are capable of being formed by means of it; and that it may be made to subserve not only the definition, but the demonstration of the scientific syllogisms. It would seem as if it had been by criticising the defects of this portion of the Platonic dialectic that Aristotle was led to think out for himself the great principles of his immortal Organon. Philosophical sciences were divided by Aristotle into two principal branches (exclusive of logic), speculative and practical. With regard to the former of these he gives the pre-eminence to the "first philosophy," called Metaphysic, from the place it occupies in his works, and dealing with the investigation of first causes or principles. These are four in number:—1. The material cause or substratum; 2. The formal cause; 3. The efficient cause; and 4. The final cause. The "second philosophy" is Physic, or the general theory of bodies. "By these two sciences," says a learned writer, "Aristotle rises to the notion of a Supreme Being, the only pure *act*, the only energy without matter, the immutable and infinite thought, the only motionless First Cause. But it is only as a final, not as an efficient cause, that this prime mover acts upon the world, which he is not even cognisant of. It is the world which of itself is eternally aspiring towards the final supreme cause, towards the absolute good." The Aristotelian Physic investigates three properties of bodies — Matter, Form, and Privation. This last is so called from the fact that matter, though susceptible of all forms, is at the time limited to its actual form. The drift of the Physic is to explain the passage from one form to another, that is to investigate motion, which presupposes a prime immovable mover, and which comprises change of quality or bulk as well as place. Aristotle is here guilty of the mistake of considering the laws of nature matter for *à priori* speculation, based on arbitrary principles, and worked out by a hasty induction. The services he has rendered to zoology are pronounced by competent judges to be of the highest order, and he has been styled the creator of the science of Comparative Anatomy. His Psychology occupies itself less with the soul proper in particular, than with the principle of life generally, vegetative in the plant, vegetative and sensitive in the animal, and in man intellectual as well. The great beauty and value of the Psychology consist in the admirable description of the phenomena of life, the analysis of the sensations and passions. It must be confessed, however, that the unity and activity of the soul are both of them grievously misapprehended. In the practical sciences we find in Aristotle treatises on Ethics, Politics, Rhetoric, and Poetics. The principle of the *Ethics* is, in a great measure, empirical, being founded on the search after happiness, not on the law of duty: neither is the rule of human conduct other than vaguely defined, when we are told to keep the mean between two contrary excesses. In Politics Aristotle is equally utilitarian, and so accepts as legitimate, practices, such as slavery, abhorrent to what is now understood as the moral law. His observations, however, are singularly suggestive. The *Rhetoric* is one of the most masterly of the Aristotelian treatises, and may be said to carry out in scientific form those lofty principles of eloquence which we find scattered through the writings of Plato. In lieu of the contemptible artifices taught in the rhetoric of the Sophists we have here a profound analysis of the sentiments, passions, and characters of men, with a view to the elaborate construction of an oratorical style and of the principles of demonstration to be adopted before divers kinds of assemblies. No rhetorical treatise has ever dived so deep into the very root of the question; but scanty are the flowers which rise upon the surface. The honied tones of Plato are unknown to Aristotle. This contrast between the two is most conspicuous in the *Poetics*, where we miss that idealism which imparts so great a charm to the Platonic philosophy of the Beautiful. The Aristotelian aesthetics are in part empirical, being founded on the principle of imitation of Nature, as an end, and not merely as a mean.

From the above hasty sketch of the tenets of the two greatest geniuses that ever adorned antiquity, it will be seen that they divide Hellenic philosophy into two great branches, not wanting in points of contact with the line of inquiry pursued, as we have seen, by the Ionic and Pythagorean schools, Aristotle manifesting a disposition towards the sensualism of the former, and Plato to the idealism of the latter. This will easily be seen by any one who reflects on the exaggerated form which those tendencies assumed under their immediate successors. In the hands of Speusippus, Xenocrates, Polemon, Crates, and Crantor, the Platonic Academy became almost openly Pythagorean in its tenets. It may be remarked that while the majority of the Platonists are moralists, that of the Peripatetics consists of physicists, whose tenets respecting the soul and the existence of a God are of the most materialist character. Such was the pass to which Aristotelian doctrines were brought in a short time after his death.

With Aristotle and Plato ends the second period of Hellenic philosophy, the period which we have styled the objective-subjective. With regard to the third period, comprising the Epicureans, the Stoics, and the Sceptics, we purpose confining ourselves to a few very brief remarks, which have a bearing on a general characteristic of Hellenic civilisation more than once animadverted on in these pages. The two schools first named are indicative of a new and important movement, social and philosophical in one. What had in former systems been the background, is now become the foreground of speculation. Physic and metaphysic, dialectic and logic, are now made subordinate to the more practical question, moral philosophy. The philosophy of the *citizen* has been supplanted by the philosophy of the *man*; and if, as we have asserted, it was the office of Hellas to *educe* the *man* from the *citizen*, the general tone and tendency of philosophical inquiry in the third period are an indication that that function is rapidly approaching its completion. The Stoics were wont to compare philosophy to a garden. The enclosure was logic; the soil and trees, physiology; but moral philosophy was the fruit. The subjective has now gained the ascendency over the objective. The idea now loomed upon the minds of men that there were societies higher than those which any civil polity could frame, and bonds of citizenship which unite together, not merely a demus or a phratria, but the whole family of man. It is needless to observe how largely this change of direction in the march of philosophy was calculated to prepare the soil for the sowing of Christian seed. With regard to the general drift of the tenets set forth by the three schools — Epicurean, Stoic, Sceptic — which close our sketch of Hellenic philosophy, we cannot, we think, better conclude this chapter than by quoting the words of Zeller* :—"The general outlines of philosophical development during this period are as follows. The pervading idea of the post-Aristotelian philosophy, or the necessity that man should withdraw into pure contemplation, there to find unlimited beatitude — this idea is, in the first instance, promulgated in a purely dogmatic form, as a fundamental moral principle, and is substantiated by an equally dogmatic physic and logic, which are framed in all their parts with reference to this end. This result is arrived at by Stoicism and Epicureanism in opposite ways. Of the two attributes which constitute the essence of personality, namely, that it be, first, a reasonable, and, secondly, an individual existence, the former is as pre-eminently characteristic of the Stoic as the latter of the Epicurean system. The one places the vocation and happiness of man solely in the submission of the individual to general laws and to reason, that is, in virtue; the other, in the freedom of the individual from everything external, and in the consciousness of this independence, in the impassibility of individual existence, and in freedom from all pain. By these practical principles the theoretical views of creation in both systems are determined in their general outlines, as we shall hereafter show. However antagonistic they may appear, both in fact occupy essentially the same ground. Perfect equanimity of disposition and uncontrolled freedom of self-contemplation, are the goal to which both strive by different ways. Along with this arises the necessity of giving prominence to this common ground as the essential aim and subject matter of all philosophy, and if the scientific hypotheses of philosophical systems contradict each other, the only conclusion to be drawn is that they cannot attain their end by any definite dogmatic view — that we are justified in ignoring science generally, in order to arrive at a complacent indifference about everything and perfect equanimity of mind, from the consciousness of our *Nescience*. Thus does Scepticism follow in the wake of Stoicism and Epicureanism, as the third

* *Die Philosophie der Griechen*, iii. 1. p. 10.

form which stamps the philosophy of that period; and, after keeping a somewhat isolated direction under the auspices of the Pyrrhonists, enters with the New Academy into a wider sphere of influence."

Juno in the diplois or doubled cloak.

(From a fictile vase.)

Western View of the Athenian Acropolis.
(*From the Age of Pericles*, according to the restoration by F. C. Penrose, Esq.)

CHAPTER VII.

ARCHITECTURE.

The classical architecture of Hellas in its three branches or orders —Doric, Ionic, and Corinthian—is a subject so vast, comprehensive, and many-sided, that we think we shall best consult the interests of the student and obviate confusion of ideas, if we select from the numerous aspects which offer themselves to our view, some one which may best admit of succinct exposition, and best unfold the idea of Hellenic civilisation and the genius of the Hellenic race. Eschewing, therefore, the historical and professional or structural details, for which the student should betake himself to the pages of Müller, Stieglitz, Hirt, and Bötticher, we shall make it our leading object to bring out as strongly as we can those features and properties of Hellenic architecture which impart to it so pre-eminently the dignity of art, and to trace in the various members of the building that *expressional* element which justifies us in looking upon the entire structure as the embodiment of a latent idea, an abstract conception in a suitable concrete form.

And here we are at once met by the inquiry, what is the leading idea of the Greek temple, what the prevailing principle which runs through its construction, not so much consciously contemplated as unconsciously directive. The purport of such an inquiry may be illustrated by the answer we should give to it in the case of Gothic architecture. It only requires a glance at any tolerably complete Gothic building to enable us to perceive that the governing principle which not only supports but almost constitutes the edifice, the principle to which all others are subordinate, by which the features of the style are defined and established, is the principle of frame-work, modified indeed by the principle of wall-work in those blank and inorganic portions of the mass, such as the panels of the roof and the spandrels of pier-arches, into which it was unable to infuse itself, but neither overcome nor suppressed till the spirit of the Gothic structure was quenched and smothered, its significance lost, its elements disbanded, its organic connection broken up and destroyed, by the perversions of later styles. This idea, when couched in more popular language, ascribes the derivation of Gothic architecture to hypothetical archetypes of wicker-work, to interwoven structures of flexible boughs. Thus much by way of a general illustration of the nature of that elementary law of which we are endeavouring to trace the workings in the features of Hellenic architecture. Accordingly we resume the inquiry with which we started: what is the leading idea of the Greek temple? we answer, the principle of column-work, a principle not the less fertile in its results because it is at first sight very simple in its expression. Before we consider the various aspects under which this principle may be regarded, it may be well to give a hasty sketch of the general arrangements of a Greek temple, and of the principal members of which it was composed. The modern conception of a religious edifice has little in common with a Greek temple. This was not so much a receptacle for worshippers as the dwelling-place of the deity, in whose honour it was created. It was emphatically the "house of God." In fact it was a kind of gift-offering or ἀνάθημα, a petrified prayer, "lifted up" or erected by the Greeks to appease the wrath or win the smiles of Heaven. The rectangular oblong platform of stone on which the entire building stood may be looked upon as the altar on which this offering was placed. It might also be called the *cothurn* of the temple: for both in the drama and in architecture the significance of the additional stature and altitude imparted to the actor and edifice respectively, was eminently religious, and intended to convey ideas and associations of something akin to the divine, whether a hero or a sanctuary. This platform was called the *stereobate*; to its uppermost slab or surface—called the *stylobate* or common substratum of all the vertical or supporting members of the temple—access was gained by a number, generally an uneven number, of steps, the height of which was frequently so great as to render necessary a special set of steps opposite the entrance like the *cunei* of ancient theatres. This arrangement, however, was considered to involve a certain sacrifice of the σεμνότης or dignity which attached to the ritualistic character of the ἀνάθημα. When you reached the highest step you would find yourself occupying the space between two columns, Doric, Ionic, or Corinthian,—a space which varied in different temples according to the diameter of the column, but was the same throughout for the same temple. Both the number of columns employed and the intercolumniations adopted gave rise to systematic classifications of temples, the terms of which have been preserved by Vitruvius. Suffice it to say that the heading under which the model temple we are now describing would be placed, is the so-called *peripteral*; a designation which implies that the colonnade or portico was continued on every side of the temple, the number of columns in front being, we will suppose, six, and on either side thirteen: for the front and side of the rectangular oblong (which was uniformly the shape of the Greek temple) were, as a general rule, in the proportion of one to two. At a distance sufficiently great to allow a convenient breadth of colonnade, arose the walls of what, in a stricter sense, was the temple itself, which was frequently divided into three compartments, all of them bounded by the same lateral walls. First, you had the vestibule or πρόναος, the entrance to which was ornamented in some cases by two smaller columns, in others by square pillars placed at equal distances from the piers which bounded the extremities of the side walls. Then came the σηκός or *cella*, separated from the vestibule by a transverse wall, means of communication being provided through a door in the centre. It was here that the statue of the god was placed (ἕδος), protected in front by railings, and behind by a transverse wall, which ran across the building, and thus limited the space assigned to the cella. In the centre of this compartment, we should add, stood an altar. It has often been made matter of discussion how light found admission into the interior of the cella, as the transverse walls just mentioned would necessarily exclude any such feeble portions as might otherwise have penetrated from the open colonnade, either through the vestibule of the temple, or through the back chamber, of which we shall presently speak. One of the most important methods by which this problem was solved has given its name to the temples in which it was employed, the buildings so constructed being called "*hypaethral*," a word which literally signifies "sub dio." This epithet alludes to an open space just over the centre of the cella, to which the roof did not extend. In order to furnish the roof with an adequate substitute for that support which the ridge would have supplied had the slope not stopped short where the hole began, a double tier of columns reached from the floor of the cella to the border of the open space.

The difficulties attending this subject are too intricate to be entered on in this place. Suffice it to state, as the result very generally arrived at by the most competent judges, that all ancient temples were provided with some opening (ὀπή, ὀπαῖον: compare *metope*,—a word, however, which is only found in Vitruvius) over the middle of the cella, the epithet "*hypaethral*" being restricted to those where the part left uncovered so greatly exceeded the dimensions of an ordinary skylight as to render necessary the adventitious support of the interior colonnade already mentioned.

The cella was in some cases followed by a third compartment, called the *opisthodome* or back-chamber, which was either a repetition of the vestibule, or a closed space serving the purposes of a sanctuary or treasury. A hasty glance at the exterior of the building must complete our general survey of the Hellenic temple; fuller details being reserved for the remarks we have to make on the functions of each particular member. Waiving the distinctions which obtained in different orders of architecture, we here find the columns employed in supporting the three successive divisions of the entablature, architrave, frieze, and cornice. These are surmounted on the fore and back fronts of the building by that triangular figure called the pediment, the shape of which bears some resemblance to the outspread wings of an eagle and was thence called by the Greeks ἀετός and ἀέτωμα.* The oblique or sloping line of this crowning member of the building may be called the synthesis of the vertical and horizontal lines which are found in the supporting and supported members respectively, which we may likewise term the thesis and antithesis.

It is in the harmonious blending of the two conflicting tendencies of verticality and horizontality inherent in the supporting and supported members respectively, that we shall find the key to those peculiar characteristics which are emblematical of Hellenic architecture, and which it is the object of this chapter to impress upon the attention of the student. As it is in the column-work and entablature that these opposing principles are exhibited, we shall reserve for the last the consideration of the capitals of the different orders, as the part where the conflict is sustained, the blending effected, the transition brought about.

First, then, as regards the column. And here we are led to speak of one of the most important differences which obtained between the Doric order on the one hand, and the Ionic and Corinthian on the other. It may best be stated in the words of the Greek

* Pindar, *Olymp.* xiii. 21; Aristoph. *Av.* 1101; Pausan. viii. 45, v. 10.

lexicographer Pollux (viii. 27): στυλοβάτης ἡ τοῦ Δωρικοῦ κίονος βάσις· σπεῖρα δὲ ἡ τοῦ Ἰωνικοῦ. It is not said that the Doric columns have no base, but that the stylobate is their common base. Now the student will not need to be reminded that the peculiar tendency of ancient forms of commonwealth to absorb the personal individuality of the man in the body corporate of the state, was at once more palpable and more complete in those states of Greece where Doric institutions and habits of thought had a marked ascendency. And just as in their forms of government every individual was compelled to remain within certain prescribed limits, and forbidden to strive after personal independence, obedience to established order stifling the assertion of individual freedom, so, in their architecture, in their system of column-work, everything which might be construed into a symbol of self-dependence, was cautiously eschewed, everything which might intimate a combination of manifold energy and power for attaining one common end, was as cautiously and emphatically brought into relief. Unlike either the Ionic or the Corinthian order, the shaft extended to the very surface of that cubical platform of solid stone which ushered in our description of the Hellenic temple: from that platform it seemed to grow like the trees of God from their parent earth; nothing was allowed to intervene, neither plinth nor torus, scotia nor astragal, nor any of the elements of the Ionic σπεῖρα, which could in any way intercept the connection between the many shafts and the one base, which could in any way foster the idea that the work which each column had to do might be done as it listed, with aim independent, with power uncontrolled, that the support for which it was indebted to the common base was in any sense mediate, derivative, transmitted, instead of immediate, primary, direct.

Whimsical as this may appear to some when viewed by itself, the argument gains in weight and the illustration in vividness, when we compare the column-work of that second branch of the Hellenic family which has given its name to the Ionic Order of Hellenic architecture. For here we find that a precisely analogous parallel obtains between the social principles of the Ionic race and the structural principles of the Ionic shaft. As regards the former, the state still assumes supreme authority over the wills, and claims the undivided allegiance, of each of its members;—but the authority was no longer uncontested, the homage was no longer the unreasoning obedience of an instinct; it was looked upon, at least was acted on, as a duty of imperfect obligation. The individuality of the *man* was gradually emerging from the chrysalis condition of the *citizen*. Accordingly, in those states of Greece where Doric forms of government were overborne by the violent shocks of political convulsions, and yielded to the tide of advancing civilisation, an attempt was ever made to throw off the thraldom of the citizen and assert the freedom of the man: the state was still respected as an admirable machinery for keeping order within, and warding off aggression from without, but it was no longer regarded as one undivided moral agent; the figure without which each of its citizens was an unmeaning cipher. So that, while in both orders of architecture the cubical platform of stone forms the ground-work of the temple, in the Ionic portico an attempt is made to express a feeling of independence, and to sever that combined unity of action, to which the Doric temple owes so much of its severe grandeur, by giving to each shaft a separate base in addition to the base which underlies them all, and which now wears a secondary and subordinate significance, as if it were merely intended to give height to the edifice,—no longer the life and soul of its stability, that without which the building could not stand. But though each of the shafts in the Ionic (and we may add the Corinthian) order had separate bases, in these no distinctions were allowed to exist for the column-work of the same temple. So that it may perhaps be said that in this particular feature, unity was the characteristic of the Doric, and uniformity of Ionic architecture. The one altogether ignored, the other reconciled, diversities. In fact, whether the coincidence, the undesigned spontaneous coincidence, between the social and structural principles of the respective races—a coincidence which is perhaps rather suggested by the nomenclature of the two orders and the general march of Hellenic civilisation than susceptible of being brought home as it were to each race by elaborate proof from written texts—be looked upon as a fancy or a fact, sufficient yet remains to account for those elements of beauty by which the mind of the beholder is impressed. That it is something more than a fancy, however, we are strongly disposed to infer from a very remarkable analogy which obtains between the drama and the architecture of Greece. The three great orders, Doric, Ionic, and Corinthian, are, in respect of the considerations above advanced, a curious counterpart of that successive unfolding of human individuality which we meet with in Æschylus, Sophocles, and Euripides. Coerced and subdued by a supreme and over-ruling destiny in the first, evenly balanced between blind submission and responsible freedom of action in the second, running to wild and dangerous excesses in the third, the impressions which in each case it leaves upon the reader's mind may not unaptly be compared to those with which we take off our eyes from the masculine grandeur of the Doric, the bewitching grace of the Ionic, and the florid exuberance of the Corinthian order. When reduced to their most abstract form, these successive stages in the development of Hellenic civilisation, whether in its political, intellectual, or moral aspect, may severally be designated as :—1. The Objective. 2. The Objective-Subjective. 3. The Subjective.

We now proceed to other aspects and features of the system of column-work on which we are disposed to lay greater stress, as their truth has been very generally acquiesced in by the masters of the craft, and by writers on art. And first we would call the student's attention to what may be termed the principle of Vitality, a principle which may indeed be discerned in all the members of the building, betraying as they do a seeming consciousness of the functions assigned to them, but which is more especially transparent in that portion of the temple with which we are now engaged. How strongly, for example, is the idea of buoyancy and of organic structure conveyed by the very shape (cylindrical without being a cylinder) of each column; the axis of the shaft being as it were the central seat of life. The fluting or, as it was called, *rhabdosis* of the shaft, so far from weakening, does but bring out more strongly the principle of vitality. For the distance of every point in the striated surface from the vertical axis still bore a certain fixed ratio, when not actually equal to the corresponding distance of every other point: and this harmony of "relations" is one of the chief sources by which that impression of vitality is conveyed, that energising spirit produced, which animates every column of the Hellenic temple. But in what direction is this energy exerted—on what object is it spent? The Greek was not a man to introduce in any member of a building a symbolical display of power exerted disproportionate to the amount of power resisted. He left this to the Roman, who seems to have had a marvellous power of misapprehending the purport and disfiguring the beauty of Hellenic architecture. And this brings us to a third feature of Hellenic column-work, the principle of Ascendant Support. How beautifully this is expressed, both by the tapering of the shaft as it approaches the capital, and by the fluted lines! If in the axis, as has been observed, be contained the inner principle of life, in these features of the exterior are no less plainly to be discerned its outward signs. If in the tapering be seen the motive upward energy, seen in characters which no one can mistake, the fluting is equally symbolical of the spirit by which that energy is sustained, showing firmness and resistance to the weight imposed, giving the lie to any apprehensions lest beneath that weight the shaft should succumb. With characteristic insensibility to the meaning and beauty of Hellenic architecture, Mr. Ruskin asserts that of course the fluting was a mere imitation of the bark of a tree. Others, with less dogmatism and more sense, have dwelt upon the advantages of that play of light and shadow which the channelled lines of the fluting were so admirably calculated to produce. Both these theories, it is submitted, should yield precedence to that principle of upward and upholding energy with which the soaring striated lines, suddenly checked at the capital, are indelibly impressed. This may more readily appear if we bear in mind the comparison between the fluting of Hellenic column-work and the system adopted in Egyptian architecture. For here, in those cases where the ascendant energy was not altogether thwarted and denied by the presence of horizontal lines drawn across the shaft, the Egyptian columns had frequently the appearance of a Greek column turned, as it were, inside out; the concave fluting being here replaced by a succession of parallel convex stripes of *reeding*. The impression conveyed was as directly opposite as might be expected. Instead of power to resist, we have an evident appearance of a tendency to collapse; a tendency of which the Egyptian himself seems to have been conscious, for the shaft was girt about in various parts with circular belts, reminding one of those cylindrical bundles of reeds or bamboos which have been looked upon as the imaginary prototypes of Egyptian column-work. Had it not been for the avowed principle of Egyptian architecture to embody and exhibit the overwhelming preponderance of downward gravitating pressure, it would have been difficult to account for the fact that, whenever the decoration of the shaft assumed a vertical upward direction, it was uniformly stamped with a character of weakness and insufficiency to bear the burden imposed, the puffy convexity of the surface suggesting — if we may be pardoned such idea—that the column was *blown*. To carry on the metaphor, the fluting of the Hellenic column, alternately radiating from and converging towards the central seat of life, may be regarded as symbolical of the calm and regular action of respiration petrified. The *effortless* character of the energy thus put into play is beautifully typified by the slight bulge or swelling — thence called *entasis*—half-way up the shaft. The impression of ease and elasticity thus conveyed is much enhanced in the Ionic column by the peculiar character of the mouldings which adorn the so-called Attic base.

As, in the Doric column-work, the principle of support is asserted with greater sturdiness, by virtue of greater massiveness and inferior altitude of shaft, than in the other orders (the masculine severity of the race here contrasting itself with the more Asiatic softness and feminine grace of the Ionians), so, in the entablature of that order, we should naturally expect, *à priori*, that the superincumbent horizontal principle should wear an appearance of greater massiveness and weight in proportion to the increased means of support which are provided to encounter the burden; so careful was the Greek not to disturb that harmony of relation which regulates all the outgoings of his intellectual life and runs as a silver cord through all the better elements of his civilisation. This expectation is at once realised by a glance at the first member of the entablature called by the Greeks *epistylium*, a word denoting its incumbent position on the summit of the columns, and otherwise known by the name of architrave, a compound of Greek and Latin signifying the principal beam. For here the flat unbroken mass which meets the eye in a Doric temple, evidently conveys a far more forcible idea of solid mass than in the architrave of the Ionic order, which was commonly broken up into three so-called "faces," projecting slightly over each other, which thus divided, and by dividing diminished, that expression of ponderous bulk which is so marked a characteristic of the bold imposing front of a Doric temple. It may be observed, in passing, that we have here exhibited the same hostility to the unifying principle of the Doric race, the same assertion of individual independence, of which we have already had occasion to witness the effects in considering the column-work of the building.

Separated from the architrave by a peculiar fillet called the *taenia*, lay the second member of the entablature known by the name of *frieze*. And here the distinguishing features which belonged to the Doric temple are peculiarly calculated to illustrate that conflict between the ascendant energy of the column-work and the pendent gravitating mass of the entablature which it is our object to impress upon the student's mind. For the Doric frieze did not present a continuous surface like the Ionic, but was divided into rectangular spaces by means of a series of projections called triglyphs from a cluster of three vertical prismatic shanks, with two channellings between, and half a channelling on either side. These projections were so arranged that one was placed over each column and intercolumniation. The frieze was thus split up into a series of vertical members discharging a certain function (of which we shall presently explain the nature), alternating with a series of rectangular spaces either left vacant or subservient to purely decorative purposes. This alternation of functional and non-functional parts may be considered a kind of echo of what we meet with in the column-work of the temple, where the columns and intercolumniations present a similar succession. But the Doric triglyph has a yet deeper meaning. If, as we have said, in the fluting of the column be seen as it were the successive inhaling and expulsion of its breath, just as the ascendant energy of the column is buoyant and strong, how beautifully is this same expression carried on and continued in the triglyphs over the axis of each column, their flutings, whole or halved, being as it were an indication that the upward energy was not entirely quenched in its collision with the architrave, but had yet some force to spare with which to meet the pendent mass of the cornice: how beautifully, again, is this expression blended with the opposite expression of downward pressure which is typified in those rows of pendent conical drops or *guttae* attached by a fillet to the extremity of each triglyph.

As our main object in dwelling upon the entablature* of the temple is to bring out the contrast between the two principles of Pressure and Support, and thereby to show how the Hellenic architect fulfilled that cardinal law, and reached that highest aim of all unity, the harmonious reconciling, the *eurythmia* of diversities, it will not be necessary for us to bestow many words upon its third member the *cornice*: for there the expression of pendent mass reigns so supreme in the heavy projecting drip, the deep shadow cast on the frieze, the outjutting mouldings, and the so-called mutules fringing the soffite over each triglyph, and very generally over each metope, that it seems superfluous to institute a demonstration of what must needs appear to every one a self-evident fact. It may not be so needless to observe how beautifully the effect aimed at received its final stroke and consummation in the low pediment which surmounted the temple on the fore and back fronts of the building, forming in fact its gable ends. It is probable that the restriction of this member of architecture to sacred edifices was originally founded (though afterwards legally enforced) on the advantages of the *impluvium* in private dwellings on the score of coolness—a consideration which was of no weight in the case of temples, the rather as they were always erected on high and airy ground. On the general character, however, of the pediment we shall avail ourselves of a passage in Cicero*, so remarkable for truth of feeling and elegance of taste, that we can scarcely believe it to have been written by a man who thought it becoming indignantly to spurn the suspicion that he had any knowledge of the history, or appreciation of the beauties, of art. The course of his argument renders it necessary for him to show that what is really useful will always be found combined with more or less dignity, not to say beauty. After quoting some instances from nature, such as the motion of heavenly bodies and the structure of trees, he proceeds to art, and here he very justly alleges that in the column-work supporting temple and portico, utility and dignity run hand in hand: this is equally true, he adds, in the pediment of temples; for although its slope may originally

* *B. de Orat.* 180.

have been designed for carrying off water from the roof, no one can deny that in ministering to structural necessities it ministers to grace and dignity as well: in this case he believes that utility is swallowed up in beauty; for if the building were set up in heaven, where rain is out of the question, he is persuaded that all its dignity would be gone if the pediment were omitted. It may be well in passing to remind the student of a passage in the *Birds* of Aristophanes where a promise is held out by the founder of Cuckootown that all the houses of the inhabitants shall be provided with pediments just as if they were so many temples (v. 1109):—

> εἶτα πρὸς τούτοισιν ὥσπερ ἐν ἱεροῖς οἰκήσετε.
> τὰς γὰρ ὑμῶν οἰκίας ἐρέψομεν πρὸς αἰετόν.

It will be remembered, too, that among the divine honours paid to Caesar, the privilege of having a pediment to his house was one of the number, nor that the least.*

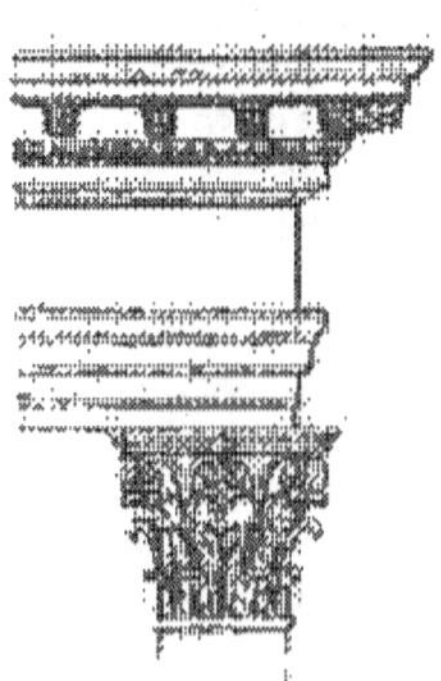

Doric and Corinthian Capitals.

We now come to that part of the column-work which we have called the point of collision between the two conflicting tendencies of pressure and support of which it has been our endeavour to bring out the expression. We allude to the capital of the column. And here, before we enter upon an examination of the details of various orders, we are prepared to expect that in all three we shall find a sturdy assertion of equality between the opposing forces, the column repudiating the suspicion of insufficient power to bear the burden with which it now comes into more immediate contact, by exchanging the strain of upward effort for an attitude of comparative ease, the entablature giving no less undeniable in-

* Cic. *Phil.* II. 43. 110; Flor. 4. 2.

dications of its downward pressure, and yet both the buoyancy and the pressure so happily blended, that the one seems as little to resist as to succumb, the other seems rather to float than to press.

Various as is the conformation of the three capitals, Doric, Ionic, and Corinthian, which may be said to epitomise the distinctions between the three orders, they all contrive in different ways and degrees to bring out the general idea which we have just stated,—the Doric in the greatest purity by the principle of Line, the Ionic by the principle of Elastic Matter, the Corinthian by the principle of Vegetable Life. The principle of line is indeed common to them all, but in the two later orders it is so over-laid and disguised by the two principles here ascribed to them, that they may be allowed to take its place. To begin with the Doric capital, we have here three members to consider. First, the plinth or abacus; second, the echinus or ovolo, with its triple annulets attached; and third, the necking or *hypotrachelium*, or small portion of the shaft contained between the lower annulet and a horizontal groove or channelling running round the shaft parallel to the annulet. The assertion of a sufficiency of power is admirably expressed by the horizontal groove just mentioned, which interrupts the soaring lines of the fluted shaft. The continuation of these lines above the groove in spite of the obstacle which vainly endeavours to arrest their passage, and that at only a short distance from the summit, where the diminution of girth might be thought to imply a diminution of strength, witnesses to a redundancy of energy in the shaft, and materially contributes to the general effect inherent in the principle of column-work. It has been remarked that the triple row of annulets which encompass with serried grasp the echinus serves to bring into relief the expanding bulge or curve by which they are immediately succeeded. Both the degree and nature of that curve varied in different buildings. In those of Athens it was almost always part of an hyperbola, in others part of an ellipse, never, as in Roman architecture, a quadrant or yet smaller arc of a circle—a distinction by the way which obtains in all the mouldings of Greek and Roman temples respectively. It has been suggested by some that this bulge may be considered as indicative of some soft matter interposed between the shaft and the abacus, and petrified while undergoing compression from the superincumbent mass. We do not see that this hypothesis helps to elucidate the particular function of the echinus. It would be more to the purpose to observe that if, at such close proximity to the ponderous mass of the architrave, the column can afford to dispense with bringing its entire force into action, we know of nothing which could convey so gracefully to the mind of the beholder that assurance of solidity which had been devised by the mind of the architect as the undulating pliancy of a curve—still further heightened by the quirk or turning inwards of the upper edge where the echinus meets the abacus — in lieu of the thickset rigidity of a straight line, so eminently symbolical of strain and effort. The final step of the transition between the curved surface of the echinus and the horizontal rectangular surface of the entablature, was fitly indicated by the third member of the capital, the plinth or abacus. In the Doric order its dimensions exceeded the lowest or largest diameter of the shaft, evidently with a view to distribute the incumbent weight over those parts most adapted for support, and to remove or lighten the pressure where the resistance was less severe.

Having endeavoured to show, in the case of the Doric capital, how that member of Hellenic architecture is intended to embody, assist, and express the harmonious transition from the upward tendencies of the soaring column to the downward pressure of the incumbent entablature, and so mitigate the violence and soften the abruptness of the collision, we shall be able to dismiss more briefly the consideration of that same member in the Ionic and Corinthian orders. The egg and dart ornament, which was only painted on the Doric echinus, is sculptured on the Ionic,—the annulets above mentioned are replaced by an astragal or bead-like fillet. But the most marked and distinguishing feature of the Ionic capital is to be found in the spiral volutes which overhang the echinus, and of which the connecting band or list is interposed between the echinus and the abacus, the latter being thinner and smaller than in the Doric capital. Though there seems little room to doubt that this most characteristic member of the Ionic capital was borrowed from Asia, it was made subservient by the Greeks — who infused their own peculiar spirit into everything they imported from other nations—to purposes very different from those which originally suggested its design, namely to the same expression of harmony between the vertical and horizontal elements of the building which we have pointed out in the Doric capital. Perhaps the actual form of the volutes, as indicative of what we have styled the principle of elastic matter, may be best typified to the mind, if we suppose a thickly quilted elastic oblong drapery, of the same width as the echinus, to be laid over that member, and then conceive the overhanging extremities to coil themselves up spiral-fashion when subjected to the pressure of the architrave. This image accounts for the inferior dimensions of the abacus;—a slab of greater surface would be less calculated to cause the drapery to roll itself up. It is needless to remark how greatly this portion of the Ionic capital, so regarded, heightens the effect of that lightness and buoyancy which distinguish an Ionic from a Doric building.

The first well-assured instance of the use of the Corinthian capital is in the temple of Athena Alea at Tegea (erected by Scopas soon after the ninety-sixth Olympiad), in the interior of

North-west View of Erechtheum, restored.

which (for the external portico was Ionic) Pausanias and Strabo inform us that Corinthian columns were superimposed on Doric. We might indeed infer, *à priori*, that the Corinthian order belonged to an age when the spirit of subjective individuality was in the ascendant, from the circumstance that it alone of the three orders traces its origin to the inventive faculties of an individual artist, not of a race. All are familiar with the story of the basket covered with a tile, around which nestled and grew, till they coiled back as they reached the overjutting corners of the tile, the leaves of an acanthus which grew by the grave of the girl in whose memory the basket was there placed. The story goes on to state that an artist of great note, Callimachus, was struck with the sight, and adapted the acanthus-swathed calathus to the purposes of columnar decoration. We have mentioned this story because we think it involves the best explanation which can be offered of the expressional features of the Corinthian capital. These are inferior in interest and significance to what we have met with in the Doric and Ionic orders, of which the Corinthian may be called the synthesis, created as it was in an age of decline, when art was passing through its eclectic phase, and compensating, by laboured combinations, for the absence of creative spontaneity. It is sufficient, however, for our purpose in the present chapter that we should call attention to what the Corinthian capital has in common with the two earlier orders, namely the office of facilitating the passage from the round and upward tendencies of the columnwork, to the rectangular and downward pressure of the entablature. The manner in which this office is discharged we have termed the principle of Vegetable Life. It should be observed, however, that while in the Doric and Ionic capitals the collision of the opposing tendencies is merged into harmony, in the Corinthian it is only masked by a meretricious mixture of foliage and volutes.

With regard to the polychromy of Greek architecture, we must refer the reader for details to the excellent treatise of Kugler on that subject, and other more detailed works on the history of architecture. On the general spirit and principles by which the Greeks were governed in the application of colour to their architecture, we feel we cannot do better than quote the words of Chevalier Bröndsted—a great authority—who asserts, with unhesitating confidence, that all the Greek temples were more or less painted. After what fashion, the following passage is intended to set forth.

"The application of colours to the decoration of architecture in the temples of Greece was of three kinds. In the first place, colour was used as a coating, without any attempt at illusion, in order to bring out the architecture properly so called, that is, to give life to the meaningless, monotonous tint of the stone; to bring together, and nearer to the eye that which in the artist's conception ought to be looked at as a whole, but which in the execution was kept apart; to give prominence to all corresponding parts, and bring them closer under the eye and observation of the spectator; in short, to heighten the effect of the whole, by giving a pleasing and distinct aspect to component parts. We must not omit the material advantage which this coating offered, as a preservative from decomposition of materials which were frequently venous and porous.

"In the second place, colour served to produce illusion in certain portions of the edifice, such as heightening the effect of light and shadow, and in giving relief and depth to plane surfaces: in a word, to make regular pictures, and, consequently, to replace sculpture in architectonic composition.

"In the last place, the application of colours to these great monuments serves as a finish to *portions strictly plastic*, when works of sculpture capable of serving an end of their own, but pressed into the service of architecture to fulfil a yet higher aim, (as for example the great groups in the pediments) were carefully painted. In this case the application of colour, regulated as it was by the laws of polychrome sculpture, had nothing to do with the architecture beyond the fact of these sculptures being an essential decoration of the building, and so far was bound to involve nothing which interfered with its aim."*

A great German critic has said that architecture is frozen music—he might have added that music was thawed architecture. If ever there were two arts which deserved to be called sisters, music and architecture are they; for they are the only arts of which the aesthetical effect is founded on measured rhythmical relations alone. To both of them might be applied the definition which Leibnitz † has given of one: "Musica est exercitium arithmeticae occultum nescientis se numerare animi." This is not the place to enlarge on the curious analogies which exist between music and architecture. Our only excuse for mentioning them at all is the admirable illustration they furnish of the distinction, the irreconcilable distinction, which prevails between Greek architecture and Gothic. The one is melody, the other is harmony. The best judges are of opinion that no traces of harmony, in the modern sense of the word, are to be met with in Greek music. And the distinction here drawn between the architecture of classical antiquity and that of the middle ages, finds a remarkable corroboration in the fact that when harmony, or the art of combining simultaneous sounds (the *ars organandi*, as it was called), received ever increasing development from the time of Charlemagne downwards, there presently arose a new form of architecture to keep pace with the progress and symbolise the transformation of the sister art.

* Bröndsted, p. 147. † *Epist.* I. 144.

Corinthian Capital.
From the Pantheon at Rome

A Modeller.
(From a bas-relief at the Villa Albani.)

CHAP. VIII.

SCULPTURE.

WINCKELMANN and Vasari should be read together. That is, the study of Greek art and the study of Italian art illustrate each other. The results obtained in the one serve to corroborate the results obtained in the other. As we compare the two together, we become sensible of a certain law of development which regulates the march, not of this art, nor of that art, but of all art. We see that the styles observable at different epochs point to the existence of an internal history, a spiritual development, an organic life, which give a significance to the outward facts and material productions of the art, fruitful of interest to the student, and suggestive of considerations which greatly sharpen his appreciation and enhance his enjoyment of the statue or painting before him. Stated in its most abstract form, this development may be regarded as the passage from the objective to the subjective, the intermediate stages being marked and distinguished from each other by the respective proportions, divers and diverse, in which these two elements are severally combined with, and predominate over, each other. Indications of such an order of succession have already been pointed out in our remarks upon Hellenic architecture; but it may be well to remark here, in passing, that to this same law of development are reducible all the aspects of Hellenic civilisation. In the political history of Hellas, for example, it marks that passage from the citizen to the man to which we alluded in our opening chapter; in the history of literature it gives us first an Aeschylus, and last an Euripides; while, in religion, it carries us on, from the symbol through the myth, to an age in which both symbol and myth fall beneath the assaults of a scepticism which made that which "each man troweth" the measure of all truth. With regard to art, however, if this law, thus stated, should seem too shadowy an abstraction, we may say more definitely that the artists and their productions range themselves under three successive heads or styles, which Winckelmann has designated as (1) the hard or archaic style, (2) the high style, (3) the beautiful style, corresponding to the stiffness, the grandeur, and the grace observable in the effects produced; but which we should prefer designating as (1) the subhuman, (2) the superhuman, and (3) the purely human styles, — such a nomenclature being more in consonance with that close connection which existed between the art and the religion of Hellas, and with the general march of the anthropomorphic spirit by which that religion was characterised. This will appear more clearly from the remarks we have to make on the subhuman style, to which — speaking with very great latitude — we may assign a period ranging from the earliest times to about B.C. 480, and comprising two portions, a mythical and an historical, separated from each other by the year B.C. 600.

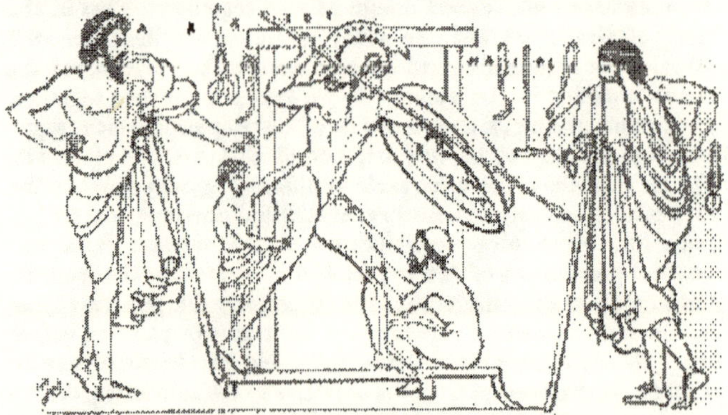

Sculptor's Shop, with workmen employed in polishing the statue of a warrior. Tools and implements hanging in the background.

(From a painted vase at Berlin.)

Pausanias emphatically informs us that, in olden times, *all the Greeks* assigned the divine attributes to, or worshipped as Gods, unhewn blocks of stone, instead of statues.* It is of great importance that the student should pay particular attention to the indications furnished on this subject by the writer just named, as well as by other ancient authorities.†

After making due allowances for the imperfections, both in

* τοῖς πᾶσιν Ἕλλησι τιμὰς θεῶν ἀντὶ ἀγαλμάτων εἶχον ἀργοὶ λίθοι. Pausan. vii. 22, 8.

† Pausan. ii. 9. 6, iii. 22. 1, ix. 24. 3, 27. 1, 35. 1. Clem. Alex. *Protrept.* iv. p. 40. Herodian, v. 182. Dio Chrys. p. 210. M., p. 230. ed. Teubner; comp. p. 238. Plutarch, *de Font.* p. 478. Tacit. *Hist.* ii. 3. Arnob. 6, 11.

conception and execution, incidental to the infancy of art, the adherence to this archaic and uncouth design in hieratic sculpture in a later age is, in itself, a proof that other causes were at work to cramp the energy of the Hellenic sculptor. These causes, we believe, are to be found not in the fetters imposed by the interdictions of a social caste, and still less in Egyptian influences, but rather in that inborn religious awe which shrunk from clothing in a human form the essence of superhuman power. That form, being the most *finished*, was the most *finite*, and, accordingly, it was felt that the less *human* was the statue the more was it *divine*. Fortunately, the Greek was preserved by his natural instinct for the beautiful from falling into that system of grotesque and unsightly symbolism which pervaded the religious sculpture of other nations of antiquity, and was content to abide by the λίθος ἀργός and the ξύλον οὐκ εἰργασμένον, till he had become possessed of the great truth πάντα θεῖα καὶ ἀνθρώπινα πάντα, and dimly foresaw what one of his own poets has so beautifully expressed.*

It is only from this point of view that we can seize the full bearing of the well-known and pregnant statement in Herodotus that Homer and Hesiod were the "makers of the Greek theogony." For in them, as in all the poets of whom their names are the types, was it first made manifest that the unseen powers who had hitherto been worshipped as stocks and stones, were "very gods" and "very men;" not only ἀνθρωποειδεῖς but ἀνθρωποφυεῖς, and in the strength of this great truth Pheidias and Plato trod together that "upward path" (that ὁδὸς ἄνω, as the philosopher calls it) which led them to discover that all the varied forms of human truth and goodness and beauty were but reflections from broken mirrors, distorted images of an unseen reality, an ideal type, which subsisted substantially within them, and thereby witnessed to something which was above them and beyond them; a lamp of fire from Heaven in the earthen vessel of clay. Again, it is only from this same point of view that we can rightly understand the spirit of those traditions which we meet with in ancient writers respecting Daedalus, the mythical forerunner of that long line of sculptors whom we have here to pass under review. Nowhere do we find so strongly indicated the first germs of what we may call that tentative anthropomorphism from the

* Ἓν ἀνδρῶν, ἓν θεῶν γένος· ἐκ μιᾶς δὲ πνέομεν
ματρὸς ἀμφότεροι· διείργει δὲ πᾶσα κεκριμένα
δύναμις, ὡς τὸ μὲν οὐδέν, ὁ δὲ χάλκεος ἀσφαλὲς αἰὲν ἕδος
μένει οὐρανός. ἀλλά τι προσφέρομεν ἔμπαν ἢ μέγαν
νόον ἤτοι φύσιν ἀθανάτοις.

Pindar, Nem. vi. 1.

development of which we have drawn our classification of Hellenic sculpture. A passage in Diodorus Siculus respecting Daedalus throws so much light upon this subject that we quote it in full.* *Εὑρετὴς δὲ γενόμενος πολλῶν τῶν συνεργούντων εἰς τὴν τέχνην, κατεσκεύασεν ἔργα θαυμαζόμενα κατὰ πολλοὺς τόπους τῆς οἰκουμένης. Κατὰ δὲ τὴν τῶν ἀγαλμάτων κατασκευὴν τοσοῦτο τῶν ἁπάντων ἀνθρώπων διήνεγκεν, ὥστε τοὺς μεταγενεστέρους μυθολογῆσαι περὶ αὐτοῦ, διότι τὰ κατασκευαζόμενα τῶν ἀγαλμάτων ὁμοιότατα τοῖς ἐμψύχοις ὑπάρχειν· βλέπειν τε γὰρ αὐτὰ καὶ περιπατεῖν, καὶ καθόλου τηρεῖν τὴν τοῦ ὅλου σώματος διάθεσιν· ὥστε δοκεῖν εἶναι τὸ κατασκευασθὲν ἔμψυχον ζῷον. Πρῶτος δὲ ὀμματώσας, καὶ διαβεβηκότα τὰ σκέλη ποιήσας, ἔτι δὲ τὰς χεῖρας διατεταμένας ποιῶν, εἰκότως ἐθαυμάζετο παρὰ τοῖς ἀνθρώποις. Οἱ γὰρ πρὸ τούτου τεχνῖται κατεσκεύαζον τοῖς μὲν ὄμμασι μεμυκότα, τὰς δὲ χεῖρας ἔχοντα καθειμένας, καὶ ταῖς πλευραῖς κεκολλημένας.* These details about "opening out the legs," and "detaching the arms from the sides," are peculiarly significative of that gradual application of the anthropomorphic spirit. What we are anxious to impress upon the student, is that course of religious development which runs parallel with the history of Hellenic art and throws a flood of light upon those peculiar characteristics of Hellenic civilisation which have been set forth in our opening chapter. It is this parallelism which has induced us to adopt the designation of subhuman as indicative of the first period of Hellenic sculpture, and as suggestive of the successive stages by which the Greek gradually became awake to the conviction that the human form was indeed divine. The general nature of this process is admirably set forth by Dion Chrysostomus in a speech which he puts into the mouth of Pheidias, and from which we give below a short extract, on which every student of Hellenic art and religion should carefully ponder.†

* Diodor. Sic. iv. 76. Compare the numerous passages quoted in Sillig's *Catal. Artif.* and in Junius *de Picturâ veterum.* Uncouth as were these Daedalian sculptures (ἀτοπώτερα τὴν ὄψιν), Pausanias seems to have gathered from them impressions of religious awe (ἐπιπρέπει δὲ ὅμως τι καὶ ἔνθεον τούτοις), ii. 4, 5. So Aeschylus, in speaking of a Paean by Tynnichus, as compared with one of his own: παραβαλλόμενον δὲ τὸν αὑτοῦ πρὸς τὸν ἐκείνου ταὐτὸν πείσεσθαι τοῖς ἀγάλμασι τοῖς καινοῖς πρὸς τὰ ἀρχαῖα· ταῦτα γὰρ καίπερ ἁπλῶς πεποιημένα θεῖα νομίζεσθαι, τὰ δὲ καινὰ περιέργως εἰργασμένα θαυμάζεσθαι μέν, θεοῦ δὲ δόξαν ἧττον ἔχειν. Porphyr. *de Abstin.* ii. 18.

† Dio Chrysost. *Orat.* xii. p. 232, ed. Teubner: νοῦν γὰρ καὶ φρόνησιν αὐτὴν μὲν καθ᾽ αὑτὴν οὔτε τις πλάστης οὔτε τις γραφεὺς εἰκάσαι δυνατὸς ἔσται· ἀθέατοι γὰρ τῶν τοιούτων καὶ ἀνιστόρητοι παντελῶς πάντες· τὸ δὲ ἐν ᾧ τοῦτο γιγνόμενόν ἐστιν οὐχ ὑπονοοῦντες, ἀλλ᾽ εἰδότες, ἐπ᾽ αὐτὸ καταφεύγομεν, ἀνθρώπινον σῶμα ὡς ἀγγεῖον φρονήσεως καὶ λόγου θεῷ προσάπτοντες, ἐνδείᾳ καὶ ἀπορίᾳ παραδείγματος τῷ φανερῷ τε καὶ εἰκαστῷ τὸ ἀνείκαστον καὶ ἀφανὲς ἐνδείκνυσθαι ζητοῦντες, συμβόλου δυνάμει χρώμενοι, κρεῖττον ἤ φασι τῶν βαρβάρων τινὰς ζῴοις τὸ θεῖον ἀφομοιοῦν κατὰ μικρὰς καὶ ἀτόπους ἀφορμάς.

These archaic sculptures of the Daedalian school were decked out with costly raiment and adorned with gaudy colours. In fact, we are explicitly told by Pausanias* that images so embellished were called δαίδαλα before Daedalus was born, or rather before he was exalted into the legendary head of the Attic school of art; for etymology alone is sufficient to show that he, in common with many of his fabled descendants (for his genealogy was kept up till the time of Socrates, who himself boasted of being a Daedalid), nay, more, with many contemporary heads of rival schools of art, are but so many personifications of periods which gave impulse to the art, their names being uniformly significative of manual skill, or borrowed from some artistic tool.

The state of sculpture, and of the arts generally, as set forth in the Homeric poems, having been discussed in an earlier portion of this volume, we pass on from the mythical to the historical section of the first period. And here we are met by such a rich profusion of works of sculpture, many of which now adorn the museums of modern Europe, that we at once ask ourselves how it was that art now attained such a sudden development, awaking like a giant refreshed with sleep from the lethargy of that trance which, for so many centuries, seems to have benumbed every limb, starting into life, like the Athene of ancient story, in all the panoply of Art's appliances and all the maturity of a ripened age. The consideration of this phenomenon may conveniently be divided into two separate heads, the comparative blank of the so-called legendary era, and the extreme productiveness of the historical era. In order to explain the contrast between the two, Egypt has by some archaeologists been called into aid. We have been told that the torpid uniformity which seems for so many centuries to have prevailed over the creations of early Hellenic art was only one of the phases of that religious thraldom which a Danaus or a Cecrops transplanted from Egypt into Greece. When we reflect that the more we go back to the fountain-head of the Hellenic race the greater is the isolation, and, as it were, the individuality which it represents, we feel disposed to retort on the advocates of this opinion, that until they can show us some Egyptian bard who served as a prototype to

"Blind Melesigenes, thence Homer called,
Whose poems Phoebus challenged for his own,"

—till they can do this, the solution they offer is singularly incomplete. To assert that no foreign influences whatever were

* ix. 3. 2.

exercised on early Hellenic art, would be to rush into the opposite extreme; but, on the one hand, when we follow these influences to their source, we find ourselves standing upon the banks of the Euphrates, not of the Nile, by the marbles of Nineveh, and not in the Egyptian court of the British Museum; and, on the other hand, the reader who has followed us thus far, will be careful not to attach to these admitted influences undue weight, taught as he has been to look for the retarding or conservative element in the progress of Hellenic sculpture, in the faltering efforts at anthropomorphism which were cramped and controlled by feelings of religious awe. It should be remembered once for all that the existence of a sacerdotal caste in Greece, so far as it may be thought to involve a hierarchical machinery of united and obstructive action, is a matter of pure assumption. Nor is this all. We believe that if we would search out any additional causes for the protracted infancy of the Hellenic art, we must betake ourselves to the workshop of the artisan. It might easily be shown that the fact recorded by Plato*, that in early times distinct parts of the town were allotted to distinct classes of artisans, when combined with other evidence, warrants the assumption that the craftsmen of early Greece existed in bodies analogous to guilds or corporations, a fact which finds its corroboration in the known practice of handing down the same art from father to son, which continued to a much later period,—for we read that Socrates (who has already been styled a Daedalid) was the son of a sculptor, Sophroniscus, and executed graces in marble before he uttered the graces of thought. It is in these religious and social features combined that we must look for the real causes of that protracted seedtime of higher art, which first put forth its buds in the days of Peisistratus, and reached its blossom in the days of Pericles.

We now come to consider the rapid progress of statuary in the century preceding the Persian war, a phenomenon which we shall fail to appreciate if we do not bear in mind the concurrent development and impulse which was then visible in every other department of the Hellenic mind. The spirit of philosophy searching out the hidden things of the universe, and unravelling the mysteries of man; the spirit of poetry beguiling the hours of the feast, and chastening the sadness of the funeral, and quickening the energies of the fight with the matchless creations of lyric song; the spirit of history discarding the childlike faith of the mythical age, and turning its keen and restless eye on the facts of historical truth; — this connection between the epochs of art, philosophy, and literature, we hold to be of paramount importance; but such large and general views must not allow us to forget the

* Plato, *Critias*, 111.

more immediate causes which brought about the extreme productiveness of Hellenic art, in the period now under discussion. We have, on the one hand, the generous emulation of rival states, the sumptuous efforts of rival sanctuaries: on the other hand, we have a larger field for art, a greater command over the materials employed. It is at the head of this historical period that the names of two artists, Dipoenus and Scyllis, are commonly associated with the first efforts in marble sculpture which deserved the celebrity they attained. This statement, which we owe to Pliny *, must be modified by the fact that a family of artists in the island of Chios, whose name may be said to have reached its culminating period about 540 B.C., in the persons of Bupalus and his sons, had, for upwards of a century previous, been engaged in works of the same material. And here the name of Bupalus reminds us of one of the most important of those causes in the enumeration of which we are now engaged. He it was who first consolidated that fruitful union between sculpture and architecture, which had been pending for nearly a hundred years, by furnishing the first well authenticated instance of marble statues in the pediments of temples. The practice of adorning this space with figures, but only with figures of terra-cotta, seems to have originated at Corinth a full century before the improvement which we have just assigned to Bupalus. The important development involved in the substitution of figures of marble for figures of clay in the pedimental space may well rank among the most critical phenomena at the commencement of the historical period. But it was not only the exterior of the temple, the pediment, the metope, or the frieze, which thus supplied an ampler field for the genius, and so stimulated the invention, of the artist. "Piety or ostentation," to use the words of Bishop Thirlwall, "insensibly began to fill the temples with groups of gods and heroes, strangers to the place and guests of the power who was properly invoked there." It was not, however, from religious or legendary sources alone that this more extended range of subjects was derived. It was about the 58th Olympiad that the triumph of the victorious athlete was first commemorated by the erection of a public statue. The influence which the gymnastic institutions and public games thus exerted on the sculpture of Greece was so rapid and potent, that we shall do well to take it into account while noting the progress of the art. There seems to be an antecedent probability that such a vast increase of subjects in the field of art would be accompanied by a proportionate increase in the number of artists employed; and that such was in fact the case the pages of Pliny

* xxxvi. 4.

and Pausanias amply testify. The limitations of the craft to particular families, and yet more to particular guilds, would now give way to the assaults of a vigorous competition, the action and reaction of demand and supply. The despotism of traditionary usages, the tenacious adherence to conventional forms, would gradually—but only gradually—be relaxed by a deeper sense of beauty and a larger exercise of individual thought.

Before we proceed to consider some of the extant remains of ancient art which belong to the period now under discussion, it may be well to enumerate the principal artists, with the dates at which they flourished.* We shall, however, extend this list down to the time of Pheidias, with whom we purpose heading the second or "superhuman" era of Hellenic sculpture. All the artists enumerated may thus be classed under the general head of Prae-Pheidiasts. Dipoenus, Scyllis, and Bupalus, have already been mentioned. To these may now be added the following artists:—Callon (B.C. 540—520) and Onatas (470—450), both of Aegina; Ageladas, of Argos (500—450), whose three greatest works were his pupils Myron, Pheidias, and Polycleitus; Canachus and his brother Aristocles, of Sicyon (500); Hegias or Hegesias, Kritios, and Nesiotes, three contemporary artists of Athens (480—450); Calamis, also, it would seem, of Athens (470); Pythagoras, of Rhegium (480); and Myron (460). A general estimate of the nature of the works of these artists, and more especially of those who open the list, may be gathered from the testimony of ancient writers.† Quintilian speaks of Callon's works as "duriora," Cicero of those of Canachus as "rigidiora quam ut imitentur veritatem," of those of Calamis as "dura quidem sed tamen molliora quam Canachi," and of Myron's as "nondum satis ad veritatem adducta." Dionysius of Halicarnassus looks in vain in the works of Calamis for the *τὸ σεμνὸν καὶ μεγαλότεχνον καὶ ἀξιωματικὸν* which he found in those of Pheidias and Polycleitus. Lucian classes all the works of the old Attic school as *ἀπεσφιγμένα καὶ νευρώδη καὶ σκληρά*. All these judgments may, we think, be summed up in the general epithet of *subhuman*, which we have assigned to the prae-Pheidian era, as indicating that conventional handling of religious art which we meet with in the Umbrian and other early Italian schools of art, and which, in the case of Greece, was prescribed by the awe at clothing in a finite human form (the exact counterpart of that

* These dates are mainly taken from Brunn's admirable work, *Geschichte der Griechischen Künstler*, *Braunschweig*, 1853. Any departure from the received chronology will there find its justification.

† Quintil. xii. 10. Cic. *Brut.* 18. Dionys. Hal. Isocr. Lucian. *Rhet. Praecept.* 9.

borne by man) the essence and attributes of the gods. Very significant on this head is the "primus nervos et venas expressit" recorded by Pliny of Pythagoras.*

These views are amply confirmed by the extant remains of ancient art belonging to the *subhuman* period, and which we now proceed to enumerate, as far as possible, in chronological order.

The so-called Selinuntine reliefs which adorned the exterior of three out of six temples erected by the ancient city of Selinus, one of the colonies founded by the Greeks in the island of Sicily, furnish us with valuable remains of three successive stages in the period now under discussion. It is in the reliefs which adorned the front of the central temple of the western hill that we possess one of the earliest remains of ancient Hellenic sculpture. They consist of two metopes or slabs of tufo-stone, which adorned the spaces between the triglyphs of the Doric frieze. The subject represented on the one is Perseus on the point of cutting off Medusa's head, Athene standing by. Medusa holds under the right arm a small figure of a winged horse, no doubt intended for Pegasus. On the other slab is found the story of Heracles carry-off the vanquished Cercopes, who had made the hero the butt of their buffoonery. In both cases the sculptures convey the idea of persons in a state of syncope, or who have not the use of their limbs. The drapery of Athene bears the conventional vertical folds so invariably seen in archaic statues of that goddess. The attitudes are stiff and angular, as if the artist had been compassed about with a dread of giving to gods the same appliances of corporeal structure and motion with which men are endowed. He seems to have felt, with Epicurus, "Hominis esse specie deos confitendum est. Nec tamen ea species corpus est, sed quasi corpus." It was left for Pheidias to discover the higher truth: "Non ergo illorum humana forma, sed nostra divina dicenda est."† The next monument we have to notice is the so-called Samothrace bas-relief. It has been supposed to form the side-slab of a throne. The subject represented was probably a council of the Greeks at the siege of Troy. The only three figures preserved are those of Agamemnon, Epeus, and Talthybius, their names being attached. From a careful inspection of this monument, we have no doubt that the Ω in the name Agamemnon, which has led others to assert that it must be posterior to B.C. 402, is the work of a later hand. We may also mention that the ornament on the upper rim of this bas-relief is found on one of the Nineveh marbles in the Louvre. The marble statue of Pallas in the Albani Villa, with aegis on breast, and a girdle of snakes around the waist; the

* xxxiv. 8. † Cic. *Nat. Deor.* 18. 32.

bronze figure of Amphiaraus, or more probably his charioteer, on the point of being swallowed up by the yawning earth; —a celebrated episode in the mythical war of the "Seven against Thebes;" the very early marble bas-relief found near Rome, but now in a private collection at Majorca, representing the murder of Aegistheus by Orestes; the bronze statue of Apollo in the British Museum; the seated figures in the "sacred way" to the temple of the Didymaean Apollo at Miletus; the marble figure of Penelope bewailing the absence of her lord; —all these remains seem to be stamped with an equal degree of antiquity, an equal want of command over the material employed. A most important addition to the sculptures of this period has been supplied by the discovery of the so-called Harpy monument at Xanthus, which is now deposited, along with many valuable works from the same quarter, in the Lycian room of the British Museum. The Harpies or "snatchers" are here represented as the instruments of sudden death, and are bearing a figure in their winged flight, which has all the appearance of a mere infant, —a circumstance which seems adverse to the generally received interpretation of these reliefs, which supposes that the Harpies are engaged in carrying off the daughters of Pandarus, who were notoriously of a more advanced age. This monument should be compared with the Albani bas-relief which Winckelmann styles Leucothea and the infant Dionysus, and which Müller, with more plausibility, takes to be a mother offering her child to a *κουροτρόφος θεά*. We now pass on to a famous group of statues which, taken all in all, their merits and their defects together, may be considered as essentially characteristic of the subhuman tendencies which we assign to this period of Hellenic sculpture. We allude to the Aeginetan marbles which decorated either pediment of a temple of Athene in the island of Aegina. They represent scenes from the wars of the Greeks, in which the Aeacidae had been the most prominent actors. On the eastern pediment we have Heracles and the Aeacid Telamon engaged in rescuing the body of their countryman Oicles, in a battle against Laomedon.* In the western pediment we have the struggle around the body of Patroclus. Such, at least, is the interpretation most generally adopted of the group last named. For our own part, we have no hesitation in preferring the view put forth by Thiersch and so ably advocated by Welcker, that it is the death of Achilles from the arrows of Paris which is here represented. If the figure of Paris had not been introduced, a very serious error would never have encumbered the history of Hellenic art. The very close

* Pind. *Nem.* 3. 67.

resemblance between the Phrygian costume worn by him and that assigned to the Persians by Herodotus gave rise to the notion that allusion was here made to the Persian war, and it was consequently thought necessary to assign to these sculptures a date differing, by nearly a century from what we believe to be the true one, namely B.C. 540. As it is, the period of one hundred years, which we have assumed to elapse between the sculptures of Aegina and those of the Parthenon, is all too little to account for the vast difference in conception and execution which their comparison presents. The rigid symmetry and equipoise, not only between the figures on the right and left of each group, but between the groups themselves, each attitude in both cases finding its counterpart in the other, Athene occupying the centre in both pediments; the archaic type in the drapery of that goddess, in the features and hair of all the figures; the vacant smile in the one, the stiff-set locks of the other, the utter disproportion of the huge armour to the naked bodies of the warriors, — in a word, the disappointment experienced in the general effect as compared with the merits of details, these and other characteristics in the sculpture of Aegina indicate a period far removed indeed from the dawn of Hellenic art, but no less distant from its meridian splendour. It ought to be remarked that the singular contrast which exists between the figure of Athene and those of the warriors is strongly corroborative of the subhuman character of religious sculpture. The artist has evidently felt himself more at liberty, and less shackled by conventional awe, in dealing with human than with divine forms.

The justice of these views respecting the Aegina marbles will more readily appear from a comparison of them with the numerous remains which belong to the close of this period. The two reliefs from another temple of Selinus in the centre of the eastern hill, representing two armed warriors succumbing beneath the attacks of two female figures (probably Amazons); the sculptures from a third temple, five in number, of which the most remarkable are the interview between Zeus and Hera (*Iliad*, xiv.), a battle between Pallas and a giant, and Actaeon punished for his temerity by Artemis, the antlers sprouting from his head as a sign of the coming change — an interesting illustration, as Goethe has remarked, of Hellenic allegorical treatment; the celebrated triangular altar of the Twelve Gods, now in the Louvre, but commonly known as the Borghese Altar; the two analogous monuments in the Museum of the Capitol at Rome; the numerous so-called choragic bas-reliefs in the Louvre; the statue of Heracles securing a stag, that of Castor taming a horse, the beautiful terra-cotta representing Alcaeus and Sappho, and illustrating a fragment in the poem of the former ("Something I have to say, but shame prevents"), all in the British Museum;—these and other remains, which we cannot here enumerate, leave us no room to doubt that, during the years immediately preceding the Persian war, Hellenic sculpture had marched with rapid strides, and had paved the way for that higher development which we find in the works of a Pheidias and a Polycleitus.

A German writer has well remarked that sculpture is essentially a "god-making art." Not Homer and Hesiod alone, but also Pheidias made the Greeks their gods. In the superhuman period, however, on which we are now entering, and which extended from the age of Pericles to that of Alexander, the relation between the statue and the god was different from that which prevailed in the period which we have just quitted. In the latter the god imparted dignity and significance to the statue; in the former the debt was repaid with usury. Most significant is the saying of Quintilian * respecting the Pheidian statue of the Olympian Zeus, — "Cujus pulcritudo adjecisse aliquid etiam receptae religioni videtur, adeo majestas operis Deum aequavit." In the first period the statues of the gods were conventional Types; in the second period they were artistic Ideals. To the purely objective creations of awe-ridden artists were now added the subjective influences of a creative mind. It may fairly be conjectured that to no other people or age will it ever be given to realise the same wealth of plastic beauty that we find in the golden age of Hellenic sculpture. And why is this? Not only because, as we have already intimated, the highest sculpture postulates those views of the divinity which are of the essence of Hellenic mythology, but because the Greeks looked on the relation between soul and body in an aspect which Christianity has once and for ever obliterated. The unbroken line of the Greek profile is symbolical of a profound truth. There is not that violent break between the seat of mind and the organs of sense which now prevails under Christian conditions of thought. Spirit informs, quickens, leavens matter. To the Greek the body was no prison-house; it sat upon the soul as an easy robe. These remarks may help to unsphere the spirit of that Idealism which is associated with the name and works of Pheidias, and to unfold the purport of that superhuman character which has furnished us with a designation of the entire period now under consideration. As subsidiary to the same end, it may be well to cast a glance at the bearings of the Socratic philosophy on Hellenic art, the nature of the influence it exerted, and of the theories it maintained. Now the

* xii. 10.

principle which underlies the aesthetical tenets of that philosophy is the same as that brought out in the *Timaeus** of Plato, namely, that like as the demiurg or creator of the visible world kept before his mind an eternal immutable idea, to which all the beauties of the universe are referable, by which they are all surpassed, so the artist, himself a creator after his kind, must beware of being sense-ridden or sense-possessed, must gaze with the eyes of his understanding upon an ideal type from which, with an organising energy kindred to that of the demiurg of the world, he must fashion the creations of his hand. "For when an artificer looks to that which hath no variableness, and, taking it for his model, brings out its idea and power in his work, that work must needs be beautiful exceedingly; but when he looks to that which is born and dies, beautiful it can never be." "Are they not as blind men," says Plato in another passage†, "who have not the knowledge of that which verily is, who have no distinct ideal in their souls to which, *like the artist*, they may keep referring as a model from which they may continually appeal." This passage from the *Republic* seems to have been present to the mind of a Roman writer whose labours in philosophy are then most valuable when they subserve the exposition of the Hellenic mind. Repeatedly requested by Brutus to put together his views on the characteristics of a public speaker, Cicero‡ thinks it well to premise that the excellences on which he means to insist may never have been found united in one man. "The like of my model" he says, "has probably never been met with." He is not going to inquire what particular excellences this man or that has attained; he wishes to determine what that excellence is which no man can surpass. Now the principle with which he starts is this, that there is no description of beauty which may not be surpassed by something more beautiful still, of which our bodily senses can see nothing but the image, but which itself can only be grasped by mental powers of thought. This principle he illustrates as follows: he has never seen anything which can surpass the excellence of the works of Pheidias, but yet, in his own mind, he can conceive of greater beauty still. This, he believes, Pheidias himself would have been the first to admit. "For when Pheidias was executing a statue of Zeus or Athene, he did not set himself to copy some specified individual as he would a likeness: no! it was in the depths of his own mind that there dwelt some matchless type of beauty; this it was on which he gazed; in this he was wholly absorbed; to resemble this he held to be the aim of art, the principle which should guide his hand." Cicero signifi-

* *Tim.* 40. C. † *De Rep.* vi. p. 484. C. ‡ Cic. *Orat.* 2.

cantly adds that the types of which he has been speaking are the same as what Plato calls *ideas.* Numerous passages from Plato might be quoted, as corroborative of the views which the above extracts so strikingly set forth; we prefer, however, winding up these illustrations of superhuman or ideal sculpture by quoting the authority of Raphael, who writes to Castiglione, with reference to his painting of Galatea, that the scarcity of beautiful women compelled him to have recourse to a "certain idea" which his imagination placed before his mind.

As we pass from the aesthetical to the historical treatment of this second period we find we have to deal with two parallel or rather transverse lines or schools, the Attic and the Argive or Peloponnesian schools,—the latter being, as it were, the bridge by which the passage was effected from the superhuman to the human period,—headed respectively by Pheidias and Polycleitus, and continued on the one side by Scopas and Praxiteles, on the other by Euphranor and Lysippus.

First, with reference to Pheidias. The general restoration of the temples and buildings which had been destroyed during the occupation of Athens by the Persians was probably commenced about the year B.C. 460. The superintendence of these works was entrusted to Pheidias. The persecution he met with at the hands of his countrymen may, in part, have been caused by jealousy at the superiority of a statue of Zeus which he had executed for the Eleians at Olympia, and which tended to eclipse the statue of Athene he had previously executed at Athens. This statue of the Olympian Zeus was considered by the ancients to be the masterpiece of Hellenic art. It was destroyed by fire at Constantinople in the fifth century, and belonged to a class of sculpture — chryselephantine, or "gold and ivory" — of which no single vestige has been preserved. Some faint idea of the effect produced may probably be formed from the attempted restoration of the chryselephantine statue of Athene, which formed a leading attraction in the Great Exhibition at Paris in 1856. Pausanias has given us a very detailed description of the Olympian Zeus, to which the student should turn. Colossal it might well be called, for it was upwards of forty feet high. Of similar dimensions were the statues of the same material which Pheidias erected on the Acropolis of Athens, in honour of Athene Parthenos and Athene Promachos. We pass on to the statues, round and in relief, which adorned the exterior of the Parthenon. We are not left here to conjecture: a visit to the British Museum will enable every man to judge for himself. They may be divided into four classes, the first comprising the sculptures — ninety-two in number, fourteen on each front, thirty-two on each side — which filled

To face page 183.

West end. Showing the commencement of the Panathenaic Procession.

East end. The reception of the Peplos and mystic utensils by the Archon and his wife between **twelve seated** Attic deities.

North side. Procession of Charioteers advancing towards the east end.

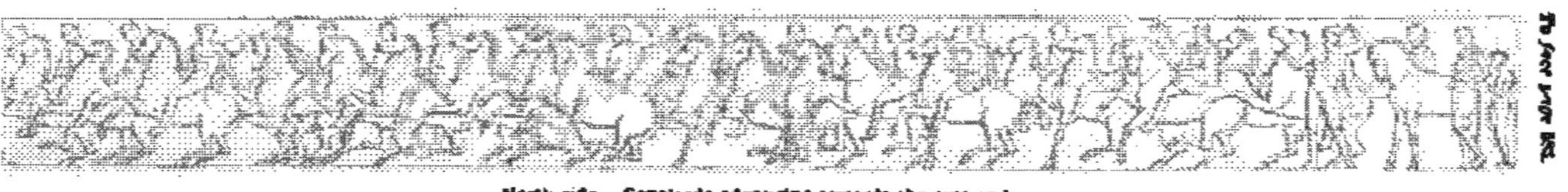

North side. Cavalcade advancing towards the east end.

the metopes, containing figures in very high relief, and representing scenes from the legendary history of Athene. Of these the British Museum possesses sixteen from the south side relating to the contests of the Greeks and Centaurs. The second class comprises four and twenty colossal round statues, from the eastern pediment of the Parthenon, representing the birth of Athene. The third class contains about the same number of similar statues from the western pediment, of which the subject was Athene's victory over Poseidon. Of these classes the Museum possesses thirteen fragments, and two occupy their ancient position on the temple. The last class of sculptures ran in very low relief round the frieze of the *cella* of the temple, and represented the procession of the greater Panathenaea. Out of the 524 feet of which this class consisted, the Museum possesses 250 of the original slabs, and 76 in plaster casts from those which have not been removed from the temple. Of the other works executed by Pheidias, our limits will not allow us to speak.

With the view of fixing the position occupied by Pheidias, we should observe that it must not be supposed that he merely freed his art from a certain degree of conventional stiffness which had blemished the works of previous artists, or, as some put it, that he merely fulfilled a natural law of development by mounting the twentieth of those steps of which nineteen had been achieved by his predecessors;—no, he belongs rather to that race of intellectual giants who, at a single stride, bridge over the gulf of centuries, and so arrive at an excellence of which their predecessors had not even dreamed. When the student stands before the pedimental figures of the Theseus, the Ilissus, or the Fates, let him observe the perfect freedom of every attitude, the lifelike character of every limb; they have not taken shape at the bidding of a dancing master; like the waves of the sea, we expect that every moment they will assume some new undulation. The beautiful flow of the drapery will remind him of Goethe's matchless expression where he calls it "the thousandfold echo of the form." There is no attempt at trickery or startling effects. So conscientiously is the work done, that those parts of his statues which, from their position, could not by any chance have met the spectator's eye, are as highly finished as those which were exposed to view. Take the back of the Theseus, for example, which Flaxman pronounced to be "the finest thing in the world," and contrast it with the dishonest negligence exhibited in the statue of a Venetian doge in the church of S. Giovanni e Paoli, on which Mr. Ruskin has animadverted, and in which one side of the forehead is wrinkled and the other, because turned to the wall, is left perfectly smooth. Nor is it only in the execution of particular separate figures that the genius of Pheidias is so conspicuous; equally sublime is the ingenuity shown in the composition of the whole as a whole. Take any group in any part of the Parthenon, and it will invariably be found that every personage introduced, every leading idea embodied, has precisely that degree of prominence, and, as it were, of emphasis assigned to it which may best assort with harmony of effect, with the subordination of each part to the whole. It may confidently be asserted that, in the Elgin marbles, in the works of Pheidias, the British Museum possesses a treasure with which nothing can be compared in the whole range of ancient art as displayed in the Vatican or the Louvre, or any other collection in Europe.

Having dwelt at some length upon some of the features most essential to a right appreciation of the best age and works of Hellenic sculpture, we feel ourselves at liberty to treat more succinctly what yet remains to be considered.

We cannot but consider it corroborative of the tendencies ascribed to Pheidias that, in the judgment of the ancients, his statues of gods and heroes were considered superior to those of men. In fact, we do not know of any well authenticated instance in which an individual, purely human, engaged his skill. A different direction was pursued by a younger contemporary, Polycleitus, who was equally as renowned for his ideal perfection of human beauty as Pheidias was for his ideal perfection of divine majesty. It was under his auspices and that of the Argive school generally, of which he was the most illustrious representative, that Hellenic sculpture began to lay aside its peculiar functions of a "God-making art." The difference in the course pursued by Pheidias and Polycleitus has been well put by Brunn.* "Pheidias started from the idea, and in his Zeus had compassed the most exalted idea of which Greek art was capable. The body, in his eyes, was only a vehicle for working out the artistic representation of this idea; and beauty of form was only so far valuable as it matched the sublimity of the Idea. Polycleitus set out from the opposite extremity; the body was his starting point; by studious reflections on its proportions and laws, he so eliminated every defect, that his statues attained a truth beyond the reach of ordinary nature, the truth which resides in normal organic formation. . . . . . With Pheidias the power of the idea was all in all: the higher that idea was, the more were his works replete with its energy, while in less ambitious efforts that artist was actually less successful. The reverse was the case with Polycleitus. Starting from the purely human, human his art remained,

* *Gesch. der Griech. Künstler*, i. pp. 226. 229.

and it was only now and then that he came up to the idea of the divinity and the dignity of the divine form." Among the most famous of the statues of Polycleitus was one called the "Spear-bearer," or Doryphoros, in which beauty of proportion was carried

Statue of Amazon.

(From the Vatican. Supposed to be a copy of the celebrated production of Polycleitus.)

to such a perfection that it was looked upon as the Canon, or normal figure, of the human body.*

We now come to the names of Scopas and Praxiteles, who head what has been called the Later Attic school of sculpture. A visible declension from the lofty idealism and majestic repose, which we find in the works of Pheidias, may now be discerned, and the germs of yet deeper decay will not escape the scrutiny of a close observer. An appeal was now made to man's lower nature: the prevailing desire after the strong excitements of sensual indulgences, which marked the age succeeding the Peloponnesian war, would find a congenial atmosphere in the studio

* Among the most important remains of the early Attic school which have come down to us should be mentioned the sculptures of the so-called temple of Theseus; those of the temple of Nike Apteros; of the Zeus-temple at Olympia; and of the temple of Apollo, known as the Phigalian marbles. On the majority of these sculptures the reader is referred to the admirable Handbook of the British Museum by Mr. Vaux.

of Praxiteles and Scopas. The predominance given in the range of subjects treated by these artists to those divinities — such as Aphrodite and Eros, Apollo and Dionysus — whose sphere of influence was more liable to the inroads of strong passions and subjective emotion of every kind, is a sufficient indication of the downward tendencies of the art. All honour, however, is due to Scopas and Praxiteles for having kept these tendencies in check. However inferior may be the copies or imitations of their works which Italian antiquaries assign to an age little short of contemporary with the originals, sufficient still remains to excite our warmest admiration. Second only to the Pheidian marbles are such glorious works as the Niobe group, now at Florence, which Pliny's contemporaries hesitated whether to assign to Praxiteles

Central figures of the Niobe group at Florence.
(A specimen of the compositions of Scopas and Praxiteles.)

or Scopas, and that matchless statue of Aphrodite in the Louvre known as the "Venus of Melos." We do not add the Venus di Medici, because its author has allowed the sensual element — to say nothing of its anatomical defects — to gain a revolting ascendency, and so has failed to catch the spirit of Praxiteles, whose statue of Aphrodite served, no doubt, as a prototype. We may, however, mention the statue of Apollo Sauroctonos in the Louvre, that of Eros in the British Museum, the numerous bas-reliefs with Dionysiac subjects in continental museums, the so-called Satyr Anapauomenos, the Apollino at Florence, the bas-reliefs from the choragic monument of Lysicrates, the Budrun marbles from Halicarnassus, the draped female figures, teeming with grace and beauty, in the so-called Ionic trophy monument, from Xanthus;—in these and other monuments will easily be recognised that grace and tenderness which the ancients assigned to the school of Praxiteles and Scopas.

The transition from the superhuman to the human period, from religious, ritualistic, and objective, to historical, monumental, and subjective sculpture, is still more marked in what may be called the Later Argive school of Euphranor and Lysippus, which stands in the same relation to Polycleitus, as the Later Attic school to Pheidias. This school seems to have all but cast aside the typical proportions of ideal human beauty which regulated the *Canon* of Polycleitus. Pliny informs us of a saying of Lysippus that, whereas older artists made men as they were ("quales essent"), he made them as they appeared to be ("quales viderentur esse"); this seems to indicate a portrait-like tampering with truth and beauty, in order to bring out, instead of eliminating, what was accidental, individual, and transient. Accurate imitation of nature, says the same writer, was carried out in the minutest details in the works of Lysippus: living images they are called by another writer, lacking nothing but breath and motion. This principle of portraiture — which can only be rightly understood when compared with the general advance of the subjective spirit in every phase of Hellenic civilisation, as set forth in a previous chapter — would naturally lead to an historical style of sculpture; and accordingly we find that Lysippus not only executed numerous statues of Alexander the Great, in all positions and at all periods of that monarch's life, but that in a large group he was represented as surrounded by warriors who had bled for his cause at the Granicus, and all of whom were accurate likenesses. Still, in his happier moments, Lysippus escaped the shackles which his theory imposed, and rose to the level of a true artist. This fact cannot be doubted by any one who has ever seen the statue of the Farnese Hercules, and the more celebrated Torso of the same hero, in the Vatican, which are both looked upon as copies of works by Lysippus. A few years ago, another statue of an Apoxyomenos, by the same hand, was discovered at Rome.

The general character of Hellenic sculpture in the Third Period, which extends from the age of Alexander to the destruction of Corinth, has been well described by a German writer.* "Art becomes more and more historical and realistic. It addresses itself to the individual rather than to the general, to the accidents of life rather than to the types of the old ideal forms. Statues of gods are still executed, but they are either reproductions of the ideal types created by the art of an earlier age, or attempts to give to those types more and more individuality, and so to make them more human. Freer scope is given to psychological analysis of character, to pathetic, exciting, and interesting effects. Along with this we see a desire to produce illusory

* Stahr, *Torso*, II. p. 65.

imitation of nature, and a fond dallying on the part of the artist with the nobler forms of animals. Portraiture rises higher and higher. The group, as well as the isolated statue, appeals to the feelings, nay, to the passions of the spectator." The description here given of the style of art prevalent in this period answers to what we have already more succinctly indicated as the ascendency of the subjective over the objective. This tendency was largely fostered by the external position of Hellenic art in the so-called Macedonian period. The numerous kingdoms which sprang up after the death of Alexander the Great, the courts of a Seleucus, a Ptolemy, or an Attalus, promoted a degraded spirit of flattery among the artists of the day, who sought to further their own aggrandisement and emoluments by ministering to the ostentation of courts and the vanity of despots. The principal focus of art, during this period, was the Rhodian school of sculpture, of which the founder was Chares of Lindus, a pupil of Lysippus, the school itself being a younger sister of that of Sicyon. He it was who executed the largest out of a hundred colossal statues of the sun, erected at Rhodes, and which is known as the famous Colossus of Rhodes. We may mention, in passing, that there is no authority for the popular notion that this statue bestrode the harbour. On the contrary, there is every reason to suppose this was not the case. To this period and this school we believe we may assign the famous group of the Laocoon, that three-act tragedy, as it has been styled. It is not improbable that the Rhodian triumvirate (for the artists were three in number, Agesander, Polydorus, and Athenodorus), in executing this group, may have had before their minds a play of Sophocles called *Laocoon*. From the time of Winckelmann downwards innumerable essays have been written on this "portento del arte"—as Michael Angelo termed it—by some of the foremost scholars, archaeologists, and literati, such as Heyne, Visconti, Welcker, Lessing, and Goethe. In these essays the student will find a rich store of most valuable aesthetical criticism on ancient art. This work is the highest of its kind; but the kind, it should be remembered, is not the highest in art. There is something obtrusive in the display of anatomical knowledge. We may rest assured that Pheidias would have eschewed the subject, and that Praxiteles and Scopas would have handled it with less study for effect. As an embodiment of physical pain, it is as remarkable in sculpture as the Philoctetes of Sophocles in the drama. To the same school probably belongs the Farnese Bull, the work of Apollonius, and Tauriscus, which, Pliny tells us, was brought from Rhodes to Rome. It is far inferior to the Laocoon. There is no central idea in the conception of the design, to reduce to something like unity of effect the medley of intersecting lines which bar the repose, and so diminish the force of the impression conveyed. Along with the school of Rhodes should be mentioned the schools of Ephesus and Pergamus. Of the latter, Pyromachus was one of the most famous artists. There is no doubt that in the Wounded Gaul (erroneously called the Dying Gladiator), and Paetus and Arria group, we have two of the works of the Pergamenian school. Both of them afford an interesting example of the mode of representing barbarians. The school of Ephesus has left us the statue of the Borghese Gladiator, unequalled, perhaps, for scientific treatment and artistic nicety of execution. During the greater part of this period art seems to have migrated from Attica and Argos to Asia Minor. Towards the close, however, a revival seems to have taken place at Athens, to which, it is believed, we are indebted (either directly or indirectly, through copies) for such works as the Belvidere Apollo and the Artemis of the Louvre, not to mention others of a similar character, which will readily occur. No one who has learned to appreciate the beauty and grandeur of Hellenic sculpture, as it came godlike from the hands of Pheidias, will refuse to make very considerable deductions from the almost lyrical outburst of enthusiasm with which Winckelmann and others have extolled the Belvidere Apollo. Apart from all anatomical defects, such as the unequal length of the legs, there is a want of repose and a marked theatrical effect about this famous statue which we must pronounce foreign to the best style of Hellenic sculpture. Schnaase has remarked that it may best be characterised as "the cleverest" work of antiquity. It is copied from a bronze, but in what marble is a disputed point.

Meagre as is the above sketch of the history of Hellenic sculpture; we trust the student will have been able to see the drift of the classification we have adopted, and to provide himself with some few of the more elementary conditions of thought under which the study of that sculpture should be approached. More than this has not been aimed at.

We must not conclude this chapter without saying a few words upon the subject of Polychromy. With regard to its application to architecture, we have already quoted the authority of Chevalier Bröndsted. On polychromic sculpture we shall content ourselves with quoting the opinion of Professor Kugler, deeming it best, on a subject so perplexing, to adhere closely to the language of those who have given much time and study to its investigation. After alluding to that kind of polychromy inherent to chryselephantine sculpture, Kugler observes as follows: * — "In statues composed entirely of marble it would appear the drapery was not unfrequently coloured all over: we may at any rate assume, as a general rule, that the hems or borders of the dress were so decorated, in order to bring them out into strong relief, as also in the ornaments of the dress, in cases where they did not consist of gilded metal. The hair, too, seems as a rule to have been covered with gold leaf. To the naked surface was applied a kind of encaustic varnish, or wax tint, which gave it a soft pale aspect. In all cases where a white material was used for the naked flesh, the pupil of the eye was depicted, either by the insertion of some dark substance, or by the application of dark colour. The expression of that organ was far too important to allow of its being passed over." The writer hastens to add, by way of guarding himself against misconception, that anything like an illusory imitation of the colours of nature was totally alien to the spirit of Hellenic art. In bronze statues, the contours of the drapery and other ornamental appendages were inlaid with gold and silver. Very frequently the white of the eye was, in them, represented by silver; the pupil by some dark material. In the earlier works, the lips were similarly decorated. These bronze sculptures place it beyond the reach of doubt that the application of colour in question was based, not on a servile copying of nature, but on aesthetical principles of decoration, as independent in their origin as they were opposite in their aim.

* Kugler, *Handbuch der Kunstgeschichte*, p. 195.

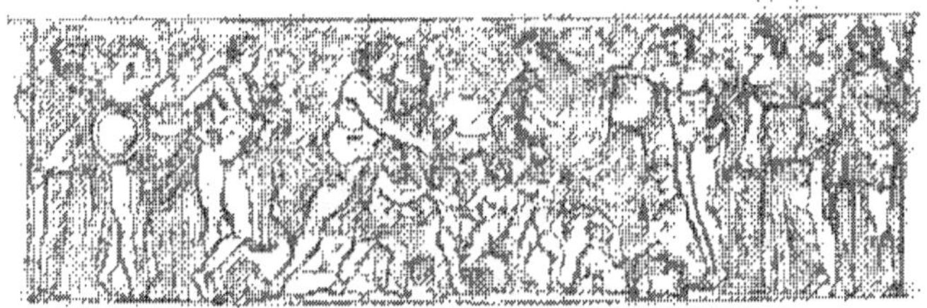

Bacchus and Ariadne attended by Nymphs and Satyrs.
(From the Casali Sarcophagus at Rome — a specimen of the luxurious style of later Athenian sculpture.)

The Muse Urania.—(From a Pompeian painting.)

CHAPTER IX.

PAINTING.

The history of Hellenic painting must be approached in a very different spirit from that in which we have discussed the history of Hellenic sculpture. It must ever be remembered that painting is as thoroughly a Christian as sculpture was essentially a Greek art. And it is very remarkable that the more the appliances and processes of Hellenic painting increased in number and in excellence, the more was the conception of the art denuded of those features which betray the influence of Greek habits of thought. In Hellenic sculpture, conception and execution reach together one and the same height of excellence, which excites at once the admiration and the despair of every other age and nation. In the person of Pheidias the mind and the hand met together. Spirit and form kissed each other. But it is not so in Hellenic painting. The supremacy is there divided. Like the "biceps Parnassus," the height of perfection to which the art culminated is a forked height. On one peak stands Polygnotus, unequalled for ideal grandeur of conception, on the other, Apelles, noted for his dexterity in the manipulation of the advanced appliances of the art and for the grace with which he disguised the absence of mental power and masculine thought. No one can be surprised at this peculiar position of the art who reflects that painting bears the same relation to sculpture as the romantic drama to the classical drama, the subjective to the objective, expression to form, harmony to melody. To the Greek a whole world of emotions, thoughts, passions, which to the Christian are familiar, were utterly unknown. They were begotten of that disruption between soul and body, that antagonism between sense and faith, spirit and matter, that looking forward from a finite present to an infinite hereafter, which moulded to new shapes and coloured with new hues all the conditions of thought and feeling of Christian men. Our sculpture will never be anything more than a feeble, soulless, imitation of an art which is not our own: but in painting we are more than conquerors; it is an inheritance which belongs to us by virtue of our Christian profession.

Thus much for the general aspect under which Hellenic painting should be regarded. Before we pass on to review the history of the art it may be well to say a few words on the methods and processes which are comprised under the word painting when considered as a branch of Hellenic art. It was not till painting became something more than sculpture in colour that the mural paintings of Polygnotus were in a great measure superseded by easel pictures, executed on panels, which were generally made of larch primed or prepared with a ground of white, probably plaster. These, when finished, were encased or let into the walls. This substitution is a fact of great importance for the right understanding of Pliny, our chief authority for the history of Hellenic painting. It coincided with such an advance in the material or technical appliances of the art—the only feature which it was Pliny's object to bring into relief—that we must not allow his well-known statement—"nulla gloria artificum est nisi qui *tabulas* pinxere,"*—to blind us to the sterling merits of the mural paintings of Polygnotus and his contemporaries. This, however, is a point to which we shall presently revert. We should bear in mind that the two main classes of paintings were mural paintings on stucco, either al fresco or in distemper, and easel pictures on wood panels,—corresponding to those two departments of excellence, ideal and technical, which we have associated with the names of Polygnotus and Apelles respectively. The methods were two:—water-colour painting, and, in the later times of the art, encaustic painting. On the process employed in the former no serious difference of opinion exists. The colours were combined either with the various glutinous vehicles known under the general name of distemper, or with wax and resin when these were converted into a water-colour medium. In fresco wall-paintings the water-colours were laid on the last layer or coating of plaster before it was dry. Encaustic painting, which did not come into general use till after the time of Alexander, may be divided into the three following processes.† The colours—called by the Romans *cerae*, and kept, says Varro, in partitioned boxes—were moistened by some oily fluid, and laid on the panel with a hair-pencil. The most important part of the operation yet remained: the toning down (ἀπόχρωσις), the fining off of the colours,

* Plin. xxxv. 118.

† The statements here made on encaustic painting are mainly borrowed from Welcker's masterly essays on the subject in his *Alte Denkmäler*, iii. pp. 412—428, to which the student is referred.

by applying, at a distance more or less remote as occasion required, a red-hot iron rod (ῥαβδίον), which ensured far greater facility and nicety of execution than either the *cauterium*, an iron pan filled with coals, or the flame of a candle, which were used in covering fresco walls and statues respectively with a wax encaustic varnish. It may be mentioned, as corroborative of this view, that Pliny speaks of a painting representing the interior of an encaustic artist's studio, where a boy was seen blowing the fire, no doubt for heating the rod in question; and, in an allegorical picture of the genius of encaustic painting found at Pompeii, we see introduced all the materials employed in this process,—the palette and brushes, the rod or ῥαβδίον, the wax-colour, and the pan or vessel for its solution. The importance attached to this finishing process may be gathered from the fact that it gave its name to the whole,—paintings bearing the inscription ἐνέκαεν, ἐνέκαυσεν, instead of the ordinary form ἔγραψεν. They painted, as it were, with fire: so greatly did the hot rod enhance the finish of the hair-pencil. The second process of encaustic painting was applied to ivory. The design was etched in with a sharp-pointed instrument called the *cestrum*; wax-colours were then applied to the interstices, and the whole was toned down as before with the ῥαβδίον. The whole process had some analogy with copper-plate engraving, and yet more with the niello-works of mediaeval art. The third encaustic process is scarcely worth mentioning: it was used in painting ships, and is thus described by Pliny*:—"Hoc tertium accessit, resolutis igni ceris penicillo utendi, quae pictura navibus nec sole nec sale ventisque corrumpitur."

A further preliminary has yet to be disposed of. What remains have been preserved of that period of Hellenic painting which forms the theme of the present chapter? To this inquiry it is scarcely too much to answer, none whatever. It is true that in the museums of Europe there exist upwards of fifty thousand Greek fictile vases, which have been exhumed during the last two centuries; but, however valuable these may be, as furnishing indications of the progress of design at different epochs, we are compelled to exclude them from our consideration, not only because they would require an entire chapter to themselves (so intricate are the perplexities which attach to their origin and history), but also because it would be as unreasonable to infer the style and merits of a Polygnotus, a Zeuxis, or an Apelles from the masterly sketches — for masterly they undoubtedly are, but more than sketches they are not — on these vases, as, in the art of modern Europe, to take the Della Robbia ware as anything like

* Plin. xxxv. 149.

an adequate substitute for the paintings or an index to the mind of Raphael. The purely manufactural character of their production excludes them from the domain of art proper, within which we are circumscribed, however much it may excite our surprise and admiration that such great things should have been accomplished in so subordinate a sphere. Equally foreign to our limits, by virtue of the age to which they belong and of the place at which they were discovered, are the wall-paintings of Pompeii and Herculaneum. There is no doubt that in an exhaustive treatise on Hellenic painting these remains would be made use of on account of the illustration they afford, collaterally and by implication, of the condition and capabilities of the art under purely Hellenic influences and at an earlier age.

From these remarks on the general spirit, technical appliances, and extant remains of Hellenic painting, we pass on to the history of the art itself: and here we are arrested at the very threshold by a phenomenon which serves to corroborate what has already been stated respecting the adventitious character of this art as a branch of Hellenic culture. We find no trace of that tendency of gathering the first faint efforts of the art around some mythical personal centre which we meet with in the case of sculpture, and, we might add, in every other department of Hellenic life. The names of the earliest painters are not, like Daedalus, representative epitomes of an entire epochal era, they evidently belong to certain specified individuals, whose existence rests more or less on an historical basis, however difficult it may be to assign their dates or arrange in due order the facts related concerning them. Between the first rise of the art and the Persian war, we meet with no artist of sufficient importance to arrest our attention. So that, passing over the first attempts at *Skiagraphy* (or the "umbra hominis lineis circumducta") and monochrome paintings, which are principally connected with Sicyon and Corinth, we come to an artist named Eumarus (Ol. 60–79), who stands at the head of that fuller development of the art which is identified with the name of Polygnotus. Pliny speaks of him in the following terms *: — "Qui primus in pictura marem a femina discreverit Eumarum Atheniensem figuras omnes imitari ausum,"—which seems to allude, first, to that distinction in the colouring of the two sexes which is a marked feature of vase paintings, and, secondly, to the indication of age and station, which we find, from the same evidence, was not originally attended to. The improvements introduced by Cimon are thus recorded †: "Hic catagrapha invenit hoc est obliquas imagines

* Plin. xxxv. 56. † Plin. l. l.

et variè formare voltus, respicientes suspicientes vel despicientes, articulis membra distinxit, venas protulit præterque in veste rugas et sinus invenit." By "catagrapha," when coupled with the context, there is no doubt that we must understand paintings in profile. In old vase-paintings, while the face is in profile, the eyes are frequently left full face. Cimon introduced the desired uniformity between the two, and we have no difficulty in conceiving how this must have enhanced the variety of expression which Pliny designates as the "variè formare voltus." To this we may add an increased attention to superficial anatomy and to massiveness of drapery artistically distributed so as to echo the form beneath. The improvements here enumerated paved the way for those more exalted triumphs achieved by Polygnotus, the greatest of the Greek painters when regarded from a Greek point of view. Flourishing as he did during the interval which elapsed between the Persian and Peloponnesian wars (for his birth coincided with the battle of Marathon), he was enabled to profit by the same external advantages which had furnished so ample and so brilliant a field for the genius of his great contemporary Pheidias. Employed by Cimon, the predecessor of Pericles in the administration of Athens, to decorate the buildings for whose erection the spoils of the Persian war had furnished the means, he both executed a part himself and gave general superintendence to the remainder of a series of *mural* paintings for the temple of Theseus, the Poecile or painted portico, the Anaceium or temple of the Dioscuri, and the hall or chamber adjoining the Propylaea. Whatever may have been the merits of these works they were surpassed in the estimation of the ancients by the paintings he executed in the Lesche of the Cnidians at Delphi, a kind of cloistered court of which Polygnotus decorated the walls on the right and left of the two principal colonnades. On the one was represented the taking of Troy and the departure of the Greeks; on the other, the descent of Odysseus into Hades. They were called by the ancients the Iliad and Odyssey of the painter. Pausanias has left us a very detailed description of them. It would not appear that Polygnotus's principles of composition had anything in common with those on which modern art relies, and which the powerful auxiliary of a finished perspective enables it to carry into practice. It seems rather to have been based on what we may call a kind of architectonic symmetry,— the various groups being arranged in parallel rows one above the other, and the spectator being left to infer the relative nearness or remoteness intended by the artist from the degree of elevation assigned. Pliny's statement of the improvements made by Polygnotus is couched in the following words *: "Primus mulieres tralucidâ

* Plin. xxxv. 58.

veste pinxit, capita earum mitris versicoloribus operuit, plurimumque picturae primus cortulit, siquidem instituit os adaperire, dentes ostendere, vultum ab antiquo rigore variare." Pliny, it must be remembered, occupies himself more with technical and material accessories than with the higher morals and aesthetic beauties visible in the works of Polygnotus. These last, we gather from other sources, were of the very highest order. Pheidias and Polygnotus were the Homers of their respective arts. A painter, indeed, Polygnotus cannot strictly be called. His works were so pre-eminently *statuesque* that they might with greater justice be called, as we have already intimated, sculpture in colour. Dionysius of Halicarnassus* has left us a valuable comparison between the paintings of the ancient and later schools, which throws considerable light on the position occupied by Polygnotus. To the like effect are Quintilian's † remarks on the "simplex color" of that artist, which he admits, though not without surprise, found greater favour with some crotchety connoisseurs than the more finished works of later painters. In a word, the works of Polygnotus were as deficient in point of technical development and appliances, as they were supreme in moral beauty. We are left in no doubt on this head from the statement of Aristotle ‡ that, as compared with Polygnotus, the works of Zeuxis had no ἦθος at all. He calls him a "good ethographer." Those who are at all conversant with the aesthetical diction of Aristotle will not need to be told that by *Ethos*, the author of the *Poetics* understands the refined expression and repose of ideal character, as opposed to the display of subjective emotions, — that kind of idealism, in short, which clothes with awe and majesty the works of Pheidias. So again in another passage of the *Poetics* §, he tells us that Polygnotus represented men as "better than they are,"—free, that is, from the individual accidents, shortcomings, and imperfections which in the world of reality

* *De Isaeo*, 4. tom. v. p. 809. ed. Tauchnitz. Εἰσὶ δή τινες ἀρχαῖαι γραφαί, χρώμασι μὲν εἰργασμέναι ἁπλῶς, καὶ οὐδεμίαν ἐν τοῖς μίγμασιν ἔχουσαι ποικιλίαν, ἀκριβεῖς δὲ ταῖς γραμμαῖς, καὶ πολὺ τὸ χάριεν ἐν ταύταις ἔχουσαι· αἱ δὲ μετ' ἐκείνας, εὔγραμμοι μὲν ἧττον, ἐξειργασμέναι δὲ μᾶλλον, σκιᾷ τε καὶ φωτὶ ποικιλλόμεναι, καὶ ἐν τῷ πλήθει τῶν μιγμάτων τὴν ἰσχὺν ἔχουσαι.

† Quintil. xii. 10. 3.

‡ *Poet.* 6. Ὁ μὲν γὰρ Πολύγνωτος ἀγαθὸς ἠθογράφος, ἡ δὲ Ζεύξιδος γραφὴ οὐδὲν ἔχει ἦθος.

§ *Poet.* 2. Πολύγνωτος μὲν κρείττους, Παύσων δὲ χείρους, Διονύσιος δὲ ὁμοίους εἰκάζει. Compare what Sophocles said of himself with reference to Euripides (*Poet.* 26.). Σοφοκλῆς ἔφη αὐτὸς μὲν οἵους δεῖ ποιεῖν, Εὐριπίδην δὲ οἷοι εἰσί. The rise, progress, and decline of the Hellenic drama furnishes throughout the most valuable illustrations of corresponding stages in the sculpture and painting of Hellas.

impair the beauty, moral and physical, of the typal man. To artists who seek to compass the highest order of truth in the idealising spirit of a Pheidias and a Polygnotus, may be applied the saying of Plautus,

> "Poeta tábulas quom cepit sibi
> Quaerit quod nusquam géntiumst, reperit tamen:
> Facit illut veri símile quod mendáciumst."

What though the artist's ideal creation be nowhere to be found (nusquam gentium) it is not the less conformable to nature when considered (to use Shakspeare's expression) as "square in all her parts," and to truth when looked at from high. Idealism, rightly understood, is verily and indeed the most sterling of all realities.

It may at first sight seem difficult to reconcile the exalted position we have assigned to Polygnotus, as the Pheidias of painting, on the authority of Aristotle, with the somewhat feeble praise awarded to that artist by Pliny. It should be remembered, however, that the main object which the Roman encyclopaedist proposed to himself was to trace the progress of the technical appliances of the art. In these, Polygnotus, as we have seen from Quintilian and Dionysius of Halicarnassus, was decidedly deficient. Accordingly, as the advancement in this particular coincided with the introduction and general adoption of panel or easel pictures, the mural paintings of Polygnotus found less favour in the eyes of Pliny, wholly bent, as he was, on the "gloria penicilli" and the "tabula." He distinctly states: "Nulla gloria artificum est nisi qui tabulas pinxere." * Aristotle, on the other hand, who looked higher and deeper than the somewhat superficial and matter-of-fact Roman, descried in the works of Polygnotus a moral grandeur, an ideal beauty, for which the more finished efforts and feeble elegance of a Zeuxis and an Apelles were but sorry makeweights. On these grounds we have no difficulty in reconciling the statements of the two writers and of arriving at a proper estimate of the merits of Polygnotus.

Among the contemporaries and immediate successors of this great master may be mentioned Micon, his collaborator in the Theseium, Anaceium, and Poecile (his skill in painting horses did not preserve him from the ridicule of Simon, a jockey of the day, for having painted eyelashes to the under eyelids of one of his chargers); Panaenus, a cousin of Pheidias, and also one of the artists engaged in the Poecile; and Dionysius of Colophon, and Pauson, whose names the reader has already seen mentioned by Aristotle in contrast with the higher style of Polygnotus. From

* Plin. xxxv. 118.

that style the two artists last mentioned exhibited a visible declension; but the passage from the school of statuesque painting to that of painting proper was greatly accelerated by Agatharchus* (Ol. 80—90), whose assiduous and successful cultivation of the science of perspective and the art of scenography turned the efforts of his contemporaries and successors into a different channel, and brought to rapid maturity those illusory effects and other features of the art which distinguish a Zeuxis or an Apelles from a Polygnotus. First among the artists who profited by the suggestions of Agatharchus was Apollodorus, whose increased attention to gradation of light and shadow, the union of local colour, demi-tint, and shade (φθορὰν καὶ ἀπόχρωσιν σκιᾶς †), won for him the epithet of σκιαγράφος. To the like effect is Pliny's statement concerning him: "Hic primus *species* exprimere instituit (*i.e.* to produce illusory effects on a flat surface), primusque gloriam *penicillo* jure contulit . . . . neque ante eum *tabula* ullius ostenditur, quae teneat oculos." ‡ Sufficient has been said on the point of view from which Pliny regarded the art to enable us to seize the meaning of this passage. His position as the founder of that Ionic or Asiatic school of painting proper on which we are now entering, may be gathered from what Pliny subjoins in words immediately following the passage just quoted: "Ab hoc artis fores apertas Zeuxis Heracleotes intravit." The principal representatives of the Asiatic school are Zeuxis and his contemporaries Parrhasius and Timanthes. (Ol. 86—100.) In an adroit choice of taking subjects and moving incidents, in an overwrought affectation of smoothness and softness, in skilful achievements of illusory effects, Zeuxis seems to have sought, and sought in vain, for a substitute for that severer ideal beauty which induced Aristotle to give the precedence to Polygnotus. From the Asiatic school onward to the close of the period we have to pass under review the history of Hellenic painting declines in interest just in proportion as the art itself seems to the superficial observer to enlarge its borders and take a wider grasp. With Polygnotus there died away that truly Hellenic spirit which informed with beauty the works of Pheidian sculpture, that truly Hellenic art. In the absence of those peculiar conceptions and habits of thought which are of the essence of painting, and which it was left to Christianity to found and to foster, nothing remained but a feeble anticipation, on the part of a highly ingenious and quick-witted

* On the date of Agatharchus, see Brunn, *Gr. Künstler*, ii. p. 51.

† Plutarch, *De Glor. Ath.* p. 346. A.

‡ Plin. xxxv. 60.

people, of those technical appliances on which modern art relies for her success. That particular development of the art towards which Zeuxis contributed seems to have resided in the adaptation of colour to the exigencies of light and shade; so much so that Quintilian awards him the title of inventor: "Luminum umbrarumque invenisse rationem traditur." *

The celebrated story of the contest between Zeuxis and Parrhasius, which relates how birds came and pecked at some grapes which the former had painted, and how Parrhasius was requested by his rival to draw aside a curtain, which proved to be nothing but a painting, is a proof that whatever skill both these artists possessed was subordinate to the vulgarest of all aims, the mere illusion of the senses. As Goethe has remarked, it is only in uncultivated minds, the sparrows of the intellectual world, that suchlike illusory effects of art, whether bunches of grapes or painted curtains, can raise any feelings of gratification or convey any impression of sterling excellence or mental power. While Zeuxis excelled in the peculiar handling of light and shade, Parrhasius seems to have addressed himself more particularly to the accurate delineation and indication of form. "In lineis extremis palmam adeptus," says Pliny †, and he explains this triumph (which he calls "picturae summa subtilitas") in the following words: "Ambire enim se ipsa debet extremitas et sic desinere, ut promittat alia post se, ostendatque etiam quae occultat." From this it would appear that whereas, in the case of Zeuxis, contrasts of light and shade were mainly subservient to modifications of colour, with Parrhasius they were made use of for modifications and accurate rendering of form; so that the latter artist has been held by competent judges to have had some cognisance of what is now known as chiaroscuro. Along with this technical dexterity was coupled what we may believe to have been an exaggerated display of psychological analysis of the emotional side of human character. This we may infer, as from other grounds, so especially from Pliny's description of his painting of the Athenian Demos ‡: "Pinxit demon Atheniensium argumento quoque ingenioso: ostendebat namque varium, iracundum, injustum, inconstantem, eundem exorabilem, clementem, misericordem, gloriosum, excelsum, humilem, ferocem fugacemque *et omnia pariter*."

* Quintil. xii. 10. 4. † Plin. xxxv. 67.

‡ Plin. xxxv. 69. The Bamberg manuscript has "ostendebat," not, as in all editions, "debebat." Sillig's note on this is important: "Imperfectum posuit Plin., quia significat Parrhasium demon ostendere voluisse, quo sensu illud tempus etiam alibi apud Plin. legitur uti 36, 20, et 36, 96."

On the manner in which Parrhasius treated this subject we are left to conjecture. Pliny merely informs us that Parrhasius endeavoured to compass it, and this is sufficient to warrant our inference that his strength lay in the portraiture of conflicting passions, rather than in the more subdued expression of character, or ἦθος. To Timanthes, with whom we close our notice of the Ionic school, ought in justice to have been awarded that meed of glory which has settled on very doubtful grounds around the persons of Zeuxis and Parrhasius. He seems to have studied with considerable success something higher than the trickeries of illusory imitation of natural objects. In the "ingenium," or "invention," ascribed to him by Pliny, and which we take to mean that suggestiveness in the choice and treatment of his subject which awakened the sympathies of the spectator ("in unius hujus operibus intelligitur plus semper quam pingitur," Plin.), Timanthes found the means of snatching a grace beyond the reach of those mere technical artifices by which his contemporaries appealed to the senses rather than to the intelligence and feeling of the public. His famous picture of the Sacrifice of Iphigenia, in which the face of Agamemnon was veiled ("quoniam summum illum luctum penicillo non posset imitari," Cic.), so as to leave every one to estimate for himself, as Quintilian puts it, the greatness of that grief which smote the father's heart, is not only a valuable illustration of the delicacy of that "ingenium" of which we have been speaking, but is further interesting from the store of aesthetic criticism to which it has given rise in the hands of Lessing, Herder, and Goethe.

That the showy trickeries and sensual tendencies of the Asiatic school did not cause as rapid a decline of the art as we might reasonably have anticipated, was partly owing to the healthy reaction set on foot by the Sicyonic school. The direction there followed has considerable analogy to that of the Argive or Peloponnesian school of sculpture. The founder of the Sicyonic school was an artist named Eupompus (Ol., 90—100); but the title might with more propriety have been awarded to his pupil, Pamphilus (Ol. 97—107), who might be called the Leonardo da Vinci of antiquity, from the scrupulous attention he paid to the scientific elements of the art. Pliny says of Pamphilus: "Primus in picturâ omnibus litteris eruditus, praecipuò arithmetica et geometria, sine quibus negabat artem perfici posse."* On the important bearing of such studies as arithmetic and geometry, on perspective and proportion, and other resources of the art, it were

* Plin. xxxv. 76.

needless to insist. Of his paintings we know little; as is also the case with his pupil, Melanthius, who held a distinguished place in the judgment of the ancients for his skill in "dispositio," *i. e.*, grouping, or composition generally. Even Apelles admitted that, in respect of composition, he must yield the palm to Melanthius. Such a merit was peculiarly characteristic of a school which founded its claims to reputation on its mathematical training. The theoretical instruction imparted by Pamphilus seems to have been put into practice with signal assiduity by his pupil, Pausias. His skill in foreshortening, in executing designs on vaulted ceilings, in bringing to perfection encaustic painting, and in executing artistic problems of every kind is dwelt on at considerable length and illustrated by forcible examples in the pages of Pliny.

Several of the artists who have yet to be enumerated before we come to Apelles, and who have been classed by Brunn under the general head of the Thebano-Attic school, seem to hold in painting the same place as Scopas and Praxiteles in sculpture. Among these may be mentioned Aristeides (Ol. 100—110), of whom Pliny tells us: "Is omnium primus animum pinxit et sensus hominis expressit, quae vocant Graeci ethe, item perturbationes, durior paulo in coloribus." * As Polygnotus was notoriously the painter of ἦθος, it is clear that the ἤθη and πάθη (for we so might re-translate "perturbationes"), with which Pliny associates the name of Aristeides as "omnium primus," must mean something different from the ἦθος of which we have all along been speaking. We are left in no doubt on this point by the terms which Pliny conjoins as equivalents, namely, "animum et sensus," and by the juxtaposition of πάθη, or "perturbationes," as something *ejusdem generis*, or differing less in kind than in degree from the ἤθη. The ἦθος is the ἤθη in the bud; the ἤθη are the ἦθος in the blossom; the ἤθη are potentially in the ἦθος; they are the variations of which the ἦθος gives the theme; they are outward manifestations of that compact and inward body of character which constitutes the ἦθος. A passage in the rhetoric of Dionysius of Halicarnassus places the whole matter in the clearest light.† The writer's object is to show how the ἤθη ought to be handled by the orator, and for this purpose he takes the ἦθος as a kind of sub-

* Plin. xxxv. 98.

† *Ars Rhet.* x. 1. Οὕτω δὲ δεῖ καὶ τῷ λόγῳ ἓν μὲν ἦθος ἐκεῖνο τὸ μέγιστον, ὁ ἐκ φιλοσοφίας (such too was the ἦθος of Polygnotus), ὥσπερ λαμπρὸν ὑποκεῖσθαι τῷ λόγῳ· τὰ δ' ἄλλα ἐπάγειν, τὰ θυμικὰ λέγω, καὶ τὰ οἰκτρὰ, καὶ τὰ ἀστεῖα, καὶ τὰ μικρὰ, καὶ τὰ ἐπίφθονα, πάντα ταῦτ' ἐκείνου ἐξηρτημένα, καὶ ἀλλήλοις συγκεκραμένα κατὰ τὸν τῆς χρείας λόγον. On this passage see Brunn, *Gr. K.* ii. p. 175.

stratum on which the ἤθη are to be erected as the design of the orator may require. In mathematical language the ἦθος is the constant factor, the ἤθη are the variable quantities. The following description of a picture by Aristeides will elucidate any obscurity which yet hangs over this question. Pliny tells us that it represented a mother dying in storming of a town, and holding away her child from her wounded breast, for fear lest with the milk it should imbibe the blood. We can easily understand how nearly akin to the πάθη were the ἤθη, which this heartrending situation would call into play.

The direction followed by Aristeides was liable to be perverted under less favourable auspices, and to lapse into a coarser realistic appeal to the senses, heightened by an ostentatious display of physical development. Such was the case with Euphranor (Ol. 104—110), and in a less degree with his pupil Antidotus and with Nicias (Ol. 108—118). The μεγαλότεχνον καὶ ἀξιωματικόν, which in the last chapter we found predicated of Pheidias in a higher sense with reference to idealism of character, were embodied by the artists just named in mere massiveness of body, which was *extra naturam*, without being, as with Pheidias, *supra naturam*. The remark of Euphranor that, while the Theseus of Parrhasius seemed to have been fed on roses, his own was fed on beef, is significant of the kind of burly beauty which he sought to compass in his pictures, and to which Pliny seems to allude when he says: "Hic primus videtur expressisse dignitates heroum." *

We now come to the greatest master of Hellenic painting, properly so called, the famous Apelles (fl. Ol. 112), whose personal character, if we may judge from the numerous amiable anecdotes related concerning him, was even more worthy of admiration than his artistic ability. He seems to have combined all that was best in the elegance and refinement of the Asiatic school of Zeuxis with the severity and scientific accuracy of execution which belonged to the Sicyonic. His precision of hand is set forth in an anecdote related by Pliny, which is so famous that we cannot omit it from our pages. Protogenes lived at Rhodes. As soon as Apelles had landed from a ship which had touched at that island, he hastened off to the studio of that artist, all eagerness to make himself acquainted with works which he knew only by fame. Protogenes himself was out, but had left in charge of an old servant a panel of considerable size all ready for work. The servant asked who he should say had called. "I will tell you," said Apelles; and,

* Plin. xxxv. 128.

taking a hair pencil, he drew an excessively fine-drawn line across the panel. Protogenes, on his return, was told what had happened. He immediately gathered from the delicacy of the line that his visitor was Apelles, for he knew that no other artist could compass so high a finish. He then took another colour and drew a still thinner line longitudinally superimposed on, and lying within, the former. He desired his servant to tell Apelles, if he called again, "Hunc esse quem quaereret." Apelles did so: "et vinci erubescens, tertio colore linias secuit, nullum relinquens amplius subtilitati locum." These words seem to mean that, with a third line, Apelles bisected *longitudinally* that second line by which Protogenes had in like manner bisected the first. That this story should be taken in the literal sense of the words in which it is couched by Pliny, is evident from his adding that it was principally with artists that the feat excited admiration. The student of Italian art will remember a somewhat similar story which is related of Giotto, and which serves to illustrate and to corroborate what has here been stated concerning Apelles. When negotiations were going on with Giotto for some decorations to be executed at Rome, the Pope desired him to send some proof of his talent; Giotto did nothing but trace a large O on a board, which he desired to be given to his Eminence. Hence the Italian proverb: "Tu sei più rondo che l'O di Giotto," as denoting a person dull of intellect. We have selected this anecdote out of many which are highly characteristic of Apelles, as indicating that delicacy and perfection of execution by which, as we have already stated, Apelles carried painting proper to the same height of excellence to which statuesque painting was brought by the idealism of Polygnotus. "The peculiar characteristic," says Kugler, "of the works of Apelles (a characteristic in which all antiquity awarded him the palm) was grace. This was no doubt manifested in fullest measure in his famous painting of the Anadyomene, the Goddess of Love, emerging from the waves of the sea, and with her fingers disentangling her dropping hair. So, again, in a second painting of Aphrodite, and in a picture representing one of the three Charites. It was, however, scarcely less conspicuous in his paintings of heroes, and especially in his idealised portraits—a field for which the historical relations of his time furnished him ample scope. It was principally Apelles who was the painter of Alexander the Great, and great fame was attached to the picture in which he depicted that monarch with the thunderbolt in his hand."

Other artists might yet be named, both during the time of Alexander and under the Diadochi. Protogenes, so conspicuous for his elaborate finish and photographic reproduction of natural objects, has already been mentioned. We may add the names of Theon and Antiphilus: the latter carried to excess those realistic tendencies which we have already had occasion to condemn in the progress of this chapter. We are not, however, solicitous about crowding the conclusion of our remarks on this branch of Hellenic art with the names of painters whose labours had no material influence on the progress and opened out no new phases of the art. Polygnotus and Apelles, it should be remembered, are the two leading types of excellence which Hellas was able to produce in the respective departments which each of them adorned,—statuesque painting, and painting proper. Such is the idea which we are desirous the student should carry away with him from the perusal of these concluding pages,—an idea on which we do not now think it necessary to enlarge, as we have already said sufficient to elucidate our meaning in the remarks which usher in the present chapter. Great as may be our admiration of Polygnotus, we must not be sparing of our admiration of the merits of Apelles. Whatever those merits may be when viewed independently, or when contrasted with the higher mental power exhibited in the works of Polygnotus, we must not forget that everything which painting proper could achieve in ante-Christian times, Apelles did not leave undone. Nay more, those merits are immeasurably enhanced when we remember the position he occupies in the history of Hellenic painting. We must not forget that he may be said to close the rank of that army of artists worthy of the name who have here been passed under review, and that he and his friend, rather than rival, Protogenes, do not come forward on the stage of our history till the concluding act has commenced; and if he has succeeded, not only in keeping up, but rousing anew, the attention of the spectators on whom the realism of his immediate predecessors had begun to pall, surely he deserves a worthy place in our esteem when the drama is over and the curtain drops. Were it to rise again, it would only display the grimaces of vulgar clowns and the ribaldry of an unseemly farce; and to such a spectacle as this we do not deem it essential that the attention of the student should be directed. This language may seem severe; but, as far as we are able to judge, the obscenity, trickery, and caricature, which entered so largely into the paintings of the Greeks from the time of Apelles and his contemporaries down to the destruction of Corinth by Mummius (the event which bounds our inquiries), can scarcely be redeemed by the few exceptions which that period presents,—by pictures of barbers' shops, and cobblers' stalls, and other efforts of a like nature, which we are wont to associate with our ideas of the Dutch school, in this respect the lowest school of all. Surely there must have been some sterling healthy principle which moved the thoughts and guided the pencil of Apelles, if, on the verge of a decline so rapid, on the brink of a precipice so steep, his eye did not lose its precision, his hand did not forget its cunning, nor his mind let go its grasp.

Lady applying fucus, or rouge, to her face.
(From a fictile vase.)

Tambourine Player.
(From a Pompeian painting.)

(From Pompeian painting.)

(From a Pompeian painting.)

CHRONOLOGICAL TABLE.

B.C.

Pelasgian æra.
Cecrops, Danaus, Cadmus, and Pelops.
Extension of the Hellenic nation.

1400—1200. The heroic age.
Heracles.
Theseus.
Minos.
Jason. The Argonautic expedition.

1194—1184. The Trojan war.

1124. About this time, extensive migrations take place in various parts of Greece, the most important being that of the Dorians.
Conquest of Peloponnesus by the Heracleids.
Codrus, king of Attica.
Dorian colonies in Crete.

1104 or 884. The legislation of Lycurgus. The latter date is that adopted by most modern writers.

1068. Medon, first archon for life at Athens.

900—800. Age of Homer and Hesiod.

776. Commencement of the Olympiads.
War between Sparta and Arcadia.

743—724. The first Messenian war.

735. Theocles leads a colony to Naxos in Sicily.

734. Syracuse founded by a Corinthian colony under Archias.

731. Aristodemus chosen king of the Messenians.

726. Aristodemus defeats the Lacedaemonians at Ithome.

724. Termination of the war. Conquest of Messenia.

708. Tarentum founded by Lacedaemonian colonists, called Partheniі, under the command of Phalanthus.

690. Gela in Sicily founded by Cretans and Rhodians.

685—668. The second Messenian war.
Aristomenes, the leader of the Messenians.

683. First annual archon at Athens.
Tyrtaeus, a martial poet, sent by the Athenians to Sparta, where his poetry revived the sinking courage of the Lacedaemonians.

682. The Messenians fortify mount Eira.

668. The war concluded by the capture of Eira, and conquest of Messenia.

658. Byzantium founded by a colony from Megara.

650. Psammetichus, king of Egypt, invites the Greeks to settle in that country.

637. More Greeks settle in Cyrene, and reform the constitution.

629. Selinus in Sicily founded.

B.C.

624. Draco's legislation at Athens.

623—612. War between Lydia and Miletus. In the last year a treaty of peace and alliance between the two states was concluded.

617. Alyattes ascends the throne of Lydia, and delivers Asia from the ravages of the Cimmerians.

612. Conspiracy of Cylon to overturn the government of Athens and make himself tyrant. War between Athens and Megara.

604. Solon recovers Salamis from the Megarians.

600. Massilia founded by the Phocaeans.

597. The partizans of Megacles banished from Athens.

595. Epimenides, the Cretan, invited by Solon to come to Athens.

594—585. The Crisaean or first Sacred war.
have lasted ten years

594. Solon appointed archon, with power to frame a new constitution and code of laws. Institution of the senate of Four Hundred, and of the Heliaea. Foundation of the Athenian navy.

582. Agrigentum founded.

572—562. Solon is said to have been absent from Athens, and to have visited Asia Minor, Cyprus, and Egypt.

570. Pythagoras.

560. Pisistratus obtains the tyrannis at Athens.
Croesus ascends the throne of Lydia, and subdues the greater part of Asia Minor.

559. Death of Solon. Pisistratus compelled to quit Athens.

554. Return of Pisistratus to Athe s.

552. Second expulsion of Pisistratus.

550. Pherecydes of Syros, the first prose writer in Greece.

546. Croesus taken prisoner in Sardis by Cyrus.
War against the Greeks of Asia Minor begun by Cyrus, who ultimately established his sovereignty over the whole country.

542. Pisistratus returns to Athens, of which he continues to be the ruler until his death.

538. Babylon taken by Cyrus.

536. Xenophanes, the founder of the Eleatic school of philosophy, emigrates from Colophon to Elea.

532. Polycrates, tyrant of Samos, at war against Miletus.

529. Cyrus defeated and slain by the Massagetae. He is succeeded by his son Cambyses.

527. Death of Pisistratus.

525. Egypt conquered by Cambyses.

522. Death of Polycrates at Sardis.

521. Death of Cambyses, and accession of Darius, who organised the Persian empire.
Conquest of Samos by the Persians.

516? Revolt of Babylon, and its conquest by Zopyrus.

514. Conspiracy of Harmodius and Aristogeiton against Hippias and Hipparchus, the sons of Pisistratus.

513 or 508. Darius invades Scythia.

510. Expulsion of Hippias and his family from Athens.
Destruction of Sybaris by the people of Croton.
Cleisthenes introduces important changes into the Athenian constitution, which increase the power of the people. Ten local tribes instituted in place of the four ancient tribes.
Cleisthenes withdraws from Athens, which is occupied by the Spartan king, Cleomenes.

508. Cleisthenes returns in triumph.
War between Athens and the Spartans with their allies, the Corinthians, Boeotians, and Chalcidians.

B.C.

504. Insurrection of the commonalty of Croton against the government and the Pythagoreans.

501. Failure of Aristagoras, the tyrant of Miletus, in his expedition against Naxos.

500. Aristagoras induces the Greek cities in Asia Minor to revolt. He applies to Sparta and Athens for support against the Persians.

499. Sardis burnt by the Athenians and Ionians, who were afterwards defeated, and returned home.

498. Second year of the Ionian revolt. The Persians recover Caria and Cyprus.

497. Third year of the Ionian revolt. Fall of several cities of Ionia and Aeolis. Death of Aristagoras in Thrace.

496. Fourth year of the Ionian revolt. Histiaeus arrives at Sardis, and thence escapes to Chios.

494. Sixth and last year of the revolt. The Ionians defeated in a naval battle off Lade, and Miletus taken by the Persians.

493. The subjugation of Ionia completed. Miltiades quits the Chersonesus, and settles at Athens.

492. Mardonius invades Europe. The Persian fleet wrecked off Mount Athos. Mardonius returns to Asia.

491. Darius sends heralds to Greece to demand tokens of submission. War between Athens and Aegina. Demaratus, king of Sparta, being deposed by the intrigues of his colleague, Cleomenes, goes to the Persian court.

490. Second invasion of Greece by the Persians, commanded by Datis and Artaphernes. Capture of Naxos, Delos, and Eretria. Battle of Marathon, in which the Persians were completely defeated by the Athenians under Miltiades, and retreated into Asia.

489. Miltiades attacks Paros, is wounded, and obliged to return to Athens; there he was impeached, condemned, and thrown into prison, where he soon afterwards died.

486. Egypt revolts from the Persian empire.

485. Death of Darius and accession of Xerxes.

484. Xerxes subdues Egypt.

484—480. Preparations are made by Xerxes during these four years, for again invading Greece. A bridge made across the Hellespont; and a canal cut through the isthmus of Mount Athos.

483. Aristides sent into exile. Themistocles becomes the leading man at Athens.

480. Xerxes begins his march into Europe. The battles of Thermopylae and Artemisium. The Persians repulsed from Delphi. The Athenians abandon their city, which is occupied by the Persians. Battle of Salamis, in which the Persian fleet is utterly defeated. Retreat of Xerxes, who leaves Mardonius to conquer Greece.

The Carthaginians defeated at Himera in Sicily, on the same day as the battle of Salamis was fought, on which, also, Euripides was born.

479. Mardonius occupies Athens, which had again been abandoned by its inhabitants. He negotiates with the Athenians, but his offers are rejected. He retreats into Boeotia, whither he is followed by the Greeks under Pausanias, who gains a great victory over the Persians at Plataeae. Mardonius slain, and succeeded in the command by Artabazus, who at once retreats into Asia.

In the battle of Mycale, said to have been fought on the same day as the battle of Plataeae, the Persian fleet was routed by that of the Greeks.

478. Sestos taken by the Athenians. Rebuilding and fortification of Athens. Themistocles causes the three harbours of Athens to be fortified.

B.C.

477. The fleet of the allied Greeks, commanded by Pausanias, takes possession of Cyprus and Byzantium. Pausanias offends the allies by his tyrannical conduct, and the supremacy is offered to the Athenians. Aristides organizes the Grecian confederacy. Pausanias recalled to Sparta. The supremacy of Athens lasted seventy-three years, B.C. 477—404.

476. Cimon, the Athenian general, conquers Eion and Scyros.

471. Themistocles banished, retires to Argos.

468. Death of Aristides.

Sophocles gains the victory with his first play.

467? Death of Pausanias.

466. Themistocles flees from Argos to avoid being arrested by the Athenians and Spartans; he goes first to Corcyra and Epirus, and thence to the court of Persia. Naxos conquered by the Athenians.

465. Xerxes assassinated. Cimon defeats the naval and military forces of the Persians in the battle of Eurymedon.

464. Revolt of Thasos from the Athenians. Earthquake in Laconia, and insurrection of the Helots and Messenians. Pericles takes an active and leading part in public affairs at Athens.

464—455. The third Messenian war. In the last year Ithome surrendered, and its defenders quitted Peloponnesus.

463. Cimon subdues Thasos.

461. Ephialtes carries a law, depriving the Areopagus of a great portion of its authority. Cimon banished from Athens. Pericles succeeds him at the head of affairs.

460. Inarus in Egypt revolts against the Persians, and is assisted by the Athenians. Commencement of the siege of Memphis, which lasted five years, and was at last abandoned by the Athenians.

457. War between the Athenians and the Corinthians, assisted by other Peloponnesians.

Myronides, the Athenian general, defeats the Corinthians at Megara. The battle of Tanagra, in which the Lacedaemonians conquer the Athenians. The building of the long walls of Athens is vigorously prosecuted.

456. Myronides gains a brilliant victory over the Thebans at Oenophyta. Completion of the long walls. Surrender of Aegina.

Death of Aeschylus.

455. The Athenians gain several advantages over the Peloponnesians, and capture Naupactus.

Euripides produces his first play.

454. The Athenians undertake the restoration of Orestes, but are defeated and compelled to retreat from Thessaly. Pericles repulsed from Oeniadae. Assassination of Ephialtes.

453. Cimon recalled to Athens: an armistice for three years, followed by a truce for five years.

449. Death of Cimon at Citium in Cyprus. The Athenian fleet defeats that of the Phoenicians and Cilicians. Amyrtaeus.

448. War between the Delphians and the Phocians respecting the superintendence of the oracle of Apollo. Sparta supports the Delphians, Athens the Phocians.

447. The Athenians under Tolmides defeated by the Boeotians in the battle of Coroneia. The ascendancy of Athens in Boeotia destroyed.

445. Expiration of the five years' truce. Revolt of Euboea and Megara. Invasion of Attica by the Peloponnesians. Subjugation of Euboea. A truce for thirty years concluded between Athens and Sparta.

444. Thucydides, the leader of the Athenian aristocracy, sent into exile.

441. The power of Pericles at its height. He carries a law excluding nearly 5000 persons from the rights of citizenship.

B.C.

443. The colony of Thurii established.

440. The revolt of Samos. Sophocles general. Its conquest by Pericles. Byzantium also taken by the Athenians. The sovereignty of Athens over her allies established.

438. Death of Pindar. Perfection of the Attic drama.

438—432. Pericles adorns Athens by the erection of the Parthenon, Propylaea, &c.

435. A war breaks out between Corinth and Corcyra respecting Epidamnus.

434. The Corcyraeans defeat the Corinthians in a naval engagement near Actium.

433. The Athenians conclude a defensive alliance with Corcyra, and send a fleet to its assistance.

432. Battle of Sybota between the Corcyraean and Corinthian fleets. Thucydides regards this battle as the first occasion of the war between Athens and Corinth.

Prosecution and death of Phidias. Accusation and acquittal of Aspasia. War between Perdiccas and the Athenians. Revolt of Potidaea and other Chalcidian towns. Defeat of the Corinthians under Aristeus by the Athenian general Callias. Meeting of the Peloponnesian confederates at Sparta, and declaration of war against Athens. The commencement of the Peloponnesian war.

431. First year of the Peloponnesian war. The Thebans attack Plataeae, but are repulsed. The Spartan King Archidamus invades Attica, and besieges Oenoë. Meantime the Athenians land at Methone, from which they are repulsed by Brasidas. Aegina and Cephallenia occupied by the Athenians, who also form an alliance with Sitalces, and devastate Megaris.

430. Second year of the Peloponnesian war. The plague breaks out at Athens. Second invasion of Attica. The Athenians ravage the coast of Peloponnesus. Surrender of Potidaea.

429. Third year of the Peloponnesian war. Continuance of the plague; death of Pericles. Commencement of the heroic defence of Plataeae. The Athenian fleet under Phormio defeats that of the Peloponnesians in the Corinthian gulf. The allies make an incursion into Salamis.

428. Fourth year of the Peloponnesian war. Third invasion of Attica. Revolt of Lesbos from the Athenians. First imposition of a property tax at Athens.

427. Fifth year of the Peloponnesian war. Fourth invasion of Attica. Surrender of Mytilene, and conquest of Lesbos by Paches. First appearance of a Peloponnesian fleet in Asia Minor. Surrender and destruction of Plataeae. Cleon appears as a leader of the Athenian people. Civil war in Corcyra. Nicias takes and fortifies Minoa. The Athenians begin to interfere in the affairs of Sicily. The plague breaks out again in Attica.

426. Sixth year of the Peloponnesian war. Earthquakes deter the Spartans from entering Attica. The Athenians are successful in Boeotia, Locris, Aetolia, Sicily, and southern Italy.

425. Seventh year of the Peloponnesian war. Fifth invasion of Attica. The Athenian general Demosthenes takes and fortifies Pylos, which is besieged by the Spartans both by land and sea. The Athenian fleet arrives and blockades the Spartans in Sphacteria. Negotiations for peace. Cleon takes Sphacteria, and conveys all the Spartan prisoners to Athens. Nicias lays waste the coast of Peloponnesus.

424. Eighth year of the Peloponnesian war. Continued success of the Athenians. Nicias takes possession of the island of Cythera, and ravages the coast of Peloponnesus. General pacification of Sicily. Brasidas prevents Megara falling into the hands of the Athenians.

B.C.

Battle of Delium, in which the Boeotians completely defeat the Athenians. Brasidas takes Acanthus, Amphipolis, and many other towns in Chalcidice.

423. Ninth year of the Peloponnesian war. A truce for one year concluded. Revolt of Scione and Mende from Athens. Recapture of Mende. Brasidas repulsed from Potidaea.

422. Tenth year of the Peloponnesian war. Cleon commands in Chalcidice, captures Torone, and lays siege to Amphipolis. Battle before Amphipolis, in which Brasidas and Cleon are killed, and the Athenians defeated.

421. Eleventh year of the Peloponnesian war. A peace, commonly called the peace of Nicias, concluded for fifty years. An offensive and defensive alliance between Athens and Sparta. The Argives put themselves at the head of a new confederacy. The Spartans conclude a separate treaty with the Boeotians.

420. Twelfth year of the Peloponnesian war. The Argives form an alliance with Athens. Alcibiades takes a prominent part in public affairs. The Spartans excluded from the Olympic games.

419. Thirteenth year of the Peloponnesian war. Hostilities between the Argives and the Epidaurians. Peace is formally maintained between Athens and Sparta.

418. Fourteenth year of the Peloponnesian war. The Lacedaemonians invade the Argive territory. The Athenians assist Argos. The Argive confederates invade Arcadia. The battle of Mantinea, in which the Spartans gain a decisive victory. Conclusion of a treaty of alliance for fifty years between Argos and Sparta.

417. Fifteenth year of the Peloponnesian war. The popular party at Argos prevails, and renounces the alliance with Sparta. Renewal of the war between the two states.

416. Sixteenth year of the Peloponnesian war. Alcibiades being sent to Argos, strengthens the popular party by carrying away 300 of the oligarchs. The Athenians besiege and conquer Melos. Ambassadors from the Sicilian town of Egesta come to Athens to solicit aid against Selinus.

415. Seventeenth year of the Peloponnesian war. The Athenians resolve to send an expedition to Sicily. The mutilation of the Hermae. Charge brought against Alcibiades. Arrival of the fleet in Sicily. Alcibiades recalled to Athens, but escapes to Peloponnesus. The Athenians commence the siege of Syracuse. Battle of the Anapus. Gylippus sent by the Spartans to Syracuse.

414. Eighteenth year of the Peloponnesian war. Siege of Syracuse continued. Battle of Epipolae gained by the Athenians. Death of Lamachus. The circumvallation of Syracuse completed. Arrival of Gylippus at Syracuse. Reverses of the Athenian army. Hostilities in Peloponnesus.

413. Nineteenth year of the Peloponnesian war. The Spartans under their king Agis again invade Attica, and establish themselves at Decelea. Naval engagements at Syracuse. Demosthenes arrives in Sicily from Athens with large reinforcements, but is totally defeated by Gylippus. The siege of Syracuse raised. The Athenians retreat, but are pursued and compelled to surrender. Nicias and Demosthenes put to death. Conclusion of the Sicilian war. Sparta becomes a maritime power. The allies of Athens make preparations for revolt.

412. Twentieth year of the Peloponnesian war. Alcibiades goes with a Spartan fleet to Asia Minor. Chios and other Ionian states revolt from Athens. First treaty between Persia and Sparta concluded. The Athenians recover many of their possessions in Asia Minor. Alcibiades deserts the Spartans, and acquires great influence over

B.C.

Tissaphernes. He intrigues for the purpose of procuring his recall to Athens.

411. Twenty-first year of the Peloponnesian war. Oligarchical government established at Athens. Democratic reaction in the Athenian army at Samos, which recalls Alcibiades, and elects him its general. The oligarchy at Athens overthrown by the people, who send commissioners to recall Alcibiades. Battle of Cynossema. The Peloponnesians defeated in the battle of Abydos.

410. Twenty-second year of the Peloponnesian war. The Lacedaemonians defeated at Cyzicus by Alcibiades, who recovers many places in Asia Minor. Thrasyllus repulses Agis in Attica. Siege of Lampsacos.

409. Twenty-third year of the Peloponnesian war. The Athenians gain possession of Byzantium.

408. Twenty-fourth year of the Peloponnesian war. Alcibiades returns in triumph to Athens, and conducts his fellow-citizens to Eleusis. Goes to Andros and Samos. Lysander appointed the Spartan commander in Asia Minor.

407. Twenty-fifth year of the Peloponnesian war. Siege of Phocaea. Battle of Notion, in which the Athenians are defeated. Alcibiades, deposed from the command, retires to Chersonesus. Conon appointed in his stead.

406. Twenty-sixth year of the Peloponnesian war. Callicratidas succeeds Lysander as Spartan commander, and is killed in the battle of Arginusae, in which the Athenians defeat the Lacedaemonians. Six of the Athenian generals put to death. Lysander again assumes the chief command.

405. Twenty-seventh year of the Peloponnesian war. Lysander totally defeats the Athenians at Aegospotami, and subdues nearly all their possessions in Asia: he then sails to Attica, and invests Athens by land and sea. Negotiations for peace, the terms of which are finally submitted to by the Athenians.

404. Lysander enters Athens, and sets up the government of the Thirty Tyrants. He takes Samos and returns to Sparta. Death of Alcibiades.

403. Thrasybulus makes himself master of Piraeus. The government of the Thirty overthrown, and democracy re-established. The Solonian constitution restored and revised.

401—400. Expedition of Cyrus against his brother Artaxerxes, the king of Persia; terminated by the battle of Cunaxa, in which Cyrus was killed. Xenophon conducts the retreat of the 10,000 Greeks.

399. War in Asia Minor between Persia and Sparta. Dercyllidas commands the forces of the latter.

Trial and execution of Socrates at Athens.

399—398. War between Sparta and Elis: in the second year the latter is defeated by Agis and compelled to accept a humiliating peace.

398. Dercyllidas goes to Lampsacos and Chersonesus. Death of king Agis, and accession of Agesilaus.

397. Dercyllidas takes Atarneus, and concludes a truce with the Persians.

396. Conspiracy of Cinadon at Sparta. Agesilaus assumes the command in Asia Minor, and winters at Ephesus.

395—387. The Corinthian or Boeotian war.

395. Agesilaus defeats the Persians on the river Pactolus, subdues nearly the whole of Asia Minor, and makes preparations for penetrating into the interior of the Persian empire. A league against Sparta formed in Greece. War between the Locrians and Phocians. Lysander killed before Haliartus. The Spartan king Pausanias goes into exile.

394. Agesilaus recalled to Greece. Battle of Corinth. The Spartan fleet

B.C.

destroyed in a battle off Cnidos by the combined forces of the Athenians and Persians. Agesilaus defeats the confederates at Coronea.

393. Massacre at Corinth. The Spartans take possession of Lechaeon, Sidos, and Crommyon. Iphicrates introduces various changes in the armour of the peltasts. Conon and Pharnabazus ravage the coast of Laconia, and take Cythera. Conon goes to Athens, and begins the rebuilding of its walls.

392. Agesilaus is repulsed from Corinth by Iphicrates, who recovers most of the places lost the year before. The walls of Athens completed.

391. The Spartans send Antalcidas to negotiate terms of peace with Tiribazus. Agesilaus conducts a successful campaign in Acarnania.

390. The Acarnanians form an alliance with Sparta. Agesipolis invades Argolis. The Spartan Teleutias defeats an Athenian squadron under Philocrates. Thrasybulus gains several successes over the Lacedaemonians, but is slain by the Aspendians.

389. Iphicrates defeats the Spartan Anaxibius at Abydos.

388. The Spartans take Aegina and harass the Athenian territory. Teleutias surprises Piraeus. Antalcidas again offers terms of peace to Tiribazus, and blocks up the Euxine.

387. The peace of Antalcidas concluded, which sacrifices the freedom of the Greek cities in Asia. The Lacedaemonians endeavour to obtain supremacy over the whole of Greece.

386. The restoration of Plataeae.

385. Mantinea destroyed by Agesipolis.

384. Phlius compelled by the Lacedaemonians to recall the exiled oligarchs.

383—379. The Olynthian wars, in which Sparta assists Acanthos and Apollonia against Olynthos.

382. The Spartan Phoebidas seizes upon the Cadmea at Thebes. Death of Ismenias. Pelopidas escapes from Thebes to Athens.

The Lacedaemonians defeated by the Olynthians in two engagements. Teleutias killed.

381. Agesipolis assumes the command of the Spartan army and marches against Olynthos. Agesilaus besieges Phlius.

380. Death of Agesipolis in Pallene. Phlius surrenders to the Spartans.

379. Polybiades compels the Olynthians to sue for peace, to conclude a treaty with Sparta, and acknowledge her supremacy. In this year the power of the Spartans was at its highest point. Pelopidas, assisted by the Athenians, liberates Thebes from the dominion of Sparta.

378—362. The Theban war.

Cleombrotus invades the Theban territory. Sphodrias makes an inroad into Attica. The Athenians prepare for war, and form an alliance with the Boeotians. A new confederacy formed against Sparta. Agesilaus invades Boeotia. Death of Phoebidas.

377. Agesilaus again makes an inroad into the territory of Thebes.

376. Cleombrotus compelled by the Athenians and Thebans to retire from Boeotia. The Lacedaemonian fleet defeated by Chabrias off Naxos.

375. The Spartans defeated in a battle near Orchomenos by the Thebans, who establish their supremacy in Boeotia. Timotheus the Athenian gains many successes over the Spartans.

374. Peace concluded between Sparta and Athens. Plataeae, Thespiae, and Orchomenos destroyed by the Thebans. Timotheus gains over Corcyra to the Athenian confederacy. Renewal of the war between Athens and Sparta. Iphicrates accompanies Pharnabazus to Egypt.

373. The Lacedaemonians lay siege to Corcyra. Their general Mnasippus is slain, and the siege raised. Iphicrates sent to take the command in the Ionian sea.

About this time the custom of employing mercenaries began to prevail in Greece.

B.C.

371. Peace concluded between Athens and Sparta. Cleombrotus invades Boeotia, but is totally defeated by Epaminondas in the battle of Leuctra. Mantinea rebuilt. Megalopolis, the capital of the Arcadian union, founded.

370. Unsuccessful expedition of Agesilaus against Megalopolis. Jason, the tyrant of Pherae, assassinated.

369. The Thebans and their allies commanded by Epaminondas and Pelopidas invade Peloponnesus. They fail in an attack on Sparta, but restore the independence of Messenia. The Athenians send Iphicrates to the assistance of the Spartans.

368. Second expedition of Epaminondas into Peloponnesus. He defeats the Spartans and Athenians, but is repulsed from Corinth. Pelopidas makes two expeditions into Thessaly; in the second of which he is taken prisoner by Alexander of Pherae.

367. The Arcadians defeated by the Spartans under Archidamus in the "tearless battle." A Theban force under Epaminondas compels Alexander to liberate Pelopidas, who is afterwards sent to Susa to conduct negotiations with the king of Persia.

366. Third expedition of Epaminondas into Peloponnesus. Achaia gained over to the cause of Thebes, but soon afterwards lost.

365. Peace made between the Athenians and Arcadians. War breaks out between Arcadia and Elis. The Arcadians overrun Elis.

364. Archidamus defeated by the Arcadians at Cromnus. The Eleans attack the Arcadians and Argives during the Olympic games, and defeat them. Pelopidas gains a victory over Alexander at Cynoscephalae, but is himself slain. Alexander is compelled to enter into an alliance with Thebes.

363. The Thebans endeavour to arrest the Arcadian leaders at Tegea.

362. Epaminondas enters Peloponnesus for the fourth and last time. Agesilaus repels the Thebans from Sparta. The battle of Mantinea, in which each party claims the victory; but Epaminondas is killed.

361. A general peace concluded. Independence secured to the Messenians. Sparta alone refuses to agree to the peace. Agesilaus conducts an expedition to Egypt, and dies on his return home.

360. Timotheus repulsed by the Olynthians at Amphipolis, which falls into their hands. An Athenian fleet defeated by Alexander of Pherae.

359. Accession of Philip to the throne of Macedonia. He is opposed by the pretender Argaeus, whom the Athenians support. Philip defeats them near Methone, and soon afterwards concludes a peace with Athens.

358. Philip conducts a successful campaign against the Illyrians; takes Amphipolis and Pydna; and assigns Potidaea and Anthemus to the Olynthians.

357. Timotheus prevents the revolt of Euboea. Chios and many other places throw off the supremacy of Athens, and thus give rise to the Social war (B.C. 357—355). Expedition against Chios and death of Chabrias.

356. Second year of the Social war. Iphicrates and Timotheus deposed from the command, which is entrusted to Chares, who forms connections with Artabazus. Birth of Alexander the Great. Philip interferes in the affairs of Thessaly.

355. The Social war concluded by a peace, which deprives Athens of most of her allies, and of a great part of her revenue. Commencement of the Sacred war (B.C. 355—346), waged in the first instance by the Thebans against the Phocians.

354. The Phocian Philomelus defeats the Locrians and Thebans near Delphi.

353. Defeat of the Phocians at Neon, and death of Philomelus, who is suc-

B.C.

ceeded by his brother Onomarchus. Sparta makes war against Megalopolis and Argos. Olynthos allies itself with Athens.

352. Philip defeats Phayllus; but is soon afterwards himself defeated in two battles by Onomarchus, and retires into Macedonia. In a second campaign in Thessaly, Philip gains a complete victory at Magnesia over Onomarchus, who is slain. Phayllus succeeds him as commander in chief of the Phocians. Philip repulsed from Thermopylae.

Demosthenes delivers his first Philippic.

351. The Phocians continue the war in Boeotia. Death of Phayllus.

350. Philip establishes tyrants in Euboea. Expedition of Phocion to Euboea. Philip lands at Marathon.

349. Philip marches against Olynthos. The Athenians send an army to assist the Olynthians.

347. Olynthos and many other Thracian and Chalcidian towns fall into the hands of Philip, who razes them to the ground.

346. The Phocians defeat the Boeotians at Coroneia. Philip concludes a peace with the Athenians and marches into Boeotia. The Phocians submit: their towns are destroyed and their country laid waste. End of the Sacred war.

344. Philip begins to interfere in Peloponnesus. The Athenians negotiate a peace between the belligerents in Peloponnesus. Philip makes a successful expedition into Illyricum.

Demosthenes delivers his second Philippic.

343. Philip continues his conquests.

342—341. Philip's expedition into Thrace. Selymbria taken.

340. Philip lays siege to Perinthos and Byzantium. The Athenians resolve on war.

339. Phocion compels Philip to raise the sieges of Perinthos and Byzantium. Philip defeated by the Triballians.

338. Philip appointed commander in chief of the forces of the Amphictions. Commencement of the Amphissian war. The Athenians form an alliance with the Thebans. Battle of Chaeroneia, in which Philip gains a decisive victory. Peace concluded by Philip with Athens and Thebes. Phocion at the head of affairs at Athens.

337. Congress of the Greek states on the Isthmus of Corinth. Philip elected commander in chief of the Greeks to conduct the war against Persia, for which great preparations are made.

336. Festivals celebrated by Philip at Aegeae. Assassination of Philip, and accession of Alexander the Great, who compels all the Greeks, except the Spartans, to acknowledge his supremacy. A permanent congress of deputies appointed to meet at Corinth.

335. Alexander makes expeditions against the Triballi, Getae, and Illyrians. In consequence of a report of his death, many Greek states revolt. Alexander storms Thebes, which is razed to the ground. He accepts the submission of Athens.

334. Alexander sets out on the expedition against Persia. Battle of the Granicus.

333. Battle of Issus. Agis III. forms a confederacy against Macedonia, which the Athenians refuse to join. Death of Memnon.

332. Alexander takes Tyre. Alexandria founded.

331. Battle of Gaugamela. Alexander enters Babylon. Agis defeated and slain by Antipater near Megalopolis. The Spartans submit.

330—328. Alexander engaged in conquering the East.

324. Nicanor sent by Alexander to the Olympic games to command the restoration of the exiles. Harpalus escapes from Asia to Greece, and is slain in Crete. The Harpalian inquisition occasions the exile of Demosthenes.

323. Alexander dies at Babylon. Confederacy of the Greeks against Mace-

B.C.

donia. Its general Leosthenes defeats the Boeotians and Antipater, whose overtures for peace are rejected. Death of Leosthenes.

322. Leonnatus defeated and killed in a battle gained by Antiphilus, the successor of Leosthenes. Antipater defeats the confederates near Crannon, and compels Athens to surrender; the Athenian constitution changed. Death of Demosthenes.

321. Murder of Perdiccas, and redistribution of the countries conquered by Alexander.

318. Death of Antipater, who is succeeded by Polysperchon: he proclaims the independence of Greece. Nicanor takes possession of Piraeus.

317. Death of Phocion. Athens submits to Cassander, who appoints Demetrius of Phaleron its governor. His administration lasted for ten years (B.C. 318—307).

315. Cassander commands Thebes to be rebuilt.

314. Antigonus and his rival Ptolemy declare the Greeks to be free.

315—311. War of the Macedonian generals against Antigonus, concluded in the last year by a general peace, which divided the empire of Alexander among four rulers, and guaranteed the independence of Greece.

312. Demetrius Poliorcetes defeated near Gaza.

308. Cassander makes terms of agreement with Ptolemy.

307. Demetrius Poliorcetes becomes the master of Athens, and restores to the people its ancient freedom and constitution. Demetrius of Phaleron leaves the city.

306. Demetrius Poliorcetes defeats Ptolemy off Cyprus, and conquers the island. Five generals of Alexander assume the title of king.

304. Demetrius lays siege to Rhodes, and compels it to conclude a peace: he returns to Greece and overthrows the government of Cassander, who had been repulsed from Athens by Demochares. Demetrius comes to Athens.

301. Battle of Ipsus, in which Antigonus is defeated and slain. Demetrius refused admission into Athens.

300. Demetrius allies himself with Seleucus, and is successful in Asia.

296. Death of Cassander. Athens besieged by Demetrius: its surrender to him. He goes into Peloponnesus and defeats Archidamus.

295. Civil war in Macedonia. Demetrius takes possession of Athens.

294. Demetrius kills Alexander, mounts the throne of Macedonia, and for seven years exercises sway over nearly all Greece.

291. Revolt of Thebes.

290. Subjugation of Thebes by Demetrius.

287. Demetrius dethroned by Pyrrhus, who becomes king of Macedonia. Athens recovers her freedom. Return of Demochares from exile.

286. Pyrrhus expelled from Macedonia by Lysimachus.

283. Death of Demetrius Poliorcetes, and of Demetrius of Phaleron.

281. Lysimachus defeated and slain in a battle near Sardis gained by Seleucus.

280. Greece invaded by the Celts. Foundation of the Achaean league.

279. The Celts routed at Delphi.

278. Antigonus Gonatas ascends the throne of Macedonia.

274—272. Pyrrhus king of Macedonia. In the latter year he is repulsed from Sparta, and killed soon afterwards.

269—262. Antigonus besieges Athens, which is at length compelled to submit to the Macedonians.

251. Aratus elected strategus of the Achaean league.

244. Agis IV. becomes king of Sparta, and endeavours to introduce many reforms.

243. Aratus expels the Macedonian garrison from Corinth, and extends the power of the Achaean league.

241. Agis put to death.

B.C.
236—220. Cleomenes IV., king of Sparta.
229. The Macedonian garrison quits Athens.
226. Aratus strategus of the Achaean league for the eleventh time. Cleomenes carries into effect the measures proposed by Agis. He commences war against the Achaean league. The Aetolians conclude a treaty with Sparta.
225. Cleomenes takes Metydrion. Accusation of Aratus.
224. Aratus strategus of the Achaeans, who resolve on war. They are defeated in several battles by Cleomenes, and implore the aid of Antigonus Doson, to whom they give up Acrocorinthus.
223. Antigonus enters Arcadia.
222. Cleomenes takes Megalopolis, and invades Argolis.
221. Antigonus enters Laconia. Battle of Sellasia, in which the Spartans are utterly routed, and Philopoemen distinguishes himself. Cleomenes flees to Egypt. Antigonus takes Sparta and restores the ephoralty.
220. Death of Ptolemy, king of Egypt, and suicide of Cleomenes. Lycurgus makes himself sole king of Sparta. An alliance formed between the Aetolians and Sparta, which led to the second Social war. Aratus defeated by the Aetolians.
220—217. Second Social war.
219. Philip V. of Macedonia invades Aetolia, Elis, and Arcadia: the Aetolians invade Achaia.
218. Philip again invades Aetolia, and defeats Lycurgus near Sparta. The Aetolians take the Panachaicon.
217. Philip concludes a peace with the Aetolians. End of the Social war.
216. Philip prepares for war with the Romans, and enters into an alliance with Hannibal.
214. The Roman general Laevinus invades Illyricum and defeats Philip.
213. Death of Aratus.
211. The Romans enter into a treaty with the Aetolians. Laevinus takes Oeniadae and Zacynthus. Death of Lycurgus: Machanidas becomes first tyrant of Sparta.
210. Laevinus takes Anticyra.
208. Philip defeats the Aetolians near Lamia; but is himself defeated in Elis. Fruitless negotiations for peace. Philopoemen becomes strategus of the Achaean league.
207. Attalus of Pergamus takes part in the war. Philopoemen defeats Machanidas near Mantinea.
206. The Romans cease to take part in the war.
205. The Aetolians obliged to make peace with Philip.
204. Peace concluded between Philip and the Romans.
202. Philip makes war on the Rhodians and Attalus.
201. Philip offends the Aetolians by attacking their allies.
200. Philip invades Attica and lays siege to Athens. Commencement of the second Macedonian war.
199. The consul Villius Tappulus fails in an attempt to invade Macedonia.
198. The consul Flamininus gains successes over the Macedonians, and secures the aid of the Achaeans; he concludes a truce with Philip, and winters in Phocis and Locris.
197. Flamininus completely defeats Philip in the battle of Cynoscephalae, and compels him to sue for peace.
196. Peace ratified by the Romans, who reserve to themselves the right to occupy Acrocorinthus, Demetrias, and Chalcis. Flamininus proclaims the freedom of Greece at the Isthmian games.
195. Flamininus makes war on Nabis, tyrant of Sparta, and compels him to accept terms of peace.
194. The Roman garrisons withdrawn from the three fortresses. War between Nabis and the Achaeans.

B.C.

192. Philopoemen defeats Nabis near Pleiae. Nabis is killed by the Aetolians. The Achaean league embraces the whole of Peloponnesus. Antiochus of Syria arrives in Greece.

191. The Romans defeat the Aetolians and Antiochus at Thermopylae. The king flees to Asia.

190. A truce for six months between the Romans and Aetolians.

189. War recommenced, but finally terminated by the consul M. Fulvius Nobilior; the power and influence of the Aetolian confederacy annihilated.

188. The Achaeans declare war against Sparta. Philopoemen conquers the Lacedaemonians and abolishes the constitution of Lycurgus.

183. The Messenians revolt from the Achaean league. Philopoemen taken prisoner by the Messenians and put to death.

181. Sparta again incorporated with the Achaean league.

179. Death of Philip: his successor Perseus prepares for war with the Romans. Callicrates begins his intrigues for the dissolution of the Achaean league.

171. Commencement of the third Macedonian war.

168. The Romans completely defeat Perseus in the battle of Pydna. End of the war.

167. One thousand of the principal Achaeans, including Polybius, sent to Rome; 550 distinguished Aetolians put to death at Rome.

155. The Athenians send three ambassadors to Rome.

151. Return of the Achaean exiles to Greece.

148. The consul Metellus makes war against the pretender Philip of Macedonia.

147. The Achaeans declare war against Rome. Metellus defeats them at Heracleia and Scarpheia, and destroys Thebes. Diaeus rejects all proposals of peace.

146. The consul Mummius defeats the Achaeans in the battle of Leucopetra, and takes Corinth. Death of Diaeus. The Achaean league dissolved. Henceforth the Romans were the virtual rulers of Greece.

Female with Lyre.
(From Pompeian painting.)

Cyclopes at work.

(From a bas relief in the Museum of the Capitol at Rome.)

Hippo-camp.
(From a Pompeian painting.)

INDEX.

A.

B.

C.

F.

G.

H.

R.

S.

T.

V.

W.

X.

Z.

Rustic clothed in the Exomis.

(From a bas-relief in the Barberini Collection at Rome.)

www.ingramcontent.com/pod-product-compliance
Lightning Source LLC
Chambersburg PA
CBHW021220300426
44111CB00007B/381